KINGDOM
in the
WEST

The Mormons and the American Frontier

Will Bagley, series editor

VOLUME II

U.S. Senator Sam Houston of Texas, Mormon Friend

Houston's long relationship with the Mormons began with Joseph Smith's unfulfilled hopes for an LDS Texas colony. During the Utah War, he was Brigham Young's most prominent non-Mormon supporter because of mutual friendships, affinity for the underdog, shared enmity with Albert Sidney Johnston, and political ambivalence about Buchanan. As photographed here in 1857, Houston often wore a signature Cherokee blanket and white beaver hat, prompting the label "magnificent barbarian." *Charles De Forest Fredericks photo courtesy of Sam Houston Memorial Museum, Huntsville, Texas.*

At Sword's Point, Part 2

A Documentary History of the Utah War, 1858–1859

Edited by
William P. MacKinnon

THE ARTHUR H. CLARK COMPANY
An imprint of the University of Oklahoma Press
Norman, Oklahoma
2016

Library of Congress Cataloging-in-Publication Data
At sword's point / edited by William P. MacKinnon.
v. cm. — (Kingdom in the West: the Mormons and the American frontier; v. 11)
Includes bibliographical references and index.
Contents: pt. 1. A documentary history of the Utah War to 1858 — pt. 2. A documentary history of the Utah War, 1858–1859
ISBN 978-0-87062-353-0 (v. 1 : hardcover : alk. paper) —
ISBN 978-0-87062-354-7 (v. 1 : collector's ed. : alk. paper) —
ISBN 978-0-87062-386-8 (v. 2 : hardcover : alk. paper) —
ISBN 978-0-87062-387-5 (v. 2 : collector's ed. : alk. paper) —
1. Utah Expedition, 1857–1858. 2. Mormons—Utah—History—19th century. I. MacKinnon, William P.
f826.m13 2007
973.6'8—dc22
2007036588

At Sword's Point, Part 2: A Documentary History of the Utah War, 1858–1859 is Volume 11 in the Kingdom in the West series.

The paper in this book meets the guidelines for permanence and durability of the Committee on Production Guidelines for Book Longevity of the Council on Library Resources, Inc. ∞

Published by the University of Oklahoma Press, Norman, Publishing Division of the University.
Manufactured in the U.S.A.

---

1 2 3 4 5 6 7 8 9 10

For Patricia H. MacKinnon

who stayed the course with a love
that made all things possible

Contents

Illustrations 11
Foreword 13
Acknowledgments 17
Editorial Procedures 25
Introduction 29
Our Story Begins: 1857 — Apostolic and Soldierly Musings — What's Past Is Prologue: 1858

1. "Great Disaster Might Befall the Command": War Spreads to New Mexico 39
Getting Up a Private Stampede: Marcy Family Anxieties — Laying Up High and Dry: Captain Marcy's Volunteers — Sincere Thanks to the Almighty: Marcy's Southbound Trek — Instigating the Different Tribes: Sounding the Alarm — A Diversion in Your Favor: General Garland's Offer — The "Good Spirit" Would Protect Them: Enter Kit Carson — A Kilkenny Cat Fight: The View from Santa Fe — Look upon the Bright Side: More Cheer from George McClellan

2. "Our East Boundary Should Be at Laramie": Mormon War Strategy 65
All into Ashes: Russian Thoughts — Right Kind of Men: The Standing Army's Origins — They Bring Important Intelligence: Return of the Captives — As Simple as Practical: Brother Bertrand Views Mormon Strategy — Unsuitable Cavalry: General Ferguson Views 1858 — Let the Pen Flow Freely: War of Words

3. "Measures to Thwart Them": Johnston Reacts . . . 87
Espionage Complete and Successful: Spy Catchers — To Rely upon the Indians: Protecting Captain Marcy — Reaching Here Unmolested: Warning Marcy — A Long and Perilous Journey: Courier Browne — Intercepting the Caballada: Countering Mormon Plans — Conduct Most Reprehensible: Magraw Savages Forney — Little or No Dissipation: Magraw Lobbies Douglas

4. "A Channel of Communication with Utah": Rio Colorado 113
Two Missions: Ives and Marcy — Ives and His Report — Ives Organizes: Robinson's Landing and Fort Yuma — Very Unpleasant Feelings: Disruptive Upstream Rivalry — Stern Duties and Pressing Cares: *Explorer* Steams North — Brought Us by Madam Rumor: Mormon Intelligence — Bad Day at Black Rock: Striking the Head of Navigation — Casting Discredit upon My Expedition: Ives Reports and Defends — My First Real Experience at Espionage: Thales Haskell in the Lion's Den — In the Face of Certain Death: Mojave Mood Shift

5. "Exert Yourself to Counteract It": West Coast Defenses 143
To Do All That May Be Necessary for Your Defense: General Clarke Acts — Hardy Pioneers and Mountain Men: California Volunteers — Perceptions and Self-Defense

6. "To Mask the Real Movement": Pacific Adventures, Presidential Intrigue 159
Hornets Raging, Hell Boiling: Mormon Anticipation — Contrary to All Strategic Principles: General Scott's Strange Behavior — A God Send to the Country: A Star for Sidney Johnston — The Real Object: Utah, Manifest Destiny, and Presidential Billiards

7. "So Gloriously to Run the Gauntlet": Kane's Passage to Utah 187
Everyone Bore a Title of Some Kind: To San Bernardino as Dr. Osborne — An Angel in Disguise: Harassment and Rescue in San Berdoo — I Am on No Fool's Errand: Last Leg to Salt Lake

8. "At Young's Very Gates": Kane among the Mormons . 215
I Come as an Ambassador: Kane Begins His Mediation — To Avoid the Calamities of War: Kane Reports to Buchanan — On the Town: Kane as Schmoozer — Backdrop for Kane's Departure: Attack at Fort Limhi

9. "Remedy Worse Than the Disease": Raising Regulars, Volunteers, and Sam Houston . . 245
My Bones Have Burned for Weeks: Completing the Standing Army — Hurrah for the Ohio Volunteers!: Organizing by Units — I Would Rather Be in Utah: Individual Hopefuls — The Best Materials to Work With: Lobbying Sam Houston — To Murder an Innocent People: Major Blair's Letter — A Magnificent Barbarian in Action: Houston Takes the Floor — Of Mormons & War, and Profligate Scoundrels: Houston's Self-Assessment — Turning Away That Fearful Storm: Houston's Impact

10. "He Fell as a Bombshell": Kane and Turmoil at Camp Scott 275
The Bearer of Overtures of Peace: The Trail to Bridger — A Self-Constituted Ambassador: Mixed Receptions — An Absence of Proper Deference: Kane Meets Johnston — That Abominable Camp Business: Kane Beleaguered — Cowards, Assassins, and Bullies: Major Porter's Influence — Narrative of My Disappointment: Kane Reports to Buchanan — Friendly Personal Relations: Dueling in the Snow — They Should Know Nothing: Communicating with Brigham Young — The Storm, So Long Impending: Kane Reports Mixed Results — The Gentleman Referred To: A Hint of Success

11. "Blessed Be Nothing": The Mormon Move South . . 309
To Take into Consideration: The Decision to Flee — When You Have Dispersed the Saints and Their Seraglios: Young Encircled — The Sheep Are to Follow the Shepherd: Announcing the Move — Somewhat Loth to Volunteer: Counsel Ignored, Guidance Followed — From the North Pole on Half Rations: Executing the Move — Be Careful to Save the Nails: Moving "Built" Utah — On the Animal's Backbone: Beyond Provo

12. "Proceeding to Salt Lake City":
The Mountain Moves to Mohammed 347
Attachment Amounting to Enthusiasm: Among the Quaking Aspens — It Is All Over Now: Euphoria, Reportage, and Preparation — Mr. Kane, You Strive to Hide Your Game: Army Consternation — He Would Obey Me in Every Respect: With Cumming in Tow — Ashamed to Feel So Near Happiness!: Road Trip — Of Clean Sheets and a Fishlike Governor: Ecstatic Arrival

13. "To Try and Settle the Matter": The Players Maneuver 383
Find Facts, Return Indictments: Eckels Pokes the Bee Hive — An Accurate and Just Statement of the Times: Fighting the Public Relations War — Barren and Desolate in the Extreme: To the Colorado with Apostle Lyman — A Fermentation of Ideas: Buchanan's Next Gambit — Greatly Annoyed by the Utah Difficulties: The Buchanan-Bernhisel Chats — Fallen like a Clap of Thunder: Buchanan's Secret Proclamation — That Moderation Will Prevail: Captain Van Vliet Re-enters the Fray — Commissioners and Correspondents West: Odd Couples in Motion — I Belong to the Cabinet: "Sisterly" Advice for the President

14. "The Final and Decisive One":
The Testing of Alfred Cumming 419
The Programme to Be Pursued: Reception Committee — More Frenzy Than I Had Expected: Cumming Takes the Stand — Precursor to the Tabernacle: The Backstory of 24 April — An Occasion of Intense Interest: Beginning of the End — For Once I Am Happy: Kane Savors the Moment — The Dread Report: News of Judge Kane's Death — Our Mutual Friend Going Home: Closing Up His Mission — Cumming Deals with the Disaffected: Aid and Duplicity — Has No Connexion to the Church: The Fay Worthen Problem — Under Kane's Influence: Cumming, Worthen, and the Growth of the War-Peace Myth — I Cannot Be Responsible for Their Safety: Starting Young's Divide-and-Conquer Strategy — Adding Fuel to the Fire: Final Arrangements — He Seemed Considerably Affected: Departures — Acting Egregiously: The Staines Mansion as Honey Trap

15. "All That Is Required":
The Differing Needs of Johnston, Buchanan, and Kane 467
On the Verge of the Grave: General Smith and More Leadership Ambiguity — To Keep the Ball A Going!: Of Quartermasters and Columns — Take a Tap, Pard: Utah Expedition Hard Cases — The Difference of a Week: Buchanan's Shifting Political Sands — Home at Last: Tom Kane Revisits the White House

16. "Man from the Moon": Enter the Peace Commissioners 505
"A.B.C." and "O.H.O." Trail the Commissioners: Insider Reporting — Our Present Position a Critical One: The Meetings of 11–12 June — Freely and Fully Pardoned: Executing Buchanan's Proclamation — Beyond the Jordan: Of Timing and Commitments — Keep the Wax out of My Ears and the Dust out of My Eyes: Spying on Cumming — Surprise That Unease Is Felt: General Johnston Responds — A Great Deal of Interesting Conversation: The Commissioners' Walk-About — Correct as Far as I Can Recollect: A First Draft of History — Cart before the Horse: From the Sublime to the Ridiculous

17. "The Most Beautiful Place I Ever Saw": The Army Arrives 555
A Place Abreast of Lewis and Clark: Recognizing Captain Marcy — All the Home We Had: Leaving Camp Scott — High Water as Well as Hell: Regrouping on Bear River — Rejoicing in Green Peas and Strawberries: In the Eye of the Storm — A Knight or Two: Romantics on Horseback — The Devil's Choice Flock: Mormon Straws in a June Wind — An Approaching Army: Mormon and Gentile Reflections at the Brink — Houses a Strange Sight to Many of Us: City Passage — In Deathlike Silence: Watchmen on the Tower

Conclusions 599
Defining the Utah War: What Was It? — Leaders' Accountability — A Conflict Irrepressible or Preventable? — Winners and Losers — The War's Significance

Epilogue 623
First Encounters: Mutual Misery and Bitterness — Warfare by Other Means: Utah's Reconstruction — The War's Impact on Individuals: Heroes and Villains-in-Waiting

Bibliography 651

Index 675

Illustrations

U.S. Senator Sam Houston . . . . *frontispiece*
Map of Utah War's Sprawling Geography 28
Map of Marcy Route, Fort Bridger, Utah Territory, to Taos, New Mexico 38
Marcy's Detachment en Route to New Mexico 46
Mariano Medina 49
Brigham Young 67
1st Lt. Lawrence A. Williams 101
Col. Albert Sidney Johnston 106
Ives Expedition aboard *Explorer* 112
Heinrich Balduin Möllhausen 117
Map of Ives Expedition's Colorado River Route 118
Sir William Gore Ouseley 179
Map of Kane's Route, San Pedro to Salt Lake City 188
Thomas L. Kane 214
William C. Staines and Mansion 235
Maj. Seth M. Blair 267
Maj. Fitz John Porter 279
Sgt. George Austin Beardsley 302
Brigham Young Family Compound, Provo 338
Gov. Alfred Cumming 346
Map of Region between Fort Bridger and Salt Lake City 349
Brig. Gen. William H. Kimball 350
President James Buchanan and Cabinet 402
Lafayette Shaw (Fay) Worthen and Family 447
2nd Lt. Robert L. Browning 479
Fort Leavenworth, Kansas Territory 480
Seventh Infantry Fording South Platte River 483
Maj. Ben McCulloch 506
Utah Expedition's March through Salt Lake City 587

Foreword

As the Yale historian Robin Winks noted half a century ago, a historian must deal with questions of evidence, and "collect, interpret, and then explain his evidence by methods which are not greatly different from those techniques employed by the detective."[1] Rather than being dull, the pursuit of history is an adventure demanding relentless investigation, careful evaluation of personalities and events, and conclusions derived from neither popular legends nor the accepted wisdom, but from the facts. In our quest to determine what happened, historians must rely on the process of discovery to reject false hypotheses and muddled stories to arrive at the best explanation of what happened—and why.

As this work attests, William P. MacKinnon may be the most relentless historical detective of his generation. He has dedicated much of the past six decades to investigating the conflict known as the Utah War, the nation's most extensive and expensive military commitment in the period between the Mexican-American War and the American Civil War. One result of this tenacity is dozens of pathbreaking articles that expanded, challenged, or demolished the war's standard interpretation. The two volumes of *At Sword's Point* showcase the most important of his documentary discoveries, set in a connecting narrative of incisive analysis.

More than half of the Kingdom in the West series' sixteen volumes deal with some aspect of the Utah War; all have included new documentary evidence and most introduced reinterpretations. Yet much of Mr. MacKinnon's highly anticipated volume is new. Among its important discoveries are Christopher "Kit" Carson's reports of "emissaries from the Mormons of Utah," trying to persuade Colorado's Utes to "forfeit their allegiance to the

[1]Robin W. Winks, ed., *The Historian as Detective: Essays on Evidence* (New York: Harper & Row, 1969), xiii.

United States"; and the army's exploration of the Colorado River as a possible supply route and Apostle Amasa Lyman's expedition to also investigate it. Further revelations include details about Brigham Young's Standing Army of Israel; Porter Rockwell and Bill Hickman's independent companies of picked men, all "well mounted, expert riders, and dead shots"; Mormon plans for a spring campaign to "use up this army first" at Fort Bridger and then "use up the others before they get to the South Pass"; and an exposé of James Buchanan's fantasy that a "quasi-military colonial system," using the flight of thousands of Mormon refugees to northern Mexico as a vanguard, could deliver Cuba and Sonora to the U.S. slavocrats and save the Union.

Among this volume's entertaining revelations are Sgt. Maj. William Porter Finlay's tale of the non-coms' Christmas ball held at Camp Scott: "without the faintest attempt at anything almost in the feminine line," it "ended in a perfectly free fight, involving the loss of the supper and the destruction of the grub"; John Fell Squires's priceless boyhood account of driving his family's pig to Nephi during the vaunted "Move South" that left the twelve-year-old's dirty dad looking "like he had come from the North Pole on half rations"; and the use of the elegant mansion built by the late Almon W. Babbitt and by then owned by William C. Staines to entangle Utah Territory's portly new governor in an intelligence-gathering "honey trap." Not so amusing is MacKinnon's chilling tale of cardsharp Charley Hart sweeping silver and gold "chicken feed" off a Camp Scott monte bank with revolver drawn. "Charley" was William Clarke Quantrill, soon to be the Civil War's most notorious guerrilla.

This volume confirmed many of this veteran skeptic's views of the Utah War but called others into question. Gov. Alfred Cumming's intelligent and professional remarks to his fellow citizens at Salt Lake in spring 1858 forced me to reconsider his role and competence. The ample evidence from Kane family documents confirmed my suspicion that "darling" Thomas was as concerned with indulging his need to control and manipulate as he was with helping the downtrodden. Kane comes across as remarkably uninterested in justice for the victims of Mountain Meadows and their survivors or in the welfare of the tattered Mormon refugees of the Move South. *At Sword's Point* enhanced my admiration of the discipline and integrity of America's best soldiers but challenged my views on knaves, fools, and religion.

The concluding volume of *At Sword's Point* may mark the capstone of a remarkable career, but I doubt we have heard the last from one of the most talented, generous, and insightful historians of his time. MacKinnon and I may go to our graves debating what the Utah War meant and means, but this book and its companion volume speak for themselves about his enduring contribution to the history of the Mormons and the American West. Together, they are a masterwork.

Will Bagley
Salt Lake City, Utah

Acknowledgments

In 2008 I acknowledged a large number of people who helped me to complete *At Sword's Point, Part 1.* During the intervening years, a plethora of additional documents have welled up through discoveries in ten countries on six continents. It is a diaspora illustrating one of my principal findings—that the Utah War was an event with international as well as regional sweep, rather than a conflict confined to Utah Territory and Washington. With this good fortune goes a need to thank those who have supported this second volume.

I am especially indebted to historians James J. Barnes and Patience P. Barnes of Crawfordsville, Indiana, for my awareness of the most exciting of this new material, the "private & confidential" diplomatic dispatches describing President Buchanan's war aims written from Washington by Sir William Gore Ouseley to the British Foreign Secretary, Lord Clarendon. Thanks also to the former owner of these reports, George Edward Laurence Villers, the Eighth Earl of Clarendon, and their custodian, Collin Harris, Superintendent, Department of Special Collections Reading Rooms at Oxford University's Bodleian Library.

With respect to alarm by the British cabinet, Hudson's Bay Company, and Royal Navy over the possibility of a mass Mormon exodus to the Pacific, I acknowledge the assistance of London librarian-researcher Catherine Cooke, who helped me to plumb the depths of the British National Archives, Kew; and Bronwen Quarry and Marie E. Reidke at the Hudson's Bay Company Archives in Winnipeg, Manitoba.

I have been able to assemble the sprawling story of William Porter Finlay, the Volunteer Battalion's sergeant-major, through the help of professionals in multiple countries: Paul Carter and Margaret Makepeace of the Oriental and India Office Collections and India Office Records, respectively, at the British Library, London; Peter B. Boyden, assistant director (collections), National Army Museum, London; historian-genealogist Helen D. Harris of Victoria, Australia; Professor Donal McCracken of the University of Kwa-Zulu, Durban, South Africa; genealogist Colleen Hardman of Newtowngore, County Leitrim, Republic of Ireland; Angus Trumble, director of Australia's National Portrait Gallery in Canberra; and Rob Mitchell of Capetown, owner of the campaign medal awarded to Finlay for his participation as a young lieutenant of British territorial forces in South Africa's Kaffir Wars.

Equally dispersed, but closer to home, are the letters of another little-known Utah War participant, Brevet Maj. Thomas Williams, Fourth U.S. Artillery, the officer detailed to establish Camp Walbach to guard Bridger's Pass, Nebraska Territory, at the end of the Utah conflict. In the late 1950s, LeRoy and Ann Hafen dropped plans to include some of Williams's letters to his wife in their *The Utah Expedition, 1857–1858* and, with Roy Hafen's death in 1985, this material essentially disappeared. In 2008 these letters surfaced, Lazarus-like, thanks to David J. Whittaker, then Curator, Nineteenth-Century Western and Mormon Americana in L. Tom Perry Special Collections at Brigham Young University's Harold B. Lee Library. With the help of Northville, Michigan, researcher Ruth McMahon as well as Detroit archivist Mark Patrick, I was able to access the balance of Major Williams's correspondence in the Detroit Public Library's Burton Historical Collection, a find supplemented by typed transcriptions of some of this material provided by librarian Mary Robinson, Harold McCracken Research Library at Cody, Wyoming's Buffalo Bill Historical Center. My thanks to all of these far-flung professionals.

Several people enriched my understanding of 1st Lt. Joseph C. Ives's war-related exploration of the Colorado River and its Grand Canyon. For access to typescripts of Ives's letters to his wife Cora, I express my appreciation to Peter Michel, director of special collections at the University of Nevada–Las Vegas's Lied Library, and to Kenneth M. Ives (no relation) of Nokesville, Virginia, who transcribed this material and provided photographs of Lieutenant Ives and his wife. Equally helpful has been the diary kept during Ives's journey by his Prussian sketch artist and naturalist Heinrich Balduin Möllhausen. This journal has been unavailable in English, but David H. Miller of Sand Springs, Oklahoma, translated and generously shared it, together with an English version of several of Möllhausen's letters to his wife Carolina. Professor Miller's contribution to my grasp of this aspect of the Utah War is second only to his help with two other events relating to the conflict: the six-hundred-mile route traversed by Capt. Randolph B. Marcy between Fort Bridger and Taos, and the Utah embroilments of the army's Steptoe Expedition during 1854–55.

I thank Steven K. Madsen of Sandy, Utah, who alerted me to the importance of the letters written from the field by Dr. John Strong Newberry, Ives's physician-geologist. With the help of Tad Bennicott, assistant archivist at the Smithsonian Institution's Archives, several of Newberry's letters have enriched this study's discussion of the Utah War's Ives Expedition. Mr. Madsen's published work also provides an understanding of the linkage between Ives's 1858 explorations and those of U.S. Army captain John N. Macomb, who a year later probed the rugged area between Santa Fe and the Green River's junction with the Colorado.

For a better appreciation of Mormon concerns about the Ives Expedition, the surveillance activities of LDS missionary-explorer Jacob Hamblin, and the explorations of Amasa M. Lyman to the Colorado River and Col. William H. Dame and George Washington Bean to the White Mountains, I am indebted to Todd M. Compton of Cupertino, California; Edward Leo Lyman of Leeds, Utah; and Clifford L. Stott of Orem, Utah, respectively.

The quarterly "sanitary" reports of Assist. Surg. John B. Moore, Fifth U.S. Infantry, are accessible in published form, but his personal correspondence from the Utah War remains unexploited. I express my appreciation to Matthew J. Grow, Director of Publications at the LDS church's Historical Department, for alerting me to this material at the Gilder Lehrman Institute of American History at the New-York Historical Society as well as to Tom Mullusky, special collections librarian at that repository.

Also to Dr. Grow, Thomas L. Kane's latest biographer, I am indebted for insights into his complex subject. Also invaluable to my understanding of Kane's Utah War role has been the advice of my intended collaborator, the late Richard D. Poll of Provo. After visiting Philadelphia, Dick urged me to focus on the Kane materials at the American Philosophical Society. He was prescient in doing so; Kane's unpublished memoranda and letter drafts found there provide an unparalleled glimpse into his actions and the Kanesean behavior that Brigham Young and I have dubbed wire-working.

I very much miss Professor Poll, appreciate his guidance in the 1990s, and marvel at the wisdom available in the vast research files he left to the University of Utah's Marriott Library. Thanks also to David Whittaker for access to BYU's trove of Kane family papers, especially Elizabeth's diary and Thomas's reports to President Buchanan. Ms. Polly Armstrong of Stanford University Libraries has been generous in helping me with those of Kane's papers lodged there, especially the invaluable trail diaries covering much of his Utah mission.

To the late Archibald Hanna, Jr., a marine veteran of the Pacific War and founding curator of the Yale Collection of Western Americana, I am indebted for my awareness that a lone but unidentified marine officer accompanied the Utah Expedition's Fifth U.S. Infantry as an observer. Serendipitously, I was able to determine that this was 2d Lt. Robert L. Browning, and through the tenacity of Harold D. Langley of Alexandria, Virginia, I was able to access Browning's Utah reports in the National Archives. Having found an 1852 daguerreotype of Lieutenant Browning, I became the beneficiary of Santa Barbara photographer Roger P. Craton's ability to transform this image into a publishable illustration. To Archie, Harry, and Roger go belated thanks, as well as a posthumous "Semper Fi" to Colonel Hanna.

In 1964, during the early stages of this study, I had the pleasure of reading in the New York Public Library most of the multivolume pocket diaries kept by Capt. John Wolcott Phelps, commander of the Fourth U.S. Artillery's Light Battery B. From inception, my plan was to include segments of this Phelps material to complement the excerpts previously published by the Hafens, and I did so in part 1. In 2011 two heretofore missing Phelps diaries covering the period June–October 1858 surfaced in private hands. Jeffrey Walker, Esq., of Salt Lake City acquired them, and I am grateful for his permission to use portions of his transcriptions while I completed part 2. This material, together with the Phelps diaries in New York and the captain's unexploited personal correspondence at Princeton University's Firestone Library, enabled me to understand one of the Utah Expedition's most able but eccentric officers.

For the little-known Texas aspect of the Utah War involving U.S. senator Sam Houston, Nauvoo Legion major Seth Millington Blair, and Buchanan peace commissioner Ben McCulloch, I am indebted to historian and Houston descendant Madge Thornall Roberts of San Antonio; John B. Bond of Roy,

Utah (Blair's great-great grandson); and Thomas W. Cutrer of Texarkana, Texas, McCulloch's biographer.

Thanks also to Brigham Young University's Dr. R. Devan Jensen for a better understanding of the Mormon Move South and one of its more over-burdened refugees, Cynthia Jane Park Stowell, his family's forebear. In surfacing and sharing the story of Mrs. Stowell's flight toward Provo, if not Sonora, in charge of more than a dozen youngsters including her newborn, Professor Jensen helped me to shed light on the price paid by Mormonism's women and children as well as by the troops involved.

Just as it seemed that the cupboard of unexploited documents was bare, Ephriam D. Dickson III, then curator of Salt Lake City's Fort Douglas Military Museum, alerted me to the typescript of a diary kept by Pvt. James M. Uhler, Company G, Tenth U.S. Infantry, in the holdings of the U.S. Military History Institute at Carlisle Barracks, Pennsylvania. From this lead came access to a variant copy held by Duane Elliott of Cedar Hill, Tennessee. My thanks to Messrs. Dickson and Elliott for their generosity in shedding light on this journal. Since moving to the Museum of the United States Army at Fort Belvoir, Virginia, Mr. Dickson has continued to surface primary sources about little-known units and other anonymous individuals to which he has directed me with unparalleled hunting skills and unfailing generosity.

To Wade Allinson of Ferron, Utah, go my thanks for sharing his fortuitous discovery of the Utah War's least accessible "document." I refer to the cryptic etching on a rock face in the Rafael Swell near Emery County's Cottonwood Wash done by 1st Sgt. Francis Mullins of Company G, Fifth U.S. Infantry, a few weeks before he committed murder and suicide. With this cryptic record, a troubled Frank Mullins left the Utah War's precursor to World War II's ubiquitous graffiti, "Kilroy was here." Apparently some aspects of an army on the march never change.

As with Wade Allinson's discoveries in the field, I am indebted to Duane A. Byland of Eagle Mountain, Utah, and Sgt.-Maj. James F. Martin, U.S.M.C. (Ret'd.) of Tremonton, Utah, for their willingness to share the results of their successful work to pinpoint the sites of Old Camp Floyd and Camp Scott, respectively. Through their skill and all-weather tenacity with metal detectors and trowels on what is now private ranch land, students of the Utah War are now able to locate the winter and summer bivouacs of individual regiments within Albert Sidney Johnston's Utah Expedition and to see some of the material culture they left behind.

One of the surprises associated with editing part 2 has been my receipt of photographs of Utah War participants from their descendants—strangers who somehow become aware of my research and thoughtfully surfaced ancestral images for this study. As often as this has happened, there is still a thrill with the first glimpse of a person about whom I have been researching for decades. I deeply appreciate the willingness of Jon Worthen and Master Sgt. Christopher D. Harlow, U.S. Army (Ret'd.), of Pueblo, Colorado, to volunteer such photographs of Lafayette Shaw (Fay) Worthen and Sgt. George Austin Beardsley of the Volunteer Battalion's Company A, respectively. My inbox runneth over.

Aside from the friends and colleagues who made these special finds possible, I am also indebted for recent leads, suggestions, documents, and inspiration to (alphabetically): Mary (Polly) Aird, Kenneth L. Alford, Curtis R. Allen, Bill Anderson, Lavina Fielding Anderson, Penelope A. Barrott, Gary James Bergera, David M. Carroll, Matthew Catalano, Brad Cole, Jeffrey M. Flannery, Lt. Col. Sherman L. Fleek, Samuel W. Fordyce IV, Lt. Rick Gabbitas, James Gerencser, William (Will) Gorenfeld, Kevin Henson, Harry Hewitt, Scott Hibbard, Michael W. Homer, Albert L. Hurtado, Scott G. Kenney, Todd M. Kerstetter, Michele Margetts, Alan Maschek, Steven L. Mayfield, John Gary Maxwell, M.D., Patricia Moss, Dennis Northcott, Shannon A. Novak, Amy Oakes, Steven L. Richardson, Brent M. Rogers, Joseph Soderborg, Vaughan Stanley, Thomas A. Sutak, Elaine Thatcher, Gordon E. Tolton, John G. Turner, and P. Bradford (Brad) Westwood.

I am especially grateful to historian David L. Bigler of Roseville, California, a colleague whose research about the Utah War also started in the 1950s and whose family connects to the conflict through Jacob Bigler, wartime bishop of Nephi. To Dave I owe my first awareness of Brigham Young's Standing Army of Israel and the significance of the Indian raid on Fort Limhi, as well as a better understanding of the theological drivers behind Young's actions and rhetoric. Thanks to Dave Bigler for these insights and his constructive suggestions as an independent reader for part 1.

One of my greatest obligations is to three historians who during 2014 read and suggested improvements to the entire manuscript of *At Sword's Point, Part 2*. Among them is Dave Miller, who performed this service in addition to his help years earlier with the draft chapters covering the exploits of Captain Marcy and Lieutenant Ives. Richard E. Turley Jr., the LDS church's assistant historian and recorder in 2008–16, read not only part 2 but the entirety of part 1, a clear case of going the extra mile, for which I am deeply grateful. The third such reader is William Grant (Will) Bagley, the KINGDOM IN THE WEST series editor, who steered me to unexploited documents, made invaluable suggestions, spotted errors of fact, and offered alternate interpretations of controversial events. In the process, Will made me a better writer. In 2010, before leaving the University of Oklahoma Press, Robert A. Clark of Pullman, Washington, read the first five chapters of this volume and provided deft guidance for this part of the manuscript, as he had for part 1.

Foremost among those organizations deserving my thanks is the Mormon History Association, especially the members of its Board of Directors with whom I served two non-consecutive three-year terms. Much of *At Sword's Point* took shape (and occasionally paused) while I was in the midst of these wonderful, welcoming colleagues. Although I was privileged to serve as MHA's president during 2010–11, I have a strong sense that I learned more than I led. This study and I are the better for such an experience. I feel the same way about the Utah State Historical Society at Salt Lake City, an organization that I joined in 1963 and now serve as a fellow as well as honorary life member.

Of all these professional benefactors—individual and organizational—none warrants my gratitude more than historian–author–genealogist–newspaper columnist–internet blogger Ardis E. Parshall, an invaluable companion-in-discovery during 1999–2013. Only Bob Clark and Will Bagley were with me longer than Ardis in my efforts to surface the story of what the Utah War was, who was involved, and what they documented.

Transforming my rough manuscript into a publishable typescript was the work of three professionals whose help has been indispensable to moving this long project forward while preserving my sanity. For the wonders they worked, kudos to Ms. Parshall and Sarah Allred of Salt Lake City and Debra Brittain of Santa Barbara.

To Messrs. Clark and Bagley as well as a wise, patient Charles E. Rankin, editor-in-chief of the University of Oklahoma Press, I owe thanks for their wisdom, encouragement, and long-term perspective with respect to my involvement with the KINGDOM IN THE WEST series. I threw in with this merry band in 1996 and feel fortunate indeed to have *At Sword's Point,*

Part 2 as a volume in this landmark series of books about Mormons on the American frontier. Also at the University of Oklahoma Press, thanks to my editor, Steven B. Baker, the possessor of a deft hand and consummate good judgment. I have been blessed to have Ariane C. Smith of Spokane as copy editor and designer of this volume as she was for the first. Galen Schroeder deserves my appreciation for his skill in creating the index for part 2, as does Polly Aird of Seattle, who along the way taught me what a first-rate index should be. To all of these professionals, thanks for their skill in turning a typescript into the quite different reality of a beautiful book worthy of the work that Arthur H. Clark (the man) began in 1902.

Finally, I acknowledge with deep appreciation the continuing support and love of my wife, Patricia H. MacKinnon. Her editorial insights, common sense, and concern for my wellbeing have contributed enormously to the completion of this study as well as to its earlier stages in the 1990s—a long march indeed that has included our relocation from Michigan to the West. To Pat I attribute much of the inspiration and many of the strengths of *At Sword's Point*; responsibility for the shortcomings, unintended as they are, belongs solely with me.

William P. MacKinnon
Montecito, California
February 2015

Editorial Procedures

"Well, well, MacKinnon is a good fellow," said Holmes with a tolerant smile. "You can file it in our archives, Watson. Some day the true story may be told."

Arthur Conan Doyle, *The Adventure of the Retired Colourman*

This volume uses the same editorial methodology employed for the study's first part.[1] Rather than repeat these procedures, the following material explains only a few new editorial challenges peculiar to the documents presented in part 2.

To begin with, there has been a need to understand the significance of both the "Private & Confidential" designator with which Sir William Gore Ouseley marked some of his Utah War diplomatic dispatches from Washington to Lord Clarendon and the means by which he couriered them to London. At stake is a proper assessment of the importance as well as the candor of Ouseley's reports of his sensitive conversations with President Buchanan about prosecution of the Utah War. Buchanan's awareness of this elaborate British system of diplomatic communication means that his own use of the "Private & Confidential" notation signals a need for special consideration of his letters so marked.

Other editorial judgments have run to such mundane matters as descriptive labels for institutions, groups, and even events. Part 2 uses them for the Native peoples from more than a dozen tribes that are part of this story. In most cases I identify such nations by specific name (such as Shoshone or Southern Paiute). When a generalized term is necessary, I have used "American Indian" consistent with the practice of the University of Oklahoma Press,

[1] *At Sword's Point, Part 1*, 29–33.

many academics, and various federal agencies. Because of its familiarity, I use the term "White House" interchangeably with "Executive Mansion" for the name of President Buchanan's residence and office, although the latter was the official designator until Theodore Roosevelt changed it in 1901.

Albert Sidney Johnston's promotion from colonel to brevet brigadier general was dated retroactively for pay and seniority purposes to November 1857 but did not become effective until the spring of 1858 when he signed a new oath of allegiance at Camp Scott. This final step in the promotion procedure followed a prolonged process of executive nomination and senatorial confirmation aggravated by a months-long lag in mail service between Washington and Utah. For part 2 I have described Johnston as colonel until he formally notified the adjutant general of his acceptance and began to use his new rank in April.

As in editing part 1, I have had to pick my way carefully through a plethora of fascinating but bogus Utah War documents beckoning for use by the unwary. These range from the claims of disengaged bystanders clamoring for recognition as heroic participants in the Marcy trek to Mexico to the stories invented by Utah Expedition deserters to cosmetize the circumstances of their departure from the army. Perhaps the most provocative such hazard is the Nauvoo Legion order of 18 April 1858 directing the Mountain Meadows–like execution of a large group of civilian non-Mormon teamsters, an enduring forgery attributed to James Ferguson that surfaced five years after the war to plague its documentary record. Bypassing Peter Sinclair's journal account of the Move South has been another such necessity—in this case because of the document's problematic association with forger Mark Hoffman.

The most complex editorial decisions peculiar to this volume have involved the evaluation and use of the widely dispersed primary materials relating to Thomas L. Kane's Utah mission. Kane generated diaries, essays, and letters either contemporaneously in Utah or within a few months after his return to Philadelphia in June 1858. Much of this material was illegible, encrypted, jumbled, impressionistic, undated, misdated, non-sequential, or fragmentary. Other portions of it are written in Kane's schoolboy French. Determining its likely timing, meaning, and intent has been difficult as well as important. On these editorial judgments have hinged an accurate understanding of Kane's arduous round trip between Salt Lake City and Fort Bridger and his convoluted interactions in those places with Brigham Young, Alfred Cumming, and Albert Sidney Johnston. Similarly, it has been necessary to assess critically the narratives that Kane drafted during a postwar illness for use in a published account of his Utah mission. These essays never became public; like Kane's earlier dispatches to Buchanan, they flowed from ulterior motives as well as the manipulative side of Kane's character.

Equally challenging has been the use of Elizabeth Kane's diary and a substantial body of Utah War–related narratives that she also drafted with an eye to publication. The most intriguing such material generated by Elizabeth described Thomas L. Kane's private meetings with President Buchanan and Brigham Young—unverifiable accounts that have come to us only after passage through the vivid, expansive imaginations of first Thomas and then Elizabeth Kane, a problematic combination in terms of the documents' reliability.

Despite the substantial challenges associated with these Kane family materials, they are uncommonly valuable in understanding Thomas L. Kane's psyche, distinctive operating style, and substantial insider's contribution to the Utah War's resolution. By indirection, these sources also shed light on the behavior, if not gullibility, of key players with whom he interacted.

Some aspects of the Utah War story were multiyear in character. Rather than devote chapters in both volumes to these subjects, I present them in only one for purposes of simplicity and orderliness. Accordingly, although Captain Marcy's trek to New Mexico, Lieutenant Ives's ascent of the Colorado River, the evolution of the LDS Standing Army of Israel, the formation of volunteer units to reinforce the Utah Expedition, and the Mormons' pleas to Sen. Sam Houston all began in 1857 and continued during 1858, I largely confined these events to part 2. Principal exceptions to this methodology for organizing materials are the chronologically sprawling stories of Thomas L. Kane's Utah War involvement and military atrocities committed by both sides.

Although I have contributed substantial narrative comments to introduce chapters, sections, and documents, the war's participants largely speak for themselves. *At Sword's Point* seeks to present a balanced explanation of the Utah War through its participants' voices, not win an editorial argument. I have tried to leave verdicts to the reader's judgment, although on crucial issues or matters of significant historical reinterpretation, my own assessments are evident. In addition, I have provided a concluding essay in narrative form to address what I think are the major questions about which readers are most apt to expect an editorial summing-up, after my nearly sixty years of research and reflection on this subject and these two volumes of primary source material.

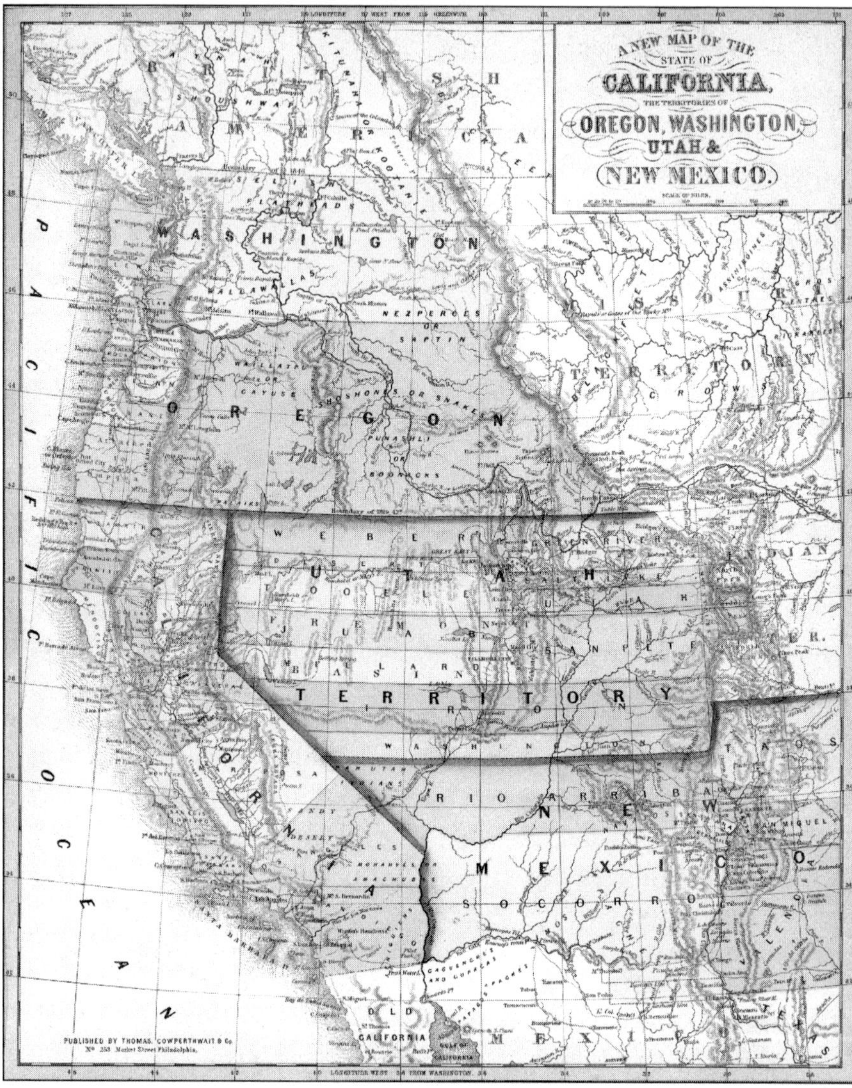

Scope and Sweep: The War's Sprawling Geography

By early 1858 the Utah War's action encompassed virtually the entire trans-Mississippi West with supply lines twelve hundred miles long and more than two thousand miles from Washington. Internationally, Mormon and federal plans impacted the Pacific Coast possessions of Russia and Great Britain as well as northern Mexico, Cuba, the Hawaiian Islands, and Dutch East Indies. *Map by Thomas, Cowperthwait & Company of Philadelphia, 1853, from editor's collection.*

Introduction

Can you point me to that portion of Scriptures in which a man is said to have scattered arrows firebrands & death & then exclaims am I not the spirit.

President James Buchanan to Rev. Smith Pyne[1]

This second and concluding volume of *At Sword's Point* continues the story of the Utah War from January 1858 until the conflict's uneasy resolution during the following summer. As with the 1857 phase of this remarkable territorial-federal confrontation, it is a complex tale rich with the interconnection of individuals, societal forces, and dramatic events that played out in such colorful venues as the Grand Canyon of the Colorado River and the quarterdeck of a British warship off Hawaii. This complexity makes it important to begin an examination of how 1858 unfolded with a brief reprise of the conflict's origins and escalation during 1857.

Our Story Begins: 1857

The year 1857 had opened with Gov. Brigham Young's attempt to use his most influential non-Mormon friend, Thomas L. Kane, as an intermediary with President-elect James Buchanan. Through Kane, a Philadelphia humanitarian, Young sought to extend his term as governor, an appointment that had expired in 1854 but remained in effect through the precarious mechanism of a day-to-day continuance. During the third week of March 1857, less than

[1]Buchanan to Pyne, undated letter written during Buchanan's presidency, accessed 2 March 2004, http://www.antebellumcovers.com/newlist303.doc. Pyne was rector of St. John's Episcopal Church (opposite the White House), where Buchanan frequently attended services but was not a communicant. The biblical verse which the president paraphrases is Proverbs 26:18 (King James version).

a month after Buchanan's inauguration, Kane attempted to make the case for retaining Young in office indefinitely. Kane's effort was burdened by the national furor over Mormon polygamy as well as nearly ten years of conflict between Utah's civil-religious leadership and virtually every department of the U.S. government. Aggravating this friction was the new administration's receipt during 17–20 March of a flurry of negative reports about Young's stewardship and loyalty from President Franklin Pierce's federal appointees in Utah. Almost all of these officials would flee the territory on 15 April 1857, the second such mass departure in less than six years.

At the heart of the problem was Utah's image as a violent, out-of-control territory led by a governor prone to inflammatory, anti-federal rhetoric. Even more corrosive were conflicting philosophies of governance. Governor Young viewed Utah as a millennially focused, quasi-independent theocracy—the "Kingdom of God"—operating under his autocratic, divinely sanctioned and inspired leadership. The U.S. government treated Utah as an American territory intended to function under republican principles as a ward of Congress. Therein lay a disconnect from which a bloody armed confrontation would arise.

By the end of March, Buchanan had privately decided to supersede Young and to send west a successor escorted by a substantial army expedition to re-establish federal authority. Despite the reservations of the general in chief, this concept jelled with the army's 28 May announcement of a Utah Expedition. The 2,500-man force was organized hastily and late at Fort Leavenworth, Kansas Territory, during the summer under the command of Brevet Brig. Gen. William S. Harney. Simultaneously Buchanan continued the search for Utah's new governor. After refusals from multiple prospects, Buchanan appointed Alfred Cumming. A St. Louis–based Indian superintendent from Georgia with mediocre talents, scant executive experience, and limited physical mobility, Cumming had a history of prickly interpersonal relationships and a fondness for alcohol. The conventional wisdom was that Cumming was an unexceptional appointee who had accepted an essential but unmanageable task.

Although Buchanan never formally communicated Cumming's appointment to Young, by late May, if not earlier, intelligence agents had alerted Young to the likelihood that the president would supersede him, as well as to the probability that the War Department would establish a garrison in Utah. Such changes alarmed Young, who interpreted them as precursor to a renewal of the persecution experienced by Mormons in the Midwest that had included the assassination of their founding prophet, Joseph Smith, Jr., in 1844. The governor also dreaded a continuation of the threat to Mormon women experienced during the sojourn of the U.S. Army's Steptoe Expedition in Salt Lake City during the winter of 1854–55.

The result during the summer of 1857 was Young's decision to contest his replacement and to mobilize Utah's territorial militia (Nauvoo Legion); send mounted patrols into Nebraska Territory to monitor the army's westward march and assist Mormon emigrants; and recall European and other missionaries to the Salt Lake Valley. He would also roll up the outlying settlements at Carson Valley, San Bernardino, Las Vegas, and San Francisco; arrange Indian alliances; obtain arms and munitions from California, Missouri, and Great Britain as well as by local manufacture; reinforce the mission at Fort Limhi, Oregon Territory; fortify key mountain passes; and proclaim martial law. The latter decree forbade movement into and across Utah by non-Mormon civilians as well as the approaching Utah Expedition, thereby halting transcontinental migration to the Pacific Coast. Young's proclamation of martial law not only created a nightmarish travel disruption, it was behavior by a sworn territorial governor intolerable to the Buchanan administration. In the midst of these provocations—on 11 September 1857—Mormon troops and Indian auxiliaries in southern Utah committed the war's worst atrocity, the massacre at Mountain Meadows of 120 disarmed non-Mormon emigrants en route to California from Arkansas. There soon followed a series of additional murders throughout the territory, smaller in scale than the unprecedented bloodshed at Mountain Meadows but comparable to the contemporaneous, unrelated carnage in Utah's eastern neighbor, "Bleeding Kansas."

With Mormon awareness in mid-September that the army would push beyond Fort Laramie and an early-October realization that the Utah Expedition might even reach Fort Bridger, if not the Salt Lake Valley, Brigham Young escalated the Nauvoo Legion's aggressiveness. During 3–6 October 1857 the Legion burned Fort Bridger, the Mormon trading post on Blacks Fork, and nearby Fort Supply; and destroyed seventy-six unguarded government supply wagons. There followed multiple raids on army livestock, the burning of grass throughout what is now southwestern Wyoming, and an episodic exchange of gunfire between the Utah Expedition's pickets and mounted patrols of both sides.

The Nauvoo Legion conducted this harassment under written orders from Brigham Young and Lt. Gen. Daniel H. Wells, the Legion's commander. They authorized Legionnaires to kill federal troops if they moved west of Bridger to approach the Salt Lake Valley. Combined with the enormity of the Mountain Meadows massacre and other atrocities that fall, such orders targeting fellow Americans belie 150 years of mythology characterizing the Utah War as a "bloodless" affair.

On 3 November Col. Albert Sidney Johnston, Harney's successor, reached his new command west of the Continental Divide, just within Utah Territory's northeastern frontier at Hams Fork, a tributary of Blacks Fork and Green River. Although the expedition was only thirty-five miles from Fort Bridger, there followed a brutal two-week march to that destination in blizzards and sub-zero weather. The carcasses of more than four thousand draft animals, dragoon mounts, battery horses, and beef cattle littered the army's passage up Blacks Fork. Thus harassed by Legion patrols, plagued by snowstorms, and weakened by the impact of massive animal losses and earlier troop desertions, Johnston overrode the zeal of some of his subordinates. He ordered the expedition into winter quarters at the charred ruins of Fort Bridger, near which he built an enormous bivouac of tents, huts, and dugouts dubbed Camp Scott in honor of the general in chief. There, Utah's new chief justice surveyed his ramshackle quarters, contemplated Brigham Young's actions, and empaneled a federal grand jury that returned treason indictments against Young and virtually the entire Mormon hierarchy.

When news of the Nauvoo Legion's raids on army supply trains reached Washington in mid-November, the result was embarrassment for the Buchanan administration and national alarm over the army's vulnerability, Mormon military capabilities, and the prospect of escalating federal expenditures. Two of Secretary of War John B. Floyd's leading generals recommended a gargantuan expansion of the army—in one case a doubling of its size. In his 8 December 1857 annual message to Congress, President Buchanan presented a more cost-conscious solution to the Mormon problem that involved continued application of force through a four-regiment (20 percent) expansion of the army.

Soon thereafter, on 5 January, Thomas L. Kane departed New York for a mission to Utah via Panama and California. There, for a plethora of complex humanitarian and personal reasons, he hoped to mediate the conflict and prevent further bloodshed. Unasked to do so by either James Buchanan or Brigham Young, Kane resigned his livelihood, made scant provision for the well-being of his wife and two young children, and at his own expense embarked on a hazardous mission of uncertain length and outcome. Kane did so over the objections of his parents and on behalf of a reviled people whose religion and most controversial marital practices he did not share.

If Kane's family was ambivalent and puzzled about his messianic mission, so too was President Buchanan. In March 1857 he had declined to discuss Mormon-federal affairs with Kane, and had met only inconclusively with him in early November. In late December 1857, though, Buchanan altered course and decided to meet with Kane at the urging of Philadelphia's U.S. attorney, James C. Van Dyke, one of Buchanan's most influential political advisors. At least two factors other than Van Dyke's counsel swayed Buchanan's decision: the national uproar in mid-November triggered by news of Mormon resistance to the Utah Expedition, and the return of a truculent Congress to Washington in early December. Legislators were anxious to probe the necessity and execution of a costly, apparently faltering military campaign undertaken to replace Brigham Young without their knowledge or sanction. With the country experiencing its worst economic dislocation in twenty years, Congress was edgy.

From the secret year-end Buchanan-Kane meeting came conflicting understandings of the discussions, especially about the authority under which Kane would travel to Utah and the substance of what he would say and do there. The president viewed the Philadelphian's mission as a personal humanitarian effort undertaken without government standing or financial support and despite Buchanan's cautions about hazards to his personal safety. The perceptions of Kane and his family were quite different than the president's.

As Thomas L. Kane saw it, he headed west with written expressions of presidential good wishes as well as informal authorization to recommend (and withhold), as he saw fit, executive pardons in individual cases. Kane's wife, Elizabeth, was both suspicious and apprehensive. She viewed Buchanan's tepid, limited support for her husband's mission as more a matter of what today's intelligence community calls "plausible deniability" than simple presidential ambivalence. Furthermore, based on her husband's comments, Elizabeth believed Buchanan had promised Kane an attractive but problematic diplomatic appointment upon his return. Judge John K. Kane added an even more extraordinary perception based on what son Thomas told him after visiting Buchanan: he intended to broach to Brigham Young the advisability of Mormon flight from Utah.

Kane's mission was a straw in the wind. If grasped discreetly, his mediation might run to the advantage of a secretive president who seemed to have no plan for resolving a costly, embarrassing Utah conflict beyond massive military pressure. But as neither Van Dyke nor Kane realized, at year-end 1857 Buchanan had a hidden reason for wanting to put Kane and Brigham Young together in early 1858. Unwittingly, both men were to be the instruments for scratching two presidential itches: resolution of the nation's Mormon problem, and James Buchanan's byzantine pursuit of American Manifest Destiny through a series of billiardslike maneuvers.

One can imagine cautious hopes in the Executive Mansion as a newly resigned court clerk boarded a Panama-bound steamer to travel incognito as "Doctor A. Osborne," an itinerant Philadelphia scientist in pursuit of botanical specimens. It was a guise devised by Kane as protection from the anti-Mormon mobs of California as well as the edgy Latter-day Saints in isolated southern Utah. Whether Kane's nom de guerre and assumed persona hoodwinked the equally unemployed banker, William Tecumseh Sherman, aboard S.S. *Moses Taylor* is an intriguing imponderable, especially since this desperate fellow passenger was bent on prosecuting the Utah War from California and would soon become one of the greatest American soldiers of the nineteenth century.

Apostolic and Soldierly Musings

In Salt Lake City, two thousand miles west of James Buchanan's Executive Mansion, Mormon apostle Wilford Woodruff finished the year 1857 and began 1858 as he usually did—by spending time with his journal, one of the great primary sources of Mormon historiography. Woodruff was not a military man; he was the Latter-day Saints' assistant church historian. Unlike apostles Daniel H. Wells, George A. Smith, and John Taylor, who spent time during the Utah War in the midst of the Nauvoo Legion's operational affairs, Woodruff immersed himself in farming, counseling the church's beleaguered leaders, and in recording the history of Mormonism as it unfolded. Woodruff's year-end journal entries provide a glimpse into senior Mormon leaders' views of their armed confrontation with the U.S. government as a religious drama rather than just a military campaign.

In thinking about the year just ending, the apostle concluded, "1857 will be the year on histories page which will be dated the Commencement of the down-fall of the United States For it is during this year that they have entered the field as the open Enemies & persecuters of the saints of the Most High god and have sent an Armey of 2,500 men 1,000 miles for the purpose of laying a foundation for the destruction of the Church of Jesus Christ of Latter Day Saints called Mormons." The next day Woodruff turned to the future with optimism as well as faith: "Let us watch the signs of the times of 1858 and we shall find that the Lord will soon Come out of his hiding place and in his fury he will vex the Nation and in his hot displeasure he will begin to Cut off the wicked and unjust stewards and appoint them their portion with hypocrites and unbelievers. Let the Saints of God prepare for that which is to come."[2]

Not surprisingly, Maj. Fitz John Porter's perspective was far different than Apostle Woodruff's. As Albert Sidney Johnston's adjutant, confidant, and tent mate, Porter was a well-informed army insider. At year-end 1857 he shared thoughts about the campaign with Col. Samuel Cooper, the army's adjutant general in Washington and Secretary Floyd's closest military advisor. In confidence and unofficially, Porter set forth his recommendations for the prosecution of the coming spring move on the Salt Lake Valley, including his enthusiasm for "extermination" of the Latter-day Saints. It was an extreme approach widely suspected by Mormons but not one advocated by Albert Sidney Johnston or even his violence-prone predecessor, General Harney, let alone their civilian masters.

Anticipating that the spring thaw would bring a continuation of guerrilla warfare and then a massive Mormon assault on the Utah Expedition, Porter predicted it would be "an attack never equaled, and will require strong and vigorous action to overcome. They are armed for the fight and no gentle action will quell them, and the rebellion will only be quenched by thorough extermination. They are monsters in minds and morals, their children are worthy of their sires, and all from their youth are familiar with murder, robbery, and crimes of the darkest kind, and unless exterminated,

[2]Kenney, ed., *Wilford Woodruff's Journal*, 31 December 1857–1 January 1858, 5:145–51.

the country will be infested with highway robbers and assassin, a species of livelihood their religion inculcates, while their system encourages the migration of scoundrals to this land. This people . . . deserve no mercy at the hands of Government."[3]

What's Past Is Prologue: 1858

And so Washingtonians, Philadelphians, Camp Scott's troops, Legionnaires in Echo Canyon, and residents of Salt Lake City made their traditional New Year's Day calls on friends, comrades-in-arms, co-religionists, and neighbors. They did so oblivious to the burdens carried by many of the Utah War's principals: a president maneuvering to turn an unprecedented political-military muddle to his advantage; a general in chief tasked with a fool's errand intriguing to Great Britain's diplomatic establishment; a seaborne reformer seeking to prove himself while preventing further bloodshed; a frustrated army colonel unaware that he was to become a brigadier while possibly losing his command; and a superseded but defiant territorial governor seeking the tactical advantage and divine guidance to lead his again-beleaguered people to millennial triumph.

It was a scene of vivid human stories in addition to its broad geographical sweep. Participants included an eclectic mix of heroes, bravos, and villains. Among those involved were Texas's Sam Houston, helping Mormonism on the floor of the U.S. Senate while draped in a Cherokee blanket; Mormon and federal Indian agents maneuvering in the wilderness for tribal allegiances; former Texas Rangers serving both sides; frontiersmen Jim Bridger and Kit Carson scouting for the U.S. government; Jenny Goodale, the Shoshone princess who endured the most arduous winter march in American military history; and guerrilla-in-waiting William C. Quantrill, honing his skills as an army teamster, camp cook, and card sharp. It included thousands of Mormon noncombatants, streaming south from the Salt Lake Valley in the continent's greatest flow of refugees since the American Revolution; 1st Lt. Joseph Christmas Ives, who ascended the Colorado River to lead unwittingly the Anglo rediscovery of the Grand Canyon; 2d Lt. William H. F. ("Rooney") Lee, who dropped out of Harvard for the action in Utah over

[3]Porter to Cooper, 31 December 1857, Letters Received, Records of the Adjt. Gen., RG 94, National Archives and Records Administration (hereafter NARA).

his distinguished father's objections; 2d Lt. Robert L. Browning, the U.S. Marines' one-man contribution to an otherwise all-army campaign; and ubiquitous guide Benjamin Franklin Ficklin, Utah's interim U.S. marshal and a subsequent owner of Thomas Jefferson's Monticello. There was also John C. Bennett, former assistant president of the LDS church, who lobbied for an army commission from the perch of an Iowa chicken ranch; Russian tsar Alexander II, who reacted to rumors of a Mormon rush to the Pacific Coast by trying to sell Alaska; and Queen Victoria, who responded to speculation about the same threat by creating the crown colony of British Columbia while sending the Royal Navy to protect the Kingdom of Hawaii.

Here was a wartime atmosphere in which the exotic flourished—one in which President Buchanan was virtually besieged by amateur strategists of wildly varying stripe: Elizabeth Craig, a vivacious Georgia widow who moved into the White House to pursue matrimony while urging the summary execution of Brigham Young; James Arlington Bennet, an eccentric Brooklyn cemetery developer and inactive Nauvoo Legion major general; and "Captain" Walter Murray Gibson, a charming felon of ambiguous background bent on arranging a presidentially sponsored Mormon exodus to an island in the Dutch East Indies. Perhaps most unusual of Buchanan's unsolicited visitors was William Smith, erratic brother of Mormonism's martyred founder.

With hindsight, even those American military men who were uninvolved bystanders lent a certain flavor of opportunism, desperation, and adventure to the conflict from its sidelines. As was the case with civilian Thomas L. Kane, this later-famous group of former or active army officers viewed the possibility of entering the Utah War as the ideal remedy for boredom, unemployment, or a stalled career. Small wonder that as 1858 opened, these talented officers strained with thousands of other adventurers to cast off their frustrations and restlessness to join the fray in Utah.

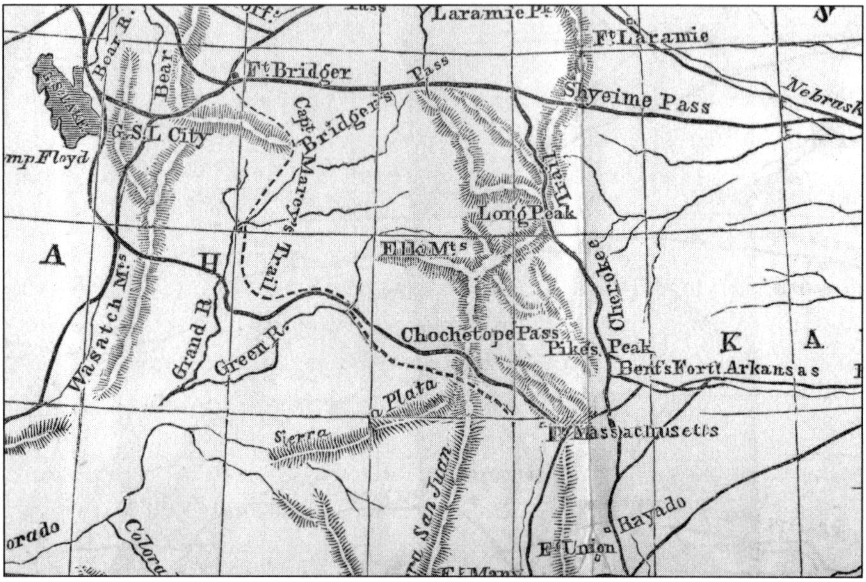

Captain Marcy's Trek,
Fort Bridger, Utah Territory, To Taos, New Mexico

From 27 November to 18 January, Marcy's all-volunteer detachment of sixty-three soldiers and civilians trekked six hundred miles down the spine of the continental divide to Fort Massachusetts just north of Taos. The most arduous winter march in American military history, it was undertaken to buy a thousand horses and mules essential for the army's spring move on the Salt Lake Valley. On this southbound march, Marcy lost one soldier; during the return by a more easterly route (the Cherokee Trail), three civilian herders died in an April blizzard. *Map detail from Marcy's* The Prairie Traveler *(New York, 1859).*

Chapter 1

"Great Disaster Might Befall the Command"
War Spreads to New Mexico

I would have cheerfully given at one time all I have in the world to have been safe out of the mountains. I never during the course of my life suffered so much mental agony.

Capt. Randolph B. Marcy to Nellie Marcy, 26 January 1858

I may, if practicable, create a diversion in your favor by throwing a column of men, not less than 800 into the country of the Utah Indians, who are becoming impudent. A rumor has reached me [in Santa Fe] that these Indians are being tampered with by the Mormons, and I am inclined to believe it.

Brevet Brig. Gen. John Garland to Col. Albert Sidney Johnston, 24 January 1858

As 1857 passed into 1858, events unfolded rapidly, illustrating in the process the breadth of the Utah War's geographical sweep. None of these episodes did so more dramatically and with a higher cost in lives than Capt. Randolph B. Marcy's 1,500-mile trek from Fort Bridger to New Mexico and back. Marcy's was the most arduous winter march in American military history. Through this trek, the war spilled into New Mexico Territory and beyond.

On 24 November 1857, Albert Sidney Johnston had ordered Marcy and a small detachment of regulars to Taos to ensure the Utah Expedition's survival as well as its mobility. Marcy's mission was to purchase two thousand Spanish mules and sheep, as well as a supply of salt. Although a vastly experienced western explorer, Marcy and others underestimated the rigors of such a trek in winter.

Among the most over-optimistic of the Utah Expedition's officers was Capt. John H. Dickerson, the quartermaster whose prescient 24 November assessment of the need for horses, mules, and sheep had spurred Johnston to order Marcy to New Mexico later that day. Unfortunately, in the process of providing advice on procurement, Dickerson placed Marcy in harm's way by giving Johnston assurances about the trek's feasibility and duration that were grossly wrong on all counts. Without firsthand knowledge of the terrain, weather, or Mormon military intentions, the quartermaster commented, "The route from here to New Mexico is believed to be entirely practicable at this season of the year. Herds of sheep have been brought through in the winter season, or, at least, started sufficiently early to get to Henry's fork by the last of April. And there does not appear to be any obstacle to our having animals brought through by the 15th of May, and arrive here in good condition. There are guides here, familiar with the route, who are willing to conduct the party, if one should be sent."[1]

On 20 November, uncertain if he would actually be ordered to New Mexico, Marcy had reassured his daughter Nellie, "We have a long winter before us and shall no doubt find it exceedingly dull, but if I remain here I shall read a great deal. If I go I shall be much more comfortable there than here."[2] Capt. Jesse A. Gove was so oblivious to what his brother officer would face that he tasked one of his corporals who had volunteered to accompany Marcy with bringing back a New Mexican pony for his young son, then in New Hampshire.[3]

Equally unforeseen was the consternation that a rumored Mormon-Ute-Navajo alliance would create when speculation about it reached New Mexico coincident with Marcy's arrival in Taos. It was an alarm that would draw Indian agent Christopher "Kit" Carson into a role in the Utah War that has been largely unrecognized.

---

[1]Dickerson to F. J. Porter, "The Utah Expedition," House Exec. Doc. 71, 100–102.

[2]Marcy to Mary Ellen (Nellie) Marcy, 20 November 1857, McClellan Papers, Library of Congress (hereafter LC).

[3]Gove to Mrs. Gove, 30 November 1857, in Gove, *The Utah Expedition,* 102.

Getting Up a Private Stampede: Marcy Family Anxieties

If at Fort Bridger Captain Marcy seemed unconcerned about his safety, his wife and older daughter in New England were apprehensive, even without knowing that a mission to New Mexico was in the offing. A week after news of Lot Smith's raid had reached the Atlantic Coast, word of Mary and Nellie Marcy's anxiety had drifted to the captain's protégé, George B. McClellan, who had resigned his army captaincy on 16 January 1857 to become chief engineer and then vice president of the Illinois Central Railroad.

Eager to calm his mentor's family while rekindling his romance with twenty-seven-year-old Nellie, McClellan wrote to Mrs. Marcy, confident that she would share his letter with her daughter. McClellan's reassurances from Chicago reflected how little the nation then understood the Utah Expedition's peril, the readiness with which Americans demonized Mormons, and the eagerness of a former officer to re-enter the army for the glory of the campaign in Utah.

McClellan to Mary M. Marcy, 21 November 1857, McClellan Papers, LC.

I am sure that you & Miss Nellie must now be more or less anxious because the Capt. is so far away & in such a place, & I feel that a letter from an old friend will be acceptable to both of you.

It is my usual hour of leisure now—after midnight—so I can afford some time to write to friends whom I embrace so much. Candidly & sincerely I think that you need not be at all alarmed about affairs in Utah—the result will probably be that the Army will winter on Bear River unless it is found that the Mormon opposition vanishes into the air. In the final case they will remain where they are until reinforcements reach them in the summer. If there is fighting then the result cannot be doubtful—it will require but little effort on the part of our old set to dissipate these fanatics. The great reasons for writing [to you] at all about the matter is that I saw in one of the papers a day or two past a notice of the fact that you had received letters not very encouraging from the Capt., & I feared that you two women would amuse yourselves by getting up a private stampede for which there can be no necessity. If affairs take a turn at all serious I have determined to give up my present position, with all its advantages of high pay &c, & re-enter the service at least until the trouble is over. I cannot bear the idea of my old friends being in campaign without me.

Do let me hear from you. Tell Nell I want to hear what mischief she has been at lately. Whenever you are low spirited write to me.

Having received encouragement, McClellan undertook to write directly to Nellie. Again he offered assurances of the army's safety—this time somewhat playfully and chauvinistically—while shedding additional light on the growing uneasiness of American attitudes toward the Utah War. McClellan wrote on 8 December, the day that James Buchanan sent his first annual message to Congress. It is unlikely that McClellan had read the full text of the president's message, although rumors and early reports of Buchanan's intent to expand the army had probably reached Chicago and caught McClellan's attention.

McClellan to Mary Ellen (Nellie) Marcy, 8 December 1857, McClellan Papers, LC.

Every one in turn is but fair, Nelly, so I will write to you this time. Your mother's letter & your own reached me this evening. As they were written on "my day" I suppose I ought to report them as very acceptable birthday presents—acceptable they certainly were.[4] What a pair of foolish frightened women you are. I am half ashamed of you. A soldier's daughter & a soldier's wife scared half to death on account of a march of a few hundred miles [to Utah] against a set of heathenish vagabonds! Has not the Captain often been through scenes far more dangerous than this will be? Were not he, & I, & 88 others scalped, & everything else once before?[5] Do not borrow trouble—heaven knows it comes often enough without one making it.

I would rather make a dozen campaigns in Utah than one in Florida.[6] You thought but little of that because it was an old story. Indians & Everglades were household words in the Army. Both of you had seen Indians & many of your friends had served in Florida, but because Utah is far away & a new thing, because you believe that very vulgar antagonist Brother Brigham to be something more than the ordinary run of man, his Danites (I'll wager them to be as cowardly a lot of cattle thieves as ever went unharnassed) a species of anthropology, you are very unhappy. . . .[7]

---

[4]McClellan turned thirty-one on 3 December 1857.

[5]A reference to lurid press accounts about Marcy's and McClellan's 1852 expedition to explore the Red River of Louisiana and Texas.

[6]Marcy and the Fifth Infantry had been fighting Seminoles when ordered from Florida to the Utah Expedition in May 1857.

[7]In a subsequent letter to McClellan, the Utah Expedition's Major Porter would use similar language: "The Mormons are an infernal set of cowards like all assassins." Porter to McClellan, 28 February 1858, McClellan Papers, LC.

That the Army will experience discomfort, cold, & perhaps even privation is possible. That the monotony of a winter camp in those distant regions may be less pleasant than the gaiety of Washington is very certain. That there is danger in Utah is very probable, but to them it is [like] walking down [New York's] Broadway, between the omnibuses & the dozens of leaves falling on one's head. There is not much more in the one than the other. Little Lady, I have seen you much alarmed in crossing from the Battery to Governor's Island [in New York Harbor]. How much real danger was there then?

Now Mrs. M. & Nell—no more of this stampede. It is very natural, but it is nonsense. There are some 1500 gallant men in that Army, led by officers as good as any that ever served. Can any great harm befall such men? Do you not well know what they are capable of doing, what privations they can cheerfully endure & what odds they can overcome? Do you not know as well as I do that should the very worst that can be imagined happens the Capt. stands as good a chance as anyone, & far better than many, & that the chances are a thousand to one in favor of any individual? I do not think Brother B[righam] will fight. I think that if he does fight, he will be soundly whipped, & I have a lively faith that my friend Marcy will come out of the affair safe & with great credit.[8]

Laying Up High and Dry: Captain Marcy's Volunteers

The soldiers who volunteered to accompany Captain Marcy shared his lack of concern about the hardships ahead. They were drawn to Marcy's national reputation as an explorer-leader and repelled by the boredom and discipline of garrison life—what correspondent Albert G. Browne called "the prospect of inactivity throughout the Winter." When the call for volunteers went out to the Utah Expedition's regular infantry regiments, the response was extraordinary. In the Tenth's Company A alone, every private stepped forward.[9] One of the Tenth's non-volunteers, Pvt. James M. Uhler of Company G, viewed their prospects wistfully and wholly unrealistically: "They calculate to get across to Fort Taos, N.M., in twenty-one days and then have a good time laying up high and dry in good warm barracks with comfortable fire and plenty to eat and drink until spring while we will have

[8]McClellan's phrase "great credit" and his assessment that Young would not fight resonated with Marcy's own language about his New Mexico assignment.

[9][Browne], "Late from the Utah Expedition," Dispatch, 26 November 1857, *New-York Daily Tribune*, 18 January 1858.

to nearly starve and perhaps freeze in this cold country. Well, so much for wanting to be a soldier."[10]

Originally Marcy expected his detachment to include three officers and one hundred men, the strength of an infantry company. Instead he was to be the only officer commanding a total of sixty-three people, including himself: forty-one soldiers (sixteen from the under strength Fifth Infantry and twenty-five from the Tenth) and twenty-two civilians. The identity of these people has been one of the mysteries of the Utah War, notwithstanding their remarkable ordeal. At the end of 1858 even the secretary of war muddled the number of people who had accompanied Marcy to New Mexico, and he never mentioned their names.[11] In many respects, the members of Marcy's detachment were to remain as anonymous as the troops in Lt. Col. Barnard E. Bee's independent Battalion of U.S. Volunteers.

Of Marcy's troops, historians are aware that Corp. Ralph Pike was among them and would become the most famous casualty of the Utah War as well as the catalyst for the longest-running case in Utah's criminal justice system. Twenty years later another member, Pvt. William Gentles, would mortally bayonet Sioux chief Crazy Horse in 1877. Little else is known about the other thirty-eight enlistees, although Marcy provided one tantalizing tidbit in telling his wife, "I have a man in our party who has been a Mormon at Salt Lake but left them after being robbed of all he possessed and is now returned to try to get his property again. He tells us many things which shows them to be very bad people."[12] Among the twenty-two civilians in

[10]Uhler Diary, undated entry, p. 23, typescript in editor's possession courtesy of Mrs. Vernona G. Elliott.

[11]In his annual report, oblivious to the participation of one woman (Jenny Goodale) and wrong about the number of guides, Floyd wrote of "a detachment of men to New Mexico" and described it as "a command of forty enlisted men, and twenty-five mountain men, besides packers and guides." "Annual Report of the Sec. of War (1858)," 7. The Tenth's Private Uhler thought that Marcy left Fort Bridger with thirty-two rather than forty enlistees. Marcy added to the confusion by stating in a dispatch written midway through his trek that he had a total of seventy men in his detachment. In writing about his experience years later, Marcy used a headcount nearly matching the sixty-three people detailed by special orders no. 50 of 24 November 1857, the directive that served as his expedition's charter. This document is the definitive source for the size of the group and provides the names of the military people and guides involved but not those of the packers and herders.

[12]Pike's 1859 assassination in Salt Lake City and the search for his killer is most recently examined in Sadler, "The Spencer-Pike Affair," 79–93. A probing analysis of the traditional story of Gentles's responsibility for Crazy Horse's violent death is Dickson, "Crazy Horse: Who Really Wielded the Bayonet that Killed the Oglala Leader?" 2–10. For the unidentified former Mormon in the detachment, see Marcy to Mary M. Marcy, 25 January 1858, McClellan Papers, LC.

the detachment, the names of only five people have survived: prominent frontiersmen-guides Jim Baker and Tim Goodale; Goodale's Shoshone wife, Jenny; Mariano Medina; and Miguel Alona.[13]

Marcy's was an eclectic group of infantrymen, civilians, European immigrants, native-born Americans, Caucasians, Hispanos, and an American Indian who was also the detachment's sole woman. Their backgrounds and postwar experiences mirrored those of the Utah Expedition's troops and civilian camp followers generally, even in the sense that one of Marcy's soldiers returned from New Mexico to a military insane asylum, some would stand trial before courts martial later in their careers, and others would die on Civil War battlefields. What set Marcy's troops apart from their peers was their willingness to volunteer and ability to endure extreme hardships under superb leadership.

On 24 November Johnston's headquarters issued Captain Marcy's eagerly awaited orders, and he left Fort Bridger three days later.[14]

Sincere Thanks to the Almighty: Marcy's Southbound Trek

The only firsthand accounts of what Marcy's command experienced during its early winter trek to New Mexico are the several narratives written by Captain Marcy during 1858 and over the subsequent three decades.[15]

The four official reports that Marcy generated during 1858 varied in length as he tailored them for diverse readers. All of this material appeared in published government documents. In addition, a few days after arriving in New Mexico, Marcy wrote shorter, private letters to his immediate family, and in 1859, he included several vignettes of his New Mexico experience in

[13]For biographical material about Tim and Jenny Goodale, see McGill, *Rediscovered Frontiersman: Timothy Goodale.*

[14]Special Orders No. 50, Head Quarters, Army of Utah, 24 November 1857, Records, U.S. House Committee on Military Affairs, RG 233, NARA. A published version of this order, without the names of individuals assigned to Marcy's command, appears in Hamilton, "History of the Mormon Rebellion, 1856–57," 4:590–91. An analysis of the bogus claims of participation in this march by James J. DeForrest and James Sweeny appears in MacKinnon, "Loose in the Stacks," 66–67, 81nn69 and 70.

[15]By the end of January 1858 a thirdhand account based on remarks by Tim Goodale had appeared in the Santa Fe newspaper. "Latest News from Utah—Arrival of Capt. Marcy from Fort Bridger," Dispatch, *Santa Fe Weekly Gazette,* 30 January 1858, 2/1, transcription in Hollon Papers, Canaday Center, University of Toledo.

Captain Marcy's Detachment
en Route to New Mexico, December 1857

Hampered by deep snow in the mountains, Marcy proceeded slowly with teams of soldiers to break trail for the rest of the detachment and their animals. Rationed for a trek of thirty-five days, Marcy survived on mule meat for more than fifty. Their rescuers from Fort Massachusetts were shocked when they saw how emaciated and ragged the troops were. Marcy's superb leadership and success drew unusual public recognition from General Scott. *Engraving from Marcy's reminiscences* Thirty Years of Army Life on the Border *(New York, 1866).*

a travel guide that he published commercially with the War Department's sanction.[16]

Marcy's most comprehensive narrative was the long, exciting account that he published as several chapters in his autobiography shortly after the Civil War, a conflict in which he rose to brigadier general while serving on

[16]For his various official reports, written in 1858, see Marcy to Cooper, 2 January; McDowell/Scott, 23 January; Porter, 12 June; Floyd, 25 November; all in Floyd, "Annual Report of the Sec. of War (1858)," 40–41, 187–95, 220–23; Marcy, *The Prairie Traveler,* 98–131. The best chronology, summary description, and itinerary for the southbound and northbound legs of Marcy's trek, as well as reprints of most of his official reports, is White, "Randolph B. Marcy, 1858," 183–211. The most reliable modern, on-the-ground assessments of landmarks and trail segments associated with this journey are to be found in the decades-long work of three historians who are also hikers and trail preservationists: Jack W. Nelson of Montrose, Colo., David H. Miller of Sand Springs, Okla., and Jack E. Fletcher of Sequim, Wash. See especially Nelson, "Marcy's Ordeal along the North Branch of the Old Spanish Trail," 28–30, and *Forgotten Pathfinders.*

the staff of McClellan, who was then his son-in-law and commander of the Union's Army of the Potomac. In this 1866 account, Marcy was able to quote from a trail journal (since lost) while providing details, anecdotes, and even names unmentioned eight years earlier in his official reports.[17]

That version, *Thirty Years of Army Life on the Border*, is easily available elsewhere, but what appears below are three quite different narratives: Marcy's 27 December 1857 field dispatch seeking aid from the post commander at Fort Massachusetts; his letter to daughter Nellie on 26 January written soon after arrival in Taos; and a rarely encountered Marcy magazine article published in February 1888, shortly after his death at age 75.

Marcy's note of 27 December was written exactly a month after he departed Fort Bridger; it pleaded for provisions, shoes, and animals at a point when his expedition was at the end of its tether. The message was intended for an officer whose name, rank, and regiment were unknown to Marcy; all that he understood was that this officer commanded a post that was crucial to his mission—Fort Massachusetts, an isolated garrison named after his native state and sited in the shadow of Mount Blanco at the north end of New Mexico's San Luis Valley. On the day that he wrote, Marcy and packer Miguel Alona had ascended a peak from which Alona was able to point out a dip in a distant range of snow-covered mountains that was key to their survival, Cochetopa Pass.[18] Once successfully through the pass about a week later, Marcy selected the expedition's three strongest mules, assigned them to Alona and Medina, and dispatched them to courier his letter to Fort Massachusetts.

Marcy to "Sir," 27 December 1857, Transmitted as Enclosure for Bowman to Nichols, 8 January 1858, Letters Received, hq Dept. of New Mexico, rg 393, nara.

I am bound for New Mexico on very important business for the Army for Utah and I have nearly exhausted my subsistence[,] my Animals are broken down and I leave a large percentage on the road daily. I shall soon be reduced

[17]Marcy, "Expedition across the Rocky Mountains," 198–221.

[18]To his presumed rescuers, Marcy described his location as "Camp on Eagle Tail River about 30 miles west of Roche-Tope [Cochetopa] Pass," in what is now Colorado. David H. Miller notes that the maps of the 1850s used the term "Eagle Tail" for a variety of streams and rock formations in this general area. Based on Marcy's indication of his distance from Cochetopa Pass, Miller believes that he was then camped near the junction of Razor and Tomichi Creeks. Miller, e-mail message to MacKinnon, 28 July 2013.

> to [eating] my mules for subsistence all of which has been brought about by being obliged to leave Fort Bridger with jaded mules but the best that could be obtained. I shall continue to move slowly on as long as my mules last and I desire you to send out subsistence for my command for ten (10) days. I have seventy (70) men.[19] I will also thank you to send me some Animals for some few of my men to ride who have frozen their feet and have become sick (six or 8). Ten or twelve pair of large shoes and stockings are much needed. I have encountered snow about 2 feet deep for the last (100) miles and I am unable to get any grass for my Animals so that you will perceive they cannot last but a few days longer without forage. If I find I am to loose [*sic*] them all I shall stop and kill them and await relief from you, but if they hold out I shall push forward as far as possible towards your post. My men have suffered much from over work and we shall all look forward with great anxiety for relief from you.
>
> The snow is light and with fresh Animals there will be no difficulty in coming to us particularly if the Animals have a little grain. I shall follow the trail made by the bearer Mary Ann.[20] So that the party that comes to us Cannot miss us one or both of the men I send will return with the party. You will be able to learn more particulars from Mary Ann.

On 7 January Marcy's couriers reached Fort Massachusetts. A week later they and their rescuers rejoined the main party at the edge of the San Luis Valley, and on 18 January they all reached the safety of the fort commanded by Capt. Andrew W. Bowman, Third U.S. Infantry.

By 26 January Marcy was in Taos, where he wrote to daughter Nellie after sending summary reports of his trek to Gen. Winfield Scott and his wife, Mary. To Nellie the captain communicated the impressions of a

---

[19]Why Marcy indicated a strength of seventy rather than sixty-three is a mystery, especially since his narratives in later years approximated the authorized headcount. Marcy may have used an approximate round number, or he may have deliberately exaggerated his actual numbers in order to ensure that his rescuers brought adequate provisions.

[20]Medina had several nicknames, including "Mary Ann" and "Marianne." That Marcy mentioned him by name twice in his letter but did not identify Miguel Alona as the second courier is puzzling, as is Marcy's willingness to pass over the extent to which Jim Baker and Medina, his official guides, failed in locating Cochetopa Pass. For example, in an essay on big game hunting that Marcy published in *Outing* during November 1887, just before the appearance of his "Ramblings in the West" piece, he again omitted reference to Miguel Alona, but described Baker, who by then was famous, as "a man of very little education, but with fair natural ability, and a generous, noble-hearted specimen of the trapper type, who would make any sacrifice for a friend." In the same essay he heaped praise on Medina as "another of my mountain guides [who] was a half-breed named Mariano. . . . He was a capital guide, a successful hunter, and full of ready resources for every emergency." Marcy, "Guides, Hunters, and Trappers," 136–37. After the Utah War, Medina became even better known as the founder of Loveland, Colorado, while Alona all but disappeared from historical notice. Gates, *Mariano Medina: Colorado Mountain Man.*

MARIANO MEDINA,
MARCY GUIDE AND COURIER
Although he earlier provided intelligence to the Mormons, Medina (with Jim Baker and Tim Goodale) guided Captain Marcy's trek from Fort Bridger to his native New Mexico. When they failed to find Cochetopa Pass into the San Luis Valley, obscure mule skinner Miguel Alona located it to save the detachment from disaster. Medina later couriered urgent dispatches to Bridger, reporting Marcy's safe arrival, fears of a Mormon-Indian alliance, and General Garland's offer to reinforce Johnston from New Mexico. Immediately after the war, "Marianne" Medina returned south to found Loveland, Colorado. *Photo ca. 1870 courtesy of Henry E. Huntington Library, San Marino, Calif.*

survivor beginning to enjoy the rudimentary comforts offered by tiny Taos after experiencing a near-fatal ordeal in the wilderness. He also returned to the familiar theme of his disgust with the family separations inherent in frontier army postings.

MARCY TO MARY ELLEN (NELLIE) MARCY,
26 JANUARY 1858, HOLLON TRANSCRIPTIONS, CANADAY CENTER,
UNIVERSITY OF TOLEDO, AND MCCLELLAN PAPERS, LC.

I wrote a letter to your mother yesterday and as I have a little leasure time this evening I will devote it to my darling Nelly:

Since my arrival here I have been very busy indeed in purchasing horses and mules so that I have hardly had time to write or do anything else except eat, which I have done a great deal of ever since I lived upon mule meat. It seems as if I should never make amends for the poor fare I had upon the march. I am staying with a merchant here who gives me a nice carpeted room with sofa and other civilized furniture and you cannot imagine how much I enjoy it after sleeping and living out doors for six months. On our march over the mountains I had no tent for a great part of the distance and we camped in the cold open air and I generally made my bed in 3 or 4 foot of snow. I labored very hard as well as my men or we should never have got through and for two weeks I considered it very doubtful if I ever saw the faces of my darling families again. But most providentially we were enabled to conquer the formidable difficulties we had to contend with and are at length safe. I would have cheerfully given at one time all I have in the world to have been safe out of the mountains. I never during the whole course of my life suffered so much mental agony, and I believe I lost (20) pounds of flesh during two weeks.[21] I knew I was responsible for the lives of 70 men and I really had serious fears that all would perish, yet I never let them know there was the least danger and they all behaved most nobely, seeming to have the utmost confidence in my ability to carry them through safe. Poor fellows, they little knew the danger they were in.

We shall not start back until the snow goes off and shall take another and better route. There will be no danger in returning in the spring and I expect to have a pleasant trip.

You cannot imagine how much I want to see your dear face again and press you to my heart. This separation is most desolate and I every day regret being in the army where I have to lead such a miserable life. I find the service more and more disagreeable every day.

The mail leaves in a few minutes and I must close with ten thousand tender embraces for yourself, dear mother and sister. Ever your fond father.

Although lacking the immediacy of Marcy's letters to family and his official reports, the captain's 1888 magazine piece has several merits: thirty more years of perspective; the author's access to all of his previously published accounts, and his ability to draw upon whatever unpublished information and memories had come to him since mid-century. With the space limitations of magazine format confronting him, what Marcy produced for publication as "Ramblings in the West" was a distillation of what he then considered the highlights of his life's greatest leadership challenge. It was to be his last word on the subject.

Marcy, "Ramblings in the West," *Harper's New Monthly Magazine*, February 1888, 397–405.

We reached Fort Bridger about the middle of November [1857], having been nearly four months upon the road. This, with the destruction of our trains, consumed the greater part of our winter supplies, and as they could not be replenished from the Missouri River before the following June, General

[21]Years later, Marcy described his total weight loss during the fifty-one days of the southbound trek as forty pounds.

Johnston, the commander, determined to send a detachment directly over the mountains to New Mexico, from whence it was believed supplies could be obtained earlier than from further east.

I was detailed to conduct this expedition, and with an old mountain guide [Jim Baker] and forty enlisted men, with sixty-six pack-mules, we left Fort Bridger on the 24th [27th] of November, and arrived at the base of the mountains near Grand River without difficulty, finding but little snow, and plenty of grass for our animals for the first 200 miles. But in advance of us the prospect did not appear so encouraging, as the lofty peaks of the Rocky Mountains rising into the clouds directly across our course were covered with snow. As from this point onward we encountered the most formidable obstructions, perhaps the mention of a few incidents relative thereto may not overtax the reader's indulgence.

We here met with a band of Digger Ute Indians, and endeavored to hire their chief to guide us to the summit of the mountains, offering him the price of four horses. But he refused, saying he would not attempt it for everything we possessed; that he crossed these mountains in the autumn and found snow two feet deep then, but it might be six feet now. He would therefore advise us to remain with him through the winter, or go back where we came from, as we would inevitably perish if we continued on.

Notwithstanding his gloomy prediction, we resumed our march the following day, but soon struck snow that materially impeded our progress, and it continued to increase as we advanced, until after a few days it became so deep that our mules could no longer wade through it, and obliged me to place the men in advance to break a track for them.

The snow at this time was five feet deep, and so dry and light that a man could not walk upright without sinking to his waist, at every step; neither could snow-shoes be used; and the only alternative was for the leading men to lie down and crawl over the snow, placing their hands and feet in the same holes, so that when four or five had started in single file the track bore up the others walking upright, and after all had passed, the snow became sufficiently packed to support the mules. Thus we struggled on at the rate of only three or four miles a day, until at length our provisions were consumed, and our poor animals, having no forage but bitter pine leaves [needles], began to falter and die from starvation. But they thus secured us from starvation, as we had no other sustenance for fifteen days save the lean flesh cut from their dead carcasses. We had no sugar, tea, coffee, salt, or tobacco, but suffered most for want of the last two.

While thus forcing our way onward, and encouraged by the confident assurances of our guide that we would soon reach the summit of the mountains, one of our herders, a half-breed Mexican, who was accidentally picked up just as we were leaving Fort Bridger, came to me, and said if I was aiming for the "Cochetopa" Pass, we were then going directly away from it; that he had been there before, and was familiar with the country.[22]

This startling announcement, as may be imagined, caused me most serious apprehension and alarm, as up to that time I had placed implicit reliance upon the knowledge of our guide, whom I at once called up and questioned closely, and he finally admitted that as he had never passed over these mountains except in summer, their appearance now, enveloped in deep snow, was so different from what it was whenever he had seen them before that he was not altogether certain he was upon the right course; still he believed he was correct.

This evidence of a lack of confidence on his part was to me a matter of the most intense perplexity and anxiety, as I had the best reasons for believing the pass we were aiming for to be the only one for several hundred miles where these mountains could be crossed in midwinter. Indeed, General [John C.] Fremont, some years before this, in the winter season attempted the passage of this range of mountains forty miles south of the Cochetopa Pass, and lost all of his animals and several of his men, obliging him to abandon the enterprise and return to Taos, the point of his departure. In view of the momentous consequences involved in the dilemma, I asked the herder if he was absolutely certain as to the correctness of his statement. If so, and he was willing to act as guide, I would give him fifty dollars in addition to his wages.[23] "But," I added, "If at any time I discover you are not leading us right, I shall hang you to the first tree we come across as certain as you are living." He replied that he was willing to risk his neck upon it, and he was received as our guide from that time, and doubtless saved all our lives, as without him we would all inevitably have starved to death.

Shortly after this, from the summit of an elevated peak, he pointed out to me a depression in the mountain chain to our left, about thirty miles distant, which he said was the Cochetopa Pass we had been so anxiously looking for. But it required ten days of the severest labor to reach it. We had not for twenty days seen the least indication of a road or trail, but here we discovered evidences that a white man had been here before us in some distinct blazes smoothly cut by a white man's axe upon the trees in the pass.[24]

---

[22]This was Miguel Alona, who was unnamed here, in Marcy's 1858 official reports, and his family letters, though he was identified in Marcy's 1866 autobiography. Martin, "Miguel Alona: The Hero of Cochetopa Pass"; and Mumey, *The Life of Jim Baker.*

[23]In his 1866 autobiography, Marcy indicated that he promised to make Alona "a handsome present for his services, provided he conducted us in safety to New Mexico." The fifty dollars indicated here was a substantial sum—equivalent to four months' pay for an infantry private—but only one-tenth of the five hundred dollars the captain paid Medina, Alona's peer, for his services on the southbound leg. In view of the great contribution of both mountaineers to Marcy's survival, the "fifty" indicated for Alona was presumably a misprint in 1888.

[24]The gap through which Alona guided Marcy was named by Utes for the buffalo herds that migrated through it seasonally and is today's North Cochetopa Pass (elevation 10,149 feet). David H. Miller believes

In looking east from the summit of the great "continental divide" at this point, we saw in the distance a vast plain bounded by a chain of lofty mountains, extending south as far as the eye could penetrate, and this our guide informed us was within the valley of the Rio del Norte [Rio Grande River], now called San Luis Park [Valley].

He also pointed out a far-distant peak [Blanco Peak], at the foot of which, he said, Fort Massachusetts (now Fort Garland) was situated; and as this was the first place from which we could expect to procure supplies, I despatched two men [Medina and Alona] with the only serviceable mules we had, giving them orders to hurry through to the fort, with a note to the commanding officer urging him to send us relief as soon as possible, as we were starving. They started at once, the snow having diminished a little in depth, and we followed on as fast as the crippled condition of our animals would permit, and at length reached the plain we had seen from the top of the mountains.

Ten days had now elapsed since our messengers left for the fort, and as nothing had been heard from them, and fresh snow had obliterated their tracks, I was fearful they had perished or lost their way; but about sunset two horsemen were discovered in the distance rapidly approaching, and to our great relief they soon came galloping into camp on fine fresh horses, and proved to be our long-looked-for messengers, and I have never witnessed such an exhibition of joy as was evinced by the party on that occasion. . . .[25]

We resumed our journey the following morning, and during the day met the supply wagons, which were at once turned into camp, when soup was made for the party, and a guard placed over the provisions to prevent the men from overeating, which in their famished condition might have serious consequences.

The commanding officer at Fort Massachusetts had kindly sent me a jug of brandy, and as soon as we reached camp I gave each one of the men a small drink, which in a short time made them very drunk, but the soup soon sobered them.

Notwithstanding my precautions, five of the men got at the provisions during the night, and were almost insensible the next morning from excruciating

---

that this was Marcy's route rather than nearby South Cochetopa Pass (10,032 feet). Today, New Mexico Highway 114 passes through the north pass, while an unimproved road of the U.S. Forest Service affords passage through the south pass. Miller to MacKinnon, e-mail messages, 12 August 2010 and 24 July 2013.

[25]At this point, Marcy was probably camped along the Siawatche or Saguache Creek where it flows from the canyon of same name into the northern end of the San Luis Valley. David H. Miller, e-mail message to MacKinnon, 24 July 2013. In 1866 Marcy described the scene and his own emotions: "Some of the men laughed, danced, and screamed with delight, while others (and I must confess I was not one among the former) cried like children. I had not slept half an hour at a time for twenty days and nights, and was reduced from 170 to 131 pounds in weight, and, of course, my nervous system was not at that juncture under very good control. My joy was too great, under the circumstances, to find utterance in noise or levity; on the contrary, I mentally offered up sincere thanks to the Almighty for delivering us from the horrible death of starvation." Marcy, "Expedition across the Rocky Mountains," 243.

pains in the stomach, the effects of their imprudence. Medicine was given for their relief, but one of them, Sergeant Morton—a most excellent soldier—of the 10th infantry, died during the day, and it was with great difficulty that the lives of the other four were saved.[26]

Four days afterward [on 18 January] we marched into Fort Massachusetts, receiving a hearty welcome from the officers and men of the garrison. But, judging from the quizzical expression of their countenances and their manifest efforts to smother their risible impulses, they evidently looked upon us as the most lean, ragged, untidy, and scantily uniformed specimens of "regulars" they had ever encountered, which was not at all surprising, as but few of the party had any caps, their shoes were worn out, and their feet bound up with mule-hides or fragments of blankets, their trousers worn off below the knees by the snow-crust and brush, and the few great-coats remaining were materially razeed [cannibalized] for repairing rents in other garments.

We had been fifty-one days in making the journey from Fort Bridger, about 500 miles, the greater part of the way over elevated mountains buried in deep snows, without the slightest trace of a road, pathway, or trail, and not a white man or house was met with during the entire trip. We were all greatly emaciated, and twelve of the soldiers had their feet and legs frozen so badly that they had to be carried upon the poor mules, only eighteen of which remained alive at the terminus of our journey.

From Fort Massachusetts we proceeded on to [Taos and] Santa Fe, and after securing such supplies as were required for our operations in Utah, set out on our return by a different route.

In writing his report of army operations for 1858, Secretary Floyd described Marcy and his expedition with superlatives: "It may be safely affirmed that, in the whole catalogue of hazardous expeditions scattered so thickly through the history of our border warfare, filled as many of them are with appalling tales of privation, hardship, and suffering, not one surpasses this; and in some particulars it has been hardly equaled by any. Their mission was one of extreme importance to the movements of the army, and great disaster might befall the command if these devoted men failed to bring succor to the camp. They had one and all volunteered for this service, and, although they might freeze or die, yet they would not complain."[27]

---

[26]The fatality, the only one of the trek's southbound leg, was Sgt. William H. Morton, Company E, Tenth Infantry, a thirty-one-year-old native of the British Isle of Jersey, who had enlisted at New York City in 1855. Morton died on 14 January 1858 at a place army records described tersely as "camp on headwaters of Rio Grande." In their 1858 reports and orders mentioning Sergeant Morton's death, Captain Marcy and Colonel Johnston went out of their way to shield the soldier's reputation from the unattractive aspects of the gorging incident. They attributed his death only to the privations of exposure and exhaustion.

[27]Floyd, "Annual Report of the Sec. of War (1858)," 7–8.

Instigating the Different Tribes: Sounding the Alarm

As Captain Marcy arrived at Fort Massachusetts and nearby Taos, he entered an isolated, newly Americanized territory both indifferent and titillated by the conflict in neighboring Utah. In Santa Fe, Capt. John N. Macomb's letters to his wife omitted all reference to the arrival of his brother-officer's command and the broader conflict of which it was part, although in mid-1859 he commented that "ever since Marcy came through here 18 months ago and bought up all the spare stock[,] animals have been scarce here."[28] Elsewhere in the same town and weeks before there was any awareness of Marcy's mission or the trail conditions he had encountered, the newspaper editor was anxious to see local volunteers dispatched to Utah.[29]

As news of Marcy's arrival drifted into Santa Fe from the north, rumors from the west alleged a Mormon plot to forge an anti-government Indian alliance. At the heart of this conspiracy theory was the counterintuitive notion of tribal cooperation between the Utes and Navajos, traditional enemies. The catalyst for these rumors was the arrival at Fort Defiance, New Mexico, of a lone Ute bearing a Mormon baptismal certificate as well as fantastic stories of intrigue. Foundational to the shockwave that followed was the long-standing controversy throughout the West of Mormon Indian tampering fueled by awareness of Southern Paiute involvement in the Mormon-led Mountain Meadows massacre of the prior September. Fort Defiance's commander sounded the alarm.

Capt. W. T. H. Brooks (Fort Defiance) to Brevet Capt. W. A. Nichols (Santa Fe), 12 January 1858, Letters Received, HQ, Dept. of New Mexico, RG 393, NARA.

About the 4th of this month an Indian, whose mother is Navajo & father is said to be Utah, living in the direction of the Moqui Villages, came into the post, and reported that he was on his return from a visit to the head men of the Navajo people, whither he had gone at the instance of some Utah chiefs who desired to make peace with the Navajos. These Utahs he reports, were from near the Great Salt Lake in Utah Territory; they had gone to him sometime in November, and were only ten days from Salt Lake City. They reported that there had been some fighting between the people of Salt Lake,

[28] Macomb to Ann Minerva ("Nannie") Rodgers Macomb, 19 June 1859, Rodgers Family Papers, LC; Madsen, *Exploring Desert Stone*, 229.

[29] "The Mormon War," Editorial, *Santa Fe Weekly Gazette*, 8 January 1858, 2/4, Hollon Transcriptions, Canaday Center, University of Toledo.

and troops from the States; and that they were sent out to make peace, with their Indian enemies.

The Indian who came here, has been to Salt Lake City and carries a certificate of baptism & membership in the Church of Latter-day Saints.

I have not seen any of the Navajo chiefs to inquire [about] the result of this Indian mission. The Indian himself reported that the Navajos were discussing of making peace, and were about to send a delegation to visit the Utahs.[30]

A Diversion in Your Favor: General Garland's Offer

Alarmed by Captain Brooks's dispatch, Gen. John Garland immediately drafted a secret letter to Albert Sidney Johnston alerting him to reports of a conspiracy that he accepted at face value. To combat this threat, Garland offered Johnston the equivalent of a regiment to reinforce the Utah Expedition. The arrangement was for Mariano Medina to courier this message north, a daunting one-man assignment for which the army would pay Medina the prodigious sum of five hundred dollars.[31] So sensitive did General Garland consider the matter of reinforcing Johnston that he directed his adjutant to omit reference to his letter in the department of New Mexico's correspondence log and to file the retained copy in his own desk.[32]

Garland to Johnston, 24 January 1858, "Annual Report of the Sec. of War (1858)," 281–82.

Our mail from the States is just in, and brings information of your determination not to enter Salt Lake valley this winter, but to take up a position on Green river, there to wait reinforcements and supplies. With a hope that it may be in my power to render you aid to some extent, I have deemed it expedient to . . . [open] communications with you.

If consistent with your views, please inform me of your designs, in order that I may, if practicable, create a diversion in your favor by throwing a

---

[30]One of Brooks's subordinates at Fort Defiance offered a similar description of this incident to his family in Oswego, N.Y. 1st Lt. John Porter Hatch to father, 20 January 1858, Hatch Papers, LC.

[31]Garland would have been presumably unaware of the extent to which Medina—caught in the middle of the war—had provided the Nauvoo Legion with detailed information about the Utah Expedition's strength and movements during the preceding fall. Wells to Young, 2 October 1857, LDS Archives.

[32]The late Eugene Hollon has argued that it was Miguel Alona whom Garland sent on this northbound mission, but it was Medina, not Alona, who was paid off at Camp Scott as a newly arrived "expressman" during the third week of March. Porter to Dickerson, 19 March 1858 (no. 161), Letters Sent 1857–1861, Vol. 1, Dept. of Utah, Records of the War Dept., RG 98, NARA; Hollon, *Beyond the Cross Timbers,* 224.

column of men, not less than 800 (eight hundred) into the country of the Utah Indians, who are becoming impudent. A rumor has reached me that these Indians are being tampered with by the Mormons, and I am inclined to believe it. A copy of this dispatch will be forwarded to the Secretary of War.

Wishing you all success in your present expedition, I am, colonel, most truly yours.

In forwarding a copy of this letter to army headquarters, Garland reprised the Fort Defiance incident and commented, "there is reason to believe that the Utahs have been tampered with, by direction of *Brigham Young*, whose object also is to extend his relations into the Country of the Navajoes."[33] Recognizing the unconventional cross-department character of Garland's initiative to reinforce the Utah Expedition, General Scott later endorsed this dispatch with the laudatory note, "This letter is highly honorable to the judgment, patriotism and zeal of Brig. General Garland.—Respectfully submitted to the Secretary of War."[34]

The "Good Spirit" Would Protect Them: Enter Kit Carson

Independent of this consternation within the army's hierarchy in New Mexico, the territory's small Indian Affairs organization had already swung into action. It did so in response to Commissioner of Indian Affairs James W. Denver's earlier warning from Washington about the perils of Mormon subversion. As Denver wrote to Mexico's Superintendent James L. Collins, "The [Taos] location of [Ute] Agent [Kit] Carson will make his position, in the present emergency, a very important one, and he, particularly, should be cautioned to leave nothing undone to carry out the wishes of the government."[35] Upon arriving in Washington and meeting with Denver, Collins wrote to Carson to inform him "the Secretary of the Interior is apprehensive that the Utah Indians are being tampered with by the Mormons, and that they may be induced to take part with the Mormons in the rebellion now

[33]Garland to Lt. Col. Lorenzo Thomas (N.Y.), 31 January 1858, Letters Sent, Dept. of New Mexico, RG 393, NARA.

[34]Scott to Floyd, 6 March 1858, Endorsement on Garland to Thomas, 24 and 31 January 1858; McDowell to Garland, 6 March 1858. All in Letters Sent, HQ of Army, RG 108, NARA. Two months later, Scott nominated Garland to fill the vacancy created by the death of Gen. Persifor F. Smith, an assignment that Floyd gave to General Harney.

[35]Denver to Collins, 24 November 1857, "The Utah Expedition," House Exec. Doc. 71, 188–89.

going on against our Govt. in that Territory." Collins directed his agent to pick up an army escort at Fort Massachusetts and to meet with one wavering band "immediately and to warn them against having any thing to do with the Mormons. . . . they will be among the tribes to whom presents are made next spring or summer, provided they remain in good faith with our government."[36] The territory's acting superintendent of Indian affairs in Santa Fe, Samuel M. Yost, also ordered Carson into the field.[37] There is no sign that Collins or Yost coordinated their actions with General Garland, an independence reflecting years of interdepartmental rivalry even in the isolation of Santa Fe.

YOST TO CARSON, 12 JANUARY 1858,
LETTERS SENT, NEW MEXICO SUPERINTENDENCY,
RECORDS OF THE OFFICE OF INDIAN AFFAIRS, RG 75, NARA.

Apprehensions are entertained that an attempt may be made by the people of Utah Territory, known as Mormons, to estrange the Indians of this Superintendency, bordering on that Territory, from the U.S. Government, and ally them with those misguided people in their hostility to the people of the United States. These apprehensions are well grounded, when the proximity of the Tabamenatche [Tabaguache] and Muataho bands of Utah Indians to the Mormon settlements, is taken into consideration. There is almost constantly a communication between the Salt Lake Utahs, and those situated on Grand [Colorado] River—all of whom speak the same language. You are, therefore, instructed to use all diligence, tempered with extreme caution, to ascertain the feelings of these bands of Utahs, toward our government, and let no occasion pass, or prudent effort be neglected, to secure their friendship to our government, and prevent their co-operation with the Mormons. To this end, you are hereby instructed, if you find it absolutely necessary, to increase their allowances of provisions, especially of meats, over your annual estimates. It will be expected, however, that the greatest care and economy be practiced by you, in your expenditures, and that in all cases, you be conscious that the increased allowances are called for by the interests of the government.

Much is left to your discretion and caution. Should the means here indicated fail in accomplishing the desired object of the government, then, it will become your duty to endeavor to direct their hostile movements against such other Indians as may be at war with our people.

---

[36]Collins to Carson, 4 January 1858, Kit Carson Collection, BYU.

[37]For an understanding of Kit Carson's functioning as an Indian agent during this period, see Moody, "Kit Carson, Agent to the Indians in New Mexico," 1–20.

> You will, should you find any stronger indications than now exist, of a hostile policy on the part of any of the bands of your agency, communicate such information immediately to this office, so that the Government at Washington may be regularly and correctly informed of the disposition of the Indians of this Superintendency, in the present anticipated emergency.

Agent Carson responded just as an agitated General Garland moved to report the Fort Defiance incident to army headquarters. Carson communicated his apprehensions about the Utah War while describing a scene of relative quiet despite the eclectic mixture of tribes then visiting northern New Mexico:

> During the first half of the month but few Indians of Muahuache band of Utahs come to the Agency. I feared the emissaries from the Mormons of Utah had been among them for the purpose of endeavoring to cause them [to] forfeit their allegiance to the United States. On the 18th, after my return from Santa Fe, having received your instructions in what manner to act in regard to the Utahs, I proceeded in the direction of their village which I was informed was situated on the west side of the Sier[r]a Blanco, a short distance from Fort Massachusetts. . . . The Indians of this agency are apparently very well satisfied and friendly disposed towards the government, and I have strong hopes of their remaining so even if urged by the rebels of Utah to commence hostilities.[38]

Newspaper accounts of Carson's activities and findings—starting with those in the *Santa Fe Weekly Gazette*—keyed more to his early apprehensions about Mormon influence than to his assurances. Such press reports took on a life of their own as they circulated throughout the United States, fueling rather than allaying fears of Mormon provocations and embroidering an already complex scene replete with Indian fantasies of magic Mormon rivers as well as of LDS machinations among the tribes of Sonora and Chihuahua in addition to New Mexico.[39]

By February 1858 the shared alarm of General Garland and Superintendent Yost had produced cooperation. The two leaders sent Carson and a detachment of troops to visit one of the principal Ute bands within the jurisdiction of the Taos agency to build a back fire of sorts—a peace arrangement between Utes and Navajos to counter any similar alliance sponsored from Salt Lake City. Given the conflicted history of relations between these tribes, Carson considered this gambit risky, if not undesirable.

[38]Carson to Yost, 28 January 1858, Letters Received, New Mexico Superintendency, RG 75, NARA.

[39]"From Santa Fe," *Pittsfield* (Mass.) *Sun*, 18 March 1858, 3.

Carson to Yost, 28 February and 31 March 1858, Letters Received, New Mexico Superintendency, Records of the Office of Indian Affairs, RG 75, NARA.

From the 1st to the 10th I issued provisions as formerly, receiving your instructions regarding the manner in which the Indians should be treated during the war with the Mormons caused me to increase the amount. Daily are they here and all that they require I give, apparently they are well satisfied. . . .

I complied with your request and of the Genl. Comdg. the Dept. by proceeding to Santa Fe, N.M. with men of the Utah Indians empowered to act for their nation to make peace with Navajoes, a tribe with whom war has been and is now in prosecution.

The Utahs have no desire to make peace. They say the Navajoes, asking for peace, were at the same time of making that application, committing depredations, such as stealing stock, murdering citizens of the U.S. & committing depredations in their (Utah) country—I am of opinion, for the benefit of the Utahs, that no treaty was concluded for it will prove more beneficial to them, and the same time be the cause (by those tribes being at war) of the Utahs not joining the Mormons. As by your direction I have been ordered to use all means in my power to prevent the Utahs, I have done all in my power to comply.

Indians from Utah have been among those of this Agency requesting their aid for the Mormons and at the same time stating that they would run no danger by rendering such aid. The Mormons have a stream in their country, so says those Indians, over which the U.S. troops have to pass which causes instant death by their drinking of it, and for Indians it is healthy and the "Good Spirit" would protect them.

With Carson's reassuring assessment in hand, General Garland relaxed and sent Albert Sidney Johnston word that reports of a Mormon conspiracy among the irreconcilable tribes were unfounded.[40] Absent any response from Fort Bridger, Garland dropped further consideration of intervening in the Utah War by reinforcing Johnston with a regiment from New Mexico. Instead he turned to arranging a battalion for the more limited duty of escorting Captain Marcy to Fort Bridger.[41]

[40]Garland to Johnston, 13 March 1858, "Annual Report of the Sec. of War (1858)," 286–87.

[41]Independently, Johnston had concluded that he had the Utes under control (perhaps through Agent Garland Hurt) and had sufficient reinforcements in transit from Kansas to deal with the Mormons. Without explicitly referring to General Garland's offer of an eight-hundred-man "diversion," Johnston deflected it in general terms while thanking him for his help to Marcy. Johnston to Garland, 28 April 1858, Letters Received, HQ Dept. of New Mexico, RG 393, NARA.

A Kilkenny Cat Fight: The View from Santa Fe

This escort consisted of soldiers from three distinct commands: Marcy's own detachment, augmented by a locally recruited group of civilian packers, herdsmen, and teamsters; a reinforced company (K) from the U.S. Mounted Rifles; and three companies (A, E, and F) from the Third U.S. Infantry. In total there were 420 troops and armed civilians, including an entrepreneurial faro dealer who traveled north with this battalion to establish a gambling den at Fort Bridger.[42] Much to Captain Marcy's chagrin, Garland assigned overall command to Col. William Wing Loring, the valorous, one-armed leader of the Mounted Rifles.[43]

With these arrangements to deal with the perceived Mormon threat to Marcy, the editor of Santa Fe's newspaper pronounced himself satisfied with New Mexico's long-distance entry into the Utah War and its likely impact on Brigham Young.

Undated [early March 1858] editorial, *Santa Fe Weekly Gazette*, reprinted *New-York Times*, 15 May 1858, 1/1–2.

If it is really true, and we have every reason to believe it is, that the Mormons desire to cut off the supplies Captain Marcy has in charge, they will find a rather warm and unexpected reception. In addition to the 400 or 500 regulars who will constitute the escort, there will be almost as many private citizens in company, who, in an emergency would shoulder the musket and do effective service. The fact is, the Saints and New-Zion are getting into a hot place, and every indication seems to foreshadow an early record of their downfall.

We are informed by the monthly reports of Agent Carson . . . that there is no probability of a peace between the Utahs and Navajoes. The former are determined upon an active prosecution of hostilities until they are satisfied. . . . The Arapahoes, between whom and the Utahs, recently, a peace was ratified, and the Cheyennes of the plains, have notified Agent Carson that they do not desire peace with the Utahs. . . . These indications promise a rather spirited engagement, and render the probability of their affiliation with the Mormons more remote than ever. A Kilkenny cat fight[44] among them, would not be of incalculable loss to humanity, or a serious retardment

[42]Phelps Diary, 28 July 1858, Walker draft typescript, 37.

[43]The strength of Marcy's escort is summarized in Garland to Thomas, 1 May 1858, Letters Sent, HQ Dept. of New Mexico, RG 393, NARA.

[44]A saying based on an ancient limerick about the mutually destructive fight between two cats in Kilkenny, a city and county in southeastern Ireland.

to civilization, while it assuredly would cut off all hope of assistance to Brigham from any of these nations.

Meanwhile from Mora, New Mexico, the center of his mule-buying efforts, Marcy described to his daughter plans for the return march to Camp Scott.

MARCY TO MARY ELLEN (NELLIE) MARCY, 6 MARCH 1858, HOLLON TRANSCRIPTIONS, CANADAY CENTER, UNIVERSITY OF TOLEDO, AND MCCLELLAN PAPERS, LC.

Since I wrote to you last I have been occupied all the time in purchasing horses and mules and I now have about 1200 which I will set out with for the Army in Utah, about the 10th of this month.

I have had no time since my arrival in the territory to do anything, as all my time has been taken up in the duties of the army pertaining to the purchasing of animals. . . .

I take a hundred men with me from here besides the forty men that came with me from Utah, so that I shall have about 250 men in my party when I return. I shall have a very heavy responsibility in the charge of the large number of animals that I take back, but if I am fortunate in not loosing [*sic*] many of them it will be much to my credit as they are of the utmost importance to the future movements of the Army of Utah.

I shall take wagons with me and a very fine carriage which a gentleman has presented me here so that I shall be very comfortable. I shall have tents and shall take sufficient provisions so that I will not be under the necessity of eating any more mules or horses. I shall probably be at Fort Bridger in about two months from the time I leave here.[45]

I shall apply for a leave of absence as soon as the war in Utah is over which I think will be early after my return and I shall go directly to where my dear family is. I am more anxious to see you than I can express, and I shall be unhappy until the time comes when I can embrace you all once more. This army life is one of continual hardships and privations and I hope before many years to be able to leave it. It is a perfect state of banishment from all the comforts of civilized life and society. The more I see of the posts now occupied by the army the more I am convinced of the truth of this and I shall be most unhappy to see you compelled to bury yourself at a garrison when you are so well fitted to adore [adorn] society in the civilized country. It does very well for some girls who have but little education or accomplishments to marry in the army but I would never advise any of my friends to do so.[46]

---

[45]Due to bad weather and a month's delay in awaiting Colonel Loring's reinforcements, Marcy did not arrive at Fort Bridger until 9 June 1858.

[46]Notwithstanding her father's advice, in 1860 Nellie married his protégé, George B. McClellan, who re-entered the army a year later for the Civil War.

> Embrace your dear mother and sister for me. Tell them how much I love them and receive ten thousand fond embraces from your devoted father.

Despite the tone of this letter, there was gaiety to Captain Marcy's brief sojourns not only in Taos, Santa Fe, and Mora but in the hamlet of Rayado, a town founded by Lucien Bonaparte Maxwell in 1849 east of the Sangre de Cristo range. There, Marcy paused, consolidated his vast herd of livestock, and enjoyed several days of fandangos staged by Maxwell in his honor before heading north.[47]

Look upon the Bright Side: More Cheer from George McClellan

Four days after news of Marcy's safe arrival in New Mexico reached the nation's newspapers, George McClellan again undertook to place the captain's accomplishment in perspective for his family while reassuring them about his safety.

McClellan to Mary Ellen (Nellie) Marcy, 17 March 1858, Hollon Transcriptions, Canaday Center, University of Toledo, and McClellan Papers, LC.

> I give you many thanks for your letter of the 12th with an extract from your Father's letter. He has made the most difficult journey ever made by an army officer, and I do not see how they can avoid promoting him if new regiments are raised [for the Utah War]. What a contrast his conduct presents to that of [John C.] Fremont.
>
> Now that the real danger is over do not go to work and rack your brain to invent new dangers. His return march will be attended by no difficulty from the elements, and he will be out of reach of the Mormons.[48] Even with his route in much greater proximity to them. I know him too well to feel the slightest alarm. You know that I could not deceive you—so you will believe what I say. I feel very keenly for you and your mother in the anxiety you have felt—but hope that you will now look upon the bright side of things and

[47] Marcy to Dr. E. E. Marcy, undated letter [late March 1858 from Arkansas River], excerpted in "From the West. Interesting Letters from Captain Marcy," *New York Times*, 1 July 1858, 2/2–3. Lucien Maxwell, who was half French-Canadian, then owned 1 million acres of New Mexico and was on his way to accumulating a total of 1.7 million acres.

[48] Marcy still faced danger. On 29 April 1858 a violent sixty-hour snowstorm hit his party while camped on West Kiowa Creek near Point of Rocks, at the divide between the Arkansas River and the South Fork of the Platte. Three civilians froze to death and hundreds of animals stampeded—some running for fifty miles, although with great effort nearly all were recovered and the march resumed on 5 May.

> not invent difficulties which do not exist. So little do I apprehend any real danger that I would gladly exchange [places] with your father now.

A northbound Captain Marcy echoed McClellan's confidence while camped along New Mexico's Purgatory River. To Garland's headquarters he wrote, "I would state for the information of the General that . . . the Mormons may try to stampede my animals but they will never molest us in any way. They will not give us a fight, it is all gas as sure as you are born. Nevertheless it is very well to keep a good lookout for them."[49] At about the same time Marcy shared a similar view with his physician-brother in New York: "I do not believe the Mormons dare attack us, and, if they do, I believe we can whip them. . . . The Mormons boast a great deal of what they intend to do, but they do not execute their boasts."[50]

---

[49]Marcy to Nichols, 22 March 1858, Letters Received, HQ Dept. of New Mexico, RG 393, NARA.

[50]Marcy to Dr. E. E. Marcy, undated letter [late March 1858 from Arkansas River], excerpted in "From the West. Interesting Letters from Captain Marcy," *New York Times,* 1 July 1858, 2/2–3.

Chapter 2

"Our East Boundary Should Be at Laramie"
Mormon War Strategy

The president I believe knew of the meditated attack on Bridger before I left home; but the attack on Laramie marked out for April [1858] and which could hardly have failed of success—I am confident no one in Washington ever dreamed of.

Thomas L. Kane to U.S. senator Richard M. Mason, 20 April 1860

So important was Captain Marcy's mission to the Utah Expedition's mobility and sustenance that intercepting him was an integral part of Brigham Young's military plans. Although Marcy did not realize it, within days of his departure from Fort Bridger, Young's scouts had reported to Salt Lake City his mission, destination, likely route, and even the name of at least one of the several civilian mountaineers engaged to guide him. Mormon intelligence capabilities were such that on 6 January 1858 Young informed his business agent in St. Louis,

> We do not anticipate that they [the army] will be able to make a very early [spring] movement in any direction, especially if they wait for the return of Tim Goodall [Goodale] and Capt Marcy whom it is said have gone to Taos New Mexico for a fresh supply of animals. We trust that their way may continue to be hedged up and that this and all other attempts to subvert the liberties of a free people may signally fail and that our enemies may be confounded and utterly wasted away while this people shall abide in strength and power.[1]

[1]Young to Horace S. Eldredge, 6 January 1858, LDS Archives.

What was Young's overall strategy? Notwithstanding his braggadocio and vague public allusions to military preparations, as 1858 began Brigham Young had only a sketchy notion for conducting the campaign. His style ran to improvisation, not the development of a comprehensive plan. Rather than a military genius, President Young was an unschooled leader with scant militia experience but well-developed instincts and excellent organizing skills. Some of Young's ad hockery was effective, while other gambits were problematic and occasionally disastrous. Whatever his educational and experiential shortfalls, though, Brigham Young had an uncommon ability to organize and move large numbers of Mormons great distances across daunting terrain.

The wellspring for Brigham Young's early 1858 view of how best to conduct the Utah War was, like Wilford Woodruff's, Mormon millennial belief that the turmoil of the conflict signaled the imminent Second Coming of Christ. What was to accompany this "end of days" was the protection and guidance of divine providence and active military help from American Indians (sometimes termed Lamanites) serving as a Mormon-directed "battle axe of the Lord." As early as 4 August 1857 Young had instructed one of his agents in Nebraska Territory about how best to deal with the tribes:

> We look upon the taking away of our mail [by the government], and the sending forth an army against us as strong indications that the Lord is hastening his work, and that the "Redemption of Zion draweth nigh." Make yourself acquainted with the Indians and let them understand that they must be our friends, have the brethren learn their language that we may have free communication with them. If they permit our enemies to kill us they will then kill them also. Let them understand this, but move in wisdom and be discreet in all you do, not to bring them nor yourselves into [public] difficulty but open up communication with them as fast as you can conciliate them and make them your friends, for the prospect is *that all Israel will be needed to carry on the work of the last days.* We trust that they will give our enemies plenty to do for the present and thereby hinder them from troubling us.[2]

Beyond these foundational religious beliefs, Young spoke early and often about the concept of a scorched-earth policy. This approach was, in turn, rooted in his basic familiarity with two incidents in Russian history a half-century apart: the destruction of beleaguered Moscow during the Napoleonic

[2]Young to William Felshaw, 4 August 1857, LDS Archives.

Brigham Young, Strategic Improvisor

In early 1858 Young approached war strategy through instinct, improvisation, and reliance on divine guidance. Defensively, he stuck to his Russian (Sebastopol) scorched-earth plan and spy network. Offensively, he worked to intercept Captain Marcy and strengthen tribal alliances. Highest priority was on completing the Standing Army of Israel, a thousand-man cavalry brigade to spearhead the Nauvoo Legion's spring attack on Fort Bridger and Fort Laramie. Simultaneously, he moved in multiple ways to influence national public opinion. *Image of Young ca. 1857 (age 56), courtesy of Special Collections, Marriott Library, University of Utah.*

Wars, and the similar fate of Russia's Black Sea port of Sebastopol in the recently concluded Crimean War. Even while the latter conflict was still in progress, Nauvoo Legion colonel George A. Smith had met with the U.S. Army's Lt. Col. Edward J. Steptoe in Salt Lake City to seek his professional view of Russian tactics. Brigham Young, in turn, sought information in Liverpool as to the whereabouts of Latter-day Saints who had served in the Crimea with the British Army.[3]

By late December 1857 Young had supplemented this defensive interest in the Crimean War with the pursuit of two other thrusts: creation of a parallel regular (standing) military force to reinforce the Nauvoo Legion's less stable militia character; and a campaign to influence American public opinion. These were defensive and aggressive behaviors unprecedented for an American territorial governor. Precisely how, when, and through whom these tactics would play out were the unknowns preoccupying the Latter-day Saints' supreme leader as 1858 began.

All into Ashes: Russian Thoughts

Early clues as to Brigham Young's thoughts about scorched-earth tactics may be found in his first comments about the likely conduct of the Utah War. He had focused his important Sunday discourse of 16 August on what would soon evolve into his Russian-inspired intent to destroy Utah's infrastructure:

> [H]ow many is there of the elders of Isreal [*sic*] and this community that will go with me . . . do as I do and take the road I shall travel? I will tell you what it is, before I ask you to do it or not. If they come here, and if it is necessary I will tell you what I shall do. I shall lay this building in ashes, I shall lay my dwelling house in ashes, I shall lay my mills in ashes, I shall cutt every shrub and tree in the Valley, every pole, every inch of board, and put it all into ashes. I will burn the grass, and the stubble and lay it waste, and make a worse Moscow of every settlement, and then I guess we will make a Potter's field of every Canyon the enemy go into.[4]

A month later, Young and General Wells reinforced this intent with Col. William H. Dame, LDS stake president in Parowan and commander of southern Utah's Iron County Military District:

[3]Historian's Office Journal, 28 December 1854; Young to Orson Pratt, 1 March 1857, both LDS Archives.

[4]Young, Discourse, 16 August 1857, Van Wagoner, ed., *Complete Discourses of Brigham Young*, 3:1315–23.

> The plan of operations is supposed to be about these. In case the U.S. Government should send out an overpowering force [in 1858], we intend to desolate the Territory and conceal our families, Stock, and all of our effects in the fastnesses of the mountains, where they will be safe while the men waylay our enemies, attack them from ambush, stampede their animals take the supply trains cut off detachments, and parties sent to Kanyons for wood, or on other service. To lay waste every thing that will burn, houses, fences, trees, fields grass, that they cannot find a particle of any thing that will be of use to them, not even sticks to make a fire for to cook their suppers. To waste away our enemies and lose none, that will be our mode of warfare.[5]

Brigham Young had shared these thoughts at a time when he believed it unlikely that the Utah Expedition would march west of Fort Laramie during 1857. When it became clear that the army would not winter at that post and would push on to Fort Bridger or perhaps even as far as the Salt Lake Valley, Young again improvised.

Right Kind of Men: The Standing Army's Origins

What arose to supplement the defensive Sebastopol strategy was the notion of organizing a new offensive force, the Standing Army of Israel. These were to be mounted troops available for indefinite service beyond the short-term character of the Nauvoo Legion's mission. Implicit in the Standing Army concept was the reality that such a regular force would be a Mormon creation rather than an arm of the federally established militia system. If Brigham Young were indeed forced to vacate the governorship in 1858, command of the Legion but not the Standing Army would pass to his successor. As governor, Young had occasionally dared to employ Nauvoo Legion detachments and individual militia officers on operations beyond Utah's borders; as a church leader commanding a private non-governmental force, he would be less inhibited about Mormon military thrusts ranging widely throughout the West.[6]

The first known exposition of the Standing Army concept appeared in a long mid-October dispatch from Young to General Wells and his two apostle-advisors, John Taylor and George A. Smith. Here Brigham Young

[5]Young and Wells to Dame, 14 September 1857, LDS Archives.

[6]It is ironic that Young adopted the term Standing Army even though Americans had traditionally used that label negatively in connection with British colonialism or a militarily intrusive force created by the central government.

also explicitly abandoned his August–September policy of avoiding bloodshed by authorizing lethal force against the Utah Expedition.

YOUNG TO WELLS, TAYLOR, AND SMITH,
17 OCTOBER 1857, LDS ARCHIVES.

> It has been suggested to my mind, so soon as our fall's work is pretty well got along with, and while [food] caches are being prepared, &c., to select some 2000 of the right kind of men, have them provided with excellent rifles, and let them furnish themselves with good bows and plenty of arrows, and learn to be as adept in their use as in sharpshooting with the rifle, and organize them into a standing army to be most or all the time on duty in the field, and so apportioned in the different feasible approaches to our Territory as circumstances may from time to time require, each [church] Ward supporting so many families, so that our soldiers can be perfectly free.
>
> About 100 on the southern route to California, about 200 on the [St.] Mary's [Humboldt] river route, 100 north to watch for Oregonians, and the remainder to watch the different eastern routes, the latter so placing their stores and rendezvous that they can operate together or apart. This we have written to you, so that you can have something to talk about, when you have nothing more profitable to occupy your attention, though we do really think that 2000 men of the right stripe can prevent all the armies of the world from coming in here.[7]

Having exposed the concept of a Standing Army to his closest military advisors on 17 October, Young shared his thinking with a broader audience the next day during a Sunday discourse in Salt Lake City's tabernacle: "This Territory and people are perfectly able to defend themselves, with the help of our God. They are perfectly able to set apart men of the right stripe, and maintain a standing army that can keep off the armies of our enemies."[8]

A week later, General Wells and Apostles Taylor and Smith left their headquarters in Echo Canyon to attend a war council in Salt Lake City. At this meeting, Brigham Young's closest colleagues learned not only of his thoughts about using the Standing Army to deal with the Utah Expedition in 1858 but, surprisingly, of his intent to expand Utah's borders. Young urged a return to those boundaries that he had unsuccessfully claimed in 1849 for the provisional State of Deseret—from the crest of the Rockies to

[7]One of the first modern discussions of the Standing Army and its Utah War significance was Arrington, *Great Basin Kingdom*, 179–80, followed by Bigler, *Forgotten Kingdom*, 183–84; Bagley, *Blood of the Prophets*, 194–95; and Bigler and Bagley, *The Mormon Rebellion*, 271–74.

[8]Brigham Young, Discourse, 18 October 1857, *Deseret News*, 28 October 1857, 268/4.

San Diego Bay—and beyond. As Apostle Woodruff recorded his remarks, Young's approach was one that later army doctrine would call taking the war to the enemy.

Kenney, ed., *Wilford Woodruff's Journal*,
25–26 October 1857, 5:114–16.

The [First] presidency and Twelve were in Conversation all the forenoon at his office upon the subjet of the war. President Young said That the United States Government was looseing their National greatness & wisdom is departed from them and we need not have as much fear of them as we would of an Army of Grasshoppers. If they take away our Charter from us & divide up our Territory it will be unconstitutional as evry thing they do against us. I told Brother [John M.] Bernhisel that if they took away our Charters to Come immediately home as soon as He Could & we would Organize our State Government & fall back upon our Original Boundaries. Our East Boundary should be at Laramie the west the summit of the Siera Nevada & run to the pacific Ocean &c & we would defend it. . . . [9]

The U.S. may do as they please. We will do as the Lord wants us. One young officer of the Army said that Old Jesus Christ Could not keep him out of salt Lake City. But they will find out who rules on Earth & in heaven. Another Officer said the United States would wipe us out another year. Should they send an Army of 20,000 men it would take more than 20 miles for their armey & train to move at all and the more there is of them the worse off they will be. Many other remarks were made. . . .

President Young said if an army comes to help them [Johnston's troops] in the spring we will use up this army first & then we will use up the others before they get to the South Pass.[10] In the spring we must ask [Col. Edmund B.] Alexander what He intends to do. Inform him He must not stay there untill He gets reinforcements in the spring and if they will not leave in the spring we will use them up first the best we Can. In 10 days we can put 2,000 men around them which would soon use them up. I do not believe that they will have 500 fighting men in the spring. They are in a vary Critical situation. They say they have no other way to get a living for their families but to [wage] war. I think it is better to let the Army alone this winter. They will die many of them and others desert & many be weakened with the scurvey & in the spring we will wipe them out if necessary if they do not go away.

---

[9]For Young's instructions to territorial delegate Bernhisel on what to do in the event that Congress rescinded Utah Territory's organic act ("charter"), as was being debated, see MacKinnon, "'Like Splitting a Man Up His Backbone,'" 110. Young's discussion here of borders is confusing inasmuch as the Mormons' "original" (1849) claim as their easternmost boundary had been the crest of the Rockies or Continental Divide, not Fort Laramie, which was several hundred miles farther east.

[10]The term "use up" was one of multiple slang terms in Utah for killing.

> We do all of our Business in the name of Israel's God and they in their own way. The whole matter can be summed up in these few words. We are here at home by our own Fireside while they are a great way from home. I intend to send those teamsters to the south whare they cannot get Back to the Armey.[11]

A month later Young discerned little or no progress and perhaps a lack of enthusiasm for pursuing his suggestions. He reminded General Wells of the need for a Standing Army and again urged that he equip it with the long bows of Indian warfare plus a touch of medieval European weaponry: "We want to be picking out our men and fitting up our bows, crossbows, &c. in readiness for another year."[12]

They Bring Important Intelligence: Return of the Captives

When the Mormons released teamster Charles W. Becker, another unidentified teamster-captive, and Pvt. Henry Feldman of the Tenth U.S. Infantry at Christmas, they returned to Fort Bridger with both an intelligence windfall and alarming news: there was to be a new Mormon military force, the Standing Army, tasked with intercepting Captain Marcy's detachment as it returned from New Mexico. Fearful that the army would view his months-long absence as a case of desertion rather than involuntary capture, Feldman was especially anxious to relate what he had heard in Salt Lake City about LDS military plans, information that he knew would be of high interest to his officers.

Who was Private Henry Feldman? Army records indicate that he was born in Hanover, Germany, and had enlisted in Buffalo, New York, in 1855. When recruited, Feldman gave his occupation as laborer; when captured by the Nauvoo Legion, he was in his late twenties and was serving as a hospital steward or orderly, a duty that he had performed in the military service of the Dutch East Indies Company for seven years before joining the U.S. Army.[13]

---

[11]It is not clear whether Young's comment about teamsters was a benign plan for dealing with the flow of army contractor employees who defied Johnston's ban on westbound travel by crossing into the Legion's lines, or whether "send those teamsters to the south" (like "send 'cross lots" and "send home the short cut") was another euphemism for killing.

[12]Young to Wells, 26 November 1857, LDS Archives.

[13]Feldman military service record and Register of Absent Enlisted Men, Tenth Infantry, November 1857, NARA. Information about his pre-1855 Dutch service appears in papers relating to his 1860 appointment as hospital steward at Fort Garland, New Mexico. Capt. Cuvier Grover, endorsement on Asst. Surg. C. M. Alden to Cooper, 26 October 1860, Letters Received, Office of Adjt. Gen., RG 94, ibid.

The intelligence that Feldman brought back from Mormon captivity was reported by an unidentified correspondent at Camp Scott whose dispatch found its way into the columns of a western Massachusetts newspaper as well as by Albert G. Browne, Jr., of the *New-York Tribune.*

"STATEMENT OF THE SOLDIER TAKEN CAPTIVE BY THE MORMONS," *PITTSFIELD (MASS.) SUN,* 25 MARCH 1858.

The following is a narrative of Henry Feldman, of Company F, 10th Regiment U.S. Infantry, who was taken prisoner by the Mormons on the 30th of October last. It is highly interesting:

I left the camp of the 10th Infantry on the 30th of October, '57, for the purpose of going to an adjoining camp of a detachment of the 10th Infantry, and seeing some friends. On my way to that place I was suddenly surprised by three men on horseback, who wanted me to stop and deliver up my arms immediately, (I had my rifle and my side arms along with me.) Not having the least intention to part with my arms, I defended myself the best way I could, and wounded the first horse which approached me, so as to dismount the horseman; I ran my bayonet into the breast of the second horse and broke it, and likewise brought the rider to the ground. In the meantime there came three other horsemen, whom I did not mention before, and seeing their friends already dismounted and their horses killed, at least one of them came to their assistance, when they were joined by the third man of the first party. These four men on horseback now tried to catch me with the lariet, but unfortunately their lariets did not catch; and while I was turning towards them the other two dismounted men threw their lariets from different sides, which brought me to the ground; and they then took away my arms.[14] They then took me to Fort Bridger. After having one day's rest in that Fort they escorted me on the second day through the canons to Great Salt Lake City.

On my arrival at that place I was immediately brought to prison, with a regular guard of two men always around me. I was not brought before any of the authorities in the city, nor had I any communication with any one in relation to the intentions or strength of the U.S. troops in the Territory.

After having been fourteen days confined, I contrived to escape, and being at the distance of thirty miles from Salt Lake City was caught, brought back, and confined in another prison. From here I had another opportunity to escape again in about five weeks. While two of my guards were asleep,

[14]Feldman's account of his capture and escape attempts is hyperbolic and unsupported by Nauvoo Legion sources. The army did not issue sidearms to privates. His embellishments were minor compared to the lurid and wholly bogus account of Mormon captivity and torture retailed by civilian Charles J. Humbert, who falsely claimed service with a non-existent "Third Dragoons." Humbert to Nolen family, 30 November 1857, "Extraordinary News if True," *Democrat* (Belleville, N.J.), 16 January 1858, reprinted in *New York Herald,* 22 January 1858, 1/1–2.

I knocked the third one down, took a revolver, and a horse I found in the yard, and galloped off as fast as I could. I changed horses twice on the road, and on the second day, being within about 20 to 30 miles of the camp of the U.S. troops, I noticed that I was followed by about thirty horsemen—who, as soon as they were near enough, fired at me incessantly, killed my horse at last, and coming up to me took me prisoner, and brought me back to Great Salt Lake City again.[15]

I was conducted to prison and kept there till the 26th of December, when I was released and brought with an armed escort, consisting of four men, to Bear River, from there to find my own way to camp.

During my last confinement I found out and heard many things, which in my belief are of some importance, the most of these things having been preached in church by Brigham Young and his adherents.

The Mormons say: That no regular troops would act as we do, that the whole U.S. force here is nothing but a mob, and that all of us, before spring opens, will be starved to death on account of not having sufficient provisions along with us. That the officers keep the soldiers in total ignorance about their sadness and sorrow, and persuade them to consider and treat the Mormons not a particle better than they would murderer and robber bands.

That *per force* they (the Mormons) can bring an army into the field amounting to 20,000 men (all between 15 and 50 years of age,) and as a party among them (which calls itself half Mormon) says, it would only require about 6000 regular troops or fighting men to defeat the whole of the Mormon force.[16] They are very badly equipped, and the firearms in their possession are in the same bad condition; they have other [either] old condemned U.S. rifles, muskets—percussion and flint lock—or Mississippi rifles and revolvers. They have no cartridges at all. Every Mormon carries a powder-horn and [loose] bullets. They have got six or eight old brass pieces (cannon) and some iron [ones]. Their calibre I don't know anything about. I never saw them.

They are organizing a corps of two thousand so-called regular troops, half horse and half foot; the cavalry armed with rifles and revolvers, and the footmen with muskets. This force they intend to station as soon as the road to Salt Lake opens between the camp of the United States troops and Great Salt Lake City in the mountains.

They are informed of all that occurs in our camp, and of all the movements of the United States troops in Utah Territory. They sent companies out from Great Salt Lake City along the road to New Mexico, to stampede the animals and destroy the Government property under charge of Capt.

---

[15]Throughout the 1850s (and beyond), stories of pursuit by groups of shadowy Mormon horsemen—often described as "Danites"—were staple fare in escape narratives from Utah. Private Feldman's fantastic story is in that tradition.

[16]It is unclear what group Feldman described as "half Mormon."

Marcy, and they have likewise sent out parties between Salt Lake City and Laramie, for the same purpose.[17]

They receive regular mails and are in constant communication with the States and California, and they are in league with the Cheyenne Indians in Kansas Territory, and all other Indian tribes, North, South, and West, in Utah Territory. That any Mormon can pass through any of the Indian districts unmolested, but that other people will be killed surely.

There was a party of six men coming from California with the intention of passing through Salt Lake City and visiting the camp of the United States troops. They were not allowed to pass through the city, and were afterwards taken prisoners. After some days' confinement they were released on condition that they should return to the place from which they came. Accordingly four of them started to return to California by the Southern route, but never reached their destination. They were killed on the road, as the half Mormons express themselves, by the "painted Indians."[18]

As Simple as Practical: Brother Bertrand Views Mormon Strategy

Louis Alphonse Bertrand, a French convert who had emigrated to Utah in 1855, had an even better view of Brigham Young's aggressive plans for 1858 than did the low-level captives Charlie Becker and Henry Feldman. He spent much of the war in Salt Lake City as a civilian growing fruit trees and sending dispatches defending Mormonism to French and American newspapers. Bertrand apparently had good access to Brigham Young, and subsequently claimed to have interviewed Col. Albert Sidney Johnston, Gov. Alfred Cumming, and Thomas L. Kane. In addition to spending time with

[17]On this point, correspondent Browne reported: "They [the returned captives] bring the important intelligence that the Mormons are already fitting out an expedition to intercept Capt. Marcy on his return from New Mexico in the Spring, stampede and seize his mules and destroy his escort. . . . He is an officer admirably adapted for the service which he has in charge, having a previous and thorough knowledge of the country through which he must pass; and being aware that the result of this year's campaign depends in great measure on the success of his expedition, he will encounter no hazard which a prudent man would avoid. It will, therefore, be practicable for news of the [Mormon] movement in preparation against him to reach General Scott in time to allow arrangements to be made to secure him against any force which the Mormons can detach to operate in his direction. It is probable that a similar effort will be made to intercept the droves of horses which may be sent down to the army from Oregon. I believe that I wrote to you that Mr. [B. F.] Ficklin was dispatched to that Territory at the beginning of December, to purchase horses with which to remount the dragoons." [Browne], "Mormon Hostilities: The Danites and Their Murders," Dispatch, Camp Scott, 3 January 1858, *New-York Semi-Weekly Tribune*, 2 March 1858, 1/1–6, 4/1–6, 5/1.

[18]Here Feldman describes accurately the capture, imprisonment, release, and assassination of the Aiken party in October–November 1857. Bigler, "The Aiken Party Executions," 451–70. "Painted Indians" refers to Caucasians disguising themselves as American Indians, as had been done by Nauvoo Legionnaires at Mountain Meadows less than four months earlier.

these leaders on both sides of the war, Bertrand obtained important Mormon documents from General Wells (and perhaps Young), who introduced him to the church's business agent in San Francisco as "a very excellent French gentleman from Paris who wishes to publish in his own country and in his native language the documents enclosed as well as others of like character which perhaps he may deem proper to translate. It is all right to forward these papers according to his request."[19] In 1862 Bertrand published his views as a book, *Mémoires d'un Mormon.*

Michael W. Homer, one of the Frenchman's most recent chroniclers, argues that "Bertrand had a unique insider's perspective on the Utah War and is the earliest [published] account of the conflict from a Mormon perspective. He presents [in his book] an entirely different interpretation of events than the one subsequently repeated in faith-promoting annals, which had a misunderstood Brigham Young working assiduously to make peace. The reality was quite different, with Young outlining an aggressive strategy for a spring campaign in 1858 and creating an elite standing army to implement these plans." According to Homer, "Bertrand's history reveals how close this aggressive campaign plan came to becoming a reality."[20]

Bertrand, *Mémoires d'un Mormon* [Memories of a Mormon], Typescript Translation by Gaston Chappuis, LDS Archives.

The months of January and February 1858 were spent in making our last war preparations. The only task unfulfilled was the organization of an armed body large enough to take the offensive in the spring. Twelve squadrons of mounted riflemen of one hundred each were recruited and equipped in a few days. Each supplied with two horses, a revolver and carbine, and sufficient food for six months, these twelve hundred cavalrymen, the cream of our youth, constituted an imposing body of elite. Our campaign plan was as follows: seize South Pass militarily to intercept any reinforcement of troops and supplies coming from the United States through this channel; assign two squadrons to the task of overtaking the horses and mules Captain Marcy was to bring back from New Mexico; then resume positions along Devils Gate, that steep mountain chasm straddling the road just ahead [east] of the Sweetwater and offering a series of formidable strategic points.

---

[19]Wells to Dwight Eveleth, 5 February 1858, LDS Archives.

[20]Homer, *On the Way to Somewhere Else*, 103. Homer's presentation of Bertrand's narrative blended Gaston Chappuis's and Hugh MacNaughton's translations in the Moorman Collection, Weber State University. The Bertrand text presented here is from Chappuis's original translation in LDS Archives. Another discussion of Bertrand and his episodic sojourns in both France and Utah appears in McClellan, "Not Your Average French Communist Mormon," 3–24.

> This plan, as simple as it was practical, would no doubt have been crowned with success. And we, French historian of this strange military epic, would have had to relate how General Johnston with his sixteen field guns and three thousand heroes at Fort Bridger, accompanied by Chief Justice [Delana R.] Eckels and other federal officers, closely tracked by the Mormons and by hunger driven to the last extremities, would have found himself in the dire necessity of surrendering without even the satisfaction of having fired a single [percussion] cap.

Two years after the Utah War, Thomas L. Kane commented briefly to U.S. senator Richard M. Mason on Mormon plans for such a spring offensive that went beyond the thrust described by Louis Bertrand. Based on what he had heard in Utah, Kane described a projected Mormon attack on Fort Laramie, the post that Brigham Young had identified in late October 1857 as marking Utah's intended new eastern border: "The President [Buchanan] I believe knew of the meditated attack on Bridger before I left home; but the attack on Laramie marked out for April [1858] and which could hardly have failed of success—I am confident no one in Washington ever dreamed of."[21]

If Buchanan did not anticipate a Mormon raid on Fort Laramie, the garrison at Camp Scott did expect one. By the end of 1857, even a newspaper as distant as Maine was repeating rumors about "the meditated attack upon Fort Laramie."[22]

Unsuitable Cavalry: General Ferguson Views 1858

Among the Mormon military leaders best equipped to understand what lay ahead in 1858 was Brig. Gen. James Ferguson, the Nauvoo Legion's adjutant general. Ferguson, age 30, was a Mormon convert born in Belfast, Ireland. He was a man of enormous talent and personal appeal with some practical military experience, having served as sergeant-major of the Mormon Battalion during the Mexican War. Subsequently, as a lawyer, Ferguson participated in some of Utah's most bruising legal disputes of the late 1850s. After the Utah War, he would co-found a newspaper, *The Mountaineer,* in Salt Lake City and die tragically of acute alcoholism in 1863 at age 35.

In early January 1858 Ferguson wrote a long report to summarize for Brigham Young the activities of his and other staff departments during 1857. He also

---

[21]Kane to Mason, 20 April 1860, enclosure to Kane to Buchanan, same date, James Buchanan Papers, HSP.

[22]"Utah—Volunteer Forces," *Daily Union* (Bangor, Maine,), 29 December 1857, 2/2.

assessed future needs. Ferguson's fluency, senior perspective, and functional responsibilities gave his report the sweeping character of a mini-history of the war, complete with the most reliable insider's description available of the Legion's troop strength and weaponry. Ferguson also provided some surprisingly frank observations about Legion weaknesses that had important implications for 1858. With varying degrees of directness, he touched on the inability of Mormon raiders to halt the Utah Expedition's westward march during the fall of 1857; the performance shortfalls of several of his peers; the impracticality of some of Young's own military suggestions; and what Ferguson perceived as an over-reliance on cavalry for mountain warfare. It is impossible to know whether Ferguson's boldness reflected an alcohol-fueled loosening of inhibitions or simply self-confidence. His observations constituted a unique insider's account to which Albert Sidney Johnston would have relished access.

FERGUSON TO YOUNG, 7 JANUARY 1858, LDS ARCHIVES.

It is particularly desirable that the energy and ability in the Surgical, Ordnance, Commissary and Quarter Master Departments should be encouraged. If the service of our troops is much called for, the two latter Departments should be put at once under good working order, and the necessary assistants, including a good accountant, attached to them. The duties of these two Departments devolved almost entirely during the last campaign, upon Genl [A. P.] Rockwood. Of the ability with which these were discharged, having been under your own personal inspection, you are the judge. Col. J. C. Little was assigned to the charge of these Departments in the field, of whose untiring energy and promptness in the discharge of his duties I cannot speak too highly.

I would respectfully and most earnestly request a close attention to the report of the Chief of Ordnance. The Public Gun Shop should be encouraged. By a little careful nurture with a view to its enlargement, and the supply of material, it would soon be able to supply the Territory with all the arms necessary. The more necessary is its encouragement from the fact that the unquestioned judgment and experience of Col. [Thomas] Ellerbeck, and the superior skill and ability of [foreman] Mr [Nathan] Davis and the employees in the shop, guarantee an issue of arms of a quality far superior for our use to the arms imported from the East. The dilapidated state of the [Salt Lake City] Arsenal should have immediate attention. The addition of strong timbers as props to the walls, would make it safe and could be so put up as to answer the purpose of wagon sheds, which are very much needed. At present, instead of securing, it rather endangers the public arms.[23]

[23]On 5 April 1887 the arsenal exploded with a catastrophic blast as the result of an accident involving boys hunting birds.

If bows are to be introduced, I have yet to see an improvement on the light an[d] effective weapon used by the Indians; and will respectfully submit the suggestion that not only was the Cross-bow peculiarly and almost exclusively adapted to the days of heavy armor and clumsy club fighting; but can only be introduced at the expense of the rifle; for the material and time to manufacture both are not on hand.[24] I consider a good Indian Bow and quiver of arrows an unburthening and valuable addition to the arms of a mountain trooper.

I may probably be one of a most limiting minority in suggesting the propriety of putting our light cannon into a suitable condition for service: (It requires but little time and expense to do this.) and provide a reasonably small supply of ammunition for them. Infantry is in fact the army, the real fighting part of it. Cavalry and Artillery are its assistants. Cavalry is necessary to reconnoitre, and harass our enemy, but alone, has too many appendages, and entirely unsuited to occupy the most desirable positions of resistance.[25] It is proved that powder can be made here. Why is it not brought into market?[26]

It is as yet a matter of great uncertainty what course the invading army will pursue in the Spring. That the Administration will insist upon establishing a Military Department in Utah I fully believe. I am of the opinion, however, that they will establish their posts near their present encampments with a view either to compromise or future vengeance.[27] Still they may advance upon our settlements in the Spring. With this probability before us, explorations should at once be set on foot, under the direction of the Corps of Engineers; that the Lieutenant General may have before him a knowledge of all the practicable routes.[28] The works in Echo [Canyon] are very good and reflect much skill upon their superintendence. Still, if the enemy come that way, the

[24]Here Ferguson treads on one of Brigham Young's personal interests, the introduction of long- and crossbows for use by the Legion.

[25]Three weeks after Ferguson sent this report to Young, General Harney wrote to President Buchanan to criticize General Scott for using mounted troops rather than infantry in the mountains of Utah. Harney to Buchanan, 30 January 1858, James Buchanan Papers. Ferguson's criticism of cavalry may have been a camouflaged swipe at Young's resource-straining Standing Army concept with its emphasis on mounted troops. After the Utah War, Thomas L. Kane commented with respect to the Standing Army, "When I was in Utah, it seemed as if any attention paid to their infantry was little better than a sham, while of horse—to the number probably of about one thousand—they had a force of picked men—which it had evidently cost them time and money to get into condition and which was plainly intended for severe active service." Kane to Mason, 20 April 1860, enclosure to Kane to Buchanan, same date, James Buchanan Papers, HSP.

[26]With this question, Ferguson pandered to Young's preoccupation with establishing a capability to manufacture gunpowder in-territory. By early 1858 such capability did exist in southern Utah, but only on an insignificant scale that did not impact the war effort.

[27]Ferguson's predictions were partly accurate and partly off-target. In the spring of 1858 Albert Sidney Johnston did designate Fort Bridger a permanent military post, but his main concentration of troops would be at Camp Floyd in Utah's Cedar Valley.

[28]As Ferguson wrote, a small Mormon group led by Indian Agent Jacob Hamblin was preparing to monitor the ascent of the Colorado River by 1st Lt. Joseph C. Ives of the U.S. Army's Corps of Topographical Engineers.

barricades are not now sufficient. They will want repairs and additions. Nor is it well, let them come which way they will, to depend upon one position. They should be annoyed for many miles; and to this end positions should be selected and examined on all the routes at an early date. The enemy have skillful guides and doubtless are making the best possible use of their time in gaining additional knowledge of the Country. *But God is with us!*

The rumors of immense armies preparing to approach the Territory at different points the coming summer are very idle [inaccurate]. Mad as mankind are about the Mormons, individuals could not be found to invest private means to fit out Volunteers to any extent for the purpose; and none but homeless penniless vagabonds would volunteer. Should it be attempted by the Administration, it would require a longer time than one short summer, and the establishment of well garrisoned depots would be necessary on the routes selected for the march of the Army. It is not presumed that an Army would come here with less than a year's supply of provisions. Ten thousand men thus supplied would in their march occupy nearly fifty miles of country, and be ill prepared to take care of themselves en route. It is not unworthy of observation that the disposition of the Regular Army of the United States, during the past year, has been rather of a menacing nature; and that they are now concentrating in the most available positions, if an invasion of Utah were contemplated.[29]

We are at peace with the Indians, thanks to the mild and pacific policy of your Excellency.[30]

Let the Pen Flow Freely: War of Words

As General Ferguson finalized his report, Brigham Young and Utah's legislative assembly completed another component of the Mormons' offense for 1858: propaganda. In this case, it was a memorial adopted by the assembly and intended for delivery directly to Congress and the White House via the California-Panama mail. Unlike the memorials sent to Buchanan a year earlier, there would be no opportunity for the president to suppress this document. If anything, the phrasing of the memorial adopted on 6 January 1858 was more defiant and combative than the earlier ones, which on 19 March 1857 Secretary of the Interior Jacob Thompson had characterized as a Mormon declaration

[29]Ferguson badly misjudged the extent to which scores of volunteer companies were spontaneously forming for Utah service in California as well as in virtually every state east of the Mississippi River.

[30]The extent to which Young's Indian policy during the Utah War was "mild and pacific" is still debated by historians. Less than two months after Ferguson wrote, a war party of Northern Shoshones and Bannocks attacked and forced the abandonment of the Mormon mission at Fort Limhi, Oregon Territory, while the other tribes raided Mormon ranches west of Salt Lake City for livestock to be sold to the army.

of "war." Young knew that this new document was also provocative, although he probably did not anticipate that it would draw wholesale federal treason indictments. On the day of the memorial's adoption, Young alerted Asa S. Calkin, president of the British Mission, to controversy ahead, writing "the Legislature are in Session, and you may expect to see some spicy Documents in print in the U.S. Papers before long." To Calkin's letter Young then added the cheeky notation, "to the Postmasters in the U.S. will you be kind enough when you have read this note, to forward it."[31]

Unsent to Washington with the new memorial (but published in the *Deseret News*) was even more confrontational material—a set of hyper-assertive resolutions adopted by the legislative assembly on 21 December as a follow-on to Brigham Young's faux gubernatorial message of 15 December. These resolutions, in turn, stoked similar expressions of anger at local indignation meetings held in virtually every significant town in Utah. Among the more provocative language used in the assembly's 21 December resolutions was a promise that:

> We will continue to resist any attempt on the part of the Administration to bring us into a state of vassalage by appointing, contrary to the Constitution, officers whom the people have neither vote nor voice in electing; nor shall any persons appointed to office for Utah by the present Administration either qualify for or assume, and discharge, within the limits of the Territory, the functions of the offices to which they have been appointed, so long as our Territory is menaced by an invading army nor so long as such appointees are so pusillanimous as to require a numerous armed force to attend their beck.

After the war, correspondent Browne reprised these resolutions—a virtual repudiation of the American territorial system—and commented sarcastically, "These were sweet-scented blossoms to blow so early on the tree of Squatter-Sovereignty, at that time scarcely four years old!"[32]

So prolix was the 6 January 1858 memorial and so similar was its rhetoric to that adopted by Utah's legislative assembly a year earlier, its text is not reproduced here.[33] Significantly, Brigham Young's instructions to delegate Bernhisel for the handling of this document were virtually to bludgeon Congress with it. When Bernhisel received this material, he promptly complied with Young's instructions and reported the results:

---

[31]Young to Calkin, 6 January 1858, LDS Archives.

[32]"Resolutions," *Deseret News*, 23 December 1857, 332/3-4; Browne, *The Utah Expedition*, 477. Browne refers to the Kansas-Nebraska Act of 1854.

[33]The complete text of this material appeared in "Memorial to the President and Congress," 6 January 1858, *Deseret News*, 13 January 1858, 4/3–4, 5/1–2.

> The [6 January 1858] Memorial of the Members and officers of the Legislative Assembly of the Territory of Utah to the Congress and President of the United States was on the 16th instant presented to the House of Representatives, read, ordered to be printed and laid on the table. The House refused to refer it to any committee. One member Mr Wilson asserted that the memorial was insulting, insolent and defiant. It has been published in the Washington Globe, New York Tribune, New York Herald, and will no doubt be by other public journals.[34]

The *New York Herald,* to which Bernhisel referred, reported:

> The reading of the memorial which was submitted to the House by Speaker Orr, from both branches of the Utah Legislature, caused quite a sensation. (The document appeared in the Herald of the 16th instant.) Frequent efforts were made to suppress its reading. The reading was listened to with much attention. Some of the language caused laughter, while other portions induced members to move that further reading be dispensed with. The memorial, however, was read to the end, including the names of the signers. Mr. Bernhisel, the delegate from Utah, left the hall when the Clerk commenced reading the memorial.[35]

Correspondent Browne described the memorial as "nothing more than an infuriated tirade" and noted sarcastically that "it was honored in both Houses by reference to the Committees on Territories, from which it received all the consideration it deserved."[36] When the text of the 1858 document reached Camp Scott shortly after adoption, a federal grand jury convened at Eckelsville and returned treason indictments against every legislator who had signed the memorial, including Brigham Young.

In addition to the formal, somewhat legalistic approach to influencing congressional and public opinion through legislative memorials, the Mormons also employed multiple informal channels of communication. All of these aggressive thrusts included common themes: indignation over the U.S. government's colonial treatment of Utah; reminders of Mormon Battalion service during the Mexican War; the worthlessness of non-Mormon federal appointees; Mormon military capabilities and determination to use them; and the promise of catastrophic, pyrrhic results of any forced entry into the Salt Lake Valley by the Utah Expedition.

Many of these mantralike themes were relatively successful communications initiatives if measured by the national newspaper coverage that

---

[34]Bernhisel to Young, 18 March 1858, LDS Archives.

[35]"The Mormon Memorial in the House," Dispatch (from Washington), 16 March 1858, *New York Herald,* 17 March 1858, 4/5.

[36]Browne, "The Utah Expedition," 477.

followed. Public and congressional acceptance was another matter, although it is clear that by the time he reached California in late January 1858, Thomas L. Kane had convinced himself that the Utah Expedition was vulnerable and at Brigham Young's mercy.

Contemporaneous to the Utah legislative assembly's display of bluster, there was a Mormon campaign of disinformation, featuring a mysterious "Mr. Wingate," that drew substantial press interest in Mormon military capabilities and intentions. Who Wingate was, if he existed, is unknown. The editors of Mormon-controlled newspapers in Iowa who originated the Wingate story described him as a traveler of unspecified background and incomplete name who had departed Salt Lake City on about 25 January 1858, bypassed Fort Bridger, and crossed the plains to Iowa bearing tales of Nauvoo Legion troop strength and Mormon weapons manufacturing capabilities. The information attributed to Wingate was almost entirely bogus or exaggerated, but as he disappeared from Iowa to pursue unspecified "important business" in Chicago, his interviews with Mormon editors rippled across the United States. Hungry for fresh news about the Utah War, dozens of midwestern and eastern newspapers reprinted the Wingate interviews indiscriminately.

There is no documentary evidence linking Mormon leaders to the Wingate material, but the timing and nature of these interviews, the familiarity of their hyperbole, Mormon ownership of the newspapers in which they initially appeared, and Brigham Young's proclivity for press manipulation makes such a connection likely. In May 1858 Young would lay the foundations for an extensive campaign to influence the eastern press through Mormon newspaperman T. B. H. Stenhouse. At the end of the Utah War's active phase, Young made clear his fondness for such a strategy, and later would sanction monetary payments, if not outright bribes, to cooperative editors.[37]

The Wingate thrust bore the hallmarks of a carefully crafted effort to influence non-Mormon views about the war while simultaneously exploiting a second cousin of disinformation: intimidation. This was done by raising the specter of Mormon-instigated arson. Brigham Young's vision of a desolated Nebraska, Kansas, Iowa, and Missouri, as described by Wingate in his interviews, echoed Young's earlier threats to burn California and midwestern cities. On 13 September 1857, two days after Mountain Meadows, he had alluded to the consequences of a possible invasion by volunteer troops from

[37]Young to Stenhouse, 8 May 1858, and Young to Eldredge, 20 October 1858, both LDS Archives; Bagley, "'Buyin' Papers Well Grounded in Mormon Lore," *Salt Lake Tribune*, 10 December 2000, B1.

California in a conversation with Capt. Stewart Van Vliet, a U.S. Army quartermaster visiting Salt Lake City:

> If the Government Calls for volunteers in California & the people turn out to come to destroy us they will find their own buildings in flames before they get far from home & so throughout the United States. Again if they Commence the war I shall not hold the Indians Still by the fist any longer for white men [emigrants] to shoot at them but I shall let them go ahead & do as they please and I shall Carry the war into their own land and they will want to let out the Job before they get half through.[38]

The Nauvoo Legion's medical director, Dr. John L. Dunyon, repeated these threats to travelers, and they found their way into eastern and presumably California newspapers. In the spring of 1858, an alarmed Illinois newspaper quoted an unidentified Mormon refugee at Camp Scott as saying: "Brigham Young threatens, in case the President does not 'back out' from the position he has taken in his [annual] message that he will send his 'destroying angels' on a mission of incineration to burn St Louis, Keokuk, Chicago, New York, and even the capital of the United States. These cities, and many others, are to be fired simultaneously."[39] After all, as Young had informed Bernhisel, there were Mormon "boys who are shrewd enough to go when and where they please and can dodge an enemy. There are plenty of them yet in the States."[40]

> Latest News from Utah—Mormon Preparations for War, *Philadelphia Standard Bulletin*, 20 March 1858.
>
> The Council Bluffs [Iowa] *Bugle* of the 3d inst., says: Mr. Wingate has just arrived in this city, *en route* for Chicago and other eastern cities, and only thirty-one days from Salt Lake City. He reports no snow in Salt Lake Valley at the time he left, and but little snow in the mountains. He came by a route known only to the Mormons and mountaineers, by which horsemen in single file can pass the army without being discovered. This route passes between a range of perpendicular rocks for thirteen miles, and in many places is not over three feet wide and completely covered over with a rock roof.[41]
>
> The Mormons are making great preparations for defending all the passes to the valley, and are manufacturing small cannon with percussion locks, and

[38]Kenney, ed., *Wilford Woodruff's Journal*, 13 September 1857, 5:96–97.

[39]"A Mormon Threat," *Vermont Watchman and State Journal* (Montpelier), 8 January 1858, 4; MacKinnon, "Buchanan's Thrust from the Pacific," 233–34; "Brigham Young Threatens to Burn Chicago and Several Other Small Towns," *Weekly Courier* (Alton, Illinois), 22 April 1858.

[40]Young to Bernhisel, 6 January 1858, LDS Archives.

[41]There were back trails that bypassed the high plains on which Camp Scott had been built, but nothing of this fantastic nature.

telescope sights. These cannon carry a two pound ball, and from their peculiar construction will do execution at a distance of a mile and a half, with as much certainty as our common rifles will at a hundred and twenty yards. They also have a manufactory of revolvers, where five hundred are turned out per week.[42]

They are also manufacturing a coarse powder, which they calculate to use in the construction of mines, by which they expect to be able to blow up a [wagon] train without running any risk themselves.

The Mormons and some of the picket guards of Col. Johnson's [*sic*] command have had a skirmish, in which the Mormons lost two killed and five wounded,[43] and he says that it is reported that four of Col. Johnson's men were killed. He also reports that Col. Johnson's mules and oxen are nearly all dead, and that it is believed by the Mormons that Johnson will not have a "hoof" alive in the spring.

Brigham Young preaches upon that subject or the war every Sunday. He says that Brigham is willing for Gov. Cummings [*sic*] and the civil officers to come into the territory and enter upon the duties of their offices; but if the army attempts to enter the valley, they will everyone be cut off.[44]

The 24th of January, the day before Mr. Wingate left the city, Brigham preached to over nine thousand people, and after the sermon he requested all who were in favor of giving the troops h—ll, in case they attempt to enter the valley, to raise up—every man, woman and child rose up. "Now," said Brigham, "I am satisfied. The Lord is with us, and if we determine of one accord to give the troops h—ll the powers on the earth and hell cannot prevail over us, for I have it revealed to me that not a blade of grass, or other green thing will be left on the plains for the support of the beasts of our enemies. Nebraska, Kansas, Iowa and Missouri will be made desolate, and a famine will prevail over the land of our enemies. Brethren be of cheer, God is with us and hell cannot prevail against us."[45]

We could not learn upon what business Mr. Wingate was despatched from the city, but have no doubt but he has important business with the Mormons in the States, "which will be made manifest in due time."

---

[42]These descriptions of sophisticated Mormon weapons and manufacturing capability were gross exaggerations at best and total fabrications at worst. For example the Sabin-Naylor pistol manufacturing operation in Salt Lake City had a capacity to copy twenty-five Colt's revolvers per week, not five hundred.

[43]These Mormon casualty figures coincidentally matched those sustained not in conflict with the Utah Expedition but from the Northern Shoshone and Bannock attack on Fort Limhi on 25 February 1858. A traveler departing Salt Lake City before the second week of March could not have known of this incident.

[44]Throughout the fall of 1857, Young and General Wells issued multiple instructions to the Legion to bar Cumming and other federal appointees from reaching the Salt Lake Valley and exercising their responsibilities. See *At Sword's Point, Part 1*, 367–69.

[45]The 24th day of January 1858 was indeed a Sunday, but there is no record that Brigham Young delivered a discourse that day. The reported audience of nine thousand people would have been more than three times the capacity of any Salt Lake City auditorium of the time. Van Wagoner, ed., *Complete Discourses of Brigham Young*, 3:1393–1454 (1858).

Chapter 3

"Measures to Thwart Them"
Johnston Reacts

For some weeks it has been contemplated to make use of the Uintah Indians as allies against the Mormons in case the latter attempted to interfere with our movements in the Spring, or threatened the safety of the caravan under Marcy, when returning.

Maj. Fitz John Porter, diary entry, 14 January 1858

Colonel Johnston reacted immediately to what he had learned of Brigham Young's plans from returned captives and other sources. Anxious to avoid a repetition of the damage done by Lot Smith's October raid, in which three large army supply trains were burned, Johnston tightened the security of his perimeter. He detailed more sentries and patrols and began the use of passwords while stressing camp vigilance. Johnston's most dramatic measure was to appoint an energetic provost-marshal, 1st Lt. Cuvier Grover of the Tenth Infantry.

Grover's task was to ferret out Mormon agents circulating within the sprawling bivouacs of Fort Bridger, Camp Scott, and Eckelsville, as well as those lurking about the Second Dragoons' isolated herdsmen on Henrys Fork. With dramatic flourish, one officer described Grover, with eight provost sergeants to assist him, as possessing "unlimited power as such. Life and death is in his hands. He is precisely in the capacity of secret police and these sergeants are detectives. They are relieved from all [other] duty, go and come when they please, have a warrant of their appointment, and examine everybody that comes in or near camp. They are to be on the watch day and night, report everything to Lt. Grover that they see and hear. Our camp has been full of Mormons for a long time. Vigorous measures are being taken and these scoundrels must keep off at a proper distance."[1]

Subsequent to Grover's appointment, Johnston formed a small company of civilian spies and guides paid at the same rate as an infantry sergeant ($14.50 per month plus rations). This detachment was commanded by Ben Ficklin, who in December had served briefly as interim U.S. marshal for Utah. If Johnston tasked Grover's uniformed detail with maintaining garrison security, he expected this supplemental civilian detachment to conduct the army's wider-ranging intelligence efforts, as with Ficklin's December–April foray into the Flathead country of Oregon Territory.[2]

Johnston's measures produced results. The dispatches of correspondents Finlay and Browne brimmed with accounts of Brigham Young's emphasis on intelligence gathering and the Utah Expedition's use of Lieutenant Colonel Bee's volunteers to counteract his probes. Together, these efforts illustrate the difficulty of maintaining security for the nation's largest garrison even when snowbound in a wilderness. Unreported to the newspapers was Johnston's greatest worry: the safety of Captain Marcy's mission. On his success hinged the Utah Expedition's ability to survive the winter and then move rapidly on the Salt Lake Valley in the spring.

Espionage Complete and Successful: Spy Catchers

In early December 1857 Johnston had recruited a battalion of volunteer infantrymen for two reasons: to provide employment and discipline for the expedition's unruly civilian teamsters, and to reverse the disastrous impact of summer desertions among the regulars. By the beginning of 1858 Bee's 350-man Battalion of U.S. Volunteers had taken on a semblance of military order and constituted approximately one-quarter of the Utah Expedition's total strength. Its four companies were as large as the ten depleted companies of the Fifth Infantry.

How best to use these raw volunteers? Johnston often assigned Capt. W. M. F. Magraw's troops in Company A to engineering and construction duties, work consistent with their earlier labors with the Pacific Wagon Road project. To the former teamsters of Companies B, C, and D fell details as

[1] Capt. Jesse A. Gove to Mrs. Gove, 6 January 1858, *The Utah Expedition*, 113.

[2] Porter to Dickerson, orders no. 106, 115, and 135 Army of Utah, 12, 14, and 31 March 1858, Letters Sent, Records of the War Dept., RG 98, NARA.

sentinels, guards, pickets, scouts, and wood hawks, the same duties assigned to the Utah Expedition's regular regiments. In one of his covert dispatches for a St. Louis newspaper, the Volunteer Battalion's Sergeant-Major Finlay described an early example of such duty.

[Finlay], "Life in Camp—Experience of a Volunteer—Capture of a Mormon Spy," Camp Scott, Dispatch, 31 January 1858, *Saint Louis Leader*, 23 March 1858, 2/4.

Since my last nothing of any importance has occurred. We are still encamped in our old spot, and have had neither arrivals nor departures of any moment. The command and the army in general continue surprisingly healthy, and the only complaints are of the shortness of the rations and the dullness of camp life. An arrival of a quantity of salt [from Fort Laramie] is the principal feature in the month's events, and although only sufficient to give each man a very scanty allowance, still it was most welcome. It is now all gone, and when we shall see any more is very problematical. . . .

On the 8th inst. we had quite a little excitement in the shape of an expected Mormon attack. Col. Bee sent me out in charge of a small patrol early in the evening, to proceed up Black[s] fork and search the scrub and bluffs in the neighborhood for a Mormon camp, which was reported to have been seen by some individual, whom we hope to see some day soon properly rewarded for making such asses of us. It was very dark, no moon, and the pleasure of wading over sage brush and rocks, on a January night amongst the Utah mountains, with a couple of feet of snow on the ground, must be tested to be appreciated. I went about 14 miles or so at a rattling pace, saw nothing, found no fresh trails, and returned to camp, where I learnt that two other larger parties under Lieutenant [James] Deshler, 10th infantry, and Lieutenant [James F.] Bennet[t], of the volunteer battalion, had started immediately [after] I had left camp; the former returned on the following day, after a fatiguing night march, but the latter was out five days, the men carrying rations for that time.[3]

It was pretty hard licks walking over these plains in deep snow and camping out at night with only a single blanket for bedding and tent. Many of the men were more or less severely frost bitten. Their reconnaissance was also unable to discover the least trace of any enemy. . . .

Strong suspicion has arisen that the Mormons have spies, and good ones too, in our midst. [One Mormon captive] asserts that they know everything that passes, and I, for one, believe it.

---

[3]2d Lieutenant Deshler of Alabama (West Point, Class of 1854) from the Tenth U.S. Infantry's Company E was part of the four-officer regular army cadre for the Volunteer Battalion. He was the unit's quartermaster. Deshler had earlier commanded Capt. Stewart Van Vliet's escort to Salt Lake City during the summer of 1857. 1st Lieutenant Bennett was a volunteer officer of the battalion's Company B. Well-respected, Bennett's peers had originally elected him to be the company's captain, but at age 19 he felt it more appropriate to cede command to an older officer (Daniel McLaughlin).

For his New York readers, correspondent Browne limned a more complete picture of Camp Scott's security problems.

[Browne], "Mormon Hostilities. The Danites and Their Murders," Dispatch, 3 January 1858, Camp Scott, *New-York Daily Tribune*, 1 March 1858.

One of their [Danite] number was taken prisoner to-day in our own camp. I passed him an hour or two ago, sitting on the sod in front of the 5th Infantry's guard tent smoking a pipe as composedly as if a noose was not dangling over his neck. His name is either James or John Thompson.[4] He is a Mormon elder, and a Thug or Danite. He came to camp this morning, accompanied by a Cherokee Indian called Jim (who has visited us twice before), leading a mule loaded with butter and eggs, the first which have been seen by us since the summer. Although disguised in soldier's clothing, he was recognized while disposing of his butter in the store of Messrs. Gilbert & Gerrish; and information being conveyed to headquarters, he was promptly placed in arrest by Major Porter, the Assistant adjutant-General. His avowed object was to discover what mails, expresses and bearers of dispatches were to leave the camp, and about the time of their departure to send word to a band of Mormons who are lurking somewhere in our vicinity, so that they might cut them off. In this project he probably intended to employ Cherokee Jim as the messenger between himself and the Mormon band; but there being no proof of this intention, Jim was dismissed with a warning both from Col. Johnston and from Dr. [Jacob] Forney, the [new] superintendent of Indian Affairs, that he will be immediately arrested if found again within the precincts or in the vicinity of our camp.[5]

Thompson's employment during the Summer and Autumn had been to forward to Salt Lake City information of the movements of the troops.

[4]Called variously John, Nathaniel, and James Thompson in contemporary newspaper reports, the prisoner styled himself as Mathew Thompson. Browne described Thompson as a Mormon, but what, if any, standing he had in the LDS church is difficult to determine. Mormon sources indicate only that Thompson had arrived in Salt Lake City in September 1857 from the west with a group traveling from Carson Valley. He married a Mormon woman en route but was divorced by her for desertion in 1859. Otherwise he appears nowhere in the standard Mormon biographical sources for this period. Later in January 1858 a grand jury sitting at Eckelsville indicted Thompson for treason along with Brigham Young and others. In July 1858 he wrote from Fort Bridger to Brigham Young to describe his imprisoned and destitute condition and to say, "I Know of no other alternative but for me to abide the pleasure of the civil Authoraties unless some of you would do me the favour to pr[o]cure a writ of Habeus Corpus for me to be brought before Judge Eckels. So that I May avail myself of the Presidents Proclamation." Thompson to Young, 7 July 1858, LDS Archives.

[5]The documents relating to the expulsion of "Cherokee Jim" from Camp Scott may be found in Utah State Archives, Salt Lake City, which implies that Jim turned over this material to the Mormons after leaving the army's camp. The Mormon side also had concerns about the reliability and loyalty of Cherokee Jim, whom they sometimes called "Calendar." See, for example, George W. Hill to Col. N. V. Jones, enclosure to Taylor to Young, both dated 25 November 1857, LDS Archives. Although most of the American Indians around Camp Scott during the winter of 1857–58 were Washakie's Shoshones, there were also Indians as individuals or in small bands from a variety of other tribes. Jacob Forney, like Garland Hurt, was a physician.

> For this purpose he stationed himself at John Richard's trading post at the Platte Bridge, about 120 miles west from Fort Laramie [before heading west in November after Cooke's dragoons had passed].
>
> Immediately after Thompson's arrest, Captain [1st Lieutenant] Grover of the 10th Infantry was appointed Provost Marshal of the camp, and to-day he has entered upon the discharge of the duties of that office. . . .
>
> The system of espionage practiced toward this expedition by the Mormons has been complete and successful. Not a single detachment of troops, nor a train, nor hardly even a party of civilians traveling across the plains either on business or for pleasure, left the Missouri border during the Summer without being accompanied by a Mormon spy in some subordinate capacity, such as teamster or cook.[6]

Newspaper correspondents were not the only people commenting on Mormon intelligence gathering in the midst of the Utah Expedition. Writing to President Buchanan from Camp Scott in mid-March 1858, Thomas L. Kane depicted Chief Justice Eckels as "surrounded by persons who report and misrepresent his every word and action. [These] cunning rascals are Mormons in communication with Salt Lake City."[7] After the war, in comments headed *Curious advantage in favor of the Mormons in 1858* and sent to U.S. senator Richard M. Mason and President Buchanan, Kane confirmed the accuracy of Finlay's and Browne's reporting:

Kane to Mason (and Buchanan), 20 April 1860, James Buchanan Papers, HSP.

> I can add a fact or two from my private experience to the consideration of this [spying] question. I was much impressed by the secrecy with which the Mormons were able to cover their movements as contrasted with the perfect acquaintance which they seemed at all times to possess respecting our own. I have a difficulty in recollecting which of our own plans and projects they do not seem to have been aware of. I might almost have suspected the existence of a traitor in high place, if I had not observed what numbers of their converts they managed to introduce into subordinate positions and employments. It is notorious that they had men of their own among the teamsters whose wagons were burned: they have them now unquestionably among the non-commissioned officers at Camp Floyd: they must have had them in great numbers in Camp Scott.

---

[6]Not all of the Latter-day Saints at Camp Scott were spies. Some, not yet under the control of Brigham Young and the Legion, had become legitimate civilian employees of the army at Fort Laramie in 1857 after having dropped out of the handcart emigration of the previous fall. One such lad, George ("Beefsteak") Harrison, was an army camp cook and later a famous Utah restaurateur. Orton, "The Mormons in Johnston's Army," 24–27.

[7]Kane to Buchanan, ca. 15 March 1858, Kane Collection, BYU.

> I remember once Young (Brigham) speaking derisively of the exposed position of the forces at [this] latter point, and being tasked [challenged] by me with having spies there, boasted that it was the fact, and by way of volunteer evidence of it furnished me with a complete diary of the life of the General commanding. He told me what had been my own daily course of life in camp, and with respect to a distinguished civilian my next tented neighbor, gave me the humorous proof of when and where it was his habit of visiting the willows [as a latrine].[8]

As often happens during wars, by 1858 tales of Mormon spying prowess—as with rumors about Utah's weapons manufacturing capabilities—reached lurid, even mythic proportions. While Browne was reporting to the *New-York Tribune* on spy-catching at Camp Scott, his genteel mother in Salem, Massachusetts, was beset by fears of LDS intelligence operatives. To her sixteen-year-old daughter, Sarah, Mrs. Browne likened the Mormon spy apparatus to "a spider with eyes on all sides, [which] is the *horror* of *horrors*." Marveling at the Mormons' apparent knowledge of frontier mail movements, she lamented, "No doubt the Mormons knew of the time when it was to leave the States. The whole body of them seems to me Argus-eyed and I have the same shuddering at the information they receive by their spies, that I have at the movements of a six eyed spider in close proximity to an unconscious, fearless child."[9]

While Mrs. Browne fretted about Mormon spies at work on the frontier, LDS intelligence gathering continued apace closer to home. On 6 January Brigham Young told Horace S. Eldredge, his business agent in St. Louis, "we want you in connection with our brethren in the states to watch the movements of the Government and keep us timely advised of every act pertaining to the movement of troops appropriations for raising and supporting them as well as all that can possibly in any way concern us, for we want to be prepared for the worst though hoping for the best."[10]

---

[8]The distinguished civilian was presumably Governor Cumming. No such intelligence diary of the type described by Young has surfaced.

[9]Sarah Cox Browne to Sarah Ellen Browne, 18 May 1858, Browne Family Papers, Schlesinger Library, Radcliffe Institute. It would have aggravated Mrs. Browne's anxieties had she known that, during the previous fall, Delegate Bernhisel had reported to Young not only her son's assignment to cover the war for the *Tribune* but the specifics of his salary; or that in an 1855 discourse, Young told his audience, "I am watching you. Do you know that I have my threads strung all through the Territory, that I may know what individuals do?" Bernhisel to Young, 2 November 1857, LDS Archives; Young, Discourse, 8 October 1855, *Journal of Discourses*, 3:122.

[10]Young to Eldredge, 6 January 1858, LDS Archives.

To Rely upon the Indians: Protecting Captain Marcy

Of even more concern to Johnston than spy catching was the success of Captain Marcy's mission to New Mexico. Accordingly, Johnston took steps to alert and protect Marcy's command. First, through Superintendent Jacob Forney, he sent Indian Agent Garland Hurt and his small band of Ute protectors to the mountains south of Fort Bridger to seek aid at the Uintah tribe's winter camp.

Precisely what Hurt and Johnston expected to accomplish among the Uintahs is murky. In the spring of 1858, when Dr. Hurt's mission became controversial, the Latter-day Saints argued that he was stimulating tribal attacks upon them, one of the most incendiary issues of the Utah War in light of Southern Paiute involvement in the Mountain Meadows massacre and the Indian attack on Fort Limhi. The federal side argued that Hurt's mission was peaceful, a journey intended to assess the feasibility of Indian farms among the Uintahs much as he had already done with Utes elsewhere. The army's explanation defied common sense given the daunting snowdrifts and weather through which Hurt's party traveled, the lack of urgency then felt about Uintah agriculture, and the inescapable imperatives of the military campaign that surrounded Hurt's activities.

Months later correspondent Browne offered a revealing two-pronged explanation of Garland Hurt's January mission to the Uintahs:

[Browne], "Interesting from Utah: The Case of Dr. Garland Hurt," Dispatch, 5 July 1858, Salt Lake City, *New-York Daily Tribune,* 11 August 1858.

He remained with the army until the close of January, when, with the assent of the Superintendent of Indian Affairs, Dr. Forney, and with that of Gen. Johnston he determined upon an expedition to Uinta Valley, which lies along the river of the same name. One object of this expedition was to examine the condition of the valley at mid-Winter, and ascertain whether it would be practicable to establish a farm there and turn the attention of the tribe to agriculture.

There was another object it was reported that Capt. Marcy and his little band of volunteers for the expedition to New-Mexico, were starving in the snows of the Rocky Mountains, and were at the same time in danger of an attack from Mormon guerrillas. If this information should prove to be well grounded, it was the intention of the Doctor to communicate with him, if practicable, by means of the Uinta Indians, afford him relief and warning of his danger.

> Accompanied only by four Pah-Utahs, he started from Camp Scott on Jan. 22, and crossed the Uinta ridge through snow drifted to the depth of more than 20 feet and descended into the valley, which he reached on Feb. 6. There he remained until the close of March, and reached Camp Scott on his return on April 13. It proved to be unnecessary for him to take any action with regard to Capt. Marcy. Dr. Hurt's expedition to Uinta Valley belongs to the same [valorous] history [as Marcy's]. Its purpose has hitherto remained a secret. Perhaps the return of this letter to Utah [as a *Tribune* dispatch] will convey the first information of it to the men in whose behalf it was undertaken.
>
> I need not enlarge upon the hardships which befell him. They resulted in an illness which threatened his life for weeks, and then seemed like to lead to consumption.

A week before Hurt departed Camp Scott, Major Porter privately confirmed Browne's understanding of the military motives behind this mission.

MAJ. FITZ JOHN PORTER, DIARY, 14 JANUARY 1858, PORTER PAPERS, LC.

> For some weeks it has been contemplated to make use of the Uintah Indians as allies against the Mormons in case the latter attempted to interfere with our movements in the Spring, or threatened the safety of the caravan under Marcy, when returning [from New Mexico]. Some days since three of our men who had been prisoners among the Mormons were returned to camp from Salt Lake City. These men confirmed the information or impressions that the Mormons designed an attack upon Capt. Marcy, and were going to organize a party of some two hundred men to capture or stampede and scatter his animals. This determined Col. J. to rely upon the Indians, and as an auxiliary to the force expected with Capt. M. and had Dr. Hurt the Indian Agent of the tribe approached on the subject.

While Johnston attempted to use tribal allies to counter Mormon plans to intercept Marcy and to attack Fort Bridger (and perhaps Fort Laramie), he did not realize that the new governor of Kansas Territory, James W. Denver, was already advocating a similar measure with which to counter the Mormon threat. Writing from Lawrence at the end of January, Denver proposed to the War Department the use of tribal allies, a measure for which he had tongue-lashed Brigham Young only two months earlier while U.S. commissioner of Indian affairs. Governor Denver advocated pitting friendly Delawares against the presumably Mormon-aligned Cheyennes to protect Fort Laramie and the overland trail. Although the War Department never sanctioned such a tactic during the Utah War, Johnston would seriously consider something like it during the following March in planning to hire Shoshone warriors to operate and defend the strategic Green River ferries.[11]

Reaching Here Unmolested: Warning Marcy

Colonel Johnston also attempted to protect Captain Marcy by relaying the intelligence brought back from Salt Lake City by Private Feldman to Winfield Scott in New York. Indirect as this west-east (rather than north-south) route might seem, Johnston chose the most reliable open communications channel available, given the daunting distance, terrain, and weather separating Fort Bridger from northern New Mexico.[12] Johnston knew that upon receipt of his letter, Scott would telegraph instructions for Marcy's protection from his New York headquarters back to Boonville, Missouri, the western terminus of the wire. From there the army would courier his telegram to Fort Leavenworth, and a military messenger or small detachment would then carry it down the Santa Fe Trail to General Garland's headquarters. Accordingly, two days after the captives' return from Salt Lake City, Johnston wrote to Lt. Col. Irvin McDowell, who was serving as assistant adjutant general at Scott's headquarters.

Johnston to McDowell, 4 January 1858, "Annual Report of the Sec. of War (1858)," 34–36.

> I have just learned that a [returned] soldier . . . has brought the information that the Mormons are organizing a force to "stampede" or capture the horses and mules it is expected Captain Marcy will bring out in the spring from New Mexico.
>
> I have already requested that an escort may be sent with Captain Marcy,[13] but the amount of force will be best determined by the [new] knowledge that an attack may be expected; and I deem it of the greatest consequence, as regards the mobility of this force, that a sufficient force should be sent with Captain Marcy to enable him to reach here unmolested. He will probably leave New Mexico by the 20th March, and I have to request that the General-in-chief will at once authorize the commander of the department of New Mexico to send a force with Captain Marcy to cover his movement.

[11]Denver to Floyd, 31 January 1858, Letters Received, Office of the Adjt. Gen., RG 94; Porter to Jacob Forney, orders no. 68 and 167, Army of Utah, 3 March and 26 April 1858, Letters Sent, Records of the War Dept., RG 98, both NARA.

[12]Unsure of such delivery, on 11 January Johnston risked sending a courier down the spine of the continent with warnings addressed directly to Garland and Marcy. Johnston to Dept. of New Mexico and to Marcy, 10 and 11 January 1858, "Report of Sec. of War (1858)," 41–43.

[13]An allusion to Johnston's request of General Garland in late November via letter carried by Marcy.

A Long and Perilous Journey: Courier Browne

As the courier to deliver this dispatch to Scott, Johnston chose a civilian rather than a soldier: twenty-three-year-old Albert G. Browne, Jr., the field correspondent for Horace Greeley's *New-York Tribune.* Although Browne had been a defendant in one of Boston's most celebrated homicides—the 1854 melee to free fugitive slave Anthony Burns—he was hardly a street fighter, let alone a seasoned frontiersman. From Boston he had headed west for his newspaper assignment afoot and toting a carpetbag. Browne's B.A. and law degree from Harvard, as well as a Ph.D. from the University of Heidelberg, said more about his upbringing, background, and bearing than did his arrest record. How such an inexperienced reporter had come to accompany the Utah Expedition has been one of the war's minor mysteries.[14]

Army records contain virtually no trace of Browne's role in maintaining the Utah Expedition's winter communications link to its headquarters. Until 1877 Browne himself was publicly silent about his mission, one that nearly matched the distance and hardships of Thomas L. Kane's Utah War travels. Sometime after the war, Browne added a notation in his personal scrapbook of *Tribune* dispatches: "During my absence from the [army's] camp from Jan 5 to May 27, 1858, I was employed on a journey to the States with despatches from Gen. Johnston to Gen. Scott, and in returning."[15]

Twenty years after the conflict, Browne broke this self-imposed anonymity to describe in a quite personal way certain of his Utah War experiences. The vehicle for Browne's disclosure was *The Ward of the Three Guardians,* his novella about the war's Henrietta Polydore case.[16] This piece appeared under Browne's name in the June 1877 issue of the *Atlantic Monthly,* the same Boston-based magazine in which during 1859 he published without attribution his impersonal, three-part insider's account of the Utah War. Although *Ward*

[14]The story of Browne's assignment by Greeley to the Utah Expedition surfaced in 1907 and remains obscure. See explanation in Trowbridge, "An Early Contributor's Recollections," 586.

[15]Browne scrapbook, Marriott Library, University of Utah. Browne also carried two letters from Chief Justice Eckels to Secretary of State Lewis Cass and President Buchanan.

[16]Polydore was a young girl whose mother and aunt, Mormon converts, had taken her from England to Salt Lake City in the mid-1850s during a divorce dispute. In 1858 Henrietta's father sought her repatriation through the British Foreign Office, the U.S. State Department, and the Utah Expedition. The title of Browne's novella derived from Judge Eckels's decision during the summer of 1858 to transfer responsibility for her well-being from the prominent Mormon family with which she had been hiding in Salt Lake City to three non-Mormon guardians accompanying the Utah Expedition: Peter K. Dotson, U.S. marshal; Washington Jay McCormick, acting U.S. attorney; and correspondent-lawyer Browne. MacKinnon, "Epilogue to the Utah War," 231–34.

was technically fiction, it was highly accurate with respect to those aspects of the Utah War about which Browne had direct knowledge. As such, the novella provides an unparalleled, albeit melodramatic, account of Albert Sidney Johnston's decision to communicate with General Scott through Browne and the correspondent's cross-country ordeal in doing so.[17]

Among Browne's five traveling companions was John M. Hockaday, who knew the route to be taken intimately from his years in the mail business. He was returning east with Browne not only as a guide but to seize an opportunity to trade the role of Utah's U.S. attorney for the more familiar one of federal contractor on the Independence–Salt Lake City postal route.[18]

Left behind at Camp Scott was the friend to whom Browne entrusted the continued flow of unsigned dispatches to the *Tribune*: David Auguste Burr. He was the *New York Times*'s pseudonymous correspondent, "A.B.C."; Eckelsville's justice of the peace and coroner; and son of David H. Burr, Utah's controversial surveyor general. That Burr would write simultaneously on the same subject for two competing Manhattan dailies without alerting his readers or editors was not then unusual although it would be unethical today.[19]

Browne, "The Ward of the Three Guardians," *Atlantic Monthly* 39 (June 1877): 697–703.

On the afternoon of New Year's Day in 1858, the medley of troops, teamsters, and adventurers who composed what was called the Utah Expedition lay huddled in a dreary camp, seven thousand feet above the level of the sea, in the shallow valley of Black's Fork, a few miles south of a little stone redoubt named Fort Bridger, which is still visible from the track of the [Union] Pacific railroad. . . .[20]

Inside of a wide-spreading hospital-tent, which was pitched near the centre of the camp and loomed conspicuously above its neighbors, there was

---

[17]MacKinnon, "Vita: Albert Gallatin Browne Jr.," 48–49, and "Epilogue to the Utah War," 225–26.

[18]Hockaday's departure from the Utah Expedition's winter quarters may also have hinged, in part, on his discomfort over spending the rest of the winter in close proximity to a large concentration of West Pointers and Mexican War veterans. Hockaday had abruptly resigned as a cadet from the U.S. Military Academy in the spring of 1846 on the eve of his court martial, and had subsequently failed to obtain a commission for Mexican service in either the regular U.S. Army or a volunteer regiment notwithstanding his several years of military training. For his unsuccessful pursuit of a commission in the Sixteenth U.S. Infantry after West Point, see Hockaday to President Polk, 7 April 1847, copy in possession of editor courtesy of James C. Johnston, Franklin, Mass.

[19]Browne and Burr never mentioned publicly the latter's substitution for Browne during his trek to the Atlantic Coast and back. Evidence of Burr's role appears in Browne's scrapbook and Burr's personal correspondence in the David Auguste Burr Papers. The younger Burr may have chosen "A.B.C." as a nom de plume because his mother ran a private elementary school in Washington, D.C.

[20]The U.P.R.R. had been built through that area during 1868–69.

a gathering, this dreary afternoon, whose gayety was in merry contrast with the savage and somber scenery without. . . .

It was during the burst of laughter which greeted the revelation of the secret of the pastry [we had just eaten] that the general, tapping my shoulder, drew me aside into a corner of the tent, and startled me with the whisper, "Would you like to go to church on Easter in New York?"[21] I think it must have been a minute before I replied; for something in his manner satisfied me that he was not joking, and set my fancy wandering off across a thousand miles of snowy desert, and then floating down the Missouri River, steaming [by train] across the land a thousand miles further, and arriving at [Lower Manhattan's] Trinity Church on a sparkling morning of the early spring, when the yellow buds of the willows were swelling in the grave-yard, and a battalion of pretty girls, with dainty new bonnets, was pressing through the portal to the music of organ and orchestra and chanting children's voices.

Five days afterwards I had finished my preparations for the long and perilous winter journey to "the States."[22] Half a dozen men, selected for my companions and escort, were sworn to secrecy as to even the fact of the adventure; and its purpose was only communicated to me in confidence, lest some accident might befall the dispatches which I was to bear. The situation was indeed serious. A private inspection of the [Utah Expedition's] commissary stores had convinced the general that they were insufficient to subsist the army till military operations could be resumed against the Mormons; the dispatches contained an earnest appeal to General Scott to force a convoy of provisions through to the camp; and I was warned that the fortunes of the campaign would largely depend upon the safety and speed of my journey.[23]

It was a dark and dismal evening[24] when I raked the ashes over the embers of my camp fire, tied up the door of my tent, and crossed the ice at the bend of the creek to take supper with the general and get my last instructions. I was to set out before dawn the next morning, and, for fear of outlying parties of Mormons, instead of striking due east was to travel south along Green

---

[21]The significance of New York was that it was the location of the army's headquarters.

[22]Three years later to the day, Massachusetts governor John A. Andrew would dispatch Browne on another secret mission to enlist the governors of New Hampshire and Maine to join him in preparing their militias for the immediate defense of Washington, D.C., in the event of a Southern attack. Browne, then still a civilian, was Andrew's former law partner and private secretary. The governor unquestionably knew of Browne's 1858 trek from Fort Bridger to Washington and back. Andrew, "Special Message to the Massachusetts House of Representatives," January 28, 1862, 305.

[23]Why Browne chose not to mention here the other compelling reason for his mission—the need to warn and reinforce Marcy through Scott—is baffling. Based on his own interview with Private Feldman for the *Tribune*, Browne knew as much as Johnston did about the Mormon intent to intercept Marcy.

[24]Unwittingly or otherwise, Browne began this sentence with a variant of the then-famous—but now ridiculed—opening phrase of Edward George Bulwer-Lytton's 1830 English novel *Paul Clifford*: "It was a dark and stormy night."

River to the mouth of Bitter Creek, follow that up as far as the snow would permit, and then journey northeast, by the compass, across the table-land towards the Wind River Mountains, till I should reach the Sweetwater and the Oregon trail that leads through the South Pass.[25] At the general's table I found the famous old trapper, Jim Bridger, who had been summoned there to give me information about the route. . . .

Just here the adjutant [Major Porter] entered the tent with my bundles of dispatches, sealed, and securely bound with red tape.[26] The last farewell was soon said, and I was wandering through the camp to warn my companions to be ready betimes in the morning.

Our party was in the saddle by star-light, before the first streak of dawn glimmered above the eastern bluff, and when Camp Scott awoke to another day of its monotonous life, we were ten miles away on the trail to Henry's Fork, where we were to select our horses and pack-mules from the herds which were pasturing there near the dragoons' camp. That evening a courier from Camp Scott brought down to me another package of dispatches, and a letter from the general's aide, the young lieutenant [Lawrence A. Williams], which inclosed one of the neat little three-cornered notes in which the pass-words for the day were usually communicated to those who were entitled to them. . . . The next morning [5 January] we were far away on our bleak journey to the States,—a journey of a thousand miles through snow-drifts, in which we should find only two spots where there was a roof that sheltered a white man.

It was near sunset on a bitter afternoon early in February, when we struck the Oregon trail. For two days we had not been able to collect fuel for a fire. The snow lay so deep on this part of the route across the dreary table-land that during the whole of the preceding week we were compelled to break the crust and trample a path ourselves, to make a passage for our animals, and we were fortunate to accomplish in this way five or six miles between sunrise and sunset. This day the thermometer had marked eighteen degrees below zero at noon. Every one of us was weary and on the verge of sickness, and several were frost-bitten. But there was spirit enough left to raise a hearty cheer when Jo Brooks, who led the trampling column and had just

---

[25]In ascending Bitter Creek from its confluence with the Green River, Browne's party would have been traveling north-northeast toward the South Pass roughly paralleling the route of today's U.P.R.R. and Interstate 80.

[26]Browne may have described the bundling of the dispatches this way because of his lingering embarrassment over not realizing in January 1858 that some of the papers were intended for delivery along the way to Forts Laramie, Kearny, and Leavenworth. This mistake was not discovered until he arrived at General Scott's headquarters in New York, the address on the outer wrapper. This delivery delayed for several weeks an awareness at Laramie of how badly the Utah Expedition needed supplies from that post. Scott's adjutant later announced that "Mr. Brown[e] is not considered by the General-in-chief accountable for this error." McDowell to Cooper, 1 March 1858, "Annual Report of the Sec. of War (1858)," 39.

surmounted a swell in the table-land, pointed to some dark knolls in the distance and cried out, "The Sweetwater!"[27]

We toiled with renewed courage long after the yellow streaks of sunset had faded into gray in the gloomy evening sky. The snow became thinner after the crest of the bluff was turned which bounded southward the bottom-lands of the stream, and soon we were able to mount and press forward with increasing speed. The outlines of the dark knolls grew more distinct in the dusk, and were recognizable as the cliffs on the other side of the river. At last we crossed the frozen ruts of the broad emigrant-road, but did not rest until we reached the river-side at a bend where the current was so swift that a strip a hundred feet long was free of ice,—a welcome sight to our eyes, for ever since we began to ascend Bitter Creek, more than a fortnight before, we had obtained water only by melting the snow. . . .

I went to church in New York on Easter, and saw the pretty girls and new spring bonnets.[28]

Because Browne had written *The Ward of the Three Guardians* primarily to dramatize the Henrietta Polydore case, that piece did not provide further details of his trek. On the other hand, in his 1859 non-fiction series for the *Atlantic Monthly,* Browne included a less personal vignette of the ordeal that he, John M. Hockaday, Jo Brooks, and the others shared:

The dispatches in which these [Johnston's] anxieties were communicated to General Scott, together with suggestions for their relief, were intrusted in midwinter to a small party for conveyance to the States. The journey taught them what must have been the sufferings of the expedition which Captain Marcy led to Taos. Reduced at one time to buffalo tallow and coffee for sustenance, there was not a day during the transit across the mountains when any stronger barrier than the lives of a few half-starved mules interposed between them and death by famine. All along the route lay memorials of the march of the army, and especially of Colonel [Philip St. George] Cooke's [dragoon] battalion,—a trail of skeletons a thousand miles in length, gnawed bare by the wolves and bleaching in the snow, visible at every undulation in the drifts.[29]

---

[27]"Jo Brooks" may have been W. J. Brooks, a seasoned mail conductor on this route, or the Joseph Brooks hired by Colonel Johnston in March 1858 for his civilian company of spies and guides. "A.B.C." [Burr], "Later from Utah . . . The Weather in the Rocky Mountains," Dispatch, 18 December 1858, *New York Times,* 26 January 1859, 2; Porter to Dickerson, orders no. 106, Army of Utah, 12 March 1858, Letters Sent, Records of the War Dept., RG 98, NARA.

[28]Based on his mother's diary, Browne was in Boston, not New York, on Easter Sunday, 4 April 1858.

[29][Browne], "The Utah Expedition," 478. An additional way to understand this winter trail experience is through Charles R. Morehead's reminiscences of his and Jim Rupe's passage over the same route ten days earlier. Theirs was a freezing, wolf-plagued ordeal that Morehead recalled with horror a half-century later in sweltering El Paso. Morehead, "Recollections," 600–22.

1st Lt. Lawrence A. Williams, Johnston's Aide
Williams's role as Colonel Johnston's aide de camp has been little noted. He was an officer in Capt. Alfred Cumming's Company G, Tenth Infantry. A native of Georgetown, D.C., Williams was cousin to Robert E. Lee's wife Mary, a descendant of Martha Washington. Johnston was prone to surround himself with able, politically or socially connected West Pointers like Williams and Lee as well as the volunteers' commander (Bee), his adjutant (Porter), and his inspector general (Marcy). *Photo taken at Camp Floyd ca. January 1859 by Mills & Jagiello, courtesy of Ephriam Dickson III and NARA.*

Whatever it was that Browne endured as Albert Sidney Johnston's courier may have prompted one of his Harvard classmates to memorialize him in 1913 by attributing Browne's 1891 death to "a disease dating probably from the privations encountered in the Utah Expedition, from which he had suffered for many years with fortitude."[30]

Unaware that her son was eastbound, Sarah Browne's moods swung from semi-satisfaction that Albert was a civilian non-combatant traveling in the midst of a U.S. Army expedition to fear of his proximity to a Mormon adversary that her Protestant-Brahmin perspective considered evil, violent, and fanatic. Unlike her more worldly husband, who drew comfort from the episodic appearance of Albert's dispatches in the *Tribune,* Mrs. Browne reacted with fear rather than pride whenever the New York newspaper arrived in Salem. To her daughter, at school in Cambridge, she confided these anxieties.

[30]Unattributed, "Albert Gallatin Browne," *Report of the Harvard Class of 1853*, 46–51.

Sarah Cox Browne to Sarah Ellen ("Nellie") Browne, 30 October, 20 November, 14 and 18 December 1857, Browne Family papers, Schlesinger Library, Radcliffe Institute.

I suppose the *Tribune* news has largely occupied *your* thoughts, as well as mine. I cannot feel as comfortably about it as does your Father. There is nothing that will rouse to desperation more easily than religious controversy. A man will fight for his religion when nothing else will rouse him to strike a blow. Brigham Young is cunning and loves power. Bold in making proseylites and finding worshippers, he may be bold in the use of the sword. If a struggle comes Albert's position *may be his protection.* The dear boy! If he were at home, I would give worlds, if worlds were under my sway. All here laugh at my fears. I feel he is altogether too *good—too noble,* to be in that unchristian place. The guiding hand that leads him there, is veiled in mystery. We know it *never errs* in the wisdom of its guidance, so we must place our hands on our mouths and shut in all murmurings. Whatever may come, we are sure it comes for visible or invisible good, and the motto of our hearts must be, "Thy will, not mine."

Your brother's letter, which I shall send you, has in it no fear, like a philosopher he reasons, no biting cold, want of fuel, want of grain or Mormon menace can terrify him. The bitter cup may be his, and if need be, he *will* drink to the dregs. His letters [of introduction] to Henry Felt may be of much service to him, as Mr. Felt holds the responsible office of Treasurer among them, and is one of the famous ten, who sway in privy council.[31] Do not let my note make you low spirited, for the majority of people think there is no possibility of bloodshed. If there were, Albert is apart from the army and need not take part with them. The strangeness of his position comes over me like a dream. I ask myself what is human foresight?

I rejoiced to find that you could read *"with pleasure"* the dear boy's letter, when to me, it was fear and trembling. The news from the plains, is so full of terror to me, that I conjure up at times fearful tidings with regard to the little army, stationed there. Albert's *personal safety* may not be in the immediate danger, which threatens the soldier. If his letters to Brigham Young and other Mormons can be delivered to their destination, they may be a great protection to him, standing as he does, in the position of a reporter of proceedings on both sides.[32] We have great reason to rejoice that his heart is brave and his health good. Should his life be spared, the sight of a bloody

---

[31]Nathaniel Henry Felt, formerly of Salem, was a respected but not senior Mormon leader and municipal official as well as merchant in Salt Lake City. He was not a member of the Quorum of the Twelve Apostles as Mrs. Browne implies.

[32]Albert's mother's implication that he was an even-handed reporter was hardly the case in view of his calls for Johnston to impose martial law and the summary execution of Mormon leaders.

> conflict, even if he is no participator, will be horrible. The Mormon party is full of bitter animosity to our government, and if blood is shed, it will flow most freely. Oh! If we could gather the dear one into the family fold again without all this! But we must wait and trust the long winter through.
>
> Albert's letter to the *Tribune,* you probably have read. The Salem people call it "good news." This collision he anticipates before Christmas, is a strange definition of *"good."* Still I am grateful that the larger part of the army is to congregate together, and that altho small in number, they can act together. We must wait and be trustfully hopeful as to the result. Albert's cheerful spirit is ever manifested in all he writes. No suffering will discourage him. He knows he is on the side of the *right* and will persevere to the *end.*
>
> The article you speak of, in the *Weekly Tribune,* no doubt, refers to Albert. Poor fellow, if he *ever* comes. The long, dreary winter months are phantoms about me. Brigham is like the arch enemy in the path.—Some nights the sighing winds seem to me like echoes from the battle fields. I drive away as much as possible, sad forebodings, but it is impossible for me to think him beyond suffering, in that region of snow and ice, even if unmolested by the surrounding foe. All we can do is to *trust.*

The military dispatches carried by Browne have survived and been published, so historians are aware of Colonel Johnston's early January concern for Captain Marcy and his urgent need for provisions from Forts Leavenworth and Laramie. Unknown, though, is the fact that when Browne reached Missouri in February, he, like Thomas L. Kane in Utah, entered the realm of independent action. Before crossing the Mississippi to resume his eastbound travels by rail, Browne dashed off a note to Marcy warning him of the Mormon threat to his mission and alerting him to the fact that, through him, Johnston was also briefing General Scott about the Mormon plans. Browne sent his letter south via the Santa Fe Trail to Fort Union, New Mexico; from there it was re-directed to the northbound captain at his bivouac near the Purgatory River. Startled to receive it, Marcy immediately sent the substance of Browne's message to General Garland's adjutant on 22 March.[33]

What did not survive Browne's travels, though, were the two letters entrusted to him by Chief Justice Eckels for Secretary of State Cass and President Buchanan. Because Browne's luggage was stolen aboard a train, he reached Washington virtually empty-handed. Attempting to recover from this humiliating reversal, Browne wrote for Secretary Cass his recollection of what Judge Eckels intended to communicate.

---

[33]Marcy to Nichols, 22 March 1858, Letters Received, HQ Dept. of New Mexico, RG 393, NARA.

Browne to Cass, 15 March 1858, Records of the Territories, Utah Series, Department of State, RG 59, NARA.

I take the liberty of addressing to you this letter, in order that the substance of its contents may be more easily referred to than if it were communicated in a personal interview.[34]

I left Camp Scott, where the army of Utah is in winter-quarters, on the night of January 5th, 1858, in company with Mr. J. M. Hockaday, the U.S. Atty for Utah Territory. A chief inducement for my journey to the U. States, was the personal and urgent request of Judge Eckels that I should proceed to Washington and represent to gentlemen connected and influential with the administration, the true condition of affairs in that Territory and the difficulties which environ the new civil leaders, and especially the officers of the courts. For this purpose he requested me to take charge of two letters, one addressed by him to yourself and the other to the President of the United States, in which he discussed at length the subject to which I have referred.

These I brought safely to [army headquarters in] New York City. From there I proceeded to [Salem,] Massachusetts to see my family, from whom, owing to mismanaged mail service I had not heard for six months.[35] After passing one night at home I started for Washington via Norwich & Worcester Railroad. . . .

Under these circumstances [of theft] I have no alternative but to communicate to you personally the substance of the Judge's letters. He left them open for the inspection of Mr. Hockaday and myself, and we informed ourselves of their contents at his desire.

In the first place he represented the necessity of an immediate change of the instructions issued from the Department of the Interior to the U.S. Marshal for Utah Territory. On the subject of these instructions Mr. Hockaday [as U.S. attorney] will give you any information you may desire. The *point* of the Judge's reccommendation on this subject was, that, the Territorial treasury of Utah being inaccessible to the new civil officers, the United States should defray the expense of conducting the Territorial courts and enforcing the Territorial laws, until access can be had to that Treasury. In support of such a policy he adduced the fact that the persons and property protected by the enforcement of the Territorial laws in the Court of Utah he organized at camp, have been almost solely the persons and property of U.S. employees.

On the subject of the legality of that Court (to which he adverted,) I must again refer you to Mr. Hockaday.

In this connection he alluded to the embarrassment which the absence

---

[34]After having faced General Scott's wrath in New York, Browne may have been reluctant to meet personally with Cass.

[35]This was a gentle criticism of the Buchanan administration's June 1857 decision to suspend mail service on the Independence–Salt Lake City route without replacing it.

of his two associate justices had caused, and recommended that in case they do not purpose to start for Utah at a very early day, a commission of Judge should be forwarded by express to someone already on the ground, with whom he could cooperate.[36] As an entirely suitable person for this purpose he named Lieut. Henry B. Kelly of the 10th Infantry, a citizen of Louisiana formerly a lawyer in New Orleans;[37] and among the papers stolen from me was a memorial to the President cordially recommending his appointment, signed by Judge Eckels,—chief Justice of the Territory [and others].

He alluded to the extraordinary and unconstitutional character of many of the Territorial laws, and to the necessity of an immediate revision of them by some competent authority.[38]

To the line of policy which Dr. Forney and Dr Hurt are pursuing towards the Utah and Snake [Shoshone] Indians he gave his cordial approbation. In regard to Mr. [George W.] Armstrong, the other Indian agent, he expressed an opinion that he should be removed, on account of his complicity with the attempt by the Mormons on [the life of] Dr. Hurt. Armstrong is himself a Mormon.

He discussed the propositions of Mr. Douglas's [12 June 1857] Springfield speech concerning Utah, and expressed himself decidedly adverse to any such plan for its separation and disorganization as was there proposed.

In conclusion he referred the President and yourself, to Mr. Hockaday and myself, for the minutiae which you might desire, as being persons well acquainted with the whole Utah question and holding sound views concerning it.

Concerning the army he expressed his profound acknowledgement to Col. Johnston for the cordiality with which he had cooperated with the court, and indeed with every movement for the institution of order and civil government,—and he expressed also his confidence in his wisdom, prudence, and ability.[39]

Allow me, sir, to add a few remarks of my own to what I have written—on

---

[36]Associate justices John Cradlebaugh and Charles E. Sinclair did not reach Salt Lake City until the fall of 1858.

[37]Henry Brooke Kelly was the son of a prominent Alabama judge and U.S. senator. At age 35 he was older, more experienced, and better educated than most of the Utah Expedition's first lieutenants, having earned two degrees from St. Louis University, served as an officer in the Mexican War, and practiced law in New Orleans before reentering the U.S. Army in 1855. In 1858 he was the acting commander of the Tenth's Company A. Kelly never received appointment to the bench in Utah but, in Hockaday's absence, he briefly functioned as that territory's U.S. attorney. Later, after service as a Confederate colonel, he became a prominent attorney and judge in New Orleans. "Henry B. Kelly," obituary, George Sharswood, ed., *Report of the . . . American Bar Association*, 499–502.

[38]Congress had the power to review and reject Utah's territorial laws but theretofore had never bothered to exercise this responsibility, as Brigham Young often commented.

[39]The absence of any reference to Governor Cumming reflects the tension that had developed between him and Judge Eckels, as well as Colonel Johnston and probably Browne.

Col. Albert Sidney Johnston
Alarmed in early January by reports of Brigham Young's plans, Johnston couriered warnings to General Scott in New York and Captain Marcy in New Mexico. He also tightened Camp Scott's defenses against surprise attacks and Mormon spies, while sending Indian Agent Garland Hurt to the winter camp of the Uintas, the first of several problematic moves to establish tribal allies. This steel engraving of a plaster bust by Richmond sculptor Edward Virginius Valentine was commissioned posthumously in 1876 by Johnston's son William. He considered it the best likeness of his father, depicted here as a Confederate general. *Image from William Preston Johnston,* The Life of Gen. Albert Sidney Johnston *(New York, 1878).*

a subject to which the Judge did not allude—viz: the insufficiency of the salaries of all the territorial officers in that country. Their salaries will not cover their own personal expenses—in several instances. What inducement then exists, for a man of family, ability, reputation, and integrity to seek or to continue in an arduous employment, subject to a thousand privations and responsibilities, when his salary will not support himself to say nothing of his wife and children?[40]

P.S.—To one portion of the Judge's letters I omitted to allude. He urged with great earnestness the need of an immediate appropriation for a law library, its purchase and speedy despatch to Utah Territory. He is convinced that the U.S. library at Salt Lake City either has been burned, as is alleged, or at all events, will never come into the hands of the Court. These important indictments of treason are pending and he has *no library.*[41]

---

[40]Here Browne was unwittingly repeating one of the arguments that Brigham Young often used in advocating federal appointments for Utahns rather than from among outsiders unaccustomed to the territory's unusual culture and high cost of living. Young to President Pierce, 30 March 1853, LDS Archives.

[41]The debate over whether unidentified raiders had indeed destroyed the territorial law library and court records on 29 December 1856 continues to this day. Treason indictments against Mormons were returned by a federal grand jury as Browne and Hockaday left Eckelsville but, contrary to Judge Eckels's expectations the grand jury did not hand down additional treason indictments in April 1858.

Intercepting the Caballada: Countering Mormon Plans

As Browne and his party struggled through the snow drifts near the continental divide, Albert Sidney Johnston provided the next eastbound mail courier with a summary of the measures that he had taken to counter what he knew of Mormon intentions and activities. In this dispatch, Johnston reacted strongly to Brigham Young's annual message and the Utah legislative assembly's related 21 December resolutions. Interestingly, Johnston's use of the word "treasonable" went far beyond the lawyerly phrasing then being used by President Buchanan, but it matched that of the federal grand jury that had just returned mass indictments from its log-cabin courtroom at Eckelsville.

Johnston to McDowell, 20 January 1858, "Annual Report of the Sec. of War (1858)," 44–45.

I have nothing material to report since my last communication. Accompanying that I sent a file of the "Deseret News," containing the message of Brigham Young to the Legislature of Utah. You have in that message and the resolutions of the legislature a full confirmation of the charge of their disloyalty to the Union heretofore made against this people. My information respecting their conduct since is, that their troops are organized to resist the establishment of a territorial government by the United States, and, in furtherance of that object, they have erected works of defence in the mountain passes and near Salt Lake City. Knowing how repugnant it would be to the policy or interest of the government to do any act that would force these people into unpleasant relations with the federal government, I would, in conformity with the views also of the commanding general, on all proper occasions have manifested in my intercourse with them a spirit of conciliation, but I do not believe that such consideration for them would be properly appreciated now, or rather would be wrongly interpreted; and, in view of the tr[e]asonable temper and feeling now pervading the leaders and a greater portion of the Mormons, I think that neither the honor nor the dignity of the government will allow of the slightest concession being made to them.

They should be made to submit to the constitutional and legal demands of the government unconditionally. An adjustment of existing difficulties on any other basis would be nugatory.

Their threat to oppose the march of the troops in the spring will not have the slightest influence in delaying it; and if they desire to join issue [in combat], I believe it is for the interest of the government that they should have the opportunity.

> On the 11th of this month I sent an express to Santa Fé to acquaint General Garland with the design of the Mormons to intercept the caballada [herd] it is expected Captain Marcy will bring on from [New] Mexico, and to ask additional force to his escort. I will also take other measures to thwart them.[42]

One of the measures that Colonel Johnston put into motion related to the assets at Fort Thompson in the Wind River Mountains north of South Pass: the winter bivouac that W. M. F. Magraw had established during the fall of 1857 for the remnant of his Pacific Wagon Road crew. When an exhausted Salt Lake City postmaster Hiram F. Morrell and his guide, Sol Gee, returned to Fort Bridger via Fort Thompson on 20 January 1858 after a futile month-long attempt to join Ben Ficklin's mission to the Flathead country, they reported that Fort Thompson was in danger from the menaces of Crow warriors and, presumably, Mormons. Two days after Johnston wrote his long status report for army headquarters, Magraw informed Secretary of the Interior Thompson that he and Johnston were planning to transfer Fort Thompson's thirteen men, tools, wagons, and animals to Fort Bridger. They would do so under the protection of a thirty-man escort of "former teamsters," probably troops detailed from Bee's Volunteer Battalion.[43]

Conduct Most Reprehensible: Magraw Savages Forney

Magraw's 22 January letter to Secretary Thompson was a complex one. In it he not only reported the joint Johnston-Magraw intent to evacuate Fort Thompson but defended two of his own earlier actions: his October decision to volunteer with the Utah Expedition, and his insistence on maintaining direct communication with President Buchanan.[44] Intertwined with these

[42]The vagueness of this phrasing probably reflects Johnston's concern over Mormon mail interception.

[43][Finlay], "The Army for Utah," Dispatch, 31 January 1858, *Saint Louis Leader*, 24 March 1858, 2/3. Finlay was the only correspondent at Camp Scott with firsthand knowledge of Fort Thompson and its small civilian cadre, having been there in early October 1857 when Magraw's Pacific Wagon Road crew, of which he was then part, built it.

[44]As this correspondence indicates, maintaining a communications channel with Buchanan, either directly or through Thompson, was important to Magraw's efforts at self-promotion. An early example appears in Magraw's July 1857 letter to Thompson from Fort Kearny relaying rumors of Mormon war preparations and perceptions of Brigham Young's despotism. Although he marked the letter "Private," by the end of the first sentence he had directed Thompson to "regard this communication as official or not, just as you may see proper" while adding the request, "if you please, show this to the President," a plea that the secretary ignored by forwarding it instead to the army's hierarchy. Magraw to Thompson, 31 July 1857, Letters Received, Records of the Adjt. Gen., RG 94, NARA.

subjects, Magraw gratuitously inserted a volatile, non-military issue that would soon trigger tensions unhelpful to the war's prosecution: conflict among the Buchanan administration's federal appointees for Utah.

The means by which Magraw contributed to this internecine warfare was his covert accusation of the corruption of Jacob Forney, Brigham Young's successor as Utah's superintendent of Indian affairs. During the prior fall, Magraw had maneuvered with Forney for influence and control over Chief Washakie's Shoshones, and there are signs that in January Magraw hoped to bolster his own shaky standing with Thompson by criticizing Forney. Thus planted, Magraw's seed of doubt about Forney's probity would bring about the superintendent's recall in 1859 at a time when Magraw was fighting to salvage his own reputation from charges of drunkenness, ineptness, corruption, and abandonment of his Pacific Wagon Road responsibilities.[45]

MAGRAW TO THOMPSON, 22 JANUARY 1858,
RECORDS OF THE FORT KEARNY, SOUTH PASS, AND HONEY LAKE SUPERINTENDENCY, PACIFIC WAGON ROAD OFFICE,
INTERIOR DEPARTMENT, RG 48, NARA.

By reference to my [2 January] letter to the President heretofore alluded to, and to the contents of his, you will be acquainted with all I have to communicate on this subject at present. But there is another matter to which I feel it my duty to call your attention. In doing so, I feel it a painful duty but an imperative one. It is with regard to the conduct of one of the Appointees of your Dept who is now in this country. I allude to the conduct of Dr Forney, Supt of Indian Affairs in Utah Territory.

I have been informed by a gentleman of undeniable veracity that Mr Livingston, of the firm of Livingston & Kinkade, had boasted that "he had the dead wood or $20,000" of his funds in Dr Forney's hands. Since that time, I have been informed by Mr Wm Gerrish of the firm of Gilbert and Gerrish, who are also here, that Dr Livingston [i.e., Forney] made propositions to him for the purchase of goods to be given as presents to the Indians, on the condition that he, Dr Forney, [share] in the profits arising from the transaction, which would, Dr Forney concluded, considerably exceed the usual returns in trade.

To the credit of Mr Gerrish, he refused indignantly the offer, and I would respectfully refer you to him for a full statement of the case, and also to Col. Johnson [*sic*] for an opinion as to his capacity to fill the position he at

---

[45]The record of Forney's travails is most readily found in his papers and those of Associate Justice John Cradlebaugh, found in the Yale Collection of Western Americana, Beinecke Library. Unknown to Magraw, as he was writing to Thompson during late January, the secretary was dismissing him from his Pacific Wagon Road superintendency and replacing him with his chief engineer, Frederick W. Lander. MacKinnon, "The Buchanan Spoils System," 127–50.

present holds. This conduct on the part of an official is most reprehensible & very much to be repulsed, more particularly in one holding a position in this Territory at this time.

Allow me to suggest the propriety of keeping up Fort Thompson as an Indian Agency, for which purpose it is admirably adapted, and the cost of construction would be saved to the Government.

Little or No Dissipation: Magraw Lobbies Douglas

Having thus unburdened himself to Secretary Thompson, Magraw immediately wrote to Stephen A. Douglas, chairman of the Senate's committee on the territories. This time the subject was naked self-promotion. Realizing that his status with the Interior Department was precarious, and that his volunteer captaincy would terminate during the summer, Magraw lobbied Douglas for a long-term solution to his employment problems: an officer's commission in the regular army. With Douglas engaged in political conflict with President Buchanan—to whom Magraw had written only three weeks earlier—the captain sought to compartmentalize his communications with each politician. Accordingly, he cautioned Douglas: "You are the only one to whom I have made known my wishes. If you should mention this subject to any of my Friends, dont mention that I have written to you about it."

Magraw to Douglas, 22 January 1858,
Stephen A. Douglas Papers, Special Collections
Research Center, University of Chicago Library.

We have no news in Camp since the departure of J. M. Hockaday & Mr. Browne who left this on the fifth inst. Not a single communication either from the States, or from Salt Lake has been received since their departure. I presume you have seen Mr. H, who has given you all the news prior to that time. The Camp is quiet, and hea[l]thy. The men are contented, all anxiously looking for the opening [of] Spring, when the order "forward March," will be given. Every man will spring into his position, and start on the Road to [Salt Lake City's River] *Jordan,* and then on its banks test the strength of Brigham Young and his followers.

On account of the difficultys in this country I had to abandon the Pacific Expedition. I built a Fort on the Big Popingia [Popo Agie] River, leaving enough of men to protect the property, [and] with the rest of them, organized a Company, and Volunteered in the Army for nine months. I have turned over a large part of my Transportation to the Army, & as soon as Col Johnson [*sic*] can prudently send an Escort to Fort Thompson to protect the transit of the remainder, it will also be delivered to him. I like my new life very well, and I hope in the spring we will be able to give a good account of the Volunteer Battalion. My company is Letter "A," it being the first, the others organized about a month after. Our camp is situated about Three Miles above "Head Quarters." It may be regarded as an out post.

Our regular Army is [too] small, and ought to be increased. Should Congress conclude to do so, (I will here remind you of a conversation I once had with you, Which was, that in the Event that certain things would take place, that I wanted a commission in the Army) I would like to get into the mounted service. I would like the position of major. If you can in justice to yourself take an interest in this matter, if there should be an increase of the Army, you will much oblige me.

Col Johnsons appointment to take Command of this Army I think was one of the best that could have been made. It is one of the most orderly, and best governed camps I have ever seen, little or no dissipation of any kind, and all is quiet.[46] About four hours of each day is spent in drilling the men. . . .

I regret that I am unable to make this letter more interesting to you. The truth is, we have no news, our position is an isolated one from all the civilized world, and the Indians are off hunting Buffalo [east of the Rockies], and I have no one to write about. Dont you think it is unkind in your old friend Brigham to keep us out here this winter. We think so, and as the Yanky says, "We intend to *argue* that *pint,*" with him in the Spring. I have every reason to believe, from my own observation, and from the best information which I can gather, that we could have enjoyed ourselves in *various ways,* had we been permit[t]ed to have gone quietly along. I expect you are better posted in Salt Lake matters than we are here, as we are informed that communication is kept open with California. We have not had a single intelligent or reliable account from there since Capt Van Vliet left [in September], and Brigham had so completely bamboozled him by feasting him on Peaches, & Grapes, and showing him through his harem, and representing his strength as being so great, that I dont think the Captain did himself justice in his report.—My kind regards to Mrs. D. & the Boys.

[P.S.] If you have the time to spare, please write to me direct Army of Utah. I will write you again when I get on the banks of the *Jordan,*—provided—Congress must make some provision [appropriation] for the volunteers.

Thus while Albert Sidney Johnston struggled in a wilderness to anticipate and counter the military moves of his Mormon adversary, Captain Magraw, one of his own officers, continued to advance his personal interests at the expense of the U.S. government. Small wonder that Senator Douglas reacted with a shrewd one-word annotation on Magraw's letter: "no."

---

[46]Magraw's portrayal of Camp Scott as a quiet garrison engaged in clean living reflected either a colossal lack of perspective or a calculating attempt to parry months of reporting by others about his own drunkenness.

THE IVES EXPEDITION ABOARD THE *EXPLORER*, JANUARY 1858

1st Lt. Joseph C. Ives and his twenty-five sailors, soldiers, scientists, and Indian interpreter-guides steaming north on Colorado River aboard the prefabricated, shallow-draft iron sternwheeler *Explorer.* Here they are above Fort Yuma and opposite California's Chimney (now Picacho) Peak. Ives's mission was to find the river's head of steam navigation at low water and assess it as an invasion route into southern Utah. Worried about encirclement, Young monitored their movements while Ives fretted about shipwreck, mission failure, Indian hostility, and Mormon attack. This rare 1858 painting by the expedition's artist was the basis for the familiar lithograph of this scene in Ives's majestic 1861 report. *Contemporary watercolor and gouache on paper by Balduin Möllhausen, courtesy of Amon Carter Museum, Fort Worth.*

Chapter 4

"A Channel of Communication with Utah"
Rio Colorado

One of those who was to remain behind at the fort raised his full cup and shouted: "Think of us when the Mohave Indians lift your scalps!" "Remember us when the Mormons burn you and your fort to the ground," we retorted.
Heinrich Balduin Möllhausen, Ives Expedition, 10 January 1858

As Captain Marcy struggled through the snowpack at the Colorado River's headwaters in early 1858, 1st Lt. Joseph Christmas Ives, U.S. Topographical Engineers, steamed north through the lower reaches of the same river more than eight hundred miles downstream. The War Department had tasked Ives with finding out if the Colorado could be used as an invasion route into southern Utah. The travels of these two officers go far to illustrate the western, if not international, sprawl of the Utah War's story.

Two Missions: Ives and Marcy

Neither officer was aware of the other's mission, but Brigham Young had known of both thrusts from the beginning. In the case of the Ives Expedition, Young's strategy was watchful waiting—monitoring the lieutenant's northbound progress while evaluating its implications for his own long-standing interest in the river. As Young saw it, the Colorado had great untapped potential to facilitate both Mormon commerce and in-migration from the Pacific Coast. Then, too, there was the river's quite different value as a possible Mormon escape route to Sonora (and beyond) should the war turn hopeless. Brigham Young did not publicly discuss such an exodus in early 1858, but others did.[1]

There were, of course, some parallels between the simultaneous Ives and Marcy Expeditions, most notably a common wartime urgency that propelled both groups into an unmapped wilderness under extreme weather conditions. For Ives's expedition, the pressure from Washington to move upriver rapidly drove the lieutenant to strip his detachment of troops, gear, clothing, and essential provisions, later forcing Ives's men to barter for corn, beans, and edible lizards with the very Indians most likely to kill them.

There were also gross differences in the missions, weather, and terrain involved, as well as in the means of transportation for the two detachments. With frontier-savvy professionals for support and Fort Yuma, California, directly to his rear, Ives had resources far different than those available to his brother officer, including the ability to communicate with his superiors and even obtain newspapers. Marcy was essentially afoot and on his own with a handful of mountaineers and a few army non-coms once he left Fort Bridger. That Ives encountered restless Indians and armed Mormon scouts even along the isolated Colorado River raised an unsettling prospect of danger qualitatively different than the traditional wilderness hazards Captain Marcy faced.

Ives and His Report

Who was Lieutenant Ives and how had he come to this assignment? In many ways Ives is a cipher. He inspired no biographer, did not write his memoirs, and died early at age 40 in 1868 without winning battlefield laurels.[2] A New

[1]On 18 November 1857 the War Department had informed Lieutenant Ives, "It is surmised that the Mormons may attempt to move Southward into Sonora." Eastern newspaper editors immediately followed suit, with some speculating about a combination of the Spanish Trail and the Colorado River as the route out of Utah. *At Sword's Point, Part 1*, 426. For newspaper speculation, see "Brigham Young's Next Move," *New York Herald*, 22 November 1857, 4/4.

[2]One of the few contemporary descriptions of Ives was written by his Utah War comrade-in-arms, 2d Lt. E. Porter Alexander. See Alexander, *Military Memoirs of a Confederate*, 110–11; Alexander and Gallagher, *Fighting for the Confederacy*, 89–93. For reminiscences of the swath Ives and his wife cut through Richmond society early in the Civil War, see Clay-Clopton, *A Belle of the Fifties*, 173–77.

Yorker and Connecticut Yankee appointed to West Point after spending two years at Yale, Ives graduated high in the class of 1852, a well-educated and presumably competent officer assigned early to the army's elite corps of topographical engineers. But by June 1857, five years after graduating from West Point, he had only just been promoted to first lieutenant. Whether such an unremarkable record was primarily a matter of bad timing, a glacial army promotion system, or a lack of personal drive is an intriguing imponderable.

With respect to Ives's involvement in the Utah War, it is fair to ask whether his connection to Secretary Floyd prompted his selection to lead the Colorado River exploration. Ives's wife, the former Cora M. Semmes of Georgia and Alabama, was the secretary's niece, but several other factors make nepotism alone an inadequate explanation for Ives's assignment. For example, while serving in the Southwest as assistant to 1st Lt. Amiel Weeks Whipple in his 35th Parallel Pacific Railroad Survey of 1853–54, Ives had actually crossed the Colorado in trekking from New Mexico to California, an uncommon experience for most army officers.[3]

The lieutenant's final report of his Colorado River expedition was a pioneering, comprehensive, and beautifully illustrated volume published in 1861 as a congressional document. This volume is, of course, essential reading and an appropriate starting point for any in-depth study of the Ives Expedition. Despite the hasty redirection of Ives's mission to serve the informational needs of the Utah War, though, his final report is limited in its discussion of that conflict because by the time the government published Ives's work, the conflict in Utah had largely lost its urgency. Consequently, Ives's unpublished progress reports from the river, the little-known twelve-page preliminary assessment that he wrote in Washington in November 1858, and the unexploited personal letters and travel accounts generated by Ives and his professionals are the documents freshest and most relevant to the Utah War.[4]

---

[3]A description of Ives's role with Whipple's survey appears in Tidball, *Soldier-Artist of the Great Reconnaissance*; and Beidleman, "The 35th Parallel: Whipple and the Naturalists, 1853–1854," 256–70.

[4]Ives, *Report upon the Colorado River of the West.* The best modern narrative history of the expedition is Miller's two-part article, "The Ives Expedition Revisited: A Prussian's Impressions" and "Overland into Grand Canyon"; while the most focused account of the survey's Utah War implications is Smith, "Colorado River Exploration and the Mormon War." Context for Ives's expedition within the extraordinary work done by the topographical engineers is provided by Wallace, *The Great Reconnaissance,* as well as Goetzmann's subsequent two monographs, *Army Exploration in the American West* and *Exploration and Empire.* See also "Preliminary Report of First Lieut. J.C. Ives . . ." in "Annual Report of the Sec. of War (1858)," 608–19.

Ives Organizes: Robinson's Landing and Fort Yuma

On 2 December 1857, after months of planning and preparation, Ives, a small party, and a cargo of disassembled ship components arrived at the mouth of the Colorado by schooner. At Robinson's Landing, just north of the Sonora-Baja border, they set about assembling his steamer, the *Explorer,* a prefabricated, shallow-draft fifty-four-foot iron stern-wheeler aboard which they would explore the river. Ives had designed, built, and river-tested his ungainly vessel in Philadelphia and then disassembled and crated it for shipment by a torturous route to the Gulf of California. For the crucial reassembly work, Ives relied heavily on A. J. Carroll, the indispensable engineer who had accompanied him from Philadelphia. Later teamed with Carroll, after Ives reached Fort Yuma, was David C. Robinson. He was a vastly experienced riverman and the landing's namesake, a steady hand at the tiller whom Ives fortuitously hired as *Explorer*'s pilot just before Christmas.

The balance of Ives's professionals had travelled separately and included a physician-geologist (Dr. John Strong Newberry of Cleveland), sketch artist and assistant naturalist (Heinrich Balduin Möllhausen of Berlin), topographer-cartographer (Baron Friedrich Wilhelm von Egloffstein of Bavaria), astronomical and meteorological assistants (Paul H. Taylor and C. K. Booker of Richmond and Hampton Roads, Virginia, respectively), and a hydrographer (Casimir Bielawski, a Pole and former Austrian army officer whom Ives hired in San Francisco). In selecting this cadre of professionals, Ives chose well.

Traveling by sea from the Atlantic Coast and Europe to an initial rendezvous in San Francisco, this eclectic group was to sail south in two parties to the ports of San Diego and San Pedro and then trek overland to the Colorado to await Ives at Fort Yuma, California, 160 miles upstream at the river's juncture with the west-flowing Gila. Accompanying the San Pedro group, by way of California's Fort Tejon, was a remuda of animals driven across the desert by a rough-hewn party of unidentified Hispano muleskinners led by packmaster George H. Peacock of Independence, Missouri.

Ives's plan was an extraordinarily complex one. He aimed to ascend the Colorado from Robinson's Landing; rendezvous with these resources at Fort Yuma; acquire Indian guides, an army escort, and an artillery piece; and then together steam upriver as far as possible. Once having determined the

THE IVES EXPEDITION'S HEINRICH BALDUIN MÖLLHAUSEN
One of several Europeans and noblemen recruited by Ives, Möllhausen, an experienced western explorer, was his sketch artist and assistant naturalist. After returning to the Prussian household of Alexander von Humboldt in fall 1858, he produced the first published images of the Colorado and its Grand Canyon for Ives's report, as well as his own still-untranslated travel account and western novels, many featuring Mormon villains. *Studio photo (1854) in frontier garb from Barba's* Balduin Möllhausen, the German Cooper *(Philadelphia, 1914), courtesy of the Arizona Historical Society, Tucson.*

Colorado's head of navigation, *Explorer* was to return to Fort Yuma, dispatch messages about this crucial finding for Capt. Andrew A. Humphreys in Washington, and then steam north again to an undefined point at which the scientists, army escort, and Peacock's pack train would leave the river in cross-country pursuit of their scientific mission. This involved marching northeast in search of the Colorado's juncture with the Little Colorado River, moving on to the San Juan River, and then trekking to the confluence of the Green and Colorado Rivers. From there, this group would loop back through southwestern New Mexico Territory to Fort Yuma to rejoin those who had steamed south aboard *Explorer.* The various parties were to maintain communications through dispatches carried by a combination of steamboats and Indian runners as well as signal rockets fired aloft at predetermined times.

Ives developed this plan in Philadelphia and San Francisco without an awareness of the changes unfolding in Utah, Washington, and along the Colorado River during late 1857. Initially Ives's scheme ran afoul of a delay in his arrival at the mouth of the Colorado, mechanical difficulties in assembling *Explorer,* an arduous overland trek to Fort Yuma from the Pacific Coast, and

The Ives Expedition's Colorado River Route

From 1 January to 6 March, Ives and the *Explorer* steamed north five hundred miles from the Colorado's mouth to its head of navigation (Black Canyon, just below today's Hoover Dam), and then returned south, encountering Jacob Hamblin's Mormon scouts at Cottonwood Valley. A month later Apostle Lyman's party from Parowan, Utah, probed the rugged upper portions of this route, becoming far more pessimistic than Ives about its suitability as an invasion route linking to Las Vegas and the Spanish Trail. *Courtesy of Arizona Historical Society.*

a wave of illness that beset several of the scientists in the desert. Aggravating all of these complexities was the challenge of maintaining communications between multiple groups of relative strangers separated by daunting terrain and distance as well as a variety of languages. There were to be surprises.

Although Robinson's Landing was wholly devoid of amenities, there was no shortage of rumors, including unsettling stories of both Indian unrest and prospective competition on the Colorado River among Anglos. With respect to the tribes upriver, Ives recorded in his journal: "The rumor of the preparation of an expedition to ascend the Colorado was long ago circulated among the adjacent tribes, and has occasioned much interest and excitement. I am told that curious inquiries have been made of the troops by the Indians about Fort Yuma as to the object of the enterprise, and the half understood replies have been transmitted, with many amplifications, up and down the river, occasioning all kinds of surmises concerning our purposes and probable movements."[5]

The rumors about competition centered on the ambitions and jealousy of Capt. George Alonzo Johnson, the civilian owner-operator of two medium-draft wooden steamers (*Colorado* and *Jesup*), with which he had plied the lower Colorado River since 1851 to supply the garrison at Fort Yuma from the Gulf of California. By late 1857, Johnson was also the bitterly disappointed bidder for the mission (and army appropriation) assigned to Ives by the War Department during the prior spring.[6]

Unknown to Ives at Christmastime, Jacob Hamblin, Brigham Young's principal Indian farmer (agent) at Fort Clara in southern Utah, was writing to update Young on what he understood to be Ives's progress far to the south: "The Government is now putting up an Iron Steemer to penetrate the Colorado as far as possible, then send pack trains through to the Southern settlements of the Saints. Whatever course you would wish me to take in reference to this operation, would be gladly received as soon as possible."[7] Hamblin also reported on two of his own missionaries' nearly fatal encounters with the Mojaves along the Colorado. By the end of December, the fact that there had been Mormon-Mojave interaction of some kind was the talk

[5]Ives Journal, 17 December 1857, Ives, *Report upon the Colorado River of the West,* Part 1, 34.

[6]With minimal subtlety but substantial hopefulness, Johnson had named one of his vessels after the army's quartermaster general, Brevet Maj. Gen. Thomas S. Jesup. Notwithstanding more than five years on the river, Johnson had never ventured upstream beyond Yuma, an area that Ives had seen in limited fashion while crossing the river with the overland Whipple Expedition.

[7]Hamblin to Young, 26 December 1857, LDS Archives.

of Fort Yuma. What the soldiers, including Ives, did not yet realize was how close missionaries Ira Hatch and Dudley Leavitt had come to losing their lives, and that any whites—Mormon or "Americat"—interacted with Mojaves at their own peril.[8] At Fort Yuma, an ailing Dr. Newberry, Ives's physician-naturalist, confided to a colleague at Washington's Smithsonian Institution, "The Indians above [upstream] are very hostile, and are bound to stop us. Our party is *(entre nous!) very badly organized of bad material, and we shall have trouble among ourselves, and I fear almost a failure of this expedition. . . . It will not be my fault.*"[9]

The December letters and observations recorded by Dr. Newberry's Prussian assistant, Möllhausen, provide glimpses of the frustrations besetting the group awaiting Ives's arrival at Fort Yuma as the river level continued to drop due to drought upstream. Unlike the rest of the professional group, Möllhausen had a personal relationship with Ives rooted in their shared participation in the earlier Whipple survey, for which Möllhausen had served as principal artist. That assignment, combined with Möllhausen's far-ranging western travels with Duke Paul Wilhelm von Württemberg during 1851, made him one of the most frontier-savvy members of the Ives Expedition.[10] It was that background, Möllhausen's talent as an illustrator and naturalist, and his standing as a household protégé of Alexander von Humboldt, then the world's most prominent scientist, that prompted Ives to recruit him in the spring of 1857.[11]

---

[8]The risks also run by Hatch at about this time while encountering Paiutes along the Spanish Trail are discussed in James A. Little, "Mission to the Muddy in 1858. Written from the Verbal Narrative of Elder Ira Hatch," *Millennial Star* (Liverpool), 12 July 1870, 433–34.

[9]It is not clear to whom Newberry was referring, although his assistant, Möllhausen, did not feel that Fort Yuma's 2d Lt. John Tipton was equal to his responsibility as commander of the expedition's army escort. On 20 December Newberry described to Spencer F. Baird his desert crossing in the midst of "drunkenness & desertion of my men," and once at Fort Yuma he absolved himself of responsibility for the expedition's outcome. Newberry to Baird, 20 and 25 December 1857, Baird Papers, Smithsonian Institution Archives.

[10]Another experienced German nobleman was Baron von Egloffstein, who had participated in John C. Frémont's grueling 1853–54 expedition as well as in the 1854 Salt Lake City–California leg of the Pacific Rail Road Survey of the 41st parallel under Lt. Edward G. Beckwith in the wake of the Gunnison massacre. For the latest assessment of Egloffstein's involvement in western exploration, see Rowan, *The Baron in the Grand Canyon,* and Miller, "Baron von Egloffstein and the First Published Images of Grand Canyon," 171–77. Unlike Möllhausen, von Egloffstein intended to remain in the United States after his emigration in 1846, which, in turn, had followed service as an engineer officer with Prussia's army. He later became a U.S. citizen, serving as an officer in the Union Army and sustaining a debilitating leg wound. He eventually returned to Germany to die.

[11]Following Möllhausen's return to Germany in the fall of 1858, he spent the rest of his life in Europe publishing his account of the Ives Expedition and writing novels about the American West, some focusing on Mormons and the Utah War. From this body of work came Möllhausen's nickname later in life, "the German [James Fenimore] Cooper." For a biography of Möllhausen and description of his role with the Ives Expedition, see Barba, *Balduin Möllhausen, the German Cooper;* and Miller, "The Ives

Möllhausen, *Travels (Reisen)*, December 1857, Fort Yuma, Translation by David H. Miller, 1:108–29.

Unfortunately, open hostilities broke out between the United States and the Mormons, so instead of supporting us [and our exploring expedition] the Mormons opposed us. In the Pueblo de Los Angeles, a few Mormons suggested that, as a foreigner, I should leave the expedition if I valued my life. So an enterprise which set out as a purely scientific undertaking was taken over by military objectives, and we were to be received by the Mormons on the Upper Colorado as an armed, hostile force. Incidentally, I accept the possibility that the orders which partially transformed our expedition into a military one had been planned for a long time previously.

We reached the Colorado [from Fort Tejon] on December 19. After the United States and the Mormons had come to open hostilities, the mail was awaited with even greater anticipation. Shortly before Christmas and throughout the Christmas season, a crowd continually gathered at the day-room at Fort Yuma to study the [just-arrived] two-month-old news of the day. This was always the case right after the mail arrived. Nothing could be heard except the rustle of the huge American newspaper pages, and now and then an exclamation of surprise, followed by an important article being read aloud. . . .[12]

This was the type of news which interested us all so much, mainly because we could not know how reliable it was. I admit that we began to doubt that the expedition would actually get underway or that it would be successful, especially since important dispatches from the government in Washington arrived for Lieutenant Ives [on December 22] in the same mail. Regardless of the circumstances, they were to be forwarded to him no matter where he might be found [and this was done via the steamer *Colorado*].

Much of the ennui experienced by Möllhausen and others ran to the fact that during the mid-nineteenth century (and for decades thereafter), Fort Yuma was widely considered to be the U.S. Army's hottest, most isolated frontier post. With such a harsh ambience, it is small wonder that for the

Expedition Revisited: A Prussian's Impressions," 1–25. Möllhausen's two-volume account of his travels (*Reisen in die Felsengebirge*) remains largely unpublished in English, although the small segment covering Möllhausen's return to the Atlantic Coast after leaving Ives was translated, edited, and published sixty-five years ago as a journal article by Burzle and Taft. H. B. Möllhausen, "Over the Santa Fe Trail Through Kansas," 337–80. David H. Miller, the leading authority on the Ives Expedition, plans to publish an English edition of *Reisen* in its entirety, and it is through his generosity that translated segments pertaining to Utah War experiences appear here. For an appreciation of Möllhausen's artistic contributions to the expedition's record, see Huseman, *Wild Rivers, Timeless Canyons: Balduin Möllhausen's Watercolors of the Colorado*; and Taft, "The Pictorial Record of the Old West: Heinrich Balduin Möllhausen," 225–44. For additional background on Möllhausen and his post-1858 Mormon-related novels, see Homer, *On the Way to Somewhere Else*, 193–207.

[12]Here Möllhausen quotes from an unidentified newspaper article describing Lot Smith's raid on the Utah Expedition and speculating that "the Mormons intend to send a strong army detachment down the Colorado to keep communication open with the State of Sonora. It is assumed that if the Mormons are driven from Great Salt Lake they will retreat toward Sonora."

official record, Lieutenant Ives noted: "Fort Yuma is not a place to inspire one with regret at leaving. The barrenness of the surrounding region, the intense heat of its summer climate, and its loneliness and isolation have caused it to be regarded as the Botany Bay of military establishments."[13]

Very Unpleasant Feelings: Disruptive Upstream Rivalry

When an overland courier brought dispatches for Lieutenant Ives to Fort Yuma on 22 December, their arrival electrified the post. Without even knowing that these were Capt. Andrew A. Humphreys's two letters of 18 November re-directing Ives's mission, the post's commander, 1st Lt. William A. Winder, and Captain Johnson, owner of the steamers *Colorado* and *General Jesup*, sensed their importance and an opportunity to pre-empt Ives in first reaching the river's head of navigation.[14]

Not content to move upriver alone, Captain Johnson obtained from Lieutenant Winder a fifteen-man military escort, a howitzer, and a pick-up group of heavily armed trappers and mountaineers. After watching Johnson and 1st Lt. James L. White steam north aboard *Jesup* on 31 December, Winder apprised his superiors in San Francisco of his actions. He couched the explanation in terms that were self-serving as well as unmistakably critical of Ives for sluggishness.[15] Balduin Möllhausen recorded the demoralizing impact of this competitiveness on his party: "I would not venture to speculate about the underlying cause of this behavior. It might have been the above-mentioned jealousy between the officers of the line [artillery] and those of the Corps of Topographical Engineers. Or it might have been [other motives]. I only know that the members of the Colorado Expedition watched the *Jesup* with very unpleasant feelings as she struck her course upstream. She did not exactly take our warmest blessings with her."[16] Small wonder that in 1955 Arthur Woodward titled his account of this episode, *Feud on the Colorado.*

[13]Ives, *Report upon the Colorado River of the West,* Part 1, 43. Botany Bay was one of the notorious British penal colonies in Australia.

[14]Winder, an officer of the Third U.S. Artillery, is not to be confused with Capt. William H. Winder, who was serving in the same regiment but elsewhere. Alonzo Johnson's account of his motives and actions appears in Johnson, "The Steamer *General Jesup.*"

[15]1st Lt. D. R. Rawson, acting post adjutant, to 1st Lt. James L. White, 28 December 1857, Fort Yuma; 1st Lt. William A. Winder to Maj. W. W. Mackall, asst. adjt. gen., headquarters, Department of the Pacific, 31 December 1857, both ibid., 1–3.

[16]Möllhausen, *Travels (Reisen),* December 1857, Fort Yuma, Miller translation, 1:130–31.

Stern Duties and Pressing Cares: *Explorer* Steams North

On 31 December an anticipated tsunami-like tidal surge swept Robinson's Landing, lifting the completed *Explorer* off the mud flats at the Colorado's mouth and into the river's channel. Ives steamed north on New Year's Day. Almost immediately he encountered the southbound *Colorado* bearing Captain Humphreys's revised instructions and news of the pre-emptive actions of Johnson and Lieutenant Winder.

By 3 January *Explorer* had steamed halfway to Fort Yuma, with Ives in a near frenzy. That day he wrote to wife Cora: "[my new orders] have considerably changed all of my plans. I shall now ascend the river to the head of navigation as rapidly as possible, and return immediately to Fort Yuma [to report to Humphreys about Utah], and then circumstances must decide whether I can prosecute the [overland or second phase of the] survey in detail." After explaining that mail connections with home would soon become even more erratic, Ives turned to his own state of mind: "I would not have you burdened with my troubles, but I cannot always sit and tranquilly write as though I were in a comfortable home with my mind free and at ease. Stern duties, and pressing cares, and arduous occupations are crowding upon me. I have men to manage and control, responsible and difficult tasks to perform, constant disappointments to encounter, and disasters to avert or to remedy. Labor by day and often by night, cold, and watching and anxiety of mind I do not care for."[17]

Balduin Möllhausen's travel narrative related what happened once Ives reached Fort Yuma:

Möllhausen, *Travels (Reisen)*, January 1858, Fort Yuma, Miller Translation, 1:131–40.

Finally, on the evening of January 6, Lieutenant Ives unexpectedly appeared at Fort Yuma. He had received news of the *Jesup*'s departure. Because of this and because of the dispatches from Washington, he was induced to hurry out ahead of the steamboat [on horseback].

Our last two days at Fort Yuma were filled with work. No one wanted to burden himself with unnecessary luggage or leave anything behind which might be important for the journey. We packed, unpacked, set some things aside, added others, and before we realized it dusk had crept upon us.

We spent the evening [of 10 January] in jovial sociable association. On this

[17]Ives to Cora, 3 January 1858, Colorado River, Special Collections, Lied Library, University of Nevada–Las Vegas.

> occasion somewhat more than the usual amount of liquor flowed, which I attribute solely to the sandstorms. The songs were followed by dances; and what dances they were! Bearded men embraced one another with sinewy hands and stamped heavily to our crude music, the eternal Yankee Doodle and Scottish Horn Pipe. At last our breath gave out and our [guitar-strumming] fingers grew numb. One of those who was to remain behind at the fort raised his full cup and shouted: "Think of us when the Mohave Indians lift your scalps!" "Remember us when the Mormons burn you and your fort to the ground," we retorted. So ended our last night at Fort Yuma.

Aboard *Explorer* as she steamed north on 11 January were a total of about twenty-five people: her small crew, Ives, his scientists, several Yuma tribal interpreter-guides, and a few soldiers. Before leaving the fort, a recovering Dr. Newberry had written to Spencer F. Baird of the Smithsonian, "We may be back here within a month, and may then go home, as the Mormon War has knocked our Exped. into pi [chaos]." To another scientist he commented, "The plan of the expedition has been all broken up by the Mormon troubles."[18]

A week later, Lieutenant Ives described the expedition's progress to his wife:

IVES TO CORA, 19 JANUARY 1858, COLORADO RIVER,
SPECIAL COLLECTIONS, LIED LIBRARY.

> We are now about a hundred miles above the Fort, and are getting along very well, having thus far been so fortunate as to escape serious accident,—which is a great deal in an undertaking of this kind, and on such a river. Again I have changed my plans. The War Department wanted me to make, if possible, a hurried reconnaissance to the head of navigation and return to Fort Yuma and report the result, before commencing the regular survey. I accordingly left the mule train and most of the [army] escort behind, and took on board twenty-five persons and provisions for forty days. It was supposed, in Washington, that I would be able to ascend to the head of navigation and return in about 10 days. It is believed that the river may be navigable three or four hundred miles above the fort.[19] But people away from here have but

[18]Newberry to Baird, 10 January 1858, Fort Yuma, Baird Papers; Newberry to F. V. Hayden, 10 February 1858, Mohave Villages, Colorado River, in Merrill, *The First One Hundred Years of American Geology*, 684.

[19]Even Fort Yuma's former commander, Capt. George H. Thomas, mistakenly believed that the Colorado was navigable to within 100–200 miles of Salt Lake City, as did Brigham Young. *At Sword's Point, Part 1*, 424. David H. Miller comments that "virtually every army officer who crossed the Colorado at Yuma speculated about exploring its upper reaches. It was generally assumed that the river was navigable as far as the mouth of the Virgin." Miller notes that on 20 June 1857 the *Los Angeles Star* published Antoine Leroux's letter about his 1837 high-water float trip from the mouth of the Virgin to the Colorado Delta, an experience that prompted Leroux to conclude, "I know that the Colorado is navigable from the mouth of the Virgin down. . . . In all this traveling, nothing that I know could stop a small steamboat in going up as far as the mouth of the river Virgin (except there be some hidden rocks under the water that cannot be seen)." Miller to MacKinnon, e-mail message, 5 April 2013.

a faint idea of the "Old Colorader," or they would have no such conceptions of rapid progress upon it.

My steamboat does admirably, and yet, on some days, though we have sailed from daylight to dark, we have been able to make but five miles. But one fortunately becomes used to such things, and though, a hundred times a day, there is a liability to some disaster that might almost ruin the success of my expedition, I have an abiding confidence that everything will turn out well. The worst is over. That was accomplished when the boat was got safely to Fort Yuma. At the [mouth] of the river we had some rather risky times.

Brought Us by Madam Rumor: Mormon Intelligence

As *Jesup* steamed slowly upstream, she left in her wake not only *Explorer* but a succession of tribal villages titillated by the prospect of a clash between Mormons and non-Utahns, whom they called "Americats." Simultaneously, Captain Johnson and Lieutenant White collected along the way jumbled descriptions of visits by Latter-day Saints from the north in search of religious converts and military allies. They were stories remarkably like those of Indian tampering then stoking non-Mormon fears elsewhere throughout the American West. In turn, the unexpected appearance of *Jesup* above Fort Yuma touched off rumors and anxieties that took on a life of their own, rippling northward by Indian runner until alarming news of a gathering federal invasion found its way to Brigham Young, with wide-ranging consequences months later. This farrago of rumors shared by soldiers, rivermen, American Indians, and Mormons complicated, if not endangered, Ives's mission. In this sense, the minor plot, hatched without authorization at Fort Yuma by Johnson and Winder to upstage Ives, was a rivalry that aggravated rather than eased Utah War tensions.[20]

Brigham Young had, of course, been aware of the Ives Expedition since the summer of 1857 from newspaper accounts and perhaps his own agent in Philadelphia. In early September William I. Cox, the Mormon mission president in San Bernardino, enriched the intelligence mix. Jumbling Lieutenant

[20]Among the unintended consequences of this unsettled atmosphere was the Mojaves' attack on the unrelated civilian Rose-Baley party of Mormon overlanders in August 1858 on the Colorado's east bank at Beale's Crossing. This incident, in turn, triggered a massive, punitive reaction by the army. Baley, *Disaster at the Colorado*; Hunter, "The Mojave Expedition of 1858–59." Like so many other aspects of the Utah War, conspiracy theories have welled up to link the attack on the Rose-Baley party to Mormon wartime activities in the region. Casebier, *The Mojave Road*, 66–67.

Ives's identity and mission with that of Maj. George A. H. Blake, the army's senior dragoon commander in southern California, Cox informed Young that "Blake of San Diego (so a friend tells me) has orders from Government to proceed immediately to Fort Yuma, on the Colorado River and ascertain the practability of running Steam Boats up the said River, as it is ordered that in case there is a collision between the Troops and our people, (as it is stated they ascend as far as the mouth of the Rio Virgin) *in case such is the case, then there is to be put on the River four or five* light draft Steam Boats, which are now in readiness, which are to lend their equipage and provisions right into your midst, or into your Territory."[21]

On 1 October Young acknowledged this message and encouraged more fact gathering as Cox evacuated San Bernardino: "You are correct in furnishing all the reliable intelligence concerning certain movements so far as you can obtain it by using all reasonable exertions, and it is expected that you will continue to do so and forward it by every opportunity." He then vented anger over the planned approach of Ives's detachment as well as the continuing overland march of the Utah Expedition. Sarcastically, Young suggested that "It may not be amiss to instruct your [California] assemblymen to use his [*sic*] influence to induce the Congress of the United States to charter the Great Eastern for the navigation of the Gulf of California and the Rio Colorado, as its immense size makes it ample for accommodating a large number of troops and great quantities of provisions and munitions which the United States at present appear to wish to land in Utah. It is said that the Great Eastern can transport 10,000 troops at once."[22]

At Christmastime Jacob Hamblin had reported on the activities of the Ives Expedition from his Indian farm at Fort Clara, Utah. Four weeks later, Apostle Amasa Mason Lyman, the Mormon leader supervising the exodus from San Bernardino, provided additional intelligence to Brigham Young from Deseret Valley in southwestern New Mexico Territory.

LYMAN TO YOUNG, 20 JANUARY 1858, LDS ARCHIVES.

Of news we have none, save such as is brought us by Madam Rumor, as neither the northern nor the southern mail has reached us. The Indians

[21] Cox to Young, 7 September 1857, LDS Archives.

[22] Young to Cox and William K. Crosby, 1 October 1857, LDS Archives. The steamer *Great Eastern,* not to be confused with the deactivated British troop ship *Great Western,* was then abuilding in a British shipyard and would soon be used to lay the first trans-Atlantic telegraph cable. Unknown to Young, Ives's men would later dub their little *Explorer* the *Great Eastern.*

have brought us the news that the "Americats" are coming up the Colorado to kill off the Mormons and Indians.[23] Of this we expect to learn more, as we intend, so soon as we shall return from the present excursion, (which we hope will not be longer than three weeks) to visit the Colorado and that portion of the country occupied by the "Hyatts" [Mojaves] with a party of twenty men and four missionaries, some, or all of whom, we propose to leave there if circumstances are favorable. Hoping by these means to extend our acquaintance with the Indians and to increase our knowledge of the country. The trip, above mentioned, to the Colorado will be subject to be changed, should any instructions be received by the coming mail, rendering it necessary to make other arrangements; otherwise, we shall proceed to its accomplishment with as little delay as possible, and report the results at the earliest opportunity.

From the Colorado, Balduin Möllhausen recorded the rumors and perceptions encountered by *Explorer* at a series of riverside Indian camps during February 1858.

MÖLLHAUSEN, *TRAVELS* (*REISEN*), FEBRUARY 1858, COLORADO RIVER, MILLER TRANSLATION, 1:239–97.

We were only a short stretch above our previous camp [in the Mojave Valley on about 10 February] when we noticed a large group of natives on the left bank. We learned that José, the first [Mojave] tribal chief, was there with his subjects and wished to speak to us. Lieutenant Ives wanted to maintain good relations with the natives, especially with such a powerful tribe which was already agitated by news of the Mormon War. So he ordered us to land to take the chief on board.

In his first discussion with Lieutenant Ives, José opened by saying that he wished to learn the purpose of our expedition. The entire Mohave tribe was agitated by rumors, which seemed to come from the Mormons, to the effect that the Americans intended to oust the Mohaves and appropriate their land. He said further that the Mohave Indians wanted to live in friendship with the Mormons. But they also wanted to remain brothers of the Americans, so they wished that the Mormons be fought in their own lands, and that the war remain far from the Mohave's peaceful valley. The Mormons had admonished them to use force to keep the Americans out of their valley, but they intended to receive the Americans as brothers, and in return to be treated by them as brothers.

This was roughly the gist of José's speech. So the Mormons had sent their Indian emissaries (from the Utah Tribe) this far downstream to goad these poor savages. Naturally the Mormons had done this to win over this

[23]This report could refer to the movements of *Jesup*'s Captain Johnson, Lieutenant Ives, or both explorers.

powerful tribe as allies and to keep the Colorado open as a military route to Sonora by causing a rupture with the Americans.

The Mohave Indians followed the best and most prudent course of action, clearly a result of José's speech. They did not want to have anything to do with the outbreak of the ruinous war of other nations far from their beloved valley.

José, like the other chiefs, considered it especially important that every one of us advised them not to be hostile toward either the Mormons or Americans. They had expected that, like the Mormons, we wanted to win them as allies, so our warning against serious entanglements made a favorable impression on these simple children of nature.[24] So they understood that our expedition was in no way intended for military purposes. . . .[25]

[Farther upstream on 14 February we encountered Mojave chief Cairook and the warrior Iretéba, whom we had befriended when they guided us on the Whipple Expedition.] Using our interpreter, Lieutenant Ives explained the purpose of our journey to Cairook. He asked Cairook to inform his tribe and all Colorado Valley inhabitants that the Americans wanted friendship with all natives. He advised all of them to stay out of the imminent war between the Mormons and the Americans.

Among other things, [on February 28] Iretéba informed us that the Mormons had already been among the Mohaves and had begun efforts to convert them, and that several of the tribe including Iretéba and Navarupe [another Mojave] had been baptized.[26] Mariando translated Iretéba's account word for word. Neither could keep from laughing as they described the scene in detail in which upon their conversion the new adherents to Mormonism had their heads dunked beneath the flowing water. Navarupe cowered in our midst, listened to our conversation with a somewhat shameful expression on his face, and assured us that despite several immersions, he was a long way from being a Mormon. Generally this procedure appeared to be detrimental rather than beneficial to the new teaching. In every case the neophytes became objects of general ridicule within their tribe, because I could not

[24]In Utah, Brigham Young's advice to the tribes ranged from admonitions of neutrality to the need for alliances with the Latter-day Saints against the Utah Expedition. Young's counsel seems to have varied depending upon the tribe involved, the status of the war, and his interpretation of Mormon theology about a Mormon-Lamanite military alliance.

[25]Möllhausen underestimated the Mojaves' astuteness in assessing the meaning of a howitzer mounted in *Explorer*'s bow and the fact that part of the boat's complement wore army uniforms, the same scene presented a few weeks earlier by the vessel *General Jesup*. Lieutenant White had heard similar descriptions of Mormon behavior, was asked the same questions by his Mojave hosts, and had dispensed advice counseling Indian neutrality. White, however, went beyond what Ives was willing to say, noting in his report, "I determined to disclose to them, in a manner as comprehensible to them as possible, the full and, as I believed, truthful statement of the origin and cause of the impending hostilities with the Mormons." White to Winder, 30 January 1858, Woodward, *Feud on the Colorado*, 100–101.

[26]For an account of this chief's influence among the Mojave and decades of help to the U.S. Army, see Cravath, "Iretaba," 24–32.

recall having seen a single baptized native who considered this ceremony to be anything other than a crass joke.[27]

Upstream from this Ives-Mojave meeting, near the 35th parallel and what became known as Beale's Crossing, Captain Johnson and *Jesup* had earlier encountered Major Blake and sixty dragoons escorting road-builder Edward Fitzgerald Beale and his exotic eastbound pack train of mules and camels. The meeting took place on 23 January and was wholly accidental. Since no ferry yet existed there, Johnson offered *Jesup* as an impromptu means of crossing. After Beale and his mules reached the Colorado's New Mexico bank, Major Blake left the river and returned west with Beale's camels toward Fort Tejon, California. As Beale explained this arrangement to Secretary Floyd, "I had sent the camels back to Fort Tejon from the Colorado river, in charge of my clerk, in order that they might be used in the campaign against Utah."[28]

If on the return leg of his march Major Blake was looking for suspicious Mormon emigrants, at the end of January he found some at the point at which the western reaches of the Spanish Trail neared California's Mojave River. There, he serendipitously encountered Apostle Lyman, an old acquaintance then on his way from southern Utah and New Mexico to assist his family's departure from San Bernardino. Lyman summarized their meeting for Brigham Young nearly a month later in Salt Lake City: "Passed Major Blake and his command camped at the Sugar loaf. He informed us that the expedition to explore the Colorado had been perfectly successful, that there were three steamers on the river, that another of 5 feet draught was to be placed on it in a short time, that they had ascended within 70 ms of the mouth of the Virgin & that they expected to be able to reach its mouth with vessels of that draught. He also hinted that 3000 men wo[uld] be sent up that way."[29]

Whether the prospect of thousands of U.S. troops pouring into Utah via the Colorado River was Blake's personal forecast of campaign developments after interacting with *General Jesup* at Beale's Crossing, or was only Lyman's understanding of what he thought he heard from Blake, is significant but

[27]Ives felt the baptismal rituals had more serious ramifications than did Möllhausen. He informed Captain Humphreys: "The Mormons have not been successful apparently in conciliating the Mojaves. The latter are jealous of their approach. They have baptized many of them, and gave great offence to one of their principal chiefs, by plunging him three times into the river." Ives to Humphreys, 14 March 1858, Colorado River, Letters Received, Records of the Office of the Chief of Engineers, RG 77, NARA.

[28]Beale to Floyd, 23 March 1858, "The Fort Defiance and Colorado Wagon Road—Success of the Camels," *Republican Advocate* (Batavia, N.Y.), 20 April 1858, 1/5; also quoted in Roberts, *A Comprehensive History of the Church*, 4:371–72n29. The Utah Expedition never used camels.

[29]Lyman Journal, 31 January 1858, LDS Archives.

unfathomable. Of greater importance was Brigham Young's subsequent reaction to Lyman's report of this conversation.[30]

Bad Day at Black Rock: Striking the Head of Navigation

By early March 1858, Ives had left astern the Mojave villages and their friendly leader Chief Cairook. He was then deep into Paiute territory, hundreds of miles north of Fort Yuma and less than a hundred miles from the Mormon mission at Las Vegas, New Mexico (now Nevada). *Explorer* steamed on through the continuing perils of low water, sand bars, rocks, and the specter of Mormon Indian tampering.

Having missed the Blake-Beale entourage at Beale's Crossing, Ives had seen no one but Indians since 11 January with the sole exception of a brief river meeting with southbound Captain Johnson on 30 January. Johnson had earlier taken *General Jesup* as far north as the rapids of El Dorado Canyon at the south end of Cottonwood Valley, 320 miles above Yuma. After proceeding a short distance through the rapids in a rowboat, Johnson was unable or unwilling to proceed farther. He then returned downstream after declaring the canyon to be the head of steam navigation, an assertion to which he clung mistakenly until his death in 1903. Undaunted by Johnson's information, Ives pressed on, knowing that the shallow-draft *Explorer* could negotiate waters unnavigable for Johnson.

Thirty miles above Fort Yuma, soon after its impromptu meeting with Ives, *Jesup*'s southbound voyage ended when she struck a submerged rock and settled to the Colorado's bottom with a hole in her hull. Unfazed by this disaster, Johnson abandoned ship, declared victory, and with aplomb set out afoot for Fort Yuma with Lieutenant White's artillerymen, while White rushed a self-serving report and a map of his explorations to Gen. Newman S. Clarke's department headquarters in San Francisco.

Oblivious to *Jesup*'s misfortune downriver, Ives proceeded through El Dorado Canyon and beyond. His next letter to Cora reflected a new self-confidence as well as the extent to which the competition with Captain

[30]Unknown to Lyman, Blake was then serving in California under a reputational cloud, the result of his role as the unwitting catalyst for his company's riot and mutiny in New Mexico less than three years earlier. This imbroglio was one of the most disgraceful such affairs in the army's antebellum history. Gorenfeld, "The Taos Mutiny of 1855."

Johnson had troubled him: "I feel as though a mountain of care were taken off my mind. My steamboat enterprise has been a risky one from the moment when the steamboat was ordered to the present time, but the little craft has escaped all the perils that have so often threatened her, and has reached a place where no steamboat has ever been before."[31]

Despite his relief and optimism, on 6 March Ives also came to grief when *Explorer* struck a hidden rock at the mouth of what he named Black Canyon, several miles below today's Hoover Dam. The boat's hull was dented but intact; however, her boiler and plumbing were badly askew. While engineer Carroll (dubbed "Captain Iron") set about repairs, the expedition went ashore to camp and built crude defenses against an anticipated Mormon attack.

On 10 March Ives continued upriver aboard *Explorer*'s skiff with Captain Robinson and one of his crew at the oars, an undertaking that the lieutenant described a few days later as a "laborious enterprise, and a somewhat dangerous one, for we were gone three days in an open boat, and ran risks of various descriptions."[32] After rowing 20–25 miles, rapids forced this small party to halt at what Ives mistakenly believed to be the mouth of the Rio Virgin, the place that the War Department had hoped would be a suitable landing for troops and supplies destined for Utah.

In reality, Ives was slightly downstream from the Virgin at a slough known as the Las Vegas Wash, 525 miles above the Colorado's mouth and at a north latitude of 36° 06'. After a brief reconnaissance ashore, Ives determined that this rocky, forbidding terrain was not only unreachable by steamboat at low water but impassable for infantry. Unable to proceed further by land or water, he returned downstream to rejoin the main party, which had been engaged in collecting scientific specimens and hunting for game. Most importantly, part of the group had also been scouting below Black Canyon for a practical overland route to the Spanish Trail and Las Vegas, believed to be only about forty miles away.

At this juncture, Ives designated the mouth of Black Canyon as the Colorado River's head of steam navigation. This conclusion became the center piece of his formal preliminary report written in Washington eight months later together with his assessment that "a wagon road might be opened between the [Spanish] trail and the head of navigation."[33]

[31]Ives to Cora, 19 February 1858, Colorado River, Special Collections, Lied Library.

[32]Ives to Cora, 14 March 1858, ibid.

[33]Ives to Humphreys, *Preliminary Report, Exploration of the Rio Colorado of the West*, 1 November 1858.

Casting Discredit upon My Expedition: Ives Reports and Defends

With Ives's return from Vegas Wash, the expedition took stock alongside the river at the mouth of Black Canyon. There had been multiple accomplishments: Ives had located the Colorado's head of navigation and reconnoitered what he believed to be the mouth of the Rio Virgin; "Captain Iron" had returned a battered *Explorer* to working condition; the scientists and artists had completed their sweep of the area; and the scouting party had returned with valuable information for army road builders about the terrain between the Colorado and the Spanish Trail. With the expedition's pack train and military escort long overdue from Yuma, though, Ives lacked the food, mules, and protection to conduct the expedition's remaining overland mission eastward toward the Little Colorado. On 13 March, after living for three weeks on bartered Indian fare and no sign of packmaster Peacock and Lieutenant Tipton, Ives steamed south to find them.

The next day, Ives pulled ashore and dispatched an Indian runner to Fort Yuma with the all-important message to Captain Humphreys describing the head of navigation. In this letter Ives also included Indian reports of a Mormon threat along the river, and, perhaps with Lieutenant White's criticism in mind, expressed regret over "the impossibility of sooner obtaining the information desired by the [War] Department in regard to the practicability of this route as a channel of communication with Utah."[34]

The same courier carried a status report for Cora filled with anxieties about survival of the type that probably beset Captain Marcy three months earlier as he searched for Cochetopa Pass. Unlike Ives, though, Marcy had had no one in whom he could confide his fears, and so he kept his own counsel and soldiered on toward the continental divide.

Ives to Cora, 14 March 1858, Colorado River, Special Collections, Lied Library.

My steamboat, darling Coe, has attained as high a point on the river as I desire, and the principal part of my exploration is at last satisfactorily accomplished. You must know that for three weeks we have been living on the provisions which I bought of the Indians below, and as these were nearly

[34]Ives to Humphreys, 14 March 1858, Colorado River, Letters Received, Records of the Office of the Chief of Engineers, RG 77, NARA.

exhausted and no supply near, everyone had begun to feel anxious for some sign of the mule train. We had been a long time without bacon, flour, coffee, salt, and the most common necessaries of food, and though I could eat my corn and beans with a good appetite, most of the men were becoming sick and dispirited, and as there was not much left of the corn and beans even, were getting frightened besides.[35] Our position had really become a dangerous one, and Friday was the most dismal day I think I have ever passed. I kept up a bright face to reassure the others but on Friday evening, I went into my cabin, and an unprecedented cloud of dismals gathered about my heart. I had given orders to start back, at all risks, on the morrow, but the danger of losing the boat [in rapids], with the little provision left, so far from any succor, the uncertainty about the train, and the responsibility attending it all were all staring me in the face, and making me feel very very blue.

Having thus written to Captain Humphreys and Cora, and perused the newspapers that had just arrived by Indian runner, Ives felt a strong need to communicate with General Clarke's headquarters in San Francisco. In this case the lieutenant's main purpose was not only to provide the department commander with information about Mormon activities and the terrain between the Colorado and the Spanish Trail but to defend his professional reputation and the credibility of his expedition against misrepresentations by Captain Johnson and Lieutenant White published in the California press. Ives was acutely aware that by the end of March, the offending San Diego and San Francisco newspapers would reach Washington and with them material raising questions about his effectiveness. Accordingly, he informed General Clarke's adjutant that "the two statements are of a gross and wanton character, and were evidently fabricated, only for the purpose of casting discredit upon my expedition. Appearing under such authority, having obtained a wide circulation, and necessarily given a false impression as to the progress of my work, I feel bound to call them to the notice of the Comdg. General of the Department."[36]

[35]Dr. Newberry wrote to Spencer F. Baird: "Think of our delectable position. Provisions half abandoned [in haste] at the start, the remainder such as no one could eat with pleasure—not half enough of that taken on the present branch of the expedition urged trusting to luck to get grub of Indians who might or might not be friendly—compelled [to] live for weeks on such fare as hogs subsist on in the East—and you will not envy me my present position." Newberry to Baird, 16 March 1858, Banks of Colorado River [35th parallel], Baird Papers.

[36]Ives to Mackall, 14 March 1858, Colorado River, Letters Received, Records of the Army Adjt. Gen., RG 94, NARA.

My First Real Experience at Espionage: Thales Haskell in the Lion's Den

On 15 March Ives encountered not his pack train but a small party of Mormon scouts. Several accounts of this meeting have survived from both sides, with the longest (and most florid) written by Möllhausen, a budding novelist as well as naturalist and artist. Ives made no mention of this incident in his preliminary report to the army and in his next letter to Cora; in his final report, with the brevity of a Yankee engineer, he described what happened in a single paragraph.[37] The Mormon accounts were even more varied, written as they were by frontiersmen (one barely literate) bent on leaving a record for posterity. Möllhausen and Ives were anxious for their postwar readers in the United States and Prussia to understand how much they knew of the Mormons and how little they revealed; the Mormon accounts, not written for publication, were filled with self-satisfaction over the Latter-day Saints' ability to gain access to the Ives Expedition's boat and camp.

Both sides left a record of mutual suspicion and hostility as well as wildly differing accounts of each other's interactions with Indians, especially the already agitated Mojaves. Two of the Mormons involved had recently escaped death while in Mojave hands; before March was over, the entire Ives Expedition would share this jeopardy.

Möllhausen, *Travels (Reisen)*, 15–16 March 1858, Colorado River, Miller Translation, 1:323–27.

On March 15 we continued our journey downstream. We were very surprised to discover the fresh tracks of two horses and two mules when we landed on the right bank to take on wood. A careful examination revealed that both horses and one mule had been ridden by whites, while the other animal, which was fairly heavily packed, had ridden [trotted] alongside. The horses' horseshoes and the manner in which the animals followed one another, as well as the way obstructing objects had been removed, proved that these were tracks of whites. These tracks were made by very experienced prairie travelers, and certainly were not the signs of predatory Indians on their way home with stolen horses, as some in our party believed.[38] Naturally we concluded at once that they were Mormons, and we considered it only too likely that when we were in Black Canyon some emissaries of that fanatical

[37] Ives Journal, 16 March 1858, *Report Upon the Colorado of the West,* Part 1, 88.

[38] The Spanish Trail had long been the route by which Ute warriors rode back to Utah after raiding the livestock of California ranchos. The tribes along the Colorado were not mounted.

sect had passed by us to incite the Indians to an insurrection behind our backs. Whoever they might be, they were now between us and our [pack] train, and so in any event we would either hear of them or see them, so we continued our journey to the south without further concern.

The sun was still high above the zenith when we reached Cottonwood Valley, where Captain Robinson steered the steamboat to the beautiful grove of trees. A voice suddenly resounded from the opposite bank, and in good English said: "Fetch me over!" We immediately manned the rowboat and sent it over, and when it returned it conveyed a lone man who looked like a Mormon. He had a haggard weather-beaten countenance, and although he could not yet have been thirty, his features bore a peculiar seriousness and energy bordering on fanaticism.[39] He wore a colorful cotton shirt which was gathered around his waist with a belt. He wore buckskin leggings and moccasins. A gray worn-out felt hat rested on his smooth, dark blond hair, which like his beard was unusually long. The only weapon he had with him was a short knife in the back of his belt.

This man gave us a cold greeting and we reciprocated.

"I would like to know," he said to us, "whether the Mohave Indians are friendly toward the whites. My two companions and I intend to travel to Fort Yuma and from there to the California settlements."

"The natives have been friendly," we responded, "although the Mormons have tried to precipitate hostilities against the Americans. What led you here by this route? We gather from the tracks of your two horses and two mules that there are three of you with a pack animal who have come down out of the mountains."[40]

Not in the least surprised that we knew so much about him and about the route he had taken, he answered that he came from the Great Salt Lake, and wanted to reach the American settlements via the safest route. He denied that he was a Mormon, but conceded that he had lived among them for several years, and had only left that place because the Mormons did not allow anyone to get ahead who was not of their faith. He said that now, with the entanglement with the United States, they would only tolerate adherents of the new faith among them. When we questioned him why he had not taken the shorter and safer route to San Bernardino instead of the dangerous route down the Colorado, he said the road to San Bernardino had become too precarious due to the Ute Indians whom the Mormons had sent there.

Despite this man's flattering phrases, no one doubted that we were face to face with a spy who, with evil intentions toward us, planned to go to the Mohaves. Although he demonstrated much cunning and carefully avoided

[39] This was Thales H. Haskell, then age 24.

[40] Möllhausen's smugness shows here. In his final report, Ives reported that there were four men in the Mormon party; the correct number was five, some of whom were not visible.

> giving himself away with an unguarded word, he looked at us with a deeply-rooted hatred when he thought we were not watching. These looks did not escape us. They were complemented by his large white teeth, which he continually flashed like a snarling wolf when he spoke. We invited the stranger to share our meal, which he did with great gusto. We also offered him a pipe, but we refused his request for salt and tobacco to take with him on his travels for the simple reason that we did not have any left ourselves.
>
> We sat up fairly late and amused ourselves as the spy spoke vehement words about the Mormons, while we said only good things about them, only occasionally dropping a sarcastic remark. He responded to these comments with an artificially loud laughter, behind which so much poisonous hatred showed through. We instinctively felt repelled by the traitor. The night was too dark to take the Mormon back across the river, so we kept him with us in camp, provided him with blankets, but posted a sentry by him so we could keep an eye on him all night.
>
> Bright and early on the 16th, our guest boarded the skiff which was to take him to the other bank. He neither said goodby nor thanked us for our friendly hospitality, and perhaps he also cursed us in his heart. But we didn't exactly greet him with best wishes, for I overheard remarks which indicated that our men would rather have seen him hanging from a tree, than in our skiff. In my view the man deserved such a fate. It was not because of the Mormons that the natives failed to wipe us out later, and in their hostile appearances only succeeded in shooting a few of our mules. The Mormons had plotted their schemes with sufficient cunning, but they lost their temporary advantage when they fled upon our approach, and when we forged an understanding, admittedly with difficulty, with the natives.
>
> Incidentally, we were all familiar with the talent the Mormons possess in winning the natives over to their plans, and we knew that under the circumstances at that time, they would not have hesitated in using any means to gain possession of our steamboat and our papers. So we had the best grounds for feeling somewhat alarmed.

Who were the Latter-day Saints involved in this incident, and what was their version of the encounter? In total there were five men monitoring Lieutenant Ives's movements in mid-March; only one of whom, Thales Haskell, showed himself. None, including Haskell, were identified in the Ives Expedition's records, although all were well known to Mormons as missionary-pioneers of hardscrabble southern Utah, and they would gain notoriety because of their still-murky roles in the 1857 murders at Mountain Meadows. In March 1858 this small party was acting under the general direction of Brigham Young and perhaps Apostle Lyman, although the bold decision for Haskell to hail and visit Ives's party was opportunistic rather than a gambit carefully planned in Salt Lake City.

The group's leader was Jacob Hamblin, age 38, soon to become known as the most prominent scout and Indian missionary in nineteenth-century Utah. Accompanying Hamblin to the Colorado were Haskell, age 24; Ira Hatch, an accomplished interpreter, age 22; Samuel R. Knight, age 26; and Dudley Leavitt, age 27. All five men were members of southern Utah's Nauvoo Legion units.[41]

Jacob Hamblin, 1854–58 Diaries and Reminiscences, Typescript, 51–55, LDS Archives.

The Iyats [Mojave], (previously mentioned as having been visited by Brs Hatch and Levett) had become very anxious to see us, believing us to be their friends, sent frequent invitations to us to come and see them. March 6th [1858] brs Knights, Levett, Hatch, Haskel and myself started to visit them. On the 15th we arrived at a small village of Iyats on the Colorado. They were very glad to see us and brought out their muskeet beans, that they had gathered for food, and gave them for our animals to eat.

[16 March][42] Next day we were visited by several indians from the larger villages below [downstream]. They said that the Americans were coming up the river; and that they were afraid that they would take their lands. We saw a small steamer lying on the opposite side of the river, and the indian said that there was a great many whites coming up the river, on horse back and on foot.[43] Knowing, as I did, the feelings of the parrent government towards this [Mormon] people, I felt anxious to know the business of this boat and, if possible, to get some information in relation to the opperations of the Government of this river, Consequently, I asked Br Haskel to go opposite the boat and hail it and, if posible, go on board of it, and find all he could in relation to their business and the opperations of Government on the Colorado, that he need not tell them that he was a mormon, but if they asked him to tell them that he had relations belonging to the church and that he was on the way to California but as the indians were very bad on the Old Spanish Trail, he thought it best to keep down the river. I accompanied him to the river

[41]There are multiple Hamblin biographies, the most definitive of which is Compton, *A Frontier Life: Jacob Hamblin, Indian Missionary and Explorer.* The controversial Mountain Meadows roles of all five men are discussed throughout Brooks, *The Mountain Meadows Massacre*; Bagley, *Blood of the Prophets*; Walker, Turley, and Leonard, *Massacre at Mountain Meadows*; Bigler and Bagley, eds., *Innocent Blood*; and Turley and Walker, eds., *Mountain Meadows Massacre: The Andrew Jenson and David H. Morris Collections.* Transcription of Hamblin's diary is courtesy of Todd M. Compton.

[42]Hamblin places the date of Haskell's overnight stay with the Ives Expedition a day later than did Möllhausen and Ives.

[43]This would have been Ives's approaching pack train and military escort led by Peacock and Tipton.

opposite the boat and secreted myself in the willows until they came with a yawl and took him on board the boat. I then returned to camp anxiously awaiting the morrow and his return. Some of the brethren expressed fears that something might befal him. I told them that we should see him on the morrow about an hour by sun or as soon as he could get his breakfast.

[17 March] Next morning br Knight and myself went opposite the boat and concealing ourselves in the willows we anxiously awated the event. Bro Knight expressed some anxiety about Br Haskel, but the same yawl brought him back about an hour by sun.

He told us that the boat was commanded by Lieut. Ives, of the U.S. army and that he was exploring the river to see if supplies might not be brought to Utah up this river cheaper than they could be brought over the Plains. Lieut. Ives treated him like a gentleman. he expressed some fears that the mormons might interfere with his expedition. br Haskel told him that he need not have any fears upon that point as the mormons had enough to keep them busy to keep the Troops back on the east side of the Territory.

As brs Levett and Knight were very anxious to return home, we held a consultation and agreed for them to take all the animals and return, which they did, leaving us without the encumbrance of animals.

[17 March] Next day br Haskel and myself started down the river with our packs on our backs. We met several indians who told us that the Americans would kill us if they saw us. We also saw a number of ~~skyrockets~~ soldiers making their way up the river.

We began to feel deprest and heavy in spirits as if there was something wrong and so we returned to where we had parted with our brethren. We saw several Skyrockets which were thrown from the boat and were answered by the Pack train that was farther down the river. . . . [On the night of the 18th], some Indians came to our camp and told us that americans had heard of us and had offered a large reward for our skalps.

[19 March?] When we arrived at the Vagas [Las Vegas mission] we found brs Levett and Knight. Br Knight stated that he met one of a guard, that had been sent by Lieut. Ives on our back trail, in company with an indian.[44] The indian that was with the guard and the one with the brethren had considerable conversation. The guard asked them who the "hell." they were, and where the "hell" they were going to. Knight told him that we were mormons, sent to learn the indians to cultivate the earth &c. This in connections [*sic*] with the talk that the two indians had completely betrayed us to Ives. This revealed to us the meaning of the Skyrockets; and had we ~~rema~~ remained there another day we would have been in trouble.[45]

---

[44]The signal rockets were intended to facilitate a rendezvous between *Explorer* and its pack train, not to communicate about Mormons.

[45]This was probably a small party that Ives had sent out to examine the terrain between the river and Spanish Trail.

Thales Haskell's account closely paralleled Jacob Hamblin's with the exception of his confession that "this was my first real experience at espionage," and his observation that some of the Indians encountered "were still excited from the Mountain Meadows Affair."[46]

In the Face of Certain Death: Mojave Mood Shift

As Jacob Hamblin and his missionary-scouts headed back to Utah, the Ives Expedition continued to steam south to the Mojave Villages in preparation for its departure from the river and the overland phase of its scientific mission. There, Ives's little band unwittingly entered the most perilous phase of its mission. It was a dangerous predicament for which they blamed the Mormons, rightly or wrongly. Typically, Lieutenant Ives reported none of what happened to either his wife or to his army superior, Captain Humphreys. Möllhausen, on the other hand, did so in detail. A letter that Möllhausen wrote to his wife from Washington five months later projected the expedition's danger with an intensity only slightly muted when he published *Reisen* in Germany several years later.

Möllhausen (Washington) to Carolina Möllhausen (Berlin), 20 August 1858, Barba, *Balduin Möllhausen, the German Cooper*, Miller Translation, 173–74.

You said my last letter was written in a melancholy frame of mind.[47] You were right, my little angel, but I also believed that it would be my last, for we were only 55 men. We were camped in the woods on the bank of the Colorado and were surrounded by 2,000–3,000 Mohaves who were incited by the Mormons, [and] . . . only too clearly gave evidence of their hostile intentions. We were at our posts night and day. In my game bag lay 30 greased bullets. In my small leather pouch were 36 rounds of buckshot, and in my vest pocket 50 revolver cartridges. After I had honed a long knife as sharp as a razor I sat down with my back against a tree. My rifle was on my right arm, on my left a double-barreled shotgun, and paper on my knees. And thus I wrote you, in the face of a terrible, wild, aroused hostile horde of Indians, in the face—as I then believed—of certain death, for there were certainly too many against us few men. But although they had a better position in the thickets than we

[46]Excerpts from Haskell Journal, as quoted in Albert E. Smith, "Thales Hastings Haskell: Pioneer—Scout—Explorer—Indian Missionary, 1847–1909."

[47]This earlier letter, probably written on 22 March 1858, has not surfaced among the Möllhausen family papers in Germany or elsewhere.

> had, we would have taken at least half of them with us. However, everything turned out all right. The efforts of Chief Cairook—with whom I had made a long journey on foot years ago [1854] . . . succeeded in calming the enraged spirits, and so I am hale and hearty here [in Washington].

Möllhausen left the Colorado River with vast relief and a feeling that he had just passed through the valley of the shadow. But Lieutenant Ives projected for Cora's benefit different feelings—a sense of accomplishment and vindication, coupled with a gross minimization of the dangers ahead on his overland trek to the Grand Canyon, a wonder unseen by Caucasians since the 1770s.

Ives to Cora, 22 March 1858, Beale's Crossing of the Colorado, Special Collections, Lied Library.

> The first portion of my labors is at last accomplished. The topographic [river] survey is made, and tomorrow the steamboat pursues its way [down,] while I strike off with the mule train upon the exploration [overland] to be conducted above.
>
> So far everything has turned out well, and the main [portion] of my work is accomplished, and accomplished most successfully. My reports and maps [for Washington] go back in the steamer, and I only feel anxious now that she should get back safely. Some reports were circulated, I find, in the [news]papers, that were calculated to give the impression that I was not proceeding as successfully as could be wished, but they were pure inventions of the rival steamboat company on the river, and I have taken measures to have them contradicted. Oh! I cannot give you an idea of the load that is off my mind now that I have got through with this branch of the work. We have had as great a variety and complication of difficulties and dangers as it would be easy to imagine, but they are over. Perilous navigation, hostile Indians, Mormons, and starvation are all in the past. The land trip will be a pleasure excursion. We may suffer from heat and weariness and perhaps live on our mules for a month or so, but the weight of anxiety that I have had loaded upon me is gone, and I feel as light-hearted as possible. Little pet need have no apprehensions now about the trip, for what is left is almost devoid of danger.

After returning to Prussia and the household of Alexander von Humboldt in September 1858, Möllhausen never came back to the United States, but he could not shake off visions of his Utah War experiences along the Colorado River, in its Grand Canyon, and in Mormon country. Long before the novels of Karl May and Zane Grey appeared in Germany and the United

States to describe this region and its Mormons, Möllhausen had captured it all. Twenty-one years later, living in Potsdam, he wrote to the head of the Smithsonian Institution to ask about comrades with the Ives Expedition. When Spencer F. Baird, the scientific godfather of army exploration in the West, replied, Möllhausen realized that he too had made an enduring impression: "I often think of the time when you were in Washington, and of the interest with which I followed your adventures in the Far West. You ask for many of your old friends and acquaintances. Unfortunately a large number of these have passed away from this world. . . . Ives is dead, as also Whipple. Dr. Newberry is at present a Professor in Columbia College, New York."[48]

---

[48]Baird to Möllhausen, 8 August 1879, Barba, *Balduin Möllhausen, the German Cooper*, 176.

Chapter 5

"Exert Yourself to Counteract It"
West Coast Defenses

The property in these [southern California] counties is such as will be of the utmost importance to them if they wage a defensive war against the U.S. With the cattle and horses they can feed and mount their Indian allies and it can be quickly moved to Utah.

J. J. Warner to Brevet Brig. Gen. Newman S. Clarke,
23 November 1857

The advantage of arming and arraying against us all the Indians living on the principal routes to Utah cannot have escaped their attention; and it is more than probable that they have taken steps to effect that end.

Brevet Lt. Col. Edward J. Steptoe to Brevet Brig. Gen. Newman S. Clarke,
29 January 1858

While the War Department redirected the Ives Expedition and began planning to open a federally controlled second front from the Pacific Coast, in San Francisco Brevet Brig. Gen. Newman S. Clarke, the army's department commander, began a local initiative to defend the region against an anticipated Nauvoo Legion attack. Although there is no indication that Brigham Young was actually capable of such a strike, he had threatened California settlements with arson by secret agents during the fall of 1857. Californians paid attention to braggadocio in neighboring Utah; in San Bernardino William S. Warren, a Mormon, lamented to Amasa Lyman in Salt Lake City, "I wish the good folks up there would not write any more than they actually know, down hereto their Apostate friends . . . and not write to such men . . . [about] killing for powder & lead revolvers & &."[1]

In large part General Clarke was responding to settlers' demands for protection against Mormon-Indian alliances in the wake of the Mountain Meadows massacre. By October 1857 news of that atrocity had inflamed anti-Mormonism first in southern California and then throughout the state, including the isolated mining camps in the Sierra. Oddly, Mormon efforts to evacuate the large LDS colony in San Bernardino only stimulated non-Mormon nervousness. Rather than prompting local relief, the exodus to Utah stoked fears of Mormon gun running, the perception being that Latter-day Saints were shipping inordinate quantities of arms and munitions east to supply the Nauvoo Legion for raids on southern California's livestock and granaries. Ute bands had hit the region's ranches for a half-century, and the fear during 1857–58 was that Mormons would do likewise.

Two letters from southern California captured the anxieties and activities on both sides of the Utah War: a report to Brigham Young from William I. Matthews, a Mormon leader in San Bernardino, and unsolicited advice for General Clarke from Los Angeles by the prominent pioneer rancher, J. J. Warner.[2]

MATTHEWS TO YOUNG, 7 OCTOBER 1857, LDS ARCHIVES.

> The news of the murder of the train of emigrants [at Mountain Meadows] is beginning to cause an excitement against us as they say the Mormons are the cause of it, and from every appearance your predictions will shortly be verified, as they are making threats to stop the Salt Lake mail and blockade the Cajon Pass to prevent any one from passing, they have also made threats to send [military] companies to the [Salt] Lake to inquire into this matter, but we heard from the Mento [El Monte] and Los Angelos last night that they would wait until they heard the truth of the matter and then pitch in. However in case of any thing of this kind we will send an express in time to give you the necessary information. In regard to the matters we talked of in counsel, I will proceed to let you know how they are getting along. The guns are considerably scattered but I think we can get them together shortly. Have to work exceedingly careful to avoid suspicion.

[1]Warren to Lyman, 6 October 1857, LDS Archives.

[2]"Colonel" Juan José (formerly Jonathan Trumble) Warner was a Connecticut Yankee who arrived in Mexican Alta California in 1831, changed his name and citizenship, and in 1849 established Warner's Ranch in what became San Diego County along the Southern Emigrant (Gila River) Trail. This rancho was the most famous civilian way station in the region between New Mexico and the Pacific Coast. Earlier in 1857 Warner had lost title to this property and moved to Los Angeles.

Warner to Clarke, 23 November 1857,
Letters Received, hq Dept. of the Pacific, rg 393, nara.

On my return to this place I find that the Mormon citizens of San Bernardino are sacrificing their homes as well as all their property not easily transported for the confessed object of moving to Utah. It is reported that the orders have been issued from Young that all must repair to Salt Lake and they are obeying the mandate.

It is the general belief here that the Mormons will attack the troops under Col. Johns[t]on; and it is my opinion that if they attack and defeat that command, a Mormon army will be in this valley immediately.

The property in these counties is such as will be of the utmost importance to them if they wage a defensive war against the U.S. With the cattle and horses they can feed and mount their Indian allies and it can be quickly moved to Utah.

There is in this and S. Bernardino Counties about 1-1/2 million pounds of barley and wheat. There is also a large quantity of corn. Young must know the importance of the cattle & horses to himself & as well as the very great importance of all these articles in this neighborhood to the U.S. Army which would be compelled to operate from this point against him.

His Eastern frontier being protected during the winter by frost he could [re-]occupy San Bernardino with a military force while he savaged the country removing what could be driven or transported; advancing to the coast to attack such small bodies as he could overpower, harass larger ones, and when compelled, return upon his supplies at Utah, becoming a desolate waste to be occupied by his enemies. Of so much importance do I consider this point in the event of a protracted war that I trust you will excuse the liberty which I have presumed to take in addressing you on this subject.

By early December 1857 Brigham Young remained nervous about the possibility of a volunteer invasion from California fueled by the Los Angeles *Star*'s reporting on the Mountain Meadows massacre. Consistent with his efforts to influence newspapers in the Midwest and East, Young instructed William I. Cox in San Bernardino to contact the *Star*'s editor, Henry Hamilton, so as to communicate what would become the staple Mormon explanation for the atrocity: bad behavior by the victims and justifiable retaliation by the Paiutes. While he was at it, Young again threatened southern Californians: "Please inform the 'Los Angeles Star' that, unless he ceases publishing such infernal lies about Utah and her people, his lies may, to his utter astonishment, become truths. Also give all mobs and 'Vigilance Committies' and companies to understand that they had better far stay at home and mind their own affairs, for the 'Mormons' are determined to resist usurpation and preserve Utah's soil and society free from the awful contaminations of modern civilization, God being their helper."[3]

Without knowing of this correspondence, Hamilton, pressed on with his massacre-driven criticisms of Brigham Young and Mormonism. A historian of his newspaper's earliest years has noted: "A strategic contribution to the Mormon War was Hamilton's suggestion that troops be sent from southern California toward Salt Lake City. Thus the soldiers would be able to use the easiest route available. A cavalry force could be raised in the southern counties, he added, that would be the best in the world, and it was only by using southern California as a base that the rebellion could be speedily suppressed. The editor's views were reinforced by other local opinion, as well as by an eastern paper, which declared that California could furnish 'hardy pioneers and mountain men,' inured to hardship and well fitted to combat the guerrilla warfare which would be waged by Young."[4]

To Do All That May Be Necessary for Your Defense: General Clarke Acts

Key to General Clarke's defense strategy was redeployment of the first U.S. Dragoons, a regular regiment scattered by companies between posts in California and the Pacific Northwest. In mid-December 1857 he ordered Maj. George A. H. Blake, acting regimental commander, to transfer the unit's California headquarters from San Diego to Fort Tejon, a key post closer to San Bernardino, where he also established a small temporary dragoon garrison. At the same time, the Department of the Pacific—prodded by Secretary Floyd—directed Blake to escort road-builder Edward Fitzgerald Beale and his pack train of mules and camels to the Colorado River for the first leg of their return march to New Mexico. One of Blake's collateral duties during this trek was to watch for Mormon shipment of weapons and gunpowder between southern California and Utah.[5] Thus it was that Major Blake encountered *General Jesup* at Beale's Crossing of the Colorado River on

[3]Young to Cox, 4 December 1857, LDS Archives.

[4]Rice, *The Los Angeles Star, 1851–1864*, 194–95. Hamilton's changing views on Utah's Mormons are discussed in Ekins, *Defending Zion*, 436–37.

[5]Contrary to subsequent folklore, there was no explicit reference in Blake's orders to Mormon affairs, but from internal department documents, it is clear that Clarke expected such vigilance. Linkage between these concerns and Blake's orders may also be inferred from their directive that, once on the road to the river, he was "to observe the country thru which you march with attention," and that, having seen Beale's

23 January, an unplanned meeting that, in turn, led to Blake's comments to Apostle Lyman a week later at the Mojave River about the significance of the Ives Expedition and its linkage to an imminent federal invasion of Utah from the Colorado River.

CLARKE TO THOMAS (NEW YORK), 18 DECEMBER 1857, LETTERS SENT, HQ DEPT. OF THE PACIFIC, RG 393, NARA.

I enclose herewith the Proceedings at a meeting of citizens in Southern California, a perusal of which will serve to show a great deal of uneasiness and excitement.[6]

A civil answer has been sent to these people.[7] Meantime to serve the double purpose of allaying the excitement and of reassuring the inhabitants and of escorting Mr. Beale, Superintendent of the wagon road from Fort Defiance to the Mohave and the camels, the property of the United States, entrusted to him, I have detached Major Blake, with [sixty] Dragoons to proceed with that object to the Colorado and remain, after Beale shall leave him, on the banks of that river for a day or two then to return to Tejon or its vicinity.

Besides I have it in contemplation to assemble at San Bernardino or neighborhood, the two companies of artillery intended to relieve two of the same corps at Fort Yuma, the relieved companies it being contemplated to halt for a time at the point at which the two former may be assembled as above mentioned.[8]

I avail myself of this occasion to say that if perchance it becomes difficult or impracticable to communicate with [the Utah Expedition's] Colonel Johnston, or Colonel Alexander, from the East, communications at least verbally could be made from this side [of the continental divide].

Major Daniels late of the Army, perhaps known to the General-in-Chief as having served in Mexico, is ready to undertake to be the bearer of any

---

party safely across the Colorado, Blake was to remain at the river for an additional day or two to act as rear guard against an unspecified threat to Beale. Floyd's involvement in Blake's orders is described in an adjutant's notation on the copy retained in San Francisco; his brother, William Floyd, accompanied Beale as a physician. Mackall to Blake, 14 December 1857, Letters Sent, Dept. of the Pacific, RG 393, NARA. For the most recent claim that Blake had orders to scout the area for signs of Mormon Indian tampering and shipment of weapons and munitions, see Johnson, *The Last Camel Charge,* 184; and e-mail message, Johnson to MacKinnon, 18 July 2012.

[6]This 16 November 1857 petition by seventy-one presumably non-Mormon citizens of San Bernardino County is discussed in *At Sword's Point, Part 1,* 444.

[7]Through his adjutant, Clarke had assured the petitioners that "the state of affairs in Southern California had already attracted his attention and received his serious consideration," although "the small force at his disposal, [would require that] every movement must be well weighed." With news of Buchanan's annual message to Congress expected soon via the new westbound Butterfield overland stage, Clarke assured the group that a "few days will probably settle the question of peace or war in Utah—and should it be war the news will be received in time to do all that may be necessary for your defense." Mackall to "Gentlemen," 17 December 1857, Letters Sent, HQ Dept. of the Pacific, RG 393, NARA.

[8]A good, slightly later summary of federal troop movements in southern California appeared in "Further from Salt Lake and the South," *Daily Union* (Sacramento), 13 January 1858.

message during the winter, to one or both of the officers mentioned.[9] The Major is enterprising and sufficiently intelligent to convey any message orally, should it be deemed unsafe to transmit any written one.

With respect to his preparations to protect the Pacific Northwest as well as California, General Clarke ordered vigilance and intelligence gathering by commanders there, and he forwarded their reports of Mormon activities to army headquarters in New York.

Clarke to Thomas (New York), 1 January 1858, Letters Sent, HQ Dept. of the Pacific, RG 393, NARA, and "Annual Report of the Sec. of War (1858)," 335–39.

The following items collected from unofficial, but reliable sources, I have thought of sufficient interest to be communicated to the General-in-Chief.

A private letter from Captain [and assistant quartermaster Ralph W.] Kirkham, of December 1st from [Fort] Walla Walla [Washington], says "we have recently received from our Indians news from Salt Lake, they report an engagement between our troops and the Mormons, the information comes through the Snakes [Shoshones] who are in direct communication with the Mormons. The Snakes tell our Indians that they are well supplied with ammunition and that they can get from the Mormons any quantity that they wish, and they further tell our Indians that the Mormons are anxious to supply them, to wit, the Nez Perces, the Cayuses and Walla Walla's, with everything that they wish. I would not be surprised if the Mormon influence should extend to all the tribes in our neighborhood, and if they are determined to fight we may have trouble among the Indians on this coast again."[10]

Extract from a letter of Geo. Gibbs, Esq. of Washington Territory of November 27th.[11] "A very curious statement was recently made [to] me by

---

[9]Joseph Daniels, a Bostonian, gravitated to Texas during the revolution, serving as a prominent (but not senior) officer in the U.S. Army during the Mexican War, and was commissioned a captain of volunteers in the army. Winfield Scott would have known him as an officer promoted by brevet to major for gallantry in two of the principal battles preparatory to the capture of Mexico City. After discharge in 1848 Daniels moved to the San Francisco area to farm and operate a government sawmill, dying there in 1886 at age 77. Cutrer, "Daniels, Joseph," *Handbook of Texas Online,* accessed 9 November 2015, tshaonline.org/handbook/online/articles/fda11. In a small way Clarke's proposal to use Daniels as a confidential civilian messenger to Camp Scott paralleled General Garland's proffer of troops from New Mexico to reinforce Albert Sidney Johnston. Johnston accepted neither offer.

[10]General Clarke admired Kirkham; it is not surprising that he shared these private comments with Winfield Scott, although the Shoshone reports he forwarded were inaccurate.

[11]In 1857 Gibbs was a geologist and interpreter with the U.S.-British Northwest Boundary Survey. A Harvard-educated attorney and former employee of the American Ethnological Society in Manhattan, he went west in 1849 as a civilian artist with the Regiment of Mounted Riflemen. By the mid-1850s his studies, publications, connections with the Smithsonian Institution, and fieldwork on multiple federal railroad surveys and treaty councils made Gibbs the most widely respected expert on the Indians of the Pacific Northwest and their languages.

some of the Indians near Steilacoom. They said that the Klikatats had told them that Choosuklee (Jesus Christ) had recently appeared on the other side of the [Cascade] mountains; that he was after a while coming here, when the Whites would be sent out of the country and all would be well for themselves. It needed only a little reflection to connect this Second Advent with the [April–May 1857] visit of Brigham Young to the Flat Head and Nez Perce country [near Ft. Limhi]."

The reports from Southern California go to shew that a like influence has been exerted over the tribes of that Region; it is not to be doubted that the Mormons have cultivated friendship with the Indians, and it is scarcely doubtful that, in the recent exodus of the Mormons from San Bernardino, they have been accompanied by Indians. The Indians in this section of the state are represented as becoming more insolent and though they have as yet committed no depredations, the fear of the inhabitants are to a great degree excited.

From Carson Valley [in western Utah] we have like reports of the ill effect on the Indians, of Mormon influence.

If these things are true, and I credit them, temporary success on the part of the Mormons, may be a signal for an Indian War extending along our whole frontier. The troops in this Department have been stationed with such strict attention to the absolute wants of the service, that but little, if any reduction at any post could be made with safety to inhabitants. In Oregon and Washington Territories, East of the Cascade Range, I consider it unsafe to remove a man for service elsewhere.

My intention as intimated in my letter of Dec. 18 with reference to the relief companies for Yuma, will be carried out, and I will station a company permanently, perhaps at San Bernardino, near Cajon Pass.

I recommend instant measures calculated to detach Indians from Mormon influence. As an initial step toward that end I suggest that Headsmen or Chiefs be invited to visit Washington. As an inducement they should receive presents to a generous extent. Such visit would disabuse them of any erroneous impressions they may have received, relative to the power of the United States, by seeing for themselves how numerous and powerful our people are.

Maj. Robert S. Garnett (Commanding Fort Simcoe, Washington Territory) to W. W. Mackall, 30 January 1858, Letters Received, HQ Dept. of the Pacific, RG 393, NARA.

It seems proper that I should report for the information of General Clarke that the Indian Chief "Skloom," brother of Kamiakin, has recently sent word to me for the second time that the Mormons on one or two occasions since last December have sent emissaries among the Indians of this region to incite them to a mission with the Mormons in hostility to the United States. He states that the chiefs repel these overtures from the Mormons, but that some of the young men seem disposed to countenance them. The Mormons make them large presents of arms, ammunition, cattle &c. For myself I do not attach much importance to these machinations of the Mormons, unless our army in Utah should meet with some serious reverses.[12]

By the last half of January 1858, General Clarke had become so alarmed by reports from military commanders and excited civilians that his directives, like Brigham Young's during the previous October, began to change character from defensive preparations to an aggressive posture. On 12 January Clarke ordered a dragoon company on detached duty along the Columbia River at Fort Vancouver, Washington, to return "with promptness" to Fort Walla Walla, where Brevet Lt. Col. Edward J. Steptoe commanded.

MACKALL TO STEPTOE, 12 JANUARY 1858,
LETTERS SENT, HQ DEPT. OF THE PACIFIC, RG 393, NARA.

The General wishes you to be deeply impressed with the importance of obtaining early and full information in relation to the Indian tribes in your vicinity and South and East towards Fort Hall and the Salmon River [Oregon Territory]. Information from various sources and points on the frontier, leads him to the conclusion that thro' the Mormons the Indians are being inclined to hostility, and that a conflict in Utah may be the signal for trouble on the frontier, and it is not improbable that the Mormons may move North. He wishes you to be prepared in advance for either contingency. Full and prompt report of all information and your opinion founded thereon is desired.

STEPTOE TO MACKALL, 29 JANUARY 1858,
LETTERS RECEIVED, HQ DEPT. OF THE PACIFIC, RG 393, NARA.

I received by last mail your letter of the 12th instant. Measures were taken at once to insure the full efficiency of this command, whenever it may be required to active service. It is very difficult to determine, from any information I have now, how far the reports that have reached the general of a meditated outbreak on the part of the Indians in this direction ought to be relied upon.

That the expediency of availing themselves of this Mormon revolt to recover some real or imagined rights has been discussed amongst them I am quite sure, but doubt whether they have resolved to commit themselves to hostilities at present. If they should learn that the Mormons have obtained any marked advantage over the troops, or if the contest in Utah should be a protracted one, I would then seriously apprehend trouble with the surrounding

[12]Garnett was an officer in the Ninth U.S. Infantry and is not to be confused with his cousin, Richard B. Garnett of the Sixth U.S. Infantry. Both were Virginians and West Pointers who died as Confederate brigadiers.

tribes. Between this post and Fort Hall there are numerous families of Snake Indians, who are represented to be great friends of the Mormons, and to be well armed and provided with ammunition. I am inclined to think this is true, and that they have made some efforts to break up the friendly relations existing between the troops and Indians in the Walla Walla country, but that the latter are not disposed to involve themselves while the chances of success are so much against them. What has been said here applies more particularly to the Cayuse, Walla Walla and various petty tribes living on the Columbia River and its tributaries below. Respecting the northern Indians (Palouse, Yakima, and Spokane), there never has been a doubt on my mind that very slight encouragement would at any time suffice to revive their late hostile feelings. It is gratifying, however, to know that they are much under the influence of the Nez Perces, who are, for the most part, and have always been, strong in their friendship toward us.

Upon the whole, I do not think, in view of the large force to be here soon, that we will have a difficulty with these Indians this year. If the troops have ordinary success in Utah, the probability will be lessened, and still further if the Mormons shall be signally worsted. I have remonstrated earnestly with the chiefs against the interference of their people in the matter, and I am sure that several of the most influential are impressed with the conviction that such interference could not fail to be disastrous to them.

Having no certain information as to the sentiments of the Indians (Snakes) between this and Fort Boise, I have long intended to ascertain the truth of the matter by sending out an expedition early this spring. My purpose now is to start three companies of dragoons over the route so soon as the absence of snow and height of new grass will justify the movement, and, if possible, to dispatch a reliable Indian immediately over the same route (perhaps further) to gain information in advance. It is only about 200 miles from here to Fort Boise, and not over 500 miles to the Salt Lake by the wagon road (probably fifty miles less by the trails.) An old trapper living here, who spent many years about Fort Hall, and has often traveled the road, says that he can go with ease from this post to the Salt Lake and back in twenty days.

A half-breed Indian from Salmon River came here three days since, and states that the Mormon settlement there removed some six weeks ago to the Salt Lake, sacrificing houses and improvements, as at San Bernardino.[13] In my opinion, this is only significant as indicating further the stern resistance contemplated by the Mormons. I question much whether the idea of leaving Utah and emigrating to some other country is seriously entertained by them. But in either event the advantage of arming and arraying against us all the

[13]This report of the evacuation of the Mormon Salmon River Mission (Fort Limhi) in January was erroneous, although that did come about in March 1858 after the raid on the mission on 25 February by Bannocks and Northern Shoshones.

> Indians living on the principal routes to Utah cannot have escaped their attention, and it is more than probable that they have taken steps to effect that end.

One wonders about Colonel Steptoe's reaction to this controversy in view of the chain of events by which he had declined President Pierce's offer of Utah's governorship three years earlier.[14]

One driver for General Clarke's military preparations in Washington and Oregon territories during January 1858 was the pressure of rising anti-Mormonism. Settlers' apprehensions about Mormon-Indian relations in the Pacific Northwest were long standing. Five months after the Mormon arrival in the Salt Lake Valley in July 1847, an agent of the Hudson's Bay Company at Fort Hall reported the astonishing news that "a city has sprung up, as if by enchantment, in the midst of the desert, near the southern extremity of great Salt Lake. It contains a population of 3,000, and numbers within its precinct 600 houses." In March 1848 the company's chief clerk at Fort Walla Walla reported to a senior officer of the Oregon militia that a renegade band from the Cayuse tribe was on the road to the new Mormon settlement via Fort Hall to seek sanctuary from punishment.[15]

As the 1850s unfolded, this sense of regional alarm grew, fueled by unremitting Indian warfare and the arrival of settlers who felt victimized while passing through Utah, as well as an influx of Midwesterners with memories of the bloody Mormon experience in Missouri and Illinois and controversies over Indian issues in those states. Aggravating these perceptions was the arrival of skeptical, if not hostile, Protestant ministers offended by both Mormon proselytizing and the religion's truth claims and unique doctrines.[16] Here was a twin of the anti-Mormonism that was sweeping California, but with a ministerial stimulus not found in the godless gold camps of the Sierra.

---

[14]Four months after this warning from Clarke, a column led by Steptoe was unexpectedly engaged by an ad hoc confederation of tribes that inflicted on him the worst defeat sustained by the army in Indian warfare until the Fort Phil Kearny massacre nearly ten years later. Viewed narrowly, Steptoe's defeat, which came in the midst of tribal unrest over the incursion of miners onto Indian lands, was independent of Mormon issues, but it reflected the volatility surrounding the Mormon-"Americat" confrontation just as Mojave unrest along the Colorado in the late 1850s was similarly aggravated. Although Latter-day Saints were not present during the 17 May 1858 battle, two weeks later Steptoe commented, "There is much doubt on my mind where the Indians obtained their ammunition, of which they had abundance. My impression is that it was obtained either from the [Fort] Colville traders [of the Hudson's Bay Company] or the Mormons." General Clarke commented that Mormons had "instigated" the tribes that attacked Steptoe. Steptoe to Mackall, 29 May 1858, and Clarke to HQ U.S. Army, 2 June 1858, Letters Received/Sent, HQ Dept. of the Pacific, RG 393, NARA.

[15]James Douglas to Governor Abernethy, 15 March 1848, quoted in Gray, *History of Oregon*, 565; Josephy, *The Nez Perce Indians and the Opening of the Northwest*, 277.

[16]Goodell and Bigler, *A Winter with the Mormons*.

News of the Utah War's eruption and Brigham Young's spring 1857 visit to Fort Limhi intensified concerns in the Pacific Northwest about Mormon activities among the tribes.

As 1858 opened, Oregon's delegate in Congress, a prominent militia general and Indian campaigner, assured a constituent, "that portion of your letters in relation to the disposition of our Indians I have referred to the Secretary of the Interior, that he may know the condition of affairs, and that we may be able if possible to avert the horrors of another Indian war. I shall urge the sending of troops to our frontiers to hold the Indians in check. I have no doubt but the Mormons will incite the Indians to take up the tomahawk. Brigham must be broken up!"[17]

By the end of January these anxieties surfaced in Oregon's territorial legislature, which memorialized Congress to sub-divide the single Indian superintendency with jurisdiction over the tribes throughout Oregon and Washington. In discussing this need, the memorial noted that "an additional reason for the division of the immense district, over which the present Superintendent presides, exists in the present hostile and treasonable attitude assumed by the fanatical inhabitants of Utah. The Mormons are in a position to exercise a powerful influence over the great interior tribes east of the Cascade Mountains, and are already reported to have seduced many bands to join them by offers to supply them with ammunition. A Superintendent located east of the Cascade Mountains would be effective in controlling such mischievous influences."[18]

By March 1858 Protestant hostility to proselytizing and even a Mormon presence in the Pacific Northwest forced the church's members to gather at the Willamette River and then depart for Utah.[19] It was a small exodus largely lost to historical notice among the earlier, more dramatic roll-up of the Mormon colonies and missions in Hawaii, Great Britain, San Francisco, San Bernardino, and Carson Valley.

Having thus seen to the defenses of the Pacific Northwest, General Clarke returned to the subject of California in early February, providing through his adjutant even more action-oriented instructions to his new subordinate at San Bernardino.

---

[17]Joseph Lane to James O'Meara, 3 January 1858, Lilly Library Manuscript Collections, Indiana University, Bloomington.

[18]Memorial to the U.S. Senate and House, Nos. 8899 and 8894, 25–27 January 1858, Papers of Territorial Government, Oregon State Archives, Salem.

[19]Smart, "Oregon and the Mormon Problem," 60–61.

Mackall to Capt. Joseph Stewart, Third Artillery,
4 February 1858, Letters Sent,
HQ Dept. of the Pacific, RG 393, NARA.

In addition to the usual duties of the commanders of posts in the Department of protecting the inhabitants from the Indians, the General desires you to take advantage of your position, (stationed as you will be in a Mormon settlement, and at the point of departure for Salt Lake) to ascertain the views of the Mormons, the amount of emigration thus far from California to Utah, the kind and amount of munitions of war sent to Utah, and the influence the Mormons have exerted over the Indians of California. Should you find that they have or are exerting an influence inimical to the Government of the United States or to the citizens of California, you will exert yourself to counteract it. Report fully everything of interest you discover in reference to this subject, or that you may be able to ascertain of the state of affairs in Salt Lake and of the routes leading to Utah.

Hardy Pioneers and Mountain Men: California Volunteers

Accompanying Clarke's official actions to protect southern California was the spontaneous formation of dozens of volunteer paramilitary units clamoring for action in the Utah War. Recognized by neither the state nor federal governments, these local companies took on a life of their own, especially after the publication of President Buchanan's 8 December message to Congress requesting more troops for Utah.

Aside from what appeared to be presidential encouragement, there were multiple factors peculiar to California that fueled this volunteerism: indignation over the recent Mountain Meadows massacre; perceptions of Mormon inhospitality while traveling through Utah; experience in organizing volunteer companies for emigration and gold mining; and the presence of a young, male, single, armed, and restless population demonstrably interested in filibustering, if not vigilantism. Dealing with the expectations of these volunteers would pose challenges not only for Brigham Young but for California's governor, the Buchanan administration, and General Scott.

Once the text of Buchanan's annual message to Congress reached California in early January 1858, the formation of volunteer units accelerated. In his inaugural address on 8 January 1858, California governor John B. Weller called for military action to respond to the Mountain Meadows massacre and Brigham Young's threatened blockage of transcontinental emigration to the Pacific Coast: "Our people are certainly entitled to protection whilst traveling through American territory, and to secure this, the whole power of the federal government should be invoked. Hundreds of emigrants during the past year were inhumanly butchered. That government will, we hope, see that such bloody scenes are not reenacted upon our great highways and in our own [California] territory." Weller made it clear that he believed the responsibility for the use of such force lay with the U.S. government.[20]

As Weller took office, he was also probably aware of the summary of statewide volunteering activity published three days earlier by a San Francisco newspaper. All that was needed was an unambiguous, consistent signal from the Buchanan administration about what it wanted—regular or volunteer troops—and a reliable indication from Congress that it would reimburse states for the cost of volunteer units organized for the Utah campaign. But with the administration uneasy about the cost and complexity of a thrust from the West, a general in chief with jaundiced views on the long-distance use of untrained volunteers, and a Congress still smarting over its lack of involvement in Buchanan's initial decision to intervene militarily in Utah, no such signals came. Nevertheless, Californians pressed on.

"More Volunteers for the Utah War,"
San Francisco Evening Bulletin, 5 January 1858, 2/1.

We mentioned last week that three companies of volunteers for the Mormon war were being organized at Columbia, Tuolumne county, and were holding themselves in readiness to obey the expected speedy call of President Buchanan for volunteers from this State for Utah. Similar companies are being formed over all the country, so that there will be no lack of men when the anticipated call from Washington comes. At Visalia, Tulare county, a company of eighty-four mounted riflemen have been organized.

The [Sacramento] *State Journal* says of this force: "On 26th December, the names of the volunteers having been enrolled, the following named gentlemen were elected as officers. . . . This company has been enlisted with a view of joining the first regiment of California volunteers that shall be called out by the President for the Mormon war. Nearly all, if not the whole number, have been accustomed to frontier life, and have seen service in Mexico and Texas. This muster roll has [been] forwarded to the Hon. John B. Weller through the hands of A.H. Mitchell, Assemblyman elect from Tulare county.

[20]Weller, "Inaugural Address," 8 January 1858, accessed 10 January 2015, http://governors.library.ca.gov/addresses/05-Weller.html.

"The Captain, Armistead H. Mitchell, is a grandson of General [Walker Keith] Armistead, late of the U.S. Army, and is at present the member elect of the Assembly from Tulare and Fresno counties. He is a Texas Ranger, and has fought the battles of his country both in Texas and Mexico. Of the first lieutenants, Mr. Morris is a son of Major Wm. W. Morris, who now commands the fourth Regiment of U.S. Artillery, and who is at present attached to the command of Gen. Harney. He has been raised in camp and garrison life, and has been in Florida['s Seminole Wars]. Lt. [Redmond B.] Sagely was a sergeant in [Col. Archibald] Yell's division of Arkansas volunteers during the Mexican war, and is at present Undersheriff of Tulare county. The other officers are well known in that section of the country as celebrated Indian fighters and Texas Rangers.

"We learn on good authority, that Captain Russett, John Boggs, and a number of the best men of the county of Yolo, are rapidly organizing a company 'for service against the Mormon traitors of Utah' as they express it in their articles of association. The head quarters of this company will be at Cacheville, the county seat and agricultural centre of Yolo. Our informant, who is a resident of Yolo, thinks that the county will send at least two of the two finest mounted commands into the field that can be raised anywhere in the state."

The town of Jackson, in Amador county, has not been behind in this Mormon furore. Under the direction of Assemblyman Briggs, says the Amador *Ledger,* about fifty volunteers have enrolled their names for Mormon service.

Not all perceptions of the Mormon threat faced by Californians were serious, especially in the state's rough-hewn mining camps so anathema to Brigham Young. Here philosophers and humorists of the Bret Harte and Mark Twain persuasion lurked among the picks, shovels, and rocker Toms. Fighting a mixture of fatigue, boredom, economic uncertainty, and homesickness, N. A. Chandler, a placer miner grubbing along in Alpha, a gold camp in Nevada County, provided his wife in Vermont with a combination of news and humor: "I wish you All a Happy New Year Although it is rather late but better late than never as the saying is. Time flies very fast with me, it dosnt seem three years since I came here. The Mormons has been moving for Salt Lake and sell out cheap. The farmers live very easy here to what they do East. We expect that Uncle Sam will have a brush with the saints soon. A great many of the *Cala* Boys seem to be ready to turn out perhaps they think they may get a widow out thare as the Mormons have more than their share."[21]

[21]N. A. Chandler to Jane Chandler, 15 January 1858, Chandler California Gold Rush Era Letters, Denison Library, Claremont Colleges, California.

A day later, Mr. "J. Struggles," an otherwise unidentified miner in the newly developed goldfields of Kern River Valley, laid on a heavier attempt at humor while updating San Franciscans on his view of the Utah War.

J. Struggles to Editor, 16 January 1858,
San Francisco Daily Alta California, 24 January 1858.

As Hestron and his express will soon be along for letters, we take great pleasure in dropping you a few lines. We must apoligise [*sic*] for not having written more regularly, but we have been so intensely and practically busy playing that highly interesting game, called "root little pig or die," that we could not avoid—well, we had better stop, or the apology will be worse than the offence.

Doubtless, many persons will be uneasy for us Kern river miners, seeing that we are in an exposed part of the frontier, and liable to a combined attack from the Mormons and Piutes; but their uneasiness would be turned to astonishment could they see the cool indifference (the snow being a foot deep just now) with which the affair is looked upon here. There is scarcely a man here, so trammeled with this world's goods, but what he could soon have them all on a mule, ready for action; then there are an astonishing quantity of revolvers and rifles in circulation. There are two companies in process of formation here, namely, the Keysville Bengal Tigers, and the Greenhorn Plug-Uglies, and we are determined to give the Mormons a cool reception—turn our backs on them if necessary.

Some timid persons hint that the Mormons will take advantage of our exposed condition, make a sweep down on the stock ranches of Tule river, and the Four Creeks, burn the towns and drive off the live stock; but taking into consideration the fact that this portion of the country is chiefly populated by contributions from the State of Pike, Arkansas and Texas, it is likely they will get more kicks than cattle. We are very skeptical on the subject, and do not think much livestock will be driven off, (without the aid of mercurial ointment.)[22] The Keysville Bengal Tigers and Greenhorn Plug-Uglies will be ever vigilant, brave but prudent, remembering Brother Brigham's hint: "The man that fights and runs away, will do the same another day."

Perceptions and Self-Defense

For historians of the Utah War, assessing the character of the Mormon threat, if any, to the Pacific Coast and the defensive-aggressive reaction of

[22]Medicinal mercury was then used for the treatment of venereal disease and constipation, among other afflictions.

the region's settlers is both complex and important. It was a scene in which perceptions, accurate or not, became realities.

That during 1857–58 Mormons bought and shipped munitions from California in quantities far beyond normal personal needs, and did so covertly, is indisputable. How one interprets this unusual flow is the dilemma. In a frontier society, what is the proper balance between the exercise of one's constitutional right to bear arms and an orchestrated, centrally directed program on a far broader, institutional scale? If at times Brigham Young threatened to unleash arsonists on California settlements, how does one evaluate this example of negative leadership alongside the right to free speech, Young's penchant for hyperbole, his oath of office, and the absence of any known capability to place Mormon saboteurs among the people of Los Angeles, San Diego, or Sacramento? Then there is the well-known tendency of frontier settlers to cry wolf (or Indian or Mormon) while lobbying for the establishment of a nearby army garrison, often the greatest economic boon for which an isolated region could hope. Utah was unique among frontier states and territories in lacking a U.S. Army garrison and never requesting one. This near-universal quest for federal troops was a behavior perhaps second only to the frontiersman's scramble for rank, honors, and cash following a gubernatorial or presidential call for volunteer soldiers.

Finally, historians need to consider the actions of the region's American Indians. For their own advantage, some of the tribes were prone to play "Americats" against Mormons and vice versa. Other bands simply tried to protect their endangered rights, cultures, and traditional hunting territories by even-handedly distancing themselves from the blandishments of both sides. These differing behaviors by the members of more than a dozen tribes impacted by the Utah War were interpreted in multiple ways by Anglos lacking even a rudimentary grasp of the tribal languages and cultures involved.

Into this Pacific Coast stew of cross currents, conflicting perceptions, religious and racial prejudices, economic self-interest, and other mixed motives stepped the Buchanan administration at the beginning of 1858. The result was an immediate broadening of the Utah War's sweep and a commensurate murkiness to James Buchanan's decisions in pursuit of Manifest Destiny as well as resolution of the enduring Mormon problem.

Chapter 6

"To Mask the Real Movement"
Pacific Adventures, Presidential Intrigue

It may seem that there is little direct connection between an expedition ostensibly against the Mormons or involving relations with Mexico and plans for the acquisition of Cuba. The latter however is the real object; the other is subsidiary to it and serves to mask the real movement.

Sir William Gore Ouseley to Lord Clarendon, 15 February 1858

The War Department's redirection of the Ives Expedition in November 1857 from a scientific mission to a military reconnaissance was the opening move of a broader federal strategy under consideration at year end. The plan was to reinforce the Utah Expedition from the Pacific Coast and to strike Brigham Young in the spring of 1858 with columns converging from California, Oregon, Kansas, and Nebraska. It was an ambitious, two-front campaign remarkably disconnected from General Clarke's more modest local efforts to defend his Department of the Pacific with the regular troops already in place.

In the immediate aftermath of Lot Smith's October raid on federal supply trains, Colonels Johnston and Alexander had recommended such a pincers movement, as did Generals Harney and Persifor F. Smith in November. A few weeks later, in his first annual message to Congress, President Buchanan had offered a plan for resolving the conflict based on a continued application of military force. In requesting a four-regiment expansion of the army to prosecute the war, he purposely left unstated the route by which these reinforcements would march on Utah.[1] Silence from Secretary Floyd and General Scott on this point stimulated press speculation as to whether there would actually be a second front for the Utah War or whether the spring campaign would involve reinforcements from Kansas alone. Uninvolved in Buchanan's March 1857 decision to intervene in Utah and alarmed by its mushrooming costs, Congress demanded information about the conflict's origins and expenditures while questioning the extent of Mormon alienation.

Thus pressured, Buchanan turned inward to the secretive, manipulative side of his administrative style. In this atmosphere, unconventional schemes sprang up to flourish in close proximity to the president. This chapter probes multiple interconnected aspects of the war as it unfolded during January 1858: Buchanan's plans to move on Utah from the Pacific Coast; General Scott's quirky effort to prepare such a campaign while simultaneously changing the Utah Expedition's leadership; and a covert presidential attempt to advance American Manifest Destiny by inducing a massive southern-bound exodus of Mormon refugees. As with the concurrent Marcy and Ives missions, the geographical sweep of these neglected Utah War thrusts is stunning.[2]

Hornets Raging, Hell Boiling: Mormon Anticipation

Although General Scott opposed the raising of volunteer troops seemingly implicit in a large, rapid expansion of the army—especially for any two-front campaign—he took seriously the need to reinforce the Utah Expedition with available regulars. Consequently, by December 1857 Scott was funneling hundreds of regular troops from New York to California via the Isthmus of Panama, although he probably did so without enthusiasm.

Rumors of a Pacific Coast thrust were widespread. As he traveled home to Utah from Liverpool, Apostle Ezra T. Benson heard them while passing through New York, Panama, and California. On 5 December Benson sent Brigham Young an early warning from San Pedro, California, of large-scale federal troop movements by sea.[3] It was news consistent with reports about

---

[1] *At Sword's Point, Part 1*, 424–32, 481–85.

[2] Much of this chapter is based on four journal articles: MacKinnon, "Buchanan's Thrust from the Pacific," 226–60; "'Who's in Charge Here?': Utah Expedition Command Ambiguity," 30–64; "Hammering Utah, Squeezing Mexico, and Coveting Cuba: James Buchanan's White House Intrigues," 132–56; and "'Not as a Stranger': A Presbyterian Afoot in the Mormon Past," 21–39.

[3] Benson to Young, 5 December 1857, LDS Archives.

the significance of the Ives Expedition reaching Young from Mormon agents Jacob Hamblin, Amasa Lyman, and William Cox. Seven weeks later Benson provided extensive comments on the Buchanan administration's developing Pacific Coast build-up while preaching in Salt Lake City.

Benson, Discourse, 24 January 1858, *Journal of Discourses*, 6:177–84.

We had on board [the ship] eleven hundred and fifty passengers, two or three hundred of whom were United States troops. When we were loading up, the soldiers were driven on board, like pigs, as thick as they could stand. Government is shipping men round by the Isthmus of Panama to California and we were informed the next steamer was to bring six hundred men. There was a good deal of fault found by the officers of government because there were only two hundred and fifty along with us, but it was said they are going to ship them by thousands to California and then forward them to Utah. They said they were coming to California, but, when we asked them privately where they were destined for, they said, "we are going to Utah."

They design in their hearts to blot "Mormonism" out of existence, and they feel like using their money for the accomplishment of this object, and even go so far as to say, their purses shall be open for their means to be used in the fitting out of men for the Territory of Utah, and they say they will come from the north and from the south and from the east and surround this people by thousands and by tens of thousands, until we are wiped out.

The halters [nooses] are already made which they design shall hang the Governor, the members of the Legislative Assembly and every faithful elder in this Church; for they feel determined to swing you up between the heavens and the earth. We understand their plays and their schemes, for we have been in their midst [while traveling].

The people of the United States seem paralyzed and do not know what to do. They are waiting for the government to call for volunteers and then they say they are all ready to go. California people say they are all ready to rally, but I tell you I believe what br. Brigham has said, they will not come here. The priest in the pulpit is ready, and says, "O yes, we must go and wipe out the 'Mormons,' but do not ask me to go."

Let us do the very best we can, brethren and sisters, for the day may come when we may be thankful for every foot of greasewood and of desert country there is between us and our enemies. I am glad that we came through [to Utah] on the southern route, for I have been enabled to learn a little of the road.[4] The editors in the States are prompting government to bring their troops from the south [of California]; why they do not know [what it is really like],

[4]This route was essentially the Spanish Trail between San Bernardino and Utah's southern settlements. It was this road which the War Department hoped to access from the Colorado River and Rio Virgin.

only they are not on that route, so subject to snow storms and they can travel in the winter, but I can tell them the south route is ten times worse than the east; it is one perfect desert from Muddy creek clear through. There is now and then a patch of grass on the journey, but what can a large army do?[5]

The kanyon coming up the Santa Clara [River] is quite as good [defensively] as Echo, and some think a little better. It does seem as if those mountains and kanyons have been prepared on purpose, and we have great cause to be thankful for those natural defences.[6]

Contrary to All Strategic Principles: General Scott's Strange Behavior

By the New Year—just as Colonel Johnston was learning of Brigham Young's dramatic plans for the Standing Army of Israel—Scott acted to position reinforcements for a multi-regiment spring attack by regulars from Kansas. On 8 January he announced to the army that "with the approbation of the War Department . . . the Army of Utah will be reinforced, as soon as practicable, by the 1st Regiment of Cavalry, 6th and 7th Regiments of Infantry, and Light Companies A and M, 2d Artillery." In total 5,606 officers and men were to be committed to the Utah Expedition, more than one-third of the regular army. Without reference to any Pacific-based movement into Utah or use of volunteer troops, Scott's order referred to this move simply as "the march of the reinforcement[s] across the plains." A week later he ordered troops from two more regular units to join the Utah Expedition: Companies B and K of the Second Dragoons from Fort Leavenworth, and Company A, U.S. Engineers, from West Point.[7] Always the intelligence gatherer, Delegate Bernhisel reported these plans for massive spring reinforcements to Brigham Young, including Quartermaster General Jesup's observation that their "train, inc[l]uding I suppose the baggage and forage wagons, will reach Washington to Baltimore a distance of forty miles."[8]

[5]Feasibility of this route is discussed in Capt. Rufus Ingalls to Lt. Col. Thomas Swards, 29 December 1857, Yale Collection of Western Americana, Beinecke Library; *At Sword's Point, Part 1*, 432–34.

[6]In August 1857 Apostle George A. Smith had visited Santa Clara Canyon and pointed out its defensive merits. A few weeks later, it was allegedly the site originally selected as the place to attack the Fancher party, much as it had been with the Ambrose-Betts affair of February 1857. Parshall, "'Pursue, Retake & Punish,'" 64–86. Echo Canyon to the northeast in the Wasatch Range was the Mormons' best-known defensive position and headquarters for the Nauvoo Legion's Eastern Expedition.

[7]HQ of the Army, General Orders No. 1 and 4 of 8 and 16 January 1858; copy in editor's possession. See also Reinforcements of Utah, Circular, HQ of the Army, Letters Received, Office of Adjt. Gen., RG 94, NARA.

Soon thereafter, during the second week of January 1858, Scott's planning for a two-front campaign turned bizarre. On 13 January, without specifying which coast he had in mind, Scott sent a telegram from Washington to Brevet Maj. Gen. John E. Wool, the seventy-three-year-old commander of the Department of the East, at his Troy, New York, headquarters: "WE WANT A GENERAL TO COMMAND THE UTAH EXPEDITION, WHAT SAY YOU OR WHO DO YOU RECOMMEND."[9] For Scott to risk sending such a volatile message by public telegraph rather than by confidential mail or army courier signals extraordinary urgency. Intriguingly, there is no evidence that Scott's superiors in the War Department and the White House were aware that he was sending such a question to Wool, although Scott's presence in Washington rather than New York and use of "we" in his wire makes it difficult to believe that he was acting unilaterally.

Compounding the risk of public awareness, General Wool replied by telegram on 15 January, indicating in the process not only the urgency of the matter but Wool's uncertainly about the crucial issue of who was behind this unexpected offer of command: "IF IT IS YOUR DESIRE OR THAT OF THE ADMINISTRATION I WILL WITH PLEASURE TAKE COMMAND OF THE UTAH EXPEDITION. SEE MY LETTER BY MAIL. PLEASE ACKNOWLEDGE RECEIPT."[10] In his immediately following letter, Wool opened by repeating the text of his telegram and then raised the obvious matter of Col. Albert Sidney Johnston's probable reaction (and those of even more senior officers) to such a leadership change, as well as some concerns of his own about finances. Not surprisingly, Wool requested a meeting with Scott.[11]

Scott's sudden offer to Wool is inexplicable. In addition to being even older than Scott, Wool had recently been relieved as commander of the Department of the Pacific—replaced by General Clarke—because of his acrimonious clashes with governors and then–Secretary of War Jefferson Davis over the prosecution of Indian campaigns, including Wool's reluctance to use volunteer troops. Wool's reassignment from San Francisco to command the Department of the East had been a political accommodation

[8]Bernhisel to David O. Calder, 18 January 1858, LDS Archives. Calder, who lived in Salt Lake City, was used as a "cut-out" through whom Mormons in the East and Europe could send mail to Young without fear of interception by federal authorities.

[9]Scott, Telegram to Wool, 13 January 1858, Wool Papers, State Library of New York, Albany; Records of the HQ of the Army, Letters Sent, RG 108, NARA.

[10]Wool, Telegram to Scott, 15 January 1858, Wool Papers.

[11]Wool, Letter to Scott, 15 January 1858, ibid.

to save his career. In addition to these liabilities, during the winter of 1858 General Wool was in fragile health as a result of the lingering effects of a leg injury sustained during 1857 while returning east across the Isthmus of Panama. Such was Wool's condition in late March 1858, less than two months after Scott had tendered him command of the arduous Utah campaign, that he was immobilized by rheumatism and unable to comply with the War Department's order that he travel from Troy to Carlisle Barracks, Pennsylvania, to preside over the court martial of Col. Edwin V. Sumner.[12]

From a twenty-first-century perspective, Scott's telegram—proposing an arrangement that would supersede Albert Sidney Johnston with a controversial, over-age officer in questionable health—would ordinarily suggest several other background factors: deep concerns about Johnston's competence, the projected complexity of the Utah Expedition's next organizational phase, and the shortage of talent in the army's top echelon available and fit for such a difficult assignment. In view of Scott's high regard for Johnston, it is most unlikely that his proffer of the senior Utah command to Wool reflected a negative view of Johnston's capabilities.

While Winfield Scott shopped for a senior commander to spearhead the war's projected second front, Secretary Floyd continued to search for information and advice about the Pacific Northwest beyond what his general in chief provided during his episodic visits to Washington. Floyd was a limited man but one who knew that in the military realm there were things he did not know, as reflected by his 1857 debriefings of Ben McCulloch, Maj. Samuel P. Heintzelman, and General Smith.[13] Early in 1858 Floyd's next source was 1st Lt. John Mullan, Second Artillery, an officer on medical leave from the Pacific Northwest with whom he met in Washington on 19 January. Mullan had vast knowledge of the region from his participation in the army's Pacific Railroad survey and other explorations. What Floyd wanted from him was information for "a new line of military operations in the Territory of Utah," the sort of intelligence he expected Lieutenant Ives to furnish about approaching Utah from the south. Mullan obliged the same day with an eleven-page report commenting on the use of the Columbia and Missouri Rivers, their tributaries, and interior valleys to channel supplies and troops in support of the projected campaign from the Pacific Coast. It was a document of panoramic

[12]Wool to Cooper, Telegram and Letter, 6 March 1858, Letters Received, Office of Adjt. Gen., RG 94, NARA.

[13]*At Sword's Point, Part 1*, 173–77, 426–30.

sweep provided to Floyd alone, who let it marinate in his desk for another two months. Eventually the report led to construction of what became the famous Mullan Road connecting Fort Walla Walla and Fort Benton.[14]

On 23 January 1858, about a week after the first exchange of messages between the two generals, Wool sent Scott another memorandum from Troy dealing with tactical aspects of the Utah campaign.[15] Strangely, this document lacked any hint that Wool had been offered and tentatively accepted a major role in the Utah War. It was as though both generals had agreed to ignore Scott's invitation and Wool's positive response by wire and letter. Apparently the meeting with Scott requested by Wool to discuss the Utah command never took place.

Thus, Scott's proposal that Wool should command a Utah campaign expanded in both size and scope died a quick, quiet death. The paper trail shedding light on this affair ends with Wool's puzzlingly detached 23 January letter to Scott. The plethora of leaked documents and contemporaneous newspaper speculation about other aspects of the Utah campaign contained no reference to this episode. There is no indication that Colonel Johnston ever became aware of Scott's proposed change, although in mid-April his quartermaster officer noted with relief that "he is not to be superceded in the command."[16]

At least two factors may have prompted Scott to drop his embryonic plan to alter the Utah Expedition's command structure: a realization that the nation was warming to Albert Sidney Johnston as a field commander, and second thoughts about the viability of congressional support for any move to subordinate Johnston to General Wool.

Unknown to Scott, just as he was about to offer this command to Wool, the Philadelphia *Press* ran an editorial coupling comments about the importance of sound leadership for "the difficult and delicate responsibilities of the present Utah Expedition" with a laudatory profile of Johnston and his career. The piece concluded that "he seems to have filled ably every part to which he has been cast. Not only has he been able, but his ability has been

---

[14]Mullan to Floyd, 19 January 1858, Letters Received, Records of the Office of Adjt. Gen., RG 94, NARA. For a recent discussion of Mullan, his career and the annual Mullan Road Conference, see Julie Turkewitz, "On a Trip through Time in Montana, a Name Demands Notice," *New York Times*, 24 May 2015.

[15]Wool to Scott, 23 January 1858, Records HQ of the Army, Letters Received, RG 108, NARA.

[16]Capt. John H. Dickerson to W. A. Gordon, 16 April 1858, Manuscripts Department, Bancroft Library, University of California, Berkeley. Dickerson probably had General Harney rather than Wool in mind as a possible succession threat to Johnston.

accompanied by the esteem and respect of all communities, civil and military, into which he has been thrown."[17]

Whether the *Press*, an anti-Buchanan paper, was simply reacting to the first reports describing Johnston's effective execution of the trek to Fort Bridger or was building an editorial backfire to counter anticipated criticism of him, this piece had impact. During the next few days multiple small-town newspapers as well as those of leading cities like Baltimore and New York reprinted it. Just as General Wool considered Winfield Scott's telegraphic surprise, adversity in Utah transformed Colonel Johnston from a relatively unknown officer to a military leader of national interest.

Coincident with the public's growing awareness of Albert Sidney Johnson's capabilities was a reawakening of the controversies dogging General Wool's reputation. On 26 January 1858 public dismay over an earlier exchange of insults between Jefferson Davis and Wool spilled into the congressional debates about expanding the army for the Mormon campaign. The House of Representatives passed a resolution requesting "that the President communicate to this House, if not incompatible with the public service, so much of the correspondence between the late [former] Secretary of War Davis and Major General John E. Wool, late commanding the Pacific department, relative to the affairs of such department as has not heretofore been published under a call of this House."[18]

With Davis then chairman of the Senate's committee on military affairs, and Congress restless about reinforcing the Utah Expedition, Scott, if not Buchanan and Floyd, may have concluded that late January was not the time to supersede Johnston with John E. Wool to lead the U.S. Army's most sensitive command. The *Press* had emphasized that the Utah Expedition must be led by an officer "possessed of superior civil qualifications to guide his dealings with the ungoverned people who are represented as denying the authority of our constitution." Johnston, Jefferson Davis's protégé as well as Scott's, was just such a leader.

With Wool no longer in the Utah picture and Johnston not yet a general, Scott resolved to go west. On 23 January 1858 his aide informed Colonel Johnston, "the General-in-chief himself, will set sail for the Pacific Coast, in the steamer of the 5th proximo [February], clothed with full powers for an effective diversion or cooperation, in your favor, from that quarter. It is not

[17]"Col. Johnston, the Leader of Our Army in Utah," Editorial, Philadelphia *Press,* 11 January 1858.

[18]"Correspondence between the Late Secretary of War and General Wool," U.S. Cong, House Exec. Doc. 88 (35-1).

desired, however, that this information shall modify the instructions heretofore given you, in any degree, or delay your movements."[19] It was remarkable news given Scott's age, medical problems, and general immobility. At age 71, the general in chief weighed about three hundred pounds, was unable to mount a horse, and at times had difficulty walking. Less than five months earlier, ill health had prevented Scott from traveling less than one hundred miles up the Hudson River to visit General Wool's headquarters in Troy.[20]

Almost certainly Scott's plans to travel to the Pacific Coast were in response to pressure from Buchanan and Floyd. Manhattan lawyer and insider George Templeton Strong, one of the city's inveterate gossips, came to this conclusion based on comments attributed to the general's daughter and her husband, General Scott's aide de camp. To Strong, such a journey was a virtual death sentence for "Old Fuss 'n Feathers": "General Scott yields to the prayers of the Administration and has made up his mind to go to California, there to organize a campaign against Utah. . . . The General is a grand old fellow, too old for the fatigue and exposure of such an expedition. It's not likely he will ever return. We must get up a graven image of him on the other side of Union Square to balance Colonel Jem Lee's copper Washington."[21]

No doubt aware of Scott's travel plans and plagued by his own ambition and long-standing feud with Scott, General Harney wrote an emotional letter to Buchanan criticizing Scott's leadership and loyalty to the president. It was a letter both insubordinate and ruthless.[22] Without mentioning by name Scott's protégé, Albert Sidney Johnston, Harney was trying to sweep away Johnston's career prospects while destroying Scott's standing with Buchanan:

Harney to Buchanan, 30 January 1858, James Buchanan Papers, HSP.

I believe your Excellency has confidence in the sincerity of my friendship, and in this belief, I deem it my duty to state some facts which you should be advised of. This I would have done last summer, but a desire not to annoy [you], if possible, restrained me from so doing.

An ill-will of long standing towards myself on the part of Gen. Scott, has

[19]Lt. Col. George W. Lay to Johnston, 23 January 1858, "Annual Report of the Sec. of War (1858)," 33.

[20]Scott to Wool, 2 September 1857, Wool Papers.

[21]Nevins and Thomas, eds., *The Diary of George Templeton Strong*, 25 January 1858, 2:383. The massive bronze (not copper) equestrian statue of Gen. George Washington had been installed in Manhattan's Union Square in 1856 and remains there. In an attempt to save face, Scott later told Albert Sidney Johnston's brother-in-law that the notion of a Pacific Coast journey was his with sanctioning by Buchanan and Floyd. Scott to William Preston, 11 February 1858, Wickliffe-Preston Papers, University of Kentucky Library, Lexington.

[22]The Scott-Harney feud is discussed in *At Sword's Point, Part 1*, 164–65.

> caused him to attempt, upon every occasion, he could turn to his purpose, to defeat any operation with which I have been charged—at the same time, his orders are studied to mortify and lower me in the estimation of the army and my friends in civil life—Personally, I care nothing for this, but as the interests with which I have been lately charged, are of the utmost importance to the successful administration of the affairs of the country, and as Gen. Scott[']s prejudices have always been too strong for an impartial consideration of any subject in which his prejudices are involved, I most earnestly call your Excellency[']s attention to Gen Scott[']s course of conduct since the commencement of your administration.
>
> From the commencement of the Utah Expedition, to the present time, he has opposed or ignored every useful suggestion I have made to him and his own plans are so faulty, I assume very little, in predicting a decided failure, should they be attempted to be carried out. He is sending Cavalry to act in a mountainous country where the expense of supporting them renders their efficiency an impossibility, and places a fine Regt of foot troops in depot on the plains, to be laughed at by mounted Indians.[23] Has it ever occurred to your Excellency that neither ignorance or imbecility, but a settled plan to defeat and confuse your administration are the motives of such conduct?
>
> Whoever you may be pleased to send to Utah, let him throw his reputation and his life upon the die, but give him the sole responsibility of his actions. The campaign to Utah cannot be planned in Washington or New York—
>
> Your Excellency is very popular in the army and it is due to the feeling that your rectitude of character will not permit injustice to be done to any one—Persons in exalted positions, seldom hear the unvarnished truth. I have spoken plainly to your Excellency—my sincere desire is to serve you to the best of my humble abilities, & not the least of this service is to tell you of your true friends, & to point out the disagreeable ones.

Less than a week after Harney sent this remarkable message to the Executive Mansion, Scott cancelled his travel plans. On 4 February, the literal eve of his scheduled departure for Panama, Scott's aide again wrote to Johnston: "I am desired by the General-in-Chief to inform you that it is no longer probable that he will go to the Pacific Coast, or that any expedition against or towards Utah will be despatched from that quarter."[24] There was no further explanation of this change for Johnston or the public, which was well aware of the general in chief's journey.

On the day that Winfield Scott unpacked and the Panama-bound packet

[23]Ironically, the Nauvoo Legion's General Ferguson came to a similar conclusion in January 1858 about Mormon forces and their emphasis on cavalry for the coming mountain campaign.

[24]Lay to Johnston, 4 February 1858, "Annual Report of the Sec. of War (1858)," 33.

steamed out of New York Harbor without him, an infantry private at Fort Bellingham, Washington, unwittingly captured the situation in a letter to his mother in Rhode Island: "Their is at present a great deal Of excitement about salt lake here amongst us soldiers But i think all the excitement will die where it first Orriginadet i believe it to be nothing more or less than soldeirs talk for i hardly think it likely that the heads of The war department is going to sind troops way out Here to relieve us for to go to war against the mormans. the i dea is a absurd one to my mind so there is no fear Of it for it would only be an expence to the government Unnecessary."[25]

John M. Bernhisel's next report from Washington to Brigham Young was equally unenlightening about the cancellation of General Scott's journey and the administration's thinking about the West Coast: "I have had several interviews with the President and Secretary of War, and have been for sometime laboring [unsuccessfully] to procure an amicable adjustment of the Utah difficulties." Bernhisel added, "the order for General Scott to proceed to California has been rescinded. It is proposed to re-inforce Colonel Johnston [from Kansas] as early in the Spring as possible."[26] Uncharacteristically, Brigham Young appears never to have pressed Bernhisel for more details about this important change to James Buchanan's plans for the Utah War.

Meanwhile, unaware of these shifts, Capt. Pierre Gustave Toutant Beauregard sent gratuitous military advice from New Orleans to fellow Louisianan John Slidell, who was both a U.S. senator and his brother-in-law. Beauregard ridiculed the administration's plan for a two-front war. A cerebral army engineer with an unusual grasp of tactics and European military history, he viewed such a multipronged campaign as ill-conceived, overly complex, and risky in the face of likely communications lags and presumed Mormon military competence. Sidestepping considerations of overall command and Albert Sidney Johnston's future role, Beauregard lobbied Slidell for appointment to a colonelcy in the new regiments Buchanan was proposing for service in Utah.[27]

---

[25]William H. Royle to Elizabeth Royle, 5 February 1858, Royle Papers, Washington State Historical Society, Tacoma. Royle was in Company D, Ninth U.S. Infantry.

[26]Bernhisel to Young, 17 December [February] 1857, LDS Archives.

[27]The holograph original of this letter is at the Huntington Library, and another copy is included in the papers of John A. Quitman, Southern Historical Collection, Wilson Library, University of North Carolina, Chapel Hill. When Union troops captured a third copy (now lost) addressed to Jefferson Davis during the Civil War, excerpts appeared in newspapers throughout the North. A typescript made from the version at the Huntington is in Leonard J. Arrington Papers, Merrill-Cazier Library, Utah State University, Logan. Based upon Arrington's research notes there, he apparently contemplated developing an essay about the Beauregard-Slidell letter.

Beauregard to Slidell,
9 February 1858, Huntington Library.

I see it stated in the newspapers that Genl Scott is about to repair to California to take command of a Corps d'Armé to move from thence on to Utah! I wonder if this is to be done upon the recommendation of the Genl? If so, it is contrary to all "strategic" principles, if to be executed in conjunction with a similar movement on this side of the mountains—for it is impossible that two operations, from such distant initial points—should be performed with such precision & regularity as to arrive at the Utah Valley within a few days of each other—at any rate such a favorable result would be against all probabilities—It would then follow, if the Mormons are ably commanded, that they would concentrate their forces in succession against each of said columns & crush them before they could unite.

How do we know but that the Mormons may have amongst themselves a great Captain *in embryo*! Are not volunteers considered *by many* as equal if not superior to regulars in a Mountainous War?—then how much the more superior would they not be, when defending their religion & their own firesides! If I were a Mormon and amply supplied with provisions & ammunitions, I would defy ~~five~~ three times the number of troops you could send against me on the system now adopted—not one of them would ever set foot within the valley of Utah!

Now with regard to that Mormon war we ought first to know, what are their resources, and how many effective men they can bring into the field—let us say about 5,000—the rest acting as scouts, guarding the passes &c not being counted but still effective to recruit from or as a force in reserve, in case of reverses—then it becomes evident from what I have already stated—that if we march two *converging* forces against them thus: [diagram: a right angle with the points marked "a" "b" and "c"]—from *a* to *c* & from *b* to *c*—the Mormons occupying the central or strategic point *c*—we must *to be certain of success,* send each column of at least 7,000 men, for by the time they would get to *c*—besides being nearly exhausted by their long and fatiguing marches—they would probably be reduced to about 5,000 fighting men each—then success would very much depend upon the nature of the ground they are operating upon, the relative discipline of the opposing forces—the abilities of their commanding officers & other contingencies not necessary to mention here.—Now as all the probabilities are that the offensive forces, would not reach the point *c* within several weeks of each other[28]—they would necessarily be fought in succession, & the chances are, that they would get whipped all other things being equal—for the Mormons would be fresh for the fray, & fighting for their religion and their homes, would be the more

[28]The difficulties encountered in coordinating the several elements of the small Ives Expedition converging on the Colorado River in December 1857 illustrate Beauregard's point.

desperate; whereas, if *the best* of these two lines of operations, were selected for the offensive march—a force calculated to arrive at *c*, a little stronger in numbers & discipline than the enemy's forces, would have all the probabilities of success on its side—whether it would succeed or not would be "for the Gods to decide"—and the same object would then be effected with a great economy in treasure, men & materials.

Should the Army be increased by two or more Regts, [I would like] to be appointed the Col. of one of said Regts.

There is no evidence that Slidell forwarded his brother-in-law's letter to any other official in the administration, although the fact that he had served as Buchanan's campaign manager in 1856 raises the possibility that he may have spoken with the president about Beauregard's observations. For good measure, Beauregard himself sent copies of this document to Jefferson Davis and John A. Quitman, chairmen of the Senate and house committees on military affairs, respectively.[29]

A God Send to the Country: A Star for Sidney Johnston

With the Utah command for General Wool stillborn and the decision that Scott was to remain in New York while reinforcing Johnston from Kansas, the general in chief turned to the matter of Albert Sidney Johnston's rank. Promoting Johnston had long been on Scott's mind, perhaps since Johnston had been selected to command the Utah Expedition during the prior summer. Reinforcement of the expedition during 1858 to include nearly one-third of the U.S. Army, together with Johnston's superb leadership during the previous fall, provided Scott with ample rationale for promotion. On 11 February 1858 he sent a fascinating letter about Johnston's future to William Preston of Louisville, who was both Johnston's brother-in-law and John B. Floyd's cousin: "Colonel Johns[t]on is more than a good officer—he is a God send to the country thro' the army. I urged his brevet [promotion], strongly, when he was here [in August], & have repeated my instances [entreaties] to the

[29] While Beauregard was formulating his memorandum in Louisiana, another officer, Col. Joseph K. F. Mansfield, one of the two inspectors general on Scott's staff, had already developed a similar critique of the administration's two-front strategy in Connecticut. In a paper probably intended for publication and written under the French pseudonym "Nous Ver[r]ons" ("We Shall See"), he argued that sending General Scott (his superior) to California to prosecute the Utah War through converging columns was tactically unsound, dangerous, and unnecessarily expensive. Mansfield, "Army of Utah," draft memorandum, ca. January 1858, Joseph K. F. Mansfield Papers, Middlesex County [Connecticut] Historical Society.

same end almost daily, since the beginning of January either in conversation with the Secretary or the President, & I told the latter that I did not doubt he would find himself constrained, by admiration, to add a second brevet before the end of this year."[30]

For those tempted to discount Scott's laudatory comments about Albert Sidney Johnston as rhetorical flourish—in this case for the benefit of a well-connected Kentuckian—there is reason to believe that Scott was indeed sincere. At about the time that Scott wrote to Preston, Johnston's close St. Louis friend, "Captain" N. J. Eaton, visited the general in chief. In the course of their conversation, Scott described to Eaton his comments to President Buchanan about Johnston's promotability in terms almost verbatim to those that he had sent to Preston. When Eaton returned to St. Louis, he reported this conversation to Johnston in a letter that undoubtedly reached Fort Bridger weeks, if not months, before any official news about Johnston's new rank. Eaton's letter conveys Winfield Scott's regard for Albert Sidney Johnston—seemingly inconsistent with the near-coincident proffer of the Utah command to General Wool—while illustrating the loyalty, respect, and affection that Johnston had earned throughout the Utah Expedition.

Eaton to Johnston, 21 February 1858, Albert Sidney and William Preston Johnston Papers, Louisiana Research Collection, Tulane University, New Orleans.

If I had written to you as often as I have thought of you, since you started on your responsible & laborious expedition, I should have been writing to you almost every hour of the day; more particularly would this have been the fact since we heard of the destruction of a part of the train of army supplies.

While my heart has yearned to extend to you, my own worthy & gallant comrade, some of the comforts of life with which I am surrounded, & while I have felt deeply the trials with which I know you must [have] be[en] beset, during the cold weather in November, I have not for a moment doubted that you would triumph over all obstacles & come out ~~triumphant~~ conqueror. [Col. George] Crosman & myself have again & again gone over the probabilities of your ~~triumphs~~ success, and while we could not tell how you were going to overcome the inhospitality of winter & the opposition of an active enemy, we have concluded that you would do it somehow. We know your own devotion & singleness of purpose, and know the patriotism & chivalry of your associates,

[30]Scott to Preston, 11 February 1858, Wickcliffe-Preston Papers, University of Kentucky Library. Later in 1858 Buchanan would appoint Preston his minister to Spain in furtherance of his plans to buy Cuba.

and we relied upon these qualities, under the smiles of a providence, which always helps those who help themselves, to carry you through all difficulties.

I have felt indignant that you & your command should have been ordered to march so late in the season, but I now feel reconciled, in as much as I feel quite sure that the very military blunder which the administration committed has been the means of bringing you more prominently before the nation and its rulers than would have been the fact, under more auspicious circumstances.[31] I desire distinction for you because I believe that the influence which it would give, would be wielded for the national good, & not for any selfish end—and I believe too, that that distinction should be extorted from difficulties, so that no man could cavil at it.[32]

I had occasion recently to go to Washington on business, (not to ask for office, thank God) and while there I called upon that esteemed soldier, & good patriot, Genl Scott, and the manner in which he spoke of you made my pulse bound again. Both he and Jeff[erson] Davis, told me that they had told the President that he must nominate you for a Brevet at once, & Genl Scott added, to the President, that if he Breveted you a Brigadier now, he would be compelled to Brevet you a Major General before the campaign was over, for you would earn it.[33] What a pity that two such good soldiers & clever men as Scott & Davis should be enemies.[34]

I think you will have to fight but I believe you will conquer no matter what the odds, and I believe too that you will come off uninjured. This confidence in your success is not wholly the dictate of enthusiasm, but is founded in some measure, upon good reason. I feel with regard to you & your success, as I felt in regard to Genl [Zachary] Taylor, before the [Mexican War] battles of Palo Alto & Buena Vista. I have an undoubting confidence that nothing can shake that it will be well with you.

It is emblematic of the disconnect between Scott and Floyd that as Scott was writing to William Preston, he was unaware that Floyd had already sent to Buchanan the nomination of Johnston for promotion to brigadier by brevet

[31]Both Generals Scott and Harney had argued unsuccessfully during May and June 1857 that the lateness of the season should have dictated a delay in the campaign until 1858. *At Sword's Point, Part 1*, 129–32, 154–57.

[32]Eaton may be referring to carping among some army officers over then-Major Johnston's out-of-line appointment to the colonelcy of the new Second U.S. Cavalry in 1855 after being absent for years from the U.S. Army because of senior military service with the Republic of Texas. Such criticism, perhaps stimulated by General Harney, would resume in the fall of 1858 in the St. Louis newspapers over Johnston's command of the Utah Expedition and promotion to brevet brigadier. It would be rebutted by Eaton.

[33]For Davis's old-age recollection of his positive 1857 discussion with President Buchanan about the suitability of Albert Sidney Johnston to command the Utah Expedition, see "Jeff Davis's Speech. The Grey-Haired Statesman Pays a Tribute to Sidney Johnston," Dispatch, 7 April 1887, *Fort Worth [Texas] Daily Gazette*, 8 April 1887, reprinted in MacKinnon, "Rest of the Story," Letter to Editor, *Dialogue: A Journal of Mormon Thought*, xviii–xix. Notwithstanding Scott's prediction, Buchanan did not nominate Johnston for a second star.

[34]The mid-1850s feud between Scott as general in chief and Davis as secretary of war is discussed in Peskin, *Winfield Scott and the Profession of Arms*, 206–28.

"for 'meritorious conduct' in the ability, zeal, energy, and prudence displayed by him in the command of the Army in Utah to date from November 18, 1857."[35] Even though Scott claimed "I have however prepared many [members] of that [Senate] body to receive it favorably," Johnston's nomination moved through the confirmation process slowly.[36] On 24 March 1858 the Senate finally turned from its debates on the Mormon problem to confirm Johnston's promotion.[37]

Rumors about Johnston's promotion reached Camp Scott before the official notification. As early as mid-April the Utah Expedition's quartermaster wrote to a civilian friend in Washington, "We were all delighted that Col. Johnston had been nominated for the brevet of Brig. General, which indicates that he is not to be superceded in the command. He is universally popular and deservedly so. He has more good points as a commanding officer than any one I know in the Army."[38]

Notwithstanding Johnston's promotion, he was not out of the woods career-wise. The matter of which general officer was to be the Utah Expedition's senior commander would continue to plague the army throughout the spring of 1858 just as the same issue had bedeviled the expedition during the summer of 1857.

The Real Object: Utah, Manifest Destiny, and Presidential Billiards

In January 1858 the notion of a two-front movement against Utah was both a real and popular possibility, but the administration abandoned it without explanation in early February. Why was such a strategy pursued against Winfield Scott's advice and then dropped just as he was about to execute it? There are at least four obvious explanations for the decision to abandon a thrust from the Pacific Coast: the growing complexity of the campaign; the absence of a vigorous, experienced, and uncontroversial senior officer to lead a Pacific Coast thrust; General Scott's distaste for a two-front war with its personal inconvenience and lamentable (as he saw it) reliance on

[35]Floyd to Buchanan, 8 February1858, copy in editor's files.

[36]Scott to Preston, 11 February 1858, Wickliffe-Preston Papers.

[37]Floyd wrote on 3 April to inform Johnston of the good news, and a week later Adjutant General Cooper dispatched the oath of office for this commission. Cooper's letter of 10 April enclosed Floyd's of 3 April. Archivist Jessica Kratz, NARA, e-mail to MacKinnon, 22 July 2008; Johnston to Cooper, 17 May 1858, RG 98, NARA.

[38]Dickerson to W. A. Gordon, 16 April 1858, Bancroft Library.

volunteer troops; and President Buchanan's acute awareness of the financial cost of such a strategy in the midst of continuing economic upheaval. As to why planning for a Pacific Coast pincers movement had been launched in the first place, there is one unstudied driver meriting attention: James Buchanan's secret plan to use a second front for the Utah Expedition as the catalyst for triggering a billiardslike chain of events starting in California and rippling into Utah, northern Mexico, and Spanish Cuba.

When Buchanan assumed the presidency, he was not focusing on Utah but was intent on acquiring international territory to further American Manifest Destiny. With characteristic indirection, Buchanan's inaugural address included the thought that "it is our glory that, whilst other nations have extended their dominions by the sword, we have never acquired any territory except by fair purchase. Acting on this principle, no nation will have a right to interfere or to complaint if, in the progress of events, we shall still further extend our possessions."[39]

Within a few months of his inauguration—on the day that the Utah Expedition began its march west—Buchanan secretly ordered John Forsyth, his minister to Mexico, to seek a treaty with that country. By Buchanan's proposed terms, unsanctioned by an absent and uninformed Congress, the United States would pay Mexico up to fifteen million dollars to purchase a vast northern region while clarifying American transit rights earlier established to build a railway across Mexico's Isthmus of Tehuantepec. With Mexico hyper-sensitive to American pressure and teetering on the brink of revolution, Forsyth was so shocked by these instructions that he withheld Buchanan's offer to the Mexican government until forced to do so the next November by Secretary Cass. The leading historian of U.S.-Mexican relations of the period characterizes the president's quest for Mexican territory as rapacious ("despoiling") to the point of brutality.[40]

Buchanan's interest in Cuba, a slave-holding Spanish colony, predated his focus on Mexico, rooted as it was in the country's long-standing fascination with the island that began soon after the American Revolution and intensified throughout the nineteenth century. This is not the place to describe Buchanan's long interest in acquiring Cuba except to say that it arose at least as early as his service as President Polk's secretary of state; by 1857 it had grown to be the

---

[39]Moore, ed., The Works of James Buchanan, 10:113.

[40]Cass to Forsyth, 17 July 1857, in Olliff, *Reforma Mexico and the United States*, 87; Manning, ed., *Diplomatic Correspondence of the United States: Inter-American Affairs, 1831–1860*, 234–38.

intended capstone of his presidency. Buchanan's minister to Spain, Augustus Caesar Dodge, recognized this priority, and in late September 1857 wrote Buchanan from Madrid, "the acquisition of Cuba I am well aware from your early and unflagging advocacy of the measure, is one which will be cherished and promoted throughout your entire administration [but] I can see little or no probability of our acquiring Cuba by any diplomatic means heretofore employed at this court and without a change in the ways and means."[41]

In December, almost as on cue from Minister Dodge, Buchanan returned to Cuban matters and did so with an unconventional approach of the type foreseen by Dodge. It was a month of multiple challenges for the president during which Minister Forsyth was simultaneously dealing with Mexican rage over Buchanan's recently delivered treaty demands of the prior July as well as the onset of a full-blown revolution. In Washington, Buchanan was grappling with aggressive congressional demands for information about the Utah Expedition's origins and cost in the wake of the Financial Panic of 1857.

On 13 December 1857—literally as Buchanan was about to invite Thomas L. Kane to the Executive Mansion to hear of his intended mediation of the Utah War—the president met secretly with another lawyer who was Kane's fellow-townsman from Philadelphia, Christopher Fallon. In Fallon's case, the presidential plan was to dispatch him to Madrid to renew efforts to buy Cuba. Buchanan directed Fallon not only to sound out the Spanish royal family (to whom he was known) but to begin discussions with European bankers on two gambits: pressuring Spain to repay its enormous national debt, and financing an American purchase of Cuba. The latter was necessary since Buchanan had not sought congressional authorization and an appropriation for such an acquisition. It is a telltale indication of Buchanan's deviousness that he privately recruited Fallon for such a mission only five days after sending his annual address to Congress without a single reference to Spain or Cuba. In the "Private & Confidential" instructions that Buchanan handwrote, he assured Fallon that "Both you & those with whom you converse may rely with confidence upon my silence & discretion."[42]

Thus at year-end 1857 Christopher Fallon sailed east to Madrid, Thomas L.

[41]Dodge to Buchanan, 26 September 1857, quoted in Pelzer, *Augustus Caesar Dodge*, 228–29.

[42]Buchanan to Fallon, 14 December 1857, James Buchanan Papers; Moore, ed., *The Works of James Buchanan*, 10:165. For a description of Fallon and how he went about his negotiations in Europe, see Wallace and Gillespie, eds., *The Journal of Benjamin Moran, 1857–1865*, 1:209, 278, 280, 31 December 1857, 27 and 31 March 1858; Cortada, "An Elusive Cuba," 23–25.

Kane prepared to head west to Utah via Panama and California, to the south John Forsyth witnessed the slide of Mexico into the chaos of revolution, and in New York Winfield Scott worked to reinforce the Utah Expedition from the Pacific Coast after hastening Lieutenant Ives upriver to reconnoiter the Colorado invasion route.

With only a thin written record surviving to determine how James Buchanan and his cabinet functioned, the key to understanding much of what the president did during the Utah War and why often lies with notes kept by credible visitors to the Executive Mansion who interacted directly with Buchanan. In many ways, the most valuable accounts flowing from such insiders were the long, newsy but cautious dispatches written to Brigham Young at least monthly by Utah's territorial delegate in Congress, Dr. John M. Bernhisel. Yet with respect to the Utah War, Bernhisel's reports have limitations since he seemed intimidated by Buchanan, avoided contact with him at key junctures, and once even withdrew from Washington during a crucial period in the spring of 1857. At other times, Bernhisel simply did not write to Young about volatile issues for fear of mail interception, as with his murky dealings with freebooter Walter Murray Gibson about the chimera of a Mormon mass exodus to the Dutch East Indies.

Another source potentially even more valuable to historians than Bernhisel's reporting were the dispatches generated by Washington-based diplomats for the information of their foreign secretaries. During 1857–58 one of the more interesting writers of such reports was the envoy closest to President Buchanan—Sir William Gore Ouseley, an old British friend from Ouseley's posting to Washington in the late 1820s and Buchanan's assignment during 1853–56 as head of the Pierce administration's diplomatic legation in London.

In the midst of the Utah War—at about the time of Lot Smith's October 1857 raid—Ouseley arrived in Washington en route to a diplomatic post in Central America. Notwithstanding this assignment, Ouseley dallied in Washington unofficially for nearly twelve months, and quickly assumed the role of presidential confidant—even confessor—on international matters. That Ouseley succeeded so rapidly in forging such an intimate tie with President Buchanan was attributable to multiple factors: the length of their friendship; their similarity in age; the diplomat's charm and that of his American-born wife; their mutual friendship with the Roosevelt family of New York; Buchanan's loneliness as an aging bachelor in the

Executive Mansion; the multiple political pressures besetting the president; and Buchanan's significant lack of confidence in Secretary of State Cass.[43]

The medium for Ouseley's reportage from Washington was a series of episodic dispatches written to the Earl of Clarendon, Britain's foreign secretary, at his explicit invitation and marked "Private & Confidential," a formal label signaling a higher sensitivity than even those reports designated "Secret."[44] With his reports thus marked, Ouseley transmitted his dispatches directly to Clarendon through an elaborate, three-stage trans-Atlantic courier system that bypassed the public postal services of both the United States and Great Britain. It was a delivery arrangement worthy of a security-conscious Brigham Young, who adopted similar procedures for sending and receiving his most sensitive letters across the United States and Europe.[45] Understanding the technical arrangements by which confidential dispatches from Ouseley were encouraged by Lord Clarendon and then transmitted to him is crucial to evaluating the candor as well as importance of these reports.

Below are excerpts from three of Ouseley's dispatches from the opening months of 1858—those most relevant to Buchanan's most sensitive thoughts about the Utah War.[46] His reports provide a unique glimpse of a cloistered James Buchanan as he dealt with geographically separated but related events heretofore viewed by historians as unconnected.

On 25 January 1858, in the midst of all these presidential activities, Sir William Gore Ouseley confided Buchanan's plans to Lord Clarendon.[47]

---

[43]For biographical information about Ouseley and the origins and dynamics of his relationship with Buchanan, see "William Gore Ouseley," *Wikipedia*, accessed 9 November 2015, en.wikipedia.org/wiki/William_Gore_Ouseley; Barnes and Barnes, eds., *Private and Confidential: Letters from British Ministers in Washington to the Foreign Secretaries in London, 1844–67*, 182–94. Also relevant with respect to the president's dealings with Ouseley's superior in London is Binder, "James Buchanan and the Earl of Clarendon: An Uncertain Relationship," 323–41.

[44]British diplomats stationed abroad did not feel free to send such non-routine, often-personal correspondence to the secretary of state for foreign affairs (in this case Lord Clarendon) without an explicit invitation by him to do so. Buchanan, from his diplomatic days in London, adopted the British practice of labeling his most sensitive correspondence "Private & Confidential" as with his 14 December 1857 letter to Christopher Fallon about acquiring Cuba.

[45]*At Sword's Point, Part 1*, 29–30.

[46]Excerpts presented here are as drawn from Barnes and Barnes, *Private and Confidential*, 182–94, and from the originals in what Bodleian Library, Oxford University, designates the "Clarendon Deposit," 25 January and 15 February 1858, MS Clar. dep. c 83, fols. 371–74 and 385–88, respectively.

[47]Ouseley's labeling of this dispatch as "Secret and Confidential" rather than "Private and Confidential" (perhaps inadvertently) resulted in its filing in the records of the Foreign Office rather than among Lord Clarendon's personal papers, as were many of the other dispatches Ouseley sent Clarendon. See F.O. 15/98 ff. 36–39, British National Archives, Kew. A discussion of this dispatch and its text appear in MacKinnon, "Presidential Billiards Revisited," vii–x.

SIR WILLIAM GORE OUSELEY, BRITISH DIPLOMAT AND BUCHANAN CONFIDANT
As old diplomatic friends, Buchanan confided to Ouseley his complex plans to acquire Cuba involving Utah, General Scott, a second front for the war, a Mormon exodus to Sonora, and an American military protectorate over northern Mexico. Ouseley reported this scenario for American Manifest Destiny and resolution of "the Mormon problem" to Lord Clarendon, the British foreign secretary. Britain moved to counter any Mormon flight to the Pacific by stationing a warship off Honolulu and creating the crown colony of British Columbia, protected by the Royal Navy. *Portrait ca. 1860, courtesy of Heritage Images, London.*

OUSELEY TO CLARENDON, FOREIGN OFFICE, DISPATCH NO. 14, 25 JANUARY 1858, BRITISH NATIONAL ARCHIVES, KEW.

A project is on foot—I ought perhaps rather to say has been suggested—the possible importance of which must be my excuse for mentioning it with the very slight knowledge that I as yet have of it. The President, and part, at least of his Cabinet, seek some mode, some mezzo-termine [adjustment] by which to facilitate future annexations of Spanish American Territory, without the necessity of admitting Representatives of the new States in Congress. The admissions of Senators and Members of a race that they despise, on a footing of equality in the Senate and House of Representatives has been, as the President has more than once told me, the main objection to the annexation of Mexico.[48]

The departure of Genl Scott for the Pacific Coast, ostensibly with the sole purpose of acting against the Mormons, may have reference to this project, which is meant to pave the way to the incorporation of Mexico, Central America, Cuba etc by the establishment in the first instance of this probationary mode of Govt.

[48]A year later Buchanan denied rumors that he was contemplating such a quasi-colonial constitutional adjustment and rhetorically asked a skeptical Lord Napier: "What could we do with such [non-Caucasian] people? We could not incorporate them; if we did, they would tear us asunder. We can only annex vacant territory." Scroggs, *Filibusters and Financiers*, 351–52.

It is fascinating to correlate these comments about Buchanan and Mexico with the fact that on 18 January, a week before Ouseley wrote, Delegate Bernhisel had informed Brigham Young that he had visited the president and that Buchanan had unexpectedly dropped his objections to the rumored possibility of a Mormon exodus from Utah to Mexico.[49] Buchanan's motives behind this change become clearer with an understanding of his conversations with Ouseley about Mexico and its connection to General Scott's pending trip to the West, all duly reported to Clarendon.

Later on the same day, in a separate dispatch, Ouseley reported additional scheming.[50]

Ouseley to Clarendon, 25 January 1858, Bodleian Library, Oxford University.

I dined the other day with the president. This was not a private party but a large dinner. I was the only Englishman, I believe the only foreigner present. When the party was about to break up Miss [Harriet] Lane had, or affected to have something to say to my wife, and asked her to remain.[51] When the other guests were gone the President took me up to his room "to smoke a cigar" and a long interview and some apparently confidential conversation of a desultory but not an uninteresting character ensued.

Among the subjects he spoke of [was] the Mormons and the troubles in Utah. He said that he had upwards of two thousand of the "best troops" ready to act against them in the spring; that they would probably migrate into British possessions and he wished me joy of them.[52] He added that any number of volunteers were ready to march against the Mormons from California but that the Governor had decided upon not calling for their services. I asked why, he replied that "all the Mormons would be massacred if the Californians marched against them." He did not wish this and it was better to let them leave the country.[53] (Yet General Scott is about to proceed to California ostensibly to conduct operations against the Mormons). Possibly

---

[49]Bernhisel to Young, 18 January 1858, LDS Archives. Ouseley also described the extent to which prolonged congressional obstinacy over funding for an expanded Utah Expedition was unwittingly threatening the viability of this internationally oriented presidential scheme.

[50]In the previously published transcriptions of this dispatch by the Barneses, the date was inadvertently misread as 23 January 1858.

[51]Buchanan's niece, Harriet Lane, facilitated his interpersonal manipulations.

[52]Here Ouseley reports a reaction by Buchanan to press speculation of a Mormon mass exodus to the Pacific Coast in language consistent with that attributed to the president in reporting two months earlier by Ambassador Edward A. de Stoeckel to the Russian foreign minister following his meeting with Buchanan about the same rumor. Buchanan's independently recorded comments to Stoeckel give credibility to Ouseley's reporting of the same subject to Clarendon. *At Sword's Point, Part 1*, 442.

[53]Ibid., 107. Since March 1857 Buchanan had feared that a full public awareness of inflammatory language from Mormon leaders would unleash an uncontrollable, violent public backlash, especially (but not exclusively) from California.

> there is an intention of directing or forcing the movements of the Mormons so as to serve the purpose of the U.S. Government in Mexico—to which I refer in my [Dispatch] No.14 of this year.

On 15 February 1858 Ouseley reported again to Clarendon, this time to relay an account of what he had learned in confidence from Buchanan about the linkage between the president's prosecution of the Utah War and his two highest priorities other than preservation of the Union—the seizure of northern Mexico and the acquisition of Cuba by purchase or conquest.

Ouseley to Clarendon, 15 February 1858, Bodleian Library, Oxford University.

The designs of the President respecting Cuba have met with an unexpected check in the refusal of Congress to allow the increase of the army or to appropriate funds for the [Utah] expedition of General Scott to the Pacific coast *une die* [at the same time].

It may seem that there is little direct connection between an expedition ostensibly against the Mormons or involving relations with Mexico and plans for the acquisition of Cuba. *The latter however is the real object; the other is subsidiary to it and serves to mask the real movement.*[54] The intention as to the Mormons was to bring about their emigration to Sonora [Mexico] and thus to turn their rebellion to [useful] account by making them pioneers for future [Texas-like] annexation under a quasi-military colonial system, that General Scott was partly to inaugurate without however being aware of the full scope of the project for the execution of which he was to be one of the instruments.[55] His [Scott's] personal [wartime] experience and former relations with [President Antonio López de] Santa Anna and other leading men in Mexico was also to be used to the furtherance of the objects of the U.S. in profiting by the [Mexican] difference with Spain.

In all these matters, the increase of the army and a large appropriation for expenditure by the Executive, would have enabled the President when this Session [of Congress] is over to begin to carry into effect his grand object.[56] I look upon it as only deferred and should not be surprised if before Congress disperses *the President should obtain the means he covets for a purpose on which he deems absolute silence to be as yet necessary.* He will find other ostensible motives to cover

[54]Emphasis added. As early as 24 November 1857, as the administration planned to reinforce the Utah Expedition, Ouseley reported to Clarendon, after meeting with Buchanan, "the key in short to his whole system of govt. negotiations & foreign policy is to be found in the one absorbing long-cherished plan of the later years of his life—viz., *the acquisition of Cuba during the term of his own Presidency*" [emphasis Ouseley's].

[55]For the extent to which Scott was often unaware of what troop movements Buchanan and Floyd were ordering during the Utah War, see *At Sword's Point, Part 1*, 95–97, 129–33.

[56]When Buchanan initiated the Utah Expedition during the spring of 1857, Congress had just adjourned. Ouseley here anticipates that Buchanan would again undertake a military intervention, this time in northern Mexico, without the complexity of congressional involvement.

> his real object. The building and equipment of several war steamers [ships] now actively in progress, ostensibly for service on the African station [as anti-slavers] and to reinforce the Gulf of Mexico squadrons have, I more than suspect, reference to the same purpose. The real intention as to the Mormons is to buy them out which will it is said cost two or three millions of dollars, and the surplus of the appropriation would have given the Executive means for commencing the execution of its real plans [for Mexico and Cuba].[57]

Ouseley's 15 February 1858 dispatch to Lord Clarendon was stunning in the complexity and cynicism of the scheming it attributed to Buchanan. The only study known to have commented upon this report summarized Ouseley's conclusion as being to the effect that Buchanan had "hoodwinked" an unwitting Congress into considering the possibility of increasing the military budget, using the Mormon problem as a stalking horse for his real objectives to Utah's south, Mexico and Cuba.[58]

From Buchanan's comments to Ouseley, it is clear that the president believed that annexation of some or all of Mexico could follow the establishment of a critical mass of Americans in Mexico along the lines of the breakaway that had unfolded in the northern part of the gigantic Mexican state of Tejas y Coahuila during the Texas Revolution of the 1830s. As historian Donathan Olliff—an authority on revolutionary Mexico—sees it, Buchanan viewed his objectives in Mexico "as achievable by either of two methods, by purchase or by settlement of large numbers of United States citizens in the subject areas. A large Yankee population could result in annexation by the will of the inhabitants, as had happened in Texas."[59] Olliff was oblivious to the possibility of tens of thousands of Mormon refugees becoming such a Yankee influx, but James Buchanan was not. And so Brigham Young's Move

[57]For press speculation that Buchanan and Delegate Bernhisel were engaged in buy-out discussions and Bernhisel's cryptic signal to Brigham Young that he was involved in some such sort of highly secret gambit, perhaps with Walter Murray Gibson, to resolve the Utah War, see "Important from Washington," Dispatch, *New York Herald,* 2 February 1858, 4/5; Bernhisel to Young, Memorandum, 29 June 1859, LDS Archives. Probably because Gibson indeed proposed a mass Mormon exodus to an unspecified island in the Dutch East Indies to Brigham Young *after* he moved to Utah in 1859 and converted, the LDS church's assistant historian, Andrew Jenson, argued in 1900, without citing a source, that such discussions had occurred in Washington during the war. Jenson, "Walter Murray Gibson," 9–10. Gibson was a charismatic felon and confidence man of ambiguous nationality. Gould, "The Filibuster of Walter Murray Gibson," 7–32; Barrett, "Walter Murray Gibson: The Shepherd Saint of Lanai Re-Visited," 146–62; Britsch, "Another Visit with Walter Murray Gibson," 65–78.

[58]Barnes and Barnes, *Private and Confidential,* 193.

[59]Olliff, *Reforma Mexico and the United States,* 113.

South, plotted for weeks during Thomas L. Kane's visit and announced in Salt Lake City on 21 March 1858, takes on special significance.

How Buchanan could believe that a southbound Mormon diaspora to Sonora—stimulated by military pressure from a Utah Expedition reinforced by a reluctant General Scott from the Pacific Coast—would be willing to re-affiliate with the United States is a mystery. Brigham Young had already been down that road after being driven out of Illinois and migrating to Mexico's eastern Alta California (Utah) in 1847. Ten years later Young still chafed over the approach of the Utah Expedition in the face of LDS participation in the Mexican War through the U.S. Army's Mormon Battalion. To expect Young to flee to Sonora in 1858 at sword's point, and then call for annexation by the United States as Texans had done fifteen years earlier, is counterintuitive. Utah's (and potentially Sonora's) Brigham Young was not Texas's Stephen F. Austin.

Then there is the matter of Mexico's likely reaction to such a humiliating chain of events. Normally such a scenario would trigger a war between the two countries involved, as it had between Mexico and the United States in 1846 following American annexation of Texas. The chaos in revolutionary Mexico starting in January 1858 was such that Buchanan may have believed that he could risk forcing his will on that country as he had, in effect, urged Minister John Forsyth to do in July 1857.

The means by which Buchanan planned subsequently to spring from Mexico to his apparent main objective, Cuba, is even more elusive. Unfortunately, the Cuban part of this expansionist billiards game was a scenario on which Ouseley did not report further. Based on Christopher Fallon's mission to Spain and Buchanan's subsequent correspondence, it appears that in early 1858 the president planned to purchase Cuba from a financially distressed Spain. Failing that, Buchanan was willing to consider taking Cuba forcibly, perhaps in the wake of an American-stimulated uprising on the island. Notwithstanding the significant cash needs of Spain's government and royal family, Fallon's discussions failed later in 1858 in the face of hypersensitivity in Madrid over the blow to Spanish pride associated with any potential loss of Cuba. At that point, a persistent president sent to Spain as his ambassador William Preston of Louisville—Winfield Scott's confidant, John B. Floyd's cousin, and Albert Sidney Johnston's brother-in-law.

Little is known about how Lord Clarendon reacted to Buchanan's Utah War plans as reported by Ouseley, although the British government was so alarmed over the implications of an army-induced mass Mormon exodus from Utah toward the Pacific Coast that it instructed the Royal Navy "to afford the Assistance of H[er] M[ajesty's] Ships for the prevention of a violent & forcible landing of the Mormons, in the event of your being called upon to do so by HM Consul General [in Honolulu] as requested by the [Kingdom of Hawaii's] Secretary of State."[60]

Awareness through Ouseley's dispatches of presidential planning for a secret, complex chain of events designed to start in Utah and end in Cuba raises an important question. Is it possible that Buchanan initiated the Utah Expedition in March 1857 to advance international expansion—American Manifest Destiny—rather than simply to restore federal authority in Utah? The evidence suggests not. Buchanan's long-term pursuit of Mexico and Cuba, while intense, was not a factor in the Utah Expedition's origins. At that time—March 1857—replacing Brigham Young and restoring federal authority were the president's objectives.[61] However, once Buchanan realized in mid-November 1857 that unexpected Mormon military resistance was a reality requiring reinforcement of the Utah Expedition, further armed confrontation in the Rockies and Great Basin provided a field for manipulation. This opportunity led to presidential fantasies, if not scheming, about California, Utah, northern Mexico, and Cuba. The need to reinforce the Utah Expedition in 1858 provided an opportunity, one unavailable on inauguration day but that later in the year stimulated Buchanan's most devious instincts.

In early 1858 a second front for the war, through a large thrust from the Pacific, provided the means to scratch two presidential itches: Buchanan's vexing Mormon problem, and his burning need to expand the United States to fulfill its Manifest Destiny. As Ouseley and Buchanan chatted in January and February 1858, William Tecumseh Sherman, a former army captain, saw the connection. Unemployed at Fort Leavenworth and seeking to reenter the

---

[60]"Contemplated Emigration of Mormons from Utah to the Sandwich [Hawaiian] Islands," Memo from British undersec. of state for foreign affairs, 8 June 1858, found in Rear-Admiral Robert L. Baines, commander Pacific station (Peru), to sec. of Admiralty board (London), 22 July 1858; ADM 1 (Correspondence and Papers of the Admiralty, and Ministry of Defence, Navy Dept.), Box 5694, Bundle Y, Item 156, British National Archives, Kew. For the views of David L. Gregg, U.S. commissioner in Honolulu, about the possibility of an armed Mormon exodus to the Kingdom of Hawaii, see King, ed., *The Diaries of David Lawrence Gregg: An American Diplomat in Hawaii, 1853–1858*, 6 and 15 January 1858, 478, 481.

[61]MacKinnon, "And the War Came," 22–37; *At Sword's Point, Part 1*, 99–135.

army through the presumed opportunities of a reinforced Utah Expedition, Sherman wrote his congressman-brother, John, "I think in the next ten years we will have plenty to do in the war line—Mormon war, civil broils and strife, contests for political power, growing out of slavery and other exciting topics, and last a war with Spain, resulting in the conquest of Cuba."[62]

Naturally a scenario of this character also raises questions as to whether a demonstrably devious Buchanan misled, if not duped, not only Winfield Scott and Congress but also Thomas L. Kane and Brigham Young. Buchanan was indeed capable of such duplicity and proved it through his dealings with these men. At Christmas 1857 it is likely that Kane told Buchanan that when he reached Salt Lake City and met with Young, he intended to broach the subject of a mass Mormon exodus from Utah. At that time the president kept his own counsel and chose not to comment on Kane's intent, notwithstanding his own interest in seizing northern Mexico following a massive influx of southbound Mormon refugee-colonists. Thus Buchanan allowed Kane to travel west a few days later oblivious to the broader California-Utah-Mexico-Cuba scheme the president would soon unveil for Ouseley and may even have just discussed with Kane's fellow-townsman, lawyer Christopher Fallon.

Historians and Mormon commentators have depicted President Buchanan as doddering, passive, indecisive, and blundering—especially when matched against a supposedly brilliant and strategic Brigham Young. Perhaps this was the president who faltered so disastrously during the secession crisis of 1860–61, but during the opening year of his administration, notably in early 1858, James Buchanan was scheming, devious, secretive, manipulative, and—above all else—interventionist, rather than feckless.[63] Thomas L. Kane and Brigham Young may have seriously misjudged the keenness of the presidential appetite for international adventure at their expense.

Ironically, in 1861, when Young stood appalled at the early violence of the Civil War, he toyed with the notion of an international adventure to divert the nation's attention and energy from internecine warfare. He asked Kane, "under existing circumstances will it not be better to annex Mexico to the United States and then go on and annex the Central States of America, Cuba—all

[62]William T. Sherman to John Sherman, [no day] January 1858, Thorndike, ed., *The Sherman Letters,* 64.

[63]The most recent examination of Buchanan's temperament, administrative style, and actions as president is Quist and Birkner, eds., *James Buchanan and the Coming of the Civil War.* In this study, see MacKinnon "Prelude to Armageddon: James Buchanan, Brigham Young, and a President's Initiation to Bloodshed," 46–85.

the West India Islands—and Canada? What can we do to help you in this matter?"[64] Young might better have queried James Buchanan rather than Kane.

Sir William Gore Ouseley was formally accredited to several Central American states rather than to the United States during 1857–58, so historians of the American West have been unaware of his peculiar sojourn in Washington let alone any association with a military campaign in Utah. Diplomatic historians, riveted on the intrigues in foreign chancelleries, have been oblivious to the Utah War, if not Mormonism itself. Chroniclers of the Mormon past, in turn, would profit by probing the world beyond Utah, the West, and the United States. From events in that broader arena might come a more complete understanding of the Latter-day Saints' American experience, including the confidential discussions of armed confrontation in Utah between a simpatico British diplomat and a lonely bachelor over Cuban cigars and tumblers of Old Monongahela whiskey in James Buchanan's White House office. Whether Buchanan succeeded with such intrigue is important; that as president he briefly entertained such plans and pursued them manipulatively, is also significant.

---

[64]Young to Kane, 21 September 1861, LDS Archives.

Chapter 7

"So Gloriously to Run the Gauntlet" Kane's Passage to Utah

Poor fellow, I hope you are not suffering from cold, crossing mountains and deserts. And the Indians, and Mormons—God preserve and guard you through all.

Elizabeth W. Kane, Philadelphia, 6 February 1858

Ammasy Lyman arrived last night about midnight with a gentleman from the City of Washington who has come from there in a little over forty days. He calls himself Dr Osborne. He travels night and day nearly and is in a great hurry to get to Brigham but tells his business to no one.

Homer Brown, Nephi, Utah, 23 February 1858

Having celebrated New Year's Day with his family in Philadelphia, Thomas L. Kane entrained for New York with Elizabeth, and from there sailed alone for Panama—the first leg of his messianic mission to Utah. This chapter deals with the "how" rather than the "why" of Kane's journey. It was a trek with difficulties encountered by few other Utah War travelers.[1] Understanding what Kane experienced during 5 January–25 February 1858 sheds light not only on his determination to help the Latter-day Saints but on the dramatic developments that unfolded immediately

[1]Ranking with Kane's travel experience (as well as the ordeals of Marcy and Ives) were those of a dozen Latter-day Saints and non-Mormons, some of whom faced even greater danger, loneliness, distance, and winter hazards than he did: James Haslam, Charles R. Morehead, George H. Peacock, Ben Ficklin, Mariano Medina, and Albert G. Browne, Jr., as well as Ezra Barnard and Baldwin ("Baldy") Watts, the farmer-missionaries who dashed from Fort Limhi to alert Salt Lake City to the Indian attack on their Oregon mission.

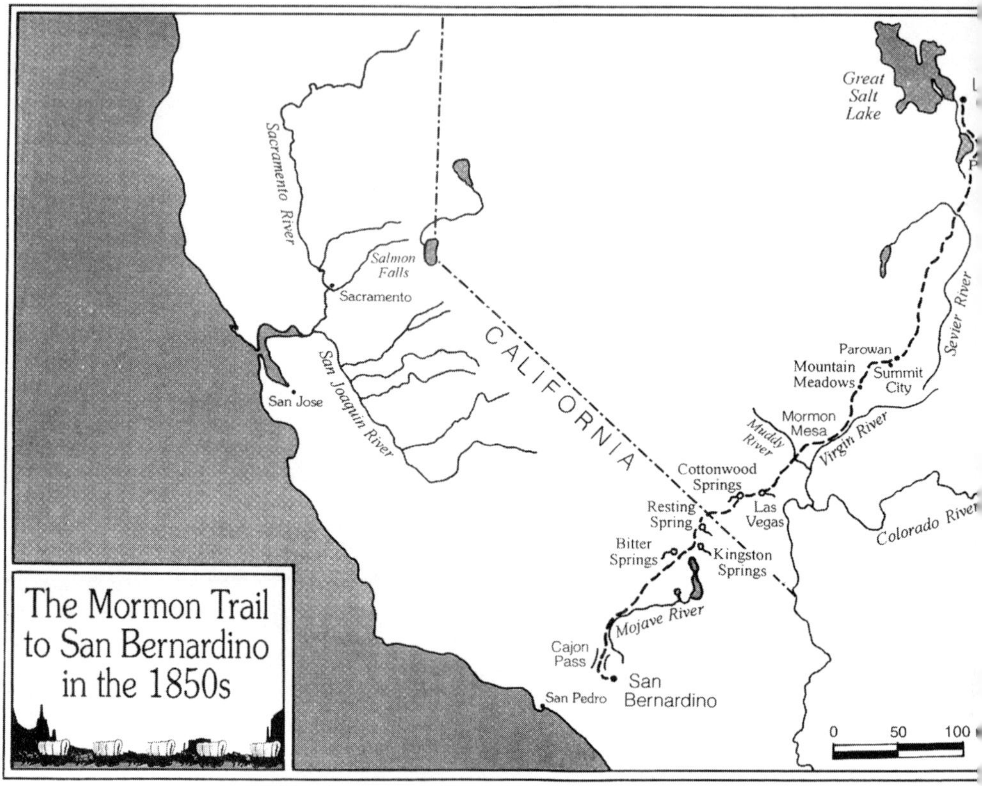

KANE'S ROUTE FROM SAN PEDRO TO SALT LAKE CITY

Ill and harassed by anti-Mormon mobs in southern California, Kane styled himself "Dr. Osborne" to make his way across the Spanish Trail to the settlements of nervous southern Utah. Key to his safety was help from the Mormon remnant in San Bernardino and refugees at the LDS Las Vegas mission, where Apostle Lyman joined Kane's small escort to facilitate reaching Brigham Young in Salt Lake City on 25 February. *Map from Lyman's* San Bernardino: The Rise and Fall of a California Community *(Salt Lake City, 1996), courtesy of Signature Books, Salt Lake City.*

after he reached Salt Lake City. It was during this journey that several key myths began to take shape in Kane's mind—views of the war that for good or ill soon impacted not only his behavior but the accuracy with which he described events in Utah to the president, congressional leaders, and the nation's newspapers. Finally, the story of Kane's trek puts into perspective the role of several courageous women whom he met along the way. Without their support, Kane's efforts to end the war's bloodshed would have played out differently.

Everyone Bore a Title of Some Kind: To San Bernardino as Dr. Osborne

Kane left few insights about his feelings upon leaving New York Harbor, but they must have ranged widely between the excitement of an unknown adventure in the American West, a dread of seasickness, and the sobering realization that he was abruptly leaving his career, young wife and toddlers, and skeptical parents for a distant mission of uncertain outcome on behalf of a reviled people. Presumably unknown to Kane, one of his fellow passengers, former army captain William Tecumseh Sherman, was also sailing to California with a mission related to the Utah War, albeit one militarily at cross purposes to his own.

We know that Kane harbored reservations about President Buchanan's reliability and, surprisingly, about his own ability to influence Brigham Young. On the last day of 1857, Kane raised these doubts with John M. Bernhisel during a meeting in Philadelphia, asking two favors, both of which the territorial delegate gently deflected. Having done so, Bernhisel recorded their conversation in a private letter to Brigham Young, and asked Kane to carry it to Salt Lake City.

Bernhisel to Young, 31 December 1857, LDS Archives.

> Colonel Kane wished me to go to see the President to make him repeat his committals with respect to his intentions, and then write to you personally my impressions in their full strength.[2] I have replied that nothing the President or Assistant Secretary of State [John Appleton] could add to the strength of

[2]A discussion of Kane's possible motives in attempting to stage a Bernhisel-Buchanan meeting before he headed west appears in *At Sword's Point, Part 1*, 503.

> my convictions on the subject.[3] I have no doubt whatever of the President's sincerity or his desire to give every power to Colonel Kane the support of whose family and political friends has at this exigency been made by the divine will of value to him. Colonel Kane has also asked me if it would not be well to write an argumentative [imploring] letter for our people at large exhibiting the necessity of their exerting themselves to make the military as comfortable as possible at Rush Valley—by building them quarters with dispatch, entertaining the sick and officers at the City, &c I have offered to write what he desires, but believe that after conversing with ~~him~~ me he prefers not accepting what would seem to reflect a doubt as to his own just influence with you. I am most fully convinced of the wisdom of Colonel Kane's far-seeing views as to our present and future interests, and believe that he is divinely guided. But he can present them to you better than any one else.[4]

Normally, Thomas L. Kane did not lack self-confidence, but with the risks he was running, he may have momentarily doubted himself while also questioning the trustworthiness of James Buchanan and perhaps even Brigham Young. Kane did not know Buchanan well, and he had not seen Young since their initial meeting in 1846. Their correspondence had been sporadic in the year immediately preceding the Utah War.

Accompanying these emotions was Kane's deep-seated need to conduct his mission in complete secrecy, an impulse shared by James Buchanan and one consistent with Kane's flair for the dramatic, as well as his preferred role as a wire-worker operating incognito behind the scenes. Then, too, there was the powerful example of his late brother Elisha Kent Kane, who had couriered dispatches covertly to General Scott in Mexico less than ten years earlier. Adding to these incentives for secrecy was the fact that Kane had reason to believe that his mission was dangerous, not only while passing through the Mormon-haters of California but even among Utah's suspicious Latter-day Saints. When Kane visited Washington just after Christmas, both President Buchanan and Delegate Bernhisel had warned him of personal dangers ahead.

---

[3]In 1857 the Department of State had jurisdiction over territorial affairs. Appleton, a Buchanan protégé, had been installed there as reliable support for Sec. Lewis Cass, whom the president considered ineffective.

[4]Richard D. Poll, one of the earliest and most astute analysts of the primary sources associated with Kane's Utah mission, has argued that this letter was intended to convey to Young a set of verbal understandings between Buchanan and Kane, especially that Kane "be authorized to suggest to Brigham Young that a peaceful settlement with the government could be had on these terms: Acceptance of Alfred Cumming as governor and establishment of a military post at some distance from any Mormon settlement in exchange for a general pardon for offenses associated with the current confrontation." There is no documentary support for this interpretation other than Kane's private assertions after he returned from Utah. Poll, *Quixotic Mediator*, 13.

Once aboard ship, Kane's precautions morphed into his assumption of the nom de guerre "Dr. A. Osborne" and the persona of a botanist collecting western specimens for a Philadelphia museum. Around 1902 Elizabeth Kane explained how this somewhat improvised guise came about: "Col. Kane sailed from New York, Jan. 5, 1858. By a fortunate accident an old servant of the family who was emigrating to California took [booked] his own passage and Colonel Kane's at the same time, and gave his own name [Anthony Osborne] in securing the stateroom. Colonel Kane found himself addressed on board as Osborne, and thought it prudent not to correct the mistake. Why the sobriquet of Doctor was added I do not know, but it seems as if at that time everyone bore a title of some kind."[5]

If Thomas Kane did not record his earliest thoughts upon leaving home, his wife Elizabeth journalized a wide range of hers. They often took the form of worries about her husband's safety and the fragility of his newfound Protestant faith; her adequacy as a wife and mother; the condition of their tangled finances; and relations with family members. Later in the year, Elizabeth would also record doubts about the steadfastness of President Buchanan and his support. Reflected in these private comments, intended for Tom to read upon his return, was her youth and dependence on him; the financial straits in which he had left her; and Elizabeth's growing awareness of the problematic aspects of Kane's behavior. During this early period of their separation, Elizabeth spent little time journalizing about the predicament of Utah's beleaguered Latter-day Saints, a lack of empathy surprisingly mirrored in the pocket diary Tom maintained to mail her from California.

Elizabeth W. Kane Journal, January–February 1858, Kane Family Papers, BYU.

6th January [1858]. My dearest husband sailed yesterday. I hope, I am sure, I did my duty to him in trying to help him and to be cheerful. Now—what can I do for him? When I think, there are so many things—I feel quite cheery to think God has mercifully given me so many things to occupy me. Thank God for my darlings! Elisha almost upset my attempts at composure today

[5]Elizabeth W. Kane, holograph transcriptions of documents and introductory notes, Thomas L. Kane Collection, MG-257, Pennsylvania State Archives, Harrisburg. Subsequently, it was through a note from the real Osborne that Elizabeth first learned of Thomas's safe arrival in San Francisco. Twenty years later, while traveling by train from Pennsylvania to Salt Lake City in the aftermath of Brigham Young's death, Kane dealt with fears of anti-Mormon assassins by again assuming an alias, notwithstanding the unexpected appearance in his Pullman car of two LDS bodyguards sent to escort him west. Grow and Walker, eds., *The Prophet and the Reformer*, 507.

by struggling forward to go to his father's room. His father! Oh my darling I can't write your name tearless. God help us to bear these weary months.

Sunday January 10. My first Sunday without my dear Tom is a very fit time to record a plan for my daily employment. In order to frame such a plan I must first think over my duties.

Tuesday. Jan 12. Worried over Tom's [financial] accounts which I cannot comprehend.

Wednesday Jan. 13. Had a long talk with Pat about Tom's accounts.[6]

Friday [15 January 1858]. Strange it is that I am so cheerful, but I scarcely feel as if my darling was absent. I have so much to do, and feel so loved by him, it seems as if he were with me. I am sure his heart is. My darling! How easy duty is when it his [*sic*] clear before one, compared to the horrible difficulties of conflicting duties. God has mercifully made my path so clear for the present, that I hope I shall be enabled to gather strength for dark days.

[16 January 1858]. Perhaps I am hard-hearted, but it is not just now *very* hard to be cheerful. Knowing that Tom felt it his duty to go, trusting that it may restore him to me in sound health, feeling that by yielding cheerfully I could say to dear Christ that I was glad to show Him a little bit of thankfulness for his great goodness in sending His Holy Spirit into my darling's heart.

Here comes one of my [morbid] puzzles, and, with no Tom to ravel it out, I shall write it down. Maybe it will ravel itself out, if I force myself to express it clearly. I often say, that were it not for the grief it would cause Tom, and the good I may be able to do the children, I would just as lieve [soon] die as live. Tom speaks of my being His instrument of some great work—of lecturing to women, etc.[7] Poor dear Tom, I wonder if he would despise me if he knew how little vocation I feel for the ideal life he plans for me.

Sunday January 17th. Tom and I must be very open hearted to each other. It is a great pain to me to find that he has so long been grieving over my disinclination to talk about the West, and that it seriously discomposed his plans.[8] It would have saved him all his bother poor darling, if he had told me of it at once, because one can make one's mind up as well sune as syne [sooner than later].

Sunday, January 24. He [Elisha] is very loving. Little Harry [daughter Harriet] is passionately devoted to a few, and has such sweet shyness about showing her fondness. They both sing a great deal—with no tune, however.

---

[6]Robert Patterson Kane, Tom's brother.

[7]In 1853, at Tom's urging, Elizabeth had begun courses at the Female Medical College. Years later she would become one of the country's early women physicians and a competent photographer.

[8]After returning from Utah, Kane began to dream of moving to the Far West, a possibility to which Elizabeth consistently objected. During the 1870s he sought appointment as Utah's governor without success. In early 1858 "West" may have meant to them northwestern Pennsylvania's Elk County, where the Kanes owned substantial undeveloped timber land.

Harry says she must go in the big ship to meet Papa. Poor father of theirs! Are you wishing to be with us this Sunday morning, my own darling? I hope my Bible is a comfort to him.

Tuesday 26th January. Today is my darling's 36th birthday. Yesterday our engagement had its sixth anniversary. God bless my darling! If Tom could only have spared time to finish it [his railroad project of the previous summer]. I hope it is not a wrong feeling of paltry ambition that makes me so very much disappointed by this. I know how much labour, what brain and ingenuity this cost, and I was very proud of his three [proposed] routes—and to have all this more than wasted—for it will pass down as "one of Tom's half-finished schemes," "one of the times when he has started with steam up on his hobby worked far too hard, and then abandoned it." I know that Tom has plenty of perseverance, and I know how many things he has done—but who will remember these, if the reputation of this sort of saying sticks to him.

Thursday [28 January 1858]. After prayers Mother and Father [Kane] began talking about Elisha and Willie [deceased sons Elisha Kent Kane and William Leiper Kane], speaking of the comfort of knowing they were Christians. So I told them my darling was one. I think they ought not to have so great a comfort kept from them. My darling—if I should die while you are away, and you read this, I would like to tell you, that I think you ought to let Johnny [brother John K. Kane, Jr.] and Pat know this. Your example has been so much thought of by them, that your influence ceasing to act *against* Christianity, may foster their spark [of faith] into a flame.

What a close tie it makes between us! I thought when I loved him we were closely drawn together, and when he was my baby's father, but yet this [religious tie] is closer and dearer than any of the links that sorrow, pain, and joy have drawn so closely round us. Either of us may die, but now we will be united afterwards.

Tuesday February 2. I was sorry to receive a bill for $10.50 from Engle for plastering. This takes away all my money but $9, which I must keep for washing bills. It seems as if I were so extravagant to have used all Tom left with me, but every bill he left has exceeded his estimate. I have a hundred and forty dollars still to pay. So I'll do my best to get along. I *wish* I could earn it!

Saturday February 6th. Little Harry said of herself last night "Dear Friend, please take care of my dear Papa, far away over the sea." Today she took a pencil and paper "to write to my darling Father." She says "she will give him her Treasure Book, and Mother Goose if he will come home." Oh Tom, if I could see you! Dear fellow, dear, dear, darling, where are you now? Oh how my heart aches for you. Poor fellow, I hope you are not suffering from cold, crossing mountains ~~and deserts~~ and deserts. And the Indians, and Mormons—God preserve and guard you through all.

Many of the details of Kane's odyssey to coastal California are available elsewhere.[9] They include not only accounts of frequent seasickness and painful neuralgia but kaleidoscopic impressions of scenery and geography encountered while crossing Panama as well as during the subsequent two-legged Pacific voyage, first to San Francisco and then San Pedro. During a brief layover in San Francisco, Kane considered and rejected the use of several routes by which to travel from northern California to Utah, including transit of California's Sierra as well as the possibility of steaming north to Oregon and then taking the overland route to Salt Lake City via Fort Hall. Kane decided on the San Bernardino route, and on 29 January he took ship in San Francisco for a one-week cruise to San Pedro, the embryonic port of Los Angeles.

Aboard this packed little vessel, Kane slept on deck in close proximity to a detachment of the Third U.S. Artillery en route to a new post as part of General Clarke's realignment of California's defenses. Kane found these troops and their loud anti-Mormonism appalling, as had Apostle Ezra T. Benson a month earlier: "And so we are here with these beasts, taking up every sheltered corner on the upper deck—a few of the choicest playing cards, the rest sea sick & disgusting—vomiting & swearing. I see but few faces that look in the least American. They appear the worst of Irish & the stupidest of Germans. I have heard them two or three times talk of their going against the Mormons. That we shd. pay such for butchering our own citizens!"[10]

An Angel in Disguise: Harassment and Rescue in San Berdoo

By 4 February Kane had landed at San Pedro, traveled to nearby Los Angeles, and then moved on to San Bernardino. There he withdrew to a hotel and took up residence as the reclusive Dr. Osborne while attempting to find a reliable (Mormon) means of traveling to Salt Lake City. He did so in the midst of a San Bernardino that was both collapsing and agitated. Beset by fatigue and a combination of ailments, Kane realized that he was about to lose his communications link to the Atlantic Coast. Accordingly, he mustered the energy to write very different letters to Elizabeth and Judge Kane.

[9]Winther, *A Friend of the Mormons*, 65–79.

[10]Kane Diary, 29 January 1858, Winther, *A Friend of the Mormons*, 76. For another description of this detachment, see "Troops for the South," *Daily Union* (Sacramento), 28 January 1858, 2/2.

Kane to Elizabeth,
5 February 1858, Kane Family Papers, BYU.

What shall I trust this threatened Mail Bag with? Words that really strive to express my adoration and so disclose to strangers the secrets of our common happiness? No;—with honest mauvaise honte [shamefulness] I send my daguerreotype, the face of a poor man who with all his 35 years of wrinkling can swear that now for two months his breast has not harbored one ignoble or impure thought.—He had no flower to gather: it is winter here—but he felt he had a right to dedicate to you such a 58 days of the life which is your own. It cost something to face that little camera lens in the staring daylight, and it cost something more not to destroy the ugly result when it first appeared clearly to view. Add $6. cost price[11]—and I know you will keep it, till I bring the crows feet and frown furrows home themselves, and my darling will kiss them as she does our own babies' beautiful dimples; and, that day, I will feel beautiful, and young—and happy, which I know I never was when young.

I am still gaining health and strength, remembering all my promises to you. My first idle man's letter will tell you how much I owe to the devotion of my Mormon friends. Words cannot express it—I was going to say—certainly they do not express it by words. Perhaps it is God inspires them to it:—perhaps you have been praying to him for me—perhaps I, even, do a little in that line—toward sunset, and only a moment or two, and when you are concerned. More I cannot say; but—we will not perhaps feel the pane of glass so cold between our lips when I return—I mean the one that said you were inside the House of G[od] whilst I stood in the Street.—Expect to hear from me by the next semimonthly mail—but be not surprised if it be not carried through. Heaven bless you, and them all.

To his father, Tom provided an update of what he knew of the situation in Utah. He also commented on what military officers aboard ship had told him of rumors flowing into General Clarke's San Francisco headquarters of a Mormon-army clash in Washington Territory.[12]

[11]The cost of this photograph would have shocked Elizabeth, who, as mentioned, on 31 January had only nine dollars in ready cash.

[12]This document, a slip of paper, was mailed encoded through a system devised by Judge Kane. The key was a London edition of the Bible each had. With a premonition of death, Judge Kane had taught Elizabeth the decryption technique before Tom went west. Many of Kane's messages from Utah were not encrypted because of their length, time pressures, and fatigue. That this message was written from southern California rather than Utah can be determined by its internal references. Years later, Elizabeth Kane described its significance: "Three months passed after my husband left, and we heard nothing, save a little slip of paper written in cipher had come to the Judge just after he was taken ill. Fever was clouding his faculties and he sent for me to decipher it, reminding me that he had foreseen the possibility of the duty falling upon me. We knew that Tom had landed in California, but that was all." Elizabeth D. W. Kane, "History of Kane [Pennsylvania]," I, chapter 3, 84–85, typescript, Kane Family Papers, BYU.

Kane to Judge Kane, ca. 5 February 1858, Kane Collection, Beinecke Library, Yale University.

Major Wise [Francis Octavus Wyse, of the Third U.S. Artillery] and others have news from Indian runners just in at Walla-Walla of engagement between the troops and Mormons, and so forth. I do not believe a word of it. If the troops have attempted an advance, they have been annihilated, but on the contrary Johns[t]on [at Fort Bridger] appears to me to be acting with judgment and discretion. At my latest advices a month ago, he was maintaining the strictest discipline and with such success that none of his men had been able to desert, as the Mormons were expecting. Johnston had cut off all communication with his camp, detaining all intruders, and completely concealing his condition from the enemy. They only know, I fancy, of his inability to retreat through the loss of his cattle, only about one mule being left to a wagon, and their own intentions these they appear to know too well.[13] I cannot honorably reveal even to you, my father, the [army's] peril. Had you known all you would not have opposed my coming here.[14] The day may be, and probably is past to make peace, but not to save our poor [army] fellows. Have no fear for my life, the [biblical] cloud and pillar will be my escort. I swear I will arrive [in Utah] in time.

Kane's last sentence ran to his greatest concern—the need to reach and influence Brigham Young before the Nauvoo Legion struck hard at what he mistakenly believed to be a vulnerable, over-matched Utah Expedition. As Elizabeth Kane later put it, "He knew that if the Mormons overwhelmed the little U.S. Army encamped there, they in turn would inevitably be overwhelmed, crushed out of existence by a nation bent on vengeance."[15]

Kane's reclusiveness in San Bernardino had the unintended consequence of generating intense curiosity, speculation, and indignation about who he was and why he was intent upon crossing the desert to Mormon Utah in the dead of winter. The result was a volatile atmosphere of the sort that multiple missionaries passing through the area had reported to Brigham Young.

Shortly after Kane left San Bernardino for Salt Lake City, William A. Wallace, editor of the Los Angeles *Star* and pseudonymous correspondent ("Yo Mismo") of San Francisco's *Daily Alta California,* reported Dr. Osborne's tumultuous passage through southern California. The newspaper ran Wallace's dispatch under the heading: "Arrival of a Supposed Mormon

[13]Kane's understanding of conditions at the Utah Expedition's winter quarters were, as he later discovered, highly inaccurate. Desertions were rife and security porous.

[14]A reference to Judge Kane's 4 January letter, hidden by Elizabeth in Tom's trunk as he left home. See *At Sword's Point, Part 1,* 510–11.

[15]Elizabeth D. W. Kane, "History of Kane [Pennsylvania]," I, chapter 3, 77, Kane Family Papers, BYU.

Emissary—Said to be a Brother of Dr. Kane, with Letters from the President—Haste to Get to Salt Lake."[16]

[WALLACE] "YO MISMO," DISPATCH, 17 FEBRUARY 1858,
SAN FRANCISCO DAILY ALTA CALIFORNIA, 10 MARCH 1858, 1/2.

On the [steamer to San Pedro] . . . there arrived a young man [of] lively and prepossessing appearance, who was made known to me as a devotee to botany and the natural sciences generally. When I met him, he was on the point of starting for San Bernardino, and asked me what I thought of his prospects for botanical and geological discoveries. I told him it was bad, and tried to persuade him to remain here and take chances with me in ranging the mountains, &c. But he could not stop. He wanted to be on the ground, where he could lay out his work. After some hesitation he gave me his address as "A. Osborne, Esq., Philadelphia," and said he was travelling under the auspices of the Academy of Natural Sciences of that city. He bade me a very cordial good-bye, and hurried away, upon a contract that he should be put down in San Bernardino, 60 miles, the same evening, he paying $145 for the ride.[17]

He arrived at his destination, and was received with open arms by Mr. [Ebenezer] Hanks, the Mormon leader there, and others of that sect. After this interview, a young man was offered $100, and all his expenses, to drive Mr. Osborne through to Salt Lake, in fifteen days. The offer was declined as impracticable. Here, also, Mr. O. announced himself as a botanist, and in pursuit of science generally. When it became known that he wished to be expressed through to Salt Lake, and that he had made very liberal offers of payment, the suspicions of the citizens were aroused. The people of this outpost are very easily excited, whenever the Mormons are in question. Many of them have been Mormons, and they are more watchful than other communities. They wish to revenge themselves upon the whole sect for the delusion which once seized upon themselves.

They called a meeting, and appointed a committee, who waited upon the botanist, and, demanding his business, charged him with being a Mormon emissary. He denied all their charges; but the demonstrations were so decisive, that he deemed it prudent to exhibit several letters of identification purporting to be from James Buchanan. He also declared that his name was Kane, a brother of the Arctic explorer, and that he was travelling on government business. He was but 23 days from Washington, and wished to be in Salt Lake at the earliest possible moment.[18] The people were not satisfied with his

[16]Unfortunately Wallace's diary for the period in the Yale Collection of Western Americana, Beinecke Library, contains no discussion of his early February meeting with Kane.

[17]Such a large fee alone would have attracted attention to Kane in Los Angeles.

[18]For Kane to have abandoned his Dr. Osborne cover and brandished Buchanan's letters (as well as the 31 December letter from Bernhisel to Young) indicates that he was under extreme pressure.

explanation, but as there was no proof against him, he was not watched very closely, and, before the public were aware of it, he had started for Deseret. Mr. Hanks had obtained a team of four of the fastest and best mules in the county, and these, before a good express wagon, were waiting for Osborne (or Kane) on the outskirts of the town, and so soon as he could get to it unobserved, away he went.

After he had gone, on being asked, several of the Mormons said they knew him well—that he was a brother of Dr. Kane, and was baptized a Mormon about eight years since, and was still faithful to the church.[19] They also report him to be a gentleman of learning, and of great energy. His appearance and departure gave rise to much talk, and a thousand suppositions were uttered as to his mission. That which gained credence was, that he was bearing important intelligence from Bernheisel [*sic*] in Washington to Young in Salt Lake.

Great is the mystery of godliness, and the mystery of Mormonism must be equally as great, when it will induce the owner of the famous name of Kane to discard it to subserve the unworthy purposes of polygamy and treason. This is one side of the story, and the side I hardly care to believe, because I dislike to think meanly of a man who wins my confidence. Mr. Kane was too much of a gentleman, and too sincere a student to be a Mormon.

I like the other story far better than the above. It is, that Kane or Osborne was actually an agent of government bearing terms to Young. It has been known, for some time past, that Bernheisel has been in treaty [negotiation] at Washington for the relinquishment of all Mormon claims to land in Utah, and their improvements thereon; and that upon the payment of one or two millions of dollars, they will evacuate the United States territory, and seek a home somewhere else.[20] It is said that no more overt act of treason can be proved against Utah than has been committed, in times past, by Georgia, South Carolina, Massachusetts and Pennsylvania, and that if Mormon intolerance and licentiousness can be got rid of by buying up their improvements, it will be far cheaper than by going into a war of extermination with them.[21] It is believed, by well-informed persons, that Mr. Kane is bearer of dispatches to this effect from Washington to Young, and the delay of the government in its military operations, and the neglect to send troops through Los Angeles, whence, only, Deseret can be reached in the winter, makes it probable that there are really some negotiations in progress.

---

[19]Kane never was a Latter-day Saint, although many people thought he was in 1858. In 1846, while visiting the Mormons in Iowa and gravely ill, his caregivers had baptized him "for health," a ritual of compassion that was not equivalent to joining the church.

[20]A reference to speculation that Bernhisel and freebooter Walter Murray Gibson were discussing such a scheme with Buchanan involving migration to a haven in the Dutch East Indies.

[21]Presumably references to the Nullification Crisis, Shays's Rebellion, and the Whiskey Rebellion of earlier years.

Later, Kane told Elizabeth a version of his brief but turbulent sojourn in San Bernardino, which she recorded.

"The Truth of His S. Bernardino Adventures," Elizabeth W. Kane Journal, 29 June 1858, Kane Family Papers, BYU.

His quarters at the tavern, where he was lying sick, were so miserable, that he went to an empty building formerly the house of Amasa Lyman to lie down in peace. (At the tavern while he lay on the floor in the dark, a row began in the next room, the combatants finally bursting in and falling over him.) Two speculators who had bought Lyman's house let him go there, and sleep in their room. This house was a very large one (fifteen windows on a side) and was divided by party walls, and separate entrances into several domiciles. At one end some people were living, a man and woman and a sick mountaineer whom they were nursing. Tom used to get the woman to boil milk for him, and doctored the mountaineer with the contents of his little [travel] medicine chest.

These people, however, he thought evidently distrustful of him. It was part of his policy to make the Anti-Mormons distrust him that their enmity might be a passport to the confidence of the Mormons. In this he succeeded only too well. The coming of the Vigilance Committee's Committee of arrest was changed by his bold front into the visit of a Committee of Inquiry. He bluffed them off and made a partial confidant of District Attorney Mann. The lead man [William] Pickett he scared into remaining outside the town all day telling him that he had three fellows watching who would shoot him if he made his appearance in the town that day.

At night feeling anxious about the safety of his trunk, left at the tavern, he made a circuit outside the town and came into the tavern where he actually was while the Vigilance Committee were holding a meeting there. When he got back to the deserted house, he affected to go to bed, but felt uneasy because his speculator companions lay down on either side of him. He determined therefore if possible, to rid himself of the valuable papers he had with him. His companions fell sound asleep and he rose and stole out of doors. Whichever way he went he found himself dogged, the house was entirely surrounded by spies. He was forced to go back, and had to stay awake all night as he was unacquainted with the house and did not know where he might not expect an attack. From the sounds some one was evidently up all night watching in the building.

With the earliest light he was up walking in the garden and saw at one of the windows a woman's face watching him; the woman who lived at the end of the building.[22] She looked not unfriendly so he greeted her, and she made him a sign to come near. When he came in, she closed the door behind him

[22]This was Frances Swan Kimball Clark.

> and falling on her knees with clasped hands said "If I know you, I'll never say that I know you. Oh, Dr. Osborne can't you be saved yet?" Then she told him she had recognized him as the companion of their flight from Nauvoo (By the bye Pickett recognized him) that she had made her husband go on the Vigilance Committee. He started with them, for they had dispatched another Committee of arrest last evening, slipped ahead, told her "For God's sake, hide that man down the well." She found Tom absent, he was then at the tavern, but hid away his valise, and when the committee arrived, told them he was away, and had had no luggage there.

In later years, Thomas and Elizabeth Kane drafted descriptions of this scene characterizing it as a highly confrontational and threatening experience. Writing with an eye to publication as well as to posterity, their retrospective accounts of Utah War events, including this more contemporary one, were tinged with hyperbole and melodrama.[23] In trying to understand the conditions Kane faced in San Bernardino, one must also consider a letter written on 6 February 1858 to Apostle Lyman by Ebenezer Hanks, the Mormon agent charged with selling the remaining church property in San Bernardino. This document, carried by Kane as he left town under cover of darkness, was a letter of introduction to Lyman should Kane encounter him on the Spanish Trail.

Hanks to Lyman, 6 February 1858, Kane Family Papers, byu.

> I hastily pen you these few lines, by way of Express, which I have diligently and successfully accomplished agreeably to the instructions of Doctor J. M. Bernhisel from Washington.[24]
>
> The bearer, D[r]. Osburne, of whom you will learn more fully on an interview with that gentleman, has been here three days. His appearance has created an alarming excitement among the people, particularly the anti-Mormon, a Mr. [William] Pickett of Los Angeles, (who now resides in this County) their ringleader, who immediately convened a Mass Meeting formed a Committee, adopted resolutions to visit this stranger, and know his designs, which they believed were strictly opposed to the views of the General Government, and to prevent his passing through.
>
> The conduct of the gallant Doctor throughout has gained the applause of the respectable portion of this community, and Mr. Pickett foreman of

[23]For a discussion of the unrest in San Bernardino generated by Kane's presence as well as the Kanes' later discussion of this scene, see Grow, *"Liberty to the Downtrodden,"* 166.

[24]It is not clear why Bernhisel's name was mentioned here unless Hanks intended it to signal that Osborne came from Washington. Kane had earlier brandished the envelope containing Bernhisel's 31 December letter to Young as a way of establishing his bona fides when confronted by the vigilance committee in San Bernardino.

this committee was fully satisfied of the integrity and uprightness of this Gentleman in the brief interview of an hour and a half and delivered his report to the meeting who were anxiously expecting the same and resulting in the unanimous voice of God Speed Him.[25]

I desire that you will send me back my carriage and team, if you can release the same, and expedite the thing for this gentleman.

The Ranch sale has been effected, of the unsold lands and writings are being executed for the $18000.00/100.

Perhaps the greatest impediment to a clear understanding of what took place during Kane's brief sojourn in San Bernardino is the confusing nature of his own unpublished postwar writings about this episode. Of special relevance is an undated, untitled, four-page narrative drafted in Kane's distinctive hand to summarize his travel experiences during the period 4 January–6 February 1858.[26] It is a strange document, couched in the third person and phrased in the detached "voice" of what historian Richard D. Poll described as "a possible news release to be published by an ostensibly neutral journalist, describing his experiences in California in early February."[27]

Such indirection would have come easily for Kane. He preferred to operate as a behind-the-scenes agent, who advanced his own views of Mormon affairs by projecting them onto some other, more visible player whom he cast in the role of front man. In 1852 it had been Kane rather than Apostle John Taylor who wrote many of the pamphlet attacks on Utah's "runaway officials" published in the *New York Herald* under Taylor's name. Historian Poll suspected that it was really Kane, not James C. Van Dyke, who crafted the 9 December 1857 Van Dyke letter to Buchanan, suggesting a White House meeting to discuss Kane's intent to visit Utah.[28] At year-end 1857 Kane had tried to shape Bernhisel's correspondence with Brigham Young; his papers for 1858 are loaded with fragmentary material ghostwritten while attempting to channel the personae of Brigham Young and Alfred Cumming.

What is most unusual (and puzzling) about this San Bernardino "press statement" is Kane's striking depiction of his travels through southern California as a struggle against Mormons in good standing who were secretly

[25] Hanks's description of these proceedings as civil and with a favorable outcome may have softened the dynamics of what actually happened in anticipation that the letter might be read by an unfriendly stranger.

[26] Kane, undated, untitled holograph narrative in file labeled "Concerning the Mormons," Thomas Leiper Kane Papers, American Philosophical Society, Philadelphia (hereafter APS).

[27] Poll, holograph research notes of 17 February 1984, Poll Collection, Marriott Library, University of Utah.

[28] Poll, "Thomas L. Kane and the Utah War," 112–35.

aligned against Brigham Young for unspecified reasons. In drafting this document as he did in other postwar documents, Kane attempted to bolster the questionable notion that he would float with President Buchanan and Alfred Cumming in March 1858—the conspiracy theory that, as champion of a peace party in Utah, Brigham Young was constantly at odds with a coterie of unidentified war hawks in his inner circle.[29]

For these reasons Kane's San Bernardino narrative began with the cryptic observation that "The Mormons may be true patriots at heart, and sadly wronged, but there is something unquestionably behind the curtain. There are very bad men among them whom they countenance and support or else they are playing a deep game, the moves of which are to say the least incomprehensible. They ascribe to others the obstacles which were offered [by them] to Colonel Kane's proceeding to Salt Lake City." From this thought, the memo proceeded to relate that Kane's "secret [identity and mission] was betrayed by Hancks [*sic*] a trustee of the Mormons to sell their property in San Bernardino" and that the San Bernardino vigilance committee confronting Kane was chaired by "a Mormon who married the widow of one of Joe Smith's brothers[30] and three of its most active members were Mormons, two of them known to be in high standing at the present time, one of them the son of a distinguished Mormon bishop, and another a leading elder, now high in the confidence of Brigham Young."

In his detached voice, Kane then explained: "When Young called in so unhesitatingly the saints in California and elsewhere to come to Zion and help him fight the United States, he perhaps did not anticipate that he was forming around him a party who would oppose his efforts to make peace, when he turned his coat as suddenly as he appears to have done. Their tails being cut off in the trap, these men thought it but fair that the rich landholders of the [Salt Lake?] Valley should be reduced to the same condition as themselves."[31]

---

[29]Poll reached a similar assessment: "His stop in San Bernardino was marked by an altercation with anti-Mormons, some apostate Mormons among them that he later used to support his public relations thesis that a war faction among the Mormons tried to block him in order to precipitate a fight with the army." Poll, *Quixotic Mediator*, 16.

[30]Don Carlos Smith.

[31]E. Leo Lyman, the leading authority on the Mormon presence and departure from San Bernardino, argues that Kane's story of a war party bringing pressure to bear on Young and composed of highly placed evacuees from southern California was "a total fabrication" and certainly not consistent with the attitudes of San Bernardino's leaders of the time, Apostles Amasa M. Lyman and Charles C. Rich. Lyman, telephone interview with MacKinnon, 31 October 2012. For Kane to have referred to Mormonism's founder disrespectfully as Joe Smith and to Brigham Young as a turn coat also rings false unless he was purposefully attempting to establish that this piece was not pro-Mormon.

The narrative ends with the assertion that upon fleeing San Bernardino on 6 February, "Col. Kane was pursued after this by Mormons who knew his real name," and that he concealed himself from any Latter-day Saints encountered on the road, since "he probably knew better than to trust the Mormons by that time."

Two courageous Latter-day Saints in San Bernardino, along with Ebenezer Hanks, came to the aid of Thomas L. Kane at his greatest peril: "Colonel" Alden A. M. Jackson and Frances Swan Kimball Clark. Both generated documents conveying a sense of danger quite different than Hanks's lower-key description but consistent with Kane's dramatic postwar reconstruction of the events that occurred during the first week of February 1858.

The exciting role played by Colonel Jackson, his wife Caroline, and their thirteen-year-old daughter, Augusta Joyce, is described in a charming, evocative essay that Augusta wrote for a prominent Mormon magazine soon after Kane's death in 1883.[32] At that time Augusta was age 41, an accomplished writer, and the plural wife of George W. Crocheron, a highly respected Latter-day Saint in St. George, Utah. Because this piece is accessible elsewhere, it is not included here. Suffice it to say that Colonel Jackson's principal service to Kane was to provide him with moral support and meals from Caroline Jackson during his stay in the San Bernardino hotel, and to spirit him to the temporary refuge of the Clark home when the threat of mob action made that arrangement untenable. It is typical of the melodramatic style of both Augusta Joyce Crocheron and Thomas L. Kane that she recorded the end of their reunion eighteen years later in St. George in language evoking both his role as a Mormon protector and his fondness for a flourish: "Looking from the doorway on the light within and the stormy night without, he said: 'This looks like our political horizon. Stay you in camp, eat roast beef and rest, I will go out in the storm and stand on picket guard for you.' He extended his hand, repeated thrice, 'good night,' and was gone."[33]

The couple to whose home Colonel Jackson spirited Kane were George Sakerman Clark and Frances Swan Kimball Clark. Mrs. Clark was a Scottish convert who had emigrated to Nauvoo, married Heber C. Kimball in 1844, and migrated with him to Utah in 1848. Frances left Kimball, Brigham Young's first counselor, in 1852 or 1853 for the Mormon settlement at San Bernardino,

[32]Augusta Joyce Crocheron was Colonel Jackson's stepdaughter. An autobiographical sketch of her life appears in Crocheron, *Representative Women of Deseret,* 97–108. Much of Crocheron's narrative for *The Contributor* may also be found in Zobell, *Sentinel in the East,* 111–13.

[33]Crocheron, "Reminiscences of General Kane," *The Contributor* 6 (1884–85): 475–77.

where she married George Clark.[34] Mrs. Clark had several reasons for helping Kane as she did. One of them, as Kane later told his wife, was to try to repair her damaged relationship with the LDS church: "She was one of Kimball's many wives, but had run away with George Clark. But they were unhappy the curse was on them; their little one died, she knew that for their sin George and she could have no children. But she said 'If by saving you, I could do a service to God's Church on earth, I would feel that I did not need a drop of water to cool my tongue when I shall lift up my eyes being in torments.' "[35]

Nearly three months after Kane abruptly left her home for Utah under the protection of George Clark and two other Mormons, Frances Swan Clark mustered up the inner resources to do what she had been intending to do all spring—write to Elizabeth Kane, a total stranger, to describe her husband's brief sojourn with her family.

FRANCES SWAN CLARK TO ELIZABETH KANE,
ELIZABETH KANE JOURNAL, 2 MAY 1858, KANE FAMILY PAPERS, BYU.

My dear Friend—I have seated myself to attempt to write to you to fulfill my promise to your noble husband, Col. Kane, & I only wish I was I was [*sic*] more capable of performing the task of writing a Letter to one that is a stranger to me, although I have never beheld your face, yet in imagination I have often held intercourse with you. I should have been very glad to have written to you before, but my weak nature is such that if any care, or especially anxiety is in my mind, I cannot direct my mind in such a channel as I desire, and although I am aware how great your anxiety must be for you have parted with your husband, the Father of your two beautiful children to undertake an arduous and tedious Journey to endeavour if possible to make peace with a people and their government so much like the self sacrificing race of the Kanes willing always to undertake any hardship for the good of their fellowman.

When the Dr arrived at San Barnardino his health was very poor I endeavoured to render him all the assistance I could, although he was travelling incog. I recognized in Dr Osburne, Col. Kane whom I had seen 12 years ago, when I found out who was going to accompany him to Utah I knew they were not suitable men to take care of a sick person. I perposed to the Dr to let my husband go along with him, as I thought him more suitable as he

[34]For the most comprehensive account of Frances Swan Clark's life and communications with Elizabeth Kane, see Ardis E. Parshall, "Frances Swan Clark: A Kindness Remembered," essay posted 18 May 2008, accessed 10 November 2015, http://keepapitchinin.org/2008/05/18/frances-swan-clark-a-kindness-remembered-redux. Thanks to Ms. Parshall for surfacing this story and providing the unusual letters exchanged by these women.

[35]Elizabeth W. Kane Journal, 28 June 1858, Kane Family Papers, BYU

had had a great deal of sickness in his own Family your husband refused to take him away from me, knowing my lonely situation, I insisted on it, telling him that it was no worse for me than yours. They started on the sixth of Feby. (and I was also somewhat afriad [*sic*] of the Dr being overtaken) many a prayer I endeavoured to offer up for their safety & success.[36] My husband accompanied him to Little Salt Lake and returned by the Dr's request to San Barnardino on business.

When he left him he had improved very much in health and I earnestly hope by this time that he is enjoying the society of his family, and helping to comfort his bereaved Mother, for I saw by the papers the death of the Hon. Judge Kane. I know how to sympathise with you in your deep affliction, for I have been sorry afflicted.

None but a mother can fully realise my only precious child has been taken from me and although nearly a year has passed away my loss seems greater to day than it did the day the grave veiled her from my sight; sweet little Daughter language fails to express the feelings of my heart, and the big tears of regrets flood freely down my cheek when I reflect She is gone. The loss of our parents is a severe trial, but the loss of our parents after we have arrived at the age of maturity and away to ourselves, is nothing in comparison with that of a promising child the only invaluable treasure you are in possession off. Our parents bided their time had their joys and their sorrows their cares & their disappointments and we could not in reason suppose they would or could desire a much longer life, but our children, we do not expect them to die, they are ful[l] of promise & hope and it hardly seems right that they should be taken from us, although we know our little cherub child has passed deaths gloomy portal. . . .

Although my dear Friend we are called by providence to be separated [*sic*] by Death from our dear Friends, yet their is something cheering in the thought that they are freed from sorrow pain & death, but I must draw to a close on this subject, for I am afraid I have wearied you now. I am very anxious to hear what success the Dr had at Utah & how he is. I see by the papers that he had left Utah will you be kind enough to answer this letter and give me some information excuse this hasty Epistle and now may the very God of peace & consolation rest & and abide with you all is the prayer of your affectionate Friend Frances Jessie Clark.

Elizabeth received this letter on 31 May and noted in her journal, "A very fatiguing day. I had a long ~~walk~~ letter[37] from a Mrs. Clarke [*sic*] of S. Bernardino telling me about Tom's being there, and her husband's accompanying

[36]Kane's companions on the dash out of San Bernardino were George S. Clark, Joseph Smith Tanner, and John Mayfield. Roberts, *A Comprehensive History of the Church*, 4:343; Zobell, *Sentinel in the East*, 115.

[37]Years later, Elizabeth referred to Mrs. Clark's letter less sympathetically, describing it as "strange" and "disconnected." Elizabeth D. W. Kane, "History of Kane [Pennsylvania]," I, chapter 3, 85.

him to Salt Lake, about her baby's death etc. I am asked to write her news of him. God grant I may have good news to give!" Elizabeth responded promptly and copied part of her letter into her journal ("that Tom may see if I have committed a terrible gaucheries in my answer") while pasting alongside this material Mrs. Clark's earlier note.

Elizabeth Kane to Mrs. Clark,
Elizabeth Kane Journal, 2 June 1858,
Kane Family Papers, BYU.

> I received your very kind letter with great pleasure, and hasten to reply to it by first opportunity, though perhaps it would be better to wait till I have news of your friend, my husband, to send you. Our last letters were dated March 24th, and I suppose you already know much more about him and the result of his labors at Salt Lake than I do. He speaks most highly of those who escorted him to Salt Lake, of whom your good husband was one; and both his mother and I are greateful for the devotion shown him by them, and by his old friends ~~at~~ in Deseret. I shall be sure to tell Mr. Kane, if he is spared to return, among the first things, how pleasant an acquaintance I have formed in S. Bernardino. And then he will tell me more of you than your letter does.
>
> I could not love my own little children so much without feeling grieved that you have lost your little darling.[38]
>
> I suppose you must have many a lonely hour, for you are far from the home and friends of your childhood. But is it not . . .[39]

When Elizabeth Kane later learned more from her husband about the extent of Mrs. Clark's help, she commented, "I am glad I wrote to her so warmly."[40]

Despite his ordeal in San Bernardino, Kane left town on 6 February with an appreciation of the area's beauty as well as the kindness of the Jackson and Clark families:

> Adieu to the Beautiful Valley, the beautiful mountains round the rim, the beautiful cultivated fields, the town shining like forms of crystal in the distant plain. Soon alas adieu to the flowers. This primrose I have plucked, with a violet—senecirs & peonies are overcome by the sands as we approach the Mts. and are replaced by oldman and wormwood & chamisse. A shrub dense white with flowers of a bitter fragrance adorns the avid thicket, but we are bidding goodbye to freshness, spring and flowers. We turn round

[38]Mrs. Kane may have misunderstood Frances Clark's ambiguous reference to her loss. Mrs. Clark's daughter died in August 1846 when only a few months old, rather than in close proximity to her writing.

[39]At this point, Elizabeth stopped copying her long letter to Mrs. Clark. For the latter's response from her new home in northern California, see Frances Clark to Elizabeth Kane, 12 July [1858?], Kane Family Papers, BYU.

[40]Elizabeth W. Kane Journal, 28 June 1858, ibid.

> the hills down upon the plains which confront our course, and discover that they impeded our view of a wave billow, a wonderful depression in the mighty mountains—the Cajon Pass.

When she later read this entry in her husband's diary, Elizabeth Kane noted with a biblical flourish, "So he went forth into the desert. May the God whom he served and who blessed his work with success, call him indeed one of the 'Children of God.' "[41]

I Am on No Fool's Errand: Last Leg to Salt Lake

The accounts of Kane's arduous, relentless movement from San Bernardino to Salt Lake City, are fragmentary. For example, on 12 February his party encountered Apostle Amasa Lyman and his family, also en route for Salt Lake, at Cottonwood Springs outside Las Vegas. There Kane's party partook of trailside home cooking while Lyman's daughter-in-law, Rhoda Ann Lyman, fashioned leggings and mufflers for his hands and arms from a buffalo robe.[42]

One of the more unusual such vignettes was provided a day later at the Las Vegas mission by diarist Caroline B. Crosby, a refugee from San Bernardino also bound for Utah.[43] She described Kane's party, now accompanied by Apostle Lyman, as it encountered the first settlement after leaving San Bernardino a week earlier. For Thomas L. Kane, it was another unexpectedly domestic scene in the desert that reminded him of his own family while prompting one of his rare displays of humor.[44]

Journal of Caroline Barnes Crosby, 13–14 February 1858, LDS Archives.

> *Sat 13th* Quite an excitement among the brethren and indians. Two horses taken [by Indians] last night. Ellen [Pratt] and I washed [clothes]. PM came Joseph Tanner. Said bro Lyman would be in in a couple of hours. I ironed. Just at dusk came bro Lyman. E[llen] was ironing. I was sitting by the stove holding the babe. I hardly knew him on account of his long beard. I looked at him for sometime, and then said I believe it is bro Lyman I can tell if I hear you

[41]Ibid.

[42]"Journal of Elder Francis M. Lyman," 12 February 1858, LDS Archives, cited in Roberts, *A Comprehensive History of the Church*, 4:343–44.

[43]For her life and travels before fleeing San Bernardino in January 1858, see Crosby et al., *No Place to Call Home*.

[44]Transcription courtesy of E. Leo Lyman of Leeds, Utah.

> speak, he then spoke and I said yes. A Dr Osborn was in company with him, also George Clark and John Mayfield. We had no introduction to him, but he commented (that is the Dr) and observed that it was quite a contrast between travelling as he had done with men, and sleeping out doors, and then coming into the fort and seeing us women, sitting by the stove, ironing clean white clothes. Said he should about as soon have expected to see his mother behind a bar in San Bernardino. We had little chance to converse with him, as the brethren soon gathered around the large fire, and Ellen and myself repaired to our wagons, to read letters from Sister Pratt, her mother. Bro Lyman invited us to sing. We sang, Come, Come ye saints, and he then prayed.[45] We all felt edified, and comforted with his remarks. 10 oclock retired to bed.
>
> *Sun 14th* After breakfast I got out of my wagon, found Dr. O. and bro Lyman standing by our fire. Bro Ly— introduced him to me. He spoke very politely, and enquired how I slept the last night. I told him well, and that I slept as well in my wagon, as I had done at home. At ten oclock, they left. After they were gone, I understood that the aforesaid Dr Osborn was no less than Col Kane, who has formerly proved himself a friend and wellwisher to our people. He came and shook hands with us on leaving, expressed some regret at not having an opportunity of becoming better acquainted with us, and hoped we might meet again. After he left, I understand he was a sketcher, making delineations for a paper.

Unknown to Kane at this time, a less domestic scene was unfolding in the mountains near Las Vegas: the mining and smelting of ballistic lead for the Nauvoo Legion. Before Brigham Young had closed down this operation in March 1857, Mormon miners had extracted 8,500 pounds of lead, enough for about 119,000 bullets. In early February 1858, pressed by the urgency of war, Amasa Lyman, Col. William H. Dame, and a detachment left Parowan to reactivate the mining-smelting effort on a more modest scale. On 17 February, the day after Kane exited Las Vegas, Colonel Dame reported: "Myself and ten of the brethren went with Bro. Lyman as far as the Vegas. There we left five to smelt some lead; 300 lbs. of ore, brought 140 lbs. of good lead (made in a little adobe furnace)." It was a yield equivalent to nearly 2,000 bullets.[46]

Another fragment, published in 1870, described the aftermath of Kane's stay in a roadside cave during a snowstorm, an incident on the trail between

[45]"Come, Come, Ye Saints" was a Mormon hymn composed during the 1846 exodus from Nauvoo. During the Utah War (and continually thereafter), it was sung as a source of comfort and inspiration at LDS gatherings.

[46]*At Sword's Point, Part 1*, 256; Dame to George A. Smith, 17 February 1858, Journal History, same date, LDS Archives, as discussed in Hunter, *Brigham Young the Colonizer*, 332; Jacob Hamblin to Young, 14 February 1858, LDS Archives.

Las Vegas and Fort Clara that included his interaction with Mormon Indian missionaries Ira Hatch and Thales Haskell before their encounter on the Colorado River with the Ives Expedition. During the course of this brief meeting, Kane gratuitously directed the missionaries to make arrangements, if not a treaty, with the local tribes for the protection and comfort of future travelers.[47] Here was an example of Kane's penchant for unauthorized interventions that would later create difficulties in Salt Lake City, Camp Scott, and Washington.

Thomas L. Kane's escort, Amasa Lyman, was also willing to engage in directive, if not interventionist, behavior while passing through Utah's southern settlements. On 20 February the party stopped in Parowan to spend the night, probably with Col. William H. Dame, the local stake president and senior Nauvoo Legion officer.[48] It is likely that during this visit Dame knew Kane's identity, but his young adjutant, 2d Lt. James Henry Martineau, did not, recording only that "to day Elder A. Lyman arrived from the south accompanied by a man direct from Washington upon Urgent business, the purport of which is unknown to us. He went to Salt Lake City with great expedition, [intent on] changing horses at every town."

Immediately following their departure from Parowan, Martineau recorded: "To day Col. Dame informed me that I am appointed to be one of a party of 20 men who are going on a trip among the I-ats (O-ma-ha-vem they call themselves) on the Colorado river. My outfit is to be two mules, arms, and two month provisions."[49] What was the purpose of the mission? In view of the timing involved, it is likely that during this brief stopover Lyman confided to Dame the details of his alarming encounter with Major Blake less than a month earlier and that, as a result of this news, Dame took immediate action to form an expedition to the Colorado. This move presumably anticipated Lyman's soon-to-follow discussion with Brigham Young in Salt Lake City about the need for such a reconnaissance.

---

[47]James A. Little, "Mission to the Muddy in 1858, Written from the Verbal Narrative of Elder Ira Hatch," *Millennial Star* (Liverpool) 32, no. 28 (12 July 1870), 434.

[48]While passing through Parowan, a bemused Kane told seventeen-year-old Joseph Fish of his difficulty in communicating with Hatch in English, a language in which the missionary was awkward because of his immersion in tribal dialects. Dr. Osborne struck Fish as "quite a small man, rather delicate, with keen, bright eyes." Fish, "Autobiography of Joseph Fish, 1840–1926," 83.

[49]Godfrey and Martineau-McCarty, eds., *An Uncommon Common Pioneer,* 20 and 21 February 1858, 143–44. Later, Martineau added the notation: "Col. Kane's arrival." There is no evidence that during this brief visit Kane or Lyman discussed with Dame the Mountain Meadows massacre, for which his troops were responsible five months earlier.

Kane left two contemporaneous accounts of the last leg of his trek to Salt Lake City, neither of which he published. The first, a letter written to President Buchanan from Brigham Young's office a week after Kane arrived in Salt Lake City, is businesslike in tone and reflects the fact that he did not yet know the results of his mission. The second document, describing the same journey from San Bernardino, was a narrative written to brother Robert Patterson ("Pat") Kane a month later from Fort Bridger. It is full of not only sibling playfulness and bravado, but Kane's sense in early April that he was making progress.

Kane to Buchanan, 5 March 1858, Kane Family Papers, BYU.

I left St. Bernardino, California, on the evening of the 6th of February, ult, and reached Williams' or *Cottonwood* Camp, a short distance from the Mormon Fort and Settlement of Las Vegas, early on the morning of the 14th. At the former point I was able to communicate directly with Mr. Amasa Lyman, a member of the Council of "the Twelve" stationed there; but three days more elapsed before I arrived within the Mormon settlements strictly speaking.[50] On the 17th I wrote to Governor Young the following:

"My dear Sir:

I trust you will recognize my handwriting. The date of my letter will apprise you of my journey hither. That I have made it in 6 weeks from New York, may persuade you that I am on no fool's errand, and have no want of confidence in my ability to convince you what is the true feeling of our people and the President toward yourself and the good citizens of Utah. I send this to you by express, to urge you to postpone any military movement of importance until we meet and have a serious interview. If you cannot see the expediency of doing so on other grounds, I entreat it as a favor—in requital of the services which I rendered your people in their less prosperous days—the name of the sincerity with which I remain

Their friend to serve them faithfully
A. Osborne."

My expectation was that this would be delivered to Governor Young at Salt Lake City on the morning of the 20th. I have not been assured that

[50]On 23 February, probably in Nephi, Juab County, Homer Brown, a member of the new Standing Army, recorded the arrival of Kane and his small escort: "Ammasy Lyman arrived last night about mid night with a gentleman from the City of Washington who has come from there in a little over forty days. He calls himself Dr Osborne. He travels night and day nearly and is in a great hurry to get to Brigham but tells his buisness to no one. He is a very small man and seems rather delicate for he had to ride on horseback from the house to the carriage; distance being about two or three rods, but he did not step on the ground as it was quite wet, he wears a Scotch cap, and a mustachio." Homer Brown Journal, 23 February 1858, LDS Archives.

this was the case; but from the expedition with which I found that Indian runners had passed through intermediate points upon the road think it most probable that Governor Young learned that a friend was traveling with all haste to communicate with him as early as the 19th. Afterwards ascertained to be the fact.

On the morning of the 20th violent snow storms set in, and before the day ended I was assured by those most competent to speak upon the subject that it was evidently not limited in its range. With the close of the 21st there was no longer room to doubt that all the passages of the Wahsatch range were so blocked up as to render any military movements for the time out of the question. I was thus reconciled to the extreme slowness of my own advance. I halted one day at Cedar City to change mules and men and rest myself,[51] but using the best despatch and travelling both night and day—no matter what track was followed, so encumbered proved the way, that it was matter for congratulation that I was able to reach great Salt Lake City on the 25th.[52]

Arrived within a few miles of the City, I sent forward to Gov. Young the following:

"My dear Governor:

"Your friend of old times is now within an hour's march of your dwelling where he asks you to name an early hour for the interview which he has travelled so far to seek; and, so near you, having no more occasion for the name of his *colored servant Osborne,* signs himself

Yours truly
Thomas L. Kane"

A polite note from Gov. Y. was delivered at my lodgings not long after appointing 8 o'clock of the same evening for our interview.

KANE TO PAT KANE, 4 APRIL 1858, KANE FAMILY PAPERS, BYU.

What a time I have had you may conjecture from your not hearing from me anything about it. I am within reach of trusty mails now, and *it is all over,* and growing in my mind to pass for an interesting story, but I must rest, and must give it my overtasked brain its holiday too—and I see no help

[51]Joseph Smith Tanner, one of Kane's escorts from San Bernardino, reported that this change took place on 20 February in Parowan rather than Cedar City and that he, Clark, and Mayfield returned home. From Parowan, Kane continued on to Salt Lake with Amasa Lyman, Edward T. Mills, and Joseph Mathews, with the latter supplying two of their four mules. Tanner, "Reminiscences," ca.1907, typescript, LDS Archives. Although Kane and Tanner left no record of it, in response to Kane's note Young sent William S. Godbe, a trusted lieutenant (but later one of Mormonism's most prominent dissenters), to join Kane's escort south of Salt Lake City. Zobell, *Sentinel in the East,* 117.

[52]While Kane was in southern Utah on 21 February, Judge Kane died in Philadelphia of pneumonia at age 62. Atlantic Coast obituaries mentioned that the judge was the father of Elisha Kent Kane, the recently deceased Arctic explorer; typically there was no reference to the judge's other sons. "Obituary. Death of Judge Kane," *New York Herald,* 23 February 1858, 5/3.

> for you against meeting in me one of the most insufferable of bores—with everything on hand to tell you—unable to tell anything well. Too hard a scuffle, Patty, for a man to have an eye to first and second positions, and the pattern of the paper hanging on the wall. But you and [brother] Johnny must both humour me, and remember that I shall miss Elisha to report to, who, I do not know why always used to listen to me so patiently.
>
> I hope you understood from my cipher letter to Father the manner in which the malice of my enemies at Saint Bernardino helped me so gloriously to run the gauntlet through the Mormon-Indian country of the Desert. I assure you that this was but one of half a hundred providences which seem to have on occasion specially interposed in my behalf. I seem to myself to have had a charmed life. And the strongest argument on which I base my more than hope that I shall yet win a peace is: what other less important purpose has such a stock of miracles been spent for? The Lord continue the mercy—I have never needed to shoot a poor copperskin [Indian] yet. I think I can always baffle, or intimidate, or ride away from them. And though it has been often pointed, I think I shall bring home your precious little rifle innocent of all shedding of blood.

One of the hallmarks of Thomas L. Kane's life was his fondness for entering a new setting with a flourish in attention-getting fashion, sometimes in alarming medical condition. Whether stress induced, psychosomatic, sympathy evoking, or simply coincidence, such behavior accompanied many of the major events of his life before and during the Civil War. In 1858 such was certainly the case with near-collapses upon his arrival in San Francisco, San Bernardino, and Utah's southern settlements. So, too, for Kane's entrance into Salt Lake City in the late afternoon gloom of 25 February. Although his traveling companion, Amasa Lyman, made no entry in his diary about Kane's physical condition, Kane later emended the 4 April memo that he had written to Pat Kane to give his brother (and a potential publisher) a far more alarming description of his health during the last leg of his trek to Salt Lake City: "Fatigue, what is termed sleeping with one eye open pretty well used me up as you may imagine, by the time I got to Salt Lake. This is an old story for myself, still it is the real drop curtain, but I hope that the good Mormons who turned in to give me a lift from the lower settlement[s] to Salt Lake city, will live to tell you how little chance they thought there was of my getting through. There was some shocking thing in the way of a [eye] hemorrhage that particularly distressed me."[53]

[53]Kane to Pat Kane, ca. summer 1858, "In Re Mormons" File, Thomas Leiper Kane Papers, APS.

As Tom Kane hurried to his evening meeting with Brigham Young on 25 February, Elizabeth Kane had already closed her journal entry for the day: "Oh my dear Tom, to think that yesterday, dear friend, our [Kane] father's body was laid in Laurel Hill [Cemetery]. Yesterday was horrible. None of the holy quiet of the farewell to his soul. All that makes death dreadful we had. Mother would see every one who came and detailed his sickness and death a dozen times. She is unnaturally cheerful I should think if they did not tell me it was the case when [her son] Willie died."[54] On the same day, almost four hundred miles north of Salt Lake City, the traumatized leaders of Fort Limhi, the Mormon mission and Nauvoo Legion outpost on Oregon's Salmon River, paused to count their dead and wounded, casualties of that morning's assault on them by Bannock and Northern Shoshone warriors.

---

[54]Elizabeth Kane Journal, 25 February 1858, Kane Family Papers, BYU.

Thomas L. Kane

Once in Salt Lake, Kane pursued his mission with a self-confidence and improvisation matching Young's, minus his religious fervor. In winning over Young and skeptical apostles, Kane strayed far beyond what the president would have sanctioned by apologizing on his behalf, committing to executive clemency, and permitting Brigham to read, if not shape, his presidential reports. Here began Kane's campaign to "sell" Young to the Buchanan administration and nation as a trustworthy leader beset by a warlike Mormon opposition. Kane is shown here photographed early in the Civil War as a lieutenant colonel of Pennsylvania volunteers, the "Bucktail Rifles." *Mathew Brady Collection courtesy of the Library of Congress.*

Chapter 8

"At Young's Very Gates"
Kane among the Mormons

I will say one thing more with regard to Osborne, he has pleaded with me on behalf of our common country for me not to chaw up the army which is out here; he wishes them to have the privilege of living. They are in our hands and government know it. What we shall do is not to be told yet; certain circumstances and time will tell.

Brigham Young, Sunday discourse, 28 February 1858

The Salt Lake City that Kane entered on 25 February 1858 was locked in winter, a community at war but trying to divert itself with sleigh rides, dances, theatrical performances, and religious meetings. With the knowledge that the army would surely reinforce the Utah Expedition once the snow melted, Utahns awaited the guidance of divine providence as revealed to their prophet, Brigham Young.

Among those in Salt Lake City attempting to pursue the normal rhythms of life was nineteen-year-old Joseph F. Smith, a son and nephew of the martyred Hyrum and Joseph Smith, a recent returnee from the Hawaiian Mission, a Nauvoo Legionnaire awaiting orders, and a future president of the LDS church. Smitten by the charms of a fifteen-year-old first cousin whom he barely knew, Smith was oblivious to the events unfolding around him, including the arrival of the mysterious Dr. Osborne.[1]

Beneath this prosaic surface, there were reminders that an armed confrontation with the U.S. government still threatened, with a need for the community to root out its backsliders and enemies. As Tom Kane began

[1]Smith to Levira Smith, 26 February 1858, Scott G. Kenney Collection, MS 0587, Special Collections, Marriott Library, University of Utah. They would marry in 1859.

his discussions with Brigham Young, elsewhere in town "several persons disguised as Indians entered Henry Jones' house and dragged him out of bed with a whore and castrated him by a square & close amputation."[2] One hundred miles to the east, a small, fifty-man detachment of Legionnaires monitored the Utah Expedition from frigid posts in the mountains, while Brigham Young pressed on with his intent to launch a spring offensive by completing the Standing Army of Israel.

I Come as an Ambassador: Kane Begins His Mediation

Precisely what Kane had in mind as he began his reunion with Brigham Young is unclear. Elizabeth Kane's later recollection of his intent sounds credible: "Tom's plan was to go in disguise to Utah by way of California, winter though it was, and to make his unexpected appearance at Young's very gates, relying upon his own mental force and Young's knowledge of the sincerity of his goodwill to the Mormons. He actually intended to turn a whole people's will, and make them ask for peace in the hour of their triumph."[3]

Apostle Amasa Lyman attended the meeting, perhaps accompanying the colonel from his comfortable guest quarters in William C. Staines's mansion. Whether Kane anticipated meeting with Brigham Young privately or in a group is also unclear. Lyman described their arrival in town and the session's beginning: "Reached Salt Lake City where about 4 P.M. This evening had an interview with the Governor, Col. Kane was present and had a kindly greeting with his old friends of '46, at which time he visited us at Council Bluffs."[4]

It is unknown whether at this meeting Lyman hung back—ceding the floor to Kane—or in some way briefed Brigham Young about the Ives Expedition and Major Blake's forecast of invasion from the Colorado River. If Lyman used this forum to report on southern events, the news would have impacted attendees' reaction to Kane's comments.

Historians differ as to how concerned Lyman was about what Blake had told him on 31 January. Lyman's biographer argues that he was remarkably relaxed about this encounter near the Mojave River, and that the tone of what he reported to Brigham Young would have been commensurately low key.

[2]Brooks, ed., *On the Mormon Frontier,* 27 February 1858, 2:653.

[3]Elizabeth D. W. Kane, "History of Kane [Pennsylvania]," I, chapter 3, 76.

[4]Amasa Lyman Diary, 25 February 1858, LDS Archives.

On the other hand, historian Melvin T. Smith describes Lyman as "greatly shaken by this supposed confirmation of the evil rumors they had been hearing." Clifford L. Stott, another historian, has argued that "on February 25 Lyman and Kane arrived from the south and went into conference with Brigham Young. Certainly Apostle Lyman informed Young of the gloomy picture in the south as painted by Major Blake. Lyman's revelation no doubt served to darken the already dismal scene and confirm earlier rumors and reports that had found their way to Salt Lake City."[5]

However Brigham Young received Amasa Lyman's report, it prompted him to delay for a few days his long-standing interest in finding oases of refuge near the unexplored "White Mountains" of Utah's western deserts. It is likely that Lyman advised Young to order a somewhat different reconnaissance—one to the Colorado River to understand better its potential as both a federal invasion route and a Mormon asset for settlement, building an alliance with the Mojaves, or escape. It was just such a survey that Lyman had urged on Colonel Dame when he and Kane had stopped overnight in Parowan four days earlier. Young ordered Lyman to return south to reconnoiter the Colorado. In Parowan Lieutenant Martineau recorded that "Amasa Lyman arrived from the north [on 19 March]. He is appointed our Military leader for the South. Our duty is to hold the South part of the Territory for the Saints."[6] With plans for Lyman's return to Parowan ordered, Young returned to his meeting with Kane and then to the task of organizing two exploring expeditions to the White Mountains.

If Amasa Lyman's description of the Kane-Young meeting on 25 February was terse, Wilford Woodruff's record was extensive, as one might expect from the LDS church's assistant historian.

KENNEY, ED., *WILFORD WOODRUFF'S JOURNAL*,
25 FEBRUARY 1858, 5:168–71.

> Governor Young Called a Council of the Presidency and Twelve at his house at 7 oclok when the following Persons were present: Presidents Brigham Young Heber C Kimball and Daniel H. Wells Of the Twelve Apostles Orson Hyde W. Woodruff John Taylor, A. Lyman C Rich, Also A[lbert] Carrington.
>
> At 8 oclok the Messenger was introduced to us By Joseph Angel Young [Brigham's son] as Dr Osborne which was Col T. L. Kane. He was vary formal

[5]Lyman, *Amasa Mason Lyman*, 260; Smith, "Colorado River Exploration and the Mormon War," 216, 221–22; Stott, *Search for Sanctuary*, 52.

[6]Godfrey and Martineau-McCarty, eds., *Uncommon Common Pioneer*, 19 March 1858, 144.

in his introduction. He was vary pale and worn down having travelled night and day. He was seated in an easy Chair. His arival was at 8 oclok.

He addressed us in the following language (though he had great difficulty in speaking): Govornor Young and Gentlemen I Come as an ambassador from the Cheif Executive of our Nation and am fully prepared and duly authorized to lay before you most fully and definately the feelings and views of the Citizens of our Common Country and of the feelings of the execative towards you relating to the present position of Officers of this territory and the armey of the United States now upon your Borders. And after giving you the most satisfactory evidences in relation to matters Concerning you now pending I shall then Call your attention and wish to enlist your sympathies in behalf of the poor soldiers who are now suffering in the cold & snows of the mountains and request you to render them aid and Comfort and to assist them to Come here and to bid them a Hearty welcome into your hospitable valley.

Governor Young may I be permitted to ask a private interview fr a few moments with you? Gentlemen please excuse my formality for a few moments.

They were about 30 minutes in secret session. They then returned to the room. Col Kane Then said that Capt Van Vleit made a good report about us [in the fall] and used an influence to have the Armey stop East of Bridger and had done a great deal in our behalf. . . . You have bourn your part manfully in this Contest. I was pleased to see how patiently the people took it.

Govornor Young asked how the Presidents [December] message [to Congress] was received. The Dr said as usual in his appointments he has been Cruelly impartial. So far he has made an excellent president. He has an Excellent Cabinate. They are more united and work together better than former Cabinets have done. President Young said I suppose they are united in putting down Utah. Col Kane said I think not. Buchanan made one Balk in the spanish affair and in the Black warrior affair.[7] The Canses [Kansas] affair is not setled as yet and I hope it may grow worse untill the people will take it in hand. . . .

Col Kane Said I wish you knew how much I feel at home. I hope I shall have the privilege of Breaking bread with these my friends. Gov Young said I want to take good care of you. . . . Col Kane said that I fear that I Can endure more than I could 10 years ago for I feel that my life dont pay and I feel like going away as soon as it is the will of God [to] take me.

President Young remarked I know to take this life as it is and as men make it it does not appear worth living in but I well tell you that when you see things as they are you will find life is worth preserving and blessings will follow our living in this life if we do right. Now if God should say I will

[7]A muddled reference to two controversial diplomatic incidents involving the United States, Cuba, and Spain that occurred during the Pierce administration, when Buchanan was U.S. minister to London.

> let you live in this world without any pain or sorrow we might feel life was worth living for but this is not in the economy [plan] of God. We have to partake of sorrow affliction and death and if we pass throug this affliction patiently and do right we shall have a greater reward in the world to come. . . . It is not in the power of the United States to destroy this people, for they are in the hands of God and so are we. And he will do with us as he pleases and if he does right God will preserve us. . . .
>
> He [Young] then said Brother Thomas the Lord sent you here and he will not let you die. No you Cannot die till your work is done. I want to have your name live with the Saints to all Eternity. You have done a great work and you will do a greater work still. We then parted and went to our homes.

What Kane and Young discussed during their half hour alone is important but murky. Only one firsthand account of this crucial conversation has surfaced. It was written by Kane, perhaps while in Salt Lake City, as an undated, untitled, one-page statement couched in the voice of Brigham Young and intended for an unspecified purpose. That Kane would draft such a document for use by another person would be consistent with his method of operation. Given this background and the fact that Young apparently never used this material, the key question is whether its content can be taken at face value. If the statement is accurate, it is understandable why Kane later refused to disclose to President Buchanan what he and Young had discussed during this private segment of their first meeting: "The particulars of our conversation upon this and on subsequent still more deeply interesting occasions, I defer communicating until favorable results certain of which I hope I am not over sanguine in anticipating privilege me to do so."[8] According to Kane, the following were Young's comments.

STATEMENT BY BRIGHAM YOUNG DESCRIBING HIS PRIVATE CONVERSATION WITH THOMAS L. KANE, 25 FEBRUARY 1858, "CONCERNING THE MORMONS" FILE, THOMAS LEIPER KANE PAPERS, APS.

> In the course of our conversation which I was requested by Col Kane to consider as strictly confidential and of which I only record the essential particulars, he admitted that the action of Government in relation to the affairs of Utah had been so precipitate as to be legitimately open to misconception and expressed his surprise at learning, as he said, for the first time, that no adequate explanation had been before offered of the intentions of the Administration in ordering the army to Utah, that I had received no

[8] Kane to Buchanan, 5 March 1858, Kane Family Papers, BYU.

> notification from Government that my official conduct in any respect was open to censure or to misconstruction—and that there had not even been transmitted me a notification that a successor had been appointed in my place and that I ~~was no longer~~ should no longer act as Governor of Utah Territory. Colonel Kane admitted that this was a grave omission and one that but for the habitual negligence of the officers of the Departments at Washington might justly be regarded as an act of injustice to the Mormon people and of personal contumely to myself. "But," he remarked ["]it ought never to be too late between persons of honor and good intentions to remedy a mere misunderstanding["] and begged me to believe and to accept his assurance of the fact that no disrespect had at any time been contemplated or intended me by the President of the United States. He then exhibited me the subjoined letter for my perusal.[9]
>
> The letter and further explanations from Colonel Kane received my due consideration. Though tardy I accepted them as the personal apology of Mr. Buchanan.[10]

There are several additional accounts of Brigham Young's discussions with Kane during February–March 1858, but it is unclear whether this material relates to the private session on the evening of 25 February or to subsequent meetings between the two men. Several of these documents appear here to convey the likely tone of the confidential conversation between Young and Kane four hours after Kane arrived in Salt Lake City.

Among the most significant of these undated fragmentary accounts was Young's postwar claim that "when Col Kane Came to visit us He tried to point out a line of Policy for me to persue but I told him I should not turn to the right or left or persue any Course ownly as God dictated me. I should do nothing ownly what was right and when he found that I would not be influenced ownly as the spirit of the Lord led me he felt discouraged & said he would not go to the armey. But He finally said if I would dictate he would execute."[11] If accurate, the comment Young attributed to Kane was a stunning description of their relationship; if not, it sheds light on the extent to which Young as well as Kane fell victim to overreaching.

---

[9]Here Kane apparently intended to but did not insert the text of one of Buchanan's 31 December letters to him.

[10]Two weeks after Kane left Utah to return home, Apostle Woodruff recorded: "While speaking of Col Kane President Young said Col Kane did say to President Buchannan [*sic*] that he owed Gov Young an apology for sending an army to Utah in the way he did and persuing the course he had towards the people of that territory and He should make that apology to Gov Young for President Buchannan and he was an agent sufficient to do it." Kenney, ed., *Wilford Woodruff's Journal*, 25 May 1858, 5:190.

[11]Kenney, ed., *Wilford Woodruff's Journal*, 15 August 1858, 5:208–209.

In another document, Kane described for Buchanan late winter conversations in which Mormons leaders expressed their greatest fears and he, in turn, responded with an amazing assurance of executive clemency unsupported by any known authorization by the president.

KANE TO BUCHANAN, CA. 15 MARCH 1858,
KANE FAMILY PAPERS, BYU.

The *(real)* fears of the more reasonable Mormons [were]—the *soldiers* and the *courts*—that they would have Illinois & Missouri over again with them. That the soldiers would be drunken, quarrelsome and licentious—and that the Judges would not punish them. That the Courts would issue process to all who sued for it, vexing the prominent men, with arrests & prosecutions without end, and that the soldiers would support them in this course. That with regard to the recent acts of treasonable . . . insubordination, the officer commanding the army of the U.S. here, would proclaim martial law, by which they would be punished summarily; or else that the Judges would approve the finding of Bills by grand juries summoned from their enemies alone, and try them with juries composed of other enemies, and finally, would call on the soldiers "to see every man hanged the Saints loved, or they chose to have a mind to."[12]

In reply to this I offered Young himself, and his immediate friends the assurance of pardon "for meritorious service to the U.S." on the strength of our interview confidentially communicated: to others I sought to prove the groundless character of such apprehensions.[13] (I had my own misgivings with respect to the questions of free admission to Bail, and Martial Law, and did not press on Mr. Young a Proclamation which I however went so far as to draught for him ["]enforcing on all who respect my Authority" &c, immediately to admit our forces.) I told them frankly that I could not promise them that Martial Law might not have been declared in Green River County, but said that I knew I could assure them how soon it would be at an end after the announcement of their submission and I pledged myself that

[12]In July 1857 General Harney had unsuccessfully sought the power to proclaim martial law in Utah and, in the fall, as the army crossed into the territory from Nebraska, junior officers debated the desirability of such an action.

[13]When Kane visited Buchanan in June 1858, he recorded that the president had confirmed that his (Kane's) powers of pardon while in Salt Lake City were identical to those granted in the spring of 1858 to Buchanan's peace commissioners, Lazarus W. Powell and Ben McCulloch. Historian Richard D. Poll seems to have accepted Kane's assertion at face value, but such a claim is counterintuitive given these factors: the absence of independent supporting documentation; Buchanan's extremely cautious operating style, especially in dealing with Kane during 1857; Kane's own comment in this same letter that while in Utah he was "without official position"; and the fact that neither Kane's wife nor father recorded discussion of such pardoning power when Tom returned home in late December to report on his meeting with Buchanan. Poll, "Thomas L. Kane and the Utah War," 123.

if I found a different state of things from that which I assured them of, that I would either send them word in terms to stay their hands from war no longer, or, (this in case of a less decided show of facts) cross the mountains again and place myself in their hands. This I did emphatically and upon my honor as a gentleman.

"Thomas L. Kane Notes," Kane Collection,
Beinecke Library, Yale University.

Here is his [Young's] language in continuation ~~verbal lit~~ as spoken on impulse: As a private individual I consider Mr. Buchanan an honorable good citizen, but in his public capacity his conduct has proved him both injudicious and hasty. I thought him a man of scrutiny, a man who knew a man when he had a man to deal with and not a man of straw. But his action respecting the affairs of Utah shows that he can act in blind conformity to the prejudices of others, if they are not to be believed his own—a thing unwise and unsafe in any statesman, but in the President of the United States both contracted and unjust.—I give you this example, taken down by me while I am writing in his room here—to show you how it differs from that which is currently reported and published of Young's speeches.

During the summer of 1858, after he had returned home from Utah, Kane developed for his brother Pat a seven-page narrative of how his discussions with Brigham Young had unfolded during the previous winter. Ill and worried about the growing public controversy over his Utah mission, Tom Kane wanted his brother to have a private explanation of his side of what he had done and with whom. Among other ambiguities is whether the Mormon positions that Kane described in this document were expressed on the evening of 25 February, later during this visit, or subsequently in the course of Kane's second sojourn in Salt Lake City during April–May 1858. With another brother, Elisha, and his father recently dead, and with his wife restive over his continuing involvement in Mormon affairs, Tom Kane was running out of people in whom he could confide.

Kane to Pat Kane, n.d. (ca. Summer 1858),
Untitled Ms., "In Re Mormons" File,
Thomas Leiper Kane Papers, aps.

You will want me to speak of public affairs. As I told the President, I am no believer in diplomacy if diplomacy means lying. I believe I displayed some talent in exhibiting to the Mormons, what was very clear to my own mind, that their interests and those of my other countrymen were inseparable. But my main strength lay in my character—in their knowledge of it, and the belief that I had not risked my life and dragged myself, half-dying in among them, to change it and betray them to their own ruin. I did a number of little things, such as apologizing to Brigham Young for a personal insult which I thought myself he had received, but the main performance of my embassy was that I gave Brigham Young and some of his best friends, my word of honor, and told others of them the same thing *upon the square,* that the President of the U.S. was not a liar.

Party lines were fully formed; battles were fought in the various [Mormon] quorums of which you must know nothing—(for to the outsiders, the Mormon church is a unit—more fools the members of it to say so). Young and his friends in a clearly ascertained majority, and he and I found it a short horse soon curried—to determine [while meeting] in my pretty little sleeping-room what were the practical measures to be taken. Why was not this the conclusion of the whole matter? The answer is, why is it not ended now, four months after? There were others beside the President and those whom he thin[k]s he commands at Washington, to drive off the track and keep from laying their infernal trains.

Young and the ~~other~~ very best men told me I should find a frightful state of feeling at Bridger. I asked them to let me invite the army in instantly. They said they could not, unless I saw the state of things there for myself, and then recommended them to receive my [military] fellow-citizens there. You may be sure I had no doubt of what I should do, and although I had hardly a doubt of Young's sincerity, and believed entirely that he had told me the truth in saying that he had stopped the Mormon movement against our troops, yet the moment of my triumph was achieved at Salt Lake, I was all haste to go over to our people. I had an additional motive prompting me to this however. I saw how near a tie the conservatives and destructives were, and I was afraid of some screw coming loose, and interfering with what every nerve in my body tingled to feel, was so great a result, and I told Young and our friends, I mean the patriotic men, that I would engage that they should have soon something from camp [Scott] that would give them a lift and corroborate their power. But to the Mormons at-large, I went very simply under this understanding; that they had my word of honor that if I found the state of things there, other than I had represented them to be when I carried my point with them, I would return to Salt Lake city and place myself a hostage in their hands, to be dealt with according to that which they should determine to be my deserts.

The conclusion of my writing to-night, which I have been urged to because I am sick and I feel a little anxious to get out such facts as will enable you to link my few papers together—I am glad, I say, to conclude my remarks for you, dear Patty, to whom I now speak more freely than to any other

> living person, that next to myself—this is modest—our country owes more to Brigham Young than to any other human being in our generation. The efforts he has made to save us, have perhaps before this, cost him his life.

The most intriguing part of this narrative for his brother was Kane's cryptic, atypical comment about wrongdoing on Young's part: "All we, like sheep, have gone astray. B. Young, painter and glazier also went astray at one time—but if not since a certain day last fall, at least since the 1st of March 1858, he has been laboring for his salvation upon his knees, without the honors of a noble Christian." Whether this was a reference to the Mountain Meadows massacre of the prior 11 September is impossible to determine.[14]

On 25 February Apostle George A. Smith was in Provo and so missed the hastily arranged session with Kane to which Brigham Young had invited the church's other available leaders. Upon returning to Salt Lake City, Smith caught up on the news and reported his reactions to Col. William H. Dame, the senior ecclesiastical and militia leader in southern Utah: "It turns out that Col Kane's message is an unofficial one, he designs our good & is a warm friend, but he wants us to spare the lives of the poor soldiers camping about Bridger. Mr. Buchanan would like us to feed them, and not destroy them until he can get sufficient reinforcements to them to destroy us. This is as near I can learn the design of the President of the United States. Bah!"[15] Whether other Mormon leaders shared Smith's skepticism is unknown, but Kane later went out of his way to spend time with this apostle, even sharing gossipy anecdotes with Smith about the sexual peccadilloes of early American leaders.[16]

To Avoid the Calamities of War: Kane Reports to Buchanan

Kane's own report to the president of the 25 February meeting took the form of two letters written on consecutive days a week after the session. During this interval Kane was able to process what had taken place that evening, as well as his subsequent thoughts and interactions with senior Mormon

[14]The significance of 1 March is also unclear. It may be linked to Kane's belief that on or about that date Young intervened to abort a major Mormon attack on the Utah Expedition, a perception foundational to Kane's argument that Young was the expedition's de facto protector.

[15]Smith to Dame, 3 February [March] 1858, William Horne Dame Papers, LDS Archives.

[16]Historian's Office Journal, 2 March 1858, LDS Archives.

leaders. For example, on 4 March Kane received from Wilford Woodruff a memo that the apostle described as "a lengthy communication to Col. T. L. Kane giving a reason of our hope and faith and the cause of our defending ourselves in these vallies of the mountains. It contained 6 pages of foolscap." It would be interesting to know how, if at all, Woodruff's arguments (now lost) entered into Kane's thinking and perhaps the comments he was drafting on the same day for James Buchanan.[17]

The 4–5 March timing of Kane's messages to the president was driven by the inflexible schedule by which the monthly westbound California mail departed Salt Lake City for the next steamer leaving San Pedro. Kane's need to write multiple letters rather one, and the grossly different tone in which he couched them reflected several factors: the byzantine circumstances under which he wrote; the volatility of the subject; and the near-paranoia about secrecy and mail interception that afflicted so many Utah War principals, especially him.

Kane to Buchanan, 4 and 5 March 1858, Kane Family Papers, BYU.

4 March

(private)

The hazard of entrusting letters to the mail here is so great, that I must confine my writing to that which is matter of notoriety [common knowledge]—at least in the circle with which I am at present associated. A communication of a more formal character [dated 5 March] will be posted along with this to your address.

I think that I hazard nothing in conveying you the gratifying intelligence that you will be rewarded for the humane efforts you have made to avoid the calamities of war. I have the highest authority here indeed for stating that my timely coming has prevented the effusion of blood, and contributed to strengthen the hands of those—and they are not few here—who seek to do good and whose patriotism is as elevated as any which labors elsewhere to confirm the bands of the Union. As regards the immediate emergency, if I were to say as I would like to, that the presentation of your autograph letter and message operated emphatically to prevent an impending movement hostile to our troops in Green river Co[unty], I might perhaps seem to detract from the merits of a gentleman, whom I am gratified to name as my friend, since I discover how much our country is indebted to him: I allude to Governor Young.

---

[17]Kenney, ed., *Wilford Woodruff's Journal,* 4 March 1858, 5:173.

From the commencement nearly of the unhappy difficulties between Utah and the United States, his commanding influence has been exercised, to assuage passion, to control imprudent zeal, and at all risks, either of his own person or that of others, to forbid and ensure a just condemnation for bloodshed. Not only last Autumn, when the Mormons were repeatedly (and I may conclude upon examination quite unnecessarily and unwisely) fired upon, but without remission since, it has been his care to protect our soldier from perils which he had better reason than others to know were menacing them.

It is scarcely the language of hyperbole to say that since the cold weather set in—there has not been an hour in which our army has not been in danger—though they have lived and slept in peace through the whole winter guarded by his arm. This is not a fact which I would state on Young's authority. Such is the violence of feeling among those opposed to the Administration, that they volunteer me evidence against themselves (upon a trial for High Treason), rather than miss an opportunity to vent their feelings of dissatisfaction at the restrain[t] imposed upon them [by Young].

To prevent Indian outbreak, also, I have reason to believe that Governor Y's influence has been directly exercised in favor of our army. Upon this head, however, I must remember that I am in possession of evidence derived solely from the Mormons themselves. Had I had the necessary time at my disposal, I could have well employed it in examining into the entire question of the relations of the Mormons with the Indian tribes around them. I confess I am not satisfied with regard to more than one matter which has been the subject of public discussion.

In my other letter, I have mentioned to you my intention of endeavoring to cross the Mountains if possible to communicate with Governor Cumming. He has it in his power to lend me assistance at this juncture with which I will hardly be able to dispense, and no effort of mine, believe me, shall be wanting to command success. (*Note*) But the snow is unusually deep upon a portion of the range of mountains which separates us, and my health has been somewhat impaired by my journey to this place, which was attended by a more than average share of adventure and fatigue. It is in contemplation of my inability to get through, that I commit this to the chances of the [Salt Lake] Post Office—to leave behind me to be placed among your private records my parting intimation of the true position and intentions of the mistaken [misunderstood] Brigham Young.

The last news from Bridger was highly favorable. Our troops were still in a state of good health and discipline, and such of their cattle as survived the storms of last fall were fat and heavy. The winter had proved an unusually open one, and the "range" for stock of all kinds excellent.[18]

---

[18]Kane's description of grazing conditions and the Utah Expedition's herds was highly inaccurate.

5 March

[On 25 February] I found the Governor surrounded by a large circle of friends and advisers—by whom I was more or less cordially received according to the character of my acquaintance with them—and said to him:

"Governor,

I have come as a citizen of our common country to bring you authentic information concerning the state of things near the seat of government as they affect the interests of Utah. I have it in my power to satisfy you fully of the present attitude of the people of the United States and the intentions of the Federal Executive towards you. This duly accomplished, I may turn you to think of our soldiers who are among the snows outside of these mountains. I might say I would intercede for them, invoking the memory of our former friendship and mutual confidence:—But I am persuaded that before our conversation reaches this point, your own patriotic impulses will move you; to take immediate measure to insure their safety, supply their wants, and bid them all a cordial welcome to your hospitable valley.

Governor Young, may I solicit the honor of a private interview?"

Governor Young retired with me agreeably to my invitation. The particulars of our conversation upon this and on subsequent still more deeply interesting occasions, I defer communicating until favorable results certain of which I hope I am not over sanguine in anticipating, privilege me to do so. As soon as the progress of affairs here may invite the step, I shall set out for Fort Bridger to communicate with Governor Cumming and our other friends there. Though my next opportunity of writing from this place therefore will be by the mail leaving for California Mar. 20 inst. I shall probably be unable to avail myself of it. The snow upon the mountains immediately East of the valley is stated to average 5 feet, and in places has the unusual depth of 25 feet for a considerable distance. But I confidently anticipate being able to send letters from *Bridger* home, across the Plains.

Aside from Kane's failure in early March to inform Buchanan that he had apologized on his behalf to Brigham Young, the strangest aspect of these documents is that they omitted disclosure of three stunning liberties taken by Kane and not admitted to Buchanan until mid-March, after he had reached Camp Scott: that the letters of 4 and 5 March had been written with Brigham Young's participation rather than as Kane's private and confidential views; that he had promised executive clemency to Brigham Young and his immediate associates; and that under certain circumstances he was considering giving Brigham Young what would be a tacit blessing to resume hostilities.

No record of the president's reaction to this material is included in James Buchanan's personal or official papers. Accordingly, historians are at sea in assessing the president's likely reaction to such bald manipulation and unsanctioned freelancing as well as the questions they raise. Had Buchanan known of all this, under what circumstances could he now accept at face value Kane's actions and recommendations? How credible was the notion—first floated at this time by Kane—that Utah was split by conflicting factions advocating war and peace, with Brigham Young leading a peace party while holding at bay unidentified leaders straining to attack the Utah Expedition? Was Brigham Young a misunderstood, valiant guardian of a supposedly vulnerable army, as Kane asserted, or did he play a different role?

Kane was a man confident that he could deal with all comers—even Indians—through quick wits and improvisation: "I can always baffle, or intimidate, or ride away from them."[19] How such a style would play out in dealings with Brigham Young and James Buchanan, accomplished manipulators in their own right, remains to be seen. Perhaps the most important thing to understand about Kane's distinctive operating style is that it was not a set of behaviors improvised during 1858 in Utah. All of its features—generosity, energy, theatrics, focus, wire-working, control urges, selective use of information, readiness to draft letters and press statements for other people, planting of anonymous stories in a wide range of newspapers, delusions of grandeur, and lapses into half truths if not mendacity—had been a part of his work on behalf of the Latter-day Saints since the beginning of their symbiotic relationship in 1846. If ascension to the presidency had permitted James Buchanan's penchant for deviousness and the oblique to emerge full blown in the Executive Mansion, Kane's Utah mission provided a new, bigger stage-in-the-wilderness upon which to exercise a set of skills already well developed elsewhere.[20]

While Kane wrote his dispatches for Buchanan, Brigham Young worked on his own correspondence for the next California mail. On 5 March he wrote similar letters to delegate Bernhisel in Washington and mission president Asa Calkin in Liverpool. To both men Young gave a perfunctory account of Kane's arrival as well as a single comment detached from the substance of the surrounding news: "We have our eyes on the Russian possessions." Whether this sentence signaled that Kane had indeed broached the subject

[19] Kane to Pat Kane, 4 April 1858, Kane Family Papers, BYU.

[20] See Grow and Walker, eds., *The Prophet and the Reformer.*

of a mass Mormon exodus to the Pacific Coast or elsewhere is unknown. There is reason to believe that Kane intended to discuss this subject, as he had told the president and his father in December. If so, Young's cryptic comment to Bernhisel and Calkin would indicate that perhaps at Kane's urging he was at least thinking about the matter, albeit fleetingly.[21]

Having finished these letters, Brigham Young turned to finalizing two military matters: regarrisoning the abandoned Mormon fort on Oregon Territory's Blackfoot River, and completing the organization of the Standing Army. With Kane then close at hand and participating in a running dialogue with Young, it is reasonable to assume that he became aware of these issues as Young dealt with them. If so, they would surely have added to Kane's apprehensions about the likelihood of a late winter or spring attack on the Utah Expedition.

The Nauvoo Legion had built the Blackfoot River post during the late summer of 1857 near the Salt Lake–Fort Limhi trail and the present community of Blackfoot, Idaho. It was unusual to construct such a remote settlement at a time when the Mormons were withdrawing from missions overseas and all of the LDS settlements in the United States. Fort Limhi and Blackfoot Mission, then, were exceptions to this roll up. David L. Bigler argues that both settlements were, in effect, part of an escape route for a possible Mormon exodus to what is now Montana's Bitterroot Valley or the Pacific Coast in the event the war went badly. When the Utah Expedition moved west of Fort Laramie in October, the Legion commander at Blackfoot, Col. Andrew Cunningham, argued that the post was vulnerable. With Brigham Young's acquiescence, Cunningham withdrew his settlers to Utah and abandoned the post, leaving the buildings intact rather than burning them as with Forts Bridger and Supply.[22] Five months later, with Kane virtually at his elbow, Brigham Young reversed this decision, and on 6 March asked William Miller to succeed Cunningham, reassemble the original settlers, and reactivate the Blackfoot River fort.[23]

On the same day that Young directed this move, he and General Wells announced the Standing Army's final organizational structure and the names of its senior line commanders and staff officers. Unlike the draft list prepared in haste on the evening of 18 January, this roster included officer assignments for men who, in the interim, had returned to Utah from missions in

[21] Young to Bernhisel and Calkin, 5 March 1858, LDS Archives. The matter of Kane's earlier discussion with Buchanan and Judge Kane about a Mormon exodus appears in *At Sword's Point, Part 1,* 501.

[22] Bigler, *Fort Limhi,* 266.

[23] Young to Miller, 6 March 1858, LDS Archives.

Hawaii and California—people who had not experienced the hardships of the Legion's fall campaign. For the first time, this directive specified recruiting quotas for each of Utah's military districts, the mechanism by which a brigade of a thousand cavalrymen was to move from concept to reality. Strangely, the implementing orders directed these arrangements without reference to the Standing Army they created. Presumably to avoid legal and financial liability, these orders directed the establishment of a private military force through the administrative apparatus (and protective cover) of a public territorial militia. Young and Wells issued these orders from the Nauvoo Legion's headquarters and signed them jointly as that force's governor-commander and lieutenant general, respectively. The designated military districts from which troops were to be levied were those created in 1857 for the revitalized Nauvoo Legion; the Standing Army's brigade, regiments, battalions, and companies were referred to opaquely as "details."[24]

To Kane, these preparations for the Standing Army of Israel and the reactivation of the Blackfoot River post would have signaled the extent to which Brigham Young had not yet accepted his advice to seek an accommodation with Albert Sidney Johnston or relinquish the governorship. From these circumstances may have flowed the jumbled diary entry that Kane made shortly before he left the territory in mid-May: "But in 4 weeks [*illegible*] s[ai]d they saved them from st[anding army?] The det[achment] from the regular organization was made in January. They were cavalry picked men to support the infantry. The assault upon the Army at Bridger *was under discussion* till about the middle of January. It was determined to make an end of them before supplies c[oul]d arrive—if the attitude [*illegible*] appeared to continue hostile."[25]

On the Town: Kane as Schmoozer

Although the initial meeting of 25 February was cordial, it was inconclusive. What, then, did Kane do during the following several weeks? There were subsequent private meetings with Brigham Young to discuss serious matters,

[24]Young and Wells, General Orders No. 1, Head Quarters, Nauvoo Legion, 6 March 1858. Holograph copies are in Newell K. Whitney Papers, L. Tom Perry Special Collections, Lee Library, Brigham Young University; and Yale Collection of Western Americana, Beinecke Library. A typed transcription is in Utah Militia Records, Series 2210, Utah State Archives and Records, Salt Lake City.

[25]Kane, "Diary III (1858)," undated, 77.

but also a substantial amount of socializing. Kane wrote dispatches, relaxed, tried to regain his health, and renewed friendships with those leaders whom he had first met in 1846 as the Mormons prepared to move west.

Notwithstanding George A. Smith's initial skepticism about Kane's mission, the warmth of a meeting between the two men on 2 March did much to transform Smith from a doubter ("Bah!") to a supporter, albeit one unwilling to send supplies to the Utah Expedition. By 4 March Apostle Smith was back in Provo to address a meeting of that community's Utah Stake at which he and Apostle Benson were positive about Kane.

MINUTES OF MEETING OF 4 MARCH 1858, UTAH STAKE, EDYTH ROMNEY TRANSCRIPTION, MS 2737, 774–76, LDS ARCHIVES.

Prest Geo A Smith said the people were anxious to here something from the dispatch from the Prest of the U.S. which is said to have pass'd through the Settlements. Col Kane came from Washington on his own recources & on his own responsibilities he came here to help his old friend Prest Buchanan out of a hobble, he has come here no doubt to do us good—he is our friend & has always been. He is going over to see the [U.S.] Troops [at Fort Bridger]—the Col weighs 104 lbs. Dr Bernhisel has taken his seat in Congress without any opposition—from all the News from the States shows that the most of the people are our bitter enemies—we understand from Col Kane that if this War is prosecuted the army out here must be Sacrificed.[26]

Elder Ezra T Benson said he was glad to hear the report of Bro Geo A Smith, it seems that the report is favorable—at all events it looks as if their was a God in Israel—I met Col Kane at Payson [Utah] on my Journey South I had an interview with him he trusted he had come to do us good, but I think he will find himself between two fires for it is as much as our Elders can do to stand [still], with all the faith they can muster—but if God has raised up a man to do us good I am glad of it—I am willing that God should rule—I belive that the little Col. has been blest with a portion of the Spirit of God for truly he has been blest & I felt to bless him inasmuch as he had come here to do us good. But I do not feel verry well disposed towards Old Buch. . . . I went to see [Ute chief] Arropeen & heard him preach[27] & if he ever was right he is right now—Some of my men [he said] are leaving me & are going to the American Camp [at Bridger] they are giving them Guns & ammunition & Blankets but they do not give them any bread Aropeen feels

[26]To the contrary, in the U.S. House of Representatives there was prolonged debate in January as to whether Delegate Bernhisel should be permitted to take his seat in view of Utah's conflict with the government. The "sacrificed" phrase reflected Kane's fear that the Utah Expedition was at the Nauvoo Legion's mercy.

[27]Arapeen had been baptized a Latter-day Saint.

first rate I will fight for the Mormons for I agreed to. I want Bro B[r]igham to give me a Mormon wife[28] & some tobacco & then he would be comfortable. Arapeen says he ask'd the Lord if we was agoing to have a fight this summer & the God he serves tells him that we shall have peace so he says we can go ahead & raise grain—Ev[er]y weapon that is raised against Mount Zion shall not prosper.

Bro Geo A Smith said he was [only] a Citizen here, But I feel to talk a little I want to give you my testimony concerning Bro Bensons remarks Col. Kane is a friend to this people—he used an influence with his father who is Judge of the [U.S.] D[istrict] Court of [Eastern] Pa & the principle supporter of Buchanan & Col. Kane wrote to Gov Young by the last Mail [of 1857] & wrote to him that he had given up all hopes of making anything of Buchanan—for says he, he had rather give up an old tried friend for some down East Editors[29]—Mr Buchanan informed Col Kane that no information had been given from the [State or War] Department, to this Territory in relation to an army coming here. They begin to realize that to support an army in U.T. is becoming a matter of Dollars & Cts—Col Kane has been inspird to come out here to do us good—& I believe that he will. Prest Young has predicted, that the [confrontational] course we was taking would do more towards preaching Mormonism than ever has been before—for the Largest papers in the U.S. are now publishing our Sermons, at full length without comments. The great hobby [horse] has been about polygamy—& they cannot bring anything to bear against that[30]—The finest Army ever fitted out—came against us but if the [government] send another we will make them go into Winter qua[r]ters further back[31]—We are in the midst of a Vast Desert—surround[ed] by Mountains—While all of the Nations of the earth are at war we will be at peace I pray that we may be enabled to overcome the world & live our religion. Amen.

In addition to cordial, even frivolous, sessions in Salt Lake City, Kane presumably attended the Sunday religious service on 28 February during which President Young touched on his visit in highly opaque fashion. From these remarks Kane learned what Young was willing to say publicly about the purpose and prospects of his mission. Young went out of his way to discourage hope that the Utah War was over.

---

[28]Brigham Young's advice to Anglo Mormon missionaries among the tribes in the Green River district and at Fort Limhi was that they should take Indian wives, if so inclined. This counsel resulted in Indian demands for reciprocity.

[29]*At Sword's Point, Part 1*, 135.

[30]There was then no federal statute barring polygamy.

[31]Perhaps a reference to Mormon plans for a spring offensive as far east as Fort Laramie.

Van Wagoner, ed., *Complete Discourses of Brigham Young*, 28 February 1858, 5:1408–11.

I apprehend, and I understand that the cause of the crowd here at the early hour today is that they are expecting, and are anxious to hear some news. If you will be patient, I will give you the news, all that we have from the outside of the cup, or this platter.

It is true our mail facilities are very scanty. There has a rumor gone through the town and the country that there is a gentleman come here on business, but what that business is, is unknown to the people; it is unknown to me at present. But as for it being of much interest to you or to me is a matter that time must determine. At the present I can say it is of no moment to me. This person or gentleman who has come here under the name of Dr. Osborne makes us a visit on his own responsibility, at his own expense, to see us, to learn us, and peradventure he may have an opportunity of presenting our case before our Great Republic, in a different attitude than he could have done if he had not paid us a visit. The result of his visit is in the future.

Many may be led to inquire is this gentleman sent by the government? Has he come to say that our government are willing to apologize and withdraw their armies? He has no such errand. Has he come to say we are in the wrong and they in the right? He has no such word for us. Has he come to say that the government have failed in their attempts and that we should push forward to our injury or the injury of the honest? He has no such errand, but calculates that they shall know the truth; consequently if you can understand my words, and get my ideas that the errand of this gentleman is of no particular moment to you or to me, I am satisfied.

You wish to know what the feelings of our government are. He does not know any more than you and I knew long ago. This gentleman, as far as he is concerned we do not care, this is not the object, but to knowing the particular object of the people and the government towards us, we know better than any man upon the earth.

If the brethren and sisters will be satisfied with these few remarks with regard to our Stranger, I am satisfied. Still there are a great many questions that if the people had the opportunity, they would doubtless ask them, but I have told you all that concerns us at present.

This gentleman will visit the army, and will return this way, and go home by California. What the result of his visit to them will be we shall learn. What the result of his visit here will be must appear at a future time.

I will say one thing more with regard to Osborne, he has pleaded with me on behalf of our common country for me not to chaw up the army which is out here; he wishes them to have the privilege of living. They are in our hands and government know it. What we shall do is not to be told yet; certain circumstances and time will tell.

Meanwhile, Kane continued discussions with Young, who facilitated their private sessions by insisting that Kane move from the Staines mansion for a few days to stay with him in the Lion House.[32] Some of what the two men discussed focused on non-controversial matters of common interest, while other subjects were more sensitive. There is no indication that Kane probed the Mountain Meadows massacre, reports of which had reached Philadelphia by mid-November and with which southern California was awash when Kane passed through nearly three months later. What Kane heard or observed as Amasa Lyman guided him through the area of Mountain Meadows in February is unknown. On the eve of his departure from Utah in mid-May 1858, Kane recorded in the last of his Utah diaries a nightmare: "[Sk]eleton dream in which I pushed past the bones of the one that had the black blue [clothing?]." Immediately following this cryptic diary entry, he wrote two phrases that one could interpret as questions relevant to accountability for the massacre: "Were there no white men at the killing[?] The Indian there [by] himself[?]"[33]

Even if Kane did not raise the subject of the massacre, Brigham Young must have been anxious about it, knowing the likely legal jeopardy that lay ahead once the army arrived. Possibly for this reason, Kane's 4 March report to the president, drafted in some way with Young's involvement, went out of its way to describe him as a restraining influence on the tribes.

In reporting all of this to the president once he reached Fort Bridger, Kane again advanced the notion that Young was a misunderstood leader with whom Buchanan (through him) could work. The vehicle for illustrating the so-called risks that Young was running with his own people to help the army was a revisiting of the salt incident of late November 1857.[34] On 25 February,

---

[32]After nearly two months of rough traveling, Kane relished his accommodations in Salt Lake City, telling his brother Pat, "My friends in Salt Lake city were hospitality itself to me. I was boarded with a Mr. William Staines, who kept the Globe Restaurant and Coffee house, but who has become a fine character for abuse with the newspaper letter-writers since I asked of him the favor of receiving Governor Cumming also. But when things were got into shape Brigham Young took me to his own house, and there I really did know what comfort and good living were." Kane to Pat Kane, ca. summer 1858, untitled ms., "In Re Mormons" File, Thomas Leiper Kane Papers, APS.

[33]Kane, "Diary III (1858)," undated, 76–77.

[34]A week after the Utah Expedition had gone into winter quarters, Brigham Young sent eight hundred pounds of salt to Albert Sidney Johnston, whose troops badly needed this item. Much to the disgust of the frostbitten Mormon packers who had delivered this load, Johnston rejected the proffer. He did so with a curt message that he did not accept gifts from rebels and that the bearers of future such gestures would be treated as intruders. After the packers abandoned their load in the snow outside *(continued)*

William C. Staines and His Salt Lake Mansion

The house, construction of which was started in 1855, was owned in 1858 by English convert Staines, a talented horticulturist and Brigham Young's gardener as well as territorial librarian. Young used the mansion to lodge prominent visitors, including Kane and soon thereafter Governor and Mrs. Cumming. During April–June 1858 Staines and Mormon agents monitoring his house reported to Young on Cumming's personal habits and private correspondence, as well as his interviews with disaffected Mormon visitors. *Image of Staines and house when later known as Devereaux Mansion, courtesy of Utah State Historical Society.*

as Kane entered Salt Lake City, Sam Houston was criticizing Albert Sidney Johnston on the floor of the U.S. Senate for his role in this affair. Subsequently, perhaps after reading Kane's dispatch, the president told delegate Bernhisel that "Colonel Johnston should not have sent the salt back."[35]

Kane to Buchanan, ca. 15 March 1858, Kane Family Papers, byu.

I remained a day and a half longer, after they [the dispatches of 4–5 March] were written, the intimate of Young's mansion, during which I was pleased to observe, as I believed the effects which even so guarded a committal had upon the minds of the Ex-Governor and his circle of intimates. Unless the most consummate and astute of hypocrites, they were familiarising themselves with the thoughts of Peace. The Pacific Railroad—a project of my own for artesian wells at certain points along the Southern Desert route to both the Tejon & Cajon Passes, &c., a great Express Mail Contract for carrying the mails from Independence to S. Francisco in 26 days:—such seemed to be the points to which their conversation most profitably and easily turned. Mr. Young's remarks to me grew additionally frank and confidential, and it seemed to me, more independent [free] of the fear that I would misconstrue them myself or misrepresent them to others.[36]

He volunteered to ask me if I would not like some letter in his handwriting "before going over to some of your people in the [army's] Camp"—some writing of authority from me yourself."

The evening [before I departed for Bridger and] I left the house (I *think* it was) he spoke out for the first time on a matter which I had not touched upon. He confessed to me that he had regarded the "sending that salt" in the light of an overture. "Wasn't that to be taken as a waiver of my [defiant] position expressed to Van Vliet [in September]? Wasn't it so represented here by those who opposed my doing it? Hadn't I a right to think it would be a

---

Johnston's encampment, entrepreneurial Indians salvaged it and reaped a windfall selling it to his troops. The story of the incident circulated widely in Utah as emblematic of army hostility. Once newspaper correspondents at Bridger filed dispatches describing the incident, it became a minor cause célèbre, with some people supporting Johnston's decision, while others criticized it as a missed opportunity to open a relationship with Brigham Young. Because of time lags, Kane would not have been aware of this incident until he arrived in Salt Lake City. For the Mormon side of this story, see Young and Wells to Johnston, 26 and 30 November 1857, 2–5, "Utah Expedition," House Exec. Doc. 71, 110–11. The army version appears in Porter Diary, 2 December 1857, Porter Papers, LC. As late as 1862, at least one group of Mormon travelers crossing the plains still talked about Albert Sidney Johnston's rejection of Mormon salt. Homer Duncan to Young, 22 August 1862, LDS Archives.

[35]Bernhisel to Young, Memorandum, June 1859, LDS Archives.

[36]Behavioral scientists of the twenty-first century would argue that highly sensitive discussions, among even old friends such as Young and Kane, would begin with neutral or non-threatening subjects such as a Pacific railroad and only then would progress to more volatile, less safe topics.

lead to my sending in other supplies, and the inter-change of good offices and feelings? What am I to do?" he said. "How much am I to submit to be railed at all round?" After this, I remember he broke out into a tirade of the most unquestionable sincerity. "And how was it—*it* received? How was the men, the man with the bad frost-bite just the same—the men who had lugged it [the salt] all that way through the snow received? Was it *gentlemen* [who] told them to turn about and go back—told them if they once showed their faces again they would be shot?—*Gentlemen,* don't tell me that! What was said about that by some not a hundred miles from here?[37] I know well enough what was said." Etc. Etc.

The same night [8 March] he escorted me to my [Staines] boarding house and bade me Goodnight and Godspeed with an effusion that was deeply touching.

Backdrop for Kane's Departure: Attack at Fort Limhi

While Young and Kane met for the last time before Kane's departure for Fort Bridger, news of an Indian attack on Fort Limhi 380 miles to the north arrived in Salt Lake City.[38] Accompanying word of the assault by a party of about two hundred Bannocks and Northern Shoshones was the Mormon casualty list: two dead (George McBride and James T. Miller), three (later revised to five) wounded, and a loss of approximately 250 head of cattle and horses. There was also speculation, originating with Limhi's settlers, that in some way, perhaps through mountaineer allies, Ben Ficklin's detachment from Fort Bridger and the Utah Expedition had provoked, if not instigated, the attack.

The message that couriers Ezra Barnard and Baldwin ("Baldy") Watts brought out of Fort Limhi at great risk was in the form of a long letter

[37]In his retained copy of this letter, Kane inserted here a cryptic annotation: "Those who were opposed to sending the salt whispered 'What did Brigham send that salt all the way up to the Mts. for?' 'You goose—to put in the snow to help to make it freeze. I think it was a heap though for one man's [frostbitten] heel and toes.'"

[38]Reasons for the raid were complex and the result of forces at work for several months, but with a Utah War catalyst. The mission on the Salmon River was highly vulnerable because of its dangerous location at the crossroads of a variety of warring tribes competing for natural resources. Although the Latter-day Saints worked to maintain a position of even-handedness among the Bannocks, Northern Shoshones, Nez Perce, Flatheads, and Pend d'Oreille, the Bannocks perceived a Mormon partiality for one or more of their tribal enemies. Also at work was Indian resentment over the missionaries' practice of shipping large quantities of salmon to Utah, a loss of a food source that angered all of the tribes. Into this volatile environment arrived Ben Ficklin and his small party of civilian stock-buyers from Fort Bridger.

from Fort Limhi's mission president and Nauvoo Legion commander, Col. Thomas L. Smith, the leader whom Brigham Young had visited during his April–May 1857 trek to Oregon's Salmon River country. After describing at length the history of Indian relations at the mission and the details of the 25 February raid, Smith concluded:

> We Consider ourselves Safe while we are in the fort but Cant Get out to farm any the Indians are watching every Movement we make & I dont Consider it safe for to leave the fort with the teams until some assistance Can be rendered us, either to Go or Stay as You think best, but I think it is of no use to try to maintain this place with the force we have here at the present. Powel [John W. Powell] a Mountaineer was with the Indians and helped them to drive off the Cattle, & from every Circumstance that we are acquainted with, this whole affair has ben Concocted last Summer at Soda Springs between the Mountaineers & Indians. In Conclusion I feel to say that we have tried to Carry out all the Councils that has been give us by you and have at all times when we have had a Chance, talked to them [Indians] and Councilled them how to act and have tried all reasonable terms to Get wives from amongst them & have tried to live as faithful as we Could, & to all appearance there has not been as much unity heretofore on the Mission as there has been during this winter past.[39]

Brigham Young's immediate response was a decision to close down Fort Limhi in orderly fashion and to evacuate its settlers to Utah with an escort from the Standing Army.[40]

Kane was not party to any of these discussions and was oblivious to what had happened in Oregon Territory until after Young had dropped him off at the Staines mansion. There Kane first heard discussion of what he initially viewed as a relatively minor affray. Upon reaching Fort Bridger, Kane collected his thoughts, evaluated what he heard from Cumming and other camp sources, and reported to President Buchanan what he knew of the Fort Limhi affair, including a brief allusion to Mormon speculation of army involvement. Whether Kane was yet aware of Ben Ficklin's December mission to the Flatheads, who were neighbors of the Mormon mission, and Dr. Garland Hurt's January trek in the opposite direction, to winter with the Uintah tribe, is unknown. Kane did not say so in his report to the

---

[39]Smith to Young, 28 February 1858, LDS Archives. During his spring 1857 visit, Brigham Young had advised the missionaries to marry into the local tribes as he had done with Mormons called to Utah's Green River region near Fort Supply.

[40]Young to Smith, 8 March 1858, ibid.; Bigler, *Fort Limhi*, 229–31, 265–66.

president, but Albert Sidney Johnston's hands were not entirely clean with respect to Indian relations.

Kane to Buchanan, ca. 15 March 1858,
Kane Family Papers, BYU.

> Arrived at my boardinghouse where I had a number of visitors at once, I saw that something had transpired which occasioned astir in the community, and soon learned that news had been received of a massacre of the Saints at Salmon River. It was a small affair, I fancy, since I could only obtain the names of two, ("Brothers McBride & Miller") as killed, & three others wounded, but of course it was exaggerated out of its true proportions and by the excited attributed, of course, to the United States.
>
> Brigham Young called upon me the next day to see me off according to promise. I thought his manner dry and he alluded to the matter too tersely to please me. After this during my progress through the Salt Lake Valley to Ogden, and in fact until I left behind me the last Mormon settlement, it was "Salmon River" here, "Salmon River" there to such an extent—men and women all wishing to regard it in the light of a Wyoming, or Miss Jane McCrea murder, that I several times questioned myself if his views were perhaps affected somewhat by the popular excitement.[41]

Notwithstanding these mid-March comments by Kane, as he and his escort had cantered out of Salt Lake City a week earlier, Kane was not yet fully focused on the implications of what had unfolded at Fort Limhi.[42] Until the party began to ascend the Weber River, the weather was good, and, judging by the fragmentary impressions jotted in his trail diary, Kane's mood was almost light hearted: "Leaving the city where the children [were] playing and householders laying out their gardens, and mill wheels turning—the women hanging out clothes still [spoke?] to all the others within doors. Blacks[miths] came forth and received our retinue. Then we came to the supply [?] country where men [were] ploughing [*blank*]. I enjoyed the holiday freedom of sunshine and peace."[43]

[41]These were references to famous Indian massacres of the Revolutionary War involving British provocateurs. Wyoming refers to a valley in Kane's native Pennsylvania after which the new territory to Utah's northwest would be named in 1868.

[42]There has been recent and thorough analysis of the brief Mormon sojourn at Fort Limhi during 1855–58 and the Utah War significance of its termination. Accordingly, this study does not rehash the details of the raid here. Bigler, *Fort Limhi*; Bigler, "Mormon Missionaries, the Utah War, and the 1858 Raid on Fort Limhi," 30–43; Hartley, "Dangerous Outpost," 135–62.

[43]Thomas L. Kane, "Diary II (1858)," 3, ca. 8 March 1858, Thomas Leiper Kane Papers, Special Collections, Stanford University Libraries. Unless otherwise noted, quotations from this document (and citations) are from a typed transcription of it contained on a microfilm copy available at LDS Archives.

Among the ambiguities surrounding the Fort Limhi attack, what is clear is that news of the incident galvanized Brigham Young's willingness to deal differently with Albert Sidney Johnston. Within hours of Kane's departure for Fort Bridger with an escort of Mormon frontiersmen, Young sent couriers after him with a remarkable note addressed to Kane but intended for Colonel Johnston. In effect, Young proffered huge quantities of flour and beef cattle to the Utah Expedition. Forgotten was the two-day-old completion of the Standing Army as a powerful offensive force; swept aside was the grudge over November's salt incident; newly evident was the influence of Thomas L. Kane's humanitarian advice.[44] Accompanying Brigham Young's apparent willingness to try Kane's way was his resolve to run whatever risk was implicit in George A. Smith's skeptical initial assessment of Kane's mission.

Young to Kane, 9 March 1858, LDS Archives.

We have just learned through the southern Indians that the troops are very destitute of provisions.[45]

Mr [William] Gerrish, a Merchant [of Gilbert & Gerrish] formerly of this place and who is now supposed to be detained in Col. Johnson's camp has quite a herd of cattle here and for which he would doubtless, like a market.[46] We know of none that would be equal to the Army of the United States now encamped within our borders, we have therefore concluded to send this herd consisting of near 200 head of cattle, a portion of which are tolerable good beef. In addition to the foregoing we shall send out fifteen or twenty thousand pounds of flour to the Army to which they will be made perfectly welcome or pay for just as they choose, all of which will be forwarded in a few days so soon as the necessary arrangements can be made & the snow will admit. If after your arrival you learn that Col. Johnson will not receive the flour, we will be obliged if you will be at the trouble of communicating the fact to those who attend you, that we may be saved the trouble.

I send this by my son Jos. A. and George S Kingham. Trusting that you are rapidly regaining your health, and that success may attend you,

[44]In much the same vein, Brigham Young simultaneously issued orders to Fort Limhi's rescuers to extend gifts of cattle to the Indians who had attacked the mission: "In reflecting upon your present difficulties with the Indians, we have considered it wisdom for you to avoid as much as possible having any difficulty with them even at the sacrifice of the [live]stock in their possession. We would prefer for you to say to the Indians if they have not got enough of the Mormon's cattle to come and get some more." Young to Cols. Cunningham and Smith, 10 March 1858, LDS Archives; Bigler, *Fort Limhi*, 267.

[45]No such report has surfaced. Indians along the Colorado River and eventually southern Utah may have been aware that the Ives Expedition was ill provisioned but not that the army at Camp Scott was hungry.

[46]When Johnston later read the letter he was offended by the word detained. Gerrish's firm was sutler to one of the Utah Expedition's regiments.

Kane described his reaction to this unexpected turn of events to the president while continuing to merchandise to Buchanan the notion of a war-peace split in Utah: "It was with great gratification therefore that as I was leaving one of my camping places about 45 miles from Gr. Salt Lake City, I saw two horsemen come up who had been riding all night, and who, dismounting from their horses (which had been badly hurt by falls on the ice) gave me the letter which I copy. My own opinion was then, and still is: that Young intended by this note to say: 'Go on. Things have not changed. I am still strong enough and confident enough of my power to wish and work for peace.' I delighted to receive it. I send [*sic*] him by his own son as encouraging an answer as I could frame."[47]

Upon receipt of Young's letter, Kane gave Young's son an oral reply filled with more verve than what he later reported to Buchanan. As with most of the entries Kane made in his field diary for this period, the one on this subject is disjointed and open to varying interpretations, although Kane's relief at thus hearing from Young is evident: "[I am] gratified especially at this juncture—such a notice of (Christian) intelligence coming from such a source, Brigham to rest assured that any grounds for his more serious conclusions must be based upon the self m authorized unauthorized indisgression [indiscretion] of our zealous subordinate agents—Said to him to say to his Father—what his reply had been to my question—was there no doubt whatever that [*blank*] evidence could be adduced in support of every one of his statements and that thereupon I had said to him that he furnished me an important reason for daring to return to the [Great] Basin. That I cd. not promise him to do so, circumstances being beyond my control—but that I wd. Make every effort to do all consistent with [*blank*]." Kane then recorded giving Joseph Young an assurance that he "wd. if possible repair to Salmon R[iver] . . . before departing home," a tantalizing commitment perhaps indicating that Kane was contemplating some sort of fact-finding side trip to Fort Limhi to probe and take east his assessment of the accuracy of Mormon allegations that the attack had been instigated by presumed army agents or allies like mountaineer John W. Powell.[48]

Although the news from Fort Limhi prompted Brigham Young to offer food, if not an olive branch, to the Utah Expedition, it also motivated him

[47]Kane to Buchanan, ca. 15 March 1858, Kane Family Papers, BYU.

[48]Thomas L. Kane," Diary II (1858)," 4, ca. 9 March 1858.

to complete that part of the Sebastopol plan featuring a fighting retreat to as-yet-undiscovered safe havens. This was the thrust briefly subordinated to the launch of Apostle Lyman's reconnaissance of the Colorado River. Having sent Lyman south, dispatched Colonel Cunningham's Standing Army detachment to relieve Fort Limhi, and ordered his son to intercept Kane before he reached Fort Bridger, Young then summoned Colonel Dame from Parowan and ordered him to lead what became known as the White Mountain Expedition. The news that the colonel's adjutant recorded upon his return from Salt Lake City was that "a [sixty-man] Company is to be sent to the desert, to explore for a place of refuge for the Saints. They are to go to the white or Lost Mountains. . . . We are to take each, a horse, 150 lbs flour, meat, seeds, tools &c including one bushel of seed wheat each. I feel thankful to be considered worthy to fill such an important mission . . . those who are called for the desert all spoke, giving their testimony for the gospel, myself one among the number."[49]

While tending to these arrangements, Young took steps to shore up his local tribal relationships, including that with Ben Simonds, the ubiquitous, opportunistic Delaware then camped near the mouth of Weber River.[50] Still styling himself as Utah's governor, Young attempted to encourage at least neutrality among Simonds's eclectic band and that of his Indian ally, Little Soldier. Shocked by the news of Indian hostilities to his far north, Young wanted to stabilize his relationship with the tribal bands wintering near the crucial Mormon defenses in Echo Canyon.

---

[49]Godfrey and Martineau-McCarty, eds., *Uncommon Common Pioneer,* 10 March and 15, 18 April 1858, 144–46. Lieutenant Martineau was free to accompany Colonel Dame, having been released from his earlier detail with Amasa Lyman's Colorado River party because of his lack of pack animals. One senses a preference by Martineau for serving under Dame, his Legion superior and fellow-townsman, rather than with San Bernardino leader Lyman, notwithstanding his higher church rank.

[50]During the war army officers as well as Mormons harbored suspicions about Simonds's motives and loyalty as he glided ghostlike between both camps to dispense intelligence, sell food, or seek economic assistance. Shortly after arriving at Fort Bridger, Major Porter recorded that Simonds "saw Brigham Young and told him all he knew of this army, which was that we were throwing something up around Bridger's Fort. Of course he (B.S.) told more,—but he is as cunning as a Mormon if he is not one. He *says* he is going for his family. He said the same before but he lied and is lying now." Six months later Porter's Legion counterpart, General Ferguson, perceived that Ben was playing a double game in supplying the army with Mormon produce as it prepared to move toward the Salt Lake Valley. After sarcastically describing the movement toward Bridger of "Simons own August person" and five wagons loaded with flour and bacon, he concluded, "I am afraid General [Wells], Ben is but a tool." Porter Diary, 7 December 1857, 6, Porter Papers, LC; Ferguson to Wells. 3 June 1858, LDS Archives.

Young to Simonds, 10 March 1858, lds Archives.

I received your letter of March 7th and appreciate the kind and friendly feelings you entertain towards me and the people over whom through the blessings of the Almighty God I am called to preside. Had my health permitted me it would have pleased me much to have seen you during your last visit to this City, but I did not know you were here till you were gone away. I should be glad to see you whenever you come.

Be assured that I am your sincere and undeviating friend, and the friend of your people and of all mankind. It is my desire to retain your friendship and that of all men who wish to do right. We expect to live and share with you a long time the free pure air of the tall mountains of our native land, and as we have ever done making war on none only defending ourselves against those who seek to trample on the rights and liberties that are the sacred heritage of all who dwell upon this land. You know that I am your people's friend, and would be glad to see them prosperous and happy, and dwell in peace among themselves and their neighbor nations. I am glad to learn that under your counsel they incline to be peaceable and honest. You do well to discourage dishonest men from seeking shelter in your camp. The enemies of this people can never be your friends. The same influence would seek to lay waste our homes and rob us of our freedom, would desolate your camp and enslave or exterminate your people. Present my love and assurance and unshaken friendship to Little Solder and the brave men of your camp; to all who have an open honest heart and love to be honorable and good. May you and they live long and become great and powerful in goodness, and dwell in peace with us in our mountain homes, and the blessings of the Great Wise God, the God of our fathers be upon you forever.

Chapter 9

"Remedy Worse Than the Disease"

Raising Regulars, Volunteers, and Sam Houston

Do as the Indians do, they take a bow and arrow, a Lariat, a Blanket and a Breech-clout, and they expect to get what they need. We want the Boys to go. Go naked and barefoot, then you are ready to fight, to run or do anything else, and you ask no odds of their enemies.

Brigham Young, Sunday discourse, 28 February 1858

Would regiments of Californians, Texans and Missourians be sent here? Would not such a remedy be worse than the disease?

Capt. John W. Phelps to Rep. John Hickman, 24 October 1857

As Thomas L. Kane tried to convince President Buchanan that Brigham Young was his army's ultimate guardian, Young accelerated efforts to field what potentially was the Utah Expedition's most formidable opponent, the Standing Army of Israel. Yet even for an autocrat, creating such a force was a hard sell in a hardscrabble territory already hard pressed to sustain the Nauvoo Legion.

The rest of the United States was alive with the grassroots formation of paramilitary units ranging in size from detachments to regiments. Once elected, their officers pressed for recognition by state governors, Secretary Floyd, and even Buchanan. Hard economic times, a national preoccupation with filibustering, and anti-Mormonism unleashed a tsunami of volunteerism. Even more of a driver was Buchanan's failure to specify whether the four new regiments were to be regulars or state-affiliated volunteers, an ambiguity that stimulated local-level hopes for military rank, payrolls, and contracting boodle. Among those seeking a place at the head of any new volunteer regiments were former and active officers who were to be among the most able of Civil War generals.

In the midst of these activities to reinforce the Utah Expedition and its Mormon adversaries, an unexpected ally of Brigham Young rose up—U.S. senator Sam Houston of Texas. He would be of more help to the Mormon cause than the entire Standing Army, an advocate for moderation and the underdog as visible as Thomas L. Kane was not. That Houston was an enemy of Albert Sidney Johnston only added to the drama surrounding his support for the Mormons. Important as Kane was to the defense of Mormonism, Houston's entrance into the fray during early 1858 was a direct reflection of Brigham Young's quiet efforts to recruit multiple allies capable of influencing the federal government as well as public opinion. Kane was a wire-worker, while Houston was a leader; yet the services of both men were invaluable.

My Bones Have Burned for Weeks: Completing the Standing Army

How did the Standing Army of Israel, a private force answerable only to Brigham Young, fit into Mormon thinking? Leonard J. Arrington viewed it almost entirely in economic terms, without probing how and why this force was to differ from the Nauvoo Legion or in what way its creation meshed with a Mormon world view.[1] On the other hand, David L. Bigler, who has done the most to shed light on this force, believes that the key to understanding the "why" of the Standing Army is a grasp of Brigham Young's all-important religious beliefs, especially as they incorporated a special role for the American Indian.[2]

In early 1858 making the Standing Army an effective fighting force was difficult, even for a leader of Brigham Young's power and motivation. Brigadier James Ferguson, the Legion's adjutant general, had politely protested in early January about the expense and questionable effectiveness of cavalry for

[1] Arrington, *Great Basin Kingdom*, 179–80.

[2] Bigler to MacKinnon, e-mail message, 7 August 2010. For other descriptions of the Standing Army, see Bigler, *Forgotten Kingdom*, 183–84; Bagley, *Blood of the Prophets*, 194–95; Bigler and Bagley, *The Mormon Rebellion*, 271–74.

mountain warfare. With the realization that a two-thousand-man mixed force of cavalry and infantry would cannibalize the leadership of the Nauvoo Legion while straining Utah's economic resources unsustainably, quiet pressures arose to reduce the size of the Standing Army. After some accommodation, Brigham Young drew the line, making clear that he expected the Mormon people to get on with the task of raising and equipping a mounted force of one thousand men.

By mid-January a committee of prominent citizens of the West Jordan Ward near Salt Lake City provided Young with a list of thirty-six families committed to supporting a total of fifteen men for the Standing Army. Acting on their own rule of thumb that "every three thousand dollars worth of property should outfit Support and Sustain One man and his family," groups of families (usually three) planned to combine their resources to equip and provision a single cavalryman. The best-known man on the list, William Adams ("Bill") Hickman, agreed to support two soldiers, one of whom may have been himself.[3]

At a community business meeting in the Salt Lake Tabernacle on 19 January, Brigham Young returned to the subject of the Standing Army for the first time in public since the previous October. His comments were short, relatively low key, and intertwined with other matters. According to the church reporter, "He also told the bishops to see to all the people in his ward had a supply of provision and preparation made to cash [cache] it in the mountains also the organization of an Army of 1,000 men. The names of the officers were read and all items of Business presented was received by the people with a shout of a loud Amen."[4] Attendees took notice of Young's comments about military affairs. Henry P. Richards noted in his journal: "Pres Young addressed the congregation upon a number of subjects, of vital importance to the Saints—among which was necessity of raising an Army of about 1000 men, for a 'Standing Army,' well Officered, and Equipped to be on hand and in readiness to protect the saints from any invasion by

[3]Joseph Harker, John Bennion, McGee Harris, William A. Hickman, and Samuel Bennion to Young, 15 January 1858, Territorial Militia Records, Series 2210, Utah State Archives and Records, Salt Lake City. In addition to Hickman, the signatories were the ward's acting bishop, the presiding elders of two dependent branches of that ward, and a son of one of these men. Interestingly, this religious-civic committee also provided Young with the name of the one man in the ward who "refused" to take part in this communal effort. Thanks to Ardis E. Parshall for analyzing this committee's membership.

[4]Van Wagoner, ed., *Complete Discourses of Brigham Young*, 19 January 1858, 3:1402.

those of our Enemies who are now on our borders, or from any who may hereafter be sent against us by the US Government."[5]

Which names Brigham Young read on 19 January as officers of the Standing Army are unknown, although a draft list created the previous evening probably provides most of the senior leaders. He described the force as a brigade commanded by Brig. Gen. William H. Kimball, a colonel in the Nauvoo Legion and son of his own first counselor. The subordinate units were regiments, battalions, and companies, although it is difficult to determine how many there were to be of each.[6]

This incomplete list and the annotations to it reflect a high degree of overlap with the Nauvoo Legion's leadership and the extent to which there were differing views among Young and his military advisors as to who was an appropriate or available officer for which role. As with the Nauvoo Legion, plans for the Standing Army exhibited grade inflation when compared to the Utah Expedition's table of organization, as well as lopsidedness in its heavy emphasis on positions for adjutants and aides de camp. Reflecting Young's focus on each man providing his own animals, arms, and other equipment, there was no apparent provision for quartermaster or ordnance officers, although A. P. Rockwood was to be the force's senior commissary officer, also his role in the Nauvoo Legion. Of Brigham Young's "b'hoys," the names of Nathaniel V. Jones, Lot Smith, Ephraim K. Hanks, and Howard Egan appeared, although those of two other trusted agents, Orrin Porter Rockwell and William Adams Hickman, were missing. As George A. Smith explained to his younger brother in England, "Porter Rockwell and Wm Hickman are getting up two independent companies. All the men selected are well mounted, expert riders, and dead shots,—armed with Rifles and Revolvers."[7]

With the completion of this roster, the biggest surprise was the absence of any apparent role for Col. Robert Taylor Burton. Presumably there either was a decision not to divert him from his senior Nauvoo Legion role or lingering disappointment over his inability to stop the advance of the Utah Expedition during the previous fall.

In Ogden, Warren G. Child recorded that on 2 February, "A meeting was called by Gen. West and assembled in the Tabernacle for the purpose of

[5]Richards, Papers, 1854–1900, Journal, 19 January 1858, LDS Archives.

[6]Officers for Standing Army, Monday Ev'g., 18 January 1858, Territorial Militia Records, Series 2210, Utah State Archives and Records, Salt Lake City. This list was later revised, finalized, and published as part of Young and Wells, General Orders No. 1, 6 March 1858, Head Quarters, Nauvoo Legion, ibid.

[7]Smith to John L. Smith, 5 February 1858, Historian's Office, Letterpress Books, LDS Archives.

selecting men and fitting them out with horses, clothing etc. for a standing army or as minute men. I volunteered to fit out one man with horse, clothing, provisions etc. Fifty young men were selected with proper officers while others volunteered to furnish them with the necessary equipment for any emergency or call which was immediately done. The 27th of Feb. I commenced plowing and putting in small grain. March 11th the minute men started for Salmon River, the Indians having made a raid on the mission there."[8]

A few days later, William Luck, a Nauvoo Legion adjutant, recorded, "Tuesday the 6th [of February], 1858, started to Ogden for a load of wheat for Sister Powell. Arrived at Ogden city on Wen. evening, the 7th stayed there one day. Thursday attended a mass meeting held there for the purpose of selecting some young men for the standing army. Saturday morning, 10th, started again for home and arrived at home in the evening, this Mon. called upon to furnish 35 men for the standing army of Utah. A tax levied to fit them up. The tax amounted to 17% my taxes amounted to $95.00. Gave some clothing, etc."[9]

In Bountiful, Joseph Holbrook, probably one of the community's more prosperous residents, listed the nature of his financial commitment to outfit two men for the Standing Army. The total for horses, pack mules, saddles, weapons, camp equipment, clothing, and provisions for a year was a staggering one thousand dollars.[10]

Despite these efforts, Brigham Young was impatient, and he said so in blistering terms in a discourse on 28 February that took to task bishops, military leaders, the Standing Army's potential recruits, and even their womenfolk.

Van Wagoner, ed., *Complete Discourses of Brigham Young*, 28 February 1858, 3:1408–11.

We have called upon Bishops and wards to sustain a certain portion of the community to act in our defense. I want to correct some mistakes, [because] reports have come to me which convince me that they have no idea of what is required of them. Some have asked what it will take to sustain one man for a year. The Bill for this has been made out for $700, including fit out of animals, arms and ammunition. This has been carried [communicated] from the Commander to the various officers; and from them to the Bishops, and the Bishops have gone to work to raise $700 to each man. This was not designed in the first place. The men that we called to go out we want them

[8]Child, "Echo Canyon War," LDS Archives.

[9]Luck, "Journal 1857–1868," entries for 6–12 February 1858, LDS Archives.

[10]Arrington, *Great Basin Kingdom*, 80; Diary of Joseph Holbrook, 2:2.

to have art enough and brain enough to fit themselves out instead of a Bishop having to furnish for 20 individuals $700 each to fit them out. I don't expect it to take [$]700 to fit them all out. But what do I learn? I learn that if a man who is called upon to go out has a horse[, mule, saddle, or coat] he shades [hides] it, and sits down and says I have nothing to do. Bishops dismiss every such man, and say I won't furnish you.

I want you Bishops to stop this raising means to encourage laziness and dishonesty. I want to correct the minds of thousands, soldiers, men and women, and to have them know and understand that we want men who will do all they can to fit out themselves.[11] Let me tell you officers, you great military men, let us please you and be dictated by you, and if you had an army at your command, fitted out as you wished it, it would be more than they could do to take care of their property. Do as the Indians do, they take a bow and arrow, a Lariat, a Blanket and a Breech-clout, and they expect to get what they need. I tell you these things are beforehand, for my bones have burned for weeks because of the ignorance and foolery of Bishops and men.

Those who go out in this army to defend us, you are required to go just as a man goes on a preaching mission. A man that does not go with his heart right before God we do not want him to go at all. Those who go in a right way will never be overtaken by an enemy, they won't be caught asleep, their horses will not be taken from them. Those who go unrighteously and do not carry out the instructions given will be delivered into the hands of our enemies, and I would rather have the room than the company of such men.

How to evaluate this discourse is challenging. So forcefully did Young deliver his message that, two years later, Kane, who apparently attended this session, was able to describe it to U.S. Senator Richard M. Mason and President Buchanan.[12] There were, of course, a small number of naysayers, backsliders, and shirkers mixed in with those Utahns supportive of the Standing Army. However, the anecdotal evidence reflected in dozens of Mormon diaries and letters for this period leads one to conclude that on 28 February Young was overreacting to individual, non-representative situations that came to his attention. Just such an overreaction had taken place earlier

[11]In contrast to Young's expectation for a self-sustaining force, non-Mormons raising volunteers elsewhere in the country viewed the war as an opportunity for adventure, glory, and financial gain at federal expense. Three weeks before Young's discourse, Jacob S. Klassen of Baltimore, a Mexican War veteran, offered to raise a mounted company of one hundred young men "of honor, & known integrity of purpose." He was willing to "meet their expenses until [the] first of March, & pay their passage to Le[a]venworth City," but expected that "Government must then furnish me with horses, two Colt Revolvers & a Minnie Rifle for each man." Klassen to Floyd, 1 February 1858, Letters Received, Office of the Adjt. Gen., RG 94, NARA.

[12]Kane to Mason, 20 April 1860, enclosure to Kane to Buchanan, same date, James Buchanan Papers, HSP.

in the month through a sarcastic letter from Young to James G. Willie, bishop of Salt Lake City's 7th Ward and leader of one of the emigration companies caught in the 1856 Willie-Martin handcart disaster. Perceiving a lack of enthusiasm for the Standing Army in Willie's ward, Young applied pressure in terms that no Mormon congregation was happy to hear or willing to resist, especially one led by a man who two years earlier had suffered an ordeal that involved the greatest loss of life in the entire American overland trails experience.

YOUNG TO WILLIE, 5 FEBRUARY 1858, LDS ARCHIVES.

> Your note of this date enclosing a Statement of the financial condition of your Ward, is just received and I lose no time in answering it.
>
> I feel to sympathize with you in your poverty, and feel to do all I can to relieve you from the burdens, requirements and circumstances which seem to weigh so heavily upon you. With this object in view—I have concluded to make the following proposition to the Brethren of your Ward through their Bishop. I will give you $25,000 for the entire property of the ward, including the houses, lands, improvements and personal property of the inhabitants of that ward, and pay you down in good available property, and will relieve you from all trouble in fitting up men for the Army. I will do that in the bargain.
>
> I want an immediate answer, as I feel anxious to compete the bargain; as I also feel assured that you will be glad to close with so advantageous an offer. I am not burl[e]squeing but [am] in earnest; and if satisfactory to you, wish to close the bargain forthwith.

Also fueling Young's anger was finger-pointing in northern Utah between a lieutenant of the Nauvoo Legion's Box Elder Military District and his commander over the requisition of shoes and beef cattle for the troops ordered to Echo Canyon. So corrosive was this supply dispute that the church's First Presidency ordered Col. Robert Taylor Burton to examine the conduct of the district's leader, Maj. Samuel Smith—who was also the mayor of Brigham City and a probate court judge, as well as the officer who had started the cash-flush Aiken party to its doom during the previous November. The court of inquiry found that Smith had exercised poor judgment, clashed with his bishop, and kept inadequate if not deceptive records. There were also innuendoes of misappropriation. The court recommended the major's removal for incompetency but not that he stand trial by court-martial. In explaining this leniency to General Wells, Colonel Burton hinted at more hugger-mugger within the Mormon military: "That Majr. Smith has been imprudent is evident . . . [but a trial] involves with it many unpleasant things in regard to others as well as Majr. Smith [that] in fact goes back to his Election to office."[13] From such atypical incidents in the Legion's operations, Young may well have inferred a widespread attitudinal problem that jeopardized the Standing Army's formation.

Quite to the contrary, resourceful, self-reliant behavior on the other end of the behavioral spectrum was exhibited by Homer Brown, a Nephi farmer and new trooper in the Standing Army. During February 1858, while witnessing the northbound passage of Dr. Osborne through Nephi, Brown engaged in exhausting farm work in a harsh environment. Nonetheless, Brown assembled the animals, weapons, and clothing he required for military operations over the next year. Brown did so in exemplary fashion by barter, his own craftsmanship, and, as a last resort, the outlay of small amounts of cash. Here was a member of the Standing Army and veteran of the Nauvoo Legion who needed no tongue-lashing from the pulpit to equip himself.[14] But entwined with Homer Brown's self-reliance and commitment to his church's military forces was a darker side already exhibited by his comrades at Mountain Meadows—a willingness to murder innocent civilians at the command of one's local religious leader. Thus it was that at the insistence of Bishop Jacob Bigler, Brown had found himself among the killers of the Aiken party along the Sevier River during the last week of November 1857.[15]

Brigham Young's volcanic discourse touched nerves throughout Utah. At a meeting in the Salt Lake Stake's North Cottonwood Ward, Col. P. C. Merrill felt it necessary to clarify that, "with regard to the words of Bro Brigham last Sunday about the fitting out the army, [they] were not applicable to our Bishop at all." Merrill's congregation then redoubled its already substantial efforts in support of the Standing Army.[16]

Within a month after Brigham Young chided the faithful on 28 February, the Standing Army was a dead issue, a casualty of a major change in his war strategy. Notwithstanding the push from atop the Mormon hierarchy

[13]Burton to Wells, 20 February 1858, Utah Territorial Militia Records, Series 2210, Utah State Archives.

[14]For a quirky proposal by a military musician to outfit a company of archers to serve in the Standing Army, see Myron Brewer to William Kimball, 5 February 1858, Myron Brewer Files, Moorman Collection, Weber State University, Ogden.

[15]Homer Brown Journal, February 1858, 24–28 November 1857, LDS Archives; Bigler, "The Aiken Party Executions."

[16]Minutes, North Cottonwood Ward, Salt Lake Stake, 4 and 7 March 1858, Minutes 1856–1859 (LR 2816 21), LDS Archives.

to recruit and equip the Standing Army, it is doubtful that this force ever campaigned offensively, although several of its small, newly formed units in the northern settlements played a key role in providing military cover and transportation for the withdrawal of Fort Limhi's settlers.[17]

Over one hundred miles to the east, the Utah Expedition's leaders did not realize these realities for some time, but since the return of Private Henry Feldman and teamster Charlie Becker in early January, Albert Sidney Johnston had been aware of and on the watch for such a force, determined to use picket posts and active patrolling to provide the warning needed to avoid a surprise attack. Accordingly, when the Utah Expedition's Edgar Brown, a thirty-year-old discharged herdsman, escaped Mormon captivity and stumbled into Fort Bridger on 2 March, he created a sensation. Brown had visited Salt Lake City and Provo and, as a prisoner, had passed through the Legion's camps in the mountains west of Fort Bridger. He warned of imminent Mormon troop movements, prompting Colonel Johnston to redeploy the Second Dragoons from herding duty to patrol the road connecting Fort Bridger to Salt Lake City and Fort Laramie. Having thus protected the Utah Expedition's front and rear, Johnston decided to relocate Camp Scott to a more defensible site on Blacks Fork adjacent to Fort Bridger's artillery emplacements.[18]

What had Brown reported? The best source is the affidavit he provided Utah's chief justice within days of returning to the Utah Expedition, a document to which covert newspaper reporter David A. Burr had access in his overlapping roles as justice of the peace for Utah's Green River County and Judge Eckels's clerk. Brown limned a portrait of Mormon cavalry on the move that unquestionably caught Albert Sidney Johnston's attention:

> There was a very general concurrence among the Mormons in the rebellion advised by their church leaders. *Three hundred* armed men were to start on the first of this month under Captains Lot Smith, Porter Rockwell, and William A. Hickman, for the vicinity of Camp Scott, to stampede and take back whatever stock was left, and then pass on the road toward Fort

[17]Understanding with certainty how the Standing Army operated, if at all, during January–March 1858 is difficult because of a paucity of records, a blurring between its activities and those of the Nauvoo Legion, and an overlap in their leadership. For the most extensive account and a positive assessment of the Standing Army's troops, see Bigler, *Fort Limhi*, 265–79.

[18]Maj. F. J. Porter to Lt. Col. P. St. G. Cooke and Maj. Henry H. Sibley, 2 March 1858, HQ Dept. of Utah, Camp Scott. Transcription courtesy of Prof. Jerry Thompson. The relocation of Camp Scott took place on 18 March but was ordered earlier in the month.

> Laramie, to cut off the mails and destroy any supplies that might be on the road. *One thousand* men, as a regular force, were to proceed about the same time, either for Echo Canon, or for this camp: deponent did not particularly understand their destination.

In acting on Edgar Brown's intelligence, one wonders how Johnston assessed the likelihood that Brown may have been nervous about the circumstances of his 1 December departure from Camp Scott for California contrary to Johnston's ban on such westbound travel. Burr commented that he had corroborated Brown's report through two other sources, although when non-Mormon merchant Abel Gerrish of Gilbert & Gerrish arrived at Camp Scott after spending several days in Provo and Salt Lake City, he reported on a number of subjects without reference to such troop movements.[19]

When Kane reached the Utah Expedition on 12 March, he became aware of the alarm that had been triggered by Brown's report a few days earlier as well as of Johnston's related defensive actions. Although there is no independent evidence that a large force of Mormon raiders took the field during late February or early March, Kane apparently believed that one did—or chose to say that such was the case. He appears to have transformed Brown's deposition, the army's flurry of defensive activity, and what he learned of the Standing Army's formation (incomplete) just before leaving Salt Lake City into one of his fanciful, postwar third-person narratives intended for newspaper publication.

Kane's draft essay described the march of an unspecified "regiment" commanded by an unidentified leader as the vanguard of the Mormon spring offensive, a force supposedly halted short of combat with the Utah Expedition near Bear River only by the last-minute intervention of a peace-seeking Brigham Young. As Kane phrased it, "This [forbearance] is known to have been done by a direct order from Brigham, and it was said among the Mormons, met with the open opposition of General Wells who was a man of high standing in their councils. But this and every other order to commence offensive operations was suspended by his Superior."[20]

[19][Burr], "Important from Utah: Escape of a Prisoner from Salt Lake City," Dispatch, 10 March 1858, *New-York Daily Tribune*, 17 May 1858, 5/6 and 6/1.

[20]Kane's draft newspaper essay is the only place that he put a name—that of D. H. Wells, Brigham Young's second counselor in the First Presidency—to a member of the alleged war faction, which he described as opposing Young's so-called peace party. Draft third-person narrative, ca. summer 1858, Thomas Leiper Kane Papers, APS. The reverse of this document bears the notation "NY correspondence *Herald!*"

One of the intriguing aspects of Kane's description of an aborted late-winter attack by the Standing Army was its part in his portrayal of a struggle by opposing war-peace factions atop the Mormon hierarchy. In the months that followed, Kane successfully merchandised this unsubstantiated story not only to news-hungry editors but to a series of influential political leaders in Washington, including the president. Kane's most recent biographer viewed this claim skeptically: "The actual existence of a 'war party,' however, seems doubtful. All contemporaneous reports of such a division stem from Kane, who never gave specifics on the war party's leadership or composition. For Kane, the division reflected more than just the perception of the situation in Utah; it was also a deliberate rhetorical construction designed to lead to a peaceful settlement. Indeed, his consistent use of the narrative in both public and private statements suggests that it was a mixture of genuine belief, misperception, and calculated creation."[21]

Perhaps through this incident, the Standing Army of Israel indeed did undertake an offensive of sorts in 1858. If so, it was a largely fictive campaign created from the alarming report of errant herdsman Edgar Brown and Thomas L. Kane's unsupported assertions.

Hurrah for the Ohio Volunteers!: Organizing by Units

As the Mormon Standing Army took shape during the first quarter of 1858, so too did scores of unsanctioned volunteer units determined to campaign in Utah for the U.S. government. For local reasons the volunteer scene in California was unusually intense but not unique. The combined impact of religious prejudice and indignation over the Mountain Meadows massacre, along with mixed signals from the Buchanan administration, economic adversity, and a restless predisposition to filibustering, spawned a volunteering phenomenon that was national. As early as October 1857, in the wake of Lot Smith's raid, the Utah Expedition's Captain Phelps had realized that spring reinforcements would be necessary, but he also recognized the disciplinary risks inherent in the use of volunteer troops, especially those from states with a history of anti-Mormonism. Writing his brother-in-law, a congressman from Pennsylvania, Phelps asked, "Would regiments of Californians,

[21]Grow, *"Liberty to the Downtrodden,"* 170.

Texans and Missourians be sent here? Would not such a remedy be worse than the disease?"[22]

The anecdotal evidence of military units formed and congressional speeches delivered indicates an eagerness to raise troops for the Utah War in the Ohio River Valley and the Mid-Atlantic region, especially in those states with tumultuous experiences with early Mormonism. Southern congressmen spoke at length about the need to suppress rebellion in Utah, but there was reluctance in that region to form units for military operations against a territory dedicated to one "peculiar institution" (polygamy) while the South had its hands full defending its own (slavery). The impact of the Republicans' "twin relics" platform plank of 1856 cut two ways.

One of the rare southern exceptions was John H. Kehler—a confirmed Democrat who offered his personal services and horse herd to Buchanan—from Greene County, Mississippi, after bivouacking with the ubiquitous, westbound W. M. F. Magraw in Nebraska Territory.

Kehler to Buchanan, 18 February 1858,
Letters Received, Office of the Adjt. Gen., RG 94, NARA.

I camped with Mr. Magraw several days on North Platte. I with my Company were enroute [east] from California. My reasons for sending this on now are that I wish to engage in the War against the Mormons. I have crossed the Plains eight times to California, and on each trip stopped amongst the Mormons one and two months. I am familiar with most of the Trails & Passes through Utah, also am acquainted with the different Tribes of Indians I have lived in California the last ten years, & can come recommended from the best Democrats of California, Virginia or Maryland.

If I could be of any benefit in any way, such as Bearer of Dispatches to and from the Army, or any appointment that would take me on the Plains I have some Forty Horses of my own that I could use at a moments warning.

I have met with harsh treatment from the Mormons. I hope that it may be to your interests to give me some appointment.[23]

If southerners were reluctant to volunteer for service against polygamous Utah, there were no such inhibitions in Kentucky, a slave-holding border state with attachments to both the South and the free states of the Ohio

[22]Phelps to Rep. John Hickman, 24 October 1857, Phelps Papers, NYPL.

[23]Document accompanied by letter of introduction, Magraw to Buchanan, 31 August 1857. Another exception to the general lack of southern enthusiasm for sending volunteers to Utah was the proffer of a battalion of either infantry or mounted troops from Savannah. Georgia governor Joseph E. Brown to Buchanan and Col. Robert B. Young to Brown, 26 March 1858, Letters Received, Office of Adjt. Gen., RG 94, NARA.

River Valley. The formation of Kentucky volunteer units—twenty-one companies eventually winnowed to a ten-company regiment—was so active and violent that in one case a fatal tavern brawl broke out in Washington County between rival officers over command of a newly formed infantry organization. To the extent that news of such behavior found its way to Brigham Young, it reinforced his perception that the Utah Expedition and its camp followers were an armed mob rather than a legitimate force of the national government.[24] Aside from the violence, what distinguished the scene in Kentucky from organizing activity elsewhere was the extent to which the legislature and governor were actively involved.[25]

In New York a downstate/upstate split developed, with a "silk-stocking" regiment-in-formation in Manhattan, while in Albany, a German tavernkeeper sought to raise a sister unit from his area's less urbane residents. What was common to both units was the heavy involvement of Mexican War veterans.[26] In Pennsylvania, President Buchanan's home state, one of his principal political allies, U.S. senator William Bigler, offered the War Department several volunteer companies from Harrisburg and Hollidaysburg, a prospect that an embarrassed Secretary Floyd had to deflect due to indecision in Congress and the administration.[27] So intense was the competition among Pennsylvania volunteers that the captain of the new Philadelphia Guards tried to advance his infantry company's claim amidst "the great struggle for 'preferment'" by noting that all of the unit's officers and non-coms had served in Mexico and that he had killed an enemy army officer there.[28]

Some newspapers deplored this rush to the colors or occasionally lampooned it. In Dover, Delaware, the newspaper reported that "[Militia] Gen. [Charles H.] Sargent, of Cincinnati, had on Monday, a formal interview with the President, and tendered a regiment of Ohio volunteers for service in Utah, supported by a recommendation from the Legislature of that State."[29] A

---

[24]Brigham Young, Office Journals, 14 June 1858, LDS Archives.

[25]Rolph, "Kentucky Reactions and Casualties in the Utah War of 1857–58"; Works Progress Administration Study, 1939, "Military History of Kentucky," 81–83.

[26]"Troops for Utah," Seward, U.S. Senate, Floor Remarks, 11 February 1858, *Congressional Globe* (35-1), 664.

[27]Floyd to Bigler, 30 December 1857, Secretary of War, "Letters Sent Relating to Military Affairs, 1800–89," RG 107, NARA. Senator Bigler's brother was a former governor of California, and his cousin, John Bigler, was a non-Mormon mountaineer at Fort Bridger who in the summer of 1858 would run unsuccessfully for a seat in Utah's legislative assembly. The flood of troop proffers from other Pennsylvania individuals and towns may be found in Letters Received, Office of Adjt. Gen., RG 94, NARA.

[28]John F. Saunton to Floyd, 3 April 1858, Letters Received, Office of Adjt. Gen., RG 94, NARA.

[29]"Washington News," *Delaware State Reporter* (Dover), 9 April 1858.

month later, prematurely anticipating an end to the Utah War, a Cincinnati paper picked up the beat to ridicule General Sargent.

"How the Mormon War Was Settled,"
Progressive Act (Coshocton, Ohio), 26 May 1858.

The Cincinnati *Times* gives currency to an apocryphal story, showing that the anticipated calling out of the Ohio Volunteers put a speedy end to the Mormon war. It says that Brigadier General Sargent, the man with the fierce moustache, after obtaining five companies from Cincinnati, and five more from other parts of the State, went to Washington taking with him his ferocious moustache for protection, and tendered the regiment to the President for the Utah service. The representative from Utah Mr. Bernhisel, hearing of the arrival of this redoubtable General, sent for him to talk over the matter, and hearing from the General a confirmation of the fact that the Ohio Volunteers were really to be called out, the M.C. [Member of Congress] from Utah instantly dispatched a messenger to Salt Lake, informing Brigham Young that the Ohio regiment, with five companies from Cincinnati, had been accepted, and that he had better come down [from his high horse] at once. And Brigham, like a sensible man, has come down.

The *Times* says: Though our gallant boys have not been brought into service, to them belongs the credit of conquering the Mormons. Hurrah for the Ohio Volunteers! Great are the Ohio Volunteers, and great is Brigadier General with the fierce moustache!

I Would Rather Be in Utah: Individual Hopefuls

There were, predictably, independent attempts by individuals to join the fray as officers in the four new regiments recommended to Congress. Of these hopefuls, the most bizarre was John Cook Bennett, former major general of the Nauvoo Legion and excommunicated assistant president of the LDS church. In January 1858 Bennett was a farmer and horticulturist living in Polk City, Iowa. On the 20th Bennett wrote to Sen. Stephen A. Douglas to lobby Douglas about a military role:

That the conflict with Utah will be more sanguinary, there is little doubt. I desire to be in the most bloody and terrible battle. You know my military capacity well. When I commanded the Legion it was the best disciplined body of troops in the Union, so admitted on all hands. I can now relead and take against them as formidable a Regiment as America can produce, if President Buchanan will only give me the *authority* to do so. Can I have your influence in procuring such authority? With my knowledge of the Mormons, there is no man living who could do the country better service. Please see the President on the subject, and write me your success.[30]

The lure of the Utah War drew volunteers not only from American states but internationally. From the Acadian Iron Mines in Londonderry, Nova Scotia, two German-born mining engineers in their early twenties, Carl F. Nordmann and Robert Schreiber, tendered Secretary Floyd their services as potential officers "in the present war against the Mormons of Utah as well as for all other times to come." In addition, they offered to recruit locally "One Hundred and more able stout men for the Service immediately, most of whom have been soldiers before and are accustomed to the hardships of field life." From the distance of British North America, these two supplicants, veterans of the Crimean War, limned a self-portrait worthy of the Volunteer Battalion's much-traveled sergeant-major, William Porter Finlay.[31]

Four former army officers who had resigned earlier in the decade also pursued volunteer commissions in 1858: George B. McClellan, a restless railroad vice president in Chicago; William Tecumseh Sherman, a failed California banker unemployed in Ohio; Simon Bolivar Buckner, steward of family businesses in Illinois and Kentucky; and Ben McCulloch, U.S. marshal for the eastern district of Texas and President Buchanan's initial choice as Brigham Young's successor. Hopeful of appointment to senior rank with these former comrades were at least two officers still in active service: Capt. Pierre G. T. Beauregard, a bored Louisiana engineering officer detailed to shore up the foundation of New Orleans's sinking custom house; and Maj. Samuel P. Heintzelman, one of the army's more entrepreneurial officers stationed in

[30]Bennett to Douglas, 20 January 1858, Stephen A. Douglas Papers, University of Chicago Library. There is no indication that Douglas responded. Bennett was not the only prominent former Mormon with close ties to Joseph Smith to offer his military services to the U.S. government during the war. Even before the Utah Expedition had been organized, Apostle Woodruff journalized that, according to an eastern newspaper, Smith's younger brother, William, had "called upon the government to furnish him with an army & money. He would Come to Utah & subdue the mormons." In mid-September 1857 a Mormon agent in New York reported to Brigham Young that William Smith had just visited the White House "where he had an interview with Pres. Buchanan, who remarked to him that '*he was going to make a clean sweep of the Mormons.*' How far it is the truth I cannot say." Kenney, ed., *Wilford Woodruff's Journal*, 31 May 1857, 5:54; Appleby to Young, 18 September 1857, LDS Archives. If Senator Douglas ignored Bennett's attempt to enter the Utah War from Iowa, three months later he favorably endorsed the availability of a volunteer regiment from Belleville, Illinois, and urged the War Department to accept its services for what Douglas termed "the Mormon campaign." Douglas to Floyd, 6 April 1858, Letters Received, Office of Adjt. Gen., RG 94, NARA.

[31]Nordmann and Schreiber to Floyd, 15 March 1858 and Cooper to same, 26 March 1858, Letters Received, Office of Adjt. Gen., RG 94, NARA.

Arizona. All of these men except McCulloch were graduates of West Point; each would later serve as a general in the Union or Confederate armies.

Notwithstanding his high status at the Illinois Central Railroad, McClellan was bored, missed military life, and chafed under the thought that his mentor, Captain Marcy, was campaigning in the West without him. McClellan also felt the lure of a senior leadership role in one of the filibustering expeditions fitting out in various American ports for adventures in Latin America.[32] Ironically, it had been to McClellan that Marcy had looked for help during April 1857 when faced with reassignment from Florida to Utah.[33] By year-end all that had changed, with Marcy en route to fame in New Mexico and McClellan fantasizing about re-entering the army. To Marcy's daughter McClellan confided, "the old lesson will not wear out. I would rather be in Utah now than anywhere else. I have no ties to bind me down to a quiet life. No reason for desiring wealth. . . . I might just as well follow the bent of my inclination as not. I am sure that my mother would prefer to see me occupy an honorable position in the service than anything else. . . . So the sage conclusion to which the ex-soldier has come is that he might just as well be in harness again, provided he can return with increased rank."[34]

McClellan had earlier written to Fitz John Porter about the possibility of leaving the Illinois Central for such military service. When Porter received this letter at Camp Scott, he reacted with alarm and tried to dissuade his friend from pursuing either alternative:

> You talk of coming out here. You never would take my advice or I would offer it now, and tell you to stay at home and mind a better business. This [campaign] is a matter of a day, and a poor one at that. What is to come will after six months longer be enmity and vexation of spirit. Do you consider a guerrilla warfare after some small party of these Mormons worthy [of] your intelligence and time? If so come out, but [if] I was [to] give any advice [it would be to] tell you that the Mormons are an infernal set of cowards like all assassins. But don't go to that other country. [Save?] your filibuster expeditions. There is nothing but notoriety to be gained by them. Honor and credit are far from there. There's only sickness. Put them in your pipe.[35]

[32]Robert May analyzes the national fixation on filibustering during this period in *Manifest Destiny's Underworld*, 101–102; and "Young American Males and Filibustering in the Age of Manifest Destiny," 857–86.

[33]Marcy to McClellan, 24 April 1857, *At Sword's Point, Part 1*, 204–205.

[34]McClellan to Mary Ellen (Nelly) Marcy, 8 December 1857, McClellan Papers, LC.

[35]Porter to McClellan, 28 February 1858, ibid. For more on McClellan's restlessness and weighing of options for returning to military action, see Sears, *George B. McClellan*, 416–17.

William Tecumseh Sherman's situation was very different. He had been out of the army four years longer than "Little Mac," and when his California bank failed during the fall financial panic, he was cast adrift at its collapsing New York branch. As early as 26 November 1857, Sherman confided to his brother-in-law, Hugh Ewing, that he was contemplating returning to the army. By mid-December a combination of idleness, dependency on his in-laws, economic desperation, and the president's annual message prompted him to approach Adjutant Gen. Samuel Cooper in Washington. Sherman asked for appointment "above the grade of captain" in the event of an expansion of the army, suggesting California as the best field for his services, as he had "helped settle the state." On 16 December 1857, the day he petitioned Cooper, Sherman also wrote to his congressman-brother, John, from their hometown of Lancaster, Ohio, to outline his plans and hopes.[36]

WILLIAM T. SHERMAN TO JOHN SHERMAN,
16 DECEMBER 1857, SHERMAN PAPERS, MANUSCRIPT DIVISION, LC.

I wrote a few days ago to my friend General Persifor F. Smith about the four new Regiments recommended by the President and Secretary of War, and which increase to the Army I think could not be for Any other considerations than the Mormon War. Of course recent events have deprived me of employment, and will consume every cent of money and property that I acquired before I left the Army and though [wife] Ellen will try and oppose it still I think rather than sit idle I will volunteer to re-enter my old business, for which I am better qualified than any other. Friends will be given priority for the highest appointments—of Colonel, Lt. Colonel and Major. Still I have very many friends among the higher officers and think by vigorous efforts I might get one of them. I will go to California on the steamer of Jan. 5, and I will if a good commission is offered me I could at once pitch in and my associates would be glad of my success.

I think one of the new Regiments will be raised in California, and if so I believe Senators [William M.] Gwin & [David] Broderick would advocate my appointment unless committed to other friends, and I feel certain I could act as rapidly and efficiently as any body in that State. I know its prospects and geography well. My Record in the Army is as good as that of any officer

[36]Hirshon, *The White Tecumseh*, 53–54. Sherman to Cooper, 16 December 1857, Andre De Coppet Collection, Special Collections, Firestone Library, Princeton University. In replying, Cooper addressed Sherman as "general," his California militia rank, in assuring him, "I have laid your communication before the Hon. Secretary of War, by whom it will be duly considered should the additional regiments recommended be authorized." Cooper to Sherman, 24 December 1857, Sherman Papers, Manuscript Division, LC.

> and Pres. Buchanan will recognize the fact that in the midst of revolution and tumult I was but in favor of the law & Constitution.[37]
>
> Keep this to yourself. I know that Ellen & [my father-in-law] Mr. [Thomas] Ewing would oppose my attempt, but I don't want to be dependent. I prefer action to the sedentary life and can stand as much exposure as anybody.

Ironically, as the S.S. *Moses Taylor* steamed out of New York Harbor for Panama on 5 January 1858, she carried at least two men who were unemployed: Thomas L. Kane, intent on mediating the Utah War, and William T. Sherman, seeking to prosecute it. There is no indication that Dr. Osborne and "Cump" Sherman met aboard ship, but the possibility is intriguing.

Perhaps while still in California, Sherman again wrote to his brother: "I think in the next ten years we will have plenty to do in the war line—Mormon war, civil broils and strife, contests for political power, growing out of slavery and other exciting topics, and last a war with Spain, resulting in the conquest of Cuba."[38] Sherman's optimism faded with the failure of his California mission and the end of the Utah War. By 1859 he was still unemployed and back in Ohio. He confessed to brother-in-law Hugh Ewing that "I have got pretty well to the end of my rope." One of Sherman's last hopes was to fall back on the economic opportunities available with the establishment of Camp Floyd, including an approach to William H. Russell to become his employee, travel to Salt Lake City, and from there trail a large herd of Russell's cattle to California. "In California I would put myself in communication with the leaders who propose to raise forces to sustain one or other of the contending factions in Mexico, and if I judge it adequate to the end proposal I would go in, though ever so much opposed to filibustering."[39]

Simon Bolivar Buckner had resigned his commission in 1855. Although essentially a resident of Louisville, Kentucky, Buckner spent substantial time in Chicago tending to the business affairs of his wife's family. He continued to attract the attention of those interested in military affairs because of his sterling record in the Mexican War. During 1857 Buckner was major of a Chicago militia unit, and during April–October 1857 he was also Illinois's adjutant general. During one of Buckner's absences from Chicago, citizens

---

[37] A reference to Sherman's role in maintaining order in San Francisco as a militia major general during the 1856 turmoil of the vigilance committees.

[38] Sherman to Sherman, [n.d.] January 1858, Thorndike, ed., *The Sherman Letters*, 64.

[39] Sherman to Hugh Ewing, 22 July 1859, William T. Sherman Papers, Ohio Historical Society, Columbus.

organized a regiment of volunteer infantry for service in Utah and elected him colonel. When Buckner returned to Illinois and discovered this turn of events, he was optimistic, telling his wife that his appointment to command the First Illinois Regiment of Volunteers in the Utah War could mean "a long step towards our return to the army with high rank."[40]

Capt. P. G. T. Beauregard was still in the service. Like McClellan, he was bored and casting about for excitement either as a filibuster or a senior officer of U.S. volunteers. That Beauregard was on duty in New Orleans, a hotbed of Latin America plots, added to his restlessness.[41] In February 1858 Beauregard wrote to his brother-in-law, Senator Slidell, to broach his interest in the Utah campaign: "Should the Army be increased by two or more Regts. . . . [I wish] to be appointed the Col. of one of said Regts (the Zouaves if possible)."[42] He sent a copy of this letter to Jefferson Davis and John A. Quitman, chairmen of the military affairs committees in the Senate and House, respectively. That Quitman was then a prominent advocate for seizing Cuba may also have entered Beauregard's calculations.

Of all the regular army officers seeking advancement through the creation of volunteer regiments for Utah, perhaps none was as opportunistic as Maj. Samuel P. Heintzelman, First U.S. Infantry. Although stationed in Arizona, throughout the winter of 1858, Heintzelman was in Washington for multiple official and personal purposes. With the president's December plans to prosecute the Utah War, Heintzelman pressed his case for promotion by visiting Buchanan to remind him that he too was a native of Lancaster County, Pennsylvania, and that in 1822 the president had supported his

[40]Buckner to Mary Jane Kingsbury Buckner, 4 April 1858, excerpted in Stickles, *Simon Bolivar Buckner,* 38. For a lampoon of Chicago militia units, including those seeking action in Utah, see Renner, "Ye Kort Martial," 376–86.

[41]May, *Manifest Destiny's Underworld,* 102.

[42]Beauregard to Slidell, 9 February 1858, Huntington Library. The U.S. Army would have no units of Zouaves, a flamboyantly uniformed infantry corps in the French North African service, until the Civil War. Jefferson Davis sent his copy of Beauregard's letter to Secretary Floyd for comment with the observation that he "is an active officer of military habits and tastes and of high professional attainments." Notwithstanding this endorsement, Floyd took no action on Beauregard's suggestions and returned the letter to Davis with the exasperated comment that "the Department is favorably impressed with the standing and reputation of Bvt. Major Beauregard, but the condition which attaches to his application—his being appointed to the command of one of the new regiments—necessarily embarrasses the Department in coming to any conclusion in the subject at this time." Thus ignored, Beauregard shifted his considerable energies and ambitions from strategizing about the Utah War to a run for mayor of New Orleans, a political race that he almost won later in 1858. Davis to Floyd and Floyd to Davis, 19 January and 24 February 1858, both in Letters Received, Office of the Adjt. Gen., RG 94, NARA.

appointment to the U.S. Military Academy. He also met with Floyd and solicited testimonial letters of recommendation from Pennsylvania's congressional delegation, including the much-lobbied Senator Bigler.[43]

Of the seven individuals discussed above—Bennett, McClellan, Sherman, Buckner, McCulloch, Beauregard, and Heintzelman—only McCulloch made it to Utah. In his case, he did so as a civilian peace commissioner rather than in his preferred role as colonel commanding a volunteer regiment.[44]

The Best Materials to Work With: Lobbying Sam Houston

Thomas L. Kane was not the only influential non-Mormon with Washington connections to whom Brigham Young turned for help during the Utah War. One of Young's skills was cultivating such people. During 1857–58 he focused on U.S. Army quartermaster Stewart Van Vliet of New York and trail-blazer Frederick W. Lander of Salem, Massachusetts.[45] Small wonder that in 1855 Apostle John Taylor had informed Young, "Col. Kane and Judge Douglass [*sic*] will certainly be the best materials to work with at the present time. Perhaps it may be better to use them and Bro. [Stephen B.] Rose to communicate with the President, than to see him myself."[46]

At a critical juncture in the Utah War, Young reached out to another such friend—Sam Houston of Texas, the most prominent of the church's non-Mormon allies. Houston, a former supporter of Joseph Smith, Jr., had written to Young as early as February 1851.[47] It is possible that Young exploited to Mormon advantage two Houston sensitivities: his long-standing, Texas-rooted enmity with Albert Sidney Johnston, and the senator's more

[43]Thompson, *Civil War to the Bloody End,* 70–71 and 370n20.

[44]Six of these men served as general officers in the Civil War. Dr. John Cook Bennett participated as a major and staff surgeon in the Tenth Iowa Infantry and Third U.S. Infantry.

[45]During 1857–58 Lander wanted Young's help in securing Mormon labor to work on his stretch of the Pacific Wagon Road, as well as his assistance in becoming Nebraska Territory's delegate in Congress. In turn, Young sought to use Lander's Washington connections. For the several two-hour meetings between these men in Young's office, see Collier, ed., *The Office Journal of President Brigham Young,* 29 and 30 August 1858, 3–6; Lander to Young, 1 June 1857 and 23 September 1858, LDS Archives.

[46]Taylor to Young, 15 July 1855, LDS Archives. Rose, a Mormon, was appointed U.S. Indian subagent for Utah in 1850; as such he had a reporting relationship to the Interior Department's Office of Indian Affairs through Governor Young.

[47]Houston to Young, 18 February 1851, LDS Archives.

recent political tensions with James Buchanan. During 1857–58 there was little awareness of these Houston-Mormon linkages.[48]

The intermediary through whom the Latter-day Saints approached Houston was Nauvoo Legion major Seth Millington Blair, a native of Tennessee, the state to which Houston migrated from Virginia before both men moved to Texas. How and precisely when Blair first met Houston is unclear, but they had been comrades-in-arms during the Texas Revolution, with Blair becoming a Texas Ranger as well as an army officer. Blair descendant John Bond believes that his ancestor may have met both Houston and Albert Sidney Johnston in 1839 when all three men, together with Blair's longtime friend Ben McCulloch, were in San Felipe, Texas. Following Blair's emigration to Utah in 1850, Houston initiated President Millard Fillmore's appointment of lawyer Blair as the territory's first U.S. attorney. In 1857 Blair's status within the Mormon leadership appears to have been that of a "middle-wagon man"—a person respected but hardly senior.[49] Nevertheless, in Brigham Young's hour of need, Blair was virtually the only Texan with a connection to Sam Houston at his disposal.

In 1857 Blair had turned from the law to the Utah War with an active assignment as a cavalry major in the Nauvoo Legion. By November he was contemplating the potential usefulness of his long relationship with Sam Houston and their mutual antipathy toward Albert Sidney Johnston. Major Blair resumed his correspondence with Houston on 24 November, drafting a long letter. By Blair's account, the idea to seek the senator's help was his, but the most senior Mormon leaders were surely involved.[50] After

[48]Among the earliest published analyses of Houston's connection to Mormon leaders are two works by Michael Scott Van Wagenen: *The Texas Republic and the Mormon Kingdom of God* and "Sam Houston and the Utah War," 66–78. The most recent such study is MacKinnon, "Into the Fray: Sam Houston's Utah War," 198–243.

[49]Van Wagenen's interpretation differs from this sense of Blair's middling standing in the LDS leadership. Based on his reading of Blair to George A. Smith, 2 June 1858, LDS Archives, Van Wagenen concludes that as early as 1850 Brigham Young intentionally denied Blair high status in the church's hierarchy to lower his profile and enhance his usefulness as an agent through the appearance of independence. Van Wagenen, "Sam Houston and the Utah War," 71–72. A more accurate reflection of the relationship between the two men as superior-subordinate is found in their January 1857 interactions over what was to become the B. Y. X. Carrying Company. See Young to George A. Smith, 26 January 1857, Journal History, courtesy of Mr. John Bond.

[50]Significantly, in early September Young had urged Mormon agents Horace S. Eldredge, Jeter Clinton, and William I. Appleby to gather intelligence in Washington by selecting discreetly a "true" agent knowledgeable about governmental deliberations and able to influence them. Blair's decision to reach out to Houston two months later was consistent with Young's September intent to recruit a Washington insider. *At Sword's Point, Part 1*, 278–81.

circulating his draft for comment by Apostles Smith and Woodruff, Blair finalized the letter, dated it 1 December 1857, and sent it east by way of the San Bernardino–Panama route.[51]

To Murder an Innocent People: Major Blair's Letter

Blair's litany of Mormon grievances and description of a prospective scorched-earth policy were apocalyptical. In terms of its raw emotion and ferocity, his letter to Houston stands out among a substantial body of overheated Utah War documents. As with many such Mormon polemics, Seth Blair's letter is far too repetitive for inclusion here in its entirety, but excerpts are useful in conveying his arguments and the warm, if distant, tone of the Blair-Houston relationship.[52]

Blair to Houston, 1 December 1857, *New York Herald*, 2 March 1858, 1/4–5.

> Once again, and probably for the last time, I take the liberty of addressing you.[53] Early in life I became, like thousands of others, your devoted friend from the impulse of the moment that I admired in you that which my inner senses taught me was noble—a man, a chieftain, a patriot, statesman and soldier which characteristics I yet hope are ripening in you, to come forth in radiant splendor when an honest man shall be acknowledged the noblest work of God.
>
> I am induced to write you at this time from the peculiar circumstances that I find myself surrounded with, in common with the citizens of my unhappy country, and especially of the citizens of Utah; for in my heart I believe you the only Senator who sits in the Congress of the United States who dares to lift up his voice in opposition to public opinion, and I write

[51]For the chain of events associated with drafting this letter, see Seth M. Blair Journal, and Blair to Smith, 2 June 1858, both LDS Archives.

[52]Finding the complete text of this document has been a challenge. The original letter has not appeared in Houston's papers. Blair did not retain a copy, and the copy in the church historian's office is partially illegible. The definitive text is that which the *New York Herald* ran on 2 March 1858, which, in turn, was composed from a copy of the original which Houston permitted the newspaper's Washington correspondent to make and telegraph to New York.

[53]This was neither the first nor the last time that Blair wrote to Houston. In 1850 he had written to Houston to introduce Apostle John Taylor, and in 1853, with his term as U.S. attorney for Utah expiring, Blair had unsuccessfully sought appointment as Utah's chief justice through Houston. Blair to Houston, 17 February 1850 and 30 October 1853, LDS Archives, courtesy of Mr. John Bond. On 15 January 1859 Blair would again seek Houston's help in an unsuccessful effort to remove the army from the territory.

Nauvoo Legion Major Seth M. Blair, Sam Houston's Friend
A comrade of Houston and Ben McCulloch from the Texas Revolution and the Texas Rangers, Blair converted, migrated to Utah, and with Houston's support became the territory's first U.S. attorney in 1850. In the fall of 1857, with the encouragement of Mormon leaders, Blair sent Houston a long letter setting forth the LDS view of the war and asking help. Houston reacted with a key Senate speech questioning the wisdom of the conflict, criticizing Johnston, and opposing use of regular reinforcements. In June, with McCulloch in Utah as a peace commissioner, the Nauvoo Legion's General Wells again used Blair as a liaison. *Lithograph from Whitney's* History of Utah *(Salt Lake City, 1892).*

to inform you most truly the feelings of the citizens of Utah. Under these impressions we labor and live, and for months we have been preparing for the worst, with an invading army on our frontier.

You no doubt ask, then, in your mind, what the issue will be. I will candidly answer you; it cannot be worse than to tamely submit to the illegal, unconstitutional and despotic course marked out by the administration against us. [The Mormons] will only act on the defense, and on the improved system of guerilla warfare. Ask the United States officers what they found at Fort Bridger? The same they found at Fort Supply. Query. What did they find at those thriving settlements on their arrival? Blackened desolation; ashes alone remained and as Forts Bridger and Supply have gone, so will each city, town, hamlet, village, settlement, habitation, field, altar, temple, all and every trace of civilization in these mountains go at the approach of the invading army. This is true, mark it well; as I tell you so have we determined to do.

Ever desiring peace, we have abstained from shedding the blood of these troops, and only taken that precaution to retard their progress that would afford the nation time to consider the rash act of the President. Let me assure you that not one of Johnston's command would now live to leech the public treasury or profane the name of that God who gave victory to the American

> arms; for with 100 Texan rangers, which we have,[54] not only their baggage wagons would have been burned months ago, but even their tents consumed over their heads, while the revolver would have done the execution that those entrusted with stampeding animals failed to accomplish; and without our shedding a drop of their blood they would now have been food for the wolves and vultures of the plains.
>
> I beseech you, then, as one who loves the Union and who despises the life that would tamely submit to a tyrannical rule, to raise your voice to stop the bigoted crusade of the administration against Governor Young and this people, and ask Congress to countermand the exterminating orders of the administration.[55]
>
> General, I beseech you as an honorable Senator not to despise our cause, and lend your influence to prevent the greatest of all national calamities—civil war. I am done. My feelings are as they ever have been towards you, and if you are not reciprocal, it is because you don't know me better. God bless you and preserve you.

Houston received Seth Blair's plea in mid-February, perhaps as early as the 10th but certainly by the 15th or 16th.[56] The next day, Bernhisel described to Brigham Young the recent arrival of Blair's still-confidential letter, as well as his own inability to influence events: "Yesterday morning Gen. Houston sent to me for perusal a letter which he had received from S. M. Blair Esq. In the afternoon I called at the Generals lodgings but he was not in. This morning I had an interview with him in the Senate Chamber; he promised to communicate with the President on the subject of the difficulties. He is in favor of a commission [to investigate affairs in Utah]."[57]

---

[54]This exaggeration was intended for Houston's benefit as well as perhaps that of Ben McCulloch, his frequent companion in Washington. Houston would have recognized Blair's evocation of Texas Ranger involvement in the Utah War as the specter of a savage frontier guerrilla conflict. In 1858 the Rangers' image was mixed, with perceptions of freebooting, undisciplined, and brutal behavior quite different than their later (and current) sanitized reputation as an elite, orderly state police force. Collins, *Texas Devils*, 208. Writing from Texas three years later, the Utah Expedition's Sergeant-Major Finlay provided a London newspaper with his impressions of the fighting qualities of Texas Rangers independent of any Utah involvement. Finlay, "The American War. The United States' Army and the Position of the Parties," Dispatch, 24 April 1861, *Daily Telegraph* (London), 27 May 1861, reprinted *Northern Whig* (Belfast), 29 May 1861.

[55]Blair evokes the 1838 executive order issued by Gov. Lilburn Boggs of Missouri to the state militia authorizing them to "exterminate" Mormons who refused to leave the state. Neither the Buchanan administration nor Albert Sidney Johnston gave such instructions or used such language, although Johnston's adjutant, Major Porter, advocated "exterminating" Utah's Mormons in private correspondence with the army's adjutant general.

[56]Van Wagenen argues that Houston received Blair's letter in January 1858, apparently because of a reference to it in a Bernhisel-to-Young letter which is misdated 17 December 1858. From the internal evidence, it is clear that the Bernhisel-to-Young letter mentioning the 1 December 1857 Blair-to-Houston letter should have been dated 17 February 1858. Van Wagenen, "Sam Houston and the Utah War," 73–74.

[57]Bernhisel to Young, 17 December 1857 [17 February 1858], LDS Archives.

A Magnificent Barbarian in Action: Houston Takes the Floor

Late in February Houston pressed Blair's letter into service as the foundation for a long Senate speech that both opposed a substantial expansion of the regular army for use in Utah and criticized Albert Sidney Johnston's leadership of the expeditionary force already in the field. The speech came at a tumultuous time of political crosscurrents: both houses of Congress had adopted resolutions demanding the documentary evidence on which Buchanan had based his decision to intervene; the president and secretary of war had formally requested the establishment of four more regiments; proffers of volunteer units for Utah service were cascading into Washington from throughout the country; and war costs were mushrooming while the backwash from the Panic of 1857 reduced the flow of revenue to the federal treasury.

Attired in some combination of white beaver hat, Cherokee blanket, and jaguar-skin vest that prompted one observer to dub the senator "a magnificent barbarian,"[58] Houston rose to address the Senate on 25 February 1858. Coincidentally, it was the day on which Thomas L. Kane reached Salt Lake City and a party of two hundred Bannocks and Northern Shoshones raided the Mormon mission at Fort Limhi, Oregon Territory.

Speaking extemporaneously, Houston's speech became as rambling as the Blair letter that prompted it. In it, Houston came at his defense of the Mormons obliquely, easing into the subject not through a direct assault on anti-Mormonism but rather through the more emotionally (and politically) neutral subject of whether volunteers or regulars would be more effective troops in such a campaign. In this sense, Houston's approach resembled Abraham Lincoln's 26 June 1857 rebuttal to Senator Douglas's 12 June Springfield speech in which Lincoln aided the Mormon cause indirectly by attacking Douglas and Popular Sovereignty rather than by defending Brigham Young.

Houston, Floor Remarks, U.S. Senate, 25 February 1858, *Congressional Globe* (35-1), 873–75.

Mr. President, I believe the subject has assumed rather a new phase, and that this is now understood to be a proposition to increase the regular Army permanently, by this addition to the present peace establishment of the standing Army. Is it that you wish to send them out to Utah to get destroyed? I wish to do it by the employment of volunteers. We are told that there is a costliness

[58]Haley, *Sam Houston,* 296. For a description of Houston, his attire, and behavior, see Windle, "Senate Chamber—General Houston," January 1858, *Life in Washington,* 32–33.

about volunteers; that they are more expensive than regular soldiers. That may be true; but I doubt it. I could show this by the celerity of volunteers. . . . God forfend [preserve] us from such a result—and the valley of Salt Lake is to be ensanguined with the blood of American citizens, I think it will be one of the most fearful calamities that has befallen this country, from its inception to the present moment. I deprecate it as an intolerable evil.

I am satisfied that the executive has not had the information he ought to have had on this subject before making such a movement as he has directed to be made. I am convinced that facts have been concealed from him. I think his wisdom and patriotism should have dictated the propriety of ascertaining, in the first place, whether the people of Utah were willing to submit to the authority of the United States. If this course had been taken by the Executive, I am sure he would never have recommended war; and if the facts had been before the Secretary of War, I am sure he would never have made the recommendation [for more troops] which he has submitted to us.

The more men you send to the Mormon war the more you increase the difficulty. They have to be fed. For some sixteen hundred [twelve hundred] miles you have to transport provisions. The regiments sent there have found Fort Bridger and other places, as they approached them, heaps of ashes. They will find Salt Lake, if they ever reach it, a heap of ashes. Just as sure as we are now standing in the Senate, these people, if they fight at all, will fight desperately. They are defending their homes. They are fighting to prevent the execution of threats that have been made, which touch their hearths and their families; and depend upon it they will fight until every man perishes before he surrenders.

I received the other day from a very intelligent Mormon whom I knew in Texas, and a very respectable man he was, once I believe the United States district attorney for Utah, a letter of seven pages. In that letter he takes a comprehensive view of this subject. He protests most solemnly that there never would have been the least hostility to the authorities of the United States if the President had sent respectable men there. He says that Governor Brigham Young has been anxious to get rid of the cares of office, and would freely have surrendered it and acknowledged the authority of the United States; but that men have gone there, who have made threats that they would hang them, and even threats of a character that renders them more sensitive in relation to their families, and that they expect nothing but rapine and destruction to ensue on the advent of those troops if they should ever arrive there.

I know not what course will be taken on this subject. I hope it will be one of conciliation. As for troops to conquer the Mormons, fifty thousand would be as inefficient as two or three thousand. I say your men will never return, but their bones will whiten the valley of Salt Lake. If war begins, the very moment one single drop of blood is drawn, it will be the signal of extermination.

Mr. President, in my opinion, whether we are to have a war with the Mormons or not, will depend on the fact whether our troops advance or not. If they do not advance; if negotiations be opened; if we understand what the Mormons are really willing to do; that they are ready to acquiesce in the mandates of the Government, and render obedience to the Constitution; if you will take time to ascertain that, and not repudiate all idea of peace, we may have peace. But so sure as the troops advance, so sure they will be annihilated.

An act of civility was tendered by Brigham Young, and you might, if you please, construe it, under the circumstances, rather as an act of submission on his part. He sent salt to the troops. What was the message the military officer sent him back? That was a time to make peace with Brigham Young, because there is something [symbolically] potent in salt. He [Colonel Johnston] sent a message I would not have sent, and I do not think it is calculated to conciliate Brigham Young. He is too proud a man, I take it; a man of too much sense to have sent such a message as that, after an act of civility was tendered.

If the Mormons are to be conquered, volunteers can conquer them immediately the regulars, never.

Of Mormons & War, and Profligate Scoundrels: Houston's Self-Assessment

What Sam Houston thought of his own speech, as well as about Buchanan and Albert Sidney Johnston, appeared in letters to his wife that immediately followed.

Houston to Margaret Houston, Roberts, ed., *The Personal Correspondence of Sam Houston*, 4:286–87, 290–91.

26 February 1858

I had been occupied all day [on the 25th], and had just made a short speech on the army Bill to raise Regulars, and some say I defeated it. It was lost in the Senate. I apprehend you will think that late canvass [election campaign] got me in such a way of speaking, that I don't know when to stop. Well heretofore I have not spoken a great deal, and may be borne with so long as I speak sense. I will send you the [Congressional] Globe, that you may judge for yourself. The speech is clever enough to be done, as Burns says, "A free off hand."[59] So it was, and the notes of my speech, I never read.

[59] A reference to Scottish poet Robert Burns's 1786 "Epistle to a Young Friend."

Mr. Buchanan has worse than this to get over, tho. I am supporting him with great integrity of purpose, but in favor of a standing army, I can not go.[60] I am a Democrat of the true Jackson American stamp, and can not be any thing else. The army, & Navy, are to prostrate, or ruin our country. You will see in my speech mailed to you, that my mind is not easy on this subject, as well as in my former speeches!

The doings about the Mormons is all wrong, and will result in terrific disaster, or shame to the Nation, & perhaps both!

The Commander of the Expedition is *our* Genl A. S. Johns[t]on, of Texas. He will not do, and if you read my speech, you will get an inkling, of what I think of him. I have not gone back, to his *infamous* conduct in Texas, when he tried to subvert the Government, and destroy the country, for selfish ends! I propose to expose him yet!

1 March 1858

The Ball opens to day, on the admission [to statehood] of Kansas. I foresee the evil to grow out of the policy, as well as the Mormon war. I am no Mormon, & the evil of the difficulty has grown out of the policy pursued by Pierce, and kept up by Mr. Buchanan. Men were sent there of worse morals, than the Mormons. For instance, a man by the name of [Associate Justice W. W.] Drummond, who left a wife, & family in Ill[inois] starving, & from this place took a *hussy* (I will not call her a woman) and introduced her at various places, Independence Mo, & Santa Fe, and San Francisco as his wife, and at Salt Lake lived with her as such. Others were men [of] dissolute habits, and these facts were known to the Mormons.

Now my dear this Mormon war has been predicated, on the reports of such men, and the Mormons have never refused to receive federal officers, and respect them. So upon these premises, the President has sent Troops to subdue them, and Genl A. S. Johnson is sent to the work, and of all men living the least qualified for such business. If the Mormons chuse [*sic*] to do it, they can destroy the whole command. If blood is drawn, the Troops will be annihilated, and then a war will ensue. Now Dearest, after the dissertation on Mormons & war, and profligate scoundrels, I will have to close my letter.

Three weeks later Houston again spoke about the Utah War in the Senate. On 18 March he briefly interrupted California senator William Gwin's emotional but largely accurate floor speech on the Mountain Meadows massacre to raise doubts as to the assumption that Mormons were responsible

[60] Houston did not support Buchanan in 1856 and would not agree with General Scott that regulars would be more effective than volunteer troops for the Utah War. He was trying to help Buchanan by January 1858. Houston to Margaret Houston, 9 and 11 January 1858, Roberts, ed., *The Personal Correspondence of Sam Houston,* 4:267 and 271.

for the atrocity: "I am opposed to this indiscriminate warfare upon Indians, or Mormons, or any other people, until their guilt is ascertained. I want the facts as to who perpetrated the crime ascertained, and then inflict punishment according to the offense."[61]

Turning Away That Fearful Storm: Houston's Impact

Measuring the impact of Houston's 25 February speech is difficult. It is clear that the ultimate expansion of the regular army was grossly less than what Buchanan and Floyd had sought in December. No volunteers—other than Lt. Col. Barnard E. Bee's battalion—were accepted for Utah service and, within two months, as Houston advised, a presidential peace commissioner (Ben McCulloch) had been appointed who had served with Seth Blair in the Texas Rangers. In all likelihood the principal importance of Houston's February remarks lay in their symbolic, if not moral, value. It was an arresting, dramatic image—a legendary frontiersman and soldier, flamboyantly attired, rising alone in defense of a reviled, beleaguered minority group.

Decades later, Apostle George A. Smith—then Brigham Young's second counselor in the First Presidency—commented to a former U.S. senator, "In 1857 when the contractors war was fulminated against us, not a single newspaper in the whole country published a kind sentiment concerning us, and the only man of national reputation who spoke a kind word for us, was the late Senator Houston of Texas, to whose efforts under Divine Providence we owe the turning away of that fearful storm."[62]

[61] *Congressional Globe,* 18 March 1858 (35-1), 1858, 1176–77.

[62] Smith to Joseph Smith Fowler, 30 June 1872, Historian's Office Letterpress Copybooks, LDS Archives. When Seth Blair died in 1875, the *Deseret News*'s obituary commented on his 1857 letter to Houston and concluded that it "was one of the means of turning the scale of the contractors war against Utah." *Deseret News,* 18 March 1875, 3/3. Blair himself was enormously proud of his role in bringing Sam Houston to the Mormons' support. Blair to Smith, 2 June 1858, George A. Smith Papers, LDS Archives.

Chapter 10

"He Fell as a Bombshell"
Kane and Turmoil at Camp Scott

I find that I have only exchanged one set of monomaniacs for another.
Thomas L. Kane to President James Buchanan, ca. 15 March 1858

As with Lieutenant Ives's ascent of the Colorado River, Thomas L. Kane misjudged the difficulty of traveling the 113 miles from Salt Lake City to Fort Bridger. Once there, he encountered a scene far more byzantine, sordid, and confrontational than he had expected. Before leaving Washington, both President Buchanan and Delegate Bernhisel had warned Kane of danger from angry Californians and suspicious Mormons; the hostility at Bridger from troops and civilians whom Kane hoped to protect was a shock for which not even Mormon cautions had prepared him. Fear of assassination within a U.S. Army post was an unanticipated prospect that kept Kane in a constant state of agitation and Camp Scott in turmoil.

The army's winter quarters were a stage on which Kane exercised his full powers of manipulation while indulging the dramatic streak that ran through his personality. The extent to which Kane, among others, bore responsibility for inflaming tensions there is a key issue bearing on the conduct of his mission. If another friend of the Mormons, Sam Houston, had the flamboyance to sport a jaguar-skin waistcoat in the U.S. Senate, it is unsurprising that a man of Kane's temperament arrived in Utah with a tiger pelt as part of his outfit.[1] From this caldron of misunderstandings, mixed motives, and theatrics emerged Kane's signal contribution to resolving the Utah War.

[1]The items in Kane's traveling kit are listed in Kane, "Diary II (1858)," 2.

The Bearer of Overtures of Peace: The Trail to Bridger

Having acknowledged Brigham Young's proffer of flour and cattle, Kane prepared to forge on to Bridger in severe weather. During the night of 9–10 March, he wrote a letter to be delivered to Gov. Alfred Cumming in the event he did not live to reach him. Written in his pocket diary for 1858 to a man he had never met, it was a grand gesture reflecting the messianic tone of Kane's thoughts: "Dear Sir: In case of accident I write this memorandum to apprise you that I am the bearer of overtures for peace from Gov. Brigham Young. Letters from President Buchanan throwing light upon my position will be found upon my person. My other letters and effects I beg may be forwarded to my family at Philadelphia." On the diary's fly leaf, he wrote: "To the finder! Hon. Judge Kane of Philadelphia, Penna. will pay $5 for this book, upon delivery, or if sent to him by mail."[2] With these arrangements in place, Kane and his escort resumed their northeasterly trek.

Kane traveled under the protection of a few frontiersmen hand-picked by Brigham Young from among his most reliable "b'hoys": Brig. Gen. Lewis Robison, Maj. Howard Egan, Capt. Orrin Porter Rockwell, and others. Later, when Colonel Johnston asked Kane to describe this party, he replied by naming only Lewis Robison (without rank), perhaps sensing that reference to such well-known adversaries or high-ranking Legion officers would destroy his credibility with the army.[3]

Other than fragmentary impressions jotted in his diary, the only known account of this journey is a narrative written by Kane for his brother Pat later in 1858. It is a piece as florid as the elusive Mr. Wingate's fictive description of his eastbound passage through daunting mountains to bypass the Utah Expedition.

Kane to Pat Kane, ca. Summer 1858, "In Re Mormons" File, Thomas Leiper Kane Papers, APS.

Brigham Young, the fine fellow wanted me to stay [in Salt Lake City]. There had fallen my heavy snow-storm No. 2. Twenty-five feet of snow lay over the great portions of the highest part of the road. He then wanted me to let some of the Norwegians carry me with sledges and snow shoes. I went with

[2]Kane to Cumming, "Between Salt Lake Valley and Fort Bridger, March 9–10, 1858," ibid.

[3]Kane to Johnston, 15 March 1858, "Annual Report of the Sec. of War (1858)," 89.

horses and mules, and worked my way through in the inconceivably short time, not of 26 hours, but some four or five days. Twenty-six hours is stuff and nonsense.[4] They worked me in and out by doubling past compound ranges and through passes, no passes, such as I have never read of even in childrens' story books of Alpine hunters. I was under a pledge to reveal nothing of the Mormons' military plans, I was under pledge not to tell any thing of the route by which we came—but I could not have told it if I had wanted to—only I did see then, if I had doubted it before, how completely these mountaineers had our foolish herds of "soldier" at their mercy.[5]

The Mormon soldiers who took me over, believed with the Mormons at Salt Lake in what they said of the temper of Camp Scott. The first I knew of it was in an unmistakeably sincere warning as to the care I should take myself to approach our own lines. You say Mr. Egan told you of some incidents of the march, but he did not tell you of what took place after I left them.[6]

A Self-Constituted Ambassador: Mixed Receptions

If there has been a gap in historians' understanding of what Tom Kane experienced in getting to the Utah Expedition's picket lines on the evening of 12 March 1858, there is no shortage of material describing what happened immediately after he entered the camp. With Fort Bridger, Camp Scott, and Eckelsville teeming with letter writers, diarists, and newspaper correspondents, accounts of Kane's unexpected arrival and speculation about his identity, religious affiliation, and intentions flowed freely. After interviewing Kane, French correspondent Louis Bertrand reported that, upon arriving at Fort Bridger, "he literally fell as a bombshell in the midst of federal officers."[7] To his brother, Kane bragged, "I got actually into camp (probably the 12 of March) without brushing against a sentry. I will say that I could have got in among the cowards otherwise in safety."

Three days later, Kane described his arrival to President Buchanan more dramatically:

---

[4]Here Kane reacted to what must have been newspaper accounts of his travels, probably rooted in his preposterous comment upon arriving at Fort Bridger that he had ridden from Salt Lake City in twenty-four hours.

[5]Cryptic, largely illegible, and indecipherable notes and maps describing his travels appear in Kane, "Diary II (1858)," 3.

[6]Pat Kane met Howard Egan at his mother's home near Philadelphia in June 1858, while Egan waited to courier a message from his brother to Brigham Young.

[7]Bertrand in Homer, *On the Way to Somewhere Else*, 108.

> I arrived in Ft. Bridger on the evening of the 13 [12]th. Although the snow proved deeper in the drifts in the Mts. than was expected for a winter of which has the reputation of being uncommonly mild I never for more than a single day doubted that my effort wd. be successful. Having not be[e]n as practised as yr. regulars of the army & navy in recounting common place perils "on the raging canawl."[8] I only add to my mention of the fact that I did arrive as above that I thereupon directly became the debtor of the kind hearted officer commanding [the post and a company of the Fifth Infantry]. He took me off my horse and put me to bed in his own couch, and as I learn that he is notoriously a gallant and efficient officer I will write his name is Captain (W. E.)? [John Cleveland] Robinson, of Conn. [New York] whom if my word or glass of wine can ever help to promote it shall henceforth ever be forthcoming.[9]

Robinson, the senior officer at Fort Bridger, immediately sent a note to Maj. Fitz John Porter, Colonel Johnston's adjutant at nearby Camp Scott: "I have the honor to report that Mr. Kane of Philadelphia (son of Judge Kane) arrived here this evening from Salt Lake City, too much exhausted to go any farther. I only learn from him that he wishes to see the Colonel Comdg & Govr Cumming. He has gone to bed and asleep—but will proceed to Hd.Qrs. tomorrow morning."[10] Even before meeting the newcomer, Porter recorded a negative reaction in his diary: "Capt Robinson tonight reports the arrival of a son of Judge Kane of Phila. From Salt Lake City.—left the States via California 5th Jany—and been in Salt Lake City 8 days—24 hours from S.L.C.—good riding—. I cannot believe him aught else than a self-constituted ambassador from the States and comes with a proposition from Brigham as insulting as his [November] Salt Letter.—He has nothing to do with us,—as we have to go forward,—and nothing but orders can stop us when we are ready."[11]

And so from the moment Thomas L. Kane crossed into the Utah Expedition's lines, he created not only a sensation but hostility. In 1850 Kane

---

[8]"The Raging Canawl" was the title of a comic folk song written by P. Morris in 1844 to lampoon the dangers of boating on New York's Erie Canal. During flights of fancy, Kane sprinkled the phrase in cryptic fashion throughout his letters.

[9]Kane to Buchanan, ca. 15 March 1858, Kane Family Papers, BYU. Robinson, a Union general in the Civil War, was indeed "gallant," later distinguishing himself in combat at Gettysburg, the Wilderness, Spotsylvania Court House, and Laurel Hill, losing a leg and receiving the Medal of Honor. Following the war he became national commander of the G.A.R. as well as lieutenant governor of New York. In 1884 Robinson published a brief account of the Utah War in which he criticized the Mormons, repeating virtually all of the conspiracy theories about the conflict's origins and wholly neglecting to mention Kane, although they had not only shared a tent overnight at Bridger but later fought together at Gettysburg. Robinson, "The Utah Expedition," 335–41.

[10]Robinson to Porter, 12 March 1858, Cumming Papers, Duke University.

[11]Porter Diary, 12 March 1858, Porter Collection, Manuscript Division, LC.

MAJ. FITZ JOHN PORTER, JOHNSTON'S ADJUTANT AND CONFIDANT
In October 1857 Lt. Col. Robert E. Lee wrote Johnston of Porter, "I am glad you have him with you. He is an able aid[e] in the field, & valuable everywhere." The 2d Dragoons' Colonel Cooke disagreed. Porter chafed under Kane's use of his old militia rank and showiness, viewing him as a "fool" and "an ass though a gentleman." Kane damned Porter to Buchanan with faint praise as a "petite & efficient adjutant." With proximity to Johnston, Porter's criticism of both Kane and the Mormons ("thieves, cowards") reinforced the colonel's own negative views. This photo was taken at Camp Floyd ca. January 1859 by Mills & Jagiello. *Courtesy of Ephriam Dickson III and NARA.*

had garnered public admiration by rising from a sickbed to be carried into Philadelphia's Independence Hall on an unhinged door to deliver a lecture in defense of the Mormons. When he galloped virtually insensible through the gloom of Fort Bridger's defensive perimeter eight years later, the startled sentries and embarrassed officer of the day gave no credit for the dramatic flourish. Kane lacked awareness that the Utah Expedition was then both news-starved and in a state of high alert following herdsman Edgar Brown's return from captivity ten days earlier. Two days after Kane hurtled into Johnston's edgy camp, the colonel recruited four more agents for his company of spies.

Then there was the matter of Kane's image. His small stature and assertive behavior immediately attracted attention, as did the superior quality of his outfit.[12] Kane's possessions and attire were matters of great personal

[12]When Kane applied for a federal military pension in 1882 at age 58, he listed his height as 5' 4" and his weight at 122 pounds. Apostle Benson had described Kane in March 1858 as weighing 104 pounds. Matthew J. Grow, e-mail message to MacKinnon, 27 March 2006. Grow has described perceptions of Kane at this juncture as somewhat "effeminate," but to a ragged Utah Expedition he probably came across as more of what ranchers thirty years later would label a "dude."

pride, yet they generated immediate reactions of envy tinged with contempt from the Utah Expedition's threadbare garrison.[13] One officer recorded with amazement that "he appeared to have a red sash on under his over-coat"; another noted that Kane arrived "with a pack mule, splendidly mounted. His whole outfit is new and well made up."[14] Correspondent David A. Burr reported, "his attire indicated that he was by no means an ordinary expressman, as he was well and warmly clad in furs."[15] When a few hours later a trail-hardened Mariano Medina rode into Fort Bridger with dispatches from Santa Fe—alone, quietly, and probably astride an army mule—the contrast with Thomas Kane's arrival was stark.[16]

Kane's explanation that he had lingered at Salt Lake City for more than a week also created a negative first impression, as did his incredible assertion that he had ridden to Bridger in a single day. Perhaps most corrosive was the anxiety that immediately welled up among both officers and enlistees—the dread that the arrival of this stranger would somehow alter the course of the war to deny them military glory as well as the pleasure of punishing Mormons. The Utah Expedition worried that political maneuvering by Young and Kane or the arrival of federal troops from California might pre-empt Albert Sidney Johnston's opportunity to complete his mission.[17] The unknown intentions of Kane, a name dropper from a nationally famous Philadelphia family, posed a threat to the Utah Expedition's promotion-hungry, vengeful officers.

---

[13]It is unlikely that Kane arrived at Fort Bridger sporting his tiger skin, but he wore the warm buffalo clothing that Amasa Lyman's daughter-in-law made at Cottonwood Springs a month earlier. From Fort Bridger, Kane boasted to his brother (and perhaps others), "I came here with the best horse, the best mule, the best furs, the *best rifle* and luckily for me, as things have gone, the reputation of being the best shot with the pistol, in camp." Kane to Pat Kane, 4 April 1858, Kane Family Papers, BYU.

[14]Phelps Diary, 13 March 1858, Hamilton Gardner transcription, Gardner Collection, Utah State Historical Society; Gove to Mrs. Gove, 14 March 1858, *The Utah Expedition*, 134.

[15][Burr], "Highly Important from Utah. Arrival of Col. Kane at Fort Bridger," Dispatch, 24 March 1858, *New-York Daily Tribune*, 24 May 1858, 5/6–6/1.

[16]Most important of Medina's papers, of course, was General Garland's secret offer to reinforce the Utah Expedition with eight hundred troops from New Mexico.

[17]"Our present fear is that what we are debarred from undertaking [a winter march on Salt Lake City] will be accomplished from the side of California before we can move in the Spring. The 'Army of Utah' will then have had all the toil of a march unprecedented in length, through a country which it is complimentary to call a desert, and all the *ennui* of hibernation at an altitude of nearly 7,000 feet above the level of the Gulf of Mexico, at a distance of only 113 miles from Salt Lake City, only to see whatever glory was to be gained from the expedition inure to others." [Browne], "Late from the Utah Expedition. General Indignation in the Army," Dispatch, 26 November 1857, *New-York Daily Tribune*, 18 January 1858, 2/1–3.

The most comprehensive narrative of Kane's arrival at Fort Bridger and the rumors that it stoked appeared in the newspaper dispatch of David A. Burr. It was a piece in which he reported: "The most intense curiosity was thus created throughout the whole command in regard to the possible object of his mission. It was generally supposed that Brigham Young and his associates had fled, and that the remaining Mormons had laid down their arms and were ready to receive us; but by many this could not be believed, and the anxiety of all was great to have the enigma solved."[18]

An Absence of Proper Deference: Kane Meets Johnston

Emerging refreshed from the hospitality of Captain Robinson's tent on 13 March, Kane rode the two miles to Camp Scott to pay a courtesy call on Albert Sidney Johnston. It was a seemingly prosaic act of protocol, but one of which Captain Marcy had run afoul at General Garland's New Mexico headquarters. Kane wanted not only to observe military courtesy but to inform Johnston that he would be meeting immediately with Governor Cumming at Eckelsville. Unknown to him, Johnston and Cumming were at odds over several petty matters, an interpersonal tension that threatened the Kane-Johnston relationship as it began.[19] As with the matter of Kane's arrival the previous night, first impressions were powerful and, in the case of these two officers, indelible.

To an unknown extent, whatever views about Cumming that General Harney had shared with Johnston at Fort Leavenworth in September may have colored Johnston's view of Cumming (and, by indirection, Kane). Harney had clashed with Cumming two years earlier at Fort Pierre, Nebraska Territory, following the latter's treaty negotiations with the Blackfeet.[20]

[18][Burr], "Highly Important From Utah. Arrival of Col. Kane at Fort Bridger," Dispatch, 24 March 1858, *New-York Daily Tribune,* 24 May 1858, 5/6–6/1.

[19]See *At Sword's Point, Part 1,* 180, 377–78. Compounding these incidents was a convoluted, early December imbroglio in which Cumming declined to act on Johnston's request to commission Capt. Bee a lieutenant colonel as commander of the newly formed Volunteer Battalion. Finally both leaders took independent action to fashion an arrangement, which saved face for Cumming while meeting the Utah Expedition's needs. Porter Diary, 7–8 December 1857, Porter Collection, LC.

[20]Chittenden, *History of Early Steamboat Navigation on the Missouri River,* 1:356–57; Bradley, "Affairs at Fort Benton," 276. A summary of the governor's embroilments in the mid-1850s while serving as superintendent of the Upper Missouri agency, and a brief discussion of his subsequent Utah assignment appear in White, "Alfred Cumming, 1856, Indians on the Upper Missouri," 415–36.

There are two firsthand accounts of what took place at Colonel Johnston's headquarters, both privately recorded but soon fodder for camp-wide gossip and eventually national publicity. They came from Major Porter and Captain Phelps, both mature, long-serving West Pointers with unmistakable anti-Mormon biases and loyalty to Colonel Johnston.

PORTER DIARY, 13 MARCH 1858, PORTER COLLECTION, LC.

While in my tent (office) the Mr Kane rode up to the Colonel's tent, with a very self satisfied air (playing the grand in presence of a number of *teamsters* then about). The Colonel was informed by the servant that a gentleman wished to see him, and the gentleman was invited to enter. The Colonel stepped to the door, and the man said "I left the States on the 5th of January, and am the bearer of dispatches to you and to Gov. Cumming." "Dismount and walk in Sir," said the Colonel. "With your permission Sir," looking around on what he supposed an admiring audience but one laughing at his conceit and self-sufficiency, "I will see the Governor first." "Certainly Sir." "Sergeant lead me to the Governor"; and was led—like an ass—because [he is] an ass.—Quite theatrical.

Just at dinner-time today I was informed that the Sergeant above designated was still attending on the *gentleman,* and asked if I should not ask Lieut. [Cuvier] Grover [the provost marshal] to send one of his men to relieve him, that he might get his dinner and the *gentleman's* property and person be secured from violence, if he is a Mormon—and as many people of the camp would be inclined to injure or insult him. The Governor became very angry, presumed Col. J. designed insulting him, and acted very childishly and in an undignified manner,—and evidently strived to make a disturbance and bring Col. J. into trouble. If the Governor be loyal to his country, he should not be making trouble but striving to conciliate the good will of the army.—I can attribute his behaviour only [to] that of a drunken man or one furiously jealous.[21]

PHELPS DIARY, 13 MARCH 1858,
HAMILTON GARDNER PAPERS, UTAH STATE HISTORICAL SOCIETY.

I happened to be at head quarters this morning when he [Kane] came up from Bridgers' Fort. He was a short, dark complected young man and was well mounted. One of the Provost Sergeants led his sumpter [pack] mule which was a fine animal well packed.

[21]Within the boundaries of Victorian propriety, this may have been Porter's way of signaling that the Utah Expedition perceived Cumming as having an alcohol problem. He may have been aware that Cumming's nephew, a captain in the Tenth Infantry, was also struggling with alcohol. *At Sword's Point, Part 1,* 222n54.

> Without looking right or left he moved straight forward to the commanding officer's tent and seemed as if he wished to ride into it instead of stopping out side, so near did he urge his horse to the opening. Someone—probably a servant—knocked and informed the Colonel that someone wished to see him. The Col. was engaged in conversation and did not come out immediately, and this delay when compared with the man's forwardness seemed to look and be felt as a check. Presently the Col. came partly out; being stopped apparently by the man's horse whose head was nearly in the opening, and looking up in a crouched attitude, his own head being near the horse's head, said "Who are you?"
>
> "Are you Colonel Johnston," asked the man.
>
> "Yes," replied the Colonel.
>
> "I am Mr. Kane," said he, "from Philadelphia, bearer of dispatches; I ask your permission to see Governor Cummings [*sic*] first, I'll see you afterwards."
>
> To this the Colonel assented and turned back into his tent. The man immediately turned away saying—"I'll see you again Colonel Johnson.—Come on Sergeant."
>
> He seemed to speak with a short breath as if repressing excitement of some kind. He appeared to have a red sash on under his over-coat. There was an absence of that proper deference due from one of his pretended character to an officer commanding an army of the United States. In his whole bearing he seemed to attach in [an] undue importance to his mission whatever it may be. He went up to the Governor's and has remained there all day without any one knowing what news he has brought.[22]

Within a day of Kane's arrival, Captain Gove confided to his wife, "My men want to hang him.[23] Say he is a Mormon. Half persuaded that they may be right from recent developments. Yesterday, 13th, he went to the upper camp and is now with Gov. Cumming. What his business is no one yet knows. Reports are many and varied this morning. Some trouble has already arisen between the civil and military authorities relative to this man. He says his name is Kane, from Philadelphia, brother to the late Dr. Kane, that he left New York the 5th of January. He has not yet delivered any despatches to Col. Johnston, though he told him he had some for him."[24]

On 14 March Major Porter noted, "The Governor is still unpacified," and described a second brief visit to Johnston's headquarters: "Mr. Kane called

---

[22]This excerpt from Phelps's diary also appears in Schindler, *Orrin Porter Rockwell,* 285–86.

[23]One of Gove's privates, Michael McCarty, would fire on Kane from his sentinel's post as Kane rode into the Utah Expedition's lines on the night of 17 March. Nielson, *Roll Call at Old Camp Floyd,* 98.

[24]Gove to Mrs. Gove, 14 March 1858, *The Utah Expedition,* 134.

upon the Colonel this afternoon,—and in a very formal manner handed the Col. a letter from Mr Buchanan,—stating that he, Kane, had his confidence. K. said he only made a formal call, and had information which would be valuable, and would be happy to impart to Col. J. if he called. 'Good evening Sir,'—and wiggled off."[25]

That Abominable Camp Business: Kane Beleaguered

Sensing the enmity at Camp Scott, Kane withdrew to new quarters in Eckelsville's ramshackle warren of dugouts, log cabins, tents, buggies, and wagon boxes.[26] The place was a far cry from the genteel amenities of Salt Lake City's Lion House and Staines mansion, but it was in close proximity to Governor Cumming and a haven from the palpable disapproval of Johnston's garrison. From this place Kane episodically issued invitations to Johnston and Porter or sallied out to Camp Scott to conduct business at their quarters.

Once again, correspondent Burr provided the most coherent account of Kane's early days with the Utah Expedition.

[Burr], "Highly Important from Utah. Arrival of Col. Kane at Fort Bridger," Dispatch, 24 March 1858, *New-York Daily Tribune*, 24 May 1858, 5/6–6/1.

After reporting to the Colonel at his quarters, he proceeded immediately to the Governor's residence. The desire to know what could be the news now grew stronger and stronger. One, two, three hours passed, yet he remained alone in close conference with the Governor. The excitement became intense throughout the camp; it pervaded all ranks, and groups of men were gathered in all directions, discussing the merits of this or that conjecture. It was ascertained that this was the Col. Kane who had written a work favorable to the Mormons,[27] who had defended them through the press, and whose influence had secured the appointment of Brigham Young as Governor. As the day wore on, the Governor had his horses sent to the [garrison's] herd, and it was announced that he had made him his guest.

It was currently reported that he had been sent by the President to make a treaty with the Mormons, and all sorts of conjectures were rumored as the truth. Some believed that he was sent by the President as a Commissioner; others that he was a Mormon, and had forged the President's signature in

---

[25]Porter Diary, 14 March 1858, Porter Collection, LC.

[26]See the David A. Burr photograph of this scene, *At Sword's Point, Part 1*, 470.

[27]A reference to Kane's published 1850 lecture before the Pennsylvania Historical Society, *The Mormons*.

order to betray us; others again that he had no papers from the Administration, but was a Mormon emissary. The fact of his being a Mormon emissary seemed strengthened by his former connection with the Mormons—for [John] Hyde, in his work on Mormonism, states that Col. Kane was baptized into the Mormon Church in Iowa—and also from the fact, according to his own statement, of his having been able to pass through the Mormon lines and make his way to our camp unmolested.[28]

The whole day was spent by Col. Kane with the Governor, except a formal visit which he made to Chief Justice Eckels, and Dr. Forney, Superintendent of Indian Affairs. Fears were now expressed that he might succeed with his Excellency, the Governor, in making some compromise with the Mormons; and Col. Kane was openly denounced by many as a Mormon traitor and spy, who should be arrested and put in confinement.

However, the next day, his Honor Chief Justice Eckels was admitted to the conference, and that evening we were relieved to hear from these gentlemen that Col. Kane's object was a most honorable one, and that it would not probably in the least affect our movements, and also that he brought letters of introduction from Washington City. Nothing further has been divulged concerning his mission.

The general impression now is that he is favorably disposed toward the Mormons—he has always been their friend in the States—and that, seeing their impending ruin, he procured letters of introduction from Washington to the Governor and Colonel in order to give character and weight to his efforts in accomplishing his purposes; and that he is now in camp as a sort of Commissioner from the Mormons, either from Brigham Young, or some of the leaders opposed to Brigham, who are forming a party favorable to the United States Government.

His reception at Camp Scott shocked and disillusioned Kane, and he described these feelings as well as a sense of personal endangerment to his brother in terms far more explicit than he used in reporting to Buchanan.

Kane to Pat Kane, ca. Summer 1858, "In Re Mormons" File, Thomas Leiper Kane Papers, aps.

Now you come [in reading this] to that abominable camp business, which I still intend to hold my tongue upon, as long as Johnston appears to be prudent and holds his. But when you think I should be severe upon *him*, I found them all [at Camp Scott] as I described them to the President, monomaniacs, and recollect I make no exception.[29] Afterward when things thickened, when opposition itself and the development of petty party division in the camp, developed

[28] Hyde, *Mormonism: Its Leaders and Designs.* This exposé by an excommunicated Latter-day Saint became available to the Utah Expedition's officers during the summer of 1857.

[29] Kane to Buchanan, ca. 15 March 1858, Kane Family Papers, BYU.

> manhood, and taught the better part of a man what it ought to do, I gathered some elements of force about me. If I had not I might have been hung as a spy. If I had not I would certainly not have been permitted to go out [beyond the lines] to communicate with a single Mormon. As it was you know what was the effort to arrest me, you know that false witnesses were ready to swear me a horse-thief, a Mormon, or murderer . . . you know that my life was threatened, you know the precautions I had to take to protect myself from assassination.

Within this context, Judge Eckels sensed a communications vacuum and apparently attempted to assume the role of intermediary. Probably without Kane's knowledge, Eckels met at length with Johnston and Porter to explain what he understood from Kane to be his mission as well as Brigham Young's point of view. Major Porter recorded the dialogue between the principals at Camp Scott and Eckelsville.

PORTER DIARY, 15 AND 16 MARCH 1858, PORTER COLLECTION, LC.

15 March 1858

Judge Eckels called today and evidently with the design of playing the part of the [biblical] good Samaritan. We were closetted for some four hours, and many misunderstandings explained—misunderstandings on the part of the civil authorities—not on ours. He explained the object of Mr K.'s visit, and stated that B.Y. was much concerned at the troubles of the territory—regretted his letter on salt to Col. J.—and is desirous of putting an end to the clamors against them. He has again made an offer of furnishing supplies to us, and again answered by Col. J. in a manner to cause the government of the U.S. to be respected, and our army to be feared, as willing to starve rather than receive supplies from him, and if willing to do that the Mormons must fear their zeal when directed in another way.

16 March 1858

A call from Col. J. was invited by Mr Kane, and we went together to receive his communication or have a conference. The Colonel stated to me if Col. K. had any communication which he could not give in my hearing he would not receive it, and should so tell him, as he regards me as his confidential officer, and there are no secrets between us. Mr Kane received us friendly but very stiffly, and evidently officially. The citizen Colonel[30] opened his conference by stating his object of asking an interview, which was substantially to obtain

[30]Here Porter lapses into sarcasm in using the title colonel, an honorific derived from Kane's appointment for several months in 1846 as a lieutenant colonel on the staff of the governor of Pennsylvania. Porter (and Johnston) may also have chafed under the knowledge that Cumming used the title colonel while serving as superintendent of Indian affairs for the Upper Missouri, not an unusual practice among civilians (like W. M. F. Magraw) assuming senior non-military appointments on the frontier.

a reconsideration and if possible a modification of Col Johnston's letter to him yesterday. The Colonel begged then to interrupt him and state the reasons for writing as he did. He said: "I have nothing whatever to do with the political question between the Mormons and the Government. I am here in the fulfilment of special instructions from the Government, and I have on another occasion informed Brigham Young of that fact, and substantially the same as I have in my letter, & that peace or war is in his hands. I told Mr Earle[31] to inform him, that I had nothing to do with him, or his people, and that when I advance if the people stay at home and behave themselves, and do not molest me they will not be troubled—that the army is to protect not oppress, but if my advance is opposed with force I shall meet it with force—that it well became Brigham Young to consider before he acted to bring on the horrors of war—that the officers under him who had been in many battles and knew the scenes attending victory were often more horrible than those attending battle: that they did not want war—but feared not its results however horrible and avoided them not when forced upon them—that Brigham Young should consider the calamities he is bringing upon his people, in pursuing a course of open opposition" (Col. K. said he had heard all repeated and that it had its effect upon B.Y.)

Col. K. then said his object to obtain a reconsideration [of Johnston's letter] was the result of a desire for peace—that the [more recent] offer of salt, and the offer of provisions was a peace offering—that there was a large peace party in Utah and B.Y. was at the head. That he feared the answer [drafted by Johnston] would prejudice the object of his mission, and indicate no desire for peace on our side. The Col (J) told him his remarks were not designed to be harsh or disrespectful, that if he wished he could use terms to irritate—but he had carefully refrained from it.—as for instance—"He said he might have used the word restore to Mr Garrish, Mr Irvin [*sic*], Mr Radford[32] &c the property taken from them &c.—Col K. stated the object of his mission—peace—that B.Y. was anxious for it,—and designed his letter as an overture—a peace-offering—also his salt letter—Stated how B.Y. was under the influence of a power he could not govern—that two parties were in existence in S.L.C.—One military and opposed to peace—the other, and the larger a peace party. He said B.Y. was very unhappy and did

[31]Jesse J. Earl, one of Brigham Young's agents who had tried to deliver salt to the army during November, not to be confused with Wilbur J. Earl of Springville, who was deeply involved in the Potter-Parrish murders of the same month and that of Henry Jones in January 1858.

[32]References to William Gerrish, Joseph C. ("Doc") Irwin, and John D. ("Jack") Radford, whose firms accompanied the Utah Expedition as either regimental sutlers or as traders hoping to do a general mercantile business in Salt Lake City. Some of these firms lost cattle or goods during the Nauvoo Legion's raids of the previous fall. Radford was foreman of the federal grand jury that returned treason indictments against Young and dozens of his colleagues in December 1857 at Eckelsville, and Irwin was a juror on that panel. *At Sword's Point, Part 1,* 469–70.

want peace but that Col. J's answer was tending to break that tendency. His admissions of B.Y.'s weakness and of the existence of two parties was an important one to us. He believes the Mormons will destroy everything and take to the mountains—a foolish notion.

The conference was a long one but ended without the Colonel changing his opinions or reconsidering his note,—and in Mr K. agreeing to take his letter. He asked for an officer to accompany him,—or an escort, which was promised him.—The trouble as to his arrest &c settled.

Cowards, Assassins, and Bullies: Major Porter's Influence

In connection with such discussions, Major Porter's proximity to Johnston would have been both influential and perhaps inflammatory. Even thirty years later, Philip St. George Cooke, Johnston's dragoon commander, recalled, "I was long an intimate friend [of Johnston], until a connextion with one F.J.P. befell him. Then I first discovered his weakness in not marching on Salt Lake City that fall."[33] Although Porter phrased his official correspondence professionally, his personal letters to friends, several of whom were senior aides to Secretary Floyd and General Scott, were loaded with anti-Mormon rhetoric that matched Brigham Young's and General Harney's most provocative fulminations. For example, at the end of November 1857, Porter confided to a colleague at Winfield Scott's headquarters in New York, "the Mormons are a set of cowards, like all assassins and bullies," a comment that later triggered an uproar in Salt Lake City when Porter's letter was leaked to a New York newspaper and mistakenly attributed to Colonel Cooke. At year-end 1857 Porter confided to the army's adjutant general in Washington that the "Mormons are armed for the fight and no gentle action will quell them, and the rebellion will only be quenched by thorough extermination. They are monsters in minds and morals, their children are worthy of their sires. . . . This people . . . deserve no mercy at the hands of Government."[34] Two

[33]Cooke to William Tecumseh Sherman, 7 May 1889, Cooke Papers, Library of Virginia, Richmond.

[34]This sort of anti-Mormon rhetoric in the Utah Expedition was pervasive. Even in New Mexico Captain Marcy informed his wife that in the spring "we shall then have men enough to whip all the Mormons in the United States, and if there was ever a holy war it is the one to be waged against them as they are the vilest and most debased people on Earth. They are a set of murderous robbers and highwaymen and deserve to be annihilated." Five months later, with little self-awareness, Marcy would tell his daughter with astonishment from Salt Lake that "there are a very few Mormon men about here but not a single woman or child that I have seen. They must think we are barbarians if they suppose we would harm their women or children." Marcy to Mary Marcy, 25 January 1858, and Marcy to Mary Ellen Marcy, 27 June 1858, both Hollon transcriptions, Hollon Papers, Canaday Center, University of Toledo, and McClellan Papers, LC.

weeks before Kane arrived at Fort Bridger, Porter privately denigrated the Utah Expedition's adversaries to George B. McClellan as "an infernal set of cowards like all assassins."

Once Major Porter moved deeper into Utah and in close proximity to her Mormon population, his invectives intensified. In May 1859, from Camp Floyd, he informed an officer at Fort Laramie that "We have no hope of a rebellion [here]. The Mormons cannot be kicked into it. A thousand of them well armed would not face one tenth of the number of our men. They will in small parties and individually, steal, rob, lie, murder, assassinate, brag, intimidate, deny their faith, would be as humble as [*David Copperfield*'s] Uriah Heap [*sic*]. Anything to gain a point to milk a gentile, or deceive one, or to serve their prophet. Anything except suffer martyrdom, which they would like to do if it did not hurt and [they] could come back to this world again safe and sound?"[35]

With Porter as Johnston's adjutant, his "confidential officer," and tent mate, it is inevitable that the major's steady flow of comments reinforced Colonel Johnston's own jaundiced views of Brigham Young and the Latter-day Saints.[36]

Narrative of My Disappointment: Kane Reports to Buchanan

In the midst of these Kane-Johnston discussions, Kane felt a need to provide President Buchanan with a status report. In a rambling, sometimes cryptic, and highly informal document, Kane described at length his earlier sessions with Brigham Young. He disclosed to Buchanan that while in Salt Lake he had taken two extraordinary liberties: allowing Young to shape at least one of his dispatches to the president without attribution, and offering "Young himself, and his immediate friends the assurance of pardon 'for meritorious service to the U.S.' on the strength of our interview confidentially communicated." Unconfessed to Buchanan was the fact that Kane had also tendered to Young an apology on the president's behalf.

---

[35]Porter to Maj. Irvin McDowell, 29 November 1857, as discussed in MacKinnon, "Fitz John Porter's Letter," vii–ix; Porter to Cooper, 31 December 1857, Letters Received, Office of the Adjt. Gen., RG 94, NARA; Porter to McClellan, 28 February 1858, McClellan Papers, LC; Porter to Lt. Col. John Munroe, 11 May 1859, Porter Letters, Manuscript Library, New-York Historical Society.

[36]Indicative of Porter's impact was the fact that Maj. Irvin McDowell, the senior adjutant at army headquarters, often shared his letters with General Scott, who, in turn, passed them to Secretary Floyd on an unofficial basis. For example, see Scott-to-Floyd endorsements on Porter to McDowell, 13 February 1858 (about trail conditions between Fort Laramie and Fort Bridger) and September 1858 (about General Harney's demeanor), Porter Collection, LC; *At Sword's Point, Part 1*, 161.

With these stunning revelations out of the way, and the limited knowledge acquired from less than three full days with the Utah Expedition, Kane's report excoriated the behavior of the army and its camp followers, condemned Eckels's discretion and judgment, recommended a series of sweeping actions, and cast himself in the role of prospective advisor to the Mormons in a way that surely exceeded anything Buchanan would have sanctioned. It is a document as loaded with hubris as laced with the personal pronouns "I" and "me."

Kane to Buchanan,
ca. 15 March 1858, Kane Family Papers, byu.

I am more content to be limited in my privilege of writing to you than I should have been a week ago. I have found the state of affairs at Camp Scott less favorable than I had reason to anticipate, and the briefer I can make the narrative of my disappointment the less the recollection of it will give me pain. You must remember that without official position as I am here, I cannot give you the sum of many particulars in the form of brief and authoritative conclusions of my own. My chief value to you, now, is, I think, as a collector of facts, as your friend, your true and grateful friend, Sir, who can best serve you by putting himself in the witness-box, and giving you that evidence which your own directing mind can act upon. Pardon, at least, therefore, this wordy preface.

I come now to the recital which I am glad to make you briefly but a little consideration of the state of things before hand shd. have prepared me before hand for my disappt.

A mixed society of about 2,000 womanless men—soldiers officers teamsters & camp followers (professional gamblers and professional anti-Mormons who had been feeding on hard beef, whiskey and a great deal of tobacco) generally had been compelled to halt within less than the distance between Philadelphia and Washington from the little capital where they had promised themselves a Capua[37] of enjoyment and luxury and compelled [instead] to pass an entire winter in extreme discomfort and a state of idleness & inaction itself sufficiently shocking to contemplate. Imprisoned within their camp bounds—when chewing at their toughest saltless beef or swearing through their hardest oaths round the smokiest tent fire, they cd. [could] *do* nothing against the Mormons. They cd. only talk against them—Weary as I was of those who cd. talk and think nothing but the *Mormon Question* T.O. [Tired Of?] when I left the Valley. I find that I have only exchanged one set of monomaniacs for another. As is the natural course of things in such

[37]The Italian scene of several battles between Rome and Carthage during the third century A.D.

cases too, the little Mutual Admiration (and mutual detraction) Society had come to feel fully impressed of the importance of its peculiar position and the fact that it was the eye mark of the world and must therefore consent to settle the Utah question for the nation. (In the Indian country in fact we always attend to things.) Do not regard me as speaking thus censoriously of the military. To assail the enemy or in Halleck's language to "swear at least to meet them undismayed" is their first (if they wd. but believe it their only!) duty.[38]

I observe, that I am tempted to keep my language away from that which it displeases me to think of.—To the point. I am not able. I cannot in honor. I dare not take upon myself the responsibility of advising the Mormons as I did a fortnight ago, to admit this army and its followers *indiscriminately?* within their Valley.

I[.] I am *not* entirely satisfied that our officers will be able to control their soldiers—much less their disorderly retinue of Camp follower and attendants (and keep them from committing excesses & offenses against the laws.)

II[.] I am *not* satisfied that the Mormon citizens of Utah will be tried for their offenses by juries impartially chosen, or that such attention will be paid to the forms of law as will persuade the world (of our intention to do them justice) that justice will be done them.

Upon the first head I do not feel at liberty to speak diffusely—wishing to pay particular regard to the friendly personal relations at present subsisting between myself and Colonel A. S. Johnston. I simply express to you the opinion which I have formed.

Under my NO. 2. I would respectfully call your attention to a fact which sooner or later, must reach the ears of the Mormons and awaken their alarm, if I should evade admitting it to them myself.—My reading of books has not particularly informed me if the "rabble rout" which follows other armies is as dissolute and wicked as that which I find gathering around this one.[39] Gambling, stealing—fighting—stabbing it seemed last fall past hope that they would not involve themselves and the few about deserving better in the fate of the rats in the barrel. I would regard the course of the Territorial Government regard had to this matter solely as deserving of high commendation. Indeed it was a fine feat to organise this very vile material as part of the machinery of Law, and with only the assistance of one man [Judge Eckels] acting as Judge to make it try, condemn and punish itself till it became suitably afraid. This has been done,—with such thoroughness in fact that now they will not *suffer*

[38]Kane quotes from Fitz-Greene Halleck's 1819 poem satirizing New York society, "Fanny."

[39]Although Johnston was a strict disciplinarian, on 16 March he commented to Kane (for Young's benefit) that he might not be able to control his troops and camp followers and that Young should "consider before he acted to bring on the horrors of war" that "the scenes attending victory were often more horrible than those attending battle." Porter Diary, 16 March 1858, Porter Collection, LC.

themselves to commit any offence in open day except gambling which in a camp perhaps it might seem ridiculous to affect to regard as such.[40]

But now for the bad consequences of "straining a point or two." The Court organised by our *one Judge* here, in *Green* [River] *County* with its Grand Jury composed of *"inhabitants"* proceeded to indict nearly every pro Mormon citizen of Utah enjoying influence there and whom it is desirable to conciliate or reward for his patriotic feeling toward the U.S. When I last heard from the *Court* they had found 75 true single Bills with a fine prospect of getting up more.

When the Mormons hear of this, familiar as they are with the character of nearly every sportsman & professed Anti-Mormon upon the so called Grand Jury, how shall I persuade them that this is not "Illinois & Missouri over again" and that the Juries of 12 by whom their lives will be had in charge will be composed of different materials?[41] I wish to avoid all appearance even of unkind criticism in speaking of the acts of Judge Eckels. I respect in him a gentleman of both energy and mental activity assiduous to cultivate relations with me of a *flattering* character. While his two Associates [Judges Charles E. Sinclair and John Cradlebaugh] have never even left the U.S. to come out here—and while he has been without Commissioner, District Attorney, or Deputy District Attorney,[42] I have to give him credit with Governor Cumming for the entire achievement of establishing order. Indeed the "bandits and *sportsmen* in the willows" he has informed me are even now threatening his life for his efforts to pull down their tents.[43]

But your Appointee [Eckels] is, I am compelled to say, perhaps an over eager prosecutor and certainly one of the most indiscreet of speakers. Ignorant that he is surrounded by persons who report and misrepresent his every word and action—having, (a secret that would make me laugh if it were less deplorable) near him as certain witnesses for the prosecution of whom he takes counsel—(and which cunning rascals are Mormons in communication with Salt Lake City) he boasts to all the world of what he intends to do when he reaches the little capital, how A.Z. and B.Y. and Co. naming each one, cannot escape "his halter" [noose], and how convinced he is that Mercy to the Union orders that blood shall freely flow &c &c.

---

[40]Newspaper reporter Burr, who doubled as a justice of the peace, confirmed Kane's view of the gambling influence at Camp Scott and noted that even the garrison's tough military police were unsafe while patrolling such establishments. [Burr], "From the Utah Army," Dispatch, 5 March 1858, *New-York Daily Times*, 19 May 1858, 1/1.

[41]For the December 1857 federal grand jury, see *At Sword's Point, Part 1*, 468–74.

[42]John M. Hockaday, U.S. attorney for Utah, had left Camp Scott on 5 January to return to Washington to seek the role of mail contractor on the Missouri–Salt Lake City route. Upon his departure, Eckels had appointed Washington J. McCormick, a protégé, to be Hockaday's successor on an interim basis.

[43]In his correspondence Kane cryptically referred to "the willows"—the vegetation lining Blacks Fork—as shorthand for latrines as well as a variety of activities such as gambling, drinking, trafficking in stolen army supplies, and sexual activity with Indian women.

> Falsehood, Mr. Buchanan, falsehood I am sure. If I were a Mormon I think I would trust my life to him as readily as any other—especially if the District Attorney pressed unfairly for my conviction and I was without other counsel for the Defence than Judge Eckels.[44] But here on Black's Fork, you see, he too can only talk, and he does talk. And he is reported to have said among other things that—he *will in no case whatever admit to Bail a person accused of Treason.* All of which—at the present critical juncture—is Bad—Very Bad.

Crafted by a very new arrival at Camp Scott, Kane's report to Buchanan was an extraordinary document in terms of its egocentric tone, unwitting admission of indiscretions, assertive recommendations, and omissions. Chief among the latter was the absence of virtually any reference to Alfred Cumming, the man at Camp Scott whom Kane most wanted to influence. Based on Kane's operating style, his silence about Cumming reflected an unwillingness to tip his hand even to James Buchanan. It was an omission signaling something was surely afoot, if not amiss, regarding Utah's as-yet-uninstalled governor and Kane's plans for his future.

Friendly Personal Relations: Dueling in the Snow

Notwithstanding Kane's assertion that there were "friendly personal relations at present subsisting between me and Colonel A. S. Johnston," he failed to inform Buchanan of one critical incident that week. On 16 March, his fourth full day with the Utah Expedition, Kane challenged Johnston to a duel. At the root of this murky affair was Kane's belief that in his first days at Camp Scott–Eckelsville, the attentions paid to him by the provost marshal's guard had been sinister, if not menacing, and that for a brief time the army had arrested him. Considering the petty circumstances and the major importance of Kane's mission, this challenge reflected a grievous lapse in judgment. Perhaps for this reason, Kane never spoke of the incident either publicly or in his subsequent private communications with Buchanan.

Johnston, the limping survivor of a duel with a brother-officer during the

---

[44]Surprisingly, in this wilderness there were independent lawyers willing to defend indicted Mormons. One such, Charles Maurice Smith of Virginia, spent the winter of 1857–58 defending Nauvoo Legion lieutenant William R. R. Stowell, who had been arrested on 16 October 1857 with Maj. Joseph Taylor. One of the war's mysteries is how Smith, later a prominent Washington lawyer, happened to accompany the Utah Expedition.

Texas Revolution, was dismayed by Kane's written challenge, but managed to deflect it.[45] He coolly assured Kane that no such arrest had occurred, that Lieutenant Grover's provost-sergeants were attempting to protect him and his baggage rather than harass, and that no personal disrespect was intended by the army's misinterpreted ministrations. Without compromising his own honor, Johnston permitted Kane to save face by encouraging him to accept his deft explanation as "satisfaction" of the affair. Kane later represented the chain of events to his family as a triumph of gentlemanly honor in the face of unacceptable provocations by a bullying army commander, whom he ultimately claimed to have humiliated. Colonel Johnston made no reference to this incident in his official correspondence and continued to focus on leading the Utah Expedition. His tent mate and confidant, Major Porter, also chose to make no official or informal record of the incident.

Matthew J. Grow, Kane's biographer, has assessed well the behavior underlying this challenge, an act that Kane repeated a few years later during the Civil War.[46] This affair reflected Kane's exaggerated sense of honor and tense emotional state at a crucial juncture in his mission. The episode seriously damaged his relationship with Johnston, an officer whom Kane needed to influence rather than antagonize. Kane's unsuccessful attempt to draw Johnston into a duel also aggravated Governor Cumming's jaundiced view of the army's commander. Notwithstanding his own grievances with Johnston and his growing rapport with Kane, Cumming tried unsuccessfully to dissuade him from issuing a challenge and had declined to act as his second in a duel.[47] This did not preclude the farcical events of 16 March from further driving a wedge between Utah's new governor and the commander of his military escort, a split that would contribute to what later would become Cumming's psychological dependence on Brigham Young.

---

[45]Johnston's duel with Texas general Felix Huston was well-known in the army, but more obscure was folklore that in the early 1830s, while serving as a subaltern in the Sixth U.S. Infantry in Missouri, he had accepted a challenge from Lt. Jefferson Davis. This affair was averted only by the mediation of Edmund B. Alexander, later Johnston's subordinate as commander of the Utah Expedition's Tenth Infantry. Brackett, "Albert Sidney Johnston," 462.

[46]Grow, "'I Have Given Myself to the Devil,'" 352–55; *"Liberty to the Downtrodden,"* 177–80.

[47]Like Johnston, Cumming was no stranger to the code duello. His older brother William was one of the most notorious duelists in Georgia and the survivor of at least one such fatal encounter. Adding to the confusion surrounding this Utah incident, in 1878 Johnston's son asserted erroneously that it was Cumming rather than Kane who challenged Johnston. In so doing, the son described Kane as "a man of talents and restless energy, but of an intriguing and erratic temper," and observed that "it was not a happy conception in Mr. Buchanan, to intrust, in any manner, the interests or honor of the United States to the hands of a person so closely identified with the enemy." Johnston, *The Life of Gen. Albert Sidney Johnston*, 221–25.

They Should Know Nothing: Communicating with Brigham Young

Immediately following resolution of his challenge to Albert Sidney Johnston, Kane hurtled off on a new adventure—departure from the Utah Expedition's camp to rendezvous in the mountains with a mounted Mormon party. With the Utah Expedition on high alert, Kane's request for an army escort to ensure safe passage through Fort Bridger's defensive perimeter fueled suspicion and animosity. On 16 March Kane equipped himself with several pistols and his brother's rifle, drew his horse from the garrison's herd, and passed through Johnston's lines with a few federal troopers. After dropping this escort, Kane rode alone into the wilderness beyond Blacks Fork heading for the Muddy Creek mail relay station.

It is unclear with whom Kane met on 17 March, but it was probably the small party led by Brig. Gen. Lewis Robison, which had remained in the area (and occasionally drawn fire) after having guided him to the vicinity of Fort Bridger. To Buchanan, Kane described traveling "into the mountains till I was fallen in with by three men whose number was afterwards increased to six."[48] Robison knew the area intimately after years as Brigham Young's principal agent for the region. Kane shared almost no substantive information with Robison but did entrust him with a sealed letter for Brigham Young, the guarded text of which Kane had previously reviewed with Cumming.

The opacity with which Kane wrote to Young was a direct reflection of his anxiety about several uncertainties: the loyalty and discretion of the Nauvoo Legionnaires with whom he would rendezvous; the security of the message that he was about to give them; and the status of Young's struggle with what Kane perceived as a Mormon war faction. Presumably because of these concerns, Kane addressed the letter not only to Brigham Young but "to those around and near him." As discussed in a later chapter, the result was a communication so ambiguous that one wonders how Brigham Young interpreted it and the soundness of the decisions that flowed from his reactions. Kane explained this ambiguous phrasing to Buchanan:

> I reasoned that if I was to regard Mr. Young in the light of a person seeking to make peace with the U.S. at the risk of his own popularity with a portion of his people, I ought assume that it was incumbent on me to adopt every precaution not to compare the subject of a strictly private communication

[48]Kane to Buchanan, 23 March 1858, Kane Family Papers, BYU.

> between him and myself to be an instrument to be used to prejudice him in the hands of his opponents. I had no right to trust any Mormon soldiers—or the first load of Mormon soldiers whom I might encounter in their outposts with what he himself might desire they should know nothing of.[49]

Reflecting Kane's low level of trust, one of the principal requests he made of the Mormons with whom he met was one included in the letter itself—his desire to have Brig. Gen. William H. Kimball, commander of the Standing Army and Heber C. Kimball's son, serve as the communications link between him and Young at a second meeting to be scheduled for the following week. Perhaps affronted, Robison and his party initially resisted this request but then agreed to it, as Kane reported to Buchanan:

> The Mormons whom I encountered made much difficulty in the way of making me this appointment; but I have I think secured it unless they are practicing a degree of deception upon me of which I do not think them capable. It is agreed that I am to proceed next Thursday [25 March] to the distance of one full day's journey in the direction of a stream called Echo Creek, and at night-fall look out for a signal fire that is to be visible from certain elevations named. Upon discharging my piece from the vicinity of the latter I will be visited by Kimball himself or those appointed to conduct me further. Whether these precautions indicate distrust or not I cannot anticipate losing perhaps a day now in a further progress eastward. It will naturally take me two days additional to retrace my steps. I shall not probably reach camp again before the 28th or 29th [of March] but this will give me ample time to write to you by the next mail, in case I have intelligence of importance to communicate.

General Kimball's pending involvement in the process was so important to Kane that he felt it necessary to inform the president that "He is an excellent young man who rendered me many services during my illness on the Platte [River in Iowa] in 1846, who showed himself very grateful for the small return which I made him, and whom I discovered upon my late visit to Salt Lake was high in the confidence of Brigham Young."[50]

Robison immediately couriered Kane's letter to Young, reaching him on 19 March with what historians Poll and Grow argue were momentous consequences.[51] This document and Major Porter's description of Kane's near-fatal return to Camp Scott on the night of 17 March follow.

[49]Ibid.

[50]Ibid.

[51]See chapter 11.

Kane to Young "and Those Around and Near Him," 16 March 1858, Kane Family Papers, BYU.

I have heard of the wanton firing on Robinson (and others, or, and his party if there were Mormons with him) and, believe me, experience with respect to it no less a degree of indignation than yourselves or any of your people. It was the act solely of the military power unauthorized and as I am of opinion directly contrary to the instructions issued by the General Government.[52] As far as I have had an opportunity of examining, too, I am confident that there is no reason whatever for believing that the man [John W. Powell] who you were told provoked the Salmon R[iver] outrage was an authorized agent of the United States, or of any authorized and commissioned Agent for Indian Affairs or other Government officer of any kind.

Since my arrival here I have been in constant communication with Governor Cumming. He has made no secret from me of his instructions, and I give you my word without reservation that I can reiterate my assurance to you that he is the faithful and determined exponent of the views of your friend the President of the United States. He has force of character enough, too, to cause his wishes and opinions to be obeyed and respected by others. Be calm. There is no change. Justice will be done you in due time.

If you can send me William Kimball, I will converse with him in perfect confidence. I greatly desire to do so. I remain Your friend to serve you.

(Read to Gov. C. before going out in rather early morning Mar. 16, 1858.)[53]

Porter Diary, 17 and 20 March 1858, Porter Collection, LC.

17 March 1858

Mr Kane started today,—pretending or believing he was in great danger,—and returned at night. Though cautioned against firing when returning he approached Fort Bridger and fired four shots—one of which was near shooting him.—The sentinel came near killing Mr K—and when brought into the garrison—he demanded why he had been shot at—but the boot was on the other leg this time and Capt. Robinson demanded of him the reason for firing at his sentinels.

After an explanation he was sent to the Governor but was taken to the Provost Marshall who placed him under guard—till the fact was reported—when he was transferred to the Governor.

20 March 1858

Visited Eckelsville—and saw Mr Kane who I still think an ass though a gentleman—Heard his explanation of causing an alarm—and being in

[52]For the exchange of notes on 14–15 March 1858 between Kane and Johnston dealing with the firing on Lewis Robison's party, see "Annual Report of the Sec. of War (1858)," 89–90.

[53]A week later Kane wrote to Buchanan that not only had Cumming approved of this language but that he had given his "approbation" to Kane's trip into the mountains to deliver it to Young's courier.

danger—from the guards. Pity they did not rid him of life—would have saved one fool from troubling us.

The Storm, So Long Impending: Kane Reports Mixed Results

Once back at the Utah Expedition's winter quarters, Kane set about communicating with multiple players important to his mission and the pursuit of two matters of unfinished business: convincing Colonel Johnston to soften the tone of his draft response to Young's 9 March offer of flour and beef, and the army's continued impoundment of the Salt Lake City mail. Even more volatile was a third issue that had gradually taken shape in Kane's thinking—trying to arrange Alfred Cumming's assumption of his gubernatorial duties in Salt Lake unaccompanied by the army.

Little is known about what occurred in the Kane-Johnston-Cumming relationship during the week following Kane's return from his rendezvous with the Mormon party at Muddy Creek. Following Edgar Brown's debriefing, Johnston was presumably preoccupied with tightening his expedition's defenses and relocating most of the regiments at Camp Scott to bivouacs adjacent to Fort Bridger's protection on 18 March.

Meanwhile, Kane remained closeted with Governor Cumming, who was still camped at Eckelsville under the protection of a company of the Tenth Infantry.[54] With a blizzard raging about them, Kane added to the chaos of the army's relocation by informing Cumming in confidence that he was about to return to Philadelphia.[55] This news stunned Cumming, as was Kane's intent. In the course of their subsequent discussions, Kane gave the governor a formal note containing an unusual request: "May I ask you to express to me your opinion in writing that the public service demands my giving up my purpose of returning to Philadelphia?" Again beset by intimations of mortality, as had been the case on the trail from Salt Lake City, Kane explained that he wanted such a document "in anticipation of the contingencies of accident to which I may shortly be exposed [in meeting with Kimball]." He added,

---

[54]On 30 March Eckelsville's inhabitants and their military guard also abandoned this site and moved to Fort Bridger.

[55]The Utah Expedition was episodically sending mail to the East by couriering it to Fort Laramie, so Kane probably planned to return home via this route (not California as Young assumed), as he eventually did in May.

"I feel as if my Father and friends were entitled to know why I continued to remain away, with my hopes of peace no longer sanguine, and at the sacrifice of personal dignity and feeling as well as of my interests at home."[56]

While Cumming attempted to cope with this development, Johnston added to the complexities besetting the governor by informing him of General Scott's intent to sail for California on 5 February to open a thrust against Utah from the Pacific Coast. Through his adjutant, Johnston did so, "presuming it possible the Government may not have informed you of the arrangements of the different branches of the administration, for suppressing the rebellion in the Territory of Utah."[57] Faced with this news and the approaching date of Kane's meeting with William Kimball, Cumming wrote a note to Kane on 23 March that expressed his admiration and the value of his mission to a Mormon population that Cumming still considered rebellious. He implored Kane to remain in Utah. It was an important letter, one that psychologically moved Cumming closer to dependence on Kane for charting his own course in Utah.

CUMMING TO KANE, 23 MARCH 1858, KANE FAMILY PAPERS, BYU.

The storm so long impending, is now ready to burst upon the deluded inhabitants of this territory; and whilst it is my duty to enforce unconditional submission to the authority of the United States, yet, in the performance of that duty I would gladly temper justice with mercy, and prevent the unnecessary effusion of blood—especially I would shield women and children from the sufferings incident to civil war.

I am not unmindful of the great sacrifices already made by you in the spirit of exalted patriotism—nor of the perils and fatigues which you have so bravely encountered in the efforts to induce the Mormons to realize their true position, and return to their allegiance. From the partial success which had attended your efforts to procure that result, I think that it is desirable you should continue to exert your influence in teaching a rebellious population that both duty and policy indicate the necessity of immediate submission to the United States, and dictate an appeal to its clemency for immunity from past offences.

---

[56]Kane to Cumming, 19 March 1858, Cumming Papers, Duke University. Kane's decision to stay the course in Utah was apparently not a casual one, as he later wrote to this father that he prayed many times before deciding to defer his return home. It is conceivable that Kane also sought such a lawyerly letter to provide support for any claim for financial relief that his family might seek with the U.S. government in the event of his death.

[57]Porter to Cumming, 22 March 1858, ibid. This note excerpted a single sentence from the letter that Scott's aide had sent to Johnston on 23 January.

> I do, therefore, earnestly desire that you will persevere in your mission of mercy, and give up, for the present, at least, your purpose of returning to Philadelphia.

Later that night, with an awareness that the eastbound mail would be leaving the next day, Kane constructed a long report of his activities for President Buchanan. Deeply frustrated, Kane drafted but then abandoned a paragraph that lashed out at Albert Sidney Johnston:

> I wd. have to accuse him of a deliberate endeavor to thwart the negotiations for peace if I did not maintain that he is a man of such capricious vain & irritable temper to that extent which unfits him to exercise his command of an army. May God only grant that he has not thrown away the sum of all my labors—that he has not made me the means of placing things in a worse condition than they were before! I will postpone my return: I will try if matters can by any possibility be mended up again. But I can have no hope so long as this unfortunate person continues to exercise the powers he now claims. Misconduct of his may at any time undo all that Governor Cumming as much [*blank*] the work of the patriotic [*blank.*][58]

Kane then turned to his lack of progress in modifying Colonel Johnston's views as well as a series of recommendations to supplement those that he had developed for Buchanan a week earlier. Kane closed with a tribute to Cumming that was to be the first of many such crafted to bolster the president's confidence in his appointee while communicating a decision to delay his return home responsive to the governor's wishes.

KANE TO BUCHANAN, 23 MARCH 1858, KANE FAMILY PAPERS, BYU.

> I am now writing on the night of Monday [Tuesday], Mar. 23rd.[59] The reply of Col. Johnston [about proffered food for the army] has not yet been communicated by me to Brigham Young. More upon this subject [below].
>
> I have not adverted to another topic which has been a subject of conversation between myself and Col. Johnston because I am yet in hopes after a further conference to influence favorably the mind of this officer. A few words upon it however you will hardly deem or regard out of place here.
>
> I found a noticeable source of irritation among the Mormons particularly those of English extraction (who are as a general thing much more peaceably inclined than our native born Americans), the detention at Bridger of their mails. The Mormons you are aware are as a class what my New England friends would term "come Outers" that is persons who have for their religious tenets severed or impaired to some extent the ties which naturally bound

[58]Kane, "Diary II (1858)," undated entry, 20.

[59]Kane was often mistaken about dates and days of the week.

them to their relatives and friends. They may be considered too in another point of view as a little nation of emigrants.

Nor was it either adverse to the true interests of the Mormon people if I waited only until I could communicate with a messenger of standing [such as William Kimball] in respect to whose character there could be no question. Through such a one I hope on delivering my letter to do much to prepare the Mormons for the less favorable state of things which I have to disclose to them. I trust too I may be able to explain away what Young will regard as the insulting part of Col. Johnston's refusal—exhibiting it as the act of the military authority alone which had no discretion in the premises, etc. has not some matter of business on hand which he is arranging with friends or agents outside the mts. And meanwhile you will observe we are the gainers by every hour of time passed by the people of the valley in contemplation of peace releasing their order for war and turning their minds into the more natural and healthful channels of thought and a return to their allegiance.

For all these reasons the Mormons as a community are large and interested correspondents. At the present time persons excited in a particular way are always addicted to the preparations of "Memorials."[60] You will understand then why the Mormons have been freer correspondents than usual of late and why in a word they should all be capable of being wounded by idle stories which have reached them of their letters being "knocked about the camp," etc, opened and laughed over by the soldiers, etc.

Upon all military matters the Mormons leaders through their agents in the army are in the receipt of constant and probably most accurate information. Confident therefore that no objection cd. be raised on this score I encouraged an application which they asked to make through me for the mails which were arrested at this place last October or November? I thought it desirable to afford this moderate earnest of our good feeling.

On Sunday [Saturday] evening, March 13th, I delivered to Col. Johnston a package entrusted me which I was informed contained letters for the army received by the last Salt Lake mail via California and a letter addressed to Col. Johnston by the Postmaster at Salt Lake City. On Wednesday morning last just as I was about to get into the saddle for my trip into the mts., Major Porter, the petite & efficient adjutant of Col. Johnston, asked me to take charge of a letter on the subject, addressed as I understood by the Postmaster here [Hiram F. Morrell] to the P.M. of Salt Lake City [Elias Smith]. Major Porter did not inform me that this letter contained a refusal to forward the mails as proposed—but I understood the fact from another source. I felt myself at liberty to refuse to be the bearer of it—stating in a note which I hastily wrote for him (the major) that I was reluctantly compelled to refuse

[60]A reference to the Utah legislature's January 1858 memorial to Congress, aggressively reprising territorial-federal relations, which prompted a federal grand jury sitting at Eckelsville to return treason indictments against every person who signed it.

SGT. GEORGE AUSTIN BEARDSLEY, VOLUNTEER BATTALION
A New Jersey protégé of Salt Lake City's non-Mormon postmaster Hiram F. Morrell, Beardsl spent the winter in W. M. F. Magraw's infantry company at the Volunteers' "Camp Barnard." Following discharge in April, Morrell appointe him briefly as the city's deputy postmaster, in w role he took the first load of postwar mail to Sa Francisco. Like many expedition veterans, Bearc had a distinguished Civil War record as colonel a New Jersey volunteer regiment. Later he becar a successful merchant of epicurean groceries in Manhattan. He is shown here photographed in civilian garb, possibly by David A. Burr at Fort Bridger, ca. 1858. *Courtesy of descendant Christopher D Harlow, MSGT U.S. Army (Ret'd), Pueblo, Colo.*

to be the bearer of communications to the Mormons of whose contents I was not made aware. And so this matter stands.

I incline to think it was unwise to detain this mail in the first instance, Mr. Buchanan, and perhaps the subject may be one which now properly demands your personal attention.

My only set-off to so much discouraging news for you, Sir, has perhaps occurred to your mind before I call it up that I have found what Brigham Young would be willing to style in his own words, *"a Man"* [Cumming].

His views generally regarding the Mormons differ seriously from my own in more than one respect, but he has a warm heart, an intrepid spirit, and a confidence in his own practical judgment which has raised him above the influence of the unhealthy, moral atmosphere of the camp. It wd. be improper in me to state how far his views accord with mine nor will I undertake to eulogize your personal friend, Mr. Buchanan, but I will prove my good opinion of your [new] Governor of Utah by saying that I have already engaged to place my humble services at his absolute disposal, and will remain away from home for this purpose till he himself is persuaded that the last hopes of peace are at an end. The last hopes in my view resting upon him.

I may mention the fact which is of public notoriety that to Gov. Cumming's determined opposition, we owe it that martial law has not been proclaimed by the military committee. I need not say would have embarrassed matters further.[61]

[61]Unlike Harney, who twice asked Secretary Floyd for authority to declare martial law in Utah, and Young, who actually did so, there is no evidence that Albert Sidney Johnston ever considered such a move.

It wd. be unjust in me to close without bestowing my highest praise on Col. Johnston for the good order and discipline in which I find his army. I have had a better opportunity of observing it in consequence of its being kept on the alert since my arrival in consequence of an anticipated attack from the Mormons who, intelligence had been received, were on the 1st of March to put 1,000 or 1,800 men in motion from Salt Lake for a general assault.

I think I understand this, as you may. My confidence is the reliability of Young's assurances to me on this head, I must say continued unimpaired, but I am pleased to state that on [Thursday] Friday & Saturday the troops were moved from their quarters near where my own tent is at present pitched to a comparatively safe position in military point of view in the vicinity of Fort Bridger. . . .

Farewell Mr. Buchanan. I remember I was your [1856 political] opponent and feel how much I have to thank you for your confidence. I do not boast of the past—the future I think will further prove me your friend to serve you.

As an immediate after-thought, Kane drafted five more recommendations for the president.

Kane to Buchanan, 23 March 1858, Kane Family Papers, byu.

Recommended Actions

I wd. recommend—pardon the haste with which I write—where at least I ought to be dexterious:

1. That if there has been any omission in the instructions issued to the civil and military authorities here to define distinctly the relations between them and the respective powers of each that it shall be promptly and completely remedied.—Let the past go for what it is worth. I shd. give up my last hope for the future, if I had not my own apprehension of the proper place and province of the military.[62]

2. I wd. suggest also that a word in time may shape the course of the Territorial judiciary and make it conform more closely to the policy of the Adm's. A course of procedure illegal from the beginning might at a future time be of service to Mormon criminals to enable them to escape justice—but at the present when interests of greater moment are at stake it is of more importance to impress the people of Utah with the conviction that they may place reliance upon our laws and their administration as something which cannot be modified or perverted either to profit or to oppress them.[63]

3. I think it wd. be well to issue instructions to our Indian agents to use the utmost circumspection in their dealings that they may not be misrepresented

[62]For the government's conflicting instructions to Johnston and Cumming in 1857, see *At Sword's Point, Part 1*, 180–82. Kane's recommendation was a perceptive one that Buchanan ultimately had to face in 1859.

[63]In 1872 the U.S. Supreme Court would dismiss hundreds of verdicts and indictments in Utah, including those for the Utah War's Yates murder, as procedurally flawed. *Clinton v. Englebrecht* (U.S. 80:434).

as bestowing gifts or using other influences to stir up the savages to war against the Mormons.

4. Military and camp followers to be kept back. How far—?

5. Lastly I wd. recommend in general what to drop as this formal tone I will call "building bridge for the flying enemy" and that all persons having authority be counseled (Mormons) to lend their aid toward the construction of any overtures for peace whether in the form of supplies of salt, beef, flour or words of Brigham Young, shall receive a courteous acknowledgment if not acceptance. That stolen beef shall not be bought of mountaineers at $80 a head instead of the same article at $20. That language of provocation and insult shall in all cases be withheld and a rein put to all ambition of contending with the eloquent speakers of the Great Salt Lake City Tabernacle. What I mean in this connection that unnecessary firing on strangers be put a stop to and that at once. That the mails for Great Salt Lake City be forwarded so long as there is no actual war—I might number a score of instances more which will occur to you, Sir, and with regard to which the discretion of a good man might most profitably be invoked and exercised.—But alas, I forget the distance which separates us and the length of time which must elapse before our longa manus regia [long arm of the law] can reach out here. And I find myself writing fanciful recommendations for the future which before then probably as a "future" of Hope or Promise at least will far enough be swept away.

Kane transmitted this material for Buchanan with a candid cover letter to his father and brother marked "private" and "for the fire." Here one sees a bit more of Kane's manipulativeness as well as his views of Johnston and Cumming, especially his concern that the challenge to Johnston could damage his reputation.

Kane to Judge and Pat Kane, 23 or 24 March 1858, Kane Family Papers, BYU.

Perhaps you will think it better to let Mr. Buchanan read my draft over in the original.(*)[64] But you *must* have it back from him—and not leave a copy in his hands of my conversation with Young—I mean his with me.—With regard to Johnston, and his outrageous conduct in precipitating the country into this disastrous war, you see how my hands have been tied by our peculiar personal relations. Not gentlemanly propriety merely—every sense of Christian magnanimity orders me to spare a man whose apology has humbled him as much as this unfortunate's.—But, shd. he prove wanting further on his part—shd. his letter writers and newspapermen dare to falsify the facts—Call [publisher-editor John W.] Forney, Ider, Martin, Lane and all my Philadelphia friends of the Press to punish him as he deserves—the

[64]Kane note: "and your own letter to[o]—*rude* as it[s] tone appears."

more condignly, the better for our i.e. the national honor. I can probably collect evidence myself of his *setting the Indians on the Mormons.*[65] He is a fool. If he, and the Eckels man (who hunts with him) hold their peace however I had better *husband my future means of influence*—through & with them. At any rate, my hand had better not be seen in the matter.

If you have any doubt or difficulty in aceeding to my request, then, best regard the whole letter to the President as to yourself and merely let a mutual friend send it over to him merely substituting, My dear Father for my dear Sir, wherever it occurs.

Please lest I shd. be delayed here, (I *am* going to stay out till my health is strong enough to last me thirty years to come) send me your views on as many law points as you think may claim my notice; and in particular how far you think this "Court" has been legally constituted &c. I have a notion of a way in which Buchanan can be saved some trouble of Pardoning, &c. How, in case of peaceful negotiations being set on foot again—how could this bloody mouthed Judge be headed off best?—[66]

I enclose a copy of a letter to me from Gov. C, however, by which you will see combien je me suis fait prier [many times I have prayed] before giving up my purpose of returning to Philadelphia—which I announced when "the Army" began to rage like the antimormon mob of Saint Bernardino. [In showing that letter to him] Buchanan may as well understand the sacrifice I make in continuing to stay away from home.

Governor Cumming *is* my friend. And is handling the soldier man [Johnston] for his arrogation [self-aggrandizing] abuse of authority if this has to be done he may be well contrasted with Cumming. My letter to Buchanan is all true with regard to him.[67]

No [more] time [to write].

Having in quite different ways briefed the president, his father, and brother, Kane finally wrote to his wife. For her he provided thoughts of love, religion, health, and his mission, but only ambiguous references to the more volatile subject of his return home. Overwhelmingly, Kane's letter focused on Kane and his mission, rather than on "Bessie" and their two small children. These family members Kane cast as bystanders who he expected to bask appreciatively in his "honor bright."[68]

---

[65]This accusation was one of the most volatile Kane made about Johnston. It is unknown whether he was thinking of the recent Fort Limhi controversy, Garland Hurt's January trip to the Uintahs, or Johnston's plan to hire Washakie's Shoshones to operate and defend the Green River ferries.

[66]Unknown to Kane, Buchanan was probably already deeply into the process of pardoning the Mormons.

[67]Kane note: "Wait for his Imprudence. No premature flash in the pan to detract from my present high position."

[68]Kane to Elizabeth Kane, 24 March 1858, Kane Family Papers, BYU.

With the dawn of 25 March approaching, Kane wrote a few more instructions to his father for handling communications with President Buchanan and provided brief comments on prospects for his mission: "My private News for you?—Well, the Troops are saved, at least until I shake my handkerchief—which the cruel thought occurs to me sometimes I am bound in honor no longer to delay to do. And the graceless hounds themselves have chased my pretty Peace out of sight into the Mountains again,—where I pursue her, with only the faintest hope to guide me. . . . My horse and pack mule—my only companions have come—Good Bye! Heaven keep you—and (dear Elisha again?)[69] Please honor my draft from Salt Lake for $600 shd. it come soon to hand, although I will have to draw from here as I said before long. I am living *like a dog* on $5 a day—whiskey and smoking tobacco for unwelcome visitors exclusive. Your ever extravagant affectionate son."[70]

The Gentleman Referred To: A Hint of Success

Before leaving for his meeting with William Kimball, Kane had written nothing to his family or even President Buchanan about his most secretive gambit—his efforts to convince Governor Cumming to accompany him to Salt Lake City without the army. Precisely how and when during the third week of March Kane and Cumming discussed this notion is unknown, although during this period Kane recorded that they engaged in episodic meetings that included long, nocturnal dialogue. Whether libations of something like James Buchanan's Old Monongahela fueled these discussions is another imponderable, but it is not unlikely given the fact that some sessions lasted until midnight (long after Elizabeth Cumming had slipped into the glacial gubernatorial bed), the primitive nature of their camp stoves, and the governor's reputation as a heavy drinker.

In 1862 French reporter Louis Bertrand produced an account of Kane's dialogue with Cumming on this subject that was both simplistic and flippant: "After a short stay in the federal camp, the president's envoy one day told Governor Cumming: 'Leave here all this war paraphernalia, these cannons, these carbines, these revolvers, just take a tooth pick with you. I will

---

[69]The extent to which Kane's dead explorer-brother was constantly on his mind provides insight into one of the drivers behind his Utah mission—living up to Elisha's example of perseverance and sacrifice.

[70]Kane to Judge Kane, 24–25 March 1858, Kane Family Papers, BYU. One wonders how Elizabeth Kane would have reacted to such bathos, living as she was on the kindness of her in-laws with only meager cash balances on hand.

see that you conquer the impregnable Territory of Utah, Brigham Young, the Twelve Apostles, the two priesthoods, and all the polygamous and non-polygamous Mormons.' And they left alone on horseback."[71] Convincing Alfred Cumming was not that casual, and at some point in March Kane felt a need to marshal his arguments in writing.

Kane, "Reasons Which in My Opinion Justify Governor Cummings [*sic*] as a Prudent Man in Hazarding His Proposed Journey to Salt Lake," "Diary II (1858)," Undated Entry, 22.

1. Those based upon the proposed posture. His presence there might exert Important in view of the present stage of peace negotiations (1) It subtracts from Johnston's refusal of peace overture making it (and the whole matter that may be represented to belong to the Army regime) of comparatively small meaning and importance &c &c.

2. It may not only qualify and keeps this important man in the place but ~~rather~~ rally my friends and peace party generally

Important because the present a time of crisis in the popular feeling. Uncertainty ~~of expedition~~ & Expectation. The month which has transpired since my arrival assurances &c having created to say the least a favorable pause, lull of excitement every hour of which counts so much in favor of peace. ~~Partisans of extreme measures have of course~~ This so far the partisans of extreme measures have vainly sought to be counteracted by reports of the Indian outrages (Shoney [Shoshone] and Ute) But they are likely to increase and the excuses for attributing them to the United States (No disproof of them like) The presence of the Governor will be taken as the best disproof which it is in his power to furnish. If such accusations are groundless to those which may be not [*illegible*] he will be to devote his immediate attention [*illegible*]. ~~The others~~

3. In this respect as in the others the mere coming and presence of the Governor exerts a sanitary [salutary?] wholesome [*illegible*] for busy minds [*illegible*] will seem to impart something where most nothing &c.

4. The spring Semi Annual Conference begins Tuesday April 6 when representatives of all the Mormons of Utah assemble in Salt Lake and where they will not only confer upon the present state of things but expect to adopt and arrange their final course. This becomes of action. His presence alone without action or committal must have a tendency to baffle

(C) The mere presence of Gov. C. tending to allay excitement. ("il y avait une fois un Roi une Ring")[72] 2. While Gov. C. is among them they will not

---

[71]Bertrand in Homer, *On the Way to Somewhere Else*, 109.

[72]In part this hybrid of French and English phrasing translates as "there was once a king," an obscure reference presumably to Cumming.

> give up exercising and lose sight of the movement of our troops. [*scratched out with burnt matches*]

While Kane chose to remain silent on this subject, Cumming did not. On 24 March the governor placed in the eastbound mail a note to his organizational superior, Secretary Cass. Here, Cumming did for Cass what Kane was unwilling to do for Buchanan—bring him current on his travel plans. Cumming's brief letter was unlike any other that he wrote during the Utah War. After twelve days of intense proximity to Kane, it was a document deeply influenced by Kane's penchant for secrecy and cryptic phrasing, as well as his flair for the theatrical. It was a letter that also raises questions as to who, at this juncture, Alfred Cumming viewed as the enemy.

Cumming to Cass, 24 March 1858, Cumming Papers, Duke University.

> A highly respectable gentleman arrived in this Camp a few days since from G.S.L. City. Whilst there he had several conversations with Brigham Young, and other prominent persons. The gentleman referred to addressed a letter by this mail to another gentleman in Washington, which will be exhibited to you.
>
> The weather is becoming very mild. The snow will soon cease to be an impediment to mountain travel.
>
> It is my present intention in a short time to visit G.S.L. City, where I can have communication with the people before the army advances. The other civil officers will await my return.

Without commenting on Cumming's cryptic allusion to Kane and Buchanan, Cass's state department later logged in the governor's note with the laconic summary, "intends visiting G.S.L. City in a short time—and will have an opportunity of communicating with the people before the army shall have moved."[73]

Oblivious to the volatile reports that Kane and Cumming were sending east, Albert Sidney Johnston added to the same mailbag a message for General Scott that was striking in its blandness: "Nothing beside [movement of the camp], worthy of mention, has occurred, and I have now nothing special to report."[74]

[73]"Utah Affairs, 1858," State Dept. Territorial Papers, Utah Series, Vol. 1 (1853–1859), NARA.

[74]Johnston to McDowell, 24 March 1858, "Annual Report of the Sec. of War (1858)," 66.

Chapter 11

"Blessed Be Nothing" The Mormon Move South

But when they persecute you in this city, flee ye into another.
Matthew 10:23

While Kane worked at Fort Bridger to influence Alfred Cumming, Albert Sidney Johnston, and James Buchanan, Brigham Young pondered his earlier discussions in Salt Lake City with Kane. Young's thoughts ran not only to Kane's advice but a plethora of intervening events, needs, and forces: disturbing news from Fort Limhi and the Colorado River; use of the Standing Army for a spring campaign across the plains; the lingering threat of a thrust by undisciplined volunteer troops from the Pacific Coast; the specter of a reinforced Utah Expedition with its rapacious camp followers; and the hangman's noose implicit in any federal investigation of the Mountain Meadows massacre. For a religious leader of Young's prophetic calling, there were also powerful expectations of divine guidance, if not intervention.

Suddenly, without Kane's knowledge, Young announced a bold stroke. He decided to abandon offensive operations against the Utah Expedition, to abolish the Standing Army, to prepare the infrastructure of northern Utah (including Salt Lake City) for the torch, and to abandon that part of the territory through a southbound exodus of as many as thirty thousand Latter-day Saints. Their immediate gathering place was to be Provo, preparatory to a continued trek to an unspecified distant haven. All of this was to be done while retaining the capability to defend the Wasatch passes and, if necessary, to conduct a fighting retreat using the Nauvoo Legion. Compounding the complexity and ambiguity of these decisions was Brigham Young's dispatch of multiple exploring expeditions to search Utah's western deserts for oases of refuge and to scout the Colorado River to assess its usefulness to both the army and the Latter-day Saints.

This thrust—the "Move South"—was a stunning development unparalleled in North American history: the continent's greatest mass migration of refugees since the eighteenth-century expulsion of the Acadians from Nova Scotia and the British Loyalists from the new United States. The Move South would eclipse even the Mormons' own earlier flights from New York, Ohio, Missouri, and Illinois.[1]

As with many other aspects of the Utah War, the Move South was an ordeal that tested the endurance, ingenuity, faith, and discipline of Mormon women as well as their men. A generation of their refugee-children also paid a price still obscured by the folklore of exodus.

To Take into Consideration: The Decision to Flee

The greatest mysteries about the Move South are the "why" and "where" questions. Ultimately, the answers are rooted in understanding how Brigham Young functioned as Utah's supreme leader. Highlighting the drama of his decision to flee rather than fight was the abruptness of the change and the murkiness of Young's public explanations, starting with his first public announcement on 21 March.

In August and September 1857 Young had discussed the concept of a "Sebastopol" or Russian strategy. Since then, he had episodically admonished the Saints to conserve and cache grain in anticipation of a fighting retreat to unspecified "mountains." As the winter drew to a close, there were signs of the upheaval soon to follow. Late in February 1858 Young began to throw out slightly different signals to his inner circle, this time about destinations he described vaguely as "deserts." This behavior reflected Young's instinctive secrecy as well as his hazy grasp of geography. His mistaken belief was that the deserts of western Utah (now central Nevada) contained undiscovered

[1]The country would experience nothing like it again until five years later when the Union Army depopulated four western Missouri counties (twenty thousand people) in retribution for the Confederates' August 1863 raid on Lawrence, Kansas. Bohl, "A War on Civilians," 44–51.

oases capable of supporting large settlements. In the mid-1850s Young had sent David W. Evans, bishop of Lehi, to search for such places near the vaguely identified "White Mountains." When Evans failed to find such sanctuaries, Young waited a few more years and sent him out again with an equal lack of success.[2]

For Brigham Young, the lure of the White Mountains, like his long-standing interest in the Colorado River, was an itch to be scratched during the Utah War. Consequently, at a prayer circle meeting on 21 February 1858, "President Young proposed sending some men into the desert to look out habitations for this people and to plant some grain. He said if any one of the brethren wished to Join in sending a man they Could do so."[3] Three days later, Apostle George A. Smith alerted southern Utah's senior military officer, Colonel Dame, to Young's rekindled interest and the substantial manpower demands it would require: "No news from the [U.S.] army. Our standing army is rigging up rapidly, and will be ready for the field in a few days. . . . Fillmore, Beaver and Parowan will be expected to send some men into the Desert west, to find some hiding places, put in some grain &c: no doubt the president [h]as written you about it this mail, as he told me he intended to. Ten or 15 men from each settlement will probably be the number required."[4]

As Smith was writing to Dame, Brigham Young was aware that Kane was rapidly approaching Salt Lake City, but he had no insight into what news was coming. Neither did Young anticipate the report by Amasa Lyman, Kane's escort, of his 31 January encounter with the army's Major Blake or that officer's speculation about a planned militarization of the Colorado River. Lyman's briefing did not overshadow Kane's dramatic message, but it so alarmed Young that he ordered Lyman to return south to organize a party to explore the Colorado and determine the army's intentions there.

Notwithstanding this southerly thrust by Lyman and the soon-to-follow White Mountain Expedition, as late as the second and third week of March, Young was still counseling a nephew on the routine, business-as-usual expansion of Mormonism into new settlements in western Utah's Ibapah Valley.[5] At that time Young's focus appeared to be on danger from tribal raids and

---

[2]Roberts, *Bishop David Evans and His Family,* 30.

[3]Kenney, ed., *Wilford Woodruff's Journal,* 21 February 1858, 5:167.

[4]Smith to Dame, 24 February 1858, William Horne Dame Collection, LDS Archives.

[5]Colonel Dame's and guide George Washington Bean's separate forays into Utah's western deserts were essentially unsuccessful. An excellent account of this futile effort is Stott, *Search for Sanctuary.*

the need to preserve the strength of the Standing Army, not on an imminent abandonment of that force and a mass exodus from northern Utah.[6]

But as the days passed, Mormon leaders grew increasingly beleaguered. On 17 March Apostle Benson wrote to a southbound Apostle Lyman from Salt Lake City to update him on a variety of problems and initiatives. While trying to remain upbeat, Benson described Indian raids throughout the territory, problematic efforts to feed the Utah Expedition, an emergency program to mill wheat and cache flour, and the introduction of a territorial currency. Benson's most important news was that Brigham Young had called a major leadership meeting for 18 March "to take into consideration our future movements, as regards our enemies."[7]

Also on 17 March, Bishop John Rowberry of Tooele visited Salt Lake City and left a note for Brigham Young informing him of livestock losses in Utah's western settlements. Among Rowberry's bad news was the intelligence that most of the cattle and horses taken by Indian raiders were destined for the army quartermaster at Fort Bridger by way of a vast west-to-east arc that swept as far north as Fort Hall, Oregon. Although little noticed by historians, contemporary settlers viewed these raids with great alarm, ranking them with the Fort Limhi disaster in terms of the Mormon response for protecting and evacuating outlying settlements.[8]

Bishop Rowberry's report on the eve of Brigham Young's war council prompted Young to write a long letter of complaint to the U.S. commissioner of Indian Affairs. It conveys Young's growing sense of being beleaguered; the less-than-paramount significance of the Fort Limhi raid (within the context of Young's other Indian problems); Mormon perceptions that the Utah Expedition was stimulating tribal scalp hunting among the Latter-day Saints; and Young's continued insistence that he still was, as he signed the letter, Utah's governor and her federal superintendent of Indian Affairs.[9]

---

[6]Young to William G. Young, 10 and 15 March 1858, LDS Archives.

[7]Benson to Lyman, 17 March 1858, LDS Archives.

[8]Kenney, ed., *Wilford Woodruff's Journal*, 16–18 March 1858, 5:176–77; Rowberry to Young, 17 March 1858, LDS Archives. The most interesting part of Rowberry's letter was his comment that "Bro [Samuel] Bringhurst and others feel very ancious that a compa[n]y should follow the Indians and try to recover th[e]ir property; but this we do not fell [feel] to do without your counsel, as something else might occour more serious than what has already transpired. Please give us your mind on this matter and your counsel shall be carried out." This comment could reflect micromanaging atop the Mormon hierarchy or an abundance of caution by the bishop in the wake of the Mountain Meadows massacre six months earlier.

[9]Young to U.S. commissioner of Indian Affairs, 5 April 1858, Gubernatorial Letterbook, Utah Territory, 703–707, LDS Archives.

With respect to the war council of 18 March, Hosea Stout, the Legion's judge advocate, recorded one of the more extensive accounts of what took place. Significantly, he believed that the meeting's outcome was inconclusive. Young scheduled a follow-on session for 8 April, implying that in the intervening three weeks there would be more time for fact-finding, debate, and decisions.

Hosea Stout Diary, 18 March 1858,
Brooks, ed., *On the Mormon Frontier*, 2:654.

Attended a general Council at the Historians office of the first Presidency, Twelve [Apostles], and officers of the Legion The object of which was to take into consideration the best plan of opperations to be adopted to counter act the purposes of our enemies, whether to attact them before they come near us or wait until they come near, or whether it is yet best to fight at all only in unavoidable self defense or in case a large force is sent against us this spring whether to fight or burn our houses & destroy every thing in and around us and flee to the mountains & deserts &c &c &c

It appears that the course pursued hitherto by Gov Young in baffelling the oppressive purposes of Prest Buckhannan has redounded to the honor of Gov Young and the Saints and equally to the disgrace of the President & his cabinet Mormonism is on the ascendancy and now what is the best policy to maintain that ascendancy. If we whip out and use up the few troops at Bridger will not the excitement and sympathy which is now raising in our favor in the states, be turned against us. Whereas if we only anoy and impede their progress while we "Burn up" and flee, the folly, and meanness of the President will be the more apparrant and he and his measures more unpopular &c[10] This was about a fair statement of the subject matter in council There was no definite measures adopted many spoke on the subject and the council adjourned till 8th April at 2 P.M. at the Tabernacle.

Wilford Woodruff's record of the meeting was more terse and ambiguous than Stout's, leaving open to interpretation whether Young had made a decision: "Speeches were made by the [First] presidency Twelve and other Officers. Presidents Youngs plan was to go into the desert and not war with the people [army] and let them destroy themselves."[11] Surprisingly, George A.

[10]Some historians have interpreted this comment to mean that Young staged the Move South as a public-relations ploy to garner sympathy in the East and pressure Buchanan to end the war. Empathy over Mormon hardships did arise in the spring of 1858, but it is problematic to link it to Brigham Young's decision-making under uncertainty during late March. Although Kane was at Fort Bridger and not involved in Young's decision, he later told a party of westbound Mormon missionaries whom he encountered near the North Fork of the Platte River in early June that "the move south by the people was a political move but did not go into detail about it." Palmer, *James Palmer's Travels and Ministry*, 128.

[11]Kenney, ed., *Wilford Woodruff's Journal*, 18 March 1858, 5:177.

Smith, the church historian who hosted this meeting, made no record of the proceedings other than to list attendees.[12]

The next day Stout recorded the arrival of a small but important Nauvoo Legion detachment:

> The Brethren who escorted Col Kane to Bridger came in this evening, bringing 9 [army] mules "with lassos."[13] After the Col had been in the enemies camp 5 days he came to our brethren [on 17 March] who were in and around Muddy [Creek] (for they did not go into camp with him) and made arraingements for them to come home and meet him at quaken asp grove on Wednesday or Thursday next to escort him in here. He said he was kept close had to pay six dollars pr day for board can not see his friends who are in camp and so forth but did not say what progress he was making as to what he went there for.[14]

On Sunday, 21 March 1858, with no record of having further consulted his closest colleagues, Brigham Young announced the Move South in a special meeting in the Salt Lake Tabernacle. What had happened during the intervening three days since the war council on Thursday, 18 March? Apostle Smith's documentary silence and Hosea Stout's account indicate no decision had emerged from the meeting. In a landmark 1989 article, Richard D. Poll concluded, "The immediate cause of action was the prospect that Thomas L. Kane's peacemaking mission would fail. The eccentric 'friend of the Mormons' brought unofficial peace overtures from the Buchanan administration, but his documents and deportment were so ambiguous as to produce some skepticism in Utah and even more at Camp Scott. As a result, his first report to [the Mormons], who had waited nearby until 17 March, was pessimistic; [they] reached Salt Lake City with the message about forty-eight hours later. There is persuasive evidence that these tidings triggered Brigham Young's decision to implement the Sebastopol policy at once."[15]

Poll's linkage of the arrival of Kane's communication from Fort Bridger and Young's decision to launch the Move South roughly parallels a muddled

---

[12]Historian's Office Journal, 18 March 1858, LDS Archives.

[13]Members of the escort later joked with Kane about how easily they had stolen these animals from the Utah Expedition.

[14]Stout Diary, 19 March 1858, Brooks, ed., *On the Mormon Frontier*, 2:654–55. While Kane's annoyance over the cost of his living expenses seems petty under the circumstances, it was an issue important to him. As discussed above, a week later he would complain to his father, "I am living *like a dog* on $5 a day—whiskey and smoking tobacco for unwelcome visitors exclusive." Kane to Judge Kane, 24–25 March 1858, Kane Family Papers, BYU.

[15]Poll, "The Move South," 68. For this historian's other discussion of the significance of the Legion detachment's 19 March arrival, sometimes with subtle changes in his assessment, see Poll, *Quixotic Mediator*, 18; and "Thomas L. Kane and the Utah War," 129.

discussion of these events recorded in Nephi by farmer Samuel Pitchforth after hearing George Washington Bean's account of the news from Salt Lake City: "President Young has thought it wisdom to evacuate the Territory as far north has [*sic*] Provo. . . . this sudden move is on account of the news from the armey. Col. T L Kane went out and came back to the boys, who escorted him to their camp. He told them that the soldiers had had fresh supplies and were determined to come. Bro L. Robinson [Lewis Robison] was shot at 24 times but escaped. [T] L Kane did not return with the brethren, so Pres. Young to save the effusion of blood, has concluded to mov(e) and let them come in. I understand that the people are to move forthwith."[16]

Poll based his argument on two factors: his interpretation of Stout's record to mean that Brigham Young had not made a firm decision during the 18 March war council; and the proximity of his 21 March announcement to delivery of Kane's message to Salt Lake City on the 19th. Poll's analysis has had impact, influencing Grow's 2009 biography of Kane and the 2011 narrative history of the war by Bigler and Bagley.[17] Delivery of Kane's letter on 19 March and whatever verbal garnishment Lewis Robison's detachment added surely played a role in Brigham Young's decision making that week, but it is problematic to over-emphasize the impact of this document apart from its context. As discussed below, there were other issues and forces in play, and Grow's view of Kane's report as a catalyst rather than a prime cause of the Move South strikes the proper balance.[18]

When You Have Dispersed the Saints and Their Seraglios: Young Encircled

By the third week of March, Young was cornered, a leader threatened from all directions. Few, if any, historians have thought of Young in this way. Only 113 miles to the east, he faced the nation's largest military force and the

[16]Pitchforth Diary, 25 March 1858, 98, BYU.

[17]Grow, *"Liberty to the Downtrodden,"* 180–81; Bigler and Bagley, *The Mormon Rebellion*, 292.

[18]Still unexamined is the issue of what Young's decision would have been if Kane's letter of 16 March had been clearer and more direct in its message, and if Kane had dropped his wariness of Mormon escorts Lewis Robinson and Howard Egan to share with them a candid verbal assessment of the likely outlook for progress at Fort Bridger. Instead, Kane treated them as mere messengers to be kept uninformed. Here was a missed opportunity. By waiting for the arrival of a presumably more trustworthy, higher-ranking, and perhaps more polished William Kimball, Kane lost contact with Brigham Young for a week at a juncture critical to Mormon decision-making. During that period, Kane left Young ill-informed, with only the cold comfort of his opaquely written status report. In this instance, Kane's habitual indirectness, lack of clarity, preoccupation with secrecy, and love of complexity undercut his effectiveness.

knowledge that the administration would reinforce it from Kansas in the spring. To the west were hostile Californians, whose anti-Mormonism grew with indignant talk of the Mountain Meadows atrocity and hopes that the Buchanan administration would make a military move against Utah from the Pacific Coast. To the southwest, there was the presence of the Ives Expedition as part of the War Department's unclear intentions for the Colorado River. From the southeast, there was the likelihood that Captain Marcy would return from New Mexico with more federal troops as well as remounts. The attack on Fort Limhi suspended colonization efforts to the north and, to the extent the Salmon River mission had been considered part of a Mormon escape route to the Pacific Coast or the Missouri River, this exit option evaporated.

Even more importantly, the 25 February attack on Fort Limhi by Bannocks and Northern Shoshones called into question the extent to which Mormons could continue to rely on the tribes as Mormon military allies or even reliable neutrals. What accompanied this shocking betrayal by Lamanites was damage to the prophetic insight dispensed by Young in describing them as a reliable pro-Mormon "battle axe of the Lord." This painful reassessment of Indian allegiances compounded Mormon sensitivity to Garland Hurt's visit to the Uintas in January; the mid-March Ute raids in Tooele, Skull, and Rush Valleys;[19] and late-winter rumors of a multitribe alliance organized to seize the crown jewel of Mormon defenses—Echo Canyon—on behalf of the Utah Expedition. If Young's intelligence was as good as Kane and Albert G. Browne thought it was, he was also aware in late March that Johnston was planning to engage Chief Washakie's Shoshones to operate and defend the strategic Green River ferries, the Salt Lake Valley's vital link to the Great Plains and Missouri River.

Although few historians of the Move South have pursued the notion, there was an additional factor important to Brigham Young's sense of

[19]These little-studied raids on Mormon ranches in the valleys west of Salt Lake City prompted a Nauvoo Legion response nearly as extensive as the Standing Army's expedition to deal with the aftermath of the attack on Fort Limhi. On 17 March Maj. Gen. George D. Grant, a Legion officer second only to General Wells, led a mounted company of eighty-seven men, ninety-eight mules, and four wagons out of Salt Lake City on a week-long pursuit to put an end to the tribal pressure on western Utah—at a time when defense of the area between Fort Bridger and the Salt Lake Valley was Brigham Young's main concern. The scope of Grant's march and the raids that prompted it provide perspective for the debate among historians as to whether the attack on Fort Limhi was a pivotal event impacting Brigham Young's willingness to confront the Utah Expedition in the spring. A summary description of this punitive expedition to the west appears in Acting Adjt. John R. Winder to Grant, 28 March 1858, Utah Territorial Militia Records, Series 2210, box 1, fd. 44, Utah State Archives.

encirclement—his realization that when the federal judges and U.S. marshal finally entered the Salt Lake Valley with the army, he would be in mortal jeopardy of the legal consequences of the Mountain Meadows massacre. In March 1858 Young had good reason to worry. As he was aware, not only California but the entire nation was growing vengeful over what the Nauvoo Legion and its Native American freebooters had done at Mountain Meadows. What Young did not yet know was that on 6 March U.S. representative A. B. Greenwood had confronted Secretary Floyd with a demand by residents of Carroll County, Arkansas, for the army's help in repatriating the massacre's child-survivors and in investigating the role in the atrocity played by "Indians and Mormons."[20] Closer to Salt Lake City, at Eckelsville, Alfred Cumming was already pondering the accountabilities associated with the Mountain Meadows massacre, a Ute report of which (borne by Garland Hurt) had reached the Utah Expedition as early as October 1857.[21] Soon after arriving in Salt Lake City on 12 April, Cumming had alarmed Young's second counselor, General Wells, with his stated intent to embark on a fact-finding trek to southern Utah, perhaps as close to Mountain Meadows as massacre leader John D. Lee's Indian mission at Harmony.[22]

By 19 March, the day Kane's message reached Brigham Young, the Mormon encirclement was such that it was the subject of speculation in London drawing rooms. That day George Mifflin Dallas, Buchanan's successor as American envoy to Great Britain, quipped by mail to Secretary Cass, "everybody is anxiously gazing on the military movement against the Sultan of Utah. When you have dispersed the Saints and their seraglios [harems], it is possible that the Church of England may proclaim a special thanksgiving."[23]

Beset by these pressures and without effective outside counsel, an encircled Brigham Young reached a point in the war at which inactivity was intolerable. He had to do something, and so he did. After listening to his most senior colleagues on 18 March and also perhaps to a still, small voice in the middle of the night, Young acted. On 21 March he set in motion the flight of an estimated thirty thousand people from northern Utah to first Provo

[20]Greenwood to Floyd, 6 March 1858, Floyd to Greenwood, 11 March 1858, and Cooper to Johnston, 5 May 1858; all in Buchanan, *Message of the President . . . in relation to the massacre at Mountain Meadows, and other massacres in Utah Territory*, Senate Exec. Doc. 42 (36-1), Serial 1033, 3–6.

[21]Hurt to Forney, 4 December 1857, "The Utah Expedition," House Exec. Doc. 71, 199–205.

[22]Wells to Young, 24 April 1858, LDS Archives.

[23]Dallas to Cass, Dispatch No. 188, 19 March 1858, Dallas and Dallas, eds., *A Series of Letters from London . . .*, 2:5–6.

and then perhaps to the alluring but elusive "mountains and the desert." Young had unshakable faith that the Lord would guide him to a next step once he and his followers reached Provo.[24] It is by no means clear that in the third week of March Young or anyone around him knew what their final destination would be. In Mormon society of the period, guided as it was by prophetic leadership and the anticipation of imminent millennial events, this lack of clarity may not have been important. As Apostle Woodruff had so aptly confided to his diary on 10 March, "If we were to Judge from the present signs of the times we might expe[c]t an Indian and white war but all things are in the hands of God and he will govern & Controll all things right."[25] It was a confluence of forces and events bearing on the "why" of the Move South that has been long under-studied.

The Sheep Are to Follow the Shepherd: Announcing the Move

What took place in the Salt Lake Tabernacle on 21 March was both routine and extraordinary. After the delivery of several prosaic discourses by other leaders, Brigham Young rose to convene a special business council of the sort that he had used on 19 January to announce the new Deseret currency and to outline next steps in the formation of the Standing Army. This time, the subject was far more momentous—the Move South and, with it, abandonment of his plans for a regular military force unconnected to the federal militia system.

Young spoke for hours, often framing his remarks as responses to rhetorical questions that he knew were on the audience's mind. Immediately after the session, he had his text printed and sent to the territory's bishops as a pamphlet. Although his intent was to communicate, the printed version of Young's "Instructions and Remarks" were so closely held in the stakes and

[24]See familiar accounts of beleaguerment and military flight found in *The Book of Mormon*, 3 Nephi 3:20–25 and 4:1–4. Rick Grunder to MacKinnon, e-mail message, 6 November 2002.

[25]Kenney, ed., *Wilford Woodruff's Journal*, 10 March 1858, 5:174. In time, Young's penchant for ambiguity over travel destinations had trained even skeptical newspaper correspondents to accept sudden changes in itinerary as inevitable: "Brigham, with his two coadju[nc]tors, Kimball and Wells, accompanied by a select party of adherents, have started on a tour South. How far they may go before they return, may be known to the initiated, but Brigham is famous for doing two things, at times—keeping his own counsel and acting under the impression of the moment. Hence, though a programme be laid out, as like as not a sudden change will be made in it during the journey." "Our Utah Correspondence," 2 November 1860, Dispatch, *New-York Times*, 28 November 1860.

wards that misunderstandings and unwarranted rumors rather than clarity became an unintended consequence.[26] With the recent reprinting of Young's complete remarks, it is necessary here to present only key excerpts from this seminal document.[27]

"A Series of Instructions and Remarks by President Brigham Young, at a Special Council, Tabernacle, March 21, 18[5]8," LDS Archives.

We will tell you what we think the Lord wishes of us and his policy concerning this people. . . . With regard to myself I cannot say what I will do. I do not know precisely in what manner the Lord will lead me, but were I thrown into the situation Joseph [Smith] was, I would leave the people and go into the wilderness [rather than submit to captivity as he did], and let them do the best they could. Will I run from the sheep? No. Will I forsake the flock? No. But if Joseph had followed the revelation in him he would have been our earthly shepherd to-day, and we would have heard his voice and followed the shepherd instead of the shepherd's following the sheep. When the shepherd follows the sheep it reverses the natural order, for the sheep are to follow the shepherd.

I want you to understand that if I am your earthly shepherd you must follow me, or else we shall be separated. As I told the people after Joseph's death, they might cling to the Twelve and receive salvation and be led in the way of truth and holiness, or go to hell if they pleased, for we asked no odds of them. I feel so to-day. I am your leader, Latter Day Saints, and you must follow me; and if you do not follow me you may expect that I shall go my way and you may take yours, if you please. I shall expect that I shall do as the Spirit dictates me. What does it now direct me to dictate to you? . . .

["]Should I take a course to waste life?["] We are in duty bound to preserve life—to preserve ourselves on the earth—consequently we must use policy and follow in the counsel given us, in order to preserve our lives. Shall we take a course to whip our enemies? or one to let them whip themselves? or shall we go out and slay them now? We have been preparing to use up our

[26]In transmitting the pamphlet, Young counseled: "You will learn from the Circular, 2 copies of which are forwarded to you by this mail, that the present policy has varied somewhat from the past. The object in printing that Circular is to disseminate information that we do not wish the world to have just now, therefore you will be careful not to lend your copies to any one except those you can trust to return them without fail." Young to Bishop Aaron Johnson (Springville), 24 March 1858, LDS Archives. Young sent virtually identical letters on the same day to each of the other bishops and stake presidents south of Salt Lake City.

[27]See Van Wagoner, ed., *Complete Discourses of Brigham Young*, 3:1411–21. Copies of the original are rare and may be found in Special Collections, Marriott Library, University of Utah, and the Yale Collection of Western Americana, Beinecke Library. There is a typescript in the Elden J. Watson compilation of unpublished discourses by Brigham Young, LDS Archives.

enemies by fighting them, and if we take that course and shed the blood of our enemies, we will see the time, and that too not far from this very morning, when we will have to flee from our homes and leave the spoil to them.—That is as sure as we commence the game. If we open the ball upon them by slaying the United States soldiery, just so sure they would be fired with anger to lavishly expend their means to compass our destruction, and thousands, and millions, if necessary, would furnish means, if the Government was not able, and turn out and drive us from our homes, and kill us if they could. . . . But let us begin a fight with the government troops, and we shall have to leave our buildings and they will possess them, and I am in favor of leaving them before I am obliged to. . . .

"Where are you going?" To the deserts and the mountains. There is a desert region in this Territory larger than any of the Eastern States, that no white man knows anything about. Can you realize [understand] that? What is the reason you do not know any thing about that region? It is a desert country with long distances from water to water, with wide sandy and alkali places entirely destitute of vegetation and miry when wet, and small, scattering patches of greasewood, and it is a region that the whites have not explored, and where there are but few Indians. There are places here and there in it where a few families could live. . . . Probably there is room in that region for 500,000 persons to live scattered about where there is good grass and water. I am going there, where we should have gone six or seven years ago.[28] Now we are going to see whether the sheep will follow the shepherd. I do not care whether they follow me or not.

"When are you going to start?" As soon as this snow is off I am going to start part of my family. I am going to a place that I can say to our enemies, "whither I go you cannot come." They may come here, and then they will find themselves a great many miles from home and will not want to go much further.

"How many are you going to call?" Only five hundred families to leave this city immediately, though more may go now, if they wish to. . . . "We have no provision." I will relieve your minds on that point. We have received only a small amount of the tithing wheat from Box Elder and Weber counties, a very little from Utah county, not any from the counties south of that, and how much do you think we now have in the General Tithing Store, from this and Davis county? We have enough to load 1,200 teams, 40,000 bushels of wheat. And I say to the Bishops to-day, report immediately to Bishop [Edward] Hunter what your Wards need, for we are going to distribute that wheat to the people through the Bishops, and they can pay for it when they

[28]Presumably a reference to Bishop Evans's failed explorations or to the arrival of the first federal officials at about that time.

are able.[29] We are going to forward this tithing wheat and flour with Church teams and all the other teams we can procure.

Another says, "I have no cow." I have two, you may strip [milk] mine part of the time. I know that the complaints among the poor will be trifling when compared to what they will be among the rich. I have so much property around me that I am really plagued. I want to cache the doors and the windows, and the frames, and casings; and my chairs, tables, secretaries and the articles that belong to the Historian's Office and the Tithing Office, etc., and I have so much property to look after that I hardly know what to do. The caches should be made in safe and dry localities, and looking glasses, clocks, musical instruments, and perhaps some other articles should be taken with you. If I had nothing but a little day book in my pocket, I could start and run. I know that it will be troublesome to men who possess fine houses and good orchards, and you now can perceive that the rich have cares once in a while. It makes me think of the old saying, "God bless the rich, the poor can beg." God bless the rich and help them to get their property out of the way, for the poor can pick up a start where they please.

That is the policy I suggest to you, and it is the best policy I can now see to make our enemies whip themselves, as they have thus far. Have we killed any of them? No, but to hear them tell the story, they have killed many "Mormons" through the winter, and the "Mormons" have not fired a single gun at them. They are whipped so far, without our fighting them. . . .

He [Buchanan] has given orders to the soldiery to build a station "at or near Salt Lake City" in Utah territory. Those orders must be fulfilled, or both political parties of the nation are disgraced, so I am for letting them come and take "Sebastopol." . . .

Some of you may think I am imprudent in making these statements here, lest our enemies hear of them and start to come here before we are ready for them. If they do that, while we are doing all we can to get away, we shall kill the infernal scoundrels. They may have "Sebastopol" after it is vacated, but they cannot have it before, according to my present feelings. . . .

If any one sends out word that the army may come in, and that we are not going to fight them, send word at the same time that if they come in to annoy us while we are hastening away, we will send them to hell, God being our helper. . . . Our Elders are willing and many are over-anxious to fight, and I also should be for killing, if I was crowded into a corner and could not back out. But I would sooner see this city laid in ashes, than to lose one good Elder. . . . And let us go to diligently and remove the women and children and the aged and infirm and the wheat and flour and meat [livestock], to as

[29]For the crucial leadership role played by Presiding Bishop Edward Hunter of Salt Lake, see Poll, "The Move South."

far south as Provo, to begin, and retain the able bodied men as much in the vacated settlements as possible, to look after our enemies and the growing crops, &c., and when we get ready to let them, our enemies may come in, in welcome. If this city was vacated and the army here, they would not dare to go to any place only where Government has ordered them to build a station. Let them whip themselves; they are at this time whipt in a masterly manner, and they have done it themselves. . . .

"Can a Prophet or an Apostle be mistaken?" Do not ask me any such question, for I will acknowledge that all the time, but I do not acknowledge that I designedly lead this people astray one hair's breadth from the truth, and I do not knowingly do a wrong, though I may commit many wrongs, and so may you. But I overlook your weaknesses, and I know by experience that the Saints lift their hearts to God that I may be led right. If I am thus bore off by your prayers and faith, with my own, and suffered to lead you wrong, it proves that your faith is vain. Do not worry. . . .

["]Now who will go first?["] Shall we call upon those who have been driven, or upon those who have not? . . . I should decide that those who have never been pioneers shall be pioneers this time. . . . As to learning what families will go, I will hand that matter over to the Bishops. It [is for] them at their meetings to-night [to] learn how many families will go out of each Ward, and report to Bishop Hunter, that we may know tomorrow. We want about five hundred families, and then we will go to work, through the Bishops, and prepare for their going. We do not want you to burn down your houses, but leave them in the care of those that are going to stay. . . .

I am well aware that there are a few families designing to leave for California this season. . . . Will families have liberty to go? We have proclaimed from this stand for years that people were at liberty to go when and where they pleased. And last season I proclaimed from Sabbath to Sabbath, from this stand, that all who wished to go to the army, were at liberty to go, and I would help them; and all that we could then find was Mrs. Mogo, whom we sent to her husband, who was then with the army.[30] That has been the word all the time, until now; but now it is, they cannot go. And when Bishops find men in their Wards who want to run to the enemy, see to it that they are furnished work to do, and that they do it, for almost invariably such persons are those whom we have furnished means [via the Perpetual Emigrating Fund] to bring them here, and when they have been here a short time and accumulated a little property, they want to go to the devil. Such characters shall be our servants, until I tell them they are at liberty to go. I will now put an iron hand upon them. Bishops, take notice of that, and

---

[30]An allusion to Margaret Mogo, wife of assistant federal surveyor Charles Mogo, whom the Legion escorted to Fort Bridger in the fall of 1857 with her dead baby in exchange for one of Bill Hickman's brothers being held by the army.

when a man who wants to draw off his wives and children, see that he has steady work and that he does it every day; and if he don't do it, lay judgment to the line and righteousness to the plummet and make him do right. . . .[31]

We will risk ourselves further south, and if you wish to risk it where you are, you can do so, but what will be your situation if the enemy should occupy this city and are between you and us? My counsel to those in the north is to remove the women, children and provisions forthwith, as soon as the road will permit, towards the desert. . . . Get ready, so that when the army come in here we can swing our hats and say, you are welcome to Sebastopol.

The brethren want counsel in regard to property they have furnished to fit persons out for the road [Standing Army]. As that movement is abandoned, justice requires that the property be returned to those who furnished it. Bishops and military officers, take due notice and govern yourselves accordingly; it is clear in the south.[32]

Before the evening was over, bishops were conducting ward meetings to select people for the vanguard of this movement and to deal with the formidable logistical challenges confronting them. Three days later, Young

---

[31]Here, with probably only Mormons present, the gloves came off publicly to announce extra-legal, autocratic restriction on the freedom of travel and imposition of forced labor of the sort that for years had called into question the appropriateness of Brigham Young's behavior as a federally sworn territorial governor. Later sensitive to these perceptions, Young addressed the matter in Provo during June: "Last spring I wanted to detect some spirits that I could not make manifest to the people, only in the course I then took. . . . With the exception of a short time during the late difficulties, all persons have always had the privilege of going away from here when they pleased, and have been repeatedly invited to do so, if they wanted to; and a certain class did not avail themselves of the privilege; but when I said that they should not go until I gave them permission, we learned those spirits, and they have gone." Van Wagoner, ed., *Complete Discourses of Brigham Young*, 2 June 1858, 3:1437. For the definitive rebuttal of Young's assurances about treatment of the disaffected and refugees, see two studies by Aird: "'You Nasty Apostates, Clear Out'" and *Mormon Convert, Mormon Defector.*

[32]Abolishing the Standing Army was a bitter pill for Young. On 24 March he informed a bishop, "the standing army is superseded, and justice requires that property collected for our army be returned to those who furnished it, at least as far as they call for it." Young to Aaron Johnston, 24 March 1858, LDS Archives. Charles Derry, an English convert and subsequent apostate, viewed the creation and dissolution of the Standing Army with cynicism. Writing from a vantage point outside the LDS church in 1908, Utah War veteran Derry recalled, "The means were raised, the men equipped, but perhaps Uncle Sam's icy fetters were broken and the mountains of snow had melted and Brother Brigham saw the fiery determination in Uncle Sam's eye to enter those valleys if he had to wade through the blood of Brigham's hosts; for Brigham declared the Lord accepted the sacrifice and the standing army was disbanded. But Brigham's lord forgot to return the poor man's cow, or horse, etc., now that they were no longer needed. Perhaps Brigham needed them." Derry, "Autobiography," in Aird, Nichols, and Bagley, eds., *Playing with Shadows*, 239. In July 1858 an anonymous apostate complained to the *New York Times* that after "the army was abolished, and notice given that all property subscribed would be refunded, how much of [live] stock, clothing or saddlery, to say nothing of wheat and other food which each had given, was returned to the owners? Not three cents out of every ten." "A Citizen of Utah," Letter of 23 July 1858, *New York Times*, 23 August 1858, 1/1–3.

formally abolished the Standing Army though the low-profile but awkward mechanism of rescinding the Nauvoo Legion order of 6 March specifying the army's command structure. Again, to avoid compromising himself through explicit written association with the extra-legal private military force he had raised, Young signed this rescission order as "Governor & Commander in Chief of the Military of Utah" and obscured the true character of the brigade he was abolishing by referring to its troops as "details."[33]

Somewhat Loth to Volunteer: Counsel Ignored, Guidance Followed

As with so many aspects of the Utah War, the story of the Move South has been told over more than 150 years, first by tens of thousands of participants and then by hundreds of thousands of their descendants. Supplementing these often faith-promoting tales of hardship and sacrifice are the analytical comments of historians prone to view the Move South through the prism of Brigham Young's overall leadership record. On 21 March 1858 Young acknowledged that he had made mistakes and, as both church president and territorial governor during 1856–57, he indeed bore ultimate responsibility for the Willie-Martin handcart disaster and Mountain Meadows atrocity, the two deadliest episodes in the entire American overland trails experience. It is unsurprising, then, that some contemporary Utahns and later their historians came to view the Move South negatively. To them, it was another large-scale leadership misstep executed at the expense of a hardscrabble Mormon population already burdened by the economic and manpower demands of the Nauvoo Legion and Standing Army.

Historian Will Bagley has argued for years that the Move South took place to a significant extent involuntarily under armed compulsion from the Legion, but he has now tempered this view to characterize the exodus as somewhat less coercive—a "staged" and a "forced removal." Perhaps no document has prompted some historians to view the Move South as coercive in character as the 3 July 1858 report to Secretary Floyd written by Buchanan's peace commissioners:

> Two or three Mormons, who had refused to obey the order to go south, informed us that, during the first week we were there, they had been notified

[33] Young and Wells, General Orders No. 2, Head Quarters, Nauvoo Legion, 24 March 1858, LDS Archives, typed transcription in editor's possession.

> that unless they went as they had been previously ordered, the military would turn them out of their houses. We understood that a small guard was left at each of the settlements from which the families had been removed. . . . We were informed by various (discontented) Mormons who had lived in the settlements north of Provo, that they had been forced to leave their houses and go to the southern part of the Territory; that they desired to remain at their residencies, and would have done so had they not been threatened with forcible ejection. We were also informed that at least one-third of the persons who had removed from their homes were compelled to do so. We were told that many were dissatisfied with the Mormon Church, and would leave it whenever they could with safety to themselves.[34]

The scope of the Move South was so massive and its sacrifices so demanding that a pervasive, coercive enforcement of prophetic counsel by the Nauvoo Legion was simply not practicable in view of that force's other duties. There are signs that Wells was hard pressed in getting his troops to perform even their routine military functions without adding the onerous task of forcing their neighbors southward at gun point.[35] Alarmed at growing disciplinary

[34]Powell and McCulloch to Floyd, 3 July 1858, "Annual Report of the Sec. of War (1858)," 172–73. For the negative impact that the commissioners' use of the one-third estimate has had on the assessment of three of the Utah War's closest analysts, see Poll, "The Move South," 78, and Bigler and Bagley, *The Mormon Rebellion*, 294–95. Determining today how often, with what level of force, and by whose authority such compulsion occurred is an imponderable. Apostate Charles Derry recalled: "an order from Brigham was issued that every man, woman, and child north of Utah County must abandon their homes and remove into the southern part of the Territory under the penalty of having their houses burned over their heads." Once he arrived in Salt Lake City in mid-April, Alfred Cumming met with scores of Utahns seeking the aid and protection of the U.S. government in leaving the territory, recording in the process that a handful of these supplicants feared that they would be forced in unspecified ways to migrate to Provo. Derry, "Autobiography," in Aird, Nichols, and Bagley, eds., *Playing with Shadows*, 239; Cumming Papers, Duke University. In old age Nauvoo Legionnaire Nicholas Harmon Groesbeck recalled that "during March and April of 1858 the entire population was compelled by Brigham Young to move south," but he seems to have softened what he viewed as the mandatory aspects of Young's decree with the observation that it was part of his Sebastopol strategy. Groesbeck, Autobiography, 11, Utah State Historical Society, Mss A 556 c.1.

[35]For a description of a late March 1858 incident of mass absence and dereliction of duty at the Legion outpost in Provo Canyon, see Carter, "Guard Quarters," and the transcript of the related courts-martial that followed on 5 and 19 April 1858, Utah Territorial Militia Records, Series 2210, Utah State Archives. As the spring wore on, disciplinary problems in the Legion worsened, as reflected in this record for 24 May: "G. A. Smith, A. Lyman and several others visited Prest. Young in the evening [at Provo] and discussed the propriety of burning G.S.L. City and the settlements north of it. Prest. Young called upon G. A. S. at his house, about Sun down and staid about one hour. . . . When Prest. Young was at G. A. Smith's Adj. Gen. James Ferguson & [Judge Advocate] Stout arrived from G. S. L. City they started at 1 P.M. They bring letters from Gen. Wells, stating that the details in the various settlements [to tend gardens and potentially fire buildings] were very remiss in their duty not more than 10 attended role [*sic*] call. One man had deserted while on guard in Echo Kanyon; he was found in the apostate camp." Church Historian's Office Journal, 24 May 1858, LDS Archives.

problems in the Legion, Brigham Young perceived an alcohol problem and descended on Hugh Moon, one of Salt Lake City's better known liquor purveyors: "I write to request you *not* to sell any more whiskey or alcohol, or any description of spiritous liquor, no matter who may call upon you to purchase. And in case the plea is made that some one will die, unless the liquor can be had, be pleased to tell them to first call upon me and g[e]t an order for the coffin, for the liquor they cannot have. We have seen as much drunkenness about our streets as we care about seeing, and they all acknowledge that they get their liquor at 'Moon's still.'"[36]

Accordingly, some unknown number of Latter-day Saints made personal decisions to remain home and did so unpunished, although probably at the risk of being ostracized. This was the group that four of the Legion's most senior officers described to Brigham Young as "families which will not move at all in any direction," noting that "there are quite a number of that class." The officers asked Young, almost plaintively, "what shall we do with [such] families," adding "we also find much difficulty in getting men to attend to roll call [in Salt Lake] there is generally about 60 in attendance all most a general Spirit of indifference prevails on this Subject."[37]

A striking case of a Mormon family that felt free to avoid or at least delay joining the Move South was that of Cynthia Jane Park Stowell, wife of Lt. William R. R. Stowell, the Legion adjutant captured by the Utah Expedition in October and still imprisoned at Camp Scott under a federal treason indictment. In the spring of 1858 Mrs. Stowell was in the late stages of pregnancy, overwhelmed by the burden of caring for at least thirteen children and the uncertainty of her husband's fate. She was apprehensive about joining the mass exodus to Provo and "the difficulties that must attend it as they loomed up in the distance seemed quite insurmountable." While Brigham Young pursued her husband's release through messages to both Thomas L. Kane and Albert Sidney Johnston, Mrs. Stowell sought counsel from a family friend, who "kindly urged the necessity of prudence. He thought it wise not to be in too much of a hurry to leave our homes as there was nothing to enforce our leaving until the way opened before us." On 14 April Cynthia Stowell delivered her baby and a week later headed south with her large brood and a sister-wife aboard a wagon pulled by two yokes of steers.[38]

---

[36]Young to Moon et al., 19 April 1858, ibid.

[37]Grant, Kimball, Burton, and Jones to Young, 5 June 1858, LDS Archives.

[38]The Utah War Experiences of Cynthia Jane Park Stowell, 3, typescript notes courtesy of BYU professor Devan Jensen.

Others who did not move south—the most disaffected—took advantage of the distractions then besetting Utah to decamp in an easterly direction for the sanctuary of Fort Bridger and the plains beyond. As apostate George Greenwood explained it to his English sister and her husband in December 1858 from the haven of Nebraska Territory, "We left the Great Salt Lake City on the 17th of May, in company with about thirty wagons. . . . We did not make our intentions public on leaving the valley; it would not have been good policy to do so. . . . We kept on the farm to the last, and as the people were moving southward, Brigham having declared their independence, we went to the city; but instead of going southward, we took to the east."[39]

If one rejects the notion that the Move South took place at gunpoint, it would be a mistake to assume that those whom Brigham Young uprooted uniformly embraced the experience. They did not. As with the earlier call to man and equip the Standing Army, Mormons complied, but with widely varying degrees of enthusiasm that included foot-dragging. Unlike the requirement to outfit the Standing Army, the immediately following counsel to migrate south required a far greater sacrifice, involving as it did one's entire family, its dwelling place, and livelihood. At stake was not just the commitment to arm, equip, and provision a cavalryman for a year but rather the abandonment and perhaps destruction of one's home, daunting transportation challenges for humans and livestock, questionable shelter from inclement weather, and a disastrous disruption of the 1858 farming cycle.

Among the most negative recorded reactions to the Move South were those of Nauvoo Legion private David Davis Bowen, who during his earlier service in Echo Canyon had journalized similar complaints. During the Move South, Bowen commented:

> All had to move with their herds of cattles and their flocks of sheep, their piggs, geese, and chickens all they had that could walk, leveing behind them their fine farms and their exelent houses, to be distroyed by Indians or any body els that felt disbose to doo soo. Thes, the people had to sacrafice thousands of dollars werth of property to satisfied the foolish ambistion of Brigham Young, one of the most tyranical, despotical villain on the face of the earth at the present time. Evry house was filled with their friends, and Dd. H. Davies took in two families [in addition to mine]. That was Owen Robert and his wife and Edward Ashton and his wife and two children. We had a full house among us all 12 head. After that we did not have much

[39]Greenwood to Mr. and Mrs. Myerscough, 7 December 1858, "Mormons and Mormonism," *Preston* (England) *Guardian*, January 1859.

pece and comford in David house, for he wished us out of his house to give more room to the others. He thought the other parties was better than us.[40]

How did Mormon leaders react to such "push-back" from Latter-day Saints? Responses ranged widely but probably centered on grudging toleration intertwined with pressure from peers and bishops to conform and heed counsel. There are even records of behavior that can be considered understanding, if not acceptance, of individual decisions not to relocate. For example, on 21 March, in his shepherd-sheep discourse announcing the Move South, Brigham Young at times struck a pastoral tone quite different than his violent threats of the 1856 Reformation:

> In the northern counties it may be inquired, "are we to do as you are doing in this city?" You may do as you please. If the Bishops north are here and wish to ask, "shall we leave for the deserts?" You may do as you please; I will set you all an example in this city. If the people want to stay in Bountiful, at Centerville, at Freedom, and so on, to our most northern settlements, they are at liberty to do so. But we will pick up and leave this city, that the army may comply with the orders from the War Department to build a station "at or near Salt Lake City," if no other course will suit them. We will risk ourselves further south, and if you wish to risk it where you are. You can do so, but what will be your situation if the enemy should occupy this city and are between you and us?[41]

Three days later Young began to pass word of the program to church, civil, and military leaders in communities north of Salt Lake City through visitations by Col. Chauncey W. West. In tones that were more tentative than authoritarian, Young instructed West "to take this letter to the Northern Settlements and ascertain the feelings of the brethren and see if they are willing to gather up and leave for the south."[42]

A few hours after Young's 21 March discourse, Hosea Stout was startled to encounter resistance to the program in his ward: "The brethren seemed somewhat loth to volunteer." Stout responded on the spot with a public display of leadership by example: "For which reason I gave my name to go in the first Company although I did not come in that class who were called

[40]Bowen, Reminiscence and Journal 1845–1863, March 1858, LDS Archives. For Bowen's 1857 complaints while serving in Echo Canyon, see *At Sword's Point, Part 1*, 371n75.

[41]"A Series of Instructions and Remarks by President Brigham Young, at a Special Council, Tabernacle, March 21, 1858," LDS Archives.

[42]Young to officers north, 24 March 1858, ibid.

upon."[43] Even General Wells—often perceived as a disciplinarian—was at times casual rather than judgmental in mentioning to Young incidents of resistance or neglect of duty during the Move South.[44] When Wells reported the capture of a deserter from the Legion detachment in Echo Canyon, he sought counsel from Young on the disposition of the case but declined to tell him the offender's name. Instead of ordering the prisoner before a court martial, Young reacted with leniency and directed "the person who deserted his post in Echo had better be furnished a pass to leave our settlement, if he wishes to do so, and is not in debt in Utah, and will leave without stealing."[45]

Standing in contrast to Private Bowen's grumbling were the supportive views of another Legionnaire, 2d Lt. James Henry Martineau of Parowan, adjutant to Colonel Dame. Having narrowly missed involvement in the previous September's killings at Mountain Meadows, one might think that Martineau would have had enough of bloodshed. But such was the religious zeal and indignation aroused by George A. Smith, whom Martineau accompanied during his August 1857 visit to southern Utah, that the lieutenant was ready for a fight seven months later. In recording his views, Martineau signaled the confusion caused by the ambiguities of Brigham Young's announcement, especially the matter of whether the intermediate marshaling place for the Move South was to be Provo or farther south in Parowan, where Martineau lived:

GODFREY AND MARTINEAU-MCCARTY, EDS.,
AN UNCOMMON COMMON PIONEER: THE JOURNALS OF JAMES HENRY MARTINEAU, 30 MARCH 1858, 145.

> Today news came from the city, with particular of proceedings of a special conference, at which the President announced the policy adopted, to save the shedding of blood. We will retreat south, and burn and destroy everything behind us as we go, leaving nothing for our enemies to profit by. The women and children are to be removed south, no crops to be put in, north of Utah County, and Parowan will be headquarters.[46]
>
> This cast something of a damper over us—the thought of retreating

[43]Stout Diary, 21 March 1858, Brooks, ed., *On the Mormon Frontier,* 2:655.

[44]Wells to Young, 12 May 1858, LDS Archives.

[45]Wells to Young and Young to Wells, 23 and 25 May 1858, both ibid.

[46]Martineau's misunderstanding that the principal marshaling place for the Move South would focus on his hometown rather than Provo stemmed from an inexplicable phrase in Young's instructions to Martineau's bishop, Tarlton Lewis: "at present it is intended to make head-quarters at Parowan." Young to Lewis, 24 March 1858, ibid.

without a fight, and killing some of the infernal scoundrels, but I suppose it is all right, and [we] will carry out the programme.[47]

In the evening, meeting was held, and Bishop Tarlton Lewis called for all the teams and wagons to help the removal south. Twelve wagons were sent—more will be soon.

From the North Pole on Half Rations: Executing the Move

With the availability of Richard D. Poll's scholarship, there is little need to describe here much more of the "what" of the Move South. The following vignettes supplement Poll's study with the less accessible firsthand views of hard-pressed Mormon women, children, and some extraordinary husbands and fathers. It is an under-studied group worth meeting.

If, on the evening of Brigham Young's 21 March announcement, Hosea Stout had worried about reluctant neighbors and ominous, snowy weather, by the next morning, the outlook was brighter. Stout found Monday to be a "warm pleasant day, snow melting."[48] As Brigham Young perused his mail that day, he found a letter that must have lifted his spirits while reinforcing his belief that he was on the right track. It was a positive note from a plural wife of Asa S. Calkin, president of the British Mission, who had been called to remain in Liverpool with the departure for Utah of Apostle Benson. Staying behind in Utah, Mrs. Calkin was self-reliant, but she had more than a few practical questions for which her distant husband was unable to provide timely answers. Without hesitation, she sought counsel from the spouse of her friend, Zina Huntington Young, on the day after his big announcement.[49]

Marietta S. Calkin to Brigham Young, 22 March 1858, LDS Archives.

Shall I intrude too much on your precious time, and add a weight to that burden which is already heavier than any mortal can stand up under, without the spirit of God, by asking a few questions relative to our preparations for

---

[47]Here Martineau reacts to Young's bland notice to Bishop Lewis, "you will learn by the Circular, 2 copies of which are now forwarded to you, that the present policy has varied somewhat from the past." Ibid.

[48]Stout Diary, 22 March 1858, Brooks, ed., *On the Mormon Frontier*, 2:655.

[49]For an example of Mrs. Calkin's earlier search for advice on financial matters, see Marietta S. Calkin to Brigham Young, 22 January 1858, LDS Archives.

this general move, which all good saints intend to participate in?—Perhaps I am wrong in thinking that the cause, which calls for the absence of my husband, together with the debilitated state of my health, and almost helpless state of our family in not having any man to look after our affairs—is a sufficient excuse. It is what I have to offer—If I am wrong please tell me—

In the first place I would like to tell you how strong we are to move or help ourselves—We have one yoke of cattle about a dozen cows, some of which we thought might work in the yoke, will that be best?—Had we better let all the stock we do not want to use in removing, remain in the care of the man that now has them?—We have a wagon but no wagon cover, or tent, or wagon boxes. We have enough in our house to make our small family comfortable, as well as to entertain our friends when they call to stay all-night—of course it is more than we can remove at one load with our provisions—shall we go with one load and return for another?—

It has been intimated to me that a single woman would like to go with us, she has a plenty of wearing apparel, I think that is all—It would be agreeable to us all to accommodate her if we can bring it about—We have some good lumber Mr Calkin put up in a state of preservation before he left—also good flour beens [bins] and cupboards—in which we could put all we might wish to bury.

Theodore might dig the hole, though he is not very strong, and we might store them away—but to cover them, I should like some man that had good judgement and felt interest enough to direct in it so that they might indeed be preserved from wet—Looking-glasses and clocks might as well be burned at once as to be put indifferently away—and I prefer it,—For I could then say "blessed be nothing:"—[50]

I will wait for some kind of an answer if you please

P.S. Please may we locate near your family for the sake of their society.

That Marietta Calkin turned to Mormonism's supreme leader for counsel in such matters reflects a number of factors: her immediate needs, friendship and proximity between the Young and Calkin families, Brigham Young's direct responsibility for her husband's absence in England, his approachability even for parishioners seeking guidance in the most mundane aspects of life, and her elevated position in Mormon aristocracy.

Then, too, there is the matter of Asa Calkin's own temperament: at times a somewhat stern, self-centered one that may have prompted his wives to seek guidance elsewhere. The leadership of a patriarchal, Victorian society

[50]Here Mrs. Calkin takes issue gently with Young's specific advice of the previous day to preserve such fragile, hard-to-acquire items.

in motion on the frontier was not always a tender one. Asa Calkin's later letter to Lizzie, one of Marietta's sister-wives, is a model of insensitivity to the hardships of the Move South. Recovering from smallpox in what his wives, unaware of his illness, must have viewed as the urban comforts of Great Britain, he wrote:

> So, you have pulled up bag and baggage and left my house while I have gone have you? Well, how do you like "Mormonism" rough and tumble? You begin by this time to understand something about what I meant don't you? I think you once asked me what I meant and I told you it was to live in a house or a tent or a wagon or by the roadside, to eat bread or roots, to dress in cloth ~~and~~ or skins &c And from all accounts you are likely to have a taste of the whole budget. How do you like it? Its nothing after you get used to it. Only hold on to this rod of iron and it will land you safe on the other side. "The Kingdom of God or nothing" is the motto, hold on to it and it will help you on wonderfully.[51]

Asa Calkin's wives were not the only Mormon women lacking empathetic husbands during the Move South. A prime example was the behavior of Elias Smith, a man often called to roles such as Salt Lake City's acting postmaster, a judge of that city's probate court, and an editor of the *Deseret News.* From these judgmental perches and the safety of his home cabbage patch, husband Smith stirred himself from a nap one day to heap long-distance demands on his refugee-wives in Provo. Smith ended one letter with advice on loading the family wagon and an admonition: "try and fix the bedsteads and table so that they will not rub more than is necessary and do not kill yourself in packing up."[52]

The children participating in the Move South viewed the experience as either frightening or a lark, depending upon their age as well as their families' circumstances. One unidentified girl, age eleven, found it deeply unsettling to leave her home—ready for the torch—for the uncertainties of life on the road:

LEVI EDGAR YOUNG,

CHIEF EPISODES IN THE HISTORY OF UTAH, 34–35.

> We packed all we had in father's one wagon and waited for the command to leave. At night we lay down to sleep not knowing when word would come of

[51]Calkin to Lizzie Calkin, 5 July 1858, Calkin Diary, LDS Archives. For more such insensitivities, see Calkin to Marietta Calkin, 17 August 1858, ibid.

[52]Smith to Lucy and Amy Jane Smith, 1 July 1858, Franklin E. Smith Papers, Special Collections, Marriott Library, University of Utah.

the army which we thought was coming to destroy us. Mother went about the house placing everything in order and mending every bit of clothing we could find, for we knew that the time would come when we might be in great need of food and clothing. There were seven of us children in the family. We put away all our playthings, for the days found us so frightened that all we did was to follow father and mother from place to place, looking into their faces for a word of comfort and a look of cheer.

One morning father told us that we should leave with a large company in the evening. He said little more. There was packing and the making of bread. Along in the middle of the day father scattered leaves and straw in all the rooms and through my tears I heard him say "Never mind, little daughter, this home has sheltered us, it shall never shelter them." I did not understand him then, but as we went out of the yard and joined all the other people on the main road I learned for the first time that the city was to be burned should the approaching army attack the people.

That night we camped on Willow Creek in the south end of the Valley and at ten o'clock every soul with bowed head knelt in prayer to God. As I dropped to sleep I heard my mother whispering that the Lord had heard our prayers and that our homes should not be burned. I cried and cried, but at last I dropped to sleep.

As with many other children, the Move South thrust on John Fell Squires, age twelve, the role of boy-drover. For Squires, unhappily in charge of the family pig, there was none of the dignity, derring-do, and freedom experienced by eleven-year-old George Richard Hill trailing livestock south astride a Nez Perce pony obtained by his missionary-father from Indians at Fort Limhi.[53] Yet even though miserable and temporarily fatherless, Squires came to realize the depth of Mormon compassion at the hands of gruff "old" David Udall, progenitor to multiple congressmen from today's Arizona, New Mexico and Colorado.

Autobiography of John Fell Squires in Notes of Interest to the Descendants of Thomas Squires by His Son, Typescript, 5–6, LDS Archives.

Mother was left with four children and winter staring her in the face, very little food in the house, and mighty little wood outside. We burned considerable sagebrush that winter, at least [brother] Harry and I thought so,

[53]All was not adventure even for young Hill: "Mother turned my collar back and looked to see what was the matter. To her horror, she found my shirt and back covered with body lice. I shudder to think of it now. The camp stopped, the cattle were turned out, the big kettle hung on the fire, filled with water, and I was stripped to the skin and all my clothes boiled." Autobiography of George Richard Hill, MS 16123, LDS Archives.

as mother and my sister could burn it as fast as we could gather and lug it into the house.

No direct news came to us from Dad [Thomas Squires, in Echo Canyon with the Legion]. Occasionally word would be given out in ward meeting that all were getting along OK in camp and that Uncle Sam's men were snowed in and half starved one hundred miles east of them. Of course this was good news to us. Well, we managed to survive the winter one way and another, but came out as poor as crows.

Our next trouble was the call to Move South. As we had nothing to move with, we did not go. But everything comes to those who wait.

One evening in the early part of April (1858), one David Udall, an old friend of Dad's, drove up to our house [in Salt Lake City] and inquired about Father. When told that he was out in Echo Canyon, he said, "That is just what I expected, so I have come to move you south and will take you to Nephi where I live. This place is 98 miles from S.L. City and I can't take all of your belongings as my horses are very poor and the roads are out of sight. We will pile in those things most needed and leave the balance here." Mother objected as she thought we were leaving for keeps, so wanted to take along all that was movable. There was quite a discussion between the two, but this man had his way, so only the articles most needed were piled in and the remainder left behind.

Of course I was just old enough for any change, so the idea of travelling one hundred miles struck me as being a pleasure trip and expecting to ride that distance.

When all was ready to pull out, Mother said, "By the way, Bro. Udall, there is an old sow pig out in the sty. We had better turn her loose as she will starve to death if left in the pen." We went to the pen to attend to this, but when Udall took one square look at that pig and another at me, an idea struck him, so he said, "We had better take it along with us, as pigs are pigs and a very scarce article just now." Mother replied, "Why, we can[']t have that hungry, dirty thing in the wagon mixing up with us all that way." "Oh no," said Udall, "You don't have to. That boy (pointing to me) can drive it as he will have to walk anyway. We will have to travel very slowly due to the load we already have, the mud, and the poor condition of my horses."

You must remember his horses pulled through the famine, consequently there was mighty little pull left in them for our trip. I had a lurking idea that this man Udall had it in for me, having made myself somewhat fresh several times in his presence when told by him to do this, that, and the other, but this knock-out blow surely did put a quietus on my anticipated ride.

When the wagon was loaded and we were ready to start for Nephi, Bro. Udall procured a piece of rope, tied one end of [it] to the pig's hind leg, and, I was going to say the other end to one of mine. All the same, I was attached to the other end. Suddenly I was doing a two twenty clip around the sty until I became dizzy. Mother hollered, "Let the darn thing go." But I could not get loose and the pig headed for the street. We shot past the wagon and took to the sidewalk, from there I was pulled into every corral and yard on the block. The pig sampled everything in sight, then had time to pick her teeth before the wagon caught up. While our outfit covered only four miles that day, we, the pig and I, covered all the real estate between fences with our tracks. . . .

We finally reached our destination, but not until that pig had sampled every weed, old shoe, bottle, can and rag between Salt Lake and Nephi, looking into every yard and breaking the world's record for speed and high jumping on the shortest notice.

As a boy travelling to Nephi with Bro. Udall, I thought him cross and mean. As I grew older, however, I realized that was not his inherent nature. He came to Salt Lake to take us to his home just out of friendship for Father and to obey counsel. He knew that he would half [*sic*] to house and feed us after we landed at his place. I know now it was worry and anxiety over this great responsibility as well as fatigue that made him irritable. There were two small rooms in the Udall home and these good folks emptied one of them and turned it over to Mother. There she set up housekeeping. . . .

All this time we had never heard one word from Father since he left for Echo Canyon. There was little if any mail getting through and Mother often said to us children, "Another day gone and no word from your Father." One afternoon in the month of June I walked into our little room and said, "Mother Dad will be here tonight." "Why, what have you heard?" "Nothing, only he is coming." Mother did not even look up from her work, just said, "Don't say such things when you don't know what you are talking about." Well, between sundown and dark that very night, Dad loomed up on foot, tired and dirty, having walked 35 miles that day. He told us that he had walked the entire distance from Salt Lake City to Nephi but, to me, he looked like he had come from the North Pole on half rations. He had inquired so often for us along the road that his voice was almost gone when he found us.

When Dad landed in Salt Lake City from Echo Canyon, he made a bee line for our house in the 20th Ward, not knowing that we had long ago gone to Nephi. Smoke was coming out of the chimney and he said to himself, by golly, now for a surprise. When he walked in without knocking, a strange woman sprang to her feet saying, "Well, what do you want?" He got the surprise right then! After staring around and getting his breath he said, "I believe this is my house. At least it once was, but things are so muddled up of late that I might be mistaken. Do you know where the people have gone who, I think, used to live here?" The woman replied, "This place was empty, so we decided to occupy it." That was all the satisfaction he got from her, so that she soon had Dad headed south.

Be Careful to Save the Nails: Moving "Built" Utah

While Utah's bishops struggled to facilitate the movement or reception of families such as these, Brigham Young and the LDS church's more senior leaders focused on a parallel challenge not yet probed in depth by historians: removing from Salt Lake City much of Utah's irreplaceable infrastructure. For months, Young had spoken passionately of his intent to incinerate public buildings, provisions, and durable goods, as well as residences, orchards, and other property improvements rather than leave them for the army's use. The fact was, however, he was not quite done with many of these items in the spring of 1858, especially his own property. As a result, Mormons made herculean efforts to disassemble and haul south a wide variety of items, many owned by the church, as well as Brigham Young's personal possessions: the printing press, paper supply, and type cases of the *Deseret News,* which were shipped to Fillmore; the machinery for multiple grist- and sawmills; and the Salt Lake Tabernacle's pipe organ, a precious but bulky item hauled across the plains with great care. Evacuating and then burning cities and regions may have happened repeatedly in Russia, but such tactics were not part of the American military tradition.[54] When the moment of truth came, Brigham Young flinched. Notwithstanding his braggadocio, he chose to relocate rather than destroy Utah's most critical infrastructure.

What also moved south with these components of Utah's civilian infrastructure were military supplies and equipment necessary to conduct the fighting retreat to which Brigham Young alluded frequently. Among the latter were large quantities of the gunpowder acquired in California and along the Kansas-Missouri frontier during 1857 by Peter W. Conover, Howard Egan, and Nicholas Groesbeck. Also shipped were the tools and equipment from Salt Lake City's "public" machine shop, a facility dedicated to manufacturing unlicensed Colt's revolvers. In reassembling the shop in Parowan, its

[54]During the Revolution, George Washington chose not to destroy Boston, New York, or Philadelphia while evacuating these cities, and the British Army showed similar restraint in later relinquishing them. In the War of 1812, the American side withdrew from Washington without destroying it, although the British did to retaliate for the earlier American destruction of Kingston, Upper Canada. During the Civil War, the Confederates did not intend to burn Richmond as they withdrew in April 1865; it was ineptness and high winds that turned the planned destruction of a few key buildings into a general conflagration. The closest that the U.S. Army has come to involvement in anything like Young's Sebastopol Plan was its extensive planning for the destruction of the Territory of Hawaii's infrastructure in the face of an anticipated Japanese invasion during World War II. Dorrance, "Scorched Earth Plans for O'hau," 159–69.

superintendent, Nathan Davis, displayed remarkable ingenuity but pleaded with General Wells for a few missing items: "It would be quite an accommodation to the gunsmith business if we could have that small portable forge that Br Barlow had in his charge, to dress small tools temper springs &c if it cant be spared, Br Ash left one at his house in the 16th ward that will answer if thare is any chance to get it down here. We got one floor laid in the shop & have got a vice bench all along one side of the shop, & got 6 vices up & the gun smiths to work stocking guns & doing what work they can on the pistols with out the lathe. Br Phelps says there is some fifteen & twenty hundred [pounds] of pretty goo[d] cast iron at the foundry that he would like to have sent down as there is but verry little iron to be had here."[55]

In the midst of this incredibly stressful scene, rivalries among the Nauvoo Legion's officers accompanied the movement of Utah's infrastructure. In his 7 January 1858 report to Brigham Young, Adjutant General Ferguson had strayed into a gratuitous critique of the Legion's staff departments other than his own, especially Col. Thomas Ellerbeck's ordnance operation. With the Move South and its relocation of provisions, weapons, and munitions, Ferguson renewed these criticisms. He asserted to General Wells that the Legion's senior staff officers were acting in uncoordinated fashion and that only strong leadership by Wells would bring the requisite order to the militia's performance. In the process, the adjutant noted that he "would like to have a word" in determining which of Ellerbeck's artillery pieces were to be mounted on wheeled gun carriages, not a detail that usually concerned adjutants.[56]

Even barns and other buildings lost their siding, roofs, and nails so that they could be shipped south along with freshly milled lumber. Brigham Young used many of these materials to build in Provo a compound of frame cabins to house those members of his families not quartered in local hotels or private homes. While hardly palatial, the lodgings for the Youngs, who had traveled to Provo by carriage, were in marked contrast with the crude accommodations cobbled together by the rest of Mormonism's refugees, who traveled afoot, in farm wagons, or on horseback. Some refugees were lucky

[55]Davis to Wells, 17 May 1858, LDS Archives.

[56]Ferguson to "General" [Wells], 3 June 1858, ibid. Ferguson may have felt free to intervene in ordnance affairs because of his likely awareness of squabbling between Ellerbeck and Wells four years earlier over a petty non-military matter: Ellerbeck's removal of a clock from Brigham Young's office. It was a comical but corrosive affair that played out through an exchange of notes in which Wells ridiculed Ellerbeck for informing Wells "you have hurt my feelings." Ellerbeck to Wells and Wells to Ellerbeck, both 18 July 1854, LDS Archives.

"Brigham's Shanties at Provo City"

In dispatching his multiple families to Provo for the Move South, Young shipped lumber from Salt Lake to build this compound of stove-equipped cabins to house them. For Mormon refugees exposed to snow and rain in wagons, tents, dugouts, wikiups, and other makeshift shelters, these comforts symbolized an inequality of sacrifice. For non-Mormons this scene telegraphed the scope of Young's commitment to polygamy. *Woodcut engraving from photo by David A. Burr in* Harper's Weekly, *9 October 1858, courtesy of Brigham Young University Museum of Art, Provo.*

enough to lodge with relatives; thousands of others camped throughout the spring snow and rain in a wide range of makeshift shelters that included tents, wagon boxes, lean-tos, willow wickiups, and earthen dug-outs. Theirs were accommodations that made the sordid shelters of Eckelsville seem upscale.

Notwithstanding Brigham Young's earlier personal vows from the stand to flee to the wilderness and live off the land, his behavior was otherwise. When the time came, he chose to live in sheltered comfort. No sooner had he announced the Move South, Young informed the bishop of Provo, "I design to soon begin to move my family, provisions, stoves, musical instruments, and such other articles as may be needed and cannot be saved in caches, as far as Provo, and I would like to have you secure me one or two large halls in your city in which I can shelter my family, and some store rooms for my property. You may wish to know how much room I may need; from ten feet square to half of your city."[57] In the process he set a highly visible example of unequal sacrifice. Few criticisms of the Young family's comforts during this crisis have survived, but it would be remarkable if such high-profile symbolism did not stimulate envy and damage morale among rank and file Mormons, especially as the group fell prey to exposure and pneumonia. One wonders about Latter-day Saints' reactions had they known that while they coped with existential issues like miserable weather and makeshift shelters their prophet was chiding General Wells about the details of his own family's accommodations: "three of the doors sent here [Provo] are too long and too narrow for the plank shanties; the doors should be 6 feet high and 2 feet and 6, or 7k, or 8 inches wide."[58] Young's inegalitarian behavior constituted a missed opportunity for him to reinforce a sense of shared hardship among what on 21 March he had called his "sheep."[59]

The papers of Brigham Young and General Wells for this period reflect the urgency and a high level of micromanagement associated with this institutional (rather than family) relocation of Utah's infrastructure. An example of this non-delegatory behavior appears in General Wells's gentle protest to Young about his directive that the heavy cottonwood benches from the Salt Lake City Bowery be hauled to Provo. Wells believed that such items might be better fabricated and replaced at the destination, with limited wagon capacity used to transport higher priority items: "I have therefore taken the liberty to load these teams with posts and scantlings for fence, storehouses, shanties &c preparatory to sheltering people & storing grain, and will wait your instructions in regard to the benches." On these issues Young reflected and relented, informing Wells that "I approve of your views and course in regard to the Bowery benches, and the preference you have given flour, wheat, families, &c., leaving the benches until a more convenient season, even in case it should in the future be deemed best to haul them."

---

[57]Young to Elias H. Blackburn, 24 March 1858, ibid.

[58]Young to Wells, 15 May 1858, ibid.

[59]Albert Sidney Johnston was hardly beloved by all of his officers and men, but he understood leadership in the midst of adversity as well as the power of symbolism atop a military organization, especially during the Utah Expedition's November march through brutal weather on the final trek to Fort Bridger. Captain Marcy's men made the same positive point about his leadership style when they arrived in northern New Mexico in January 1858.

Yet within a week of this little show of independence, the Wells-Young relationship reverted to its customary authoritarian pattern. From the distance of Provo, former carpenter Young instructed Wells to "take the boards off from my *woodhouse,* which are good and well seasoned lumber, and make of them wheat boxes, flour boxes, and whatever else you please; be careful to save the nails, for the roof is put in with wood nails." The general responded by seeking additional counsel on a wide variety of small matters as well as important issues: "Shall we pack up the [territorial] Library and send it off? Shall Bro Staines keep his house [open] for Gov. Cumming? That was his wish before he left. Shall the Globe [Restaurant] be opened for the boarding of those who will probably accompany Gov. Cumming upon his return? Or had Bro. Townsend better furnish the accommodation? Or would it be still better to let them furnish [feed] themselves where they can get a chance? Shall we take out and board up the windows of the Tabernacle, Council House, Endowment House, Deseret Store and other public buildings, and prepare the sash for caching?"[60]

The remarkable scope of this effort is encapsulated in a status report written from Salt Lake City to General Wells by Maj. Jonathan Pugmire, Jr., one of the dependable Legion officers who had earlier constructed the defenses of Echo Canyon.

PUGMIRE TO WELLS, 3 JUNE 1858, LDS ARCHIVES.

Sir, I take this opportunity of informing you how we are getting along since you left [for Provo]—We are loading up the teams as fast as we can with wheat, but could do it much faster providing the teams from the South had wagon beds to hold Wheat without boxes. I had forwarded by Hoopers Train 2 Loads of 2 inch Pine plank, in consequence of not having boxes to load them up with wheat. There are 2 or 3 more Loads of cotton wood slabes at the Bowery & will forward them should you think proper.

The rooffs are taken of[f] the Foundry, Gun & Machine & the New part of the Stone shop. The Gun shop floor is allso taken up. The Foundry chimney is taken down for fear of accident as it was pretty much damaged.

If we get run [room] for Lumber I shall take of[f] the North side of the rooff of the Black Smith Shop & leave on the south side so that the men may not all day be exposed to the sun. I should like to know about the rooff of the carpenter's shop.

---

[60]Wells to Young, 12 May 1858; Young to Wells, 14 and 18 May; Wells to Young, 19 May; all ibid.

Please let me know if there is any Public buildings that you want boarding up. Please to enquire of Prest B. Young if I could take & use the iron that is laid up in his louft. I should like if you could forward any iron to this place to keep things moving in the Shop and get Nails for the boxes.

I think that every thing here moves along pretty well. But would feell glad to have a Letter from you with such suggestions as you may think proper for me to have. Please give my best respects to Prests Young & Kimball & yourself not accepted.

P.S. There are some good joist in the upper louft of the Machine shop. I should like to know if you wish them forwarded & What is to be done with those castings in the Foundry.

On the Animal's Backbone: Beyond Provo

As for the all-important "where" question prompted by the Move South, it is an intriguing mystery. One unsubstantiated report argued that in 1857 Young "told Capt. Van Vliet . . . he (Brigham) was on the 'backbone of the animal,' and he 'intended to stay there,' though he might not always stick to the one identical place on it."[61] Both Young and Kane floated references to Sonora, Mexico, as a likely destination at various times and in quite different ways. On 25 April Young did so through a Mormon intermediary for Alfred Cumming's benefit; for his part, Kane left a trail of innuendoes about Sonora with the newspaper reporters and editors who interviewed him in Nebraska, Kansas, and Missouri while returning east during May–June 1858. Louis Bertrand, the French convert-journalist with unparalleled access to the most senior Mormon leaders, described the Move South as heading "toward" Sonora, but he could not bring himself to use the word "to."[62]

Did Sonora mean its coast on the Gulf of California? The mountains or valleys of the state's interior? Specifics were never forthcoming, and so speculation about elusive places like the White Mountains continued. Both Young and Kane spoke about Sonora in similarly vague (even coy) terms that invite perceptions of a coordinated effort to shape public opinion. It was behavior much like first Kane's and then Cumming's effort to merchandise the notion of an undefined war-peace split atop the Mormon hierarchy.

With Brigham Young beleaguered by existential threats from all directions

[61]"From Utah," Dispatch, 24 August 1860, *New York Times*, 20 September 1860, 5/2.

[62]Bertrand, *Memoires d'un Mormon* in Homer, ed., *On the Way to Somewhere Else*, 112.

and a keen need to take some kind of action, invoking Sonora as a destination was an illusionary rather than substantive option—one intended to create the appearance of action while masking the embarrassing reality that, as the spring wore on, Young had no actionable plan for Utah's Mormons beyond the intermediate goal of rallying on Provo. As early as his mid-September conversation with Captain Van Vliet, Young had indulged in such wishful thinking: "President Young said if we can Ceep [*sic*] the peace for the winter I do think there will be sumthing [*sic*] turn up that may save so much shedding of Blood."[63]

In early May 1858 rumors and uncertainty about a destination were good enough for Legionnaire John Kay. Writing from Salt Lake City to a friend at the British Mission to update him on the Sebastopol plan and its Move South, Kay reported, "the United States' troops are expected to be in here on the first of June; but that will be if the Lord will. For over a month, the Saints have been very busy moving south with their provisions and live stock. There are not a great many families in this city. The brethren from the north and Tooele have left. Yesterday, I sent off thirty-five hundred [pounds] of flour and wheat, also two of my wives, Susan and Ellen, with their children; and in a short time we shall have everybody out of this. Then, if we cannot do better, we shall cut down our fruit-trees, set fire to our houses, and move on slowly towards Sonora, although I believe the nearest way is to proceed *via* Jackson County, Mo.[64] However, we can go any way we please: we have now the Territory on wheels."[65]

The absence of multiple necessities crucial to the success of any such mass exodus to Sonora made it impractical: a passable wagon road between the Spanish Trail and the Colorado River; a water supply en route for tens of thousands of refugees and their animals; a river landing serviceable for use in a large-scale Mormon embarkation; knowledge of the river's navigability; a fleet of shallow-draft boats by which to descend the Colorado and negotiate the Gulf of California; mutually acceptable understandings about transit rights and resource use with the hostile tribes to be encountered; language capability in Spanish, if not a plethora of Indian dialects in two countries;

[63]Kenney, ed., *Wilford Woodruff's Journal*, 26 September 1857, 5:101.

[64]A reference to Zion, or the ultimate gathering place, then believed by Mormons to be in Independence, Jackson County, Missouri, based on a revelation received years earlier by Joseph Smith.

[65]Kay to Thomas Williams, 10 May 1858, *Millennial Star* (Liverpool), 24 July 1858, 474–75.

an identified, mapped, accessible, and prepared destination in Sonora; and facilitating negotiations with the state and federal governments of a Mexico republic then wracked by revolution. The massacre of the Rose-Baley party of Mormon emigrants by Mojaves at Beale's Crossing of the Colorado in the fall of 1858 was a telltale sign of only some of the dangers awaiting Anglo travelers to the region.[66]

If one believes that Young instead envisioned an overland trek to Sonora via the interior of what is now Arizona, many of the arrangements necessary for a downriver exodus to the Gulf of California via the Colorado would also have to have been in place to pursue this option. In addition, three other essential components of infrastructure would have been necessary: a large-scale ferry system by which tens of thousands of people could safely cross the river; hundreds of miles of north-south wagon roads within Arizona; and a chain of way-stations to support an overland exodus of this scope.

Based on the record for Amasa Lyman's reconnaissance from Parowan to and along the Colorado in the spring of 1858, as well as Jacob Hamblin's harrowing exploration of the region south and east of the river during the 1860s and early 1870s, it is clear that none of these prerequisites for success were in place or even under way so as to extend the Move South into northern Mexico. Todd Compton, Jacob Hamblin's latest biographer, believes that when Kane returned to Utah in 1872, he and a still-beleaguered Young planned an overland exodus to Mexico through Arizona that depended on Hamblin's help. This possibility is not to say that the essential topographical knowledge and infrastructure were at hand fifteen years earlier to make any such gambit even remotely possible in the midst of the Utah War.[67]

It could be argued that the scope and success of the 1846–47 Mormon migration from Nauvoo to the Salt Lake Valley constituted an omen, if not a template, for the practicality of the Move South's continuation into Mexico. But it should be remembered that the earlier east–west exodus had elements of preparation, knowledge, governmental negotiation, and staging wholly missing for any Mormon plunge into another country already ill-disposed to a large-scale influx of land-hungry Americans. Evocative of such a scenario is dictator Porfirio Diaz's later lament, "Poor Mexico, so far from God, and so close to the United States!"

[66]Baley, *Disaster at the Colorado.*

[67]Compton, *A Frontier Life,* 365–66.

Since Young left nothing more than tantalizing phrases and innuendo about his thoughts on northern Mexico as a destination-haven, what is valuable, by way of indirection, are his more extensive comments and questions in May 1858 about the possibility of leaving the United States to colonize Nicaragua's "Mosquito" coast. He did so in the course of meeting with four agents of "Colonel" Henry Lawrence Kinney, a filibuster from Texas who offered to sell him thirty million acres at ten cents per acre. In the course of probing this offer with Kinney's agent, John B. Cooper, Brigham Young entered into the following exchange. It was relevant to Mexico as well as Central America:

> Gov. Young said the United States would be for annexing that tract of country. Mr. Cooper answered "the Clayton & Bulwer treaty prohibits either Eng. or the U.S. touching it." Gov. Young said they care no more for breaking treaties than a horse does to break a spiders web in his way to a feed of oats. He asked Mr. C. how we could get to Mosquito Coast. Mr. C. answered by shipping from San Diego. Gov. Y. said then we would have to leave our teams, cattle, sheep &c, Mr. Cooper said "you can buy cattle there. Mr. Kinney has a great many cattle." Gov. Young said "if you have any propositions to make I'll receive them, but as far as I am concerned; if Mr. Kinney owned all central America and would give it to me for nothing, I would not go there. I am satisfied the climate is unhealthy. . . . You must make them [propositions] in view that we will not move from this Territory as we are just where we want to be and where we intend to stay, and all hell cannot move us from it."[68] Two days later, "President Young said to Mr. Cooper what could Mr. Kenny [*sic*] mean or think of us to send to us [such an offer] as he has? Does he think we are fools? The United States would give millions of dollars to have us go to that Country for then they could lay their hands upon us. I would not go to that Country if it was Covered 15 inches deep with gold and we owned it all. We are here and here we will stay in this Territory."[69]

Thus, in the war's final month, Young returned to the comment he had made during the conflict's opening week. Within days of returning from his five-week exploration of the Fort Limhi area to the north during April–May 1857, he had responded to hypothetical questions about why the Latter-day Saints did not seek refuge in southern California, Texas, or western New Mexico's Gila River region: "We are in the happiest situation of any people

[68]Church Historian's Office Journal, 24 May 1858, LDS Archives.

[69]Kenney, ed., *Wilford Woodruff's Journal*, 26 May 1858, 5:192.

on the world. We inhabit the very land in which we can live in peace, and there is no other place on this earth that the Saints can now live in without being molested. . . . As I have often said. I am thankful to a fulness that the Lord has brought us to these barren valleys, to these sterile mountains, to this desolate waste, where only Saints can or would live, to a region that is not desired by another class of people on the earth.[70]

Two years later the correspondent of a New York newspaper informed his readers from Salt Lake City, "I am inclined to think that Brigham never seriously thought of such a thing as selling out, nor made any proposition of the kind. But I may be mistaken. Certainly, the Mormons of these parts do not look and act as if they intended, or were ready to sell out. That subject is generally met here with contemptuous turn up of the nose."[71]

---

[70]Young, discourse of 7 June 1857, Van Wagoner, ed., *Complete Discourses of Brigham Young*, 3:1271–72.

[71]"From Utah," Dispatch, 24 August 1860, *New York Times*, 20 September 1860, 5/2.

"Colonel" Alfred Cumming, ca. 1855

This pencil sketch by Pvt. Gustavus Sohon is the only known Cumming image contemporaneous to the Utah War. It depicts him as a commissioner to the treaty talks with the Blackfeet in October 1855 at Montana's Judith and Missouri Rivers. Cumming's clashes there with Gov. Isaac Stevens of Washington Territory and later with General Harney foreshadowed his poor relations with General Johnston and Utah's federal judges. *Courtesy of Washington State Historical Society, Tacoma.*

Chapter 12

"Proceeding to Salt Lake City"
The Mountain Moves to Mohammed

Gov. Cumming left this camp for Salt Lake City on the 5th inst. He took no one with him but two teamsters and Col Kane of Philadelphia who has been here for some weeks past a self constituted Ambassador & Umpire between the two High Powers. He was formerly if he is not yet a Mormon.

Capt. John H. Dickerson to W. A. Gordon, 16 April 1858

[Kane] was a man who never allowed his right hand to know what his left was doing. He was possessed of a great soul. His chief object in life was to do good.

Apostle and First Counselor George Q. Cannon, March 1884

How Kane brought a skeptical Governor Cumming to realize that his destiny lay in Salt Lake City rather than with the army, and then moved him there, lies at the heart of this chapter. It was no small feat. Almost singlehandedly he transported an unfit, obese man beset by fear of rabies across one hundred miles of deep snow, mountains, unbridged rivers, and canyons. As Kane later told it, he was also burdened by threatening camp followers, Mormons, and Indians, menaces that may have been more imaginary than real. If during the Utah War Kane's other behavior and actions opened him to perceptions of manipulativeness, this accomplishment warrants admiration. Gritty as it may seem, Kane's persuasion and delivery of Utah's new governor under such circumstances was a signal contribution to the conflict's resolution. No one else could have done it. Postwar, this adventure would be foundational to Kane's public campaign to retain a politically endangered Alfred Cumming.

Attachment Amounting to Enthusiasm: Among the Quaking Aspens

On 25 March Kane embarked on what he considered one of the most hazardous steps of this process: a rendezvous with Brig. Gen. William H. Kimball, his requested Mormon intermediary. By prearrangement the two men were to meet at Quaking Aspen Hill, a landmark well beyond range of Fort Bridger's patrols but one requiring Kane to travel alone through miles of rugged, unfamiliar terrain.[1] A similar ride two weeks earlier had nearly killed him while trying to reach Fort Bridger from Salt Lake City. The purpose of the meeting was to provide Brigham Young with a status report on Kane's discussions with Cumming and Johnston while giving Kane information about developments in Salt Lake City since 9 March. Both sides had startling news to exchange.

From LDS sources, virtually nothing is known of the Kimball-Kane meeting except what little may be inferred from Elias Smith's observation in Salt Lake City on 22 March: "I had my hands full of business all day. W. H. Kimball with 25 or 30 men started out east to meet Col Kane and escort him in, if he wishes to return, or can have permission to return to the States this way."[2]

Kane left several accounts of what took place. To brother Pat he complained about the remoteness of the meeting site while fantasizing about his peril from two threats: shadowy camp followers dogging him from Fort Bridger and potentially hostile Latter-day Saints:

> You know finally that instead of being able to hold the [easy] intercourse with the Mormons, which I had persuaded Governor Cumming of the necessity of my establishing, I was obliged to go out into the mountains to seek them where I could find them, outlaws or honest men, all the Mormons that hated

[1]At 7,315 feet above sea level, the euphoniously named Quaking Aspen Hill or Mountain was the highest point between Fort Bridger and the Salt Lake Valley and a major landmark on the Mormon Trail. It is approximately twenty miles from Fort Bridger near today's hamlet of Aspen, Uintah County, Wyoming, a stop on the Union Pacific Railroad sixteen miles east of Evanston. Because of the shelter and water it afforded, Kane and Kimball probably met at the abandoned mail relay station at Quaking Aspen Springs near the mountain's summit. John A. Eldredge, e-mail message to MacKinnon, 25 June 2013.

[2]Smith Journal, 22 March 1858, 1:58.

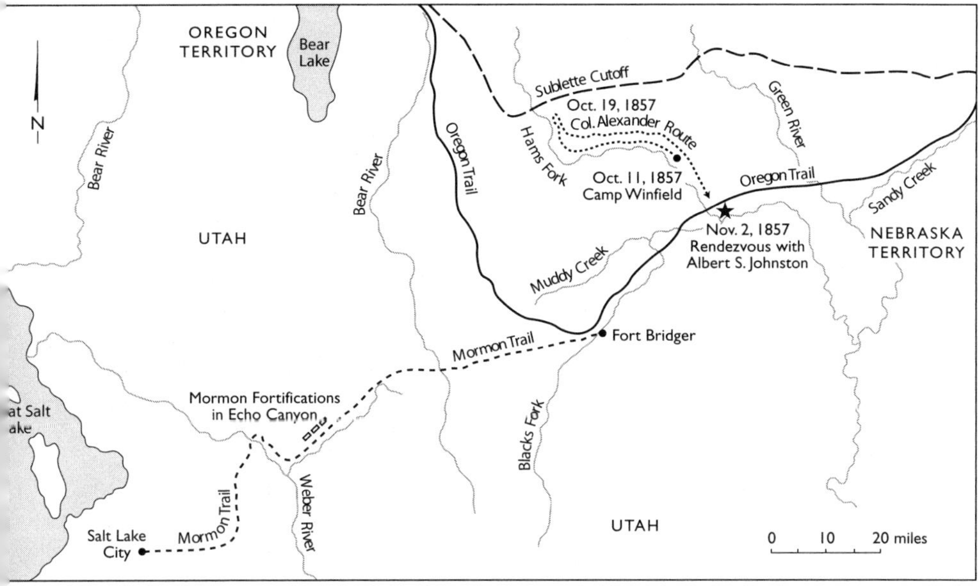

Northeastern Utah:
Region between Fort Bridger and Salt Lake City

Once Kane reached Fort Bridger on 12 March, much of the war's action centered on the 113-mile stretch of mountains, canyons, and high desert between the Utah Expedition's winter quarters and the Salt Lake Valley, the army's intended destination. It was a watershed laced by snow-fed tributaries of the Green River (flowing into the Colorado) and Bear River (emptying into Great Salt Lake). *Map drawn by Bill Nelson, Accomac, Virginia.*

me, or the Mormons that loved me, twice facing terrible snow storms, to one of which I had nearly fallen a victim, and waylaid by Indians as no power on earth will ever persuade the Mormons, not at the direct instigation of the army, as I myself think there might be some reason to fear, at the instigation of some [civilian] parties in camp.

The nearest approach to one of the vulgar stories that people like to hear from the vulgar braggarts who tell stories their own way, is of a chase I had by a party, I fancy rising up, to try to cut me off, when I was no more than 15 miles out from camp; it may be dressed up very well [in the later telling], though the truth was I knew well I had much the fleetest horse in that country.[3]

[3]Kane to Pat Kane, ca. summer 1858, "In Re Mormons" File, Thomas Leiper Kane Papers, APS.

THE NAUVOO LEGION'S
BRIG. GEN. WILLIAM H. KIMBALL
The oldest son of First Counselor Heber C. Kimball, he led the Standing Army in early 1858. At Kane's insistence, Kimball was go-between for him and Brigham Young for the crucial rendezvous at Quaking Aspen Hill near the end of March. Trusted by Kane since 1846, Kimball was one of Young's rough-hewn "b'hoys" whom Kane described to Buchanan as a "fine fellow" lending him "valuable assistance." In 1859 Kimball was disfellowshipped by the church for alcohol-related incidents, and in 1871 he was indicted (but not tried) for the Utah War murder of Richard E. Yates. Photographed here as a Legion major or lieutenant colonel in the mid-1850s, he wore essentially the same uniform as the U.S. Army officers against whom he later campaigned. *Courtesy of descendant M. Kent Larsen, Wellsville, Utah, and International Society, Daughters of Utah Pioneers Museum, Salt Lake City.*

Kane's journal includes several jumbled entries bearing on travel to the meeting. They indicate that he left Eckelsville equipped with rudimentary directions to the rendezvous and a pre-arranged regimen of gun shots and fire beacons with which to signal the Mormons. The trek was arduous, one that tested Kane's mettle. During the outbound trip, his pack animal faltered, with near-disastrous results. As he struggled on the trail, Kane's spirits reached a low ebb, and he recorded fragmentary thoughts ranging from his travails with the army to wife Elizabeth and even the possibility of suicide: "Severest trial of Temper worse than Johnston & all. The mule & Rifle broken ?? God forgive me—I thought of drawing my knife and Knelt in the snow and prayed and wrote this record of ?? [*t and reversed C symbol*]. 10 P.M. What an entry might have been made after this 'The Story of a Mule.'"[4]

Several weeks later, when Kane passed through the same area in better

[4]Kane, "Diary II (1858)," 7. The rifle may have been the one Kane borrowed from his brother Pat, a prized possession. The meaning of the symbol is unknown, but because it appears in several of Kane's letters to Elizabeth, it had some mutually understood religious or romantic significance.

weather and with companions, he spotted the site of his mishap. Now in higher spirits, he wrote of his earlier attempt to evade what he thought were Indians:

> To think that the snow was so deep that the trail nowhere blew it deep enough to see any of these bushes. This is the place I came in the other time I was lost, and there I was fooled by the big grizzly's tracks drifted over. Sure enough, I see how it was I fell so rapidly into a valley the time I turned off, to keep out of sight of those suspicious appearances to the right! Cd. it have been so short a distance further on where I ensconced myself to wait till the storm broke enough for me to see if that was smoke down yonder? Just under that bare water wasted mountain side did I first experience the pleasure of exclaiming? "Lo the poor Indian!"[5] What a calamity I thought it when back & piece I broke my [rifle's ram] rod before I had presence of mind to think of turning it into a flail. So this is but three miles from where I swore at them so frightfully.[6]

When he returned to Eckelsville, Kane described his trek to Pat Kane in dramatic tones and a survivor's sense of exhilaration:

> As for my health you can measure it by the amount of blood I have in circulation when I tell you that I was out last week in the worst snow-storm which has been experienced here since last November. I met it full in my face on an open table ridge in the Mts. and was eight hours going as many miles—so completely benumbed were my animals by the force and coldness of the wind. And yet, encountering a Mormon horseman about night-fall, I went with him to his camp about 30 miles off—slept in the falling snow that night, and the next, and the next;[7] and have actually suffered by the trip less than either my horse or my mule. Out-door exercise—with excitement enough to blunt the sense of affliction, and Mountain Air dear fellow—the Altoona [Pennsylvania], dear Patty with which you saved my life. Indeed I try to remember it and the dear ones who stood by me there—with every draught of the pure atmosphere I relish.[8]

[5]By 1858 this phrase was a stereotypical part of many discussions about Native Americans, derived from Alexander Pope's famous 1734 poem, "Essay on Man": "Lo, the poor Indian! Whose untutor'd mind / Sees God in clouds, or hears him in the wind. . . ." Later, Capt. Albert Tracy of the Tenth U.S. Infantry would relive his boredom at Camp Floyd by composing a poem about an imaginary fight between a dragoon lieutenant and a Ute brave using "Lo" in its title. Tracy, "Lo—With an Attachment," 378–80.

[6]Kane, "Diary II (1858)," undated entry [early April], 9.

[7]Kane was actually gone two nights rather than the three implied here, a confusion similar to his description about details of the trip to meet Lewis Robison at Muddy Creek a week earlier.

[8]Kane to Pat Kane, 4 April 1858, Kane Family Papers, BYU. For the Altoona adventure, see *At Sword's Point, Part 1*, 511–12.

Once Kimball and Kane came together, news of Brigham Young's announcement four days earlier of the Move South overshadowed all of these travails. The focal point of Kimball's briefing was the letter he delivered on Young's behalf. It was a strange document. Written on the day Kimball cantered out of Salt Lake City, it posed questions more logically asked several days earlier, i.e., before Young decided to launch the Move South. Kane later told his father that Young had "written in the anticipation that Kimball wd. receive bad news from me—the escort [led by Lewis Robison] which accompanied me to within 40 miles of Bridger having returned [to Salt Lake] without favorable intelligence." After allowing Kane to read this document, Kimball asked for its return. Kane complied, but had Kimball copy the crucial third paragraph into his diary.[9]

YOUNG TO KANE, 22 MARCH 1858, LDS ARCHIVES.

Your escort returned [to Salt Lake City] in safety, on the afternoon of the 19th inst.

With the miserable mail facilities extended to Utah by the Post Office Department, you are aware that any news from the East, of later date than we can expect by the Southern mail, and also to fill the gaps occurring on that route, will be very acceptable.[10]

We are now preparing to remove our men, women and children to the deserts and mountains, that our enemies may come in and complete their instructions "to establish a military post at or near Salt Lake City," if that is their only alternative. What do you think of the policy? Which is the better, that plan, or fighting? And will our enemies keep off and let us alone while we are removing, or are they so bloodthirsty that they will not be satisfied short of doing their utmost to destroy our lives?[11]

So far as we have information, their present instructions only reach to establishing a "post" in this city and acting as a "posse" when called upon; and if they come here and find neither people nor city, what will be their next move?

With your opportunities, keenness of perception and accuracy in drawing

---

[9]As a result of this restriction, the only complete copy of the letter's text is the original, which came to rest in Brigham Young's files upon Kimball's return. The excerpt may be found in two documents: Kane, "Diary II (1858)," undated entry, 20; and Kane to Judge Kane, 4 April 1858, Frank Evans Research Collection, MS 1251, LDS Archives.

[10]Young did not realize that, thanks to the still-functioning Panama-California-Utah mail link, he was better informed about Atlantic Coast news than were Kane and the Utah Expedition.

[11]These are fundamental questions similar to those about Mormon military intentions asked belatedly by Secretary Floyd in July 1857, weeks after he and Buchanan launched the Utah Expedition. *At Sword's Point, Part 1*, 173–78.

conclusions, you will, doubtless, be able to form a pretty correct judgement on these questions.

What was the report of those prisoners that were taken last fall, and escorted from this city to the soldiers' camp during the latter part of winter?[12]

When you have perused these few lines to your satisfaction, and have made such minutes thereof as you choose, will you be so kind as to hand this letter back to the bearer, William H. Kimball, and oblige, truly your Friend.

P.S. I should be much pleased if you would ascertain and send me word whether they will recieve [*sic*] the flour mentioned in my [9 March] letter to you on your way out, as the late snowstorms have prevented its being forwarded to date. Having heard [from Lewis Robison] that there is plenty of flour in the camp, I shall not send out any until the roads become sufficiently settled, which, according to present appearances, will not be until after I again hear from you. The [Gilbert & Gerrish] cattle will not be driven out unless the flour is sent.

Please learn what you can in regard to [captive Nauvoo Legion Lt. William R. R.] Stowel[l], and what their intentions are towards him.[13]

Such unexpected information and questions must have stunned Kane. At the time he left no record of his reaction to the Move South, although later he offered Young his "sincere congratulations on the wisdom of the course you have pursued. It is additional[ly] apparent to me since my return [home]."[14]

Significantly, Kane chose not to mention the massive exodus then taking place in Utah to either President Buchanan or his family. First word of the Move South drifted east to Fort Bridger, the Kansas-Missouri frontier, and then to Washington not from Kane but from Abel Gilbert, a respected non-Mormon merchant who had spent several days with Brigham Young in late March while traveling from California to the Missouri River. With such upheaval beyond his ability to control, it is as though Kane was loath to discuss a major decision made by Young in his absence. Although reluctant to admit it, Kane may have realized there were limits to his influence among the Mormons' most senior leaders. Perhaps for this reason, Kane later

---

[12]A reference to Pvt. Henry Feldman, teamster Charlie Becker, and an unidentified third captive.

[13]Young was very solicitous about Stowell's treatment, perhaps because, upon escape, fellow captive Maj. Joseph Taylor had reported attempts by the army to poison them. Earlier, Young had warned Colonels Johnston and Alexander: "If you imagine that keeping, mistreating, or killing Mr. Stowell will redound to your credit or advantage, future experience may add to the stock of your better judgment." Young to Johnston and Alexander, 26 November 1857, "The Utah Expedition," House Exec. Doc. 71, 110–11.

[14]Kane to Young, 18 July 1858, LDS Archives. Several historians have interpreted this broad statement as a belated endorsement by Kane of the Move South's public-relations value. Poll, "Thomas L. Kane and the Utah War," 129; Grow, *"Liberty to the Downtrodden,"* 184.

trivialized the Move South by characterizing it as "a political move" to a party of westbound missionaries whom he encountered on the Oregon Trail.[15]

If Young's letter caught Kane unawares, he, in turn, provided Kimball with his own surprise: news that Cumming intended to travel to Salt Lake City. In November 1857, still claiming the governorship, Young had instructed the Nauvoo Legion to detain Cumming to prevent his entry into the city.[16] Although much had since taken place, including his own arrival in Utah, Kane had not prepared Young for an appearance by Cumming in Salt Lake.

The most important guide to understanding how Kimball and Kane discussed the possibility and arrangements for such a journey is Kane's diary. Understanding this record is challenging; many of the entries are cryptic, jumbled, undated, non-sequential, and illegible. In addition, the comments attributed by Kane to the Mormon side were recorded in his own phrasing after passing through his distinct, sometimes fanciful perspective on what was or should be happening in Utah. The result is a source unique but problematic in its accuracy.

From this material, it seems likely that early in the discussions Young, speaking through Kimball, asserted that if war were to take place, the responsibility would lie elsewhere. Young then reminded Kane that in their private session on 25 February he had heard Kane's explanation of Buchanan's views, had received and accepted the presidential apology tendered on his behalf by Kane, and had even reciprocated ("equivalent given") in some approximate fashion. Young then listed several subsequent acts deserving credit: his "committal" in some unspecified fashion to Kane, provision for Kane's "safety against the war zealots"; "staying [delaying] contemplated [Legion] attack of 1st March," and "direct overtures for peace." With respect to the latter, Young listed three specific gestures: tendering salt to the army in November, releasing three army prisoners at Christmas, and offering flour and beef to the Utah Expedition in March.

Having provided this litany of positives, Young concluded that the federal response was hostile: "Overtures disdainfully refused. And the time which might have [been] employed ridding the M's [Mormons] of Johnston's command before the advance of other [reinforcing] columns—and the inclement season elapsed when they were at M's mercy—has been used simply in

[15]Palmer, *James Palmer's Travels and Ministry*, 128.

[16]*At Sword's Point, Part 1*, 367–69.

bringing all forces to bear for their destruction. This proves insincerity of President [Buchanan] or want of power to control Camp Scott people." In response to these assertions, Kane chose to distance himself from the federal side, noting gratuitously to General Kimball that one might add to this list of indignities the grand jury proceedings then under way at Eckelsville ("Indicted by the Camp") and commenting at one point, "did I not say that I was the bearer of no dispatches. That also the Prest. did not wish me to risk myself by carrying any."[17]

Kane then put two crucial questions to Kimball: "Is it important to gain time? Is there anything to be lost—position to be waived—or the like by yr admitting C[umming] and recognizing him?" The general responded "yes" and "no," respectively. William Kimball's second answer had momentous political and military implications, signaling a willingness on Young's part to accept Cumming as Utah's governor. It is unlikely that Kimball would have given such a response without pre-authorization to discuss this volatile subject—one at the very heart of the armed confrontation under discussion.[18]

With this understanding, Kane and Kimball moved from the matter of "whether" to multiple "how" issues. Kane specified two conditions essential to Cumming's involvement in the peace process: "No insult or indignity; if B.Y. wrong headed on inquiry both of us shall have honorable repulse [withdrawal]." For Kane the challenge was to preserve the new governor's self-image and safety in the event that Young or Mormons supposedly aligned against him were unwilling to see a successor ensconced in Salt Lake City. Accordingly, Kane then

> asked after C's safety. Manner in wch he wd. be received &c. I then promised to do my best to bring him on the conditions expressed—viz.: None but reliable men on outposts &c all others called in. Coming of Gov. not to be imparted [disclosed]—so that we may be in keeping [company] of reliable men, before any desygning [*sic*] Mormons can come if of their own accord. Orders given to all out [on patrol] to respect Camp near Spring. If allowed to proceed—reliable escort all the way. Guard around Governor—Don't care what anybody think or say (seems an accusation). He will understand it. He is entitled to guard of honor. And I am entitled to have wild [*illegible*] kept off me. And fools whom, he needn't seem to have anything to do with it if people raise objections. (W.H.K.) They won't. It's alright.

---

[17]"Recollection of lost memorandum of W.H.K.'s remarks," Kane, "Diary II (1858)," undated entry, 21.
[18]Ibid., 19.

To these arrangements Kane added an elaborate array of visual signals ("1 white and 1 black cuff—things not favorable; 2 white cuffs—I may be accosted. Company ride up.") for both sides to display as Cumming and he, uncertain of Mormon attitudes, approached Kimball's detachment in early April.[19] To think that they could use such complex signs, signals, and passwords on horseback in the snow-packed wilderness was as impractical as it was Kanesean.

Among the most colorful aspects of the meeting was also its most murky: a proposal to Kimball for how Cumming and Kane would deal with either a rebuff of their overture by Brigham Young or an attack upon them by Mormon interlopers. Kane recorded: "If Young not notified [of] W.H.K.'s assurance then Repulse—by a number & by authority. Four or Five unauthorized I will probably shoot at—for he [Cumming] will if I do not mistake my man." Later Kane tried to explain this proposed arrangement to President Buchanan with only slightly less opaque language. Matthew J. Grow's interpretation of what was discussed is that "Kane gave the Mormons an escape clause should Young find the plan unacceptable. In such a scenario, Young should send a large group of Mormon soldiers to forcefully, but without violence, compel Cumming and Kane to return to Camp Scott." To Grow, this arrangement "demonstrates that Kane and Young had not agreed on a scheme to induce Cumming to go to Utah [Salt Lake]; rather, Kane acted on his own initiative in conceiving and executing the plan."[20]

It is unknown whether, before this meeting, Cumming had shared with Kane his new awareness that the army was planning a Pacific Coast thrust against Utah and if, in turn, Kane passed this important information to Kimball. It is questionable that Cumming and Kane would have felt obliged to keep this information confidential, and it is likely that making Young aware of such a threat through Kimball would have suited their own purposes. Kane might reasonably have expected that such news would help to motivate an already beleaguered Young to arrange an accommodation with the Buchanan administration through him.[21]

---

[19] Ibid., 7, 19.

[20] Grow, *"Liberty to the Downtrodden,"* 184.

[21] This aspect of the pressure on Young would, of course, dissipate with his subsequent awareness that the administration had cancelled both Scott's trip to California and plans for a second front.

It Is All Over Now: Euphoria, Reportage, and Preparation

When Kane and Kimball returned to base on 27 and 28 March, respectively, they carried an agreed-upon scenario for their principals to consider. It was one as convoluted as the Utah War machinations revealed to Sir William Gore Ouseley by James Buchanan.

Major Porter noted Kane's arrival at Eckelsville tersely: "Kane returned. Nothing known of what he heard or saw."[22] Kane's diary presents a far more turbulent picture than these bland comments. He returned exhausted yet exhilarated over surviving the trek and making major progress in advancing Alfred Cumming's journey to Salt Lake City. What Kane recorded was the joy of triumphant leisure and a wide range of other emotions:

Kane, "Diary II (1858)," 28 March 1858, 8 and 8A.

And now behold my first Sunday—the first time since I embraced this work, that I have heard the Order to Halt & Stand at Ease. I have returned from a trip on which I was *successful in* making the arrangements for *introducing Governor C. into the valley,* with the feeling that I have done my last utmost, and may leave the future to a less finite power.—It shall prove for me if there is any God—other than that which nailed Him to the Cross—whose groans are still heard.

This day I might endulge in journalizing for my darling, but I have not given me a holiday from *Duty,* and [illegible] commands me to rest my weary being utterly. It will not exercise my mind to read the Mignon Bible and Sintiam [Xtian?] and the blessed leaves, and sigh over the fading, fading photographs.

I put on my day clothes the one clean change—early, this morning: I anticipated enjoying it so much.—But this must be more wearing than that which I have been confronting. Homesickness, fears for them all—and, oh, my griefs, my griefs!

—May I but return before this has changed me and I seem to the dear ones another than myself!—Elisha, my dear Elisha.

I made one of the Qrmaster's men tie me in my tent from the outside—to keep me from intruders while I lay down—and my tears fell till sun down into the cups with which I held the cold water against my frost bitten cheeks. I then arose—prayed to the memory of my Prince, and, asking forgiveness for my regrets, promised my best to *keep strong* and not to think of returning home before I saw plainly it was my duty.

---

[22]Porter Diary, 27 and 28 March 1858, 19, Porter Collection, LC.

> I ought to regret if my adventurous service is ending, for another reason. I am evidently the child of a more heathen day than my dear wife and the saintly to whom her life belongs. But, in my coarser way—while I am for Good's sake spending my life time among rude risks—I think I lift my heart as high to heaven as theirs. This is the discipline adapted for my nature, and I should have more of it. I should live in the stone fortress on the rocks of the moon till the "change of some kind comes over me."—Now, I am but on the *mournful journey,* through the wild tangled paths of the snow clad valleys.
>
> —This passage of my darling's book came into my mind on Thursday, just after I had recovered the trail and saw the storm approaching—the *magical* storm I called it—which soon broke on me in such wicked blindness. Until it compelled an active struggle with the danger it threatened it was a grand & solemn enactment productive of the highest poetical impression.
>
> Doing nothing now which it will interest anyone to read the record of—it is time that I shd, like others make entries in my Diary. Well, Monday & Tuesday Have been devoted to tasks connected with striking the tents for a removal from Camp Scott to Camp Bridger—and running conversation with the Governor.—(protracted to 12 last night). He will go with me to Salt Lake. . . .

What Kane did not record is that he found Alfred Cumming a shaken man, the victim of a "serious" dog bite within hours after he left camp to meet William Kimball. Because of the governor's prominence, the dog's attack on several people, and fears that the animal was rabid, news of the incident rippled through a Utah Expedition starved for diversions. Within the day, the Volunteer Battalion's Captain Magraw reported Cumming's misfortune to Secretary of the Interior Jacob Thompson in a letter marked "Private" and "Not Official." As soon as merchant William Gerrish returned to Missouri from Fort Bridger, he described what happened while characterizing the governor as "fearful and distressed about the matter."[23]

On the eve of his and Cumming's departure for Salt Lake City, Kane reported to Buchanan on his conference with William Kimball but made no reference to the Move South, a remarkable omission. For the president, Kane could not resist the opportunity to describe the extent to which he misrepresented Johnston's 16 March note of refusal to Young while simultaneously advising Young, if challenged, to deny that the offending document even existed. More important than these manipulations, Kane revealed to

[23]Magraw to Thompson, 25 March 1858, Pacific Wagon Road Records, RG 48, Microcopy No. 95, Roll 4, NARA; Dispatch, *Weston Weekly Platte Argus,* 14 May 1858, reprinted in *Baltimore Sun,* 24 May 1858, 1. Cumming escaped the agony of rabies.

Buchanan the news that he had broached to Kimball the possibility of Cumming traveling with him to take up Utah's governorship. Again he bent the truth by asserting to the president that such a trek was solely Cumming's idea. For Buchanan's benefit, Kane twice invoked his favorite straw man: the physical danger to Young (and now Cumming and Kane) from contending war-peace factions among senior Mormon leaders.

KANE TO BUCHANAN, 4 APRIL 1858, KANE FAMILY PAPERS, BYU.

I have the pleasure of writing to you with renewed hopes of peace.

I was successful in obtaining the interview which I sought last week with Mr. W. H. Kimball and have to report its result as of the most cheering character. I found the fine fellow all that I anticipated and he lends me valuable assistance to counteract the effect of the inconsiderate conduct of the gentlemen of the camp.

I was not able to promise his people much with respect to the Salt Lake mails but I represented their detention here as the act solely of the military authority and added that it did not meet with the approval of Governor Cumming. I stated also that Governor Cumming had taken pains to secure the mail matter from being lost or stolen and that he had caused the letters directed to Brigham Young in particular to be enclosed in a sealed envelope to prevent their circulation among curious hands.[24]

With regard to the graver matter of the refusal of the supplies of the beef and flour by Colonel Johnston I did my best to represent it as an act with respect to which the commanding officer possessed no discretion. In relation to the written reply which I was requested to communicate I asked Mr. Young that I had, since the date it bore, obtained Colonel J's authority for stating that it was not his intention or desire "to say anything either harsh or insulting to Mr. Young." Mr. Kimball not inappositely rejoins, "why was the letter communicated to him in its unacceptable form"—I in reply bade him assure Mr. Young, *from me,* that if the language of Colonel J's letter was likely to prejudice him in the estimation of his counsellors, Mr. Young need not consider it as having been communicated to him textually at all. "If the language of the letter" I said "was about to be regarded as of more importance than in my candid opinion it was entitled to,—I cheerfully assumed the responsibility of authorizing Mr. Young to announce at Salt Lake that nothing but the substance of a courteous refusal of his offer had been communicated to him by Col. Kane."[25]

[24]Kane's draft for these opening paragraphs appears in Kane, "Diary II (1858)," 4.

[25]Prevarications of this kind were not unusual among senior leaders under pressure during the Utah War. For example, on 31 December 1857, in order to prevent dockage of his gubernatorial salary, Brigham Young certified to the U.S. Treasury Department's first auditor that he had never left Utah during the year—notwithstanding his five-week trek to Fort Limhi, Oregon Territory, during April–May 1857.

But in my interview with Kimball I had another object in view in which I did not allude in my last letter, feeling hardly justified in truth by the faint expectation which I then entertained of success.

In the course of one of my dialogues with *the man* [Cumming] whom I have already thanked you for sending out here to keep these overgrown boys in awe—in more considerate language, at the close of a dispirited conversation which I had the honor of having with his Excellency Governor Cumming, he somewhat startled me by requesting my opinion of a purpose which had entered into his mind—of proceeding with me to Salt Lake City, himself.

The manner in which the brave man put his query satisfied me that one element of success will not be wanting if the fates invoke it. But the step presented itself in more than one aspect and I therefore only replied by a request for time to give it a mature consideration. Although flattered to have such a duty imposed upon me I feel the responsibility of deciding on a matter of this kind for one [by myself]. I was not long in arriving at the conclusion that it would be well for an attempt to be made and without delay—(some of my reasons I take the liberty of enclosing as copied from my private Memorandum book—though they will not repay your perusal, I may perhaps thank you to keep them within your reach for my future justification). Although it was clear enough however, that the step proposed by Governor C. was highly expedient looking to the public interest solely, it was entirely out of my power to form an estimate of the amount of personal danger to which he would be exposed. I was not only unable to judge if this would be greater than the chances of good to be done would compensate for, but in fact had no means of determining if the effort to penetrate to the valley would met with any success whatever.

I think, Sir, that my interview with Kimball has provided me with the pledge of a man of his word in reference to the result of such an attempt. I am promised that we shall either succeed in reaching Salt Lake City itself—where the friends of peace, if needful, can take us into keeping or we shall be met at an early stage of our journey by a repulse of too formidable and peremptory a character to make it incumbent upon us [not] to offer any forcible resistance to it. Mr. Kimball was informed [by me] that the opposition of no [any] party numbering as few as four or five persons or unprovided with express authority from those in power at Salt Lake should be respected by me [and we will turn back]. Mr. K. and a number of other Mormons profess for me publicly a degree of attachment amounting to enthusiasm. I am confident that upon other similar contingencies which may arise, I can in like manner enlist this affection to compel an observance of the forms of respect towards the United States as represented in the person of their excellent Governor of Utah.

I need not say to you, Mr. President, that I mention this simply with the desire of doing justice to a heroic person and not in order to relieve myself

> for the responsibility of having counselled a measure of which the result may not prove fortunate. It is true I cannot predict the future and may only absolutely promise you that in case of an event to be deplored, my father's son will not prove qualified to tell the story. Such is my confidence, however, in the soundness of the arrangements which I believe myself to have made with Mr. Kimball that I assure you I do not permit myself to divert a thought in this direction [failure]. In my opinion we shall either be turned back in a manner which will supply completely the defect in the national *joinder of issue* to which I adverted in my conversation with you of [9] November last or else we shall penetrate as far as the city itself and remain there as long as circumstances indicate it to be desirable.

Reflecting fear of postal interception or his own habitual indirectness, Kane's phrasing here is torturous to an extreme. He seems to be telling Buchanan that either he and Cumming would be intercepted and barred from traveling to Salt Lake City (thereby confirming perceptions of Mormon resistance to federal authority), or they would proceed unimpeded to take the next step in a mediation effort of uncertain outcome.

In closing his report to Buchanan, Kane attempted to explain Cumming's thinking in undertaking such a trek. In the process he emphasized the idea that the decision to journey to Salt Lake without army protection was a courageous one solely attributable to Cumming, thereby casting himself in the role of facilitator rather than instigator.

Kane to Buchanan, 4 April 1858, Kane Family Papers, BYU.

> I experienced deep gratification in communicating the result of my expedition [to meet Kimball] to Governor Cumming, who is one of those characters who are thankful to be guarded from insult and indignity though quite above the vulgar fear of death. But at the risk of seeming to infringe upon a matter of personal privilege I must beg to state at once a fact which I have since been made acquainted with. Long before my coming it was the settled purpose of Governor Cumming to endeavor to make his way into the valley with the first "grass of spring," alone, without even myself for an escort. Last Autumn, his intention was the same and had he been able to carry out the design, no one can decide how much our country would have been the gainer.
>
> (Five months nearly have our foolish [army] columns been at it since—encamped too within a distance foolishly incalculated to embolden the Mormons and doing their utmost to incense them by threatening, indicting indiscriminately, eloquently corresponding and equally promiscuously wearing and firing at them. The Mormons count over two hundred shots within "point blank range" as discharged at different occasions at various citizens

of Utah and I see no reason to question their arithmetic. Would indeed, our other weapons of offence had been employed as innocently as our firearms! The uniform inaccuracy of their aim encourages me to hope that my poor guide Robinson [*sic*] may have escaped without a wound.)

—But the elements conspired against him [Cumming]; the mortality among the drove [draft] animals in November deprived him of the means of transport and the officer in command of the army to whom he applied for means to convey him over the mountains felt compelled to state it was out of his power to supply them.[26] My knowledge of this fact I have derived from another source than the statement of Governor Cumming. . . .

As I have said, I wrote to you again in a tone hopeful of peace; it is cherished by the warmth of my intercourse and confidence in Governor Cumming. We differ as much as ever, I fancy, in regard to Mormon men and things, but if we do not agree when he has seen them with his own eyes, I am almost in a mood to admit that my own and not his judgment will prove the one at fault. I do not think he will set them in order, range them in their proper places, the Mormon men and things.

Should he not, however—should he fail in all other respects, he will consider himself well repaid for his journey by the conversation which cannot fail to attend his mission. He cannot be debarred from making up for our country that complete and perfect record of its acts which will ensure us in the future the favorable verdict of history. I have had an opportunity of again inviting Colonel Johnston to review his decision with respect to the Salt Lake mails. I have also had a most satisfactory conversation with him with regard to our relations with the Indian tribes of the region, at the camp to which I was conducted; the night upon which I had my last interview with Mr. Kimball I obtained from the Mormon Elders some unpleasant details in relation to additional outrages which had been committed against the more Southern Mormon settlements and learned that various tribes are hovering between the two armies performing with native address the part of the Skinners and Cowboys of the Revolution.[27] This fact, if inclined to doubt it—I had shortly a more than satisfactory opportunity of verifying for myself. Colonel Johnston agrees with me that too much circumspection cannot be used in our dealings with these bands—since they find it to their advantage to represent their excesses as committed by the authority of the United States and their statements, true or untrue, place a most undesirable weapon in the hands of the war party of Utah—such bands whom of all persons on earth we must agree at present in regarding as the most detestable of our enemies.

I write to you today—as I hope soon again to write to you—when

[26]Neither Cumming's records nor those of the Utah Expedition indicate such a request and refusal.

[27]During the American Revolution "cowboys" and "skinners" were Caucasian raiders or guerrillas who were pro-British and pro-Independence, respectively.

imperfectly restored from recent severe fatigue and exposure. I offer you no apologies for my style however, while convinced my words cannot disclose me as other than your faithful and respectful friend and servant.

Mr. Kane, You Strive to Hide Your Game: Army Consternation

Originally, Kane and Cumming intended to depart for Salt Lake City very soon after Kane's 27 March return from the Kimball meeting. They set 2 April as a target date but then delayed it for three days because of a snowstorm. After several days of secret planning, it became necessary to involve Albert Sidney Johnston to arrange safe passage through the Utah Expedition's lines as well as to procure transportation, provisions, and camp equipment for Cumming, two servants, and Kane.[28]

News of Cumming's intent stunned Johnston; he attempted to dissuade the governor and then, under protest, furnished the requested items. As one reporter later described this interaction: "when he [Cumming] left Fort Bridger to enter Salt Lake City, Gen. Johnston proffered him an escort, he replied: 'No, sir; if I can't enter the city without one, I can't with one.' "[29]

Of prime importance to Johnston was gauging Cumming's risk. He did so by probing whether Brigham Young had tendered an offer of hospitality to the new governor. Absent such an invitation, Johnston feared that Cumming would be traveling unprotected amidst a hostile Mormon population. Major Porter recorded Cumming's assurances that he was indeed responding to such an invitation, but Kane's diary conveys the opposite response. Almost immediately, especially as the story became politicized, a years-long debate arose over the invitation issue. On it hinged the matter of whether one should view Cumming's journey as a quasi-heroic one undertaken in the face of an uncertain and perhaps threatening Mormon reception, or as a more prosaic act by which a federal appointee simply undertook an arduous trip to assume his rightful position.

[28]A question has arisen as to whether one of the unidentified servants was Anthony Osborne, the Kane family's black retainer. He was not. Osborne had earlier left the Kanes' service and had migrated to San Francisco. His only role in Kane's Utah mission was to accompany him aboard ship, send Elizabeth Kane newspaper clippings reporting Thomas's arrival in California, and, of course, to serve as the inspiration for Kane's nom de guerre. Both servants participating in the Bridger–Salt Lake trek were the governor's employees.

[29]["Traveller"], Dispatch, Salt Lake City, *San Francisco Daily Alta California,* 5 September 1858.

Major Porter provided an insider's view of the consternation flowing from this latest twist in the Cumming-Johnston-Kane relationship. He also recorded his skepticism about both the extent of Cumming's risk and the straightforwardness of Kane's (and now Cumming's) description of a Mormon war-peace split. Porter sensed Kanesean manipulation and presumably said so to Johnston.

PORTER DIARY, 2–6 APRIL 1858, PORTER COLLECTION, LC.

April 2d—Friday

About 3 o'clock A.M. a violent storm of wind rose—threatening to carry away tents and all habitations—So violent a storm I never felt—At Reveille snow mixed with hail in large quantities fell—covering the ground till noon—Squalls of snow were passing over all day. The storm is severe upon the animals—but the moisture is good for the grass. If our animals do not improve shortly I fear we will have to resort to mule-meat—though the ration of beef is diminished to avoid such a contingency.

Gov. Cumming called upon Col. Johnston today, and in connection with his friendly visit, to refer to the following business.

"I have decided to go in person to Salt Lake City, for reasons of state, and wish to obtain assistance in transportation and that I may not be dependent upon the Mormons for supplies, I wish to procure some additional quantity from the commissary. I wish to go to Salt Lake City, to meet B.Y.—Next week a conference or convention of the people will be held in S.L.C.—and from what I have understood the matter of peace or war will be determined.[30] I have assurances that B.Y. wishes for peace,—and that he finds it difficult to rule his people. I wish to go as far at least as Echo Cañon, where I will meet with either no opposition, indicating a peaceful tendency, or a few to repel me, and which it would be useless for me to oppose."

Col Johnston asked—"Governor, am I to understand that you are expected; that there is some invitation or impression made to you that your presence is desired as without some such understanding, I should be inclined to enter my protest."

Gov. C—"Yes, Sir, there is such an understanding—I am expected[31]—and

[30]Here Cumming recites an idea originating with Kane. This refers to the Mormons' annual General Conference scheduled for 6 April, timing impossible for him to meet with the weather-related slippage in his travel schedule.

[31]Based on what Cumming later told him, Kane recorded a very different version of the Johnston-Cumming exchange: "I [Johnston] trust you have assurance from Brigham Young. If not I should certainly be inclined to protest against your going. I have no such assurances. Does Col. Kane accompany you? He will. Will Col. K. probably return to the U.S. this way or by California? I do not know. He has not spoken to me of his arrangements upon that subject." Kane, "Diary II (1858)," undated entry, 25. The Tenth Infantry's Lieutenant Colonel Smith concluded, "Col. Johnston I have reason to believe is in entire ignorance of the nature of the negotiations that have been going on and of the Governor's visit to Salt Lake City." Smith to Fanny M. Smith, 14 April 1858, in Mesch, *Your Affectionate Father*, 154.

I think it would be beneficial for the country that I go—as for my person I have nothing to fear, unless from some of those wild fanatics, who are opposed to a peace and would be glad to see a collision with the government—and who are not responsible to the authorities in S.L. V[alley]. No doubt, indeed, it is known there are some of the [civilian] employees here of the Quartermaster who are anxious for such a result and I have as much to fear from them. I therefore wish my intention kept a secret that none of those people may interfere with my progress from this camp. I will advance with only two men and a companion [Kane]—with the hope of reaching S.L. City. In the course of ten days the result will be known—either there will be peace by unconditional submission—yielding to me all the seals, keys and papers of my office and the Secretary—or the duty you will perform will be marked. If I am repulsed from Echo Cañon—of course my mission will end. In the overtures for peace from B.Y. there may be a sincerity, and as the proposition to you [for flour and beef] was not made through me, there may be no intention to recognize my authority—yet seeing only the physical force, he may have thought the ruler of that was the one to be conciliated—and thus passed me by.

I wish 8 mules and a light ambulance wagon—and a quantity of extra provisions in case I should be long delayed."[32]

Col. J—"Under the circumstances I will give you any assistance you wish and will be obliged to you to address me a note expressing your wants. [Quartermaster] Capt. Dickerson and Capt. Clarke [of the Commissary of Subsistence] will be directed to fill them. . . ."

April 6th

I hear today that Gov. C. went to Salt Lake, contrary to the advice of Col. Kane, and that he has given the impression that great risk is run by going. That no reason, no inducement other than existed last fall, has caused this trip. Too late Governor to give the impression you are heroic. You run no more risk in going—if as you said you were invited—than I do staying here—unless injured by outsiders. To give this impression Mr Kane you strive to hide your game—but no use—it is seen through. The Mormons are ordered to differ in opinion from the leaders—to create a sympathy for the latter. They say they are willing for all to enter except the army and wish to keep them out.—Of course if we go in—the people will be made to understand it is by permission. But I believe an effort will be made to keep the expedition from proceeding. . . .

Kane prepared for the trek by writing three letters to his father and brother to be entrusted to the Fort Laramie courier. The first of two for Judge Kane transmitted Thomas's report to President Buchanan while providing his father

[32]Army ambulances had an enclosed wooden body that permitted travelers like senior officers to use them rather than tents for sleeping quarters.

with a feel for the camp's shocked reaction to the governor's imminent journey as well as an intimate description of Cumming. Kane's hastily scrawled second note may not have been sent to the judge for his benefit as much as to illustrate the sort of communication that he intended to send to several Protestant journals to explain the Mormons' intended course of action. Thomas's third note was for Pat Kane; it was still different in tone and content, filled with brotherly love as well as a playful display of ego as he reveled in the belief that the worst part of his mission was over and that success was nearly within his grasp. All three letters provide insight into how Kane shaded communications for his readership: the president, his family, or the public.

Kane to Judge Kane, 4 April 1858, Kane Family Papers, BYU.

I enclose you a letter of mine to read before forwarding it to Mr. Buchanan. In an hour after placing it in the courier's hands, myself and the Governor will probably be off on our good errand. They have all been at him here—from Colonel Commdg., to volunteer aide-de-camp, conjuring him to believe that he is rushing on certain death—without the most distant hope of ever returning. &c. &c. Although we have kept the utmost secrecy as to our purposes (to prevent his being picked off by the peace-haters of the camp who might think this their shortest cut to interrupt negotiations in progress—and for other good reasons) quite a delegation of "anxious friends" have called to dissuade him from his purpose without an invitation—without authority even from Brigham Young! "madness, simple madness, &c., &c." To which the brave fellow offers but one reply: "I can see no result by which my own honor and the honor of my country will not be the gainer." To Colonel Johnston arraying a line of appalling chances [risks], he said: "In none of those cases will I have done more than is required of my honor by my country and the honor of my country by the world."

You observe from my letters how I am learning to like Cumming, in spite of his bitter prejudices against the Mormons. How can I help myself when I contrast his natural and manly character with that of the bragging, drilling, parading bugle-playing, musket-firing crowd of bravos by profession by whom he is surrounded! I assure you I do not believe there is another man in the 2400 here who cd. be persuaded to follow his example. What will come of it of course we neither of us can foretell—except that the worse the Mormons behave the more clearly he will put them in the wrong before the world.

My hero pish and pshaws the ideal—drinks whiskey, smokes pipe, and is fond of talking "Human Nature," "It comes to the same thing" and "what good will all that do us after we are dead and buried," but I do not believe a more enraptured Poet in action ever rose above the Earth, than the same man, when persuaded himself that he heard the trumpet call of patriotism, or catching sight of the particular flag which he will reject all rule of reason to follow. He is shrewd and sagacious, and sees every blunder which has been made, politically, with regard to the Mormons. He will be hard on them, I fear, if he gets the chance; but, my word for it, he will set the thing straight, as I have promised Mr. Buchanan.

He has made his arrangements with Judge Eckels, "in case of his death or imprisonment, to carry out his instructions," and I learn from his lady "set his house in order."[33]

Kane to Judge Kane, 4 April 1858, Kane Family Papers, BYU. I wished very much to write two letters by this opportunity, one to the President setting forth alternative calculations and predictions for the future, and the other to Bishop Potter,[34] or my dear old friend Barclay, respecting what I think will be the ultimate issue of the Mormon War, so called. This is a different strain, and for publication in the [Philadelphia] Episcopal Recorder, or the Observer of New York. I am convinced that, with our army in their present improved position next [to] Bridger, no such general [Mormon] assault as Johnston contemplates (or contemplated Mar. 1) will be attempted. I am sure there will be no pitched battle or engagement of importance of any kind accepted. My notion is that the Mormons will employ their force entirely in impeding the march of our soldiers and delaying their advance, till the last of the women & children are removed from Salt Lake City and whatever their Moscow fire has spared is thoroughly destroyed by other methods. [General] Kimball confessed to me that a number of families *had* already removed from Salt Lake "into the mountains" S. West, and he was the bearer to me of a letter from Young, which he wd. not allow me to retain in my possession, but of part of which I took a copy in my Mem. Book, pointing clearly enough the same way. I should premise that it was written in the anticipation that Kimball wd. receive bad news from me—the escort [led by Lewis Robison] which accompanied me to within 40 mils of Bridger having returned [to Salt Lake] without favorable intelligence, or the Mails which he, Young, expected. Still I can connect its statements with two or three facts in my possession, in a significant manner. Young says: [excerpt from Young to Kane of 22 March 1858, pp. 352–53]

I imagine some of the Mormons think they have to reproach me with tying their hands, &c.—but I am sure *Young* does not. I think he has been opposed to the effusion of blood from the beginning, and has only been glad to stave it off as long as possible. But suppose the answer to be made *in fact,* which I suggested Mr. Kimball that our *next move* would be, to issue warrants for treason and go on employing the military force in making arrests of offenders as long as a criminal was supposed to lie hid among the mountains. Suppose that,

[33]Cumming appointed Washington Jay McCormick, a young Indiana protégé of Eckels, to be acting territorial secretary to provide for gubernatorial succession in his absence.

[34]Alonzo Potter, D.D., was bishop of the Episcopal Diocese of Pennsylvania.

in this wise, or in consequence, as is more probable—of an early collision between the forces—War is once begun—I cannot tell you, dear Father, what an amount of suffering I think would necessarily be inflicted. Not upon the leading heresiarchs—certainly not among the dishonest and insincere of them whom the devotion of their adherents wd. shield as hornets are said to do their queens.—Who could instigate resistance as long as it was perfectly safe to do so, and then retire disguised at their pleasure toward any one of the points of the compass, to disappear among the dwellings of white men—or take shipping for England, the Sandwich [Hawaiian] Is. or Heaven only knows where.

Nor wd. there b[e] great suffering among "the boys" "the hunters" and "mountaineers"—the harum scarum *warriors* already in the field—whose every day lives are such that the most serious aspect in which war presents itself to their minds is that of a licensed and consecrated most magnificent *tall spree.* These love to play Indian, love to act Indian, and Indians or savages they would be, after the first season's campaign, in fact as well as name. It wd. be slow work exterminating them—one by one, them and their Indian robber allies. In the end however, with an army to each provision train and supplies furnished at a cost that wd. build the Pacific Railroad about once a year—with a nick of the woods in uniform to track up a swamp covert of them here, and a Pelissies[35] perchance by good luck to smoke out a cave full of them there—I think it can be done, and in shorter order than the Mormons prating of their *Seminole War* will believe.

But meantime

(1) What will become of the women and children? What is to be done to the dirk belted females who seemed to me uniformly the crazyest of all the crazy? What about the timid and moderate whom it is cunningly proposed to "unite in sentiment" by burning and destroying the substantial interests which incline them in favor of peace? What is to be done with those who aid and abet their husbands in rebellion in every conceivable degree, and who shall decide when they are to be treated with leniency and when with severity?[36]

---

[35]Probably a reference to Jean Jacques Pelissier, who in May 1855 became commanding general of the French army in the Crimea and a major figure in breaking the siege of Sebastopol.

[36]Kane notes: "I can give you one posed me by a woman herself: 'I'll tell you in confidence Colonel,' she said, 'where it is the women of our stake are going. Our Cache is near what we call the Valley (south of the Virgin). We've enough for one while, may be, never mind that. But we calculate to put in and raise enough for our men folks, ourselves. And when any of them that's out on the hills (soldiers) can't pick up enough hurting and helping themselves—they'll be welcome to what they want, I tell you. Now I want to know: Supposing some of your soldiers came acrost us, wd. their business be to rob us and leave us to starve the next winter. We'd tell 'em straight out, as long as we had a pint of barley it wd. be sheared with the first Saints come along.' 'Madam,' replied I, 'a good officer wd. Make you prisoners and keep you in custody, in quarters, with plenty to eat at our expense till the winter was over and your husband came in.' 'Wd. they make out to surprise us, if they carried provision enough along with them for that.' 'No,' she exclaimed with a lower throat screech of exultation (passing Irish Jenny's) 'I was in hopes, when they broke down our fences and tramped in our crops—they they [*sic*] didn't slay of us—wd. starve—we wd. all starve.' (This I took down from memory several days ago.)"

You can see what numbers of doubtful cases, and cases not doubtful, will arise, by reading over some book that will give you a true notion of toutes les gloires de la [all the glories of] France in [colonial] Algeria.

2. What will be the fate of the real abomination which we ought to wish should perish—the Religion itself—the Mormonism? This was to be the especial theme of my letters to the Bishop. I can prove with sorrowful cogency what an impulse will be given to it everywhere—what a clover of female approbation the Mormon lecturer will delight in who appears before his British audience "in deep black for his murdered wife and family," or "in the costume which he bore upon the occasion of his memorable escape from the American soldiery at [blank]," or if the veriest sneak that ever counted pins, introduced to a provincial public as "Elder Thomas Peter, so called, suspected of being really the last survivor of the massacred Council of Twelve." "The way the red scripture tickets and sixpences for spiritual tea & muffins is coming in," wd. be frightful.

The Mormon strength—for warlike purposes—overrated by the newspaper people, is greatly underrated by our military authorities. It would take so little to correct public opinion on a matter in which I perceive we are befooled by interested persons whose spanners are out to effect attachments with the Treasury. But it is too late. I have no time. And I feel that I have done wrong in spinning out so long this note which I began, as you may notice, on the half sheet only of *demy* paper. The remainder at least of this poor broken Sunday I must give to rest. For tomorrow at 9 we set out, and it is my calculation, if we meet with no respectable resistance, to hurry the Governor through with all speed. Albeit while he drives in his ambulance (as far as the snow permits at least)—I must not at any moment be out of my saddle. How my heart longs to be erdting [?] the good matters of home affairs! But I may not even spare yr. eyes by copying this off. Instead of finding fault however, you shd. rather praise me for the pains I took with my letter for Mr. B[uchanan], seeing that my hands are as stiff and sore as if all the gout of our ancestry had settled in them. The next mail I hope will convey me a letter to Mother. I wish I were good enough to pray Heaven to bless her. Perhaps I do not fall far short of it, tell her.—A Dieu [Farewell.]

Kane to Pat Kane, 4 April 1858, Kane Family Papers, byu.

What a time I have had you may conjecture from your not hearing from me anything about it. I am within reach of trusty mails now, and *it is all over,* and growing in my mind to pass for an interesting story, but I must rest, and must give it my overtasked brain its holiday too—and I see no help for you against meeting in me one of the most insufferable of bores—with everything on hand to tell you—unable to tell anything well. Too hard a scuffle, Patty, for a man to have an eye to first and second positions, and the pattern of the paper hanging on the wall. But you and [brother] Johnny must both humour me, and remember that I shall miss Elisha to report to, who, I do not know why I always used to listen to me so patiently. . . .

My dear Patty, I have probably been well rewarded for my moderation in the matter of Col. Johnston's humiliation [over the abortive duel]. It has strengthened my hands to do good, and I had besides all the satisfaction which a gentleman ought to exact. Col. Johnston's relations with me continue agreeable, though the Camp still yelps like a pack of vicious cayotas. The lower "hangers-on" even "threaten my life," &c., like natural Anti-Mormons. But I am become used to this sort of tomfoolery and know better how to keep it under [control] than I did.

Tomorrow I leave the self-tormenting crew—to guide the Governor to Salt Lake City, and there if I meet with no contretemps shall set out myself to enjoy life a little more. Make Bessie feel that henceforth I shall not be incurring danger. As I have said to you, *it is over now.* The danger is over: omne aliter visum [everything decreed otherwise]: "Raging Canawl"! I have done my work good or bad; I can leave the issue in the hands of a less finite power. . . .

This letter which has avoided so successfully the details of facts wd. be inconsistent, if I closed it with saying how constantly I think of you—how much I love you. Take care of your health, *Head of the Family;* let us have and keep a living brother to be proud of. I need not ask you to nurse your affection for Old Tommidge.[37]

He Would Obey Me in Every Respect: With Cumming in Tow

And off they went with quartermaster Capt. John H. Dickerson describing Kane as "a self constituted Ambassador & Umpire between the two High Powers,"[38] leaving behind Elizabeth Wells Randall Cumming of Boston, the governor's plucky, well-educated forty-seven-year-old wife. Because of her multiple roles as Alfred's secretary and confidante, Elizabeth Cumming, a great-granddaughter of the Revolution's famous patriot Samuel Adams, was in an ideal position to chronicle her husband's departure and plans. She did so in a letter to her sister-in-law, Anne Elizabeth Cumming Smith of Georgia.

---

[37]Kane alludes to his and Pat's loss of two older brothers and his own mortality.

[38]Dickerson to W. A. Gordon, 16 April 1858. Letters to W. A. Gordon, BANC MSS 68/49p, Bancroft Library. The Tenth Infantry's Lieutenant Colonel Smith called Kane "a self constituted minister plenipotentiary and ambassador extraordinary to heal the differences between the US and the Mormons." Smith to Fanny M. Smith, 14 April 1858, in Mesch, *Your Affectionate Father,* 153.

Elizabeth Cumming to Anne Smith, 5 April 1858, Canning and Beeton, eds., *The Genteel Gentile*, 33–36, and Cumming Papers, Duke University.

A party leaves here for the States directly. I have time very limited—Have just written home, & have a few minutes only left so will rush into the midst of matters.

I have just bid (to-day) good bye to Alfred. He has gone to Salt Lake City, where so many have sworn he never shall enter alive. Col. Kane, our guest, is his only companion, & two of our men servants go as driver and cook.

Alfred will go to the city, (unless prevented on the way there) reissue his proclamation of Novr,[39] take possession of the seals of office, & order the [Mormon] troops to disband. If any or all of these things are refused, he will have recourse to the aid of the military—but he will give them the chance of peacefully submitting to the U. States authority—other matters will be attended to, which I am not at liberty to mention at present.[40] I believe him right to do this, & I consent with my whole heart.

He has promised me, if he should be imprisoned there, to send for me immediately. He does not *anticipate* imprisonment—but it is a *possibility,* & must be prepared for. In view of this *possibility,* he has today appointed a new Scy of State—(Mr. Hartnett being absent). *He* is to remain *here*—so that if the Mormons think to confuse & baffle the new government by imprisoning or injuring in any way the new governor, they will find themselves mistaken & as he has communicated his views & intentions about Mormon matters to the new Secy so that whatever may happen, Alfred's views will be carried out in a great measure.[41]

I say *Alfred's* views, for Mr. Buchanan has given him *carte blanche* as to nearly all Utah matters.

Col Kane, in former years was a good deal with the Mormons, formed some friendships with them—& those friendships still exist. *He* is exposed to no danger in Salt Lake—for although Brigham & the elders have proclaimed that no Gentiles shall enter into Salt Lake City & live, yet *he* was received a few weeks ago as a *friend* among them. He is not a Mormon, but he is a

[39]A reference to Cumming's proclamation of 21 November 1857 in which he announced to Utah's people that he had assumed the governorship and expected obedience to federal law. The document prompted ridicule in the territory.

[40]What Mrs. Cumming meant by "other matters" is intriguing: probing the Mountain Meadows massacre, Brigham Young's gubernatorial stewardship, the behavior of federal appointees?

[41]The territorial secretary was next in line of authority. With John Hartnett's abrupt departure for the comforts of St. Louis earlier in the winter and his own departure for Salt Lake, Cumming designated Washington Jay McCormick, a young lawyer-protégé of Judge Eckels from Indiana, as acting secretary. Meanwhile, Mormon merchant William H. Hooper continued to function in Salt Lake City as acting territorial secretary, a role unsanctioned by the U.S. government but one to which Young had appointed him after the murder of Sec. Almon W. Babbitt in 1856.

friend of several, who are deeply indebted to him for former kindness, & are friendly to him. He is acquainted with *many* of them, & his knowledge of their *character* will be useful to Alfred, if he succeed to entering the city.

A man has called for the letters—& I have two gentlemen, visitors, in my tent, waiting for me to write this—I fear it is disjointed.

We are now at Fort Bridger—the army is, I mean—our tents are about quarter of a mile from camp. Col. Johnston politely offered a company for my protection—but it was declined. I have a sentinal, day & night at my tent, & two of our men servants sleep in a tent near me—so I am quite safe here—but guns & pistols are as much a part of our tent furniture as tables or seats.[42]

Elizabeth Cumming was unaware that her husband had left for Salt Lake with a companion who believed that the governor had agreed to subordinate himself in all that was to follow. Kane described this remarkable understanding: "[At first,] I would not take him with me to Salt Lake, but [I did] after I had his promise that I should sleep with him, and that he was not to miss me one moment—from his sight—that I should order him in every respect as I thought fit, and that until I brought him back to camp, he would obey me in every respect in all things implicitly. He did so as became a gallant gentleman who had given his word to that effect. But I was with him at every moment."[43] It was an admission providing one of the clearest examples of Kane's intense need to manipulate and dominate.

Even after he returned home to Philadelphia, Kane would continue to control the image of this two-man odyssey by maintaining the fiction that Cumming rather than he was the driving force behind it. Hearing this at the Kane home in mid-July, as well as Thomas's assertion that "when the true history of the Peace came to be written, B. Young would receive due credit as the peace maker," his bodyguard-escort, Howard Egan, blurted out: "I have as strong faith in Bro. Brigham as anyone, but I can't allow Mrs. K[ane] and Mr. S[tenhouse], who don't know the truth as I do, to believe that Gov. Cumming would ever have felt to enter the city without Johnston to back him, or been allowed to enter if he did without another man [Kane]." Unsettled at challenging his host's version of the trek to Salt Lake City at his own dinner table, the major added, "I had to tell the truth."[44]

---

[42]Mrs. Cumming's observation mirrors the warning to Kane by an unidentified resident of the camp: "It doesn't do to speak too plain on personal matters—here where every man wears a revolver." Kane, "Diary II (1858)," undated entry, 19.

[43]Kane to Pat Kane, ca. summer 1858, "In Re Mormons" File, Thomas Leiper Kane Papers, APS.

[44]Elizabeth W. Kane Journal, 16 July 1858, Kane Family Papers, BYU.

Ashamed to Feel So Near Happiness!: Road Trip

For Kane, his leave-taking and the easy traveling immediately after passing through the Utah Expedition's lines were a lark: "One goodby to the perfect wife and then nothing to do but shake the execrated dust off the feet of the vile camp. Sat stiff for bitter pride in Governors carriage [as we passed sentries] till abreast of Table Bluff then stepped into saddle.—Hope. Adventure. Mountain Air. A good Horse & Liberty! Felt like old [*blank*] the[*blank*]. Riding ahead to take shots. What fun! Ashamed to feel so near happiness! But things were changed in a brief 9 days. . . . Got kicked by a mule. Snow deep."[45]

The bare outline of what Cumming, Kane, and their two servants experienced between their departure from Eckelsville on 5 April 1858 and arrival in Salt Lake City on 12 April is known from one of Cumming's official reports to Secretary Cass and anecdotal accounts from their Nauvoo Legion escort. It is a brief story of a long journey filled with snow banks, unbridged stream crossings, and the complexity of Cumming's dependence on some combination of a buggy and an army ambulance, both of which were wholly unsuited for the terrain and weather. What has survived in Mormon folklore are vignettes of the Legion's respectful treatment of Cumming, as well as a proud retelling of the ruse by which the travelers' nocturnal, torch-lit passage through Echo Canyon was stage-managed to hood-wink them into grossly over-estimating both the Legion's strength and the effectiveness of the canyon's defenses. Interest and awareness of the events of this week-long trek has atrophied amidst a preoccupation with the major events that unfolded after Cumming and Kane reached Salt Lake City. Lost in the process is the unusual nature of the trip and the use to which Kane later put it to burnish Cumming's image.

The governor wrote virtually nothing of a personal nature about the journey, and what he told friends about the trek is largely lost.[46] A new picture of the Cumming-Kane trek emerges from several unpublished or underappreciated documents: General Kimball's account of the extent to which their party was threatened by Indians; passages from Kane's trail journal;

---

[45]Kane, "Diary II (1858)," [presumably 5 April], 9.

[46]One of the few exceptions is a story that he related to a boyhood friend after the Civil War. Cumming's 1857 travel from Fort Leavenworth to Fort Bridger is conflated with his 1858 journey to Salt Lake, and Kane is wholly absent from the story. Hyperbole, exaggeration, and fabrication about the Utah War were not the sole province of Nauvoo Legion veterans and a fanciful Kane. Perry, "Alfred Cumming," *Reminiscences of Public Men*, 292.

interviews with Abel Gilbert, the eastbound non-Mormon merchant who encountered Cumming and Kane on the trail; multiple newspaper accounts of the journey ghostwritten by Kane during the summer of 1858; and Kane's 1859 lecture to the New-York Historical Society, which was designed to cast their trip as an heroic ordeal while virtually canonizing his portly traveling companion.

An account of the potential Indian threat faced by Cumming and Kane before falling in with a Legion detachment on the trail appears in a report written at an unknown date for Governor Cumming by an unidentified Mormon brigadier general, presumably Kimball.[47] Mixed with this material are accounts of Indian surveillance of Kane's two earlier sallies out of Fort Bridger, to meet Robison on 17 March and Kimball on 25 March together with the brigadier's veiled allusions to Kane's non-Indian enemies.

Extracts from Report of Brig. General [*blank*]
(Copied with great pleasure for His Excellency
Governor A. Cumming), Thomas Leiper Kane Papers, aps.

At the time Genl Kimball fell in with Col Kane and Gov. Cumming near Bear River, I was on the look out for them it being the time which was named for them to be round there. . . . When Gen Kimball was upon Bear River I sent scouts to the camp of Ben Simon[d]s about 7 miles North of the road to pick up information from him and his associates. . . . The scouts learned from Ben and various other Indians there that Col. Kane had passed out West of the pickets of the Camp of the Army and had been watched by the Indians while out. What they mentioned of his conduct on two occasions of his coming out showed how closely they had watched his movements. They reported the track which he had followed &c, and mentioned the cedars he had taken shelter from the snow in &c &c—and stated that he had met such a number of white men (Mormons) had given them whiskey to drink and chewing tobacco. The whiskey they said on one occasion, naming it, was drank [*sic*] out of a bottle. They said that Kane was watched thus from the time he left the plain by the Fort till he met the men he came out to meet—and then was followed in like manner all the way back again.

They said they knew they were Mormons, the men he met, and they were different men he met each time. But said one of a knot who were talking on the subject: "you'll never see him again." Why? Judson Stoddart asked. The speaker stopped—and further questioned shrugged his shoulders. After a pause he went on to state the reasons [omitted]. These reasons made me and

[47]No other copy of this document has surfaced where it most logically should be, such as the Nauvoo Legion records in Utah State Archives and LDS Archives or in Cumming Papers, Duke University.

> my men believe that Col. Kane would not succeed in getting out to us. Besides however we saw no tracks upon the road, but 50 or 60 yards from it—saw any number of pony tracks, winding in and out among the sagebrush &c.
>
> For this cause I kept the full command with me till I came in with Col. Kane. I was out all day light hours with the boys scouting up to as far as outside Quaking Asp—and by Monday [5 April] began to adopt the painful conclusion that Col. Kane had attempted to come out on Sunday or Saturday and had been made away with—between Quaking Asp and the Camp. The relief of mind which I experienced on learning that Col. Kane and Governor Cumming had been found was [*illegible*].

Once in company with their Mormon escort, Cumming and Kane encountered merchant Abel Gilbert on 7 April in Echo Canyon. Gilbert was in mid-passage between California and Missouri via Utah's southern settlements, Provo, and Salt Lake City. During these travels Gilbert spent several days with Brigham Young, with whom he had a respectful but ambivalent relationship. As a result, he provided Cumming's party (and eventually the nation) fresh information about the grisly scene at Mountain Meadows, the Move South, and those of Brigham Young's plans that the prophet was willing to discuss for non-Mormon consumption. In turn, when he reached Fort Bridger and the Kansas-Missouri frontier, Gilbert provided news of Cumming and Kane. On 9 April Major Porter recorded his arrival at the Utah Expedition's headquarters and again questioned the motives of the governor and his companion:

> Mr. Gilbert came in today—Says the people are running from S.L. Valley—Many want the troops to come in for protection—No crops are planted this year—Met Gov. C. and Kane—escorted by Mormons. Gov. called them "my soldiers" and remarked they were good riders—One however said "they would soon teach him a different story."—Saw Judge Eckels today who confirmed the reports the Gov. and Kane had circulated about not being invited in the risk he ran &c all of which is false—Col. Kane is a Mormon and is working for the Mormons—and if he can he will work trouble.[48]

A newspaper correspondent at Fort Bridger also interviewed Gilbert and wrote a dispatch that the merchant carried east:

> Mr. Gilbert was much surprised to find on his arrival in the city that they were making preparations there for the expected arrival of Governor Cumming. *A room had been prepared expressly, and was in readiness for him. . . .* Mr. Gilbert

[48]Porter Diary, 9 April 1858, Porter Collection, LC.

> left the City on the 6th inst. and met Governor Cumming on the evening of the 7th inst., in Echo Canyon, about forty-five miles from the city; he was escorted by a guard of some thirty picked men who had been sent by Brigham to meet him, and who were paying him every attention in their power. He expected to reach the City this evening, and will no doubt meet with a flattering reception. Much may be accomplished by this visit.[49]

Of Clean Sheets and a Fishlike Governor: Ecstatic Arrival

Cumming and Kane reached Salt Lake City on 12 April 1858. How they had spent the five days since encountering Gilbert in Echo Canyon is a mystery, although the Mormon intelligence network reported that the two men delayed their arrival by episodic halts for gubernatorial hunting.[50] The confusing entries in Kane's diary indicate that he was prostrate in their ambulance during part of the journey. These fragments also spoke of awe-inspiring vistas and surrealistic rock formations as well as a stopover at the Indian camp at the mouth of Weber Canyon. Here Cumming and Kane entered an eclectic, hardscrabble bivouac of small bands from multiple tribes and individual traders of mixed blood, including part-Delaware Ben Simonds and the ubiquitous Cherokee Jim, whom Albert Sidney Johnston had ejected from Camp Scott.

If Kane was ill during the latter stages of this journey, his spirits soared upon glimpsing Salt Lake City again and descending the canyons leading into town. As had been the case when returning to camp from his forays to meet Mormon emissaries at Muddy Creek and Quaking Aspen Hill, Kane was euphoric, reveling in even the ordinary signs of civilization and the advent of spring. The Legion escorted the travelers through the city's refugee-clogged streets to pre-arranged quarters in the Staines mansion, a refuge well-known to Kane. Here, he and Cumming luxuriated much as

---

[49][Burr], "Highly Important from Utah. News Direct from Salt Lake City. Kane and His Negotiations," Dispatch, 9 April 1858, *New-York Times,* 24 May 1858, 1/1–4.

[50]Smith, Historian's Office Journal, 8 and 10 April 1858. What Cumming's Legion escort permitted him and Kane to see in Echo Canyon by flickering torches and bonfires versus what Gilbert observed in daylight is intriguing. The merchant bore a travel pass from Brigham Young and, perhaps with an eye to his future commercial relations with the Mormons, he said very little to interviewers about this segment of his travels. Kane recorded privately, "here I saw and had explained to me what I cannot in honor ever trust notes of on paper. The defences of the Mormon Nation!" Kane, "Diary II (1858)," undated entry, 5.

Captain Marcy had done three months earlier in Taos upon emerging from his near-death experience in the mountains of northern New Mexico: "The first flower found in the valley was the fragrant Heart's Ease. Reached Salt Lake City Apr. 12. Stoddarts in the valley Apr. 13. Peach blossoms and green grass—and fire side Arm chair and carpeted floor—Great tub of spring water clean sheeted bed grass butter and asparagus music of children's voices chronometer."[51] What also awaited the travelers at the Staines mansion was proximity to women, a novelty after roughing it at close quarters with an overwhelmingly male army expedition.

Apostle Woodruff was in the city on 12 April and noted the arrival of the travelers with disdain: "A. Cummings [*sic*] that would be governor of Utah arrived in this City to day with Col Kane accompanied by a small mormon Guard. When he saw the streets lined with people moving he said dont move you shall not be hurt. I will not be Govornor [*sic*] if you don't want me. The poor Devil should have thought of this principle before he started from home and not Come with an armed force to force himself as govornor upon a people who did not want him."[52]

At that time, Brigham Young was also in town to meet late into the night with his closest colleagues. In one such session, General Wells and Apostle Smith "said they disliked to have A. Cumming become by any means Governor of the Territory, in virtue of the laws of the U.S. which he would do if he came here and was sworn into office.[53] Prest. Young remarked he did not care anything about it, the Lord would overrule it for good, which soever way it happened. He did not wish to see Cummings [*sic*] unless he particularly desired an interview. If he (Cummings) was anxious to have a meeting with the people, to ascertain if they wanted him for governor, he thought it might be good to have the Tabernacle filled with women for the occasion."[54]

Church Historian George A. Smith recorded what unfolded the day after the Cumming-Kane arrival. In the process he captured a revelatory private comment made by Kane to Young about Cumming that ranks as the most cynical observation of the Utah War:

---

[51]Kane, ibid.

[52]Kenney, ed., *Wilford Woodruff's Journal*, 12 April 1858, 5:181.

[53]Bypassed in the discussion was the important fact that Cumming had taken the oath of office at Fort Bridger on 21 November 1857 and since then had been Utah's governor.

[54]Historian's Office Journal, 9 April 1858, LDS Archives.

Smith, Church Historian's Office Journal,
13 April 1858, LDS Archives.

Ben Simonds, Jim Cherokee alias [*blank*] visited. Gov. Young expressed themselves very friendly, said a white man from Johnson's camp had told his Indians that Johnson would give $150 ea. for Mormons and $1000 for Lot Smith, Cherokee Jim heard it instead of the [U.S.] Agents giving the Indians the presents promised, they gave some powder & lead & 50 lbs of Tobacco to 500 Indians but promised them big presents in a little while.

Col. Kane visited Gov. Young told him that he had caught the fish—now you can cook it as he had a mind to.[55] Gov. Cumming asked Gov Young to call on him.

Gov Young invited G.A.S. to accompany him on his visit to Cumming they walked down to Staines at 4 P.M. Col Kane introduced Gov. Young & G.A.S. to A. Cumming. G.A.S.'s first impression when he saw Cumming was that he was a toper, but on examining him with his glasses he concluded he was a moderate drinker and a hearty eater, he was well dressed in black, ruddy face & grey hairs, his head was small round the top, would think holds more chops than brains, probably weight about 240 lbs.[56] Conversation turned upon the weather, the beauty of the valley, the fruit, the improvements, some of which he had tasted, as Col. Kane had carried 4 apples off Gov Young's into the enemys camp which he gave to Mrs. A. Cumming. She divided them among the ladies, and it became quite a joke in the camp that the Gov was feeding on Mormon fruit. Elder H. C. Kimball arrived. Gov. Cumming expressed his satisfaction at the arrangements of his reception made by Gen. W.H. Kimball also at the arrangements of the illumination in the [Echo] Kanyon, which outstripped any thing he ever expected to see. Col. Kane said he never expected to see such a sight again. The effect he said could not be described.[57]

---

[55]This was not Kane's first use of a fish analogy in a Mormon context. Twelve years earlier, while writing a letter to his sister from a bivouac of the just-recruited Mormon Battalion, he gently lampooned the new soldiers milling around him admiringly as "being fresh caught salmons, green from their own camps." Kane to Elizabeth (Bessie) Kane, 23 [20] July 1846, Kane Family Papers, box 1, Clements Library, University of Michigan.

[56]A substantial underestimation.

[57]Three years later, probably after Cumming had left Utah, journalist T. B. H. Stenhouse spoke with him about this incident in which the Legionnaires in Echo Canyon had created the illusion of a large Mormon force for Cumming's benefit by covertly repositioning a small detachment under cover of darkness. In 1873 Stenhouse published this commentary: "In the course of time he discovered how the Mormon leaders had imposed upon him and amused themselves with his credulity, and he was ever afterwards unpleasantly reticent when the affair was mentioned. Although subsequently on good terms with Brigham, he could not forget the incident of his passage through the canon by night, and to the last hour that he was in the Territory he felt annoyed at having been so absurdly deceived, and held Brigham responsible for the mortifying joke." Stenhouse, *Rocky Mountain Saints*, 390.

Cumming said he would be glad if a sketch of his reception at Quaking asp creek could be taken, the illumination could not be; on finding himself in echo Kanyon the Gov said he did not know what to think, he was surrounded by armed soldiers who on his arrival presented arms in honor of his arrival, he said he did not know what to do; but he delivered a speech & he did not know but he had committed himself. Col. Kane assured him his speech was a happy effort, for an extemporaneous address.

At yellow creek gov. Cumming said he expected to get a miserable meal but Gen Kimball had made the most complete arrangements, the Gov said he was there introduced to the Mormon officers & Gen Kimballs mess, the arrangements of which was overseen by David Candland, whom the Gov. said was a superb cook.[58]

Gov Young invited A. Cumming to take a ride through the City & view the improvements. Cumming would be happy to do so in a few days when he got rested. The Gov remarked to Cumming that if he had come in last fall he would have been made more comfortable. Cumming remarked he had a crow to pick with Gov. Young in relation to that by and bye. Gov Young replied as he was a sort of a preacher he would give him a text to consider on & said "The people who know me best love me best."

Col. Kane said thats not only a text but a sermon. Col. Kane appeared quite healthy.

Elder Kimball & G.A.S. took supper with Prest. Young, then went to his office, where they were joined in conversation with D. H. Wells & A. Carrington until 9 P.M.

The interactions of Cumming, Young, George A. Smith, Heber C. Kimball, and Kane at this session found their way into Smith's office journal in fragmentary fashion over the next few days, providing a feel for these leaders at the beginning of their relationship unmatched by any other document of the period.

HISTORIAN'S OFFICE JOURNAL, 14–15 APRIL 1858, LDS ARCHIVES.

14 April

The President invited G.A.S. to take supper & while the supper was taking the Prest staid & talked with G.A.S. altho' the office was full of folks waiting for him; he said he had had an interview with Cumming, Cumming had asked him for his office, twice Col. Kane informed Cumming that Gov Youngs office was a part of his private residence.

The Gov. said he was fully satisfied from the talk he had with Cumming

[58]Brigham Young often asked Candland, proprietor of Salt Lake City's Globe Restaurant, to provide for the comfort of prominent non-Mormon visitors.

that he (C) desired the destruction of the Saints; he said Gov. Cumming came pretty near commanding him (Gov Y) to forbid the people leaving their homes; as there would be nobody left here but the renegades who followed the army for Juries.

Gov Young said to them you both are lawyers. Cumming disdained the idea but let me ask you a question. What right has an officer to issue instructions in violation of law. What particular thing do you allude to asked Cummings. Stopping the mail for instance said Gov. Young, even if the contractors had forfeited the Postmaster was required by law to let it out to carriers, but the postmaster at Independence was instructed by the Department [in Washington] not to let the mail go in the hands of a Mormon; and it has been stopped ever since; they were silent.

Gov. Young said, for this seven years the people have been at peace with the Indians, they came to our houses eat and drank with us; but Indians come now and draw their bows on our wives & take blankets from off our beds, they say the Mormons are squaws they won't fight, but the soldiers will fight and kill all the Mormons; the Indians say that Dr. Hurt is laying in Uinta valley with a body of Indians who are stealing horses and cattle coming in to plunder the settlements and they send messengers to the Indians in the settlement to incite them.

The Indians who are stealing horses and cattle are taking them to the Mericats [American] camp. The Massacre at Salmon river was led by a white man.

The Indians say they have been offered $150.00 a piece for a Mormons. A. Cumming replied it aint possible.

Gov Young answered: It will not be easy to make the people believe anything else.

Cumming agreed to let Gov. Young see his private instructions to morrow at 11 A.M.

Elder [Orson] Hyde reported that the Indians had stolen 100 mustang horses from bro. Nail, 5 miles west of Lehi. . . .

Gov Y. said he would postpone going to Provo in the morning, at A. Cummings request.

Gov Young remarked he would rather burn everything he had than submit to them 5 minutes.

15 April 1858

Gen. W. H. Kimball told G.A.S. he had learned from Kane, the remarks made by Gov. Cumming concerning the interview of the 13th. A. Cumming (who professes to be an adept in Physiology) said that Gov. Young was a man of lamb like disposition and possessed a superior brain—a mind capable of grasping everything. Prest. Kimball was a fierce, brave, unflinching, unchangeable man, and more to be dreaded than any of the others, fine determined temperament, and a very fine man; and if any of them needed hanging it would be him; Geo A. Smith possessed an unaccountable memory, would make an excellent historian and a No. 1 politician if he had a chance. They were three exceedingly fine intellectual men, and he had been deceived in what he had heard of them; he liked them.

Kane said to Cumming, You have seen three leading men, the Prest. of the church and Governor of the Territory by the will of the people, his Counsellor one of the oldest members of the church, and a Representative of the Smith family, a kinsman of the founder of the church; and you like them all. . . .

Two days after this first meeting with Brigham Young, Cumming couriered a message to Fort Bridger in which he notified Colonel Johnston:

I have been everywhere recognized as the governor of Utah, and so far from having encountered insults or indignities, I am gratified in being able to state to you that, in passing through the settlements, I have been universally greeted with such respectful attentions as are due to the representatives of the executive authority of the United States in the Territory. . . . Ex-Governor Brigham Young paid me a call of ceremony as soon as I was sufficiently relieved from the fatigue of my mountain journey to receive company. In subsequent interviews with the ex-governor he has evinced a willingness to afford me every facility which I may require for the efficient performance of my administrative duties. His course in this respect meets, I fancy, with the approval of a majority of this community.[59]

Meanwhile, elsewhere in the Staines mansion, the travelers' host and his chambermaids went about their normal duties. An intriguing unknown is the extent to which by then Staines had taken on an intelligence-gathering task for Brigham Young that unfolded during subsequent weeks: reporting about Cumming's visitors and movements, his amorous indiscretions, and the contents of the confidential correspondence lying unguarded in the governor's room.

[59]Cumming to Johnston, 15 April 1858, "Annual Report of the Sec. of War (1858)," 72–73. Kane, who often confused dates, mistakenly recorded in his diary that the first meeting between Cumming and Young occurred on 16 April.

Chapter 13

"To Try and Settle the Matter"

The Players Maneuver

I trust that moderation will prevail in your councils & that you will submit freely & willingly to the authority of the U.S. for that is your duty so long as you remain within the limits of this country. It is your duty to God, as well as to man—I advised this course when I was in Salt Lake City last fall, because it was right & I advise it still.

Capt. Stewart Van Vliet to Brigham Young, 25 April 1858

I showed Col. Kane a copy of the [Buchanan] Proclamation—a document which has fallen like a clap of thunder from a clear sky upon every man on the plains who has been personally familiar with the history of Mormon aggressions.

New York Times reporter James W. Simonton, 23 May 1858

As Alfred Cumming and Thomas L. Kane departed Fort Bridger, major developments unfolded on multiple fronts simultaneously. Leaders and agents on both sides maneuvered to win tactical advantage, if not the means to prevail, in what had become a stalemate.

Kane and Cumming passed through the Utah Expedition's pickets on 5 April. Later that morning Utah's chief justice empaneled a federal grand jury to probe the Mormon practice of plural marriage. With polygamy, Judge Delana R. Eckels took aim at a target galling him while fascinating the nation and enthralling Mormondom. It was a morass well beyond his judicial purview, one at odds with Buchanan's stated intent to confine the war's objectives to restoration of federal authority. Absent a U.S. or territorial statute banning polygamy, the judge's gratuitous charge to the jury smacked of religious persecution, a provocation that sent shock waves to Salt Lake City and Washington.

On the same day, 113 miles to the west, Apostle George A. Smith and William Gill Mills, one of Brigham Young's clerks, wrote to a Mormon employee of the *New York Herald* in Manhattan, T. B. H. Stenhouse. Racing to catch the departing California mail, Smith and Mills worked to provide Stenhouse with a summary of the Mormon position on the Utah War, justifying the Move South and waving the bloody shirt of army-sponsored tribal scalp hunting. They crafted these letters to advance the arguments with which Stenhouse would begin a campaign to influence Atlantic Coast editors.

Oblivious to these developments, Apostle Amasa Mason Lyman and a small party left Parowan heading southwest toward the rugged terrain bounded by Utah, eastern California, and northwestern New Mexico Territory. Technically Lyman did so under Brigham Young's orders of late February, but he had long intended to visit the region's Mojave bands while assessing the lower reaches of the Colorado River for two mutually exclusive uses: a potential U.S. Army invasion route and a prospective haven or exit path for Mormon refugees.

While these players pursued their missions in different parts of Utah, James Buchanan worked in secret to launch a plan to resolve the war. Without direct word from Kane during the winter, the president yielded to months-long pressure from Sen. Sam Houston, Congress, and Delegate Bernhisel to send official commissioners to the Mormons. Although Buchanan accepted the notion of dispatching government-sponsored emissaries to Brigham Young, he was determined to do so on his own terms. These involved substantial exercise of his political guile, ego, and lawyerly draftsmanship.

In 1857, without Congress's involvement or even awareness, Buchanan had superseded Brigham Young as governor, triggering an armed confrontation in the wilderness that Young escalated to the level of rebellion. In the spring of 1858, with the country still gripped by recession, the president again worked covertly to end this expensive, embarrassing conflict.

Find Facts, Return Indictments: Eckels Pokes the Bee Hive

From Camp Scott's rumor mill, Kane realized as he and Cumming departed for Salt Lake City that Judge Eckels was convening the U.S. district court for Green River County. But Kane misunderstood Eckels's intent, assuming that he was seeking additional treason indictments instead of unleashing a grand jury on polygamy. On the eve of his trek, Kane sought legal advice from his father and complained about Eckels's machinations without fully understanding what they were: "Write me, in case I shd. be kept out here longer, and suggest whatever you can to help us against this Judge. With all his flattery to me, I fear he is a bad man. . . . I do not believe as was intimated to me that [in scheduling treason cases] he desired to embarrass the peace negotiations, to *which he is opposed*; but he has been fully notified of the prejudicial influence that a trial for treason 'by [jurors of] the Camp' wd. not fail to exert at this critical season. A regard for the Governor's safety at least, ought now to teach him prudence."[1] Later, writing in the third person, Kane assessed the judge's action: "the charge [to the jury] of Judge Eckels against polygamy being in direct contradiction to what the President authorized Colonel Kane and the Commissioners to state to the Mormons, may discredit with them, even his admirable proclamation of amnesty and induce their too suspicious minds to believe that Colonel Kane, Governor Cumming and Messrs. Powell and McCulloch are in league with the President to betray and destroy them."[2]

The most complete description of the charge came from James W. Simonton, a controversial veteran correspondent whom the *New York Times* had sent west to supplement, if not supersede, David A. Burr's amateur reporting. By the time he arrived at Fort Bridger on the evening of 27 May, the U.S. House of Representatives had barred Simonton from entering its chamber because of his provocative coverage of congressional corruption. Once into Utah, his behavior grew more brash, culminating in a knife fight with a rival reporter. During his first twelve hours in camp Simonton ferreted out what he reported as copy of Judge Eckels's April charge to the grand jury.

---

[1]Kane to Judge Kane, 4 April 1858, Kane Family Papers, BYU.

[2]Untitled and undated four-page ms. (pp. 3–4) in T. L. Kane's hand (annotated on reverse "NY correspondence *Herald!*"), Thomas Leiper Kane Papers, APS.

"S" [Simonton], "Important from Utah," Dispatch, 28 May 1858, *New York Times*, 24 June 1858, 1/1–5.

. . . Judge Echol's [*sic*] Charge.

On the day Governor Cumming left Camp Scott for Salt Lake City, Judge Echol delivered the following charge to the Grand Jury in reference to polygamy:

We cannot conceal from ourselves the knowledge of the fact that certain domestic arrangements exist in this Territory at war with those which pertain to all other Christian communities, and destructive of the peace and good order of society. Polygamy exists in Utah to a very considerable extent, while it is forbidden by every other State and Territory of the Union. It is not for you to inquire where this institution had its origin, or when or what were the consequences resulting from it. It is our duty to inquire whether it is authorized by law, and if not, by what statute, if any, it is punishable.

It is understood that the United States acquired all of this Territory that is inhabited by treaty from Mexico. As the law of Mexico stood at the time of the treaty, polygamy was prohibited in this country. The municipal law in this respect was not changed by its cession to the United States. Has it, then, been altered since we acquired it? After the most diligent search and inquiry I have been enabled to make, I have found none, and presume the law is, therefore unchanged; and hence, all marriages after the first, whilst it remains in full force, are illegal and void. Is there any law in force in this Territory under which this practice is punishable? I find no statute punishing polygamy, but there is one, however, for the punishment of adultery, and all illegal intercourse between the sexes, if either of the parties have a husband or wife living at the time, is adulterous and punishable by indictment. The punishment prescribed by this statute is imprisonment for a period of not less than three nor more than twenty years, or by fine not less than $300 nor more than $1,000, or both by fine and imprisonment, at the discretion of the Jury trying the cause.

No consequence in which a large proportion of this people may be involved, in consequence of their criminal practice, will deter you from a fearless discharge of your duty. It is yours to find the facts and to return the indictments, without fear, favor, affection, reward, or any hope thereof. The law was made to punish the lawless and disobedient, and society is entitled to the salutary effects of its execution.

Although the jury declined to return indictments, its very existence damaged the administration in Mormon eyes. The fact that the judge convened the panel amidst an army and tasked it with probing Utah's "peculiar institution," undercut the court's image for impartiality as well as the credibility of Cumming's assurances that the U.S. government had no quarrel with LDS religious tenets. With this misstep, the judge created a furor that undermined any Mormon willingness to accept the army while unwittingly ceding a part of the moral high ground to Brigham Young. By embarrassing his Washington political sponsors, Eckels placed his own appointment in jeopardy. The specter of polygamy prosecutions in Utah reinforced Brigham Young's worst fears. It was an albatross encumbering Governor Cumming's and President Buchanan's effectiveness for the next two years.

An Accurate and Just Statement of the Times: Fighting the Public Relations War

T. B. H. Stenhouse had earlier worked in Manhattan for Apostle John Taylor on the defunct *Mormon,* but since fall 1857 it had fallen to George A. Smith rather than Taylor to maintain the church's relationship with Stenhouse. Smith wrote to him monthly. Not lost on the apostle was the fact that Stenhouse's new employer, the *New York Herald,* had the largest circulation of any newspaper in the United States; oddly its non-Mormon proprietor, James Gordon Bennett, was a former brigadier general in the Nauvoo Legion. Aiding Smith in maintaining this connection was W. G. Mills, Brigham Young's bookkeeper-poet.[3] Mills, like Stenhouse, was a member of the LDS church's small, articulate band of converts from the Isle of Man.

Immediately after receiving the April letters sent by Smith and Mills, Stenhouse mailed them to the church's British Mission in Liverpool. There the editor of the Mormon *Millennial Star* ran their complete text under the heading "Deseret" after assuring readers they "were written a few days before the arrival of Governor Cumming in Great Salt Lake City, and can be relied upon as giving an accurate and just statement of the times and feelings of the people, and their determination not to submit to intercourse with blackguards, thieves, drunkards, and scoundrels." Although the Smith and Mills letters commented extensively on Indian relations, they were silent on Mountain Meadows and polygamy.[4]

---

[3]For a discussion of Mills's poetry during this period, see Alford, "Latter-day Saint Poetry and Songs of the Utah War," 23–25.

[4] *Millennial Star* (Liverpool), 17 July 1858, 457–62; Smith to Stenhouse, 5 April 1858, George A. Smith Papers, and Mills to Stenhouse, 5 April 1858, Historian's Office Journal, Ms. History of Brigham Young, both LDS Archives.

Six weeks after Smith and Mills positioned Stenhouse, Brigham Young called him to the role of church publicist, an assignment to be conducted in secrecy and with generous financial support. By year-end Stenhouse would dispense cash to the East's most influential newspaper editors under the guidance of another Manxman, George Quayle Cannon, former editor of San Francisco's *Western Standard.* Brigham Young made it clear to both men that they were to work in close consultation with Thomas L. Kane.

Barren and Desolate in the Extreme: To the Colorado with Apostle Lyman

As part of the war's action played out through a church historian and a determined federal judge in Utah's snowy north, still other scenes unfolded in the territory's sunbaked deserts more than four hundred miles south of Salt Lake City. By the time Cumming and Kane left Fort Bridger, Amasa Lyman had reached Parowan, selected and equipped almost twenty men from among San Bernardino's evacuees, and started for the Colorado River, which had been explored by the army's Ives Expedition a month earlier. Not only the instructions of his prophet but the threat of three thousand federal troops steaming upriver toward southern Utah imparted a sense of urgency to Lyman. It is unknown whether Young shared with Lyman the intelligence and speculation sent to him by Mormon Indian missionaries at Las Vegas in 1855 about the formidable region the apostle was about to traverse.[5] Although the White Mountain Expeditions of George Washington Bean and Col. William H. Dame during the spring of 1858 are well-known, Lyman's Colorado River reconnaissance remains obscure.[6]

[5]See Thomas D. Brown to Young, 23 June–12 July 1855, and John Steele to George A. Smith, 1 October 1855, each with accompanying maps of the Las Vegas area and both ibid.

[6]For the most recent scholarship on this subject, see Lyman, *Amasa Mason Lyman,* 262–70, and Stott, *Search for Sanctuary,* 192. Because Young's instructions to Bean were so counter-intuitive and are not well known, they are worth noting: "We do not contemplate sending families across the Deseret this spring hence you need not hurry to send us word but send in every opportunity by those who may be coming back. . . . We do not expect you to find large extensive tracts of arable land desirable for settlements or cultivation, as the world would esteem it but rather places where nothing can be raised of consequence and exceedingly difficult of access. Good places for hiding up where there is absolutely no chance to obtain subsistence by the ordinary exertions of men." Young to Bean, 28 April 1858, LDS Archives.

Diary of Amasa Lyman, April 1858,
Romney Typescript, ms 2737, lds Archives.

[April] 3rd. Sat[urda]y. Preached to the inhabitants . . . and in the afternoon bid adieu to our friends at Fort Clara, and joined the balance of the party at the foot of the river. Names of the party. Amasa Lyman, Roby. Clift, [unnamed] Spanish Interpreter, Ira Hatch,[7] [Indian Jim] Guide & Piede interpreter Freeman Tanner, John D. Holladay, David H. Holladay. Marion Lyman.[8] Henry G. Boyle. Walter E. Dodge. Wm. S. Warren. Marcus L. Shepherd, Cunningham Mathews. Edward T. Mills. Henry Jennings. Fred T. Perris. Taylor Crosby. Norman Taylor Harvey Clark. Wm. H. Shearman. . . .

6th Tuesday. Left camp at 7 A.M. C. Mathews mule ran off about 3 miles. Reached [Paiute chief] "Isaac's" camp at 9 1/2 A.M. Stopped here for the day as there is good feed on the hills. Br Clift complained here of severe pain in his leg & foot, & of being very unwell.[9] He was in bed most of the day, and had considerable fever. In the evening gave the brn. [brethren] my views and advice with respect to the course I wished them to pursue, both with regard to their intercourse with each other, and the various duties which will devolve upon them in the course of our trip. Weather rather cool—but pleasant.

7th Wednesday. Left camp at 7 1/2 A.M. Went down the Virgin [River] about 4 miles. . . . Reached the Muddy about Sunset, where we found br. David Savage's Company camped. Dr. [William L.] McIntyre was along. Preached to the people in the evening.

8th Thursday. Remained in camp all day. Wind blowing a perfect gale all day—covering everything with sand and dirt. Very unpleasant. Towards evening had a slight sprinkling of rain. Read the President's circular [about the Move South] to the camp. . . .

13th. Tuesday. Left camp at 5 A.M. Reached the holes where Ira [Hatch] expected to find water, in about 7 miles at 7 A.M. Were much disappointed at first in not finding more than enough water to wet our lips, but by hunting round a little in the neighboring ravines we found as much as we needed for our own use—but not sufficient to water the stock. Were detained here an hour—filling our canteens Kegs &c &c when we proceeded over a very rough road for about 7 miles when we halted at 10 1/2 A.M. to get breakfast. . . . Resumed our journey at 12 m. and reached the Colorado at 3 P.M. Distance 12 ms.

The whole country over which we passed between the Vegas & Colorado is barren and desolate in the extreme, without a single spring, and scarcely

[7]Hatch, of course, had participated in Jacob Hamblin's encounter with the Ives Expedition. He was one of the few members of this party who had not lived with Lyman in San Bernardino.

[8]Francis Marion Lyman was Amasa's son. He would be called to the Quorum of the Twelve Apostles after his father's excommunication.

[9]Clift's leg had become infected.

any grass, but abounding in Cactus & prickly pear bushes which are very annoying, and indeed dangerous to the animals. The country all around the Colorado, on both sides, presents the same barren, rocky, Mountainous desert aspect, and there is no feed but brush and a little scattering dry bunch and salt grass, and that very scarce. This river is rightly named [in Spanish], for it is very red and muddy. A few hundred yards above where we struck the river, on the same side, the rocky bluffs rise perpendicularly from the shore to the height of several hundred feet—rendering it impossible to get down to the water if approached from that quarter. The opposite shore is not so bold. The water here is shallow on this side, but swift and deep near the opposite shore. Day has been very warm.

14th. Wednesday. Moved down the river about two miles to a place where there is a little grass. . . . One of the three Indians who have accompanied us from the Vegas went down to the Hyatt [Iats or Mojave] Wickyups, about three miles below, and brought up about a dozen of the Hyatts, who staid at our camp all night.

16th. Friday. Immediately after breakfast, Oat-sen-a-wantz, the principal chief, arrived, accompanied by ~~about~~ several of his minor chiefs and some 15 or 20 Warriors, making 35 in all, who were present with us.[10] They are a fine looking race of men and will compare very advantageously with the Piede [Paiute] tribes in size as well as in many other respects. The old chief was so considerate as to remain with his party some distance from our camp, when he learned we were at breakfast—until we had done—and in their deportment in Camp, and obedience to their Chief they set an example which many of our own people might imitate with advantage. We had quite a long "talk," & he expressed a desire to cultivate friendly relations & intercourse with us, and also said he intended to pay us a visit in the Settlements. Gave them flour and meat to make their breakfast, and then gave the Chief the few presents we had brought for him, consisting of a blanket, shirt, knife and piece of tobacco. . . .

17th. Saty. Morning rather cloudy, and cool enough to be pleasant. Quite a number of the Hyatts remained in our camp last night. Left camp at 7 1/2 A.M. For the first 3 or 4 miles—road pretty good—the next 9 or 10 miles over a very mountainous, rough, rocky road, through narrow defiles, down the sides of sharp, craggy rocked hills, and along the sides of precipices where a single misstep would precipitate an animal down a hundred feet or more. Noticed one place in particular, about 10 ms. from our camp this morning, which affords excellent facilities for commanding the river, as the channel is, at this point, on *this* (west) side of the stream, and the adjacent rocks & ravines afford protection and shelter for a great number of men. . . .[11]

[10]The Ives Expedition did not encounter this Mojave chief.

[11]Here Lyman was thinking of the terrain in terms of defending against any army landing.

Oat-sen-a-wantz sent us word that some of his men intended to stampede our mules if they had an opportunity, and that we had better tie them up. He also sent his War chief Totab, and two others to stop at our camp all night & see that no "mischief" was done us.[12] We hobbled nearly all the mules, and having made every precaution in our power, all but the guard went to bed. . . .

18th. Sunday. Left camp about 7 1/2 A.M. and proceeded down the river to the place where we were to meet Oat-sen-a-wantz and his chiefs, and where they have their villages on both sides of the river. . . . Soon after we stopped, Oat-sen-a-wantz made his appearance attended by a large concourse of his people both male and female. As we did not yet know what kind of a reception we should meet with, we made every preparation for either a hostile or peaceful one. We soon found, however, by their appearing accompanied by their women, and without their arms, that they were peacefully disposed. I concluded to stop all day with them, and have more talk with the Chief and ascertain further their feelings towards us. We accordingly moved down into the [river] bottom, where we were soon surrounded by about 250 of the natives—of both sexes—who had assembled prepared to have a gala day, devoted to mirth and enjoyment. . . .

Some of their women are well made & possessed of tolerably good looking features—and, in their antique dresses of bark and wool, reaching from their waist to their knees, they made quite a picturesque and tasty appearance. The most of them, however, are corrupted & polluted by the little intercourse they have had with the Americans [at Fort Yuma], and one or two are afflicted with venereal disease, which if not checked, and unless a course is taken to prevent it, will no doubt soon spread among the rest of the tribe. They judged us, at first, by what they had seen and known of the Americans who have visited them, and offered to let us have their women to use, in consideration of blankets, tobacco &c &c; but when we told them that we did not come for such a purpose—that we did not want it, and that it was wrong, they seemed much pleased and their confidence was increased. Oat-sen-a-wantz renewed his expressions of friendship and desires to have some of our people come and live with them, & assured me he would protect them. . . .

Lyman's journal for 1858 ends abruptly in early May, but it is known that he returned from the Colorado so as to reach Provo on 22 May. There he helped Young, preparing for his June meetings with Buchanan's peace commissioners, armed with the assessment that the harsh terrain between the Colorado and the Spanish Trail made the use of the river to invade Utah

[12]Totab, presumably a Mojave, is not to be confused with Toanob, one of the Paiutes present at the Mountain Meadows massacre. Walker, Turley, and Leonard, *Massacre at Mountain Meadows*, 269.

impractical.[13] Although Lyman's journal also described this region as useless for a Mormon refuge or escape route to Sonora, it is unclear if or how he shared this view with Brigham Young. Whether large havens awaited the Latter-day Saints in the deserts near the White Mountains was then still unknown, although Colonel Dame continued to tantalize Young with overly optimistic field reports holding out that possibility.

A Fermentation of Ideas: Buchanan's Next Gambit

The notion of a congressional committee to investigate Utah affairs first arose when Brigham Young learned of the Utah Expedition's launch. In a private session during the second week of September 1857, he broached the matter with army quartermaster Stewart Van Vliet, who reacted in sympatico but ambiguous fashion, stating: "the Government may yet send out one to Utah & Consider it policy before they get through with it."[14] Upon departing Salt Lake City, Van Vliet may have realized that he had been indiscreet. In writing his trip reports for General Harney and Secretary Floyd on 16 September and 20 November, respectively, he made no recommendation concerning an investigating committee and failed to mention Young had advocated one.

In January 1858 the notion resurfaced, this time in a Congress still resentful that, without its involvement, the president (and Young) had plunged the country into armed confrontation for reasons still murky. No officer of the U.S. government had seen Brigham Young since he and Captain Van Vliet parted company in mid-September. As the new year opened, Congress was unaware of "Dr. Osborne" and his mediation mission. It would be months before the president knew Kane had reached Utah, let alone what he was doing there. As the winter wore on, Buchanan asked George Plitt, one of his well-connected political operatives, for the latest news of "our friend Kane." No one had any.[15]

Meanwhile, Washington was awash with rumors of Mormon-Indian alliances, an appalling massacre at Mountain Meadows, the army's defeat, a military thrust from the Pacific Coast, and a Mormon mass exodus to

---

[13]Unknown to Lyman and Young, Ives had already shared a quite different (optimistic) conclusion with Washington based on his more superficial examination of the terrain.

[14]Kenney, ed., *Wilford Woodruff's Journal*, 26 September 1857, 5:100.

[15]Elizabeth Kane Journal, 22 April 1858, Kane Family Papers, BYU.

destinations ranging between Russian America, Vancouver's Island, northern Mexico, Hawaii, coastal Central America, and the Dutch East Indies. Alarmed diplomats asked questions, state governors lobbied for volunteer units, and the Treasury hemorrhaged cash.

Near the end of January, Congress lost patience over the ambiguity shrouding Buchanan's war and his plans for concluding it. The House adopted a resolution asking the president for "the information which gave rise to the military expedition ordered to Utah Territory, the instructions to the army officers in connexion with the same, and all correspondence which has taken place with said army officers, with Brigham Young and his followers, or with others, throwing light upon the question as to how far said Brigham Young and his followers are in a state of rebellion or resistance to the government of the United States."[16] At the same time, Rep. Isaac Morris of Illinois tried to get the House to push for the appointment of a three-man commission to negotiate a buyout of the Mormons linked to their departure from the United States.[17]

Within this context Sen. Sam Houston visited the Executive Mansion to urge presidential support for appointment of some sort of investigatory body. Delegate Bernhisel followed suit but, after rebuffs from Buchanan, he reported to Brigham Young "the proposition has not been favorably received."[18]

The model for action urged by many people—the Pierce administration's congressional committee to examine civil unrest in Kansas—was not what James Buchanan had in mind for Utah. After considering Houston's advice and President George Washington's handling of Pennsylvania's "Whiskey Rebellion" of 1794, Buchanan closeted himself during March to draft a lawyerly document by which he hoped to resolve the war.

Greatly Annoyed by the Utah Difficulties: The Buchanan-Bernhisel Chats

While thus occupied, one of the few people with whom the president consulted was Delegate Bernhisel. Buchanan left no record of these meetings, but Utah's territorial delegate later reconstructed two accounts of their conversations.

[16]The Utah Expedition," House Exec. Doc 71, 1.

[17]Bigler and Bagley, *The Mormon Rebellion,* 265.

[18]Bernhisel to Young, 17 December [ca. 17 February 1858], LDS Archives.

Both documents recorded a wide range of presidential comments about the war that soon found their way into the strategic materials he was crafting in private. It was a rare record of Buchanan's thinking during this period.

Even though at one point Buchanan urged Bernhisel to communicate with Young immediately, a fear of federal mail monitoring paralyzed the delegate during the late winter and spring of 1858. In the first of Bernhisel's subsequent accounts—a 29 June 1858 letter to Brigham Young—he prefaced his summary of Buchanan's earlier comments with a quasi-confession of what seems to have been a lack of audacity, urgency, and ingenuity in forwarding important intelligence to Young: "I did not write you so fully the past winter as I should have done, on account of the apprehensions entertained by me that my communications would never reach you, and Dr. [Jeter] Clinton seemed reluctant to be the bearer of any written matter lest he should be captured by the troops; and there was an effort made at Washington to connect me with what they called the Utah rebellion, and the New York Herald proposed that I should be arrested as a spy." As a result of these anxieties, Bernhisel denied Young a coherent, timely account of even the crucial fact that "in the winter I made propositions to the President for an amicable adjustment of our difficulties to which the newspapers have alluded, but the details of which I must reserve until I shall have the pleasure of meeting you again."[19] With this remarkable introduction, Bernhisel summarized his interactions with President Buchanan.

BERNHISEL TO YOUNG, 29 JUNE 1858, LDS ARCHIVES.

During the session [of Congress] I had repeated interviews with the President in relation to Utah affairs, and endeavored to induce him to withdraw the troops, but he refused saying that the Federal laws must be enforced. I replied that the people denied having violated any laws, or resisted any authority, and stated that the reports that the records of the Supreme court had been destroyed and other outrages committed were without the slightest foundation in fact, and that some of the civil officers sent there were very bad men. He observed that the officers now [recently] sent out were the best men they could find in the country and spoke particularly of Gov. Cumming. On one or two occasions he said that all he wanted with the troops there was to enforce

[19]The "propositions" that Bernhisel was unwilling to communicate by mail may have included his support for Walter Murray Gibson's gambit to have Buchanan execute a federal buyout of Mormon properties in Utah in exchange for a Mormon exodus to a large island in the Dutch East Indies. If some combination of Gibson and Bernhisel made such a proposal, the president rejected it.

> the constitution and laws, to keep the Indians from committing depredations on emigrants, and act as a posse if they should be required, and if everything went on quietly they [*sic*] troops would be withdrawn. He disclaimed any intention to interfere with our religion. He seemed greatly annoyed by the Utah difficulties, and on one or two occasions also, he expressed a wish that he had Brigham Young here to talk to him for about two hours. The President also said he should regret if there was a single drop of blood shed, and that he did not wish to hurt a hair of their [Mormon] heads.

A year later, back in Salt Lake City, Bernhisel developed the second summary of his discussions with Buchanan. This memo largely repeated the substance of his earlier letter of 29 June 1858 but added several important comments not previously attributed to Buchanan.

Memorandum, "Account of Conversations with President James Buchanan," Bernhisel to Young, ca. June 1859, LDS Archives.

> He had no desire to interfere with the religion of the people of Utah, and had instructed Gov. Cumming, not in his written instructions only, but orally. . . . Said he would pardon all. . . . Stated that Colonel Johnston should not have sent the salt back [in November]. Thought it would be very foolish for the people to burn their houses. Inquired where Gov. Young went last Spring [of 1857]. . . . Spoke of the report of our being about to remove to the British possessions. . . . Intimated that if the people submitted to the laws the troops would be withdrawn after a short time, except a few companies to keep open the line of travel to California, for it would be too expensive to keep troops there. Observed that he was more friendly to us than Congress. Did not favor our removal [flight]; thought that we were better in Utah than in any other part of the world.[20] Stated that he received the Deseret News and that some of Brigham Young's speeches were terrible. . . . it was a rebellion without any cause, and that he should renew his instructions to Colonel Johnston not to interfere with their religion.[21] . . . [Young had been intending] to establish an Independent Government, and had been preparing for this for years. States that Captain Van Vliet had told him that Gov. Young had informed him that he had laid up provisions for three years. . . . His Excellency was of the opinion that the war would continue for years, but that their [*sic*] could be but one opinion as to the result. The President was greatly annoyed by the Utah difficulties until they were amicably adjusted.

---

[20]In the spring of 1858 Buchanan had given up the notion of opening a second front from the Pacific Coast to force a Mormon exodus into northern Mexico.

[21]Buchanan did not do this.

As March 1858 turned into April, Buchanan's drafting progressed to the point that he shared with Bernhisel an important glimpse of his intentions. On 3 April 1858 the delegate mailed Young a terse two-sentence account of how things stood with Buchanan: "I have just had another interview with the President and I hasten to inform you that he has finally concluded to send Commissioners to Utah with the view to restore peace and harmony. The appointees are Major McCulloch of Texas, and Ex-Governor Powell, of Kentucky."[22] It is unknown how Buchanan recruited these stalwarts of the Democratic Party, but both men had agreed to serve by the time the president revealed their names to Bernhisel. Buchanan had shown poor judgment in selecting William S. Harney and Alfred Cumming for key roles at the onset of the Utah War, but with Lazarus W. Powell and Ben McCulloch he chose well.[23]

Powell was one of Kentucky's most eminent attorneys. He was "available" in the sense that he had vacated the commonwealth's governorship and would not take his Senate seat until 1859. He projected the image of a senior figure who was approachable but respected through the exercise of a keen intellect and consummate good judgment. These were attributes complemented by a low-key but resolute temperament shaped by the practical challenges of a modest background and an ability to endure hardship.

McCulloch still served as the senior federal peace officer for east Texas, but he was restless, spending a substantial amount of time in Washington with his mentor, Sam Houston. The bond between the two men was so close that on the day of the congressional resolutions about Utah, their relationship entered the senator's attempt to describe for his absent wife the romantic thoughts through which he coped with chronic homesickness: "I slept last night after the clock struck *four*, and not one minute until then. The reason was my Love, that I was thinking of you. I could if I would make you smile, and just because I can, I will do so. When I came from the Presidents Levee, a friend from Texas, an old Ranger came with me to my room, and we sat down, and as I had procured a quantity of Tobacco, as I came by Lynchburg [Virginia], I ordered some fine smoking Tobacco, of the kind which I took home! We smoked, and talked until late, and when I lay down, my mind followed the

---

[22]Bernhisel to Young, 3 April 1858, LDS Archives. Sent via the California mail, this status report did not reach Young until 20 September 1858.

[23]For a discussion of the uneven quality of Buchanan's Utah War appointments, see MacKinnon, "Prelude to Armageddon," 57–62.

train of 'smoking,' so my Dear, I thought of our *social habit* of smoking *together*, and then a train of reflections, most effectually drew sleep from me!!!"[24]

While in Washington with Houston, McCulloch read extensively about military science and lobbied for command of one of the new regiments projected to be raised for service in Utah or Texas. McCulloch, of course, had been Buchanan's initial choice to supersede Brigham Young in late March 1857, but he declined the offer, although he agreed to visit General Harney's headquarters three months later to assess the Utah Expedition's readiness. As a veteran of the Texas Revolution, the Mexican-American War, and the Texas Rangers, Major McCulloch was a man who impressed others as tough, resilient, and savvy. He possessed an independent streak, one that permitted him to forge an amicable relationship with Albert Sidney Johnston notwithstanding Sam Houston's unwillingness to do so.[25] When Henry McCulloch learned of his brother's appointment, he informed their mother: "Ben writes me that he has agreed to go to Utah as *peace commissioner* to try and settle the matter with Brigham Young without bloodshed, and will get back to Washington if there is no fighting by the first of August. I had much rather he had gone at the head of a gallant Regiment as twould better suit his taste and habits."[26]

Taken together, the two commissioners came close to personifying the Texas Rangers' informal motto adopted a half-century later: "One Riot, One Ranger." At ages 45 and 46, McCulloch and Powell were mature, vastly experienced agents able to operate on the frontier unsupported. They were men unlikely to embarrass Buchanan and unwilling to allow Brigham Young to intimidate them. Capt. James H. Simpson saw the two men passing through Fort Leavenworth in late April and commented, "the Governor is a shrewd, kind-hearted, venerable man; and though the Major has all the air of a sharp, resolute character, yet, under all this, there seems to be a deep substratum of caution, that will, no doubt, prevent his doing anything rash."[27]

---

[24]Houston to Margaret Lea Houston, 27 January 1858, Roberts, ed., *The Personal Correspondence of Sam Houston*, 4:281.

[25]In 1855 McCulloch had harbored hopes of re-entering the army as colonel of the new Second U.S. Cavalry, a command for which Sec. of War Jefferson Davis selected Albert Sidney Johnston. Although bitterly disappointed at the time, McCulloch generously commented later to a friend that Davis had made the right decision and that Johnston had done a fine job in Utah. Colonel Love to Albert Sidney Johnston, 11 June 1860, Johnston, *Life of Gen. Albert Sidney Johnston*, 228.

[26]Henry E. McCulloch to Frances L. McCulloch, 24 April 1858, Henry Eustace McCulloch Papers, Center for American History, University of Texas at Austin.

[27]"S" [Simpson], Dispatch from Fort Leavenworth, 26 April 1858, *Buffalo (N.Y.) Courier*, 4 May 1858, 2/2. Captain Simpson is not to be confused with James W. Simonton, who also signed his dispatches to the *New York Times* as "S."

Fallen like a Clap of Thunder: Buchanan's Secret Proclamation

In briefing Delegate Bernhisel on his intent to appoint commissioners for Utah, James Buchanan shared only half of his plan. Typically, while alternately stroking and lecturing Bernhisel during March, he withheld from him (as well as Congress and the public) what he intended Powell and McCulloch to do once they reached Utah. Their assignment was to extend a pardon to Utah's entire population conditional upon Mormon acceptance of terms unilaterally imposed via an accompanying presidential proclamation.

From fragments in his personal papers, it appears that Buchanan crafted this long document himself rather than delegating the task to one or more cabinet officers with jurisdiction over this complex territorial problem.[28] On 6 April, in splendid isolation, the president finalized the proclamation by which he hoped to resolve the Utah War.

What Buchanan created in such fashion was a remarkable document comprised of two sections of unequal length. The first segment reprised a long, Judge Drummond–like litany of unacceptable Mormon conduct accompanied by extensive editorial comments. It was a narrative destined to inflame the proclamation's intended beneficiaries while appalling non-Mormons. The document made no mention of Brigham Young; it used the word "Mormon" only once; but here the president used the words "rebellion" and "treason" with a vigor absent from his December annual message to Congress. Because of its length and accessibility elsewhere, only excerpts appear here.[29]

Buchanan, "By the President of the United States, A Proclamation," 6 April 1858, Moore, ed., *The Works of James Buchanan*, 10:202–206.

> Fellow-citizens of Utah, this is rebellion against the Government to which you owe allegiance; it is levying war against the United States, and involves you in the guilt of treason. Persistence in it will bring you to condign punishment, to ruin, and to shame; for it is mere madness to suppose that with your limited resources you can successfully resist the force of this great and

[28] See James Buchanan Papers, Historical Society of Pennsylvania. NARA's staff has been unable to find a trace of documents relating to the development of Buchanan's proclamation among its holdings for the office of the president, presidential pardons and executive clemency, or the records of the office of the attorney general.

[29] The text also appears in Hafen and Hafen, eds., *Mormon Resistance*, 332–37.

powerful nation. If you have calculated upon the forbearance of the United States, if you have permitted yourselves to suppose that this Government will fail to put forth its strength and bring you to submission, you have fallen into a grave mistake. . . .

Do not deceive yourselves nor try to mislead others by propagating the idea that this is a crusade against your religion. The Constitution and laws of this country can take no notice of your creed, whether it be true or false. That is a question between your God and yourselves, in which I disclaim all right to interfere. If you obey the laws, keep the peace, and respect the just rights of others, you will be perfectly secure, and may live on in your present faith or change it for another at your pleasure. Every intelligent man among you knows very well that this Government has never, directly or indirectly, sought to molest you in your worship, to control you in your ecclesiastical affairs, or even to influence you in your religious opinions.

This rebellion is not merely a violation of your legal duty; it is without just cause, without reason, without excuse. . . . But being anxious to save the effusion of blood and to avoid the indiscriminate punishment of a whole people for crimes of which it is not probable that all are equally guilty, I offer now a free and full pardon to all who will submit themselves to the just authority of the Federal Government. If you refuse to accept it, let the consequences fall upon your own heads. But I conjure you to pause deliberately and reflect well before you reject this tender of peace and good will.

Now, therefore, I, JAMES BUCHANAN, President of the United States, have thought proper to issue this my proclamation, enjoining upon all public officers in the Territory of Utah to be diligent and faithful, to the full extent of their power, in the execution of the laws; commanding all citizens of the United States in said Territory to aid and assist the officers in the performance of their duties; offering to the inhabitants of Utah who shall submit to the laws a free pardon for the seditions and treasons heretofore by them committed; warning those who shall persist, after notice of this proclamation, in the present rebellion against the United States that they must expect no further lenity, but look to be rigorously dealt with according to their deserts; and declaring that the military forces now in Utah and hereafter to be sent there will not be withdrawn until the inhabitants of that Territory shall manifest a proper sense of the duty which they owe to this Government.

As with the explosive memorials received from Utah's legislative assembly in March 1857 and his December instructions to Christopher Fallon about purchasing Cuba, the president kept his proclamation secret as long as he could. Among those uninformed about what Buchanan was doing were the Kanes. Thomas, of course, was in Utah, but his family lived in Philadelphia.

Despite this proximity to Washington and the rising volume of newspaper speculation, Buchanan never communicated to them the text of the proclamation of pardon or informed the Kanes of his decision to appoint commissioners to deliver it. This lapse in communications replicated the president's failure to inform Brigham Young of his removal from office a year earlier.

Elizabeth Kane first realized that Buchanan might appoint commissioners from newspaper rumors that reached her on 5 April, the day before the president finished his proclamation. As McCulloch and Powell moved west during April and May, her initial anxiety was that their involvement would overshadow her husband's accomplishment. This concern led her to the hope that Pat Kane and George Plitt could arrange Thomas's appointment as a third commissioner so the government would reimburse his substantial expenses. The two men apparently pursued such a proposition but without success. Meanwhile they also undertook to place stories favorable to Kane's mission in a variety of newspapers.

Buchanan's insensitivity so galled the Kanes ("Mr. B. has behaved badly") that on 19 May Pat Kane visited the White House to deliver decryptions of Tom's latest letters to Buchanan and to complain about a lack of presidential recognition and support for his brother. In a two-hour session with the president, Pat Kane confronted him with the family's anxieties about Thomas's reputation in the light of the commissioners' parallel mission. Buchanan "spoke of Tom as a noble character, etc." and then extricated himself with a patent untruth: that "the 'Peace Commissioners' were no more Commissioners than Tom himself." It was a convenient fabrication that Tom Kane later adopted in preparing an account of his mission for publication.[30] On the spot, Buchanan wrote a piece for insertion in his administration's "organ," the *Washington Union,* to clarify Kane's status. When published, the unsigned notice (couched as an editorial) stopped far short of declaring him one of the official peace commissioners or anything other than a well-intentioned, freelancing volunteer. To parry growing public speculation about Kane's religious affiliation, Buchanan's piece asserted that he was a non-Mormon.[31]

The appointment of Powell and McCulloch did not require Senate confirmation. Under Buchanan's design, they were to function as co-equals, although Powell always signed his name before McCulloch's and took the

---

[30]See Elizabeth Kane Journal, April–May 1858, Kane Family Papers, BYU.

[31]"Col. Thomas L. Kane," unsigned editorial, *Washington Union,* 21 May 1858, 2/3.

lead in public speaking. They were commissioners without a commission, reporting to the president through Secretary of War Floyd. It was an unusual arrangement in view of the State Department's responsibility for territorial affairs. Buchanan never explained this irregular reporting relationship. Presumably it flowed from the president's low regard for Secretary Cass, as well as the army's role in providing the resources necessary for the commissioners to travel and conduct their mission, and the inescapable reality that Powell and McCulloch were seeking to terminate a war.

On 6 April, as a matter of protocol, Secretary Cass authenticated Buchanan's proclamation; the next day he wrote to Governor Cumming to inform him of these appointments, transmitting a copy of the proclamation and enclosing the commissioners' instructions from Floyd. Anticipating Cumming's likely discouragement, Cass assured him "you enjoy his [Buchanan's] entire confidence, and . . . he is sure that you will heartily co-operate in carrying these measures into effect, and will afford the commissioners all the aid and information in your power." Cass made no reference to Kane and provided no guidance to Cumming for integrating the anticipated work of Powell and McCulloch with whatever understandings he and Kane had already reached with Young.[32]

In effect, Buchanan marginalized his new governor for Utah much as he earlier did with Gov. Robert J. Walker of Kansas, who resigned in disgust. It was a convoluted, Buchananesque arrangement about which Elizabeth Kane, if not the president, worried: "I hope Tom will have succeeded in making peace before the Commissioners get out there. (I hope it isn't unchristian to wish that!) If they do get out I hope they will not be empowered to revoke Tom's arrangements. I *hope* Mr. Buchanan is going to uphold Tom! I see a frightful possibility. Suppose poor Young or H C Kimball give themselves up on the faith of Tom's word and then Buchanan refuses to sustain him? My God, help Tom to act wisely!"[33]

It took another five days for Floyd to follow Cass in issuing operating instructions to the new commissioners. Perhaps the documents transmitted on 7 April were delayed because they had become the subject of wrangling within the administration, as had been the case with the prolonged completion of Harney's marching orders during June 1857. The fact that fumbling,

[32]Cass to Cumming, 7 April 1858, Hafen and Hafen, eds., *Mormon Resistance,* 329.

[33]Elizabeth Kane Journal, 16 April 1858, Kane Family Papers, BYU.

President Buchanan and Cabinet, ca. 1859

(clockwise from president's left) Secretaries John B. Floyd (War), Lewis Cass (State), Howell Cobb (Treasury), Joseph Holt (Postmaster General), Isaac Toucey (Navy), Jeremiah S. Black (Attorney General), and Jacob Thompson (Interior). When the war started, Brigham Young was in conflict with virtually all of their departments. In 1861 four of the seven became Confederate generals or Southern sympathizers. *Mathew Brady Collection courtesy of NARA.*

if not conflict, was also occurring in the cabinet is indicated by a highly unusual, unpublished letter marked "private" that Cass wrote to Cumming on 10 April. Here the secretary explained that after mailing him Floyd's intended instructions to the commissioners on 7 April, he became aware that this material was "incorrect," which presumably meant objectionable or misguided. The result was a frantic attempt by the administration to recall the War Department's offending instructions through Postmaster General Aaron Brown's agent in St. Louis and their redrafting in Washington.[34]

While the administration struggled to formulate instructions for its peace commissioners and to do so secretly, newspapermen seized upon tidbits that leaked out of the cabinet departments. On 10 April the *Chicago Daily Tribune*'s Washington reporter wrote that "the President has not yet fully determined to send Gov. Powell and the Texas Ranger, McCullough [*sic*], as Commissioners with the army of Utah. He has been recommended by the Military Committee of the Senate to do something of the kind for the purpose of bringing about a peaceful settlement; but with the mulish obstinacy which marks all of his proceedings, Mr. Buchanan has given no answer. He has no right to send these Commissioners without a law creating the office, and without a legal appointment they could effect but little of any good." Unaware of the conditional pardon which McCulloch and Powell were carrying west, this reporter speculated without enthusiasm that the administration was superseding Albert Sidney Johnston with General Harney, an officer not "over burthened with brains." As the correspondent saw it, one of the commissioners' collateral duties was to protect the administration from Harney's "blunders."[35]

In the midst of this activity, Buchanan stepped gingerly around a controversy that arose in western Utah with neighboring California's governor and state legislature acting as provocateurs: the desire of Carson Valley's disaffected non-Mormons to separate from Utah to form a new territory. This was not a new issue, but the timing was explosive. On 9 April Buchanan dealt with the issue by sending to Congress Carson Valley's latest petition for territorial status, but without either a presidential recommendation for

[34]Cass to Cumming, 10 April 1858, Domestic Letters of the Dept. of State, Vol. 48, 289, NARA.

[35]"Junius," "From Washington. Command of the Utah Expedition," Dispatch, 10 April 1858, *Chicago Daily Tribune*, 14 April 1858, 2/4.

action or editorial comments on the document's litany of complaints against the LDS hierarchy. For Buchanan this was not the time or cause for which to complicate his Utah maneuvering.[36]

Finally, on 12 April Floyd gave the commissioners their orders. They were to engage in neither investigation nor negotiations. Their sole authorization was to tender the proclamation of pardon contingent upon Mormon acceptance of federal authority and the presence of the army. It was a take-it-or-leave-it proposition. The instructions acknowledged Kane's presence in Utah, alluded obliquely to the possibility of his usefulness to the commissioners, and provided the text of two of the three letters that Buchanan had sent to Kane at year-end 1857, documents that the administration never shared directly with Cumming or Johnston, although Kane had done so soon after arriving at Camp Scott. Lazarus Powell and Ben McCulloch were now aware of Kane.

If Lewis Cass had not mentioned Kane in his instructions to Cumming, Secretary Floyd's orders to the commissioners lacked any reference to Brigham Young. Although this omission was presumably deliberate for lawyerly or diplomatic reasons, it was awkward. This ambiguity required McCulloch and Powell to grapple with the practical technicality of determining who was to speak for Utah's disaffected population and whether that person—presumably Brigham Young—would do so as president of the LDS church, as former governor of Utah Territory, or as an unelected private citizen without organizational affiliation representing tens of thousands of Mormons on an ad hoc basis. By what legal right would an individual such as Young speak for an entire territory, and what would be the standing of individuals who opted out of the pardon process or dissented from his decision? At stake with the answers to such apparently unasked questions was the continued vulnerability of dissenters to prosecution for treason if not for criminal acts such as the Mountain Meadows massacre.

---

[36]Buchanan, "Message to Congress on Carson's Valley," 9 April 1858, Moore, ed., *The Works of James Buchanan*, 10:206–207. Buchanan's reluctance to champion the cause of western Utah's separatists at this sensitive time was consistent with his refusal a few weeks earlier to become embroiled in George P. Stiles's attempt to gain reinstatement to his seat on the bench of Utah's federal judiciary—or at least understand the accusations that led Buchanan to replace him at the beginning of the year. Stiles, an excommunicated Mormon, was still anathema in the territory, and he wore as a badge of honor his claim that "I was one of the Fathers of the Military Expedition." Stiles to Jeremiah S. Black, 21 February 1858, Records Relating to the Appointment of Federal Judges . . . of Utah, Microcopy No. 680, Roll 1 (1853–69), RG 60, NARA.

FLOYD TO POWELL AND McCULLOCH, 12 APRIL 1858, "ANNUAL REPORT OF THE SEC. OF WAR (1858)," 160–62.

You will proceed with all practicable despatch to the Territory of Utah, and it is hoped you will reach the forces commanded by General Johnston, before hostilities shall have been actually renewed. You will carry with you the President's proclamation to the people of Utah, dated on the 6th instant, and give such extensive circulation to it as you may be able to effect amongst them. This will clearly point out to them the unfortunate relations in which their present attitude places them towards the government and people of the United States.

The duties committed to you by the President are of great importance, though you are not authorized to enter into any treaty or engagement with the Mormons. It is the great object of the President to bring these misguided people to their senses, to convert them into good citizens and to spare the effusion of human blood. He relies much upon your high character, patriotism, and prudence to accomplish these results, by convincing them, should the opportunity offer, how desperate is their effort to resist the authority of the government, and how much in accordance it will be with their own true interests to return to their allegiance, and submit promptly and peaceably to the Constitution and laws of the United States upon the assurances contained in the President's proclamation.

To restore peace in this manner is the single purpose of your mission. To this end, you may place yourselves in communication with their recognized leaders, should this be deemed expedient under their circumstances, on your arrival in Utah.

Much must necessarily be left to your discretion and wisdom in any communication you may have with the Mormon people. You can repeat the assurances heretofore given by the President, that the movement of the army to Utah has no reference whatever to their religious tenets or faith. Whilst they obey the laws and perform their duty as citizens, no power in this country has either the right or the disposition to interfere with their religion. In the language of the proclamation addressed to the Mormons, "If you obey the laws, keep the peace, and respect the just rights of others, you will be perfectly secure, and may live on in your present faith, or change it for another at your pleasure. Every intelligent man among you knows very well that this government has never, directly or indirectly, sought to molest you in your worship, to control you in your ecclesiastical affairs, or even to influence you in your religions opinions."

It is the duty and determination of the federal government to see that the officials appointed and sent out by the President shall be received and installed, and due obedience be yielded to the laws and to their official acts. When this shall have been fully accomplished, a necessity will no longer exist to retain any portion of the army in the Territory, except what may be required to keep the Indians in check and to secure the passage of emigrants to California.

You will communicate freely with General Johnston and Governor Cumming, and act in concert with them. At this distance it is impossible to anticipate what may be the condition of affairs on your arrival in Utah, but the President was determined to leave no effort unessayed to bring these rebellious people to a sense of their duty before it be too late.

In the month of December last Colonel Thomas L. Kane, of the city of Philadelphia, impelled thereto by ancient kind feelings for the Mormons, deemed it to be his duty to repair to Utah for the purpose of influencing that people to do their duty to the government of the United States, and, if possible to spare the effusion of blood. He acted under a deep conviction of duty, against the advice of his excellent father, Judge Kane, since deceased, and other members of his family. Having determined upon this course, the President, whilst he recognized him in no manner as a government agent, addressed him two letters under date of 31st December last, copies of which are now communicated to you. Colonel Kane is probably at this time in Utah, and if you should find him there he may render you essential service in accomplishing the object of your mission.

All orders for facilitating your journey shall be given to the officers in command of the troops and stations along the line.

With these instructions, McCulloch and Powell headed for Washington's railroad station. Before entraining, the administration recalled them for another day of unspecified consultations. Seven months later, an erratic James Arlington Bennet wrote Brigham Young to claim responsibility for this delay. In so doing, Bennet advanced one of the truly preposterous claims associated with the war's peace process: "From the beginning I opposed by letters of the strongest Character to the President & General Floyd, whom I also have long known, the sending of an Army into Utah, as I foresaw the evils that would arise from that measure, not only to the Saints, but to the Administration itself.... But when the [Senator] Douglas affair [over Kansas] arose I had the finest opportunity to send the matter home to the President and offered to go out as a peace commissioner, & on the receipt of this letter the President actually stopped the Commissioners then in the R[ailroad] Car and kept them for 24 hours to get the advice of his Cabinet on the propriety of Adding me to the number but was over Ruled (advised) in the matter."[37]

[37]Bennet to Young, 20 November 1858, LDS Archives. Here was a precursor to Bennet's bizarre offer to provide President Lincoln with up to ten thousand Mormon troops he did not command to reinforce the Union Army. Bennet to Lincoln, 22 October 1861, Abraham Lincoln Papers, Manuscript Division, LC, microfilm reel 28. A single sentence describing the commissioners' mysterious delay in departure moved

The commissioners carried a pass from Floyd explaining their mission to army officers encountered en route. It was a document in sharp contrast to the travel letters Buchanan had given Kane less than four months earlier: "It is hereby certified that Lazarus W. Powell, of Kentucky, and Ben McCulloch, of Texas, have been authorized by the President to proceed to Utah to perform certain duties more particularly set forth in instructions of this date from the War Department. They are entitled to full credence in the premises."[38]

Another document they carried west was a formal letter of introduction to Young written by Bernhisel. Addressing him as "His Excellency Gov. Young," the delegate carefully explained the titles of each man and noted that they "have been appointed by the President Commissioners to proceed to Utah with instructions to adjust if possible the existing difficulties." Bernhisel closed with the phrase he used in all such letters but one ludicrous under the circumstances: "Any courtesies extended to him [Powell] and his colleague by you and any of your friends will be received as a personal favor by [me]."[39]

On 25 April the peace commissioners arrived at Fort Leavenworth, a post then engaged in reinforcing the Utah Expedition on an unprecedented scale. There they picked up their supplies and transportation (five mule-drawn ambulances and three saddle horses) and paused to have what one reporter later described as "bushels" of Buchanan's proclamation printed on an army field press. The entourage of fifteen heavily armed soldiers and civilians included the commissioners, their six-dragoon escort (commanded by a sergeant), five teamsters, a wagon master, and a guide. None of their names are known except those of the commissioners.

That Moderation Will Prevail: Captain Van Vliet Re-enters the Fray

As this party prepared to move west from Leavenworth, the post's quartermaster, Capt. Stewart Van Vliet, handed Ben McCulloch a sealed envelope for Brigham Young. Within was both personal advice and an expression of concern of the sort that earned Van Vliet an honored place as one of

by telegraph from the capital to a Cleveland newspaper and then throughout the country. "Important from Washington," Dispatch, 14 and 20 April 1858, *Cincinnati Daily Enquirer,* 1/5 and *Memphis Daily Appeal,* 1/3. For more about Bennet's fantastic attempt to intervene in the commissioners' work, see Bennet to Buchanan, 8 April 1858, James Buchanan Papers, HSP.

[38]Floyd to [blank], 12 April 1858, "Annual Report of the Sec. of War (1858)," 163.

[39]Bernhisel to Young, 11 April 1858, LDS Archives.

Young's strategically placed non-Mormon friends. With the distractions of the war, it took Young six months to reply to Van Vliet. He did so at length, sharing a negative view of Mormon-federal relations unchanged from those he held during April 1858.[40]

VAN VLIET TO YOUNG, 25 APRIL 1858, LDS ARCHIVES.

Governer [*sic*]:

Before this reaches you you will hear of the appointment of two commissioners ~~being appointed~~ by the President to visit you—one of them, Major Ben McCulloch will hand you this.

These commissioners will tell you the views of the President & the people in regard to your present attitude towards the U.S. Government.—I trust that moderation will prevail in your councils & that you will submit freely & willingly to the authority of the U.S. for that is your duty so long as you remain within the limits of this country. It is your duty to God, as well as to man—I advised this course when I was in Salt Lake City, last fall, because it was right & I advise it still.

I also told you that I did not think that the troops would enter Salt Lake Valley ~~last~~ that year, but that this spring you would see an overwhelming force. This has come to pass: we are making great preparations & in a short time there will be 5,000 men on the road towards Genl Johnston's camp[41]—You will see that you have nothing before you but war & bloodshed, unless you submit to the Government. You may annoy our troops for some time but in the end you must be overcome. You will not be able to plant & sow & famine will visit you. You must lose a great many of your people by battle & disease; you must subject yourselves to sever[e] privations & hardships & what for? It is not for your religion certainly, for the Government has no intention of troubling it. Mr Buchanan told me [last fall] that his instructions to Gov Cumming were not to interfere or meddle with the Mormon religion in any way. If your religion cannot withstand the contact of the world, it cannot be true. If the presence of a thousand U.S. troops quartered in Rush Valley can shake the faith of your people that faith can be of little value.[42]

I spoke to you freely & frankly when I was in Utah & I now write to you in the same way. As a lover of my country it pains me to see strife & civil war.[43]

---

[40]Young would remember Van Vliet's kindness and reciprocate. A year later he secured a cadet's berth at West Point for the captain's half-brother from Utah's quota of appointments. Van Vliet to Young, 5 November 1859, and Young to Van Vliet, 6 December 1859, both LDS Archives.

[41]The scope of the reinforcements ordered to Utah was an open secret along the Kansas-Missouri frontier, but this was a remarkable disclosure to an adversary during wartime by a serving officer.

[42]In 1855 Rush Valley was the site for a military reservation recommended by Lieutenant Colonel Steptoe. In 1858 Albert Sidney Johnston rejected Steptoe's advice and chose Utah's Cedar Valley.

[43]In three years Van Vliet would find himself in the midst of the Civil War, during which he served with distinction as chief quartermaster of McClellan's Army of the Potomac.

I have friends in Utah & I do not want them to place themselves in the wrong, thereby bringing trouble & desolation ~~upon them~~ to their homes & their families.

Dr Bernhisel wanted the President to appoint me as one of the commissioners, but at that time this measure had not been decided on & a soldier should not I presume have anything to do with political matters.

Be pleased to remember me to my friends in Utah.

YOUNG TO VAN VLIET, 22 OCTOBER 1858, LDS ARCHIVES.

I feel it due to you as well as myself to reply to your note of April 25th. I admire your candor and believe that you gave your advice sincerely desiring our best good. We think however that we understood the designs of the administration, and our enemies better than you, and that the check which the Army received [in 1857] evinced to the people that we were in earnest and would not tamely submit to being used up at the dictation of anonymous and lying scribblers, corrupt officials, speculators and gamblers, upon whose misrepresentations the administration, without the consent of Congress, based hostile action against us. No person was more anxious to avoid a collision than myself, and I feel truly thankful that matters have thus far progressed without one. But Captain it is but small liberty that a people can enjoy when every officer, trader, contractor are selected from among our enemies, imported, held, backed up and sustained by the Government of this Great republic by her standing army and the train of hell which follow after. It is bad enough now. What would it have been last fall if this heterogeneous mass had been permitted to come into our Settlements without the restraint which subsequent events caused as a rein to be held over them, and checked our bitter enemies in accomplishing the base purposes which they had so cunningly devised?

You say that "If your religion cannot withstand the contact of the world it cannot be true—If the presence of a thousand U.S. troops quartered in Rush valley can shake the faith of your people that faith can be of little value." Our Religion has ever stood the test and come off gloriously victorious in its contact with the world, and for this reason, and because it is true and cannot otherwise be overthrown, it is that the world arrays their armies against us to endeavor to destroy by physical and brute force the humble and sincere votaries of principles which their best logicians and most eloquent champions have by argument and reason contended against us in vain. . . .

It is not the objectionable feature that the U.S. troops being quartered in our midst will shake the faith of the Saints. They are welcome to all they can draw off and it would be a good riddance to our community. But throwing into our midst such a mass of abandoned profligacy, licentiousness, debauchery and dissoluteness as you Captain must acknowledge so generally pervades every department and always attends the camps of the U.S.

Army. The corrupting influence of such a mass of filth might well be, and is dreaded in every well regulated community and we trust that ere another winter they will find more congenial quarters, where they can perform some practical service at less expense to the Government. I trust the next "war" the contractors and Treasury leeches get up they will seek elsewhere for the field of their enterprize. That this has been as extravagant as it is useless, none I presume will deny. If the President, his Cabinet, and the Contractors are satisfied I am glad of it, and hope that they will rest content.

If Congress and the people of the United States feel equally content and satisfied, we can only say they are senseless to the knell of departed Liberty, and will only awake to a sense of their loss when its funeral dirge shall echo in the sacred precincts of their own cherished homes.

Captain;—where is your overflowing Treasury? Where the prestige of your Army? . . .

We have learned of your Court of investigation.[44] We soon expect to hear of your successful triumph over your accusers; but if you do not, remember, Captain, there is a day when truth and integrity will prevail not only with you but us.

All is well with us as could be expected under the circumstances, as we are used to the "kicks and cuffs" of the world, but as you are aware our trust is in that power which all must sooner or later acknowledge; and who can cast down, and set up, and none shall presume to stay His hand.

May God bless you for your kindness of heart, and preserve you to live until you shall see truth triumphant and our oppressed, though innocent people obtain their Constitutional Rights.

With best respects I have the honor to remain Your Friend,

Commissioners and Correspondents West: Odd Couples in Motion

By the end of April, the commissioners had moved into Nebraska Territory. On 3 May they reached Fort Kearny, on 17 May Fort Laramie, and on the night of 29 May they rolled into the Army of Utah's headquarters at Fort Bridger. There is no indication that Powell and McCulloch had encountered an eastbound Kane on the trail, but at Sweetwater Bridge, on 22 May, Kane first became aware of their appointment and the pardon they

[44]During the fall of 1858 Floyd ordered Van Vliet to appear before an army court of inquiry probing his purchase of thousands of mules for the Utah Expedition. At the heart of this indignity was Van Vliet's resistance to Floyd's efforts to steer contracts to personal friends at inflated prices. The captain emerged from the investigation professionally vindicated but personally affronted.

carried through a chance meeting with westbound James W. Simonton, the *New York Times*'s reporter "S." Ill, exhausted, and perhaps overwhelmed by the enormity of the army reinforcements he was passing, Kane noted this news with a journal entry of only four words: "Commissioners Coming. A Proclamation!"[45] His low-key reaction to the proclamation was fateful, unleashing Simonton's suspicions of conspiracy on a vast scale, linking Buchanan and his proclamation to a clandestine plot involving the president, Young, Kane, and Cumming.

"S" [Simonton], "The Mormons. Colonel Kane's Statement on the Way Home from Salt Lake," Dispatch, 23 May 1858, Sweetwater Bridge, N.T., *New York Times*, 25 June 1858.

> We met the Colonel yesterday, about 30 miles west of this, on his way to the States, with an escort of half-a-dozen Mormons. I had only time for a few words with him. . . . I showed Col. Kane a copy of the Proclamation. He manifested no surprise at the tenor of a document which has fallen like a clap of thunder from a clear sky upon every man on the plains who has been personally familiar with the history of Mormon aggressions. He certainly seemed to have anticipated it. I have heard a rumor which I fear is true, to-wit, that Mr. Buchanan, desirous of evading the responsibility of carrying the issue with the Mormons to a vigorous end, selected Col. Kane—for his well-known sympathies with the people of Salt Lake—to go out there months ago, and prepare them for the reception of a Proclamation of a general amnesty for past treasons and seditions, such as that which the Peace Commissioners are now carrying with them. I have no time to comment on this whole proceeding, for I write this note while our mules rest for a few moments, and we are already notified that our "outfit" is ready to proceed.

The two formal reports that Powell and McCulloch sent to Lewis Cass en route provided few details of what was essentially a tedious, uneventful journey. Simonton and his traveling companion from the *New-York Tribune,* Albert G. Browne, Jr., filed several dispatches that included colorful vignettes of the commissioners as the two parties crossed paths along an Oregon Trail crowded with tens of thousands of civilian emigrants and army reinforcements. Browne, of course, was on his way back to the Utah Expedition after leaving Camp Scott on 5 January with dispatches to the Buchanan administration from Albert Sidney Johnston and Judge Eckels. He reveled in his spring return to the West and, from an overnight camp at

[45]Kane, "Diary III (1858)," 22 May 1858, 56.

Ash Hollow, informed his readers: "I challenge the whole Orient to rival the Occidental luxuries I enjoy in [lounging on] my pile of buffalo robes and pipe full of *kinnikinnik* [Indian tobacco]. In this Arcadia there is an independence of starched collars and tight boots which is delightful after a two months' sojourn among the conventionalisms of New-York and Boston."[46]

In addition to limning vignettes of a naked Ben McCulloch fording the South Platte astride a mule and commissioner Powell mending his underwear on a river bank, the two reporters provided New Yorkers with a harsh critique of what they understood to be the commissioners' mission. In their dispatches Browne and Simonton adopted a "voice" that alternated between the reportorial and editorial. It was jaundiced material, and in Simonton's case it focused on his perception of a complex transcontinental conspiracy involving Buchanan, Kane, Cumming, and Young, with the president's proclamation key to understanding it. Today such suspicions may seem excessive, but the penchant for secrecy that drove each of these major players, taken with the sub-plots that actually existed, made grand conspiracy theories easy if not inevitable. These dispatches from the frontier disposed Atlantic Coast readers to mistrust the events unfolding in Utah; later, when copies washed back into Utah in the printed pages of the *Times* and *Tribune,* they reinforced hostility toward Buchanan in army bivouacs and Mormon refugee camps alike.

[Browne], "On the Way to Utah," Dispatch, Fort Laramie, N.T., 18 May 1858, *New-York Tribune,* 12 June 1858.

The President's Commissioners, who left Fort Leavenworth on April 25, arrived here yesterday, accompanied by the first weekly [Hockaday] mail to Utah Territory, which arrived from St. Joseph, Mo., on May 1. . . . They bear with them a proclamation from the President of the United States to the people of Utah, which I have not yet seen, but which is, I presume, by this time published in the States. In my ignorance of its precise character I forbear from any comment upon it at present; but I am satisfied that if its purport is (as I understand it is) to grant a general amnesty for all offenses against the law committed by the Mormons thus far in their rebellion, it will only aggravate the unhappy feeling which the conduct of Gov. Cumming has already excited in his civil associates, and in the entire army. . . . One thing I regard as certain—that unless Gov. Powell and Major McCulloch modify determinations which they have publicly expressed [on the trail], the course taken by Gov. Cumming will not be attended by such disgrace

[46] [Browne], "On the Way to Utah," Dispatch, 14 May 1858, *New-York Tribune,* 12 June 1858.

to the National Government as might otherwise be expected. They are fresh from intercourse with the people of the States, they understand the popular feeling on this Mormon question, and I hope that they will *represent* it. Of course their power is limited. I understand that in their appointment the President undertook to follow the example set by [George] Washington, who appointed Commissioners in a similar manner with reference to the whisky insurrection in Pennsylvania. If so, they can exercise only advisory authority; but if this is exerted consistently and firmly, it will carry great weight. . . . There is no reason to believe that the position of any of the other Territorial officers or of Gen. Johnston will be modified during the interval. I think that I understand the views of all those gentlemen well enough to venture to assert that they will consent to no compromise which shall result in releasing the Mormons from responsibility for their lawless acts, or in non-fulfillment of the orders under which the army proceeded to Utah, viz: to establish three military posts in the Territory, and to assist the civil authorities as a *posse comitatus* to execute the laws. . . .

P.M. Since I wrote to you this morning I have received a copy of the President's Proclamation. The general amnesty which it grants will not be attended with such happy consequences as the President affects to anticipate, unless Brigham Young shall recede somewhat from his position, for it is accompanied by an expression of determination that the Army of Utah shall remain in the Territory, and Young has repeatedly declared that he will never consent to any adjustment which shall permit them "to camp within his boundary line." The Proclamation, as a whole, will cause disappointment to every one of the civil associates of Gov. Cumming, and to the entire army. It is a concession on the part of the National Government which they do not expect and for which they are not prepared.

"S" [Simonton], "Important from Utah. The Peace Commissioners," Dispatch, Camp Scott, Near Fort Bridger, 28 May 1858, *New York Times*, 24 June 1858, 1/1–5.

Our arrival [yesterday] even in twenty-seven days, was hailed with joyful surprise by the Army here, who had almost come to the conclusion that news from home was never to reach them in much less than about twice that time. We overtook the well-appointed train of the Peace Commissioners, Messrs. Powell and McCulloch, at the South Platte crossing, notwithstanding they had six days the start of us—and as they cannot reach here before to-morrow night, we have beaten them quite eight days. . . .

The President's Proclamation tendering a general amnesty to the people of Utah for all seditions and treasons of the past—a copy of which I brought hither—is received by the Army with infinite disgust. Indeed, during the last twelve hours it has been the butt of a continual fire of jests, which have far more of gall than humor in their composition. The idea of *tendering* pardon to a people who do not ask it, but who are still in open rebellion against the Government, defying its officers and threatening its Army with annihilation, is mournfully ludicrous to the brave men who were ready to risk their lives in maintaining the honor of that flag which the President thus trails in the dust. . . .

The course pursued by Governor Cumming—a course which seems to have been shrouded in profound mystery,—the mission of Colonel Thos. L. Kane to Salt Lake, and his mysterious consultations with Governor Cumming, and the appointment of the expected Peace Commission, were disjointed events of which the Presidential Proclamation also seems to have been the key and interpretation. You are already aware that Governor Cumming has never acted here nor attempted to act in harmony with the Judicial officers of the Territory or with the Army. . . .

To [re]capitulate briefly, these are the facts, as they now seem to stand in regular and connected sequence: From the hour of his arrival in Utah, Gov. Cumming has shrouded himself in mystery,—with a policy of his own, the secret springs of which were studiously concealed from his associates here. It is now believed that he has been acting all along, under secret instructions from the President, of which it is more than probable that Brigham Young has information. Next, Col. Thos. L. Kane, a sympathizer with the Mormon faith, and therefore necessarily a disciple and servant of its High Priest, mysteriously disappeared from Washington and turned up on Salt Lake City, *via* California, on some secret mission to Brigham Young. True, he denies having any "powers" from the President, and yet he was able to exhibit here and elsewhere "letters" from the President, which secured him at once free entrance to this Camp from Salt Lake, and free egress on his return—the confidence of Governor Cummings [*sic*], and the aid of federal officials wherever found. He was clearly an accredited agent of the President to the arch traitor of Salt Lake; and he possessed some talismanic power with him, which induced Brigham Young to recall his oath that no new Governor should enter the Territory, and to send Kane out to Bridger to bring Gov. Cumming in.

What was this talisman? And what was the subject of the several interviews between Kane and Cumming, which finally resulted in the journey of the latter into Salt Lake,—interviews and proceedings still conducted with the most insulting secrecy from Gen. Johnston and Judge Eckles [*sic*]? The proclamation is thought to furnish the key; and it is supposed that the President, in his agony lest the Mormons should either go to Sonora, and so render that Province impossible of acquisition, or else should compel him to accept the responsibility of *forcing* the people of Salt Lake to obedience to the law—determined to send a Mormon emissary to Brother Brigham, to notify him that he would soon send out Commissioners with a bushel of printed proclamations, pardoning all their past offences, provided they would only consent to sham obedience to the law for the future, and so let the federal Administration get its fingers out of the fire. Let future developments, and the light they shed decide upon the accuracy of these views.

"S" [Simonton], "Important from Utah. Arrival and Reception of the Peace Commissioners," Dispatch, Camp Scott, Near Fort Bridger, 5 June 1858, *New York Times*, 30 June 1858, 1/1–6, 8/1.

Messrs. McCulloch and Powell, the Utah Peace Commissioners, arrived at this Camp on the 29th ult., some hours after the departure of the mail of that date, and were received by Gen. Johnston, and the officers generally, with much cordiality. Although, as I have heretofore suggested, the President's Proclamation is far from popular in the Army, a very general feeling of confidence was expressed from the beginning that the Commissioners would give it an interpretation which should satisfy the people of Salt Lake Valley that they had nothing to hope but the sword unless they shall at once yield implicit obedience to the law. The sentiments of these gentlemen, frankly expressed whenever occasion offered, confirmed the conviction that in their hands the flag of the Union was not likely to suffer any degradation. After due inquiry, they fully sustain and approve the policy pursued by General Johnston and Judge Eckel[s], believing that the firm, strong hand, alone, can successfully grapple with the rampant treason which has taken possession of Brigham Young and his deluded followers. Major McCulloch has a reputation as a man of practical common sense, with abundance of nerve and decision. Gov. Powell, Senator-elect from Kentucky, seems to be a good specimen of the genial gentleman and able jurist, and an energetic, determined man, in all emergencies. It is now well understood in Camp that they intend simply to present the President's Proclamation, enforcing it with appeals to their loyalty, telling them at the same time, of the enormity of their crime against the Government, and assuring them of severest retribution if they shall now reject the free pardon tendered them by Mr. Buchanan. It is believed that they will accept no half-way penitence and reform, but will exact full, free and unconditional submission to the Federal authority. It is now ascertained beyond doubt that they have no authority, as they have no disposition, to prevent the Army from pursuing its march into the Valley, and they say that the entrance of the Army is a sine qua non [prerequisite], and will not be yielded upon any consideration.

Quick interviews and snap judgments were the province of not only newly arrived New York reporters. Based on only two days of discussions with Cumming, Johnston, Eckels, and a group of disaffected Mormons fleeing Utah, Powell and McCulloch concluded that Brigham Young had duped the governor. As they saw it, continued, expeditious pressure from the army rather than delay would be the key to their success in dealing with Mormon leaders. The commissioners never mentioned Kane, who had left the scene two weeks earlier. In their first report from Utah, they dismissed his and Cumming's efforts to resolve the conflict with a single sentence: "From information received from [refugee] Mormons and others recently from the City of Salt Lake, we fear that the leaders of the Mormon people have not given the governor correct information as to the condition of affairs in the valley; Governor Cumming having communicated the result of his visit to the Great Salt Lake City to the government we deem it unnecessary to state anything concerning it."[47]

Gone with Thomas L. Kane was nebulous talk of a war-peace split atop the Mormon leadership and the portrayal of Brigham Young as the hidden protector of a vulnerable Utah Expedition. Gone were fur-trimmed finery, splendid outfits, mysterious forays into the wilderness to meet shadowy emissaries, and unprovoked challenges to duel in the snow. What replaced such notions and flourishes amidst consternation over leaked news of a blanket pardon for Utahns, was the commissioners' expression of full confidence in the expedition's commander and support for his determination to move on the Salt Lake Valley: "It affords us pleasure to state that General Johnston most heartily and cordially co-operates with us, and has done everything in his power to facilitate the object of our mission. We find the best order and most cheerful feeling prevail in the command, and that the command have borne the severe trials and difficulties by which they have been surrounded in a manner becoming American soldiers."[48]

On 2 June the commissioners added to their party the ubiquitous Ben Ficklin, former interim U.S. marshal for Utah and Albert Sidney Johnston's winter emissary to the Flatheads. Thus fortified, the president's peace commissioners resumed their trek to Salt Lake City.

I Belong to the Cabinet: "Sisterly" Advice for the President

As McCulloch and Powell moved out, Buchanan's mail brought gratuitous advice and implied criticism from one of his recent houseguests. The president's correspondent was Elizabeth Church Craig, widow of a murdered army

[47]Powell and McCulloch to Floyd, 1 June 1858, "Annual Report of the Sec. of War (1858)," 165–67.
[48]Ibid.

officer and a socially prominent, vivacious beauty from Athens, Georgia. Upon Buchanan's inauguration, Craig signaled Sec. of the Treasury Howell Cobb, her fellow-townsman, that she intended to marry the country's most prominent bachelor. In due course, Cobb and his wife Mary Ann made the introduction. Buchanan was smitten, and during December 1857 he invited Mrs. Craig to move into the White House for an extended stay.

Although initially confessing to Cobb that dreams of Mrs. Craig were disturbing his sleep, by the sixth week of her residence Buchanan grew restless with her forceful political opinions and his suspicions that influence-peddlers were seeking to manipulate her. During this period, the president grew irascible and inattentive. In February 1858, having dubbed him "the Grand Turk," a discouraged Elizabeth Craig returned to Georgia. Wistfully, James Buchanan resumed his bachelor's regimen of Cuban cigars and Old Monongahela with Ambassador Ouseley much as, in a smoky hotel room down the street, Sam Houston and Ben McCulloch did.[49]

The last known correspondence between Mrs. Craig and the president was her letter of 1 June 1858. She filled it not with Houstonesque thoughts of romance but rather with notions of how best to dispatch Brigham Young and the need to do so summarily. Styling herself a member of Buchanan's "Cabinet" and his eternal "Sister," Elizabeth Craig dispensed the sort of draconian advice that Brigham Young long suspected was at the heart of the U.S. government's Mormon policy.

Craig to Buchanan, 1 June 1858, James Buchanan Papers, hsp.

You have been kind enough to listen (on one or two occasions) if not approvingly, at least not reprovingly to some of my plain Georgia talk—This emboldens me to write what I would say had I the power of obtaining the Ear of royalty. This mornings mail brings the news that Brigham Young has ordered his people to retire from their city, and not to fight—I wish, I cannot say hope, that the Mormons will do as they are said to promise. But my "guess" is that it is a rascally put off—a gain time and strength stratagem. They are not, I cannot believe, honest—and if I were the Government Brigham should pay the penalty of traitor before I would listen to terms—I know this may be considered presumption—ignorance, folly, want of charity, blood thirst and all that sort of slang, but I think Brigham's blood would save the blood of probably thousands—and millions of money!

The mean, disgusting scamp, to set at defiance the whole government, burn supplies, murder men, involve the country in untold expenses, and the

[49]Klein, "Bachelor Father," 297–98; Klein, *President James Buchanan*, 217, 285, 333, 436.

> Army in unappreciable hardships, and then when a sufficient force is at his doors, to put him down, become gentle as any sucking dove forsooth, and receive the U S Governor with all respect and honor! Why if a poor Devil chances to open a little mail bag of Uncle Sam's, he is shut up for life—and yet this man may burn hundreds of public wagons, and steal thousands of mules and horses, and murder unoffending travelers, and public officers in the discharge of their duties, and yet peace commissioners are sent to treat with him! Avast I say to any treat with, or any treatment of Brigham Young, but treat of a traitor's halter [noose]![50]
>
> I have not turned politician, but in years gone by I was taught Political Economy—I think it will be capital political economy to hang Brigham and a few of his choice spirits. Political Economy treats of national wealth and I think, if the old scamp had been hung some time since our Government would have found it capital economy—if they do not now lay their hands upon him, they will find it to have been one of the worst pieces of economy which has for a long time been practised. I belong to the Cabinet and think I have a right to give you the benefit of my sage reflections on this subject, and if you deem the reading of them an affliction, you may reflect that you alone have proven me a submissionist and that to me is no pleasant reflection!
>
> With many apologies for intruding upon you yesterday, today, and whenever I do.

As Buchanan had come to understand, the widow Craig spoke for neither the nation nor even the citizens of Athens, where her strong-mindedness had divided a church congregation over a matter (appropriate church music) far more trivial than the life or death of Brigham Young. In early March 1858, as Elizabeth departed the White House, one of her fellow-townsmen wrote Sen. Jefferson Davis to express thanks that Congress had not allowed Buchanan to "bayonet 'them' Mormons." Styling himself "F," Davis's correspondent added the thought that although many people condemned the Latter-day Saints, the Bible did not prohibit polygamy and the constitution protected them.[51]

---

[50]As societal background for the widow Craig's enthusiasm for hanging Brigham Young, see Shuler, *The Thirteenth Turn: A History of the Noose.*

[51]Davis, *The Papers of Jefferson Davis: 1856–1860*, 12 March 1858, 6:566.

Chapter 14

"The Final and Decisive One" The Testing of Alfred Cumming

For once I am and know myself to be happy.

Thomas L. Kane, ca. April 1858

I have reasons to hope that my intercourse with these persons has contributed to allay fears on their part which are perhaps unreasonable. I regret to have been an eye witness however to scenes of great trial & suffering.

Gov. Alfred Cumming to Secretary of State Lewis Cass, 12 May 1858

While the peace commissioners moved west, Governor Cumming and mediator Kane set about their own work, oblivious to the appointment of Powell and McCulloch, as well as the pardon they carried. How Kane and Cumming spent the spring of 1858 is a story of ambiguity, theatrics, and intrigue. For Cumming it was a period of stress, one that tested his independence and strength of character with mixed results.

For the most part, the two men were inseparable. Kane was constantly at the governor's elbow to stage-manage interactions with Brigham Young and appearances before large gatherings of skeptical Latter-day Saints. The two men engaged in fact-finding visits in Salt Lake City, Tooele, and Provo. Kane wrote most of Cumming's letters to Secretary Cass and Colonel Johnston. Brigham Young may have deflected Kane's offer to provide letters and press statements during February–March, but in April–May Alfred Cumming continued to be receptive to such services, so Kane remained his covert draftsman and strategist.

At less stressful times, Cumming was on his own while Kane relaxed, visited friends, read Mormon poetry, and gathered colorful stories for publication. All of this changed abruptly with a blow that struck Kane in early May, one bringing the realization that he belonged at home and back at the White House.

By mid-May there were glimmers of peace, but the war was far from settled, as Brigham Young informed Delegate Bernhisel. Kane was rushing east; Cumming was temporarily back at Fort Bridger; Johnston was combating Mormon accusations of scalp-hunting; Captain Marcy was still en route north; Young pressed on with the Move South; Scott continued to pour reinforcements into Kansas; and Buchanan lusted after Mexico and Cuba while awaiting news from Utah—any news.

The Programme to Be Pursued: Reception Committee

On 13 April Thomas L. Kane had cynically described Alfred Cumming to Brigham Young as a fish that he had caught and delivered to Salt Lake City. How did Young proceed to "cook" him? The record suggests a process of grilling with liberal applications of drawn butter and alcohol. Abel Gilbert, a shrewd non-Mormon observer of LDS ways, predicted the tone of Cumming's initial reception based on Brigham Young's past behavior and whatever Young told him during their time together in Provo and Salt Lake City.

Porter Diary, 9 April 1858, Porter Collection, LC.

> Mr. Gilbert came in today. . . . [he] gives the programme to be pursued when the Gov. gets to S.L.C. He is to be shown his elegant rooms prepared for him two weeks since. On Sunday he will address the people. B. Young will also and ask them who they want as Gov. Of course they answer B.Y. Then he will ask if they will receive him provided the troops are withdrawn. "Yes." The Ex-Gov and the Gov will have a pow-wow, perhaps agree to get the troops withdrawn or delayed, or fly into a passion and say he will make no compromise. He will find out that many want the troops to enter and he may come out here [to Bridger] and ask for an escort to go in with him, of sufficient size to secure protection on his arrival to any one seeking it. I presume however Col Johnston will not agree to it not willing to risk his command in detachments. The Governor cannot insist upon it, or [as] his demands are not obligatory on the Colonel.

The first major issue confronting Cumming was his part in a large meeting of rank-and-file Mormons to be held in the adobe Old Tabernacle on 25

April.[1] At Fort Bridger the governor had told Albert Sidney Johnston that he expected his first mass meeting to be a popular referendum on whether war or peace was to be the next step. As Cumming then expressed it, this would be a gathering to reveal whether the Mormons were indeed in a state of rebellion and if he could govern without military force. Once Cumming arrived, Young ceded the governorship, but only in a superficial sense and in the privacy of the Staines mansion. The pending session in the Tabernacle was intended to introduce (but not endorse) Cumming to the people he hoped to govern while doing what later marketeers would call "sell himself."

Beneath this veneer of civility lay Brigham Young's intent to throw another unwelcome visitor to the lions. The Tabernacle session was an early opportunity to test and bloody Cumming in hopes of driving him out, or at least bring him to realize Young would continue to rule, if not govern. As Abel Gilbert knew, Young was a consummate manager of such public meetings, staging them to intimidate as well as communicate.

How would a Mormon audience react to Cumming's appearance and demeanor? It was an important matter, impacting as it did Utahns' willingness to accept him as Brigham Young's gubernatorial successor. At age 56 Young was becoming portly, but Cumming, a year younger, was grossly so. Inevitably, Mormon comments ran to Cumming's girth and its presumed connection to his alcohol intake.

Apostle George A. Smith, a heavy man in his own right, initially had mixed reactions to Cumming's weight and presumed drinking habits when he met him on 13 April. Eight months later, Smith downgraded this view: "Gov. Cumming is tub built, so that he seldom can get liquor enough aboard but that he can carry it. At times, he may not be inaptly compared to a whiskey barrel in the morning, and a barrel of whiskey at night; his memory is frequently at fault in consequence of his inebriety; he is evidently the most generous, whole hearted & upright man of all the officers sent to Utah."[2]

Feminist Hannah Keziah Clapp interviewed the governor while passing through Salt Lake immediately after the Utah War. Wearing bloomers and sporting a revolver, the formidable Miss Clapp took Cumming's measure and bluntly labeled him "a superannuated, brandy-soaked, Buchanan

[1]Not to be confused with the larger turtle-shaped Salt Lake Tabernacle, which was completed in the 1860s and still used.

[2]Smith, Church Historian's Office Journal, 13 April 1858 and 1 January 1859, LDS Archives.

Democrat."[3] In early July 1858 an unidentified non-Mormon resident of Salt Lake City complained to the *New York Times* that "the common epithet applied by Mormons to Gov. Cumming is 'old swill tub' and they boast of having him constantly intoxicated. . . . such I feel grieved to hear is the way they are able to speak of a man like Gov. Cumming."[4]

Aside from an unimpressive appearance, Cumming had to deal with two other negatives: Utahns' belief that he was a Missourian and lingering reactions to his choice of words five months earlier. Cumming was the scion of a prominent Georgia family; in all likelihood, the misconception about his background arose from either Cumming's immediately prior service as U.S. superintendent of Indian Affairs for the Upper Missouri River agency based in St. Louis, or confusion over his name and that of R. W. Cummins, a Mormon persecutor in Missouri.[5] As soon as news of Cumming's appointment reached Utah during the summer of 1857, reference to him as a "Missouri ass" had appeared in one of the endless verses of "Doo-Dah," the Mormon war song composed and set to the music of Stephen A. Foster's "Camptown Races" to ridicule the Utah Expedition. Identification with Missouri was no small matter in Utah. After the Mountain Meadows massacre, Mormons justified the atrocity in part with the specious argument that the victims, a wagon train of Arkansans, included a substantial number of errant "Missouri Wildcats." For Alfred Cumming's skeptical audience on 25 April, perceptions of a Missouri background were an unfortunate liability from which few men could recover.

Cumming's second hurdle was a self-inflicted wound: the text of the 21 November proclamation by which, from the distance of the army encampment at Fort Bridger, he assumed Utah's governorship. In this document Cumming used terms such as "rebellion," "traitorous acts," and "treason."[6] The proclamation offended Cumming's new constituents when issued and still rankled five months later. In the spring of 1858, his perception of Utahns was far less skeptical than earlier, thanks to more than a month of exposure

[3]Clapp to unidentified friend, 17 July 1859, *Lansing Republican*, 6 September 1859, in Holmes, ed., *Covered Wagon Women*, 7:249.

[4]"A Citizen of Utah," Salt Lake City, 9 July 1858, "The Mormons. Interesting Letter from Utah. Interior View of Mormonism," *New York Times*, 10 August 1858, 1/3–4.

[5]Walker, Turley, and Leonard, *Massacre at Mountain Meadows*, 38.

[6]Cumming, "To the People of Utah Territory," 21 November 1857. Even stiffer accusations appeared in the letter by which Cumming transmitted this proclamation to "ex-governor" Young. "The Utah Expedition," House Exec. Doc. 71, Serial 956, 91–92.

to Kane's influence. Nevertheless, what came back to haunt Cumming in the Tabernacle on 25 April were the words of his November proclamation.

More Frenzy Than I Had Expected: Cumming Takes the Stand

Precisely how Alfred Cumming came to join Young's party on the Tabernacle stand is murky. The only known explanation is a highly egocentric one developed by Kane for his brother Pat and intended for publication. Although problematic, Kane's explanation, at bare minimum, provides a glimpse of his need to control the governor's introduction to Mormon society: "I was with him at every moment. But a lie in this morning's [Philadelphia] paper about the meeting at the Tabernacle makes me repeat that I was there with him also. I suggested that he should request to be allowed to speak there and give publicity to my (his) proclamations. The leave was granted as a favor to me. I was with him, arranged matters perfectly for his escape in case the joke was carried too far."[7]

Some attendees were obvious Brigham Young plants. How many others in the audience knew in advance that Cumming would speak is unknown. When the meeting started, he was not on the stand. An unidentified diarist noted, "Brother Brigham began to speak but was soon called away to the vestry. After a while he came forth with Mr. Alfred Cumming and introduced him to the congregation. The new Governor Mr. Alfred Cumming began to speak unto us." Cumming estimated "between three and four thousand persons were assembled for the purpose of public worship; the hall was crowded to overflowing." He reported to Secretary Cass "the most profound quiet was observed when I appeared. President Brigham Young introduced me by name as the governor of Utah, and I addressed the audience from 'the stand.'"[8] The raw, unpublished notes taken by a relay of Young's stenographic reporters provide a fascinating glimpse into what Alfred Cumming, Brigham Young, and several other speakers said during the day's morning and afternoon sessions.[9]

---

[7]Kane to Pat Kane, ca. summer 1858, "In Re Mormons" File, Thomas Leiper Kane Papers, APS. Thomas's reference to "the joke" implies his participation in stage-managing by Brigham Young.

[8]Van Wagoner, ed., *Complete Discourses of Brigham Young*, 3:1427; Cumming to Cass, 2 May 1858, "Annual Report of the Sec. of War (1858)," 95. There is no indication that Young also introduced Kane.

[9]In addition to this material, there are useful accounts left as letters and diary entries by attendees, especially Kenney, ed., *Wilford Woodruff's Journal*, 25 April 1858, 5:183–84. Kane generated several pages of jumbled notes that are in some respects more detailed but less reliable than those of Young's skilled stenographers. See box 14, fd. 16, item 1, Kane Family Papers, BYU.

Remarks in the Salt Lake Tabernacle, 25 April 1858, by Gov. Alfred Cumming, Apostle John Taylor, and Pres. Brigham Young, Brigham Young Collection, Letterbook 4, 153–88, LDS Archives.

Governor Cumming

I feel rejoiced, my friends, at this opportunity, which has been presented of meeting you face to face. I have but a few words to state to you. I have been sent by the President of the United States, with the consent of the Senate to be the Governor of this Territory. It is a source of pleasure to me that I have the pleasure of the friendship of this gentleman that has introduced me to this stand.

I am not ignorant of the gross misrepresentation that has been made by the enemies of this people with regard to you.

It is true that upon your frontiers there are a large number of armed men. I will say to you in the presence of these gentlemen, that this force is not sent for any aggression upon the Mormon people, but for their protection; remember what I say, protection against the lawless savage that has been committing depredations upon you from time to time.[10]

I come here ladies & gentlemen, but I am not an orator. I am not an educated man, and therefore cannot address you as such a man.[11] I expect to long remain with you, therefore misrepresentation would be a foolish course. I came here with the instructions to enforce obedience to the laws and powers of our common country, and this duty I will endeavor to perform temperately, and I intend to perform it strictly and to regard the law as supreme. I feel assured that I shall have the aid & co-operation of the men and women that now surround me, and that they will be willing to maintain the constitution of our common country.

You are a Territory of the United States, and there appears to have been something that has been very obnoxious to the Government, as well as some things that have been obnoxious to you; but it is common usage that the officers of Territories are sent by the President of the United States, with the consent of the Senate. I hope that you will soon be formed in the grand galaxy as an entirely independent state.

The enforcement of the law is my first duty in this Territory, and the other is, that I am to prevent the perversion of the law. It has been said

[10]For Cumming to describe the Utah Expedition's prime mission as Indian control opened him to ridicule, as it did Buchanan when he offered the same explanation. *At Sword's Point, Part 1,* 133–34.

[11]Cumming did not attend college, but his education below that level was a good one in the private academies of the South.

that those who have been in this country, have perverted the law when they should have been the fulfillers of it. This I trust, will not take place under my administration. I shall in all matters connected with my future course which I deem it necessary to pursue, consult with such gentlemen as have enjoyed, hitherto your confidence.

It is not necessary, I presume, believing, that there is not one person in this society, that need me to say, that I or the government officers who have come here or those who may be sent have nothing to do with your social habits; nothing whatever to do with your religious opinions, or the manner in which you try to serve God.[12] God is above all. He will try your hearts as well as others. But let no vain man throw an obstacle in the way of that great power.

I desire then having said these few words, to leave the matter for your consideration. I shall be cheered by the acquaintance of the strangers with whom I expect to associate and I hope that we shall be friendly together. I do not expect a path of roses, and I do not expect to attain a victory without a trial. I expect some office seeking demagogue will try to influence men's minds to thwart me in my holy work. I say fear God, & think of him when you try to thwart a good man.

I may not know you all personally, but if I ever err in my administration do not say "that old man has come with views different to ours, & we will treat him as he deserves."

I desire, friends, that you will come and counsel me. I shall not be obstinate, and it will be with the utmost pleasure that I shall receive you.

I shall endeavor to enforce the laws of the constitution of the United States. I will now close that subject.

I will now say a few words upon another subject. It has been represented to me that certain persons in the Territory of Utah have been restrained of their liberty, & would go away but cannot. To all such persons I would say it is my official duty to see that they shall not be restrained. If such persons will make an application to me properly I will enquire into the nature of their cases. I am satisfied that no good man would desire to detain any such persons in their society, & especially among so very intellectual & highly eminently religious people. . . .

To the women of this Territory I would say that I desire to be assisted with the women. My youth has passed & I cannot be expected to have the same intentions as younger men, but I trust that I shall find & meet none but friends in the common circles of life.

---

[12]With an awareness in Salt Lake City that on 5 April Judge Eckels had charged a federal grand jury with examining plural marriage, Cumming's assurance damaged his credibility.

There is a communication which I desire to have read, & then for the present I will close my remarks. (Leo Hawkins then read a notice signed Alfred Cumming &c.)[13]

My friends I am unwillingly placed on the stand before you for the purpose of asking, if there are any persons present who have wishes to present that I may wish to know. A cool dispassionate way is the only way we can get at an expression of public feeling, this is what I desire.

I desire this people to understand that I am not here to represent that miserable set of office seekers who are constantly prowling round the administration, neither am I here to have an office which I declined through diffidence & an idea of my incapacity to fill it, but I would desire and should be pleased that this congregation should by some kind of expression express their feeling of approval of my coming here in the way I have. I have come here on my own responsibility, as a self constituted commissioner believing that I should be protected. . . .

Apostle Taylor

These are strange occurrences to be taking place in our midst, here on the Sabbath day, when we have met to worship God; they are rather new in our history. However, there is very frequently something new associated with Mormonism and when we must receive as among the current scenes that are transpiring, as we pass along through this stage of existence. . . .

In relation to Governor Cumming; I know nothing about the gentleman, but I should be glad to see him courteously treated as I would every other gentleman, while he remains here. In relation to the difference of sentiment between us and him, I would say that notwithstanding that we wish to treat all men as gentlemen while they are with us, & we wish to entertain no other feeling, if we can be met on honourable terms by religious or political gentlemen. When we can do this we are ready, & we never should be found taking up arms, except our most sacred rights were infringed upon. . . .

If we had been disposed for war & bloodshed, could we not have easily cut off all supplies? Why they came straggling along in the most miserable condition. Some have said that we have been disposed to plunder & that we have taken their cattle. What have we done it for? To weaken their forces & spare their lives! For as sure as God lives if they had come a little farther they would have been dead men; & if it had not been for Govr. Young, as

[13]Hawkins was one of Young's clerks and stenographic reporters. He read: "NOTICE: It has been reported to me that there are persons residing in this and in other parts of the Territory who are illegally restrained of their liberty. It is therefore proper that I should announce that I assume the protection of all such persons, if any there be, and request that they will communicate to me their names and places of residence, under seal, through Mr. Fay Worthen, or to me in person during my stay in the city." Cumming to Cass, 2 May 1858, "Annual Report of the Sec. of War (1858)," 94.

it was they would have been dead men, & your entire army, sir, would now have been sleeping the sleep of death! He felt as a Governor should feel, & he felt that the man who had been elected to the highest office in the United States [Buchanan] had led a few ignorant men to intrude upon our rights! If they had been our enemies, who have from time to time abused us, there would not have been one left to tell the tale! No, sir, not one! . . .

Govr. Young looked upon this & felt it, and said shall we take their [soldiers'] lives because they are placed in this position by a miserable man the representative of this nation? No, says he, we will save them! What was the difficulty he had to cope with? It was the feelings of the people whose rights have been so often trampled upon. Hold on said he! Hold on said Genl. Wells, spare their lives! That is the crime that he has been guilty of. (Govr. Young: and for that they would hang me.) We had men playing around them & laughing at their imbecility & I have seen the officers come up to Genl. Wells, & say in the name of God, why wont you let us loose on those men, we will cut them off! But the time had not come, but when it does come it will spread fire & desolation wherever it goes! We are free, & we will be free! (Voices: hear hear.)[14]

Talk about an Army coming for peace; it is nonsense to think of such a thing. Govr. Cumming, we speak frankly here, & we believe there is something under that white heap,[15] something that is perfectly understood by us, & it is sung from Maine to Missouri and from Louisianna to Wisconsin, "Destroy them from the earth." (Govr. Young: Do not be so personal in your remarks.) I do not wish for any discussion, but permit me to say with all defference to Govr. Cumming.—for I have been a stranger in strange places, & I do not wish to be personal—I do not wish to inflict a wound upon any person's feelings who is a stranger. I do not want any circumlocution neither do I want to evade anything. . . . If the representatives of any other Territory of the United States with the consent of the whole people had petitioned Prest. Buchanan, and given him four or five different names for every office, I very much question but what the President would have given them their choice. Do not you think so? (Govr. Cumming: I think that prejudices have arisen against you, & I have come to disband them.) In relation to this matter I have no doubt you are right, respecting the prejudice. . . . And now with all this knowledge [of Mormon persecution in Missouri]

[14]These remarks by Taylor, who held no military rank, would have reinforced Kane's perception of a war-peace split among Utah's leaders.

[15]In "The Cat and the Old Rat," a story in the school books of generations of English and American children, a wily rat spotted a cat who had rolled herself in flour to hide in the meal barrel: "I don't much like, said he, that white heap yonder; something whispers me there is mischief concealed under it." William Scott, *An Introduction to Reading and Spelling* (1803), 42. The phrase, a favorite of Taylor's, found its way into the Utah legislative assembly's January 1858 memorial to the president and Congress.

they have appointed as a Governor from the state from whence we were driven, & most inhumanly treated (Govr. Cumming: I am a Georgian Sir, I am Georgian; I was only there holding a civil office.) The gentleman says he is a Georgian, & I am glad of it. (voices: hear hear.) but still these things took place in the state of Missouri, and were not these things known to the United States government? . . .

The catechism is very straight gentlemen, but Govr. Young is desirous that I should not go into these matters & they are truly very painful to reflect upon.

We will come to things of a more recent date. We do not wish to act impolitely or through passion, but is it not a well known fact that in every other state and Territory they have given grants of pre-emption [and permitted homesteading by settlers]? (Govr. Cumming: the Indian title [to land in Utah] has not been extinguished here.) Why has not the Indian title been extinguished here? Because, we are Mormons. . . .

(Govr. Cumming: I am desirous that the people should know that preliminary to all Indian treaties it is customary to have the surveys of all Territories. There have been reports circulated against you, but I have not come prejudiced, neither have I come Mormon, but I come here to enquire into your condition, and what do I find? I find the records of the Courts in a perfect condition. I find them all. As a self constituted commissioner by virtue of my office I have come to enquire into all these matters. Then let us get rid of all feeling of excitement. . . .

I have come for the purpose of doing good, and when the darkness comes, or if I find that I am not wanted, I shall not be found loafing about. I have come with the expectation of making my home here; my wife has come with me, my children are dead. I come not as a traveler, but I come to stay among you, & to have an interest with you, and I am pleased to hear from you and to learn that I am the Governor, of a honorable constituency who know their rights and who are willing and ready to maintain them.)

Elder Taylor resumed. As it is about time to dismiss our meeting, I will not detain you with many more remarks, but there is one thing I will say, *those troops must be withdrawn before we can have any officers palmed upon us!* (Thousands of voices responded, hear hear.)

Govr. Cumming wished to hear from the ladies whereupon one arose in the congregation[16] and said: I wish to bear my testimony to the liberty I have enjoyed in this Territory. I gathered with this people to Nauvoo, and then I moved with the Church to this city, and since then I have been twice back to visit my family in the states; I have gone there and returned at my pleasure and I have enjoyed all the liberty that I could desire or wish for, and I know that all other ladies enjoy as much liberty as I do, and in fact I have known nothing but liberty since I have been here.

---

[16]This was Augusta Adams Cobb Young, a plural wife of Brigham Young.

Govr. Cumming said: I am rejoiced to have the opportunity of hearing from the lady who has just spoken, and I am glad to know that she and the ladies here are satisfied with the liberty they enjoy in this Territory; and I will repeat again that the remarks I have made are not to make contention, but only for the purpose of guaranteeing a fair privilege to the people & to show that they have the opportunity of going away and if any persons feel disposed to address themselves to me, or to Govr. Young they can do so. I do not wish to control the matter. I hope that after the somewhat unaccustomed excitement we shall be prepared to retire to our homes, there to await till our new duties call us away again.

I presume my place of residence [the Staines mansion] is known to most of you, if it is not you can learn it from the gentlemen who are here, and you can come not under any excitement, nor under the influence of passion. . . .

Governor Cumming and Gilbert Clements[17]

After the speech of Mr. Clements; Gov. Cumming said: I would appeal to the gentleman who has addressed this congregation with such skill and evident ability, as must have been apparent to all: I would appeal to him with regard to one thing, and request that he will state to this people that no digression has attempted to be performed by the government to the exclusion of the rights of this people with those of other Territories. If the gentleman has heard what I have said, he will make the response, whether there has been any digression or not, or whether this has been the same as with all the Territories.

Mr. Clements replied: In answer to His Excellency, I would respectfully say, that for years there has been a manifest difference on the part of the Government towards us and the people of other Territories. . . .

Gov. Cumming said: May I take the [*illegible*] passing upon that gentleman's time (Voice, don't be angry.) I am not angry, but I wish to consider things coolly and dispassionately. I have not the pleasure of your name, Sir, but I wish to ask, whether there has been any digression in regard to this Territory and other Territories of the United States. (Voice: Yes, there has.) . . .

Gov. Cumming remarked: . . . I have come here to carefully investigate this matter. One gentleman gives me a suggestion to keep my temper, which I trust I shall always do. I have come here with no assurance of being treated well, but I come believing in your intelligence, and that I should be protected. I met some [Nauvoo Legion] gentlemen on the way [in from Bridger], and was treated courteously by them, (Voice, why didn't you come last fall?) but now I am here, and you have me for what I am. I can appeal to gentlemen, whose names are revered by you, when I say, that I have a desire for the promotion

[17]Clements, an accomplished Mormon debater and Brigham Young plant, spoke at greater length than Cumming, Taylor, and Young combined to rehash the long litany of Mormon complaints about treatment at the hands of the U.S. government. Only the repartee between Cumming and Clements is presented here.

and the independence of a people who have dared to strike for liberty such as is guaranteed by the constitution and the laws which emanate from it.

I do not desire to come as an interloper. I come here direct from the source of power; and I am not for the bayonets that come to enforce your respect. I trust I shall yet live to see the day, as old as I am, when I shall be glad to remember the day I first met with you. If you do not believe me to be the man that I say I am, the time may not be far remote when one not much better may be sent here, and in fact, I am assured that such will be the case, provided another should have to be appointed in my stead. I know my own heart, but I know not what may be upon the hearts of others. As to the dictation which this gentleman alludes to he knows as to the peculiar mode in which I should be received, if I were to transcend my limits. Should any unpleasantness arise during my administration, then let me be judged by my acts, and if I am then condemned let me be invited here, and have a plain, open enquiry about my conduct, and I promise that I will not be found a ragged thing hanging about your skirts when you do not want me any longer.

With these feelings I trust I shall be received as a friend.

Mr. Clements replied: I am sorry your Excellency does not understand me, for I have already stated a number of instances in which Utah has been treated differently from other Territories. . . .

President Young

I do not arise to discuss any subject, and the circumstances that brother Taylor was inclined to bring before the people I do not wish to hear them myself, and I know there are a great many here that do not, for we have already seen too much of such scenes.

I want to make statement with regard to officers of Territories. It has been the custom for the President of the United States to appoint Territorial officers, such as Governor, three Judges, Attorney, and Marshal for each Territory, and Indian Agents for the States and Territories. I wish to answer a query that will arise in the minds of the people with regard to Utah being treated different from any other Territory by saying, I presume that there never was a Territory that made choice of their officers but this Territory, or that suggested any thing of the kind to the General Government.

When a new Territory is commenced we see broken down politicians flocking to that Territory seeking for office under the Territorial government, hoping yet to gain the high honor of being appointed representative of that people in Congress. This is generally the case as we have witnessed with regard to the officers for this Territory.[18] I shall close my remarks on this point by making one statement: We have requested the General Government to appoint men

[18]Some of the first federal appointees for Utah were Mormons, including Young. Among the non-Mormons was Associate Justice Perry E. Brocchus of Alabama, who traveled to Utah in 1851 with the unrealistic ambition of being elected her first delegate to Congress.

> of our own choice to be the dispensers of the law in this Territory. This is perfectly legal; it is our right, no doubt. The United States government in its several departments has taken the liberty to pick up men who are unacquainted with us, without giving us a voice in the selection of any officer whatever. . . .
>
> It is late, and time to bring our meeting to a close. I have felt a little mortified to see so much enthusiasm manifested. I would like to see men and women cool, and not become excited upon any subject. I will take the liberty to say to my friend Governor Cumming that he may be ensured, and so may everybody, that had it not been for the influence I have over this people, it is not for me to say where the United States army now within our borders would have been this day. I have used my powers of reason, and my influence to teach the people not to do that [what] they believed to be their imperative duty. I look forward in hope that all matters will be amicably adjusted, and we shall be in peace here. It is true the people are moving, the reason of which I can explain before the congregation, or to any gentleman at any time. They are removing, and will continue to move—the result [only] God knows. . . .
>
> You have heard a Note read here from Gov. Cumming concerning persons who feel themselves restrained in the exercise of their liberties; who wish more liberty, and to withdraw from this community. What have I said to you? Have I not told you all the day long that we would help you away. If there are any such here who want protection at the hands of Governor Cumming, men or women, will you have the kindness to be manly enough, to manifest it here—if there are those here who feel to withdraw from this community, and who feel restrained in their liberty—by a show of hands. (Four persons showed hands, two of whom were not [members] in the church.)

Why did this meeting change from what it could have been—a crude display of intimidation designed to drive Cumming east—to a raucous, orchestrated debate that left Utah's new governor bruised but still standing? The answer lies with the platform demeanor of both Cumming and Young and the impact of several incidents immediately preceding the 25 April session.

On his feet, Cumming was empathetic, flexible, self-effacing, and willing to admit governmental errors, as when he criticized Buchanan's patronage system and the character of federal office seekers. He did so without giving ground on his main mission—restoration of federal authority, and handled adroitly the unexpected subject of travel restrictions on those seeking to leave the territory. Cumming was neither defensive nor combative. His flare of protest in rejecting John Taylor's characterization of him as a Missourian and other provocations from the floor played well with his audience. Cumming seems to have held his own in repartee, although he had no credible response to several of Gilbert Clements's complaints about preemption and executive appointments. Notwithstanding what must have been an unpresupposing platform presence, Cumming displayed courage, humility, grit, and determination. For this the audience gave him credit but not acceptance.

For his part, Brigham Young repeated the long, familiar litany of Mormon grievances, but, importantly, he leavened it with civility rather than stoking the anger smoldering in the audience. It could have been otherwise. Young did so by admonishing a combative John Taylor during both morning and afternoon sessions, while urging the audience to be "cool, and not become excited upon any subject."[19] Surely those present also noted Young's reference to his gubernatorial successor as "my friend" as well as his grudging willingness to cede Cumming a role in facilitating the departure of disaffected Utahns. This reversal of his earlier prohibition on such exits was stunning if taken at face value. Unquestionably impacting Young's platform behavior was his awareness that 113 miles to the east Cumming had the support of the greatest concentration of military power in North America. The meeting dynamics and outcome were far different than those involving Young's public interactions with Judge Brocchus six years earlier.

Kane was delighted with the meeting and told Pat Kane, "Brigham Young behaved splendidly—not merely like a gentleman, but like a Christian—on that as on every other occasion."[20] Governor Cumming emerged from the session in a positive mood, but the ferocity of his audience and its continuing commitment to the Move South shook him. A Nauvoo Legion major in the audience concluded, "A. Cumming would be Gove[r]nor of U.T. if he could be. Was present and addressed us but learned from an expression of the people that he was not our choice and we did not want him."[21]

---

[19]One could argue that this Young-Taylor by-play was prearranged as what today is called the good cop/bad cop technique. Wilford Woodruff seemed not to have perceived staging, commenting that "John Taylor followed [as a speaker] but being vary hard and personal to Mr Cumings was Stoped by President Young." Kenney, ed., *Wilford Woodruff's Journal*, 25 April 1858, 5:184. In 1873 T. B. H. Stenhouse described Cumming's later thoughts about the 25 April meeting: "The proceedings in the Tabernacle were all an understood [arranged] thing. . . . Brigham was seated beside the Governor on the platform, and tried to control the unruly spirits who were clamorous for their 'rights.' Governor Cumming may for the moment have been deceived by this apparent division among the Mormons, but three years later he told the Author that it was all of a piece with the incidents of his passage [with Kane] through Echo Canon. He fully comprehended it. In his characteristic brusque way he said: 'It was all humbug, sir; all humbug; but never mind, it is all over now. If it did them good, it did not hurt me. Brigham Young is a smart man—smart man, but he may yet find out that other people are not so blind as he may think they are. Smart man! But he doesn't know everything.'" Stenhouse, *Rocky Mountain Saints*, 392–93.

[20]Kane to Pat Kane, ca. summer 1858, "In Re Mormons" File, Thomas Leiper Kane Papers, APS.

[21]J. D. T. McAllister, Journal No. 2, 25 April 1858, LDS Archives.

Precursor to the Tabernacle: The Backstory of 24 April

Crucial to shaping the performance of Young and Cumming that Sunday was the positive impact of a discussion between them the previous day. Young was in Provo on Saturday and, in anticipation of the next day's Tabernacle sessions, started north at 5:00 A.M. on 24 April with First Counselor Heber C. Kimball. Despite the fatigue of this eight-hour trip, an hour after reaching Salt Lake City, Young met with Cumming and Kane. In this session the men presumably discussed some combination of their plans for the future, the status of the Move South, likely moves by the Utah Expedition, and perhaps the disposition of Cumming's intent to travel to southern Utah to inquire about Mountain Meadows.

Cumming had made known in some way that he wanted to make such a trip. With the deaths of 120 massacre victims uninvestigated and unexplained, this prospect had potentially catastrophic implications for Mormon leaders, prompting General Wells to alert Young to it on the 24th. Wells did so while linking such an investigation to his concerns about a possible assassination attempt on the new governor.

Wells to Young, 24 April 1858, LDS Archives.

> Mr Governor A Cumming returned yesterday, and intends leaving for the south Monday. They are intending to investigate the Mountain Meadows affair and will I expect go as far as Harmony. Bro Wm H. Kimball and David Candland are preparing to accompany them. He wants Brigham [Jr.] and Stephen [Taylor] to go as guard to which I consented if you was willing, they will see you and stop at Provo if you prefer for them not to go. The boys dont any of them feel much like going but he must be cared for while he remains in our midst for it would be entirely to[o] responsible a concern to go down on our hands, and I feel as though it is rather risky to let him stay so long, and hope that his life is insured long enough to last him back to camp.

Wells's note was one of the rare written references to the massacre during this period by a senior leader. Surely it added to Brigham Young's sense of beleaguerment. According to historian Ronald W. Walker, the letter's impact motivated Young to seek an understanding with Cumming by which he would delay, if not abandon, his trip to Harmony to probe the Mountain Meadows "affair." Because Wells wrote from Salt Lake City, he sent his message to Young in Provo by Legion courier. With Young having left that town at dawn, it is unlikely that he saw Wells's message before meeting with Kane and Cumming that afternoon, unless, of course, the courier had accosted him on the road. There is no record of such an interaction. Walker's assessment is directionally correct with respect to the likely alarm that Wells's note would have triggered, but it is questionable whether the general's alert reached Young in time to influence his fateful discussion with Cumming almost immediately after reaching Salt Lake City.[22]

For his part Cumming came to this meeting of the 24th influenced by not only weeks of exposure to Kane's point of view but the more recent investigatory process in which the two men engaged once in Salt Lake City. In rummaging through deserted offices, desks, and crates in mid-April, Cumming satisfied himself—but not all historians—that the territorial law library, federal district court records, and Utah's official seal were intact and available. He also drew a bead on the likely whereabouts of the U.S. surveyor general's important field notes, office records, and survey instruments. In further pursuit of facts about Utah's tangled land surveys, the governor and Kane travelled to Tooele and other locations, where they interviewed the territorial surveyor, Jesse Fox, as well as settlers with strong opinions as to the corruption and inefficiency of the federal land surveys done in Utah since 1855 under David H. Burr's supervision.[23] All of these findings shaped Cumming's disposition while vastly relieving Brigham Young by calling into question the validity of some of the accusations of rebellion swirling around his gubernatorial stewardship.

Of more visceral impact on Cumming was the sight of ill-clad refugees streaming south through Salt Lake City and every hamlet that he and Kane visited. On 24 April Apostle Wilford Woodruff commented, "when A Cummings got to Toille [Tooele] City On his way to Rush valley [during 21 April] he found all the people Moveing. He said My God have I Come to late to stop all this moving and burning of property? I must stop the burning some how."[24]

[22]Walker, *Heroes and Hero Worship*; Walker to MacKinnon, e-mail message, 4 February 2015. Walker's co-author for *Massacre at Mountain Meadows*, Richard E. Turley Jr., is persuaded by this theory and believes that Cumming cancelled his southern trip not because of an understanding reached on 24 April but rather because of the turmoil following Cumming's 25 April platform performance in the Old Tabernacle and Kane's unwillingness to travel south with him after learning of his father's death on 5 May. Turley notes that Cumming did indeed send Indian superintendent Jacob Forney on a fact-finding trip to southern Utah as his proxy, but this was not until 1859. Turley to MacKinnon, e-mail message, 5 February 2015.

[23]Cumming to Cass, 2 May 1858, "Annual Report of the Sec. of War (1858)," 93–94; Kane, "Diary II (1858)," undated entries, 10, 11, 13–14, and 16. Kane recorded these trips with the light-hearted notation "Vamosed the Ranch."

[24]Kenney, ed., *Wilford Woodruff's Journal*, 24 April 1858, 5:183. Strangely for a humanitarian, Kane's diary is silent about the misery of the Move South. At Tooele, where Cumming became distressed, Kane focused on

Also disturbing to Cumming was his first awareness of a problem involving not the Mormon faithful but the religion's disaffected: "On the morning of the 24th instant [ultimo] information was communicated to me that a number of persons who were desirous of leaving the Territory were unable to do so, and considered themselves to be unlawfully restrained of their liberty. However desirous of conciliating popular opinion, I felt it incumbent upon me to adopt the most energetic measures to ascertain the truth or falsehood of this statement. Postponing, therefore, a journey of importance, which I had in contemplation, to one of the settlements of Utah county [Provo], I caused public notice to be given immediately of my readiness to relieve all persons who were or deemed themselves to be aggrieved."[25]

With these influences as background, the 24 April discussion between Young, Cumming, and Kane unfolded in a positive way, resulting in an accommodation of sorts. Young apparently accepted Cumming's presence as a *fait accompli* and, in return, received assurances from the new governor that he would not attack polygamy. Whether there was a quid pro quo at that time about investigating Mountain Meadows is problematic. Young concluded that Alfred Cumming was a governor with whom he could in some way partner and even dominate. A highly insecure Cumming, who craved acceptance and warmed to flattery, sensed a level of respect and receptivity not evident during their previous meetings.[26] Triumphantly, Kane described this session in his diary as "the final and decisive one."[27]

That evening, Brigham Young met with Mormon leaders in his office to discuss the Fort Limhi affair, progress of the White Mountain Expedition, and army intentions. It is unlikely that he shared the decisions he had made with Cumming and Kane that afternoon, since Wilford Woodruff did not mention them in his usually comprehensive journal. During this session Young received word that Judge Kane had died in Philadelphia on 21 February.[28] For

trivia such as the features of the Lee home in which they lodged. Kane, "Diary II (1858)," undated entry, 14–15. As he left Utah, Kane made a single brief allusion to the migration. Kane to Young, 12 May 1858, LDS Archives.

[25]Cumming to Cass, 2 May 1858, "Annual Report of the Sec. of War (1858)," 94. This was another humanitarian issue with which Kane chose not to concern himself.

[26]Preservation of his dignity and an appropriate militia escort of "his troops"—from the Nauvoo Legion—had been prerequisites to Cumming's agreement to accompany Kane to Salt Lake City. Once there, the Legion laid on ceremonial pomp, as described by Kane: "[Gen. W. H.] Kimball and [Col. R. T.] Burton &c handsome in uniform. The Cavalry came in—1st Regiment (Cavalry)—300 in. The General (of Brigade) and Col. Burton of 1st Regiment, with Adjutant General Ferguson waited on Gov. Cumming in citizens (mountaineer) dress this Evening." Kane, "Diary II (1858)," 20 April 1858, 11.

[27]Ibid., undated entry, 17.

[28]Kenney, ed., *Wilford Woodruff's Journal*, 24 April 1858, 5:183.

whatever reasons, rather than communicate this bad news to the judge's son immediately, Young withheld it for eleven days. It was an important, deliberate manipulation of which Tom Kane and his family were never aware.[29]

And so the next morning Alfred Cumming and his host, Brigham Young, took to the Tabernacle's stand with dramatic results. That evening at a private devotional gathering, Young sent an optimistic signal to his colleagues. He did so through a seemingly mundane aside recorded by Apostle Woodruff: "He said I told Hiram [Clawson?] to make some thin boxes and put my windows in. Mark them so we may know whare they go for I should not think [it] strange if we used them in the same place."[30]

An Occasion of Intense Interest: Beginning of the End

A week after the Tabernacle meeting, Kane drafted and Cumming signed a long status report to Secretary Cass. What drove the timing of this document was their acute awareness that much had happened since Cumming had last written on 15 April. Kane had sent no word to the president since his last dispatch from Eckelsville on 4 April. Aside from matters of timeliness, Cumming was alarmed by the appalling hardships created by the Move South and the implications of a 25 April comment attributed to Brigham Young but not made in his presence: "I have a good mind to tell a secret here; I believe I will tell it any how; they say there is a fine country down south there; Sonora is it, is that your name for it? Do not speak of this out of doors if you please."[31]

Understanding how Governor Cumming represented his Tabernacle experience to the Buchanan administration is important to assessing what occurred during that meeting and under what circumstances. At bare

[29]The most recent analysts of this incident argue that what Young heard at this 24 April strategy meeting in his office were rumors of Judge Kane's death, the implication being that he delayed informing Kane's son until 5 May, when confirmation of the event arrived in Salt Lake City. Apostle Woodruff, who attended the meeting, recorded that "a report" of the judge's passing had been received without adding a qualifier as to the credibility of this news. Grow and Walker, *The Prophet and the Reformer*, 260.

[30]Kenney, ed., *Wilford Woodruff's Journal*, 25 April 1858, 184.

[31]Cumming to Cass, 2 May 1858, "Annual Report of the Sec. of War (1858)," 96. The unedited transcriptions generated by Young's reporters did not include this remark. George A. Smith recorded that the comment was made not in the Tabernacle, as Cumming later implied, but in the small inner circle that met that evening: "P.M. Prest Young said he would tell the people a secret; if they would keep it, that was, that there was a fine country in the north of Mexico. He said it that Cumming might here [*sic*] of it (it was taken to him before night)." Church Historian's Office Journal, 25 April 1858, LDS Archives.

minimum Cumming's dispatch of 2 May, excerpted in draft form below, conveys a sense of Mormon emotion and anger—undiminished in Kane's and the governor's memory a week after the event. It was a tone largely missing from the antiseptic phrasing of Young's stenographic reporters.

Cumming to Cass, 2 May 1858,
Draft, Kane Family Papers, BYU.

... My presence at this meeting in the Tabernacle will be remembered by me as an occasion of intense interest. ...

In a discourse of about forty minutes duration, I touched (as I thought best) *~~boldly~~* boldly upon all the leading questions at issue between them and the General Government. ...

Thus the meeting might have ended. But, after closing my remarks, I rose and stated that I would be glad to hear from any who might be inclined to address me upon topics of interest to the Community. This invitation brought forth several powerful speakers, who evidently exercised great influence on the masses of the people. They harangued. ... The Congregation became greatly excited, and joined the speakers in their intemperate remarks, exhibiting more frenzy than I had expected to witness among a people who habitually exercise great self control ... the wildest uproar ~~was the result~~ ensued. I was fully confirmed in the opinion, that this people, with their extraordinary religion and customs, would gladly encounter certain death, rather than be ~~subjected to the mockery of a trial by a jury composed of the followers of a Camp~~ taxed with a submission to the military power which they (wrongfully) consider to involve a loss of honor. ...

I now found the ~~utmost~~ greatest difficulty in explaining these points, so great was the excitement. Eventually however, the efforts of Prest. Young were successful in calming the tumult and restoring order before the adjournment of the meeting.—~~I should~~ It is proper that I should add that more than one speaker has since expressed his regret at having been betrayed into intemperance of language in my presence.[32]

For Once I Am Happy: Kane Savors the Moment

As April turned into May, Alfred Cumming was unsettled by the continuing spectacle of the Move South and the dilemma of dealing with disillusioned

[32]This draft is in Kane's hand, with minor edits by Cumming. Strikeouts by Kane appear here in italics, while strikeouts not in italics (along with associated insertions) are by Cumming. The final version is found in "Annual Report of the Sec. of War (1858)," 91–97.

Mormons, but his companion was not. Once Kane realized at Fort Bridger that Cumming would indeed accompany him to Salt Lake City without the U.S. Army, he experienced exhilaration fueled by the belief that the most difficult part of his mission was over. The successful completion of the trek to the city—no small accomplishment—and the positive aspects of what unfolded during 24–25 April added to this euphoria.

Kane had informed his brother that if he succeeded in reaching Salt Lake with the new governor, he intended to enjoy himself, and indeed he did for three days after completing Cumming's long dispatch to Lewis Cass on 2 May. In his diary Kane followed his brief notation about the successful Cumming-Young meeting of 24 April with the equally short but exuberant reminder to include a thought in his next letter home: "For once I am and know myself to be *happy.*"[33]

Kane continued to revel in visits with friends while savoring the honorific poetry sent to him again by Eliza Roxcy Snow and anew by William Wines Phelps, a Mormon intellectual who had been relegated to a post at the Salt Lake City weather office when his mental powers began a steep decline. Phelps sent a three-verse poem to Kane at the Staines mansion written, as he called it, from "the center of the 'Asylum of the oppressed,' to honor the '*tongue that forever speaks truth.*'"[34]

In addition to renewing acquaintances, Kane took time to socialize with an eclectic range of new people, including Louis Bertrand, the French horticulturist and religious convert who was sending European newspapers the first Mormon insider accounts of the war. Time spent with Bertrand provided Kane with an opportunity to relive his student days in Paris while testing his proficiency in French. As Bertrand remembered it, "I was struck by his small stature . . . after fifteen minutes of conversation we were already old acquaintances. He showed himself full of goodwill toward the Saints in general. In our private conversation he was quite communicative. His mission to Utah, at the direction of President Buchanan was not of an official nature. The secret instructions given to the federal troops had truly been of a ruthless nature. But time has not come to say any more on this subject. The following day I had the privilege of lunching with the Colonel and Governor Cumming. I was for both of them the object of an intense curiosity."[35]

It is possible that during this period, through a series of these interactions,

---

[33]Kane, "Diary II (1858)," undated entry, 17.

[34]W. W. Phelps to Kane, 26 April 1858, Kane Family Papers, BYU.

[35]Homer, *On the Way to Somewhere Else,* 111. Bertrand erred in believing there were ruthless secret instructions to the army.

Kane began to piece together a story of several of the most violent, sensational incidents of Utah's recent past: the massacre of Capt. John W. Gunnison's party in 1853 and the Mountain Meadows massacre in 1857. He recorded this material in an undated section in the last of his three Utah diaries, placing the text in quotation marks without identifying the source. It is unknown whether these important but unattributed accounts were fresh journal entries made contemporaneously in Utah from interviews and other fact finding or were a record of what Brigham Young, aided by George A. Smith, later sent him in Philadelphia as the three men collaborated to construct a defensible story to explain such killings to Buchanan and Congress while shifting blame from Latter-day Saints to others. Irrespective of the process, what ended up in Kane's Utah travel journal was the stock Mormon explanation of this violence: that Gunnison's military party unwittingly fell victim to an Indian need to avenge the cavalier killing of tribal members by civilian emigrants en route to California; and the Baker-Fancher party had provoked Indian retribution at Mountain Meadows by willfully poisoning springs and a beef carcass near the tribal farm at Corn Creek. In the case of the latter story, Kane was recording the earliest Mormon obfuscation about responsibility for Mountain Meadows: the Indians did it, and the victims deservedly brought catastrophe upon themselves.[36]

For all the time that he spent with others, Kane made little effort to communicate with his family, perhaps assuming that he might reach home before his letters. Virtually the sole exceptions were two letters that Thomas wrote on 18 April: one to his wife describing his health and weight, and the other to Judge Kane. That Kane had made the considerable effort to encrypt this latter message indicates that he probably intended his father to forward it to President Buchanan. The surviving excerpt advised: "Mr Buchanan should send out a good District Attorney. Let the administration and papers handle the letter-writing of officers without gloves. Things are working well. But for the presence of the troops the brave Cumming would have no difficulty. He has made one grave mistake, (not to be mentioned) but is right on public matters. It will be easier to save blood from being shed than the city from burning. Brigham Young is laboring in earnest, but the people are flying south by hundreds, and the Indians breaking in enough to justify their alarm. Thank God, my health is such as you have never known it."[37]

---

[36]Kane, "Diary III (1858)," undated entry, 12–19.

[37]Kane to Judge Kane, 18 April 1858, excerpt inserted into Elizabeth Kane Journal at 19 June 1858, Kane Family Papers, BYU.

Another exception was a note that Kane dashed off to Elizabeth as soon as he had finished Cumming's long dispatch of 2 May to Secretary Cass: "Accept this proof of my love—that I collect my thoughts enough in my distress to dedicate my work to you under whose invocation it has been achieved. MY PEACE. May the Prince of Peace remove us from this world of wars together!"[38]

The Dread Report: News of Judge Kane's Death

What brought Kane's idyllic interlude to a dramatic end was news that his father had died more than two months earlier. In the interim, Elizabeth Kane dreaded her husband's first awareness of this loss. As early as 3 April she recorded in her diary: "I feel intensely sad. About this time my poor Tom must receive the tidings. And I am far from him. Oh my darling, may our Father send the Comforter to bring all these sweet words of our Savior's to your remembrance, as He promised when he was here."[39]

In several subsequent accounts of her husband's Utah mission, Elizabeth wrote that the news of Judge Kane's passing "was tenderly broken to him by Brigham Young" on 5 May.[40] Her implication was that Young communicated this bad news in person. But on 5 May Kane and Brigham Young were miles apart. Kane was with Cumming in Provo, where the governor was attempting without success to moderate the Move South, and Young was in Salt Lake City. Originally Young and Heber C. Kimball had planned to spend 5 May traveling to Provo to meet with Cumming and Kane, but a combination of Kimball's poor health, arrival of the California mail the day before, and Young's realization that he probably could no longer delay Kane's awareness of his father's death, prompted a change in plans. As Mary Ellen Kimball recorded it, her husband "started [south] again to day but after seeing Brigham he returned said they concluded to send for them to come here to have the interview." Consequently, Kane's diary recorded, "Upon the 5th Day of May on the evening the two [messengers] came riding up to meet me who brought word that my Father was indeed Dead."[41]

---

[38]Kane to Elizabeth Kane, 2 May 1858, ibid.

[39]Elizabeth Kane Journal, 3 April 1858, ibid.

[40]Elizabeth D. W. Kane, "The Story of the Mother of the Regiment," Vol. 2, chapter 3, 86, unpublished typescript, ibid.

[41]Mary Ellen Harris Abel Kimball, Journal Feb. 1857–May 1863, 4–5 May 1858, LDS Archives; Kane, "Diary II (1858)," undated entry, 17. For an account of this event by Nelson A. Empey, one of the couriers sent to Kane by Young, see Nicholson, "Some Incidents in the Life of Nelson A. Empey," 16–22, LDS Archives.

Soon thereafter, Louis Bertrand found Kane "deeply grieved at the news of the death of his father, once one of the most enlightened magistrates of Philadelphia. The Colonel was sorely tried by this loss, suddenly added to that of Doctor Kane, his brother, famous for his travels into the arctic regions."[42]

Our Mutual Friend Going Home: Closing Up His Mission

Once Kane learned this news, he resolved to return home immediately via the plains rather than retrace the California–Panama–New York route. Cumming decided to join him on the first leg to Fort Bridger so that he might confer with Albert Sidney Johnston and then move his wife and household goods to Salt Lake City. Here was an abrupt change that brought further complexity to Brigham Young's staggering burdens, one that he had attempted to forestall by delaying delivery of "the dread Report." On 6 May, in a note later carried east by Kane, Young wrote to Delegate Bernhisel of "our mutual friend Col. Kane who is going home," and noted "the sad news of the death of his Father which sorely afflicts him."[43]

Initially Kane intended to depart on 10 May, but it took several additional days for him and Cumming to wind up their affairs in Salt Lake City. It had been more than ten years since Kane had seen Brigham Young, and he may have lingered in anticipation of another prolonged separation. The farewells took time.

As word spread of Kane's imminent departure, well-wishers and supplicants streamed to the Staines mansion, some of whom simply wanted to use Kane as a courier. Deep snow and war had disrupted Utah's mail service for more than a year. The unexpected availability of a reliable, Mormon-friendly traveler with safe passage was an opportunity that some letter-writers could not resist.[44]

Brigham Young's most recent letter to Bernhisel was among those Kane agreed to carry. It is a valuable summary of Young's thinking at the time.[45]

---

[42]Homer, *On the Way to Somewhere Else,* 110–11.

[43]Young to Bernhisel, 6 May 1858, LDS Archives.

[44]James Ferguson, the Legion's adjutant general, wrote: "May I ask you the favor to carry the enclosed letter for me and drop it in the letter box of some good Eastern Editor. I am told you leave tomorrow. I am one of fifty thousand whose hearts are all sad to part with you. Your gallant philanthropy in the dark midnight of our stormy experience has engraven your name in our affections, deep and indelibly, for ever. God bless you! Proud to be your friend." Ferguson to Kane, 11 May 1858, Kane Family Papers, BYU.

[45]For more insight into Young's use of such a document to present the Mormon case, see the draft memo that he developed earlier for Kane and Cumming on 17 April, five days after their arrival *(continued)*

Most noteworthy was his comment that "matters are by no means settled as yet." Young's observation that Cumming had not yet been accepted by the people, his continued pursuit of a scorched-earth policy, and fears of summary execution indicate that Young wrote candidly to his delegate in Congress. Young may have intended this document as "talking points" for Bernhisel to use with President Buchanan.

Young to Bernhisel, 6 May 1858, LDS Archives.

Your note dated Dec 17 [1857] to D[avid].O. Calder is the only ~~thing~~ one which we received from you by this mail.[46] We do not fully understand how it is that ~~you~~ we have received nothing ~~but~~ later from you. We have written to you by every southern [California] Mail the only one you are aware that we have been favored with as yet since last June. We send this by our mutual friend Col. Kane who is going home. ~~e trust that he may go~~ and is the bearer of important dispatches to the Government. The Col's health is much improved since his sojourn in the Mountains and only for the ~~afflicting~~ sad news of the death of his Father which sorely afflicts him, would now feel very well.

He visited the Army and after remaining there three or four weeks returned to this city accompanied by Gov A. Cumming who is still with him and now on a visit south but contemplates returning with the Col as far as the Army where he left his wife. He intends returning here soon and bringing his wife with him you will see his report which we trust will ~~have a tendency to~~ disabuse the mind of the President and cabinet and have a tendency to correct public opinion in regard to this people ~~He~~ The Governor seems disposed to do all he can to make things right if he can only be recognized as Governor an item which the people have not ~~by any means~~ as yet acceeded to. His course however thus far is calculated to modify their feelings and he doubtless feels quite sanguine of ultimate success.

The People North of Utah County including this city are all moving. Myself and Bro Kimball have removed the principal part of our families and effects and the Northern settlements are now principally vacated, and this city will be in a few more days. So if the [civil] officers do come in they will ~~be~~ have to chase up the people to get any subjects and if the Army comes they will find blackened desolation. Every preparation is making for the conflagration preferring to sacrifice comfortable houses improvements and

in Salt Lake City. Essentially this piece was a rehash of the familiar litany of LDS persecution at the hands of the Buchanan administration. Although Young apparently chose not to complete this paper, he unquestionably conveyed its substance to his two visitors face to face during the week preceding Cumming's Tabernacle appearance. Grow and Walker, *The Prophet and the Reformer,* 254–59.

[46]Bernhisel often used Calder as a "blind" through whom to send letters to Young.

possessions the labors of the last ten years than to sacrifice our constitutional rights, have officers thrust upon us at the point of the bayonet or submit to a military despotism.

We see by the papers that the redoubtable Judge Eccles [sic] has formed a grand jury out of the followers of the camp and gone through with the judicial ceremony of finding indictments. Tis strange that they could not wait until they fairly got into the territory [*illegible*] and organise[d] before they disclosed their purposes. We knew before that this was their plan of operations but did suppose that they might have had sense enough to have kept it in the dark a little longer. And if they or the Government think for a moment that they can hood wink us or that we will permit their [*illegible*] clutches to fasten and hold us while their assassins can slay us they will find out that they are "barking up the wrong sapling." We are not to be caught in that snare. They will have to try some other expedient that is not so palpable or that they have not practiced quite so often.

So you see that matters are by no means settled as yet but we hope that the present demonstration may be turned aside and actual collision avoided. We shall act as we always have done strictly in our own defence and that we have a right to do.

We are sacrificing much to avoid collision let them also recede from their positions which were taken in the dark based upon foul calumny and misrepresentation. Let the Government admit us as a state into the union if they would avoid such difficulties. They cannot consistently expect us to receive their officers much less their standing Army to enforce them upon us. . . .[47]

They have presumed and do yet rely upon the popular prejudices existing against us as a people on account of an [*illegible*] to sustain them but as the Editor of the N.Y. Herald [James Gordon Bennett] very properly remarked nearly a year ago, Mormonism as "political capital will not pay" and it appears from present indications that the Government is beginning to find it out. We see no other way for them to act consistently and save the Democratic party (Buchanan poor fellow is already gone) than to admit us into the union then we care nothing about their army they can do us no harm but what can be remedied or provided against.

With this object in view we have been writing to you to present our Constitution and application for admission into the union . . . you may esteem it the height of absurdity and presumption to make this application but Doctor, we do not reason as the world reasons upon such subjects. Do as we request you if you have to leave Washington within half an hour afterward and leave the event [?] with God.[48] If they reject us all right, they will most

[47]Young abolished his own Standing Army but did not give up using the term for regular troops.

[48]Since 1856 Bernhisel had declined to submit Utah's latest petition for statehood on the advice of Senator Douglas and others that submission would inflame congressional anti-Mormonism.

likely not have the privilege of rejecting us but once ~~and then we shall know what to do~~ and in time to come they cannot say you never applied. We have no feelings in the matter. If the Lord lets them reject us we are only the more happy for them to do so. If on the other hand they should entertain the idea of admitting us it may have a tendency to restrain the dogs of war a short time and if they admit us before they go to pieces still there may be an advantage in being placed in that position.

You know that we are aware that the Nation cannot last long in its present capacity ~~therefore do not be too afraid of this or that but~~ She is liable to perish in an hour. At any moment she may be dismembered and rent asunder the only wonder is that the slender thread which holds her together has not already ~~snapped~~ parted. Therefore improve the present opportunity to make our application lest another may not occur. Earnestly advocate our admission. You have a right to speak and they will hear you. Claim it as a right and bring the ~~issue~~ matter to such an issue, if possible, that each house will be obliged to vote direct upon the merits of the question of Admission or request [?] it and have the ayes & nays taken whenever you have a right to call for them on every point that they may be recorded. Tis nothing you need be ashamed of or afraid of—That God who rules and dictates in the affairs of men will witness your struggle in behalf of his People. . . .

All is well with us and enjoy our moving very much the saints are very cheerful. The Temple foundation is cached [covered with dirt] the Public wks removed except what is required to be retained in operation in order to fix wagons shoe animals make boxes &c all is stir & bustle to get away and all are [*illegible*]ing to be ready for whatever may occur.

Cumming Deals with the Disaffected: Aid and Duplicity

Alfred Cumming worked hard, although naively, to honor his high-profile commitment to facilitate the departure of disaffected Utahns. The right to travel freely was riddled with church-imposed hurdles, barriers, and indignities undercutting the assurances Brigham Young gave on 25 April. As a practical matter, Cumming was able to offer only limited help.[49] Kane appeared to have had no interest and therefore no role in this aspect of the human suffering in Utah.

On 2 May Cumming summarized for Secretary Cass what had happened since his first public attempt to reach out to Utah's disaffected in the third

[49]The most comprehensive studies of why, how, and to what extent disaffected Mormons exited the territory during and immediately after the Utah War are Aird, "'You Nasty Apostates, Clear Out,'" 129–207, and *Mormon Convert, Mormon Defector.*

week of April: "I have since kept my office open at all hours of the day and night, and have registered no less than fifty-six men, thirty-three women, and seventy-one children, as desirous of my protection and assistance in proceeding to the States. The large majority of these people are of English birth, and state that they leave the congregation from a desire to improve their circumstances, and realize elsewhere more money for their labor. Certain leading men among the Mormons have promised to furnish them flour and assist them in leaving this country."[50] Subsequently, more such visitors sought Cumming's help. Fearing retaliation, virtually all of them offered disingenuous, non-confrontational explanations for their departures. It was a behavior that they later disavowed upon reaching Fort Bridger.[51]

Where Cumming held these interviews is unclear, although it is likely that the "office" to which he referred in his report to Cass was a room in the Staines mansion. Prospective departees suspected that the privacy of their visits was compromised—if not by William Staines, by other houseguests believed to be church agents. When a group of eastbound English-born refugees reached Fort Bridger in late May, they described how this breach in trust had occurred: "the Governor was continually under espionage while among the Mormons. Upon his arrival in the City, he was quartered immediately at the house of W. C. Stearns [Staines], one of the most reliable of 'the faithful' and upon the same day, three men high in the confidence of the Church, took up their residence in the same family, ostensibly as boarders, but in reality in order to spy out the Governor's movements, and keep away from him persons whom it was not deemed prudent to permit to communicate with him."[52]

Despite the impact of this Mormon surveillance, it paled in comparison to Alfred Cumming's own indiscretion in betraying potential apostates' plans and complaints. Two days after the governor's public assurance of

---

[50]Cumming to Cass, 2 May 1858, "Annual Report of the Sec. of War (1858)," 94–95.

[51]Cumming's notes of his interviews with supplicants are in Cumming Papers, Duke University. One of the most extensive, articulate explanations of the real reasons behind such departures from Utah is in a letter written to his family by George Greenwood, an eastbound English-born refugee, several months after he reached Nebraska. See Greenwood to Mr. and Mrs. Myerscough, 7 December 1858, "Mormons and Mormonism," *Preston* (England) *Guardian*, January 1859. Using these and other sources, historian Polly Aird has compiled the most complete list available of departees from Utah during the spring of 1858, copy in editor's possession via Aird to MacKinnon, e-mail message, 11 August 2013.

[52]"S" [Simonton], "Camp Scott, Near Bridger's Fort," Dispatch, 5 June 1858, *New York Times*, 30 June 1858, 1/1–6 and 8/1. David Candland, a trusted Young agent and one of Governor Cumming's assigned escorts, confirmed this surveillance and blocking arrangement, recording that he "was on guard at Bro. Staines' as some one had on the previous evening had an interview with the Governor contrary to all order." Candland autobiography and diary, mid-April 1858, Mormon Manuscripts Collection, Huntington Library.

confidentiality, he had a "lengthy conversation" with a delegation of four senior Nauvoo Legion officers: Hosea Stout, James Ferguson, George D. Grant, and Robert T. Burton. Stout recorded the subject of this session as "those persons who are running to him dayly to lay before him their grievances. He very frankly showed us the statements of all those who had come to him which he had taken in writing which he said was all that they said. There was nothing in any of those statements which reflected sencure [censure] on the people or authorities here. They mostly were in relation to their wanting to leave here besides some family difficulties &c. He also pledged himself that where statements were made against the community or people he would hold the same open for rebutting evidence as well as hold all such statements open to public inspection. He declared himself to be our friend and he would not be in our midst any longer than he could be of use to us."[53] There is no indication that the governor displayed this material publicly, but the fact that he shared it in private with such a group reflected an appalling breach of the confidences of Utah's disaffected to curry favor with the leaders they feared.

Has No Connexion to the Church: The Fay Worthen Problem

Part of the confidentiality problem also stemmed from the governor's selection of Lafayette Shaw (Fay) Worthen, age 23, for a series of sensitive assignments. Worthen was an energetic but pliable young man from Warsaw, Hancock County, Illinois. Like Kane, he was a non-Mormon trusted by senior LDS leaders. How he balanced the ambiguities, complexities, and sensitivities of such a bifurcated situation is both revealing and problematic.

Worthen apparently arrived in Salt Lake City during 1856 to work in the store of John B. Kimball, a non-Mormon merchant-relative of his mother. With the advent of the Utah War, gentiles John B. Kimball and Fay Worthen were, in effect, trapped in Salt Lake. That the Mormons permitted them to stay as civilians and operate Kimball's business was unique. In the fall of 1857, Brigham Young had given all other non-Mormon merchants the option of either selling out to him and leaving the territory or staying and submitting to military service with the Nauvoo Legion. The exception in Kimball's case undoubtedly reflected his strong identity with the Mormon cause and family relationship, albeit distant, with Heber C. Kimball.

[53] Brooks, ed., *On the Mormon Frontier*, 27 April 1858, 2:658.

LAFAYETTE SHAW (FAY) WORTHEN, CUMMING-KANE PROTÉGÉ

A non-Mormon relative of Counselor Kimball, Worthen *(front row, far right)* was visiting Utah from Illinois at the war's onset. Starting in mid-April 1858, Cumming used him as courier, escort, and liaison with Utah's disaffected Mormons, roles in which Worthen betrayed confidences by reporting sensitive information about the army and apostates to Brigham Young. Under Kane's influence, Worthen's newspaper interviews spread the myth of a war-peace split atop Mormonism, with Young supposedly blocking attacks on the army. *Family portrait courtesy of descendant Jon Worthen.*

Fay Worthen's first known involvement in the Utah War came with Alfred Cumming's use of him and John Kimball as couriers. Within three days after arriving in Salt Lake City, Cumming had met and tasked the pair with riding to Fort Bridger to deliver word that he had reached the city and been appropriately received as Utah's governor. Cumming provided Johnston with an introduction to his messengers describing them as "engaged in mercantile pursuits here, and are represented to be of the highest respectability, and have no connexion with the church. . . . I beg leave to commend them to your confidence and courtesy."[54]

When Cumming's couriers returned to Salt Lake on 24 April, the nature of their allegiances and the governor's naïveté in selecting them for such a role surfaced in Wilford Woodruff's revealing notation, "Kimball and Worthing [*sic*] returned from the Armey and reported to President Young what they saw and heard."[55]

In his unexpected Tabernacle intervention on behalf of apostate Mormons, Cumming announced Fay Worthen's next assignment: intermediary or "gatekeeper" for those wishing to consult him confidentially about leaving Utah. This too was a role in which Worthen demonstrated a willingness to betray confidences while shedding light on Young's thirst for intelligence, cavalier attitude about the monitoring of others' mail, and disregard for his own stated commitment to protect the travel rights of disaffected Utahns. George A. Smith noted in mocking tones, "Quite a number of persons called upon Cummin [*sic*], they generally wished to see him alone; and generally their wants were a little tobacco, sugar, coffee & Tea. One man said that he thought that a thousand dollars would do to get him away from this country. Fay Worthing asked Prest. Young what he should say to those who came to him with letters for Cummin. He told him to take them and send them to him by Wm. H. Kimball."[56] With at least Smith, his clerks, and Brigham Young's office staff aware of this diversion of confidential letters, small wonder that cynicism spread about the porosity of information confided to the new governor.

---

[54]Cumming to Johnston, 15 April 1858 included in Cumming to Cass, 21 May 1858, "Annual Report of Sec. of War (1858)," 92–93. Whether Cumming was aware that Worthen was Heber C. Kimball's fourth cousin once removed is unknown. Of more concern to Johnston would have been John B. Kimball's surname, with its implicit connection to Heber C. and his son, Brig. Gen. William H. Kimball of the Nauvoo Legion. The family relationship is confirmed in Parshall to MacKinnon, e-mail message, 21 February 2009.

[55]Kenney, ed., *Wilford Woodruff's Journal,* 24 April 1858, 5:183.

[56]Historian's Office Journal, 26 April 1858, LDS Archives.

Young's interception of Cumming's mail started even before the new governor arrived in Salt Lake City. During the winter Young received and sequestered a letter written to Cumming by Augustus Ripley Burbank, a Portland businessman and member of the Oregon territorial legislature seeking news of his long-silent Mormon brother and family:

> Now in case of my brother's death by war with U.S. Troops, or other wise, I hope you will be so good as to give advice, and if possible, protection to his [five] children. Have them sent to me in Oregon. . . . I feel very solicitous for these *poor children* especially his eldest daughter whom if there is no interposing providence may be sacrificed to Brigham's harem. . . . I have long since had but little hope of [my brother's] reform, or for the chances of his children to escape the *Mormon hell.* I have no doubt but our Government will have to wage a war of extermination, to all leading Mormons. Be subdued, they must, let the cost (blood and treasure) be what it may. . . . I never have at any time been less than a constant opposer of Mormonism, we here are fearing that the Mormons may stir up the Columbia [River] Valley and other Indian tribes to wage war upon Oregon and Washington territories.[57]

Worthen moved deeper into Alfred Cumming's personal entourage with his inclusion in the praetorian guard of Legionnaires and civilians described by various observers as either protecting or isolating him from Mormon society: "Mr. [Richard W.] James states that Gov. Cumming's Mormon guard, when he visited Provo [in early May], consisted of Howard Egan, Jno. Kay, Fayette Worthen, David Candland, Wm. Kemble [*sic*], and Col. Kane. In view of such details as those, it would seem difficult to doubt that the Governor was mistaken in supposing his own movements in the Valley to have been so entirely free of espionage and restraint."[58]

Under Kane's Influence: Cumming, Worthen, and the Growth of the War-Peace Myth

A demonstration of Kane's skill in identifying and using pliable spokesmen surfaced with an interview that Worthen gave to the *St. Louis Republican* in

[57]Burbank to Cumming, 12 December 1857, LDS Archives. Burbank's brother was Daniel Mark Burbank. Nine days before his brother wrote this letter, Daniel returned to Salt Lake City exhausted, ill-clad, and hungry after campaigning as a chaplain and commissary officer with the Nauvoo Legion's cavalry in the vicinity of Echo Canyon and Fort Bridger. He and his large brood of children remained in Mormonism and Utah for the rest of their lives. A. R. Burbank's anti-Mormon views probably originated in his native Illinois.

[58]"S" [Simonton], "Important from Utah," Dispatch, 28 May 1858, Camp Scott Near Fort Bridger, *New York Times,* 24 June 1858,1/1–5.

mid-June 1858 after accompanying Kane across the plains. In the newspaper's report of Worthen's opinions, it was all there: the presence of a war-peace split atop the Mormon hierarchy, Brigham Young's efforts to moderate the aggressive inclinations of unnamed LDS leaders aligned against him, and Young's avoidance of bloodshed by courageously curtailing a planned attack on Fort Bridger at the beginning of March. So closely did Worthen's comments match the concepts and phrasing of Kane's March–April letters to President Buchanan and even the draft letters to the editor found in Kane's personal papers, one must conclude either Worthen adopted Kane's views by osmosis or was overtly primed for such an interview by his new mentor.[59]

Worthen's St. Louis comments were news, and they spread to papers across the United States with telegraphic speed. What began to take shape through this process was a perception that Mormonism was a divided rather than monolithic society, with a benign Brigham Young undertaking risk to steer a peaceful course to resolve the Utah War. By implication, this view cast Young as a reliable leader with whom James Buchanan could find common cause. It was a seductively appealing image designed to replace that of a demonized prophet stripped of his governorship, accused of murder, and indicted for treason. Below the surface, this transformation had the power to facilitate a beleaguered president's growing inclination to divert national attention from a controversial, ruinously expensive campaign against the Mormons to military thrusts against less sympathetic groups such as the tribes of the Pacific Northwest and New Mexico.

The day before departing Salt Lake for Fort Bridger, Kane helped the governor write a long, out-of-channels letter about Utah to Rep. James L. Orr of South Carolina, the new speaker of the U.S. House of Representatives. Risking the wrath of Secretary Cass and President Buchanan, Cumming confided to Orr highly sensitive views that he had not yet shared with the administration.[60] The governor and Kane may have been willing to risk bypassing the secretary because of their criticism of Eckels and realization "he enjoyed an acquaintance with Lewis Cass."[61] Although the governor authorized Orr to

[59]"Interesting Particulars from Great Salt Lake City," *St. Louis Republican*, 16 June 1858, reprinted in *New York Herald*, 19 June 1858, 1.

[60]In contrast, on the same day Cumming sent to Cass a note of only two paragraphs indicating that he had journeyed to Provo to try to allay the fears of Mormon refugees and that the road to California was now open to emigrants. Cumming to Cass, 12 May 1858, "Annual Report of the Sec. of War (1858)," 99. For a draft of this letter in Kane's hand dated 11 May, see Kane Family Papers, BYU.

[61]Furniss, *The Mormon Conflict*, 209.

use his own judgment "as to how far this note shall be circulated," he told the speaker he had decided not to send this material to the president. Nonetheless, when Kane delivered Cumming's letter to Orr in Washington on 21 June, the speaker immediately decided to send it on to Buchanan, pausing only to recopy the original to delete the names of several federal appointees in Utah about whom the governor expressed dissatisfaction: Chief Justice Eckels, Secretary Hartnett, U.S. Attorney Hockaday, and probably others such as Surveyor General Burr, Postmaster Morrell, and Indian Agent Hurt.

CUMMING TO ORR, 12 MAY 1858,
JAMES BUCHANAN PAPERS, HSP.

In our last conversation at Leavenworth you kindly invited a correspondence when I should have arrived in Great Salt Lake City. I have therefore concluded to address this note to you written in the midst of perplexing engagements, and on the eve of my departure for Camp Scott. I will endeavor to give you a brief but intelligible statement of the condition of affairs in this Territory, with my views in relation to future action and its probable results—accompanied by such suggestions as in my opinion are most likely to promote the public interest.

It will be remembered that at the date of my commission and instructions—an alleged refusal on the part of this people to receive the Civil Officers of the Territory—their expulsion of citizens on account of their religious opinions—restraining individuals, male and female of their liberty—destroying the records of the U.S. Courts—destroying or embezzling the records and other property belonging to the Government at the offices of the Secretary of State and Surveyor General, together with the Territorial Library;—purchased with an appropriation from the United States;—charges to this effect had been the origin and were the sum and substance of the (original) Utah Difficulty. That difficulty no longer exists. It has been removed without the necessity of resorting to military force. Without being accompanied by a single soldier, the Governor appointed has been received, and entered upon the duties of his office: the other Territorial Civil Officers will also soon, I trust, be at their posts prepared for the performance of their official duties.

The adjustment of the past difficulties too has been attended with sufferings certainly severe enough to impress upon this people a remembrance of the penalties of disobedience.

There is an almost universal emigration. The people have left their homes, their farms, their workshops. The highways are thronged with wagons, cattle and sheep: Women and little children are exhausted with unwonted labor; wandering they know not where, anxiously awaiting future developments, which are to determine whether they will apply the torch to their homes, or return to enjoy the comforts which they have so promptly forsaken at the "call of duty." In short we are at every moment presented with touching scenes of suffering and unhappiness.

This has become the new aspect of the Utah difficulty—involving new subjects of solicitude and calling for renewed action—to save all the improvements from being burnt, entire settlements from ruin—to prevent the inhabitants from migrating to a region beyond the limits of the Territory where it would be less advantageous to have them, and where, at some future time they would give the Government more trouble than here. These subjects occupy my thoughts and employ my utmost energies.

These people *must* be induced to return to their homes and their employments. If I am so unfortunate as to encounter such opposition as will thwart my efforts to avert the perils of a collision between the army and people and blood be spilt, we may expect a long, expensive, unsatisfactory guerilla war, in which a small band would probably perpetrate frightful acts of atrocity, whilst the mass of the community would appear to be the most loyal and pacific of men.

I am fully aware of the prejudices and difficulties I must encounter, yet I do not despair of settling this second Utah affair by a bloodless victory. But Congress and the Administration must aid me. I must have a full, an intelligent, an impartial [judicial] bench—a Secretary of State, a District Attorney; and they should not only be willing but able to give me counsel upon matters of law.[62]

You know that I am not a politician nor a lawyer. I therefore desire the advantage of consulting wise and experienced counsellors.

If the Governor is to be deprived of the benefits resulting from the presence of certain offices, he should at least escape the opposition of those who are present.

I infer from the tone of communications coming from Camp, that numerous intriguers "correspondents" and others have assailed me with bitterness. My friends at Washington will not expect me to sacrifice the public interest even for the purpose of advancing certain officers of the Army.

How far it may be [a] question of legal propriety to constitute a Grand Jury from the teamsters and other followers of the camp & employees of the Army is one of a class of subjects upon which I would like very much to be advised.

Mr. Hartnett the Secretary of State is not a lawyer, or a man of business experience; so that I am compelled to grope in the dark, especially during the absence of the District Attorney—who, by the way, has not, I believe, devoted his undivided attention to the law. Would it not be well to have

[62]An allusion to the absence from Utah of Judges Cradlebaugh and Sinclair as well as Secretary Hartnett and U.S. Attorney Hockaday.

the Attorney general [Jeremiah S. Black] furnish instructions meeting the questions which will probably arise?

There are several officers appointed who are deservedly obnoxious to the people here. [*names not given*] x x—are I think [e]specially so and it may be necessary to consider the propriety of appointing several new civil officers, and of issuing instructions to the officers already here to conform their actions to a course of policy indicated by the Governor as circumstances arise.

The great distance between this territory and the seat of Government at Washington and the altogether unprecedented condition of affairs here, lead me to counsel the utmost legal extension of the powers of the Executive.

This community is divided on the war question—there is a peace party and a war party. I esteem it to be the duty and policy of my administration to support the former & break down the latter.

Brigham Young is at the head of the peace party. There are in the community other zealots of as old a standing in the Church who have great influence among the people in leading them to action, but the spiritual influence of no one in the Territory is equal to his. He is a man earnest, intelligent & of great experience in addition to all which he is vested with the authority to announce the terrors awarded to those who sin against the "Holy Ghost" the most awful doom to which Mormon humanity can be subjected. There is a division in the ranks, probably; all fear Brigham Young; but many also hate him, in consequence perhaps of the pacific measures attributed to him. However this may be, my chief hope of control over this extraordinary people is exerted through this man. I believe that I have obtained his confidence and will therefore exercise some ascendancy over his actions. If this be true, it is of importance, especially as connected with a certain degree of personal popularity which I feel that I have acquired with the masses.

If events here should have an untoward result, so far as peace is concerned, the country may reasonably anticipate a war of several years duration, at an expense of many millions; and the terrors of war would be visited upon those who are least deserving of them. It would have the effect of confirming the dangerous spirit of this people, and extending their influence abroad.

There is an accumulation of mail matter at Bridger destined for the inhabitants of the valleys, which I hope to forward to this place in a few days. If I be not opposed in this matter, I shall have done much to appease angry feelings excited in the community.

There are at Washington many large accounts, the payment of which has been, perhaps unnecessarily, deferred. It would be wise to advance the settlements of all just accounts as speedily as possible.

Large amounts of money have from time to time been appropriated for Territorial purposes in Utah, which for some reason have not been disbursed; this matter should be enquired into.

The hostile character of the Indians of this Territory leads them to frequent depredations upon the settlements, of extensive and most annoying character. These tribes I shall be compelled to chastise, I fear. I have warned some of them of my intentions, which has already produced some beneficial effects, causing a restoration of some stolen property. There should, however, I think, be treaties held with these people, and liberal arrangements made for annuities.

When I received my instructions from the Secretary of State, he also furnished me a copy of the orders for the guidance of the officer in Command of the Utah expedition, which, I presume, have not since been materially modified.[63]

I esteem it of the utmost importance that I should be advised of any modification, which will affect the civil administration of this Territory. The military may be in receipt of instructions under which they may feel themselves compelled or authorized to act. Therefore, I would suggest that all such orders should be subjected to minute inspection from the Administration.

You will use your own judgment as to how far this note shall be circulated.

xxxxxxxxx—

It has been a question with me whether the substance of this note, should or should not be communicated directly to the President, but I have been so much and constantly engaged, I feel myself compelled to limit myself to this hasty note to yourself.

I have assumed my position in regard to Utah affairs, and unless I receive advices of an opposite character, will presume that my official conduct is approved by the President & his administration.

I have been advised by a personal friend in the Camp, that immediately after my departure from that place for this City, Chief Justice Eckels charged a jury against polygamy in this Territory. This unwise and unauthorized act, if known here, would have greatly added to the perils and difficulties of my situation. xxxxxxxxx—

Orr to Buchanan, 21 June 1858, James Buchanan Papers, hsp.

I enclose you herewith full extracts from a letter I have just received from Gov. Cumming of Utah Territory. My last request of him before his departure for Utah was that he should correspond with me relative to Utah matters our long and intimate friendship has put me in possession of the letter from which these extracts are made.

He confides to my discretion the proper use to be made of his letter and I have thought it advisable to communicate it to you rather than the press as it may contain some suggestions not already communicated to you.

---

[63]See *At Sword's Point, Part 1,* 168–71 and 180–82.

> I have the highest confidence in his judgment courage and discretion and believe that every facility should be furnished him to carry out his policy which has thus far proved eminently successful & peaceful.
>
> His letter is written in a style of manly frankness to a friend and I commend most cordially all his views and opinions to your gravest & most favorable consideration.

I Cannot Be Responsible for Their Safety: Starting Young's Divide-and-Conquer Strategy

With Thomas L. Kane deeply engaged in drafting and eventually delivering Alfred Cumming's letters of 12 May, it is likely that Brigham Young was aware of their contents if not contributing to them. George A. Smith recorded that "Cumming agreed to let Gov. Young see his private instructions," and two weeks later, while meeting with a group of Legion generals, Cumming "read to us his correspondence with Col Johnson and also his report in part which he is preparing to send to government [on 2 May], which was vindicating Gov Young's character &c." There is no reason to believe that for the drafting of important dispatches to Cass and Speaker Orr that Kane and Cumming would not have dealt Young into the process.[64] In addition to Cumming's observation that "this community is divided on the war question—there is a peace party and a war party," Young would have been most pleased with the new governor's description of division among the federal appointees—one that Cumming and Young were to widen during the summer of 1858. This split became the cornerstone of Brigham Young's long-term strategy for dealing with the federal establishment: divide and conquer.

Cumming's comments on 12 May about the shortcomings of his federally appointed colleagues may well have been stimulated by an extraordinarily critical letter Young sent him four days earlier. If this note did not threaten assassination of such officials, it communicated an indifference to the possibility akin to his earlier observation that "the Indians we expect will do as they please" at Mountain Meadows.[65] Young's letter alarmed Cumming, prompting him to raise the matter of recalling federal appointees obnoxious to the Mormons.

[64]Historian's Office Journal, 14 April 1858, LDS Archives; Brooks, ed., *On the Mormon Frontier,* 27 April 1858, 2:658.

[65]See *At Sword's Point, Part 1,* 327–28.

Young to Cumming, 8 May 1858, Gubernatorial Letterbook, 710–12, LDS Archives.

You are familiar with many, if not all, of the malicious charges which enemies to American rights and liberty have so widely and industriously circulated against the citizens of Utah, and, so far as the brief time since your arrival in our settlements has permitted, you have personally become cognizant, one by one, of the entire falsity of those charges, to the full number and extent that they have come under your observation, as have already all of the more important. You have also freely addressed a large assemblage of citizens in the Tabernacle in this City, and could discern that their bosoms actually glowed with enthusiasm in behalf of freedom of conscience, respect for the rights of man and every principle couched in the Constitution of our country.

These and other facts which have come within our observation, together with the well known important position I am understood to occupy with the citizens of this Territory, compel me, notwithstanding my full and sincere admiration of your conduct and official course and a strong desire to lend you such aid therein as may be in my power, so far as you may deem it proper to require it, to frankly inform your Excellency that I cannot be responsible for the safety of certain Government appointees, such as Dr. Garland Hurt, H. F. Morrell, [Indian Agent] C. L. Craig, and, perhaps, others which your better judgement will probably dictate, should they venture to come into our settlements where the history of their strenuous efforts and desires to bring on a collision between us and the Federal Government is understood.

Governor Cumming will observe that I do not discuss or entertain the question of the amount of danger these parties would incur in the Valley; but whether I as an individual will assume the responsibility of encouraging them to expose themselves at this time. I might, perhaps, qualify other portions of my letter, but do not consider this desired by Governor Cumming—whose purposes as I understand them, my letter best promotes by my frank committal as above. At the same time, in a country where the people are so justly esteemed sovereign, all rulers must realize that their influence and real security are and rightly should be based upon their own correct official and private conduct, which of itself insures the protection and respect of all good men, in Utah at least to as great a extent as elsewhere.

You need not to be informed that your highly commendable efforts in behalf of law, order and the extension of civil and religious rights, are most cheerfully and promptly sustained by the people as well as by myself, thereby, as Utah has already declared, demonstrating the perfect freedom enjoyed by all who are disposed to do right, and, as a direct consequence, the worse than uselessness of quartering troops within or near our settlements. From these and kindred reasons, by you well understood, you will readily perceive that the nearer approach of United States troops will at once greatly complicate and jeopardize the loyal efforts of yourself and your numerous friends, at least until a candid investigation has preceded their further movement towards our settlements.

On your way from the army to this city, you met a small number of men on duty, as a guard against Indian depredations; when your judgment dictates that there is no further necessity for their remaining to watch the hostile demonstrations of evil disposed Indians, or the movements of any armed bodies of men who will not listen to your counsels, at your request the persons now performing that duty will most cheerfully repair to their respective homes.

With Kane as scribe, Cumming responded to this mixture of threats and flattery on the eve of their departure for Fort Bridger. He ignored Young's comments about the dangers afoot for his federally appointed colleagues, warmed to his compliments, tried again to stem the Move South, and exceeded his authority by implying to Young that he had the power to influence the timing and movement of Johnston's troops. Cumming's response was as unusual as Young's letter had been unconventional. Taken together, they shed light on a critical relationship in formation.[66]

Adding Fuel to the Fire: Final Arrangements

One of Kane's greatest fears as he prepared to depart was the prospect that news from Washington might arrive via the Panama-California mail to disturb Governor Cumming's carefully nurtured (Kanesean) view of the Utah War and Brigham Young's role in it. In a sense, it was a concern about not upsetting the new status quo, not unlike that which had prompted Brigham Young to manipulate the timing by which Kane learned of his father's death. Accordingly, Kane took steps to filter what mail came to Cumming's attention in early May while arranging eastbound courier service to Fort Bridger so as to aggravate the enmity between Albert Sidney Johnston and Cumming. The following letter from General Wells in Salt Lake City to Brigham Young in Provo describes these manipulations while telegraphing a patent disrespect for Cumming he felt free to express to his leader.

Wells to Young, 1 May 1858, LDS Archives.

I visited Col. Kane yesterday. He said all things were progressing well as we could expect. He is quite anxious that the Cumming dispatches should

[66]Cumming to Young, 12 May 1858, Cumming Papers, Duke University.

> be finished and forwarded before Mail comes in no matter what the news may be and ~~for this pur~~ lest it might make some little difference with the poor old man the Col would prefer if it should come to have it detained at Provo say until Tuesday the 4 [of May] tho he hopes if they can keep among [?] company to have the dispatches off by Monday noon. He is haranguing the Old Man by telling him that he must start south Monday but he has to contend some points with him which detains him. The Col. has also got his consent to have the dispatches forwarded to Col Johnson by Mormon couriers, and wishes me to select gentlemanly Men who will civilly answer all civil questions and refuse to answer all others telling them that they did not come there to either tell or carry tales but were bearers of dispatches. He thinks that they will be perfectly safe and that it will tend to add fuel to the fire between ~~the~~ Cumming and Johnson. We have thought of sending Col [Hampton S.] Beat[t]ie and Henry Lawrence. They will probably not get off south before Tuesday.

Brigham Young responded: "I will see bro Scovil, and arrange so that the Cols wishes may be carried out, in relation to the delaying of the mail."[67]

With Kane's departure imminent, Young decided to use this protective cover to send with him instructions of wildly different stripe for Mormon agents. It was a practical use of Kane's de facto immunity from search, not unlike Delegate Bernhisel's misuse of Captain Van Vliet's hospitality to send intelligence reports to Young from the overland trail in mid-September 1857. The most important of such letters was one Young drafted to instruct Mormon newspaperman T. B. H. Stenhouse in New York on the rudiments of a campaign to "handle the public pulse very carefully" while establishing a future liaison on press matters with Kane in Philadelphia.

Young to Stenhouse, 8 May 1858, LDS Archives.

> You are more or less aware of the influence of the "press" in moulding public opinion, whether for good or evil. You are also somewhat familiar with the difficulties attending efforts to introduce truth into the columns of the periodicals of the day, more especially when the Latter Day Saints are in question. In view of these facts, and in consideration that many are ignorantly prejudiced against us through the tirades of falsehood so constantly teeming in the newspapers, it has been deemed proper to use some effort to give a right direction to public opinion, by gradually and as rapidly

[67] Young to Wells, 2 May 1858, LDS Archives. On 3 May, Mormon merchants Lawrence and Richard Hopkins (not Beattie) left Salt Lake with eastbound mail from Cumming and Kane. Three days later Albert Sidney Johnston reported their safe arrival to Cumming and, notwithstanding Young's skepticism, his commitment to forward this material via army courier. Johnston to Cumming, 6 May 1858, "Annual Report of the Sec. of War (1858)," 99.

as possible influencing that opinion in the columns of papers supported by the world and having a wide circulation, such as the N.Y. Herald, Times, Tribune, &c. From representations of yourself by Elders Geo. A. Smith, John Taylor and others, I am induced to request you to take this subject into consideration, and trust, inasmuch as the way may open, that you will take all steps in your power and judgment to ward a blow from Utah or in any way to promote the welfare of all lovers of the truth, and to defeat the evil intentions of its opponents.

The mode of conducting an operation of the nature in question can not well be minutely detailed to you, until you shall have reflected upon and moved somewhat in the matter, after which you will be better enabled to seek and receive such further counsel as may be requisite. To carry this scheme into effect may include the use of more means [money] than you may individually be able to command, which however can be provided for as economy and prudence may dictate. The objects to be first moved for are the prevention of any re-enforcement to the troops now in our borders and the withdrawal of those troops at the earliest date upon which it can compassed [*sic*], introducing such arguments therefor as the public press and pulse will bear, and then from time to time continue the labor for human progress in the path of true advancement.

You are respectfully advised to put yourself in communication with Col. Thomas L. Kane of Philadelphia, who will be able to give you counsel upon the points above named; and also to co-operate with br. Ebenezer R. Young of Westport, Con. You need apprehend no difficulty in regard to means for this work, for they will be supplied so far as prudence and opportunity suggest. Br. E. R. Young is a man of business, whom you will do well to consult on financial affairs.[68]

---

[68]So zealous was Stenhouse in responding to Young's counsel that he appeared at the Kanes' home unannounced within a week of Thomas's return and "asked for information he said he was going to write 'an interesting account saying nothing.'" Elizabeth found him to be repulsive. Upon returning to New York, Stenhouse acknowledged his instructions and told the First Presidency, "I have had pleasant interviews with Col. Kane since his return to the East, likewise with Dr. Bernhisel, both of whom I have solicited to write me and counsel my pen, when they may consider that anything I can do might be useful." Elizabeth Kane Journal, 29 June 1858, Kane Family Papers, BYU; Stenhouse to Young, Kimball, and Wells, 30 June 1858, LDS Archives. With this letter, the church's president laid the foundations for a long-running campaign to influence editors through cash payments from a substantial fund. As context, it should be noted that contemporaneous to Young's launch of this national campaign to influence the press, Abraham Lincoln engaged in similar behavior in Illinois to advance his political objectives. Relying on Harold Holzer's surprising portrait of Lincoln's covert dealings with newspapers, Fergus M. Bordewich describes him during this pre-presidential period as "a sometimes cajoling, sometimes bullying manipulator of the press, a man supremely skilled in the arts of leaking information, planting favorable news items and, when necessary, buying the editors." Bordewich, "A Cajoling, Bullying Manipulator," *Wall Street Journal*, 18–19 October 2014, D6/1. Ebenezer R. Young, a Mormon, was not related to Brigham Young. For his role in the church, see Bagley, "Note on Ebenezer Russell Young," *Catalogue 30* (Salt Lake City: Ken Sanders Rare Books, 2007/08), 15–21.

I wish you to say to all the Saints with whom you may come in contact to be of good cheer, for the way will open for their deliverance through faithfulness. If the presiding Elders have left your region of country, I wish you to take the oversight of the brethren in the Eastern churches.

In your communications through the papers, since matters appear to be turning slightly in our favor, be careful not to print any article with so much of the "Mormon" stamp on the coin as to prevent its passing, or doing more harm than good; in other words, handle the public pulse very carefully, lest more harm than good be brought about. . . .[69]

Pres. D.H. Wells,
Dear Brother:—

You may add what you think best to what is above written, and consult with Col. Kane as to his willingness to confer with br. Stenhouse, also to be the bearer of this letter.

Young was so anxious about the success of Stenhouse's newspaper mission that three days later he sent him another letter on the subject, also to be carried by Kane. This time Young added the signature of his two counselors for emphasis. Collectively, they urged Stenhouse to "do what you can for the benefit of the Saints, and use your pen in the defence of the Saints when opportunity presents; and you will do well to make use of such organs as are willing to admit a ray of truth in their columns." Simultaneously, in an accompanying note, Stenhouse's mentor, Apostle Smith, provided more of a newsletter and a lighter touch than his colleagues: "You would like to know the cause of the rise of the expedition. Ans[wer]. The Lord has revealed the truth to the L.D.S. And the Devil is determined to wipe it out of the earth, and all his servants are doing their best to aid him. The statements official and otherwise made by the fugitive officers and other scape graces which have agitated the public mind are unqualifiedly false. The officers left of their own accord without being molested, and their statements had no existence except in their own imaginations. . . . Gov. Cumming appears to be doing what is right as far as we understand his movements. We learn from the Indians that emissaries are endeavoring to incite them in the South part of the Territory to violence with some success. Indians say they are to have a price for Mormon scalps."[70]

---

[69] Young later cautioned Stenhouse to moderate his public praise for Kane lest it damage Kane's credibility. For Young's additional instructions to his agents on influencing "that mighty engine, the press, which has been so successful in the manufacture of public opinion against us," see Young to Eldredge, 20 October 1858, and Young to Hooper, 8 February 1866, LDS Archives.

[70] Young, Kimball, and Wells to Stenhouse and Smith to Stenhouse, both 11 May 1858 from Provo, Brigham Young Collection and George A. Smith Papers.

He Seemed Considerably Affected: Departures

Young next turned to the most sensitive subject of all—the matter of Kane's religious beliefs and whether at long last he would be open to a dialogue about Mormonism. At dinner with the First Presidency and George A. Smith on 7 May, Kane had telegraphed some sort of interest in religion, a signal discerned by both Heber C. Kimball's wife Mary Ellen and Apostle Smith.[71] The next day, Brigham Young followed up on the subject through a note marked "For your own eye" and addressed to "My Dear and Tried Friend." Doing so by letter rather than in person could reflect Young's wariness about raising the matter, or perhaps a desire to give Kane time and distance to consider his offer.

Young to Kane, 8 May 1858, LDS Archives.

Though our acquaintance from its commencement, which now dates from many years past, has ever been marked by that frank interchange of views and feelings which should ever characterize the communications of those who have the welfare of mankind at heart, irrespective of sect or party, as I am well assured by a long and intimate acquaintance, is a feeling signally shared by yourself in common with your best friends; yet, so far as I can call to mind, I do not remember to have ever, either in correspondence, or in familiar conversation, except, perhaps, by a casual and unpursued remark, alluded to matters of religious belief, as entertained by myself and others who are commonly called "Mormons," nor do I remember that you have ever overstepped the most guarded reserve on this subject in all your communications with me. So invariably and persistently has this peculiarity marked our friendly and free interchange of views, upon policy and general topics, that I have at times imagined, and still am prone to imagine, that you are more or less inclined to scepticism even upon many points commonly received by the religious world.

The faith embraced by the Latter Day Saints is so naturally philosophical, and so consistent with and enforcive of every valuable and true principle that should govern in every department of life, that I am strongly of opinion that a plain, candid exposition of the faith of the everlasting gospel, which I have so much at heart, cannot, probably, fail to at least interest a person of your reflective turn of mind. Such being my conviction, your permission to me to converse familiarly with you upon a subject of so much import, previous to your departure for your home, or to write to you upon your return to the society of your family and friends, will confer a highly esteemed favor upon, most truly, Your Friend and the Friend of all good and honorable men.

[71]Mary Ellen Harris Abel Kimball, Journal, 7–9 May 1858, LDS Archives.

There is no record that Kane replied. As Elizabeth Kane later realized, Thomas was struggling with whether he wanted to be a Christian, let alone a Mormon. The recent assessment of biographers Grow and Walker is that "no evidence exists that Kane accepted Young's invitation to investigate Mormonism's spiritual claims." As faithful Latter-day Saints and close observers of Kane's behavior during this period, they conclude "even in this moment after his father's death, Kane simply was not drawn to the church's spiritual message." Indeed, news of Judge Kane's passing on 5 May seems to have undercut his son's already fragile acceptance of Christianity. On 2 May Thomas had written to his wife of "the Prince of Peace"; by mid-month his thoughts about religion had turned pessimistic, with Kane recording recollections of earlier times as "those days [when] I had prayers to say." Yet if Kane kept his own counsel on this subject, it is possible that he recognized the significance and sincerity of Young's 8 May invitation to dialogue. In describing his preparations to depart Salt Lake City, Kane may have referred to Young's religious overtures in recording that he "receive[d] last words of advice on important subjects." If so, it is significant that he later characterized such otherwise unidentified advice as "prized now."[72]

If Kane was unwilling to discuss his own religious views and affiliations, he did pursue the "curse" which his San Bernardino benefactress, Frances Swan Clark, felt the church had placed on her. Elizabeth Kane recorded, "He told me that he tried in vain to have the curse erased from Frances Clark when he went to Salt Lake. Only when he was coming away Br. Young told him as a piece of news that there was a special revelation that Heaven was disposed to look leniently on Frances on account of her eminent services to the Church."[73]

Recognizing reality, Young dropped the subject of religion and turned to devising a convoluted arrangement to reimburse Kane for twelve hundred dollars' worth of expenses he incurred in Salt Lake City.[74]

If Kane's faith in Christianity waned during his last week in Utah, he did not lose his sense of euphoria over the prospect of returning home and what he believed to be the success of his mission to Utah. A full realization

[72]Grow and Walker, *The Prophet and the Reformer*, 261, and Grow to MacKinnon, e-mail message of 21 May 2015; Kane, "Diary III (1858)," 75.

[73]Elizabeth Kane Journal, 28 June 1858, Kane Family Papers, BYU.

[74]Wells to Bernhisel and Young to Kane, both 12 May 1858, LDS Archives. This effort carried on into the 1880s.

("reaction") of what he had accomplished in mediating the Utah War came upon him in stages during his last night in the Staines mansion as he listened to the "apopleptic snoring" of his gubernatorial roommate. Much as he had confided to his brother Pat in early April when he had convinced Cumming to travel to Salt Lake City without army escort, Kane journalized, "my work was over." As Kane later described it, "I packed got some [Cumming] signatures [on letters drafted] and then met those who came to me [to] say Good Bye . . . and rode away from the house the women bringing me flowers."[75]

Kane, Cumming, Worthen, Howard Egan, and three other Legionnaires departed Salt Lake City on 13 May. Within hours, William Staines had closed up his house and put his wives and children aboard wagons to join the Move South. Daniel H. Wells rode with Kane's party into the canyons east of the city and recorded their final interaction:

> Col. Kane and Gov Cumming left on the 13th inst. I rode out on horseback with the Col. a few miles; he had a good deal to say and seemed considerably affected in taking leave of the City, constantly looking back as we rode along the bench, and admiring it, but said he should never see it again.[76] The jist of his remarks seemed to be to stave off and shun by all possible and honorable means a collision either with the troops or officers and wait for time to have its effect. He was very sanguine that much could be effected perhaps all that we could desire, but it would take *time* to accomplish it. I believe him a true friend and think he will do all he can to aid us. He obtained a letter from his wife by Dr [Jeter] Clinton who arrived the day he left.[77] Bro Wm H. Kimball accompanied the Col. up into Echo [Canyon] and returned Saturday night. He said that this letter from his wife gave the Col. great satisfaction. She was well and the news of family affairs were generally favorable.[78]

Elizabeth Kane recorded what her husband told her about this parting, a discussion prompted by her query as to who D. H. Wells was: "I did not like him much, he replied. He rode 20 miles on my road back with me and on parting dropped something heavy in my lap and rode off and not stopping for all

[75]Kane, "Diary III (1858)," 75.

[76]Kane returned to Salt Lake City with his wife in 1872 and again, alone, upon Brigham Young's death in 1877.

[77]This was presumably Elizabeth's letter of 7 March, which her diary recorded she had sent "by a Mormon who is going to try to get through the army, if possible." Elizabeth Kane Journal, 7 March 1858, Kane Family Papers, BYU. Kane recorded without comment that he received Elizabeth's letter in the middle of the night from Mormon courier Thomas Wheeler while camped with his escort on the trail near Echo Canyon. Kane, "Diary III (1858)," 71.

[78]Wells to Young, 17 May 1858, LDS Archives.

my shouts. I had to give it to Mrs. Cumming [at Bridger] to take back to him. It was a chronometer watch worth at least $500 with a heavy chain and seals the latter his own daily wear." Months later, when drafting an account of this incident for publication, Elizabeth Kane commented, "the Mormons would gladly have shown their gratitude in any way Tom would permit, and he was often forced to decline their offerings at the risk of wounding their feelings."[79]

Arriving at Fort Bridger on 16 May, Kane dropped off Cumming, picked up safe-conduct passes for his escort, retrieved his gear, and headed across the plains for the Missouri River, Philadelphia, and Washington.[80] He did so amidst army suspicion and animosity while suffering from one of his episodic bouts of ill health. Mrs. Cumming was so alarmed at Kane's condition at Fort Bridger that she reminded him a month later, "you seemed so unwell the day you left us, that Mr. Cumming was very uneasy about you."[81]

For Kane, sick and unfamiliar with his surroundings, the trip was nightmarish. Beset by the hardships of spring snow in the mountains followed by heat, rain, mosquitoes, overflowing rivers, and difficult trail on the plains, he recoiled at encounters with the Utah Expedition's reinforcements ("soldiery beastry"), Mexican laborers ("greasers & jail birds"), and Indians ("stark naked"). At one point Kane considered backtracking briefly to accomplish some task but instead forged on because "a day extra of this awful return home wd. kill me." Instead of inspiring awe, the sight of one of the Oregon Trail's great landmarks triggered feverish thoughts of his own and Elizabeth's mortality and a dread that they might not survive to see one another: "Camp abreast of Chimney Rock—my devil's thumb. Will the parallel between us end here? Will I not be able to show my hands above the water before I go down!" It was an existential despair not unlike the depression Kane suffered during March in the snow en route to meet William Kimball. Although Kane seemed to take no solace in the fellowship and support of his Mormon escort, occasional encounters with returning LDS missionaries buoyed him, as did nothing other than the prospect of reaching his own home.

[79]Elizabeth Kane Journal, 5 December 1858, Kane Family Papers, BYU.

[80]Kane's escort when it reached the river at Florence, Nebraska, on 9 June, twenty-three days after departing Bridger, included Howard Egan, John R. Murdock, E. Van Ettan, Fay Worthen, and two other men named West and Knowlton. The latter were most likely Lewis A. West, younger brother of Col. Chauncey W. West, and John Quincy Knowlton, who four years later was first lieutenant of Lot Smith's Civil War cavalry company. "Arrival of Col. Kane and Escort from Utah," unattributed notice, *Millennial Star* (Liverpool) 20, no. 3 (24 July 1858): 467.

[81]Elizabeth Cumming to Kane, 25 June 1858, Kane Family Papers, BYU.

As Kane entered the Mormon Missouri River settlement at Florence, he closed his Utah diary with additional thoughts of loss and death, especially those of Apostle Parley Pratt, his brother Elisha, and their father Judge Kane. There, as he prepared to move on with Howard Egan alone, he summed up his life's work in typically cryptic fashion: "When I ask myself what I have gained and before answering Naught—I remember my wife and children. Heavy handed as well as heavy hearted though I be I remember also that these blessings have not been of my earning and seek my rest with this though[t] more worthy of a Sunday Evening."[82]

Acting Egregiously: The Staines Mansion as Honey Trap

Once back at Fort Bridger, Cumming began to act gubernatorially. He rebuked Marshal Dotson for stating that Utah was still in a state of "rebellion" and sacked Washington Jay McCormick as acting territorial secretary for participating in a posse organized by Dotson (at Judge Eckels's direction) that struck Cumming as anti-Mormon. At Bridger Cumming was beyond the sight of Mormon leaders—but surely was not out of their mind. As President Young and the apostles struggled to manage the Move South, unsettling dreams of the new governor plagued their sleep:

> On the way to Provo Kanyon Prest Young said he dreamed last night, of seeing Gov. Cumming, he appeared exceedingly friendly, and said to Prest. Young we must be united; we must act in concert; and commenced undressing himself to go to bed with him. Elder Taylor said he also dreamed of seeing Cumming; Cumming asked him if the people would acknowledge him as their Governor, if he sent the Army back. Bro. Taylor studied some time, and then answered "we have never refused to receive any officer sent by the Government." At that Cumming danced & capered about like a mountebank.[83]

Offended by what he perceived as Cumming's lechery, William C. Staines contemplated discontinuing the governor as his guest when he returned to Salt Lake City in June with Elizabeth Cumming. Staines viewed Kane as "one of the most Gentlemanly men I ever meet" but complained that Cumming was "to[o] free with the Girls about the House going to & fro from parlour to Kitchen & this is very annoying to the Girls." Here was, as Staines

[82]Kane, "Diary III (1858)," 57, 60, 61, and 67–68.

[83]Historian's Office Journal, 20 May 1858, LDS Archives.

described it, a diplomatic embarrassment resolved only when Brigham Young and Heber C. Kimball counseled Staines to continue Cumming's role as his star boarder. George A. Smith was present during Staines's discussion of this sensitive matter with Young, and recorded this version:

> Wm C. Staines had an interview with Prest. Young and G. A. Smith, in regard to keeping his house open to receive Gov. Cumming and family. Bro Staines said that while Cumming boarded with him, he acted very egregiously in trying to take liberties with his women, so much so, that they were afraid to go about the house alone, two had to go together; that did not prevent him from invading the privacy of their rooms while they were attending to their household duties, he would follow them into the dining room, Kitchen and Buttery, and seize them and try to down them. At one time he seized one of his hired girls, and pulled her down on his lap the other girl took a candlestick and told Cumming she would split his head if he did not let the girl get up, and she would call Staines. Cumming said well what of that. Staines was watching them through the window, the girl succeeded in getting away from him.[84]

In his encrypted letter to his father of 18 April, Kane may have referred to these incidents in saying of Cumming, "He has made one grave mistake, (not to be mentioned) but is right on public matters."[85]

What came with Brigham Young's awareness of his successor's personal peccadillos was another avenue for subordinating a vulnerable Cumming emotionally, if not co-opting him politically. Whether Alfred Cumming realized it while packing at Fort Bridger, Salt Lake City's Staines mansion lay waiting to serve Young as what twenty-first-century intelligence services would dub a "honey trap."

---

[84]Ibid., 22 May 1858, LDS Archives. Three and one-half years later, with no U.S. Army presence in the territory during the first year of the Civil War, Cumming's successor, Gov. John Dawson, met a quite different fate after allegedly making improper advances on a Mormon widow within weeks of his arrival in Salt Lake City. Such was Dawson's fear of exposure and vigilantism that he fled Salt Lake City on 1 January 1862. At a Wasatch stage station, he was severely beaten, if not castrated. As a battered and bleeding Governor Dawson resumed his eastbound travels, Porter Rockwell and other well-known bravos tracked down the governor's assailants and summarily executed all five men during what they characterized as escape attempts. Potterf, "John W. Dawson, Herodotus of Fort Wayne," 1–14.

[85]Kane to Judge Kane, 18 April 1858, in Elizabeth Kane Journal, 19 June 1858, Kane Family Papers, BYU.

Chapter 15

"All That Is Required" The Differing Needs of Johnston, Buchanan, and Kane

The army when the reinforcements shall have joined will probably aggregate at least 5,000. This force, doubtless, is all that will be required to place the Mormons where they should be—at the feet of the Government.

Capt. James Hervey Simpson to *Buffalo (N.Y.) Courier*, 26 April 1858

There is reason to believe that our difficulties with the Territory of Utah have terminated and the reign of the Constitution and the laws have been restored.

President James Buchanan to Congress, 10 June 1858

As Ben McCulloch, Lazarus W. Powell, and Thomas L. Kane traveled the Oregon Trail in opposite directions, they did so amidst a vast flow of men, animals, artillery pieces, and supply wagons heading west to reinforce and resupply Albert Sidney Johnston. Catalyst to this movement were General Scott's belated awareness of the Standing Army of Israel, the collapse of Secretary Floyd's thrust from the Pacific Coast, Congress's reluctance to provide new regiments, and the shocking realization that the Utah Expedition faced deprivation. Thus, while Brigham Young and James Buchanan maneuvered to end the war without further bloodshed, nearly one-third of America's regular army was in the field under orders for Utah, the nation's most extensive and expensive military effort since the Mexican-American War.

In the early spring of 1858, the size and complexity of this force prompted the War Department to revisit its organization and leadership. For the second time in 1858, Albert Sidney Johnston's command responsibilities came under review, this time not in secret—as with Winfield Scott's January proffer of command to General Wool—but in a clumsy, public way that jeopardized Johnston's morale, enraged his officers, and stoked Mormon anxieties.

Brigham Young had accepted Alfred Cumming as governor, but he persisted with the Move South to maintain pressure on the Buchanan administration while providing a contingency in the event of army misbehavior in Mormon settlements. Continuation of the Move South also reflected Young's unwillingness to appear indecisive in light of several abrupt, disruptive decisions: abandonment of San Bernardino; withdrawal from Fort Limhi; creation and then abolition of the Standing Army; dispatch of expeditions to the White Mountains and Colorado River; and launch of the Move South itself. As Kane later phrased it for anonymous publication, Young "was committed too far to retrace his steps beyond redemption. The effect of his changing his position for the third time, would have been to discredit entirely extraordinary pretensions as one receiving revelations from the Most High."[1]

James Buchanan, in turn, had dispatched Messrs. Powell and McCulloch in April to extend a pardon to an entire territory, contingent upon Mormon acceptance of federal authority. Absent more than a hope for the commissioners' success and largely uninformed of Kane's progress, the president continued to apply military force, channeling veteran regiments and raw recruits into Fort Leavenworth on an unprecedented scale.

Notwithstanding these plans, the political sands shifted rapidly for the president beginning on 9 June, when Alfred Cumming's dispatch of 2 May arrived at the state department. With Congress on the eve of adjournment, Buchanan recognized this report as a political opportunity to seize. The next day he sent a brief, hastily drafted message to Congress transmitting Cumming's dispatch and expressing his belief that the Utah conflict was over. Buchanan's message prompted both relief and ridicule in the House. On the same day, the *New York Times* undercut Buchanan's congressional gambit by publishing a copy of the president's still-secret proclamation of pardon obtained from the peace commissioners at Fort Laramie by reporter James W. Simonton. On 11 June the *Times* followed up with a sensational front page featuring Simonton's excoriation of Buchanan for issuing such a pardon.

[1]Untitled and undated four-page ms. (p.3) in T. L. Kane's hand (annotated on reverse "NY correspondence *Herald!*"), Thomas Leiper Kane Papers, APS.

With the simultaneous accumulation of Simonton's material from Fort Laramie, Cumming's dispatch from Salt Lake City, and the president's congressional message, the *Times* executed an editorial about-face critical of Buchanan. The newspaper questioned the wisdom of an expensive Utah Expedition tasked to do what Cumming, somehow aided by Kane, appeared to have accomplished single-handedly. At the same time, the *Times* expressed sympathy for the tens of thousands of Mormon refugees trekking south. For James Buchanan, the political fat was back in the fire at the very moment he so publicly declared victory in Utah.

And then, like the ghost of Banquo in Shakespeare's *Macbeth,* Thomas Kane loomed up at the Executive Mansion to confront the president with secret demands for finalizing the peace and shaping Utah's political future.

On the Verge of the Grave: General Smith and More Leadership Ambiguity

When Capt. John H. Dickerson first heard in mid-April that the army was promoting Albert Sidney Johnston, he was both delighted and relieved. Unaware that three months earlier General Scott had tried unsuccessfully to subordinate Johnston to General Wool, quartermaster Dickerson told a friend in Washington that Johnston's elevation "indicates that he is not to be superceded [*sic*] in the command."[2] If Dickerson did not know about a potential intrusion by Wool on the command scene, about whom had he been worrying? The likelihood is that the captain's concern ran to General Harney's future. Violence in Kansas had subsided and Gov. Robert J. Walker, who had demanded Harney's retention there, resigned in December. But if Dickerson's focus was on Harney, he was, for the moment, worrying about the wrong man. The threat to Johnston's primacy was Brevet Maj. Gen. Persifor F. Smith, commander of the Department of the West.

By the spring of 1858, Secretary Floyd and General Scott had settled on an arrangement to activate the long-planned Department of Utah, with Smith as its commander. Reporting to him as equals would be two brevet brigadier generals, Harney and Johnston. Under this scheme, Johnston was to retain command of the forces at Camp Scott and move them deeper into Utah; Harney was to organize and lead west the reinforcements marshaling

[2]Dickerson to Gordon, 16 April 1858, Bancroft Library.

at Fort Leavenworth. Once these troops reached the Salt Lake Valley, Smith would determine anew the allocation of responsibilities between his two brigadiers, of whom Johnston was the junior. Scott announced these changes in command on 15 April 1858.[3]

In some respects, Persifor Smith's appointment to such a major command was logical. A patrician Philadelphian with strong ties to Louisiana, he received two brevets in Mexico and was vastly experienced in campaigning throughout the West, although not in the Great Basin. As a brigadier general and major general by brevet, only Winfield Scott, David E. Twiggs, and John E. Wool outranked Smith. During late November 1857, in the wake of Lot Smith's raid, it was General Smith rather than Winfield Scott to whom Secretary Floyd turned for military advice.[4] As recently as January 1858, Rep. Charles J. Faulkner, chairman of the House committee on military affairs, sought Smith's views, an overture to which the general responded with a long treatise advocating expansion of the regular army by increasing the size of existing companies rather than creating new units.[5]

The decision to appoint General Smith drew fire, especially from opposition newspapers. The editor of the *Buffalo (N.Y.) Courier* rose to the administration's defense, denying that Buchanan and Floyd had acted in partisan fashion to punish congressional leaders who had opposed the president's failed attempt to secure statehood for Kansas under the Lecompton Constitution. In doing so, the paper challenged the notion that Albert Sidney Johnston had been "superseded unjustly," "must feel the wrong most keenly," and might even "throw up his commission" after suffering "a flagrant and wanton indignity." To the *Courier,* the selection of Smith rather than Johnston was logical rather than personal, political, or punitive: "When the exigencies of the service demanded a larger army [for Utah], the appointment of a General to command it became a matter of military necessity. No man understands this better than Col. Johns[t]on." Ignoring that the Utah Expedition's existing commander was not only a colonel but a general officer by brevet who had been leading multiple units for seven months, the newspaper went on to argue that "a military expedition must always be placed under the charge of an officer of adequate rank. A Colonel commands a regiment,

---

[3]G. O. No. 8, HQ of the Army, 15 April 1858, Robinson, "History of the Mormon Rebellion," 149; LeCheminant, "A Crisis Averted?" 41.

[4]*At Sword's Point, Part 1,* 427–30.

[5]Smith to Faulkner, 28 January 1858, Persifor Fraser Smith Papers, BYU.

or even two regiments; but when the force is increased to a Division, or a Brigade, etiquette and discipline make it imperative that the officer in command should be a General."[6]

Notwithstanding this argument, there was a serious flaw in the command structure created by Floyd and Scott: General Smith was deathly ill. As rumors seeped out of the War Department, "Junius," the Washington correspondent of Chicago's *Daily Tribune*, reported, "there is a great dispute about the command of the Utah army. For some reason or other Col. Johnston is to be superseded. Major General Smith, a very sensible and discreet officer has been ordered to take the command, but it is well known that he is too old and too infirm to endure the fatigues of the journey. He can hardly walk." Without a firm grasp on what decisions had been made, "Junius" guessed that the administration would compensate for Smith's physical limitations by using Harney as a proxy, adding that, because of the intellectual shortcomings of "Mad Bear," Buchanan would somehow use the newly appointed peace commissioners "by way of securing themselves against his blunders."[7]

Lt. Col. Robert E. Lee, Johnston's executive officer in the Second Cavalry, agreed with "Junius's" assessment. Writing on 17 May to his son Custis, an army officer in California, Lee stepped over the issue of whether Buchanan should have selected Sidney Johnston or perhaps even himself for the new command, focusing solely on the matter of officer health: "You have of course seen the orders organizing the command, and I will not repeat. General Harney and General Johnston will have to operate [in the field for Smith]. I do not think it right to commit the honor of the country and the lives of the soldiers to persons so prostrated. General Smith showed the true spirit of a soldier when he said he would rather die than not go, but other matters have to be considered."[8]

As Lee wrote while on a leave of absence in Virginia, Persifor Smith, commander of the department of Utah, lay dead at Fort Leavenworth. After roaming the country for years in search of treatment for a never-mentioned ailment, he fell victim to chronic diarrhea, an affliction probably acquired in Mexico. That the army's leaders appointed an obviously incapacitated officer to such an assignment raises serious questions of judgment. They

[6]"The Command of the Utah Army," Editorial, *Buffalo (N.Y.) Courier*, 12 May 1858, 2/1.

[7]"Junius," "From Washington. Command of the Utah Expedition," 10 April 1858, *Chicago Daily Tribune*, 14 April 1858, 2/4.

[8]Lee to Lee, 17 May 1858, Jones, *Life and Letters of Robert Edward Lee*, 92–93.

are the same issues prompted by General Scott's earlier offer of the Utah command to the aged, controversial General Wool.

Several of the officers at Fort Leavenworth viewed with dismay General Smith's appointment, arrival, and death. Brevet Maj. Thomas Williams, an artillery officer, described General Smith's passing to his wife "Moddie," the daughter of an army surgeon: "The General's decease was expected & predicted on all sides by the medical men as well as by outsiders, to be near at hand. The night he arrd here (May 14) [from St. Louis] he had to be lifted out of ~~the~~ his carriage & carried into his room, & it was supposed would not survive this the night."[9] Capt. James H. Simpson, a topographical engineer, told his fellow-townsmen in Buffalo, "I always thought it remarkable that an officer who was daily reported as being on the verge of the grave, should desire to hold on to the command of the Army, when so much responsibility was involved, and so much energy required, as was the case with ours in the prospect of a conflict with the enemy. But as soon as I saw the lineaments of his face, I could well see how such a spirit could determinedly hold on to his command, and die in the attempt to reach the theatre of action."[10]

With an army promotion system best described as glacial, Smith's death stimulated an intense campaign among senior officers hoping for the vacated brigadier's commission.[11] Even before receiving confirmation of the general's death, Scott wrote to Floyd from New York to recommend that the likely vacancy be filled "immediately," and that he choose from three colonels who were already brigadiers by brevet: John Garland and Joseph G. Totten, both veterans of the War of 1812 who had received their stars ten years earlier in Mexico, and Albert Sidney Johnson, the army's newest brevet brigadier general, who at age 55 was, respectively, eleven and fourteen years younger than the other two candidates. Noticeably absent from Scott's short list of "suggestions" was Brevet Brig. Gen. William S. Harney.[12]

---

[9]Williams to Mary Neosho ("Moddie") Williams, 16–17 May 1858, Thomas Williams Correspondence, BYU.

[10]"S" [Simpson], "Character of General Smith," Dispatch, 22 May 1858, *Buffalo (N.Y.) Courier,* 2 June 1858, 2/1–2. Support for Simpson's point appears in the plethora of orders and planning documents generated by Smith in the four weeks before his death in order to shape the Utah campaign. For example, see the detailed, seven-page memo that he dictated from Philadelphia, directing General Harney on the necessary logistics and force protection measures to be taken for the march ahead. If much of the army viewed Smith's death as imminent, he behaved otherwise. Smith to Harney, 21 April 1858, Letters Received, Office of Adjt. Gen., RG 94, NARA.

[11]See Garland to Floyd, 15 June 1858, Letters Received, Office of Adjt. Gen, RG 94, NARA.

[12]Scott to Floyd, 20 May 1858, ibid.

After a short period of deliberation, the promotion fell to Harney, a decision made by President Buchanan, presumably on Secretary Floyd's recommendation. It was a selection that delighted those anxious to see Mormon Utah brought to heel while appalling observers mindful of Harney's blemished disciplinary record and rough command style. By the time New York correspondents Simonton and Browne reached Camp Scott on 27 May, the garrison was aware of General Smith's appointment and realized that he was ill, but had not yet heard of his death. Nonetheless, the camp was alive with rumors that newly promoted General Johnston was in some way to be superseded by Harney. As Simonton reported it, the reaction to such a prospect was highly negative: "it will prove a serious blunder; breeding discontent in the army, which, however well concealed, will be none the less dispiriting and demoralizing. It certainly does seem as though the Federal Administration is doomed to serious blunder in each and every successive step of their policy in respect to Utah."[13]

Johnston made no public comment about either Persifor Smith's appointment as department commander or the speculation about Harney's preeminence. Absent orders to the contrary, Johnston, in effect, stepped over what must have been a humiliating command ambiguity and prepared to press on toward the Salt Lake Valley at the earliest opportunity. Harney, in turn, chose not to stand on ceremony and avoided treating Johnston—twelve hundred miles to the west—as a subordinate. He apparently never sent Johnston a direct order or otherwise communicated with him. During the late spring and early summer of 1858, General Harney applied all of his energies to the herculean task of organizing and equipping the Utah Expedition's reinforcements at Fort Leavenworth and following them west through Kansas toward Fort Bridger.[14]

To Keep the Ball A Going!: Of Quartermasters and Columns

To supply and transport this force, army quartermasters and their civilian contractors worked feverishly, especially those in St. Louis, Fort Leavenworth,

[13]"S" [Simonton], "Important From Utah," Dispatch, 28 May 1858, Camp Scott Near Fort Bridger, *New York Times,* 24 June 1858, 1/1–5.

[14]LeCheminant, "A Crisis Averted?" 30–45.

Nebraska City, and Fort Laramie. Mark R. Wilson, the most recent historian of the army's antebellum supply effort, describes the scope of this effort through statistics:

> In January 1858, [Quartermaster General] Jesup signed a new comprehensive two-year freighting contract with [Russell, Majors and Waddell] that provided for the delivery of as much as 15 million pounds of supplies per year, a maximum three times higher than in the previous contract. RM&W responded by expanding its operations, building a new depot in Nebraska City, and augmenting its force to include some 3,500 wagons, 40,000 oxen, 1,000 mules, and 4,000 [civilian] men. At the same time, the Quartermaster's Department hurried to procure more goods than it had during the previous year. Army manufactures and purchases for the new [reinforcing] expedition included 24,000 pairs of boots and shoes, 17,000 pairs of trousers, 14,000 shirts, 300 wagons 4,000 mules, 1,500 cavalry horses, and 200,000 iron horseshoes. . . . The operations of 1857 and 1858 would come to be known in history, declared [Illinois congressman Owen] Lovejoy, "as the war of the plunderers and contractors, instead of the Utah War."[15]

This tsunami of men, animals, and materiel was in addition to the several thousand mules, horses, and sheep on the trail north from New Mexico with Captain Marcy and his escorting battalion.

As Harney's troops moved west in six independent columns, many of their reactions echoed those of the soldiers preceding them a year earlier, but under different circumstances.[16] The April–May start in 1858 was accompanied by rain, mud, and rising rivers that had not plagued the Utah Expedition in the dry months of July–August 1857. The threat of Indian attacks had

[15]Wilson, *The Business of Civil War*, 54–54.

[16]The reinforcing regiments were the Sixth and Seventh Infantry; First and Second Cavalry; and Second, Third, and Fourth Artillery; as well as Company A of Engineers and a detachment from the army's Corps of Topographical Engineers. Accompanying these veterans were detachments of several hundred recruits assigned from depots in New York, Pennsylvania, and Kentucky. These troops were in addition to the units already at Camp Scott: the Fifth and Tenth Infantry, Second Dragoons, Phelps's Light Battery B from the Fourth Artillery, Reno's siege battery from the Ordnance Department, and Bee's battalion of volunteer infantrymen. Although Albert Sidney Johnston had declined Gen. John Garland's proffer of an eight-hundred-man regiment from New Mexico, General Scott pressured Garland into providing a northbound captain Marcy a battalion-strength escort formed from elements of two regiments, the Mounted Riflemen and Third Infantry. Thus a total of approximately five thousand men drawn from fourteen major units were under orders for Utah in the spring of 1858. The most concise compilation of army units committed to Utah, as well as their organization and the identity of their commanders, is Parks, "The Army of the Mormon War, 1857–1858," 84–87. These tabulations are especially helpful in comprehending how the six columns launched from Fort Leavenworth in 1858 were constituted, although unfortunately they do not set forth the total troop strength associated with these columns and the units already bivouacked at Camp Scott.

temporarily abated during the intervening year as a result of Col. Edwin V. Sumner's punitive expedition against the Cheyennes in the summer of 1857 and the residual impact of Harney's own Sioux campaign of 1856. Still complicating the future was uncertainty over whether the Utah Expedition would have to fight its way into the Salt Lake Valley and the nature of what awaited it once there: continuing guerrilla warfare or an oppressed Mormon population grateful for liberation.

Some of Harney's reinforcements included now-anonymous soldiers and understudied units—dramatis personae one might dub the Utah War's "lost."[17] Among the most talented soldiers of these was Brevet Maj. Thomas Williams, a company commander in the Third U.S. Artillery. At age 43, Williams was older than many of his peers and at an age that made active campaigning physically difficult. Raised in Detroit, his father was a militia major general, prosperous real estate investor, and the city's first elected mayor. A West Pointer, Williams served in Mexico as an aide to Winfield Scott and received two brevets for valor. He served at posts as widely dispersed as Florida and Lake Huron's Mackinac Island. Williams wrote frequently to his young wife, then living in Newburgh, New York, to describe his Utah War experiences.[18]

Williams to Mary Neosho ("Moddie") Williams, April–July 1858, Thomas Williams Correspondence, BYU.

17 April 1858 (Fort Leavenworth):

There is nevertheless much conjecture concerning whether it be the purpose of the *expected* orders that we should really enter Utah, or that the orders are published for their moral effect on Brigham & his people. Certain it is, an express passed thro' here about a week ago to arrest the march of Gen. Johnston, & that Commissioners are understood to have been appointed to treat with the Mormons. One would think that the President must have recd. thro' the Mormon delegate in Washington [Bernhisel] overtures of submission of an unusual character to justify negotiation with a community in open rebellion against law & authority, & that, if so, those orders for the movement of more troops into the Valley of Salt Lake, must be in the way of demonstration, or, in other words, to show the Saints the Government is determined & ready to punish them if they recede from their own overtures of submission. Again, if the Commissioners, daily, hourly expected to arrive

[17]MacKinnon, "'Finding the Lost,'" in MacKinnon, *Predicting the Past,* 23–25.

[18]For the most extensive summary of Williams's life and Utah War involvement, including his establishment of Camp Walbach, the cantonment built in late 1858 to guard the east entrance to Cheyenne Pass, Nebraska, see MacKinnon, biographical note to inventory of Thomas Williams Correspondence, BYU; and Ryan, "Camp Walbach," 5–20.

here, en route for Utah, should succeed in their mission of peace, may we not find ourselves turned back before getting to Utah? Yes, turned back before getting to Laramie, half-way? this is a consummation greatly to be hoped for. In any event, there will be troops required to occupy Salt Lake city—a strong garrison—but this garrison may be furnished by Johnston's army. On the other hand, to exhaust conjecture, if we suppose it to be intended, at Washington, that all the troops ordered to Utah should go there, shall we retrace our steps or go to the Pacific? that is the question!

Capt. [George Washington] Getty, Mrs. G.; Capt. & Mrs. De R. [Gustavus Aldolphus De Russy] & others are, of course, greatly moved, some excited & others depressed. Poor Getty, had only just gotten his wife here, after a separation of nearly 18 months! He told me this morning, that if he had 10,000 dollars he'd throw up [his commission]. [Capt. John Clifford] Pemberton, I understand is especially moved, & more in a quandary how to act than any of his neighbors. I'm told he has said from time to time, that if ordered to Utah, he'd resign.[19]

If, I can go thro' what is before me & at the end [find?] myself as well as I now am, I shall be content. Then, I think I may quit, with the prospect of comfort for wife & children & happiness for all. I do not entertain the idea of resigning under orders. Having adopted the army as a profession, I entered it to take service as it came. Having had some years of comfort, especially since my marriage, I shall not shrink from doing disagreeable or hard duty when it comes. My only anxiety touching the service is whether I am equal to its fatigues, & I am willing to make the experiment, which, if successful will be to me ample demonstration that I am perfectly restored. No small satisfaction it will be, to feel & be *sure* that I am as well as I ever have been.[20] But, my dear baby, meanwhile let us hope that there is nothing in the future we cannot meet, the ground of our hope being that we have gone thro' the past without serious mishap & with a large share [of] comfort & happiness....

Moddie dear, have I told you what I purchased towards an outfit for the plains in St. Louis? To make sure I'll repeat. 1st. a camp bedstead of wood made to fold closely together; a cotton mattress; two cotton comforters, 4 hickory seated chairs. In all, about $14—(fourteen dols) Yes, 16 dollars, for I got a trunk or box for $2 to relieve the large trunk, as the Porters complained of its great weight & wanted extra for handling it. If I take the large trunk on the plains, it is proposed that it be provided with a set of wheels, making the whole a *trunk-wagon*!!! If I get a riding-mule—saddle mule, I mean—he'll cost me about $180 or 200, with saddle & bridle! Saddle mules, are scarce &

[19]Pemberton did resign but not until 29 April 1861 to enter the Confederate service, in which as a lieutenant general he surrendered Vicksburg. All of the officers Williams mentioned in this letter were in the Fourth Artillery.

[20]Williams had apparently been ill.

in much demand. They are greatly preferred to horses, chiefly on account of being more easily subsisted. A mule will fatten, on what a horse would starve. We cannot take grain, & without it, horses break rapidly when confined to the grass of the plains. The mule, if he cannot get grass, will make out with weeds, chips &c &c. Besides for a *long* journey, a mule is far easier to the rider.[21]

3 July 1858 (Camp Near Fort Kearny):

Left camp near Ft. Kearney [*sic*] at 6 1/2 AM this morning. . . . Genl. Harney has gone on notwithstanding the letter from [1st] Lt. [Grier] Tallmadge [of Phelps's Battery] near Salt Lake with Gen. J's army to Capt. [John Porter] McCown [post commander] at Ft. Kearney which was shown him; saying that Genl. Johnston then within 50 miles of Salt Lake City, had recd. the submission of the Mormons, & in a [14 June] proclamation said, he was now as ready to support as he had been to oppose them, & that Gen J. had sent back from his army to New Mexico the companies of [Mounted] rifles & of the 3d. Infantry.[22] And, yet our orders are to push on. 25 days are given us to reach Laramie, & thence, 40 days to Salt Lake City. Having placed himself, thus unaccountably out of the way of expected orders from the east; an express with the orders of recall for a portion of the troops, we learn to be out, cannot now overtake him before he reaches Laramie. Our orders are to "push on" without regard to the supply trains. Perhaps, the purpose is (Genl. H. fearing Gen. Johnston may have a surpluss of supplies) to send on with dispatch, a force to consume the surpluss. Stupid! Stupid! Stupid! . . .

Two officers of 2d Drags from Fort Bridger passed thro' this evening on their way East. They represent matters at Salt Lake as they have already been in the letter of Gov. Cummings to the Sec. of State. And, all this movement of troops & supplies as an immense fraud on the Treasury. Ah! Moddie didn't I tell you some time since, I suspected we were in the hands of the Philistines:—contractors! jobbers! & scoundrel politicians?!!! And, now we're going on to consume provisions & the great outfit in horses, mules, wagons, &c &c provided for this army, to keep the ball a going! Thereby the contracts &c &c may have more provisions, more mules, more horses, more wagons &c &c to provide. A principal officer of the Qr. Master's Department, with the Hd Quarters of the Army told me a week ago, that if the expedition were arrested then, certain contractors whom he named, could not fail to make two millions of dollars. I wish public attention could be properly bro't to examine this infamous fraud on the country.[23]

---

[21]A mule is also less sway-back than a horse and has a different gait and temperament, so some officers preferred these animals.

[22]The report attributed to Tallmadge was inaccurate; Johnston would not order these two regiments back to New Mexico until 19 July.

[23]Here Major Williams sounds like Brigham Young in full cry about what he dubbed the "Contractors War." See MacKinnon, "125 Years of Conspiracy Theories," 219–22.

> This prostitution of the army to the basest uses, I wish some man equal to the task of exposing the big & little scoundrels; the scoundrels of every degree, concerned, would adjust himself to his work, at once. What a pity it is, for the ends of justice, that knaves are generally cunning knaves. That truth, is so easily intermingled with falsehood to the success of knaves & the mystification of honest men. It is true, indeed, that knaves are generally found out, but found out when its too late, found out after they've effected their objects! What lien have the public upon these fellows after they've pocketed the treasury's money? what sensible man ever doubted of a future retribution. I believe; this article of faith has alike entered into the religions of the rudest nations, in all times.
>
> Good night, my own dearest & best. Its 10 P.M. & I'm up at 4 in the morning.

Far more obscure to historians than Major Williams was 2d Lt. Robert L. Browning, the U.S. Marine Corps' contribution to an otherwise all-army campaign. In the aftermath of an unpleasant court martial, Browning sought a change from sea duty by petitioning commandant Col. John Harris and Secretary of the Navy Isaac Toucey for detached assignment to the Utah Expedition as an "observer." They and Secretary Floyd agreed, and Browning marched west from Fort Leavenworth with General Harney's Fourth Column. Once into Utah Browning served with the Fifth Infantry, Johnston's regiment that most needed officers. In thinking about the oddity of a naval officer ahorse in the Great American Desert, 2d Lt. George E. Ryan of the Seventh Infantry commented, "It is my private opinion that when he sees once more a ship or Marine Barracks that it will be a long while before he volunteers [again] for land service. The novelty wore off might quick with him, in fact I guess that is the case with most young fellows who join the army." Although he was almost gored while running buffalo in Nebraska, Lieutenant Browning survived the Utah War but not his next assignment. In 1860 he and all hands went down with U.S.S. *Levant* during a storm off Hawaii.[24]

Another interesting and somewhat neglected officer was Capt. James Hervey Simpson, like Lieutenant Ives a member of the army's elite Corps of Topographical Engineers. Certain aspects of Simpson's western work during the late 1850s are well known, especially his explorations and trail blazing during the fall of 1858 and the summer of 1859 between Provo Canyon

[24] Ryan to parents, 10 January 1859, Ryan Family Papers, Catholic University of America, Washington, D.C. For nearly 150 years commandants and historians at the corps' headquarters were aware that a marine officer served on detached duty with the Utah Expedition, but until 2003 Browning's name, rank, and the circumstances of his unusual assignment were forgotten. MacKinnon, "Epilogue to the Utah War," 219.

2D LT. ROBERT L. BROWNING, U.S.M.C. In the spring of 1858, Browning sought respite from the Marines by requesting detached duty as an observer with the otherwise all-army Utah Expedition. He crossed the plains with General Harney's fourth column; once into Utah he served with the under-officered Fifth Infantry. In 1860, after Utah, Browning died in a Pacific storm with the entire ship's company of U.S.S. *Levant. Daguerreotype ca. 1852 from http://www.prices4antiques.com/Daguerreotype-Photograph-1-2-Plate-Portrait-Marine-Corps-Officer-D9967088.html (accessed 2 January 2014).*

and Fort Bridger (to develop a road to bypass Salt Lake City) and between Camp Floyd and Carson Valley (to shorten the trek to California).[25] What is unknown are Simpson's perceptive dispatches written during the spring and summer of 1858 to the *Courier* of Buffalo, New York, the city in which he served during the 1840s and where his wife lived during their frequent separations.[26] Simpson's initial Utah War assignment was command of a detachment of topographical engineers and supporting civilians traveling in the midst of Lt. Col. Pitcairn Morrison's Seventh U.S. Infantry, a regiment tasked to provide leadership for the campaign's Fourth and Fifth Columns while escorting General Harney and his department headquarters.

Through Simpson's letters to the *Courier*, students of the Utah War now have a glimpse of the little-known Seventh Infantry and perhaps the most eclectic of the six columns marching to reinforce the Utah Expedition. In

[25]Beeton, "James Hervey Simpson in the Great Basin," 28–43; Peterson, *A Route for the Overland Stage*; and Simpson, *Report of Explorations across the Great Basin.*

[26]Simpson is not to be confused with Capt. Marcus de Lafayette Simpson, a staff officer (commissary) serving at Fort Leavenworth during this period, or with James W. Simonton, the Utah War correspondent of the *New York Times* who, like Simpson, signed his newspaper dispatches as "S."

FORT LEAVENWORTH, KANSAS TERRITORY, MAY 1858

The post as Buchanan's peace commissioners saw it while pausing to pick up their guides, weapons, transportation, dragoon escort, and "bushels" of the president's printed pardon. This photograph is among the first taken of the post by Samuel C. Mills of Washington, who accompanied Capt. James Hervey Simpson's detachment of topographical engineers then awaiting orders for Utah. The trooper shown was probably from Col. E. V. Sumner's First Cavalry, part of the Utah Expedition's reinforcements. *Mills & Jagiello photo, Lee-Palfrey Collection, courtesy of Manuscript Division, Library of Congress.*

addition, through the work of Samuel C. Mills, the Washington daguerreotypist accompanying Simpson, we have the first photographs taken along the Oregon Trail, including pioneering images of Forts Leavenworth, Kearny, Laramie, and Bridger as well as the troops' ultimate destination, Camp Floyd, Utah.[27]

"S" [Simpson], Dispatches, *Buffalo (N.Y.) Courier*, April–July 1858, 2/2.

26 April 1858 (Fort Leavenworth), Published 4 May 1858:

This post is all alive with the preparation necessary for the coming grand march. The absence of the General who is to command the troops, however, makes it still a doubtful matter as to the precise time when we shall get off. It cannot, I think, by any possibility, be before the 10th of May. The late very cold weather having checked the growth of the grass, to make it about its ordinary height at this season, it would not be expedient that we should start sooner.

The number of troops here, at this date, including every arm, is about 1,800; and when all shall have arrived that have been ordered, the total force will be upwards of 3,000. This probably will be the strength of the reinforcements that will join the army of Utah. The army when the reinforcements shall have joined will probably aggregate at least 5,000. This force, doubtless, is all that will be required to place the Mormons where they should be—*at the feet of the Government*; and many think that a smaller force would be sufficient for the purpose. But it is well to take into consideration their mountain fastnesses, which certainly give them no small advantage.

The Quarter Master's and Subsistence Departments are all in a flourishing condition, and their chiefs find no difficulty in procuring all the horses, mules and cattle they require. . . .

The Utah Commissioners, Governor Powell and Major McCullough [*sic*], left yesterday, with the party, all told, of fifteen persons, for the army of Utah. They have five light four mule ambulances to carry the party, and the necessary forage. They contemplate going through in thirty days. I had the pleasure of traveling with them from Cincinnati to St. Louis, and have seen them since they arrived here. They seem to be fully aware of the delicate mission they have had entrusted to them, and doubtless will wisely carry out the instructions of the Government. The Governor is a shrewd,

[27]Mills's beautiful trail and garrison photographs are part of the Library of Congress's Lee-Palfrey Collection. Published portions of these images appear in MacKinnon, "125 Years of Conspiracy Theories," 212–30; Langellier, "The William Lee Diary Account of the James H. Simpson Expedition, 1858–59," 36–47; and *At Sword's Point, Part 1*, 163 and 219. The best assessment of Mills's Utah War work is in two articles by Dickson: "On the Trail of Captain Simpson's Illusive Photographer," 3–6, and "'Shadowy Figures about whom Little is Known,'" 270–89.

kind-hearted, venerable man; and though the Major has all the air of a sharp, resolute character, yet, under all this, there seems to be a deep substratum of caution, that will, no doubt, prevent his doing anything rash.

1 June 1858 (Spring Branch, K.T., 25 Miles West of Fort Leavenworth), Published 11 June 1858:

Here I am, with the Topographical Engineer party on my way to the Army of Utah. At present I am journeying with Col. Morrison's column of Utah Forces (the 4th) but shall join Gen. Harney when he overtakes us. I have with me two young [brevet 2d] Lieuts. [Haldimand Sumner Putnam and Joseph Lee Kirby Smith[28]] and I wish to put them in the train of their duties before joining Head Quarters. Colonel Morrison's column marched out of Fort Leavenworth yesterday, at 9 A.M., and a very imposing and creditable appearance the troops made.[29] The soul-stirring drum and the martial notes of the band added not a little to the elation of the occasion. . . .

The whole command, aggregating over 600 men, and having a train of 100 wagons, loaded with subsistence for 25 days, to serve till they reach Fort Kearney [*sic*]; and half [animal] forage for fourteen days. You may readily imagine so large a number of troops make a very interesting appearance on their march; and when, with this, is combined a series of landscapes which cannot fail to move the heart of any lover of nature, you can readily call up the emotion that such a spectacle would naturally create. . . .

Capt. [William F.] Barry's Battery [2d Artillery] forms no inefficient portion of Col. Morrison's column. His men show themselves above the ordinary standard of rank and file; and finely and strongly equipped as he is, with powerful horses, and a well-appointed battery, and his company well-drilled, he cannot fail to do his part in any collision we may have with the Mormons.

2 July 1858 (Platte River Between Forts Kearny and Laramie), Published 19 July 1858:

Gen. Harney and staff moved camp yesterday at Fort Kearney, and came as far as this and we are now encamped immediately on the banks of the Platte, within a few feet of the river. As I write the water is coursing along with a strong current; and what we have not seen until we reached the valley of the Platte, there lies directly in front of us a river at least two miles

[28]Lieutenant Smith is not to be confused with Capt. Edmund Kirby Smith, then serving in the Second Cavalry under Robert E. Lee and later a famous major general in the Confederate Army.

[29]In a private letter to his superior, Capt. A. A. Humphreys, Simpson described this departure in more detail and added a personal opinion not shared with his *Buffalo (N.Y.) Courier* readers: "All the companies presented a fine soldierly appearance, and marching as they did in the order in which they are named each with an appropriate field costume, and with a firm and elastic step, they presented in epitome a very good representation of the power of the army whenever it shall be conducted against the enemies of our country. The other day both officers and men felt the relaxing effects which the late news from Utah was calculated to produce; but now that there appears to be no change in the policy of the government to hold the leaders of the Mormon rebellion to a strict accountability for their outrageous and unexcusable conduct there seems to be one spirit prevailing among officers and men, and that is to move forward." Simpson to Humphreys, 28 May 1858, Letters Received, Office of Explorations and Surveys, RG 77, NARA.

THE SEVENTH INFANTRY FORDING SOUTH PLATTE
EN ROUTE TO UTAH

A unique contemporary sketch of 20 July 1858 by an unknown participant depicting one of the expedition's understudied regiments, Lt. Col. Pitcairn Morrison's Seventh Infantry. It captures the enormity of the reinforcements under General Harney snaking across the plains in Nebraska Territory in six columns to support Albert Sidney Johnston's push to end the war and occupy Utah. *Courtesy of Utah Museum of Fine Arts, Salt Lake City.*

in breadth to the island, and possibly as much in breadth on the other side. The water, however, is not deep, not more than two feet deep, except in the channel, which appears to be quite narrow. Some of our men went in bathing yesterday, and they had to walk a great distance from the shore before they found water sufficiently deep to enable them to swim. . . .

The General is waiting, or rather progressing slowly, for the reason that different columns must protect the contractors' trains, and therefore must conform their movements to the slow movement of the trains. Besides, he is in something of a quandary in relation to the recall of a portion, or the onward movement of all the troops towards Utah. And as he wishes to have them so circumstanced that, without injury to the cause in which they are engaged, they may prove of less expense to the Government, and be less fatigued by useless marches, he at present is moving slowly, so as best to cover the whole ground of his duty.

Col. [Charles A.] May's column, and that of Col. Morrison, as well as a portion of Col. [Edwin V.] Sumner's, are encamped near Fort Kearney; but will all move on in due time, unless orders should be received to the contrary.

As affairs are now in Utah, there is a great deal of suspense and doubt. But it would seem to the writer of this, that the indications are that we have not seen the end of this peculiar drama. These Mormons, from Brigham down, are a queer sort of people, and while at one moment they are all fight and fustian to gain a point, they as quickly assume the air of the conquered, if by that means they can gain the same end—that is, the overthrow of the Government. The truth is, they require at the hands of the Government, a ruler, who, while being a humane man, is one who cannot be duped by their deceits, but will carry out firmly and legitimately the laws of the country in respect to them. May Gov. Cumming prove such.

The War Department has directed General Harney to cause a Military Reserve, 25 miles long by 20 miles broad, to be carefully surveyed and marked out about Fort Bridger; and Capt. Simpson, of the Topographical Engineers [the writer], has been directed to effect it, as soon as practicable after his arrival at the post.

[P.S.] since writing to you this morning, the Salt Lake mail, the first that has come all the way from the city since the Mormon troubles, passed our Camp a few moments since. The driver reports that he met Gen. Johnston within fifty miles of the city; a portion of the troops had got through Echo Canon; and, when he left, there were only about 50 Mormons remaining in the city. Col. [William] Hoffman [Sixth Infantry] had been left in command of Fort Bridger, with but one [two] Company. The Peace Commissioners had granted authority to General Johnston to establish posts in the Territory where he deemed necessary.

Take a Tap, Pard: Utah Expedition Hard Cases

Captain Simpson did not report for the *Courier*'s readers all that he saw, including bad behavior in the less-than-elite Seventh U.S. Infantry.[30] The regiment's commander, Lt. Col. Pitcairn Morrison, struggled to enforce discipline among his junior officers as well as enlistees. Alcohol was at the root of most of Morrison's challenges, as with the multiple, career-ending imbroglios involving 2d Lt. Jesse B. Wharton.[31] With the example of such negative leadership by their officers, the regiment's enlistees strayed into serious difficulties. On 3 June, Capt. Lewis Henry Little, commander of Company E, recorded that the Seventh's senior non-com, Sergeant-Major Robinson, was reduced in rank to private for an unspecified but grievous offense. Two weeks later, Captain Little noted a fatal affray elsewhere in the ranks: "Fifer Ewing run through with a bayonet by a Gen[eral] Pris[oner] named Smith. The men much excited & tried to lynch Smith. . . . Pris[oner] Smith died from injuries recd. in being captured & disarmed."[32]

That the Utah Expedition produced no atrocities like the Legion's Mountain Meadows massacre and Aiken party executions was due more to regular army discipline and effective leadership than inherent good behavior by Albert Sidney Johnston's troops and their camp followers. Within a few days of her arrival at Camp Scott, Governor Cumming's wife described the behavior of the civilians she encountered during the final stages of their brutal trek along Blacks Fork: "In the very cold weather, the teamsters seemed more like madmen than human beings. Much sin abounded. The cold & privations seemed to make them crazy."[33] Unaware that six months later he would be assaulted by drunken troops of the Tenth U.S. Infantry, Judge Eckels described the civilian flotsam surrounding him at Fort Bridger: "Among the immense number of teamsters discharged at this point there were but few good men. They were composed principally of W[h]arf Rats from St. Lewis [*sic*] and gamblers. Too

---

[30]The most comprehensive research and analysis of the Seventh Infantry's role in the Utah War is that of Ephriam D. Dickson III and will appear in his forthcoming study, "A Sojourn in Zion: The Seventh U.S. Infantry in Utah Territory, 1858–1860." The Seventh's Utah War problems ran largely to ineffective leadership and drunkenness and persisted during its Civil War service in New Mexico. Lowry, "Boys in the Bag," 50–53.

[31]Disposition of Court Martial Proceedings, 2d Lt. Jesse B. Wharton, Seventh U.S. Infantry, File HH-980, Records of the Judge Advocate General, RG 153, NARA.

[32]Diary of Capt. Lewis Henry Little, 3 and 18 June 1858. Document in private collection; transcription courtesy of Ephriam D. Dickson III.

[33]Elizabeth Cumming to Anne Elizabeth Cumming Smith, 28 November 1857, Canning and Beeton, *The Genteel Gentile*, 14.

many were corrupted on the way I fear. The idea was general among them, that because of the Mormon rebellion there was no law here, and larceny, forgery & their kindred vices became frequent."[34] In the fall of 1857, Captain Van Vliet reported to Secretary Floyd that Brigham Young "had no objection to the troops themselves entering the Territory; but if they allowed them to do so, it would be opening the door for the entrance of the rabble from the frontiers, who would, as in former times, persecute and annoy them."[35]

The twin scourges of alcohol and gambling created most of the Utah Expedition's disciplinary problems. For the civilians catering to such vices, the thirsty, bored, and unwary members of the garrison posed an irresistible opportunity. In all likelihood, it was this lure that prompted the six flashy, cash-laden members of the Aiken party to ride from California to Utah, where they were intercepted by a Nauvoo Legion patrol, robbed, and murdered in the company of Lts. Porter Rockwell and Bill Hickman during November 1857.[36] So powerful was the Utah Expedition's profit potential for gamblers that a New Mexican faro dealer insisted on sharing the hazards of the trek north from Santa Fe with Colonel Loring and Captain Marcy when they returned to Fort Bridger with the army's remounts. Captain Phelps later reported that once ensconced in the midst of the Utah Expedition, this worthy's "bank is in full operation every night, so that officers can fight the tiger to their hearts content."[37]

Phelps's diary provides anecdotal descriptions of sometimes fatal aspects of the scene:

> Some of the men in my Company tapped a sutler's liquor [supply] last night, and one of them drank enough to kill him. He had been an exemplary soldier. The liquor was strong Scotch Whiskey. His body and limbs remained warm & limber for the period of some eight hours after all other signs of animation were suspended. The Doctor tried to restore him by breathing into his lungs. . . . Night before last one of the Sutler's clerks on a visit to Capt. [James M.] Hawes' camp which was some two miles from here, got into difficulty with a Dragoon soldier. They whipped out their revolvers and exchanged several shots. The Dragoon was shot thro' the thigh. The

[34]Eckels to Sen. Jesse D. Bright, 13 December 1857, Microfilm Pub. M12, State Dept. Territorial Papers, Utah Series, 1853–73, Reel 1 (1853–59), NARA. With Johnston's encouragement, hundreds of these men found their way into Bee's Volunteer Battalion.

[35]Van Vliet to Floyd, 20 November 1857, "Annual Report of the Sec. of War (1857)," 38. For undisciplined behavior among the teamsters accompanying the army's reinforcements in 1858, see MacKinnon, *At Sword's Point, Part 1*, 193–96, and Beehrer, "Freighting across the Plains," 2–17.

[36]Bigler, "The Aiken Party Executions," 451–70.

[37]Phelps Diary, 28 July 1858, Walker draft typescript, 27.

> clerk has been tried by Judge Eckels court and acquitted. . . . The Dragoon who was shot in the leg the other day, died this morning from the effects of the amputation. . . . Another man was carried to the grave day before yesterday, a victim of an excess potation of liquor probably alcohol. A third, it is expected, will not recover.[38]

These and other, more serious imbroglios kept the garrison's officers busy with service on courts martial. In January 1858 such panels tried twenty-nine soldiers from regular regiments for offenses that included neglect of duty, refusal to obey orders, and conduct subversive to good order and prejudicial to military discipline; while another five regulars stood trial during that month for the capital offense of desertion. Similar breaches by Colonel Bee's volunteer troops also clogged the Utah's Expedition's trial dockets throughout the winter and spring of 1858, with three courts convened to dispose of seventeen cases involving enlisted volunteers and a fourth trial ordered to try 1st Lt. John Owens of Magraw's Company A, an officer accused and convicted of sleeping on duty.[39]

Lounging among the army's camp followers at Fort Bridger was William Clarke Quantrill, an Ohioan barely out of his teens but already a killer. Within five years Quantrill would become the most notorious guerrilla of the American Civil War as the leader of the Confederate atrocity at Lawrence, Kansas. Working as teamsters with Quantrill during 1857–58 were David Poole and George Shepherd, future members of "Captain" Quantrill's guerrilla band. Poole witnessed the October 1857 raid by Lot Smith on the Utah Expedition's undefended supply trains.[40]

---

[38]Phelps Diary, 18 December 1857, 12 and 28 March 1858, and 2 April 1858, all in Phelps Papers, NYPL.

[39]The documents convening these trials, announcing the verdicts and sentences, and setting forth Johnston's approval/alterations of convictions are among the voluminous special and general orders issued during 1858, headquarters, Dept. of Utah, RG 98, NARA.

[40]Shepherd rode with the postwar gang led by Jesse James and Cole Younger until captured and imprisoned following a Kentucky bank robbery. Quantrill would be mortally wounded by a Union Army patrol in June 1865 at age 27. Until relatively recently his skull rested in the refrigerator of an Ohio household and his other bones in a cabinet at the Kansas State Historical Society. It was an apt fate for the remains of a Utah War veteran whose guerrillas rode rough-shod over the Missouri-Kansas border with human ears and scalps dangling from their horses' bridles.

Ironically, among the corpses Quantrill's band left in the smoking ruins of Lawrence was that of Lemuel Fillmore, a local realtor and relative of President Fillmore, who during the Utah War was a field reporter for the *New York Herald* until he engaged in a knife fight with James W. Simonton of the *New York Times* at a Provo hotel. A direct consequence of Quantrill's Lawrence raid was the Union Army's punitive Order No. 11, which in the fall of 1863 depopulated four western Missouri counties, a mass exodus comparable to the Utah War's Move South. Clarke, "W. C. Quantrill in 1858," 218–23; Connelley, *Quantrill and the Border Wars*, 1–7, 66, 75–81, 87, 94–96, 99–100, 103–104, 100–10; Crouch, "A 'Fiend in Human Shape'? William Clarke Quantrill and His Biographers," 143–56; Leslie, *The Devil Knows How to Ride*, 52–63; and Ismert, "Quantrill-Charley Hart?" Also Cuthbertson, "Shepherd Was Name to Fear in Border War Era," 140.

Quantrill's behavior at an improvised Fort Bridger gambling "hell" provides historians with a vivid glimpse of the raw behavior dreaded by both Brigham Young and Albert Sidney Johnston. This account of Quantrill in action comes from the reminiscences of former cavalry private Robert M. Peck, one of Johnston's reinforcements and a veteran of Col. Edwin V. Sumner's famous saber charge against the Cheyennes at Solomon Creek, Kansas, the previous July.[41]

FORMER PVT. ROBERT MORRIS PECK,
COMPANY K, FIRST U.S. CAVALRY,
"ROUGH RIDING ON THE PLAINS 50 YEARS AGO,"
WASHINGTON NATIONAL TRIBUNE, 25 APRIL 1901, 1/1–4, 2/6.

I was a soldier in one of the two companies of 1st Cav. that formed a part of the command of Lieut. Col. Wm. Hoffman, 6th Inf., which command was sent out from Fort Leavenworth early in the spring of '58 to escort several trains—some [drawn by] mule teams and some of oxen—loaded with supplies for the command of Brvt. Brig. Gen. Albert Sidney Johnston, Commanding the Mormon Expedition, who had been snowed in all winter at Fort Bridger, or Camp Scott, as it was officially designated.

We arrived at Camp Scott in the first days of June. A paymaster who had followed us arrived about the same time and paid the soldiers off. As there were few ways of spending the money outside of Judge [William A.] Carter's sutler store, where prices were outrageously high, during the few days that intervened between our arrival at Fort Bridger and the departure of Gen. Johnston's forces for Salt Lake City, gambling was rife throughout the camp, and, as usually happens, in a short time, a few sharpers had nearly all the soldiers' money.

Among the celebrities of the camp I had frequently heard the name of Charley Hart[42] mentioned, whose notoriety seemed to be derived from his reckless bettings and phenomenal winnings. I heard it stated that he had come out from Kansas with Gen. Johnston's troops the previous fall, working as a teamster in one of the six-mule [per wagon] trains.

While sauntering through a big gambling tent a day or so after pay-day, watching the fluctuations of fortune at the various tables where chance games were being operated, I heard some one remark, "There comes Charley Hart," and having heard his fame as a wild plunger in gambling, I took a good look at him. I could see nothing heroic in his appearance, but considerable of the rowdy, as I now recall the impression I then got of him.

He was apparently about twenty-two or twenty-three [twenty] years of age;

[41]For context, see MacKinnon, "'Take a Tap, Pard': The Utah Expedition as Finishing School for Civil War Hard Cases," in Alford, ed., *Civil War Saints*, 393–96.

[42]Quantrill assumed the alias "Charley Hart" in Kansas during 1856–57 to cover his part in a spree of thefts and involvement with the slavery-related violence wracking the region.

about five feet ten inches in height; with an ungraceful, slouchy walk; and by no means prepossessing in features. He had evidently been patronizing Judge Carter's store, since he "struck it rich," for his clothes all seemed new. A pair of high-heeled calf-skin boots of small size; bottoms of trousers tucked into boot-tops; a navy [Colt] pistol swinging from his waist belt; a fancy blue flannel shirt; no coat; a colored silk handkerchief tied loosely around his neck; yellow hair hanging nearly to the shoulders; topped out by the inevitable cow-boy hat. This is the picture of Charley Hart, as my memory presents him now.

As he entered the tent he carried in his left hand a colored silk handkerchief, gathered by the four corners, which apparently contained coin. Advancing to one of the tables where the operator, or banker, as the dealer of a chance game is usually called, was dealing "Monte," he set the handkerchief on the table and opened it out, showing the contents to be gold coins, and seemingly in bulk about equal to the stacks of gold coins tiered upon the table in front of the banker.

Hart then asked, "Take a tap, pard?" meaning would the banker accept a bet of Hart's pile against the dealer's, on the turn of a card. The banker accepted the challenge, shuffled the cards, passed the deck to Hart to cut, then threw out the "lay-out" of six cards, in a "column-of-twos" style.[43] Hart then set his handkerchief of gold on a card, at the same time drawing his pistol, "Just to insure fair play," he remarked, seeing that the banker had his gun lying on the table convenient to his right hand. Keeping his eye on the banker's hands, to make sure that the deal was done "on the square," Hart said, "Now deal."

Turning the deck face up the banker drew the cards off successively. Hart's card won. As the dealer looked up with a muttered oath he found himself looking into the muzzle of Hart's pistol.

"Back out," said Hart quietly. "Don't even touch your pistol. I'll give it back to you when I rake in the pot."

The banker did as directed, while Hart, without showing any nervousness, still holding his pistol in one hand, reached across the table and with the other arm swept the banker's money and pistol over to him. Picking out the twenties, tens, fives and two-and-a-half pieces, he tossed them into his handkerchief. There still remained on the table about a double handful of small silver, (there were very few silver dollars in circulation then, the little one-dollar gold pieces being largely used in their stead), and a handful of gold dollars. Sweeping this small stuff into his hands, Hart said, "I don't carry such chicken feed as that," as he tossed the small coins up in the air and let the crowd scramble for them.

Then handing the dejected looking banker his pistol and a twenty-dollar gold piece, he said: "There, pard, is a stake for you," and gathering up his plethoric handkerchief, he meandered on seeking new banks to "bust."

---

[43]This description in military parlance reflects Peck's background as an old cavalryman.

The next day, so I was told, Hart's marvelous luck deserted him, and he lost every dollar he had; and after trying in vain to "strike it up again," he became discouraged and disgusted with gambling, joined some outfit going back to the states, and went back to Kansas dead broke.[44]

I never heard the name Quantrill used till the summer of '61, when his depredations along the borders of Missouri and Kansas were bringing the name into unpleasant notoriety. I then heard that Quantrill, the bloody-handed guerrilla leader, and Charley Hart, the reckless gambler of Fort Bridger, were identical.

Notwithstanding these disciplinary problems in the Utah Expedition, its reinforcements, and camp followers, there were countervailing pockets of exemplary, faith-based behavior within the force, most noticeably among some of its higher-toned officers. For example, as Capt. James H. Simpson marched his topographical engineers west from Fort Leavenworth in June, he brought with him a box of Bibles and hymnals with which to conduct Sunday religious services. In another small unit, Company A of Engineers, its young executive officer, Brevet 2d Lt. Edward Porter Alexander, worried about the moral example he was setting for his troops, confiding to a brother-officer, "I wish to be thought by my men to be a Christian and have their sympathy and interest during the expedition to Utah." Two days later, as Alexander's miners and sappers prepared to begin their long march to Fort Bridger from West Point, they filed into the post's chapel to receive spiritual guidance from the military academy's mathematics instructor. Among his advice was "the idea that a Christian soldier was the highest type. In him the sense of duty and contentment were combined."[45]

At times both the forces of bad behavior and moral uplift beset a military unit or party of camp followers. Such was surely the case with the thirty raw teamsters hired by Russell, Majors and Waddell to staff young George W. Beehrer's bull train during the summer of 1858. Beehrer, a German immigrant, recorded the distribution of Bibles and ban on swearing enforced by one of the firms's partners, Alexander Majors. Despite this influence, when Beehrer's crew reached Salt Lake City in September, they found a "rendezvous for the

[44]After leaving Fort Bridger in the summer of 1858, Quantrill followed the Utah Expedition west and worked as a civilian cook at Camp Floyd, until returning east in late 1859. Apparently he did not give up gambling after the encounter witnessed by Private Peck; months later a store clerk in Salt Lake City recorded "Charley Hart" leaving a sack of five thousand dollars' worth in gold at his establishment for safe keeping. Ackley, "Across the Plains in 1858," 215.

[45]Dickson, "Shadowy Figures," 279, and Howard, *Autobiography of Oliver Otis Howard*, 1:95.

vicious," where teamsters "squandered not only their money, but also their souls. Within three days, three of my train comrades were dead. Antonio was stabbed in an affray over a bar-maid. Johnny Bull was shot at a gaming table; and Red, the Missourian, was murdered in a saloon brawl." Shortly thereafter Beehrer's seasoned wagon master, Dave Wagner, lay dead in Echo Canyon, dry-gulched by teamster Charley French, a "half-breed Sioux" anxious to settle a lingering grudge.[46]

The Difference of a Week: Buchanan's Shifting Political Sands

Whoever had the duty at the state department on 9 June—perhaps the president, who had a desk there—recognized the arrival of Governor Cumming's 2 May dispatch as important. Buchanan had, of course, already received several of Kane's March reports from Salt Lake City and Eckelsville, but those were personal letters from a private volunteer whose presence in Utah he was unwilling to acknowledge until the third week of May, in response to pressure from Pat Kane.[47] Buchanan had heard nothing of substance from Cumming since his westbound departure with Kane from Fort Bridger on 5 April. Now came substance from the president's official representative in Utah, and it arrived on the eve of Congress's adjournment until the next December.[48]

The message Buchanan crafted and transmitted on 10 June was his first communication with Congress about the Utah War since being forced to disgorge documents about the conflict's origins and prosecution on 26 February. The *New York Times* ran the communication the next day under the heading "Message from the President Announcing the End of the War."

---

[46]Beehrer, "Freighting across the Plains," 16–17.

[47]The decrypted letters Pat Kane brought to Buchanan on 20 May were probably those sent by Thomas on 4 March (Salt Lake City) and 15 March (Fort Bridger). Their receipt by Buchanan is known only because of an entry in Elizabeth Kane's diary. Buchanan never made public mention of receiving correspondence from Kane, and there is no sign of these Utah dispatches in either Buchanan's personal papers or government records. Hence the great historical value of the retained copies preserved for decades by the Kane family and now at BYU.

[48]Buchanan's relief, if not euphoria, was such that when Secretary Cass acknowledged receipt of Cumming's dispatch of 2 May (as well as those of 12 and 21 May), he informed the governor, "it gives me pleasure to inform you, that, your entire course of proceedings in relation to the Mormons, meets with the approbation of the President." Cass to Cumming, 29 June 1858, Domestic Letters of the Dept. of State, Vol. 48, 500–501, NARA.

Buchanan, "Message to Congress on Affairs in Utah," 10 June 1858, Moore, Ed., *The Works of James Buchanan,* 10:217–18.

To the Senate and House of Representatives:

I transmit a copy of a dispatch from Governor Cumming to the Secretary of State, dated at Great Salt Lake City on the 2d of May and received at the Department of State on yesterday. From this there is reason to believe that our difficulties with the Territory of Utah have terminated and the reign of the Constitution and the laws has been restored. I congratulate you on this auspicious event.

I lose no time in communicating this information and in expressing the opinion that there will now be no occasion to make any appropriation for the purpose of calling into service the two regiments of volunteers authorized by the act of Congress approved on the 7th of April last for the purpose of quelling disturbances in the Territory of Utah, for the protection of supply and emigrant trains, and the suppression of Indian hostilities on the frontier.

I am the more gratified at this satisfactory intelligence from Utah because it will afford some relief to the Treasury at a time demanding from us the strictest economy, and when the question which now arises upon every new appropriation is whether it be of a character so important and urgent as to brook no delay and to justify and require a loan and most probably a tax upon the people to raise the money necessary for its payment.[49]

If Buchanan expected Congress's reaction to match his own, he was chagrined to read the *Times*'s report that "the Utah news communicated to Congress this evening, produced a profound sensation. The allusion in the President's communication to economy was received by the House with loud laughter. There is some talk this evening of ordering a Committee of Investigation on the conduct of the Utah Campaign." The Associated Press also reported a mixed reception: "The President's brief Message announcing the events in Utah, came rather unexpectedly on the House to-day. Its reading was several times interrupted by laughter. When the Clerk finished, expression rose from various parts of the Hall, 'So the Mormon war is ended?' 'I'm glad of it,' &c., &c. The indefatigable Chairman of the Committee of Ways and Means wanted to go into [session as] Committee of the Whole [to discuss it], but the House had glory enough for one day and joyfully adjourned."[50] Elizabeth Kane criticized the president's message on grounds of ingratitude:

[49]Unknown to Congress, Secretary Floyd, with Buchanan's nervous acquiescence, had financed the Utah Expedition "off the books," by paying military contractors with millions of dollars in "acceptances," promissory notes drawn on his signature without congressional authorization or appropriation. It was a highly questionable practice that led to Floyd's forced resignation in December 1860.

[50]See various dispatches from Washington of 10 and 11 June 1858, *New York Times,* 1/1–3.

"Went to town. Saw the President's message in which he says no word of Tom, though in a special message on Utah affairs a word of praise would have been, to say the least, graceful."[51]

On 11 June the *Times* ran a scathing front-page dispatch by James Simonton from Fort Laramie as an immediate follow-on to the copy of Buchanan's pardon he cadged from the peace commissioners. With this scoop, Simonton questioned the logic of offering a blanket pardon to Utah's Mormons unasked and, as the reporter viewed it, undeserved.

"S" [Simonton], "Late News from Utah. Intelligence from the Peace Commission," Dispatch, Fort Laramie, 18 May 1858, *New York Times*, 11 June 1858, 1/4–5.

I have been talking this evening with the Peace Commissioners, who now admit, for the first time, that they have with them a Proclamation from the President to the People of Utah, exhorting them to submission to the law, and granting them a general amnesty for past offences, on condition that they shall yield obedience henceforth. This is the general tenor of the document, as I understand it from the representations made to me; but I hope to inclose you a copy of the paper in this package, so that you may judge of its character and import for yourself. [This Proclamation has already been published in the Times.][52]

A rumor that some such proclamation had been authorized by the Federal Executive reached my ears some days ago, but I confess that it seemed to involve so silly a policy on the part of the Administration, as well as so serious interference with the functions of the Judiciary, that I attached little or no importance thereto—supposing the rumor to be baseless. . . .

After years of defiance of the Federal authority, the President was forced last year to take steps to compel the people of Salt Lake to bow to the law. . . . At a cost of millions of dollars an army was sent over 1,100 miles across the wilderness,—not to make war against Mormondom, but to sustain the Judicial authorities in their efforts to maintain the supremacy of the law in Utah, and to punish Young and his minions for its manifold violations. . . .

And now, just when the desperate game of Mormon "brag" has been almost played out . . . the President proposes to retire before the rebels, confesses the country powerless to subdue them, and begs them to accept pardon for the past, as the condition of a promise that they will be good boys for the future! A dignified position, truly, is this that the United States are made to occupy by its President—a position in which our Government is confessed to be a failure, because it is incompetent to compel obedience to law, except by pressing unsought pardon upon traitors.

---

[51]Elizabeth Kane Journal, 18 June 1858, Kane Family Papers, BYU.

[52]This was the newspaper's editorial note.

> What will be the result? Simply this, if I mistake not: Brigham Young will see that his neck is in a halter, and he is not quite ready yet to go to the heaven which he preaches to his followers. He will gladly seize upon this opportunity to get out of his scrape, and will subside awhile, until the army is withdrawn. When that day arrives he will resume his iniquitous practices. ... Better far to break or impair the influence of the "Prophet" Brigham over his deluded followers, by humbling him at the feet of the civil power which he has so long defied. Such a consummation would destroy his prestige, while the President's humble prayer to him for peace will but exalt him in the eyes of the "Saints" and make them more ready than ever to do his bidding. The dealings of our Government with Mormondom have been a series of blunders from the beginning, but this last blunder will prove the greatest of them all.

Within the next week, the *Times* shifted its editorial position from support for the war to an attack on the administration for plunging the country into it. Wholly forgotten was the paper's strident position of a year earlier. The vehicle for this shift was a pair of pointed editorials run on 14 and 17 June 1858. Although now as critical of Buchanan as its controversial field reporter was, the *Times*'s publisher, Henry J. Raymond, was careful not to adopt James Simonton's anti-Mormonism. Raymond was attuned, as his reporter was not, to his readers' rising sympathy for the Mormon refugees of the Move South.

"The Mormon Exodus," Editorial, *New York Times*, 17 June 1858, 4/2–3.

> No dispassionate person, whatever his political partialities, can fail to see that the various enterprises undertaken by Mr. Buchanan do not seem to prosper in his hands. He has meddled in nothing, suggested nothing, entered upon nothing, since he entered the White House, which has not ended in confusion worse confounded.... The Mormon war was as promising a little quarrel as ever an enterprizing statesman gloated over. It contained every element of success and popularity. Impudent imposture, murders, rapes, polygamy, treason, intrusion on United Stares Territory—defiance to the Government and to public opinion—nothing was wanting to convert our venerable President into a glorious crusader on behalf of law, order, morality, and nations dignity. The pudding was full of [contracting] plums. It too has failed him. Even Brigham, the Prophet, has not turned out well as was expected, and refuses to be a traitor; and when the Lord's anointed deserts our President in the time of his need, his case is indeed pitiable.
>
> The latest news from Utah places the Administration in a position marked by a singular mixture of farce and tragedy, and the whole story of the war is crowded by as much ignorance, stupidity and dishonesty, as any Government

> ever managed to get into the annals of a single year. . . . "We have made a desert, and we call it peace."
>
> Whatever our opinions may be of Mormon morals or Mormon manners, there can be no question that this voluntary and even cheerful abandonment by 40,000 people of homes created by wonderful industry in the midst of trackless wastes, after years of hardship and persecution, is something, from which no one who has a particle of sympathy with pluck fortitude and constancy, can withhold his admiration. . . . When people abandon their homes, to plunge with women and children into a wilderness, to seek new settlements they know not where, they give a higher proof of courage than if they fought for them. . . . We have certainty the satisfaction of knowing that we have to deal with foemen worthy of our steel.
>
> However this singular affair may end, nothing can release us from the responsibility we have incurred in it. . . . We, with our Bibles, our churches, our single wives, our education, our sacred family life, ought to know better than entrust the extirpation even of a creed which inculcates rebellion, to such men as General Harney and Col. Johnston; and Mr. Buchanan ought to know enough to do something at the right time, in matters of such moment. His Peace Commissioners and Governor ought to have tried the effects of confidence and conciliation before our bayonets glistened in the canons of the Rocky Mountains, and his admonitory proclamation ought to have made its appearance before the General in command had addressed language to the malcontents worthy of Bajazet dealing with a rebellious Pasha.[53] . . . Posterity must not have to acknowledge with shame that our indiscretion, or ignorance, or intolerance drove the population of a whole State from house and home, to seek religious liberty immunity from the presence of mercenary troops, in any spot of the Continent to which our rule was never likely to extend.

Not all of the nation's newspapers adopted the *Times*'s critical tone. In Buffalo the *Courier* picked up the text of Buchanan's proclamation from the *Times* but ran it in tandem with an editorial that was critical of the Latter-day Saints and laudatory about the administration and Kane, whom the paper believed had undertaken "the divinely blessed mission of a peacemaker."[54]

Home at Last: Tom Kane Revisits the White House

Having dismissed most of his Mormon escort at Florence on the Missouri River, Kane hurried on by steamboat and rail with Maj. Howard Egan, his

[53]A reference to Bajazet II, Ottoman Sultan, 1481–1512.

[54]"Proclamation of Amnesty to the Mormons," Editorial, *Buffalo (N.Y.) Courier*, 11 June 1858, 2/1.

protector on the final leg to Philadelphia. The story of Kane's unannounced arrival home on 19 June is one of the stranger aspects of his Utah mission. As Elizabeth Kane recorded it:

> Tom and I had a good deal of talk together. I said in my [earlier] diary [entry] that "I was so happy and unhappy." What made me unhappy was this. Tom told me the first moment we were alone, like my dear honest darling, that the hope that had dawned on him of being a Christian was gone.—Now what distresses me is not the same trouble as I used to have, because I am sure it is only a cloud veiling the sun. I *know* that my prayers won't fall to the ground, I *know* that he will be a Christian. . . . My grief is that the only comfort in his trouble is not his now. . . . And how hard it will be to shut up in my own breast again all the sympathies that went out to my brother Christian. He was so much nearer me! I don't know how to talk to him, for my thoughts have so mouldered [molded] themselves around that hope that I—Oh dear poor Tom! I think I must not show you my diary. It would pain you now. I am glad I did not know he had lost his staff [faith] till now. I could not have borne his absence.

After unpacking, the financially strapped couple fell to squabbling over whether Kane should seek government reimbursement for his expenses, as well as the practical implications of his unilateral decision to delay seeking employment so that he might continue to pursue Mormon affairs. Tom further unsettled Elizabeth, a homebody, by confiding to her that "they were going to offer him the embassy to [the Kingdom of] Naples, as hush money." A day later he rushed off abruptly to see James Buchanan.[55]

Kane arrived in Washington as a mysterious (even romantic) figure of national notoriety. He was the object of press scrutiny of the personal sort that he tried to evade throughout his Utah mission. In Washington, as during his return across the plains, he continued to feed reporters his version of Alfred Cumming's heroics and perceptions of a war-peace split atop a non-monolithic Mormon hierarchy. It was the same mantra he intended to dispense to the Speaker of the U.S. House of Representatives and the president of the United States.

Associated Press, "From Washington. Arrival of Colonel Kane—Governor Cumming's Dispatches," Washington, 20 June 1858, *New York Times*, 21 June 1858.

> Colonel Kane arrived here last night, bringing dispatches from Governor Cumming, whom he left at Camp Scott on the 16th of May. They were

[55]Elizabeth Kane Journal, 20 June 1858, Kane Family Papers, BYU.

delivered to the President of the United States. Their purport has not officially transpired, but it is ascertained that many of the accounts with which the public mind has been preoccupied are erroneous, and calculated to deceive the country in respect to Utah matters generally. To this fact may be attributed the uncourteous refusal of Colonel Kane to communicate with the Press.

It is understood that Colonel Kane denies the truth of the telegraphic announcement from Booneville [Mo.], intimating that the army would move on the arrival of the Peace Commissioners, when in fact Governor Cumming has requested it to remain where it is until orders shall be received from Washington.

Contrary to the reports widely circulated, Colonel Kane does not admit that there has been any such want of harmony between Governor Cumming and General Johnston as would jeopardy[ize] the public interests. He speaks in eulogistic terms of General Johnston, and the high state of discipline in which the latter maintained his forces, and of the praiseworthy spirit manifested by the army during the Winter. The friends of the Administration are much pleased with the manner in which he is understood to allude to the conduct of Governor Cumming, saying that he is deserving of the gratitude of the country.

There was great hope in Utah, as elsewhere, that the war was at an end. A peace party had been formed, and was sufficiently strong in time to arrest the march of the Mormon forces against our own last Spring. It was the impression in Utah that Brigham Young, who openly espoused the cause of the United States, would, in this respect, be able to maintain his position. There was, at one time, strong opposition to him, before emigration was resolved upon, but ever since, this feeling of hostility has been subsiding.

Other than providing Speaker Orr and President Buchanan with a copy of Cumming's 12 May memo, what did Kane hope to accomplish in visiting the Executive Mansion? The best indication is a complex document discovered in his papers, fortuitously copied by a representative of the LDS church during 1949 but since lost. Most likely, it is the retained copy of a position paper that Kane developed in Washington after meeting with Secretary Floyd to use as talking points for his meetings with the president during the last week of June. Whether Kane left this document with Buchanan or retrieved it is unknown; like all of Kane's communications for the president, there is no trace of it in Buchanan's personal or official papers. The document was vintage Kane, complete with the same offer of ghost writing and draftsmanship extended to Young and Cumming in Utah. Disjointed as it is, Kane's rambling draft has value as a guide to his thinking and a partial explanation for why the president rejected so much of his advice.

Kane, "Brief for the President," Photostat, Undated Draft Memo (ca. June 1858), Frank Evans Research Files on Thomas L. Kane, Folder 14, MS 1251, LDS Archives.

Introductory.

How we have been all at sea, and (whether we change front or not—). How the whole subject calls for a re-examination. This wretched incumbrance left by another administration. Whatever the position taken by the present executive—hostile to the Mormons or friend the *position of the late* [Pierce] *Administration altogether untenable.*

The dispatches received from Cumming are enough to settle this much. We can no longer go before the country on the old ground.

(President [Present] State of things)

Now, the Mormons who could have destroyed our scattered bands last winter—whose advance was already within 40 miles of [Colonel] Cooke's command [herding at Smiths Fork] before their march could be arrested, after my arrival—*have given themselves into our hands.* The[y] have given over fighting, given up their plan of Campaign—have virtually opened the way to our troops. Our peace is made. But this does not end the matter. Close this head by reading as follows: "In this time of general congratulation an humble individual or 'private person' should not be misunderstood. Governor Floyd remarked to me yesterday, that 'a great responsibility, &c., rested upon Governor Cumming and myself, since we had caused a change in the destination of our forces, and the withdrawal of a portion of them from Utah'—or words to that effect. If I am indeed responsible to such a serious extent for the advice I may offer, I will be pardoned for expressing beyond mistake what my opinion really is with respect to the movements of the military.

"I do not advise the withdrawal of a portion of our troops from Utah. I advise one or the other [of] two alternatives. I advise the withdrawal of them *all,* of every soldier, without exception, within a reasonable time; or I advise the administration to send forward without delay as many men, regulars or volunteers as we can possibly bring into the field.

"Inasmuch as the Mormons expect peace and fair treatment, and have no notion of resisting at the present time, these troops could probably reach Bridger, if not the [Salt Lake] valley, in perfect safety, and reinforcements could follow them (Note Bene, if Congress please) next year. They would be a *highly serviceable nucleus* for the large force which we would stand in need of to effect the subjugation of the Mormons.—Whether I regard this enterprise advisable, or the reverse, I shall, when called upon express myself with sufficient clearness.

Second Head.
(My views of Public policy at the present crisis.)
Our policy is
(A.)

1. *To prevent them from: "Going South."* Reasons why this is particularly to be deprecated. The Pres't informed by me personally of what may be its result. Mex[ico]. relations &c. At least perhaps only postponing an evil day. Imitating Pierce, who left this to his successor. I would have the Admin of Jas Buchanan *settle* the Territorial Questions, &c.

2. *Spread them—Avoid concentrating them.* To this end I would,

1. Save their improvements and keep up all their detached settlements—to harbor them.

2. Spread~~ing~~ them—rather prefer the North in the direction of [the border with British North America at] Lat. 49 [degrees]. But aim to confine them generally to *the region that will not be colonized by other Americans.* The secluded, cold, and arid valleys among the so called Rocky Mts. A definitation [*sic*] of this. Where the land is not rain watered, and cultivated successfully only by irrigation. This the case with nearly all Utah. The material advantages of which have been as much exaggerated by the Mormons as their enemies. Many of them being Western men of New England origin, prone to exaggerate unscrupulously the value of their country.
(B.)

But if we succeed in arresting the present movement of the Mormons—(make them understand me) *The Utah difficulty not ended.* (a.) Enough without my assurance of it, that wrong has been done, and wrong breeds wrong. For some time to come, a degree of distrust and alienation from the parent government must be looked for. (b.) The course of Prest. Pierce. How he played directly into the hands of our enemies and broke down—nay, directly insulted and alienated three true and reliable men [the LDS First Presidency], of conservative tendencies, and the patriotic friends of our country and its Institutions.[56] The *Query:*—"Has he managed things so well as things have turned out, that we should follow his footsteps blindly without examining into the matter for ourselves? (c) How past wrongs are a standing capital for the war men, and we cannot afford to go on breaking down and insulting and alienating the hardly rallied leaders of the [Mormon] Peace party (d) If we shirk duty, and the former make head[way] against Young himself, Papa, Pope as he is, would have to yield or go by the board (e) Why, also, a secession among the Mormons of the more violent to be deprecated.

[56]It is not clear which of President Pierce's policies prompted Kane's criticism, unless it was Pierce's botched attempt in the fall of 1854 to supersede Young as governor with a non-Mormon, Colonel Steptoe.

Third Head.
The measures to be attended to at once.
(C.)

1. A cordial support of Cumming, not real only, but proclaimed. As the part of Hamlet omitted so far. So that at least Mormons may know they must conciliate him if they expect to influence Government. [(a)] Bad effects on the Mormons of Newspapers under influence of particular interests. This to be remedied. Promise to contribute my part. The Admin must do more. (b) Better remove him than not make his words deeds with the Mormons. He should have power and instructions couched in such language as to suffer him to exhibit them to the Mormons. Showing that he has power (c) The other officers should be taught their proper places (d) Here the Attorney General can lend us important aid. (Article in Union this morning good) A *District Attorney*—a lawyer if possible; if not, an honest man. But $150 vs. 10,000.

2. An *examination* ordered, whether for appearance sake only, or better, real, into all the vexed matters of the past. If Congress will be right, (Administrations next winter, they may appoint but it may be spoken of in advance as a measure finding favor with the Administration. The Report of the Commission would support the action of the Admin based upon it.

3. The new appointments. In the spirit of the Prest's Message all new offices [*sic*] (But put in a good word for [Jacob] F[orney]) Public opinion not prepared probably for appointment of Mormons. Still, none but a good man should have an appointment at present to Utah. If any office is of too little importance to put a good man in it, throw it away. Either give it to a Mormon as a pride sop or appoint no one to it. (b) Amplify definition of *New* Difference between Fish and Fishy—I prefer mackerel to the dirt stinking of the greasy barrel. Private history of the poor devils.

4. Make the Washington Offices [federal departments] behave themselves, Accts. &c. And no abusive correspondence on the part of eloquent clerks in bureaux &c tolerated.

5. Besides taking care that the [Washington] Union and [New York] Herald write reasonable and not scandalous articles—let one article at least be published in the Union at my dictation, and another *one* at least hold out hopes which I shall bring our own papers out upon—hopes of the one thing needful. This [is item]—6

6. *Admission of Utah as a State.* Develop this fully. How little it will cost the Administration and Democratic party to lend [lead?] the agitation &c for this, important assistance—highly appreciated by the Mormons. My own determination. Where the South necessarily.

Aside from this glimpse into what Kane planned to say to the president, it is unclear what actually took place with whom during his five days in

Washington. The most colorful but fragmentary source is Elizabeth Kane's diary entry, recording what her husband said immediately after he returned home. Due to James Buchanan's known deviousness and both Kanes' proclivity for melodrama, one needs to evaluate this source cautiously.[57]

ELIZABETH KANE DIARY, CA. 25 JUNE 1858,
KANE FAMILY PAPERS, BYU.

I write down all I can remember of his interview with the President upon his return.

The President was waiting for him, he was told; he turned someone away as T[om] came into the Hall. Up there he met Mr. [Pennsylvania senator William] Bigler, however.

The President taking T's hand with effusion, "Colonel Kane!"

T.L.K. "Well, Sir, Have I been as good as my word?"

Jas. B[uchanan]. "Better—More than as good as your word." (More effusion and words of thanks) Sit down, you look fatigued. How are you?"

(Here Mr. Bigler left, the President saying he would see him some other time).

J.B. Now tell me all about it.

T.L.K. Well, it is all true, or "all so."

Being told that it was, and better than he [Buchanan] had yet heard, he thanked God with some solemnity, and immediately after, "But these poor [Mormon] creatures—is there much suffering among them? Will they be homeless (or some such phrase) next winter? Have they food enough?—I rejoice to hear it. If they had food enough—that is what I wanted to know."

He was here silent "saying grace probably" Tom said, as he was then. "Now tell me about it" he said and Tom went on. That Saturday evening and a part of Monday morning he explained a few matters of the past but the whole of the 5 days spent in Washington with the president and Cabinet were given to the exhibition of such facts as bore upon the future.

Tom explained the abuse of the newspapers by the fact that he had refused to tell them anything. He thought none the less highly of the President & Cabinet because they had altercations with him afterwards upon the subject of the course to be pursued respecting Utah in the future. He said they were honest and open differences of opinion, and if he did not convince at once, what wonder, seeing that the truth had been kept from them by designing persons and they no doubt heard it from him for the first time.[58]

---

[57]Elizabeth Kane's journal entries for the period are sometimes undated, jumbled, or non-sequential.

[58]As with the shadowy members of the war party in Utah who supposedly threatened Brigham Young's leadership, Kane never identified the "designing" persons seeking to manipulate Buchanan and his cabinet.

Aside from Elizabeth Kane's indirect record of what he told her, Kane generated a direct account of his dealings with President Buchanan during the past year for his brother Pat the week after returning from Washington. Unfortunately, after recounting his two White House meetings in 1857, Kane broke off this memorandum before describing his crucial June 1858 visit to the Executive Mansion. Nonetheless, this fragment touched on the Utah pardon and, in so doing, illustrated how far Kane's recollection of his year-end understandings with Buchanan strayed in six months from the president's own sparse account of their interactions. To Pat Kane he wrote: "My powers you have understood rightly from [your May visit to] Mr. Buchanan were the same as those of Messrs. Powell and McCulloch sent out in April as Commissioners. I know this from Mr. Buchanan reading over to me their instructions last week. The only difference between us was that they were the bearers of a proclamation of general pardon, while I had a discretionary power as pardons were to be granted upon my recommendation. I still however remember a humane expression of the President's which I wrote down at the time and afterwards repeated with good effect 'I shall be glad to pardon *the whole* of them.'"[59]

Another indirect, fragmentary account of Kane's June discussions with the Buchanan administration appears in Delegate Bernhisel's correspondence with Brigham Young. As Kane was leaving Washington, Bernhisel realized his friend was on the verge of one of his episodic collapses that might leave him unable to report to Young the results of the White House meetings. Accordingly, Bernhisel accompanied Kane home, where indeed he took to his bed and was unable to communicate with Young in writing until strong enough to dictate a note to Elizabeth on 18 July.

The focus of Kane's letter was Utah's future rather than the past, and so the message Howard Egan couriered to Young omitted any account of Kane's trip to Washington.[60] But while Kane and Bernhisel were together, they discussed at length what had transpired between Kane and Buchanan. The delegate tried to convey the gist of these conversations to Young through two letters in early July, but Bernhisel's obsession about federal mail monitoring allowed him to communicate only in cryptic phrases. Bernhisel explained,

[59]T. L. Kane to R. P. Kane, untitled and undated (ca. late June 1858) five-page ms. (p. 5) in T. L. Kane's hand, "Concerning the Mormons and Pres. Buchanan" File, Thomas Leiper Kane Papers, APS.

[60]Kane to Young, 18 July 1858, LDS Archives. In accepting this advice, Young told Kane, "it is well, as you say, to dismiss the past, and look [to] the present and future." Young to Kane, 10 September 1858, ibid.

"as I send this by mail I will not risk details by an imprudent mention of them here." This material reveals little more than Kane's assessment that his major accomplishment in Washington was saving Governor Cumming from immediate removal while sowing doubt about Judge Eckels's suitability as Utah's chief justice.[61] As with Kane's mid-March meeting with Lewis Robison at Muddy Creek, as well as Bernhisel's refusal to brief Brigham Young by mail about his January 1858 discussions with Buchanan about ending the war, the two men again limited their helpfulness to Young in June by needlessly opaque communications.

Soon Kane's view of James Buchanan's trustworthiness and reliability would become as jaundiced as his family's, but for a brief time after returning from Washington in late June 1858, he clung to pleasant memories of Buchanan's face-to-face flattery. That summer he confided to Pat Kane, "I say what you do not like to hear me say, but many a time after [my late December meeting] when I was hard driven, I was helped to carry myself through by remembering not merely the particular confidence to which it was a compliment that he admitted me whom he had never known except as his [political] opponent in our State [Pennsylvania], but numerous express kind and friendly words, rallying my pride of family, and convincing me that at least I would not be forgotten by him, if my life was thrown away."[62]

When Major Egan left the Kanes on 19 July to return to Utah, he carried not only Thomas's forward-looking message for Young but a letter to Cumming. For the new governor, Kane summarized the precarious state of his health and his view of affairs in Washington.

Kane to Cumming, [*blank*] July 1858,
Frank Evans Collection ms 1251, Fd. 17, lds Archives.

You probably received a Note from me informing you of my success at Washington. I kept up till somewhere about the date of it and I fancy until I had accomplished everything essential. But I then broke down. You must expect no more from me for some time to come. I have been so completely prostrated by my fever and its consequences that I am obliged to suffer this valued opportunity of writing to you confidentially by Mr Egan to give me the slip. The slightest mental effort flushes me and induces suffering. I shall serve you best as I shall best serve all who count upon me, by ascertaining if

[61] Bernhisel to Young, 2 and 8 July 1858, ibid.

[62] T. L. Kane to R. P. Kane, ca. late June 1858, "Concerning the Mormons and Pres. Buchanan" File, Thomas Leiper Kane Papers, aps.

I have strength enough to carry me to [the resort at] Bedford or some more quiet place among our mountains and there stay in absolute repose till the hot season has passed over.

It is no longer, I image, the interest of the Treasury leeches to assail you; but how they hate the authors of their discomfiture you must expect to see in their hired organs for some time. My family keep the newspapers from me here; but I understand that if they cannot ascribe the pacification to Johnston, they are endeavoring at least to give the credit of it to Power & McCullough [*sic*]—which gentlemen have evidently their own arrangements with the Press. Let them alone. I intend to live; and if alive next fall, will brode [? break] their wind bags and see justice done. Meantime I have a great advantage in the strict silence I have observed with regard to my personal course to the great confusion of the Press, as you will observe—but to my great fortification, as I am mortified enough to confer with the President and his Cabinet. How I wish I were able to gratify myself by indulging in the confidence of personal friendship, and telling you the ins and outs of certain of these poor creatures—that I might seem to hear you at this distance say to your noble lady "How truly has *our Friend* redeemed his pledges to us!"

But I am too forcibly admonished at this moment to close—I will still go on however to say to you that *you are all right at Washington*; and what is more I have [Sec. of the Treasury] Cobb's promise to *watch jealousy for any threatening fire in the rear and let me know immediately.*

Present me affectionately to Mrs. Cumming.

Chapter 16

"Man from the Moon"
Enter the Peace Commissioners

The Governor [Powell] is a shrewd, kind-hearted, venerable man; and though the Major [McCulloch] has all the air of a sharp, resolute character, yet, under all this, there seems to be a deep substratum of caution, that will, no doubt, prevent his doing anything rash.

Capt. James H. Simpson, 26 April 1858

If a man comes from the moon and says he will pardon me for kicking him in the moon yesterday, I don't care about it, I'll accept of his pardon, it don't affect me, one way or the other.

Brigham Young, 12 June 1858

The arrival of Ben McCulloch and Lazarus W. Powell in Salt Lake City on 7 June was vastly different than that of Alfred Cumming and Thomas L. Kane in mid-April. Gone was the bustle, dust, and noise of thousands of southbound refugees and their animals. There was no showy escort by Nauvoo Legion officers, no comforting Staines mansion, no visitation from the Lion of the Lord, no crowd waiting to intimidate on cue an unwanted visitor to the Tabernacle. Salt Lake City was the biggest city between St. Louis and San Francisco, but the place was virtually deserted, shuttered, unwelcoming, and silent. The only sounds were those of a few workmen disassembling a Provo-bound roof while snow-swollen City Creek rushed westward toward the River Jordan. As a Mormon observer reported to Brigham Young, the commissioners "expressed much surprise at the largeness of the City, and at its being empty."[1]

[1]Report attributed to Legion adjutant general James Ferguson, Church Historian's Office Journal, 9 June 1858, LDS Archives.

Maj. Ben McCulloch of Texas

A Sam Houston protégé and Democratic Party favorite of the Buchanan administration, he was U.S. marshal for eastern Texas and a veteran of the Texas Revolution, Mexican-American War, and service with the Texas Rangers. Although McCulloch preferred to enter Utah as colonel of a volunteer regiment, he agreed to serve as part of Buchanan's two-man peace commission to tender the Mormons a blanket presidential pardon. With this background, forceful personality, and role as the commission's ramrod, McCulloch was a formidable federal officer unlike any Brigham Young had encountered. Four years later he died a Confederate brigadier at Pea Ridge, Arkansas. *Charles De Forest Fredericks carte de viste ca. 1859. Courtesy Dorothy Sloan—Rare Books, Austin, Texas.*

There were other ways in which this arrival was also different. The earlier visitors had been men on their own, each beset by complex personal problems. One of them—a stranger to Mormondom soon dubbed "Old Swill Tub"—was tall, obese, alcoholic, nondescript, and a person of meager professional accomplishments. The other was short, lean, elegant, flamboyant, and manipulative—a messianic friend of the Latter-day Saints but essentially an unemployed Philadelphia lawyer overshadowed by the fame of his dead explorer-brother and father.

What followed these first visitors into Salt Lake City twenty-seven days later were emissaries, officially representing the president of the United States and long accustomed to making things happen. One, an accomplished lawyer, was the respected former governor of a major American state and its senator-elect. His companion, the U.S. marshal for the largest state in the Union, was a hardened veteran of frontier combat in the Texas Revolution, the Mexican-American War, and the Texas Rangers.

Their guide, a seasoned frontiersman, had earlier been left for dead on a Mexican battlefield; he would go on to found the Pony Express before buying Thomas Jefferson's Monticello and falling under suspicion as a member of the Lincoln assassination conspiracy. He was a man who would brace Brigham Young in his own office when he perceived an insult to fellow Virginian John B. Floyd.[2]

The party's escort was a small detachment of hand-picked dragoons armed to the teeth with the latest Sharps breech loaders and Colt's revolvers. They were the first U.S. soldiers to enter Salt Lake City since the Steptoe Expedition had done so four years earlier. Behind them, 113 miles to the east, stirred the vanguard of the largest concentration of troops in North America.

As correspondent A. G. Browne reported from Camp Scott, "these gentlemen are secure from being Steptoed by any influences which Young can bring to bear on them. Unless they modify the determination with which they left our camp, they will insist that the submission of the Mormons shall be immediate and unconditional."[3]

Exit the amateurs, enter the professionals.

The decisions made in Salt Lake City during the second week of June by James Buchanan's peace commissioners and the leadership of the Latter-day

---

[2]Minutes of Meeting: Brigham Young and Benjamin F. Ficklin, 19 July 1858, LDS Archives. "A.B.C." [Burr], "Utah. Condition of Mormon Affairs," Dispatch of 24 July 1858, *New York Times*, 24 August 1858, 1.

[3][Browne], "Letter from the Utah Army," Dispatch, 12 June 1858, *New-York Tribune*, 7 July 1858.

Saints are a part of the Utah War story that has been addressed but not fully told.[4] Not well understood is that all this took place in rapid, fairly undramatic fashion because Brigham Young recognized that for the first time he faced a serious adversary, one as smart and tough as he was. Confronting him now was a small team that was self-sufficient, focused, fearless, and powerful enough to bring about his destruction if his behavior remained unchanged. It was one thing for Brigham Young to dispatch Bill Hickman or Porter Rockwell to "use up" some troublesome visitor like Richard Yates or the Aiken brothers on an isolated trail. It was a far different challenge to sit in a room backed by a few of his closest colleagues to deal with Lazarus Powell and Ben McCulloch as equals. The change was a harbinger of things to come.

As the spring wore on, the pressures of his predicament began to take its toll on Young. Twice his sleep was disturbed by nearly identical nightmares filled with violent personal encounters involving Albert Sidney Johnston and Lt. Sylvester Mowry, the Steptoe Expedition officer whom Young had threatened with death in 1855. Both of these dreams involved injury to one of Young's fingers, the member that he crooked at meetings to signal displeasure—if not a person's imminent destruction. The clerk on duty in the Church Historian's Office recorded the latest version a week before the commissioners entered Salt Lake City:

> In the night Pres Young dreamed that he was in the midst of the U.S. troops, and heard them laying plans to kill him. Col. Johnson [*sic*] saw him through his [spy] glass, he said "I suppose now, Brigham Young will know whether we have come for peace or not." He discovered Lt. Mowry who swore that it was his privilege to kill Brigham Young; there was a general rush, howling and shouting "now we have got old Brigham Young," they came up to him and passed by as though they could not see him. After they had gone he discovered a small hurt on the side of the little finger of his left hand, near the point.[5]

The greatest threat to Young's physical wellbeing during this period came not from the army but an obscure member of his own extended family. On 4 June 1858, near Provo, James Valentine Young, a nephew-in-law,

---

[4]Roberts, *A Comprehensive History of the Church*, 4:420–40; Hafen and Hafen, eds., *Mormon Resistance*, 327–59; Furniss, *The Mormon Conflict*, 194–97; Bigler and Bagley, *The Mormon Rebellion*, 311–20.

[5]Church Historian's Office Journal, 16 April and 30 May 1858, LDS Archives. For Lieutenant Mowry's peccadilloes in Salt Lake City, see MacKinnon, "Sex, Subalterns, and Steptoe," 227–46. Mowry showed his capacity for such violence a year later when, as a civilian, he fought a duel with an irate newspaper editor in Tubac, Arizona, using carbines at forty paces. "Interesting from Arizona," Dispatch, 9 July 1859, *New York Times*, 5 August 1859, 1.

unexpectedly struck his uncle several times, administering "a whipping" until bystanders subdued him. Shaken and embarrassed, Brigham Young dealt with this episode by directing that his assailant "be furnished with a horse and necessary equipment to let him have his desire which he had cherished for some time of going to the States." Thus disgraced and banished, James Valentine Young rode for Fort Bridger and dropped from historical notice.[6] Ironically, the Utah War principal most at risk from U.S. troops was not Brigham Young but Chief Justice Eckels. Drunken soldiers of the Tenth Infantry roughed up the judge during a nocturnal visit to his Fort Bridger "establishment" a week after James Valentine's attack on Young.[7]

By the second week of June 1858, Young was cornered, out of options, short on divine guidance, and confronted with competent, powerful federal appointees. In selecting commissioners for Utah, the president, with Sam Houston's help, had taken more care and exercised better judgment than in forming his own cabinet. In June these higher standards had major consequences. Through these dynamics, more than the tribal raid on Fort Limhi, the war changed, and the territorial-federal balance of power began to shift in a way that transformed Utah forever.

"A.B.C." and "O.H.O." Trail the Commissioners: Insider Reporting

The peace commissioners did not linger at Fort Bridger. After less than three days of rest and fact finding, they departed on 2 June. Correspondent Browne reported that the day they left, "the President's proclamation was read . . . to the various regiments and corps of the army at dress parade. The feeling concerning it remains unaltered, that it originated in a mistaken view of the political designs and social system of the Mormons. The most comprehensive criticism which I have heard made on it was the remark of a gentleman that 'the amnesty with which it ends is a most illogical deduction from the premises set forth in its preamble.' "[8] Captain Phelps saw the

[6]President's Office Journal, 4 June 1858, LDS Archives; Documents of David Candland, 2–9 June 1858, Utah State History Collection. James Valentine Young was the son of Jemima Angell Young, the sister of Brigham Young's wife, the former Mary Ann Angell. With his father dead, James had traveled to Utah with his mother in 1848 under the protection of Brigham Young's wagon train.

[7]Phelps Diary, 12 June 1858, Phelps Papers, NYPL.

[8][Browne], "A Week Later from Utah. Arrival of the Peace Commissioners," Dispatch, Camp Scott, 3 June 1858, *New-York Tribune*, 1 July 1858.

pardon in more practical terms, describing it as a sign of permissiveness that reduced a fear of punishment among his artillerymen while encouraging them to risk the penalty for desertion: "The intention of a considerable number of men to desert has evidently been bringening [burgeoning] in the company for a long time. This, however, might have been defeated had not the broad pardon of the Mormons for all their crimes against the United States been granted by the President."[9]

Ben McCulloch's persistent case of mountain fever slowed progress, but they made better time than if they had been encumbered by Alfred Cumming, his wife, and their baggage, as originally planned. Delayed by the need to repair a broken wagon, the gubernatorial entourage and a mountain of withheld mail entrusted to postmaster Morrell traveled separately, trailing a day behind McCulloch and Powell.[10]

As the commissioners traveled, Gen. James Ferguson assembled and distributed intelligence reports on their movements from Legionnaires in the field. On 3 June he reported to General Wells that the commissioners had arrived at Fort Bridger; he did so based on his personal questioning of a detainee who said he was a deserter from the Utah Expedition.[11] A few days later, as the entourage of federal appointees neared the city, Ferguson sent additional details of their progress to Wells. His report contained several revealing passages, the first an assessment by Mormon merchant Henry Lawrence that "Cumming talked friendly [on the trail] and from what Henry says seemed determined to carry out the President's (B.Y.'s) policy, or at least do us justice." Then Ferguson asked a telltale question, one that betrayed the ad hoc, improvised nature of Brigham Young's war planning at this critical juncture: "How shall we receive the Commissioners?"[12]

---

[9]Phelps Diary, 26 July 1858, Walker draft typescript, 36.

[10]Accompanying Cumming, his wife, and servants were Jacob Forney, U.S. superintendent for Indian affairs; Morrell; and David A. Burr. Also traveling with the governor was newly freed Nauvoo Legionnaire William R. R. Stowell, whose treason indictment was dropped after he signified his acceptance of the presidential pardon by taking the oath of allegiance to the United States. In effect, Lieutenant Stowell was the first beneficiary of this amnesty and the only individual case in the midst of the blanket pardon granted to the territory's entire population. Judge Eckels had planned to travel with Cumming, but at the last moment decided to distance himself from the governor, choosing to enter Salt Lake City with the army several weeks later.

[11]Ferguson to "General" [Wells], 3 June 1858, LDS Archives. The man calling himself Private Sawyer was a civilian using a military identity to bolster his credibility and ease his passage through the Legion's lines to California. The records for the Second Dragoons during this period contain no reference to a soldier by this name. Nielson, *Roll Call at Old Camp Floyd*, 109–48.

[12]Ferguson to Wells, 6 June 1858, LDS Archives.

A few days later Brigham Young provided guidance to Ferguson and the other senior officers remaining in Salt Lake City. His counsel was a mixture of tortuous ambiguity seasoned with bravado that telegraphed insecurity:

> It will probably be well to call a meeting of the few male citizens in Great Salt Lake City, who are not actively engaged in the operations necessary for speedy removal [of southbound materiel] and appoint one or more Delegates to call upon His Excellency Governor Cumming and learn his wish and instructions in regard to their waiting upon Commissioners Powell and McCullough, also upon such other matters as His Excellency may be pleased to offer his suggestions, instructing the Delegation to emphatically inform whomever it may concern, that conferences for a more happy understanding of matters which now are at least so very differently proclaimed, if not by many differently understood, cannot, consistently with the spirit which should actuate American freemen, be held at the bayonet's point and cannon's mouth, and that pending all such conferences and their results, the United States troops ordered to Utah must in strict good faith refrain from advancing any nearer to the settlements in Utah than are the comfortable quarters at Camp Scott.[13]

With historians preoccupied with the commissioners' subsequent meetings in Salt Lake City, there is little awareness that theirs was virtually the first passage by non-Mormons through the Nauvoo Legion's most formidable defenses since the Utah War began. The circumstances of Cumming and Kane's westbound travel through Echo Canyon in early April had produced impressions that were jumbled, if not misleading by intent. Eastbound merchant Abel Gilbert, who passed Cumming and Kane on the trail, was a keen observer but one who for business reasons did not discuss the fortifications in Echo Canyon.[14] What did Lazarus Powell and Ben McCulloch see?

Neither commissioner nor any member of their official escort left an account of this segment of their mission, but two civilian travelers close to them generated contemporaneous, detailed descriptions of this portion of

---

[13]Young to Ferguson, George D. Grant, and others, 7 June 1858, ibid.

[14]Several months later, Gilbert learned a lesson about the business risks inherent in offending Brigham Young. The day after the army marched through Salt Lake City, Young complained to James Ferguson, "I understand that Mr. Gilbert is raving about, before the [Peace] Commissioners and others of my not having dealt fairly by him, and that I am owing him large amounts and that he is going to put me through &c. &c." When Gilbert sought a meeting with Young to resolve the controversy, Young refused, informing him that "your remarks and conduct, of late, as reported to me through what I deem reliable channels, have been of such a character as to preclude my granting the interview you requested." Thereafter Young intended to deal with Abel Gilbert only by letter. Young to Ferguson, 27 June 1858, and Young to Gilbert, 2 July 1858, both in LDS Archives.

the trail. The first was written by David A. Burr, who was well qualified to comment on how Echo Canyon and Salt Lake City had changed since 1857, having passed through the area many times since arriving from Washington in 1855 with his father, Utah's controversial surveyor general. The two Burrs had fled Utah in April 1857 with other federal officials. David A. was returning to Salt Lake with Cumming in June 1858 to find and secure David H. Burr's surveying instruments and field notes. What the younger Burr did not disclose to Cumming was that, before leaving Fort Bridger, he had undertaken a secondary mission—to provide a description of what he saw to the two New York newspaper reporters left behind with the Utah Expedition, Messrs. Simonton and Browne.

The three reporters understood that Browne and Simonton would later incorporate Burr's descriptive material into their own dispatches to the *Tribune* and *Times*, respectively, with Burr's authorship anonymous. He was willing to defer to Simonton because of their common linkage to the *Times*, for which Burr was a "stringer" (as "A.B.C.") since the summer of 1857. In Browne's case, Burr was presumably motivated by some combination of friendship and cash, which prompted him to stand in for Browne with anonymous dispatches to the *Tribune* during Browne's five-month mission to the East.[15] To an unknown extent, Burr also deferred to the other reporters because of the difference in their ages, although his winter dispatches to New York's *Times* and *Tribune* hardly lacked self-confidence. In the spring of 1858, Burr was nineteen years old, while Simonton and Browne were thirty-five and twenty-three, respectively. It is unlikely that Alfred Cumming was aware of any of Burr's newspaper arrangements, as he had earlier banned travel of correspondents to Salt Lake City to avoid journalistic provocations.

Burr's memorandum for Simonton and Browne provides a unique document bearing on the brief, eerie period between the evacuation of Salt Lake City and arrival of the Utah Expedition—the proverbial calm before the storm. It covers a description of Echo Canyon and its defenses after withdrawal of the Nauvoo Legion, the appearance of Salt Lake City abandoned and ready for the torch, and an outsider's limited view of the talks between Mormon leaders and President Buchanan's peace commissioners.

---

[15]For an example of the reporters' nearly verbatim use of Burr's description of Echo Canyon's fortifications, see [Browne], "Important from Utah," Dispatch, 17 June 1858, *New-York Tribune,* 19 July 1858.

David A. Burr to Browne and Simonton, June 1858, Burr Family Papers.

I propose to give you the particulars of our journey this far as much in detail as possible, and you can use for publication such portions as you may deem suitable.

After leaving the camp on the 3rd inst [June] we travelled on as far as the Big Muddy where we camped at about three o'clock in the afternoon. We met on the bench near the spring Sam Worthen[16] & the other Mormons with [the stolen] Gilbert & Gerrish's Cattle, who informed us that they met the Commissioners that morning between 8 & 9 o'clock near the Quaking-aspen hill travelling very rapidly. Upon reaching camp the Governor finding his mules weak and unable to travel farther that evening, determined to send on an express to these gentlemen requesting them to wait for him in Echo Canyon or on the Weber River, and as Dr. Forney & I were the only persons who had extra animals, requested of us the loan of them. As I was anxious to go on so as to be with the Commissioners I offered to take the express myself and accordingly started on at six o'clock accompanied by Stowell and the Indian Jim as an escort.[17] I took a note from the Gov. to Messrs. Powell & McCulloch and had also a note to Major [E. D.] Wooley who commanded the [Mormon] militia on the road, in the event I should meet any of them. I travelled on at a sound pace and reached Bear River that night at 10 o'clock and to my great satisfaction found here the Commissioners camped for the night, having been waiting since 11 o'clock that morning for the Gov. [Jesse] Jones & [Hiram F.] Morrell had gone on to Yellow Cr. with the mail.

Fearing that they might go on Gov. Powell determined the next morning [4 June] to start at daylight with his train & overtake the mail, and he accordingly went on to Yellow Cr. to breakfast, & there found Morrell with the mail. We now however thought it would be very tedious to wait a whole day here for the Gov. as we could not fish, nor had any shade trees to lounge under & therefore concluded to go to the Weber River that night & there wait for his Excellency. On entering Echo Canyon we looked about anxiously for signs of Fortifications, camps etc., but in vain. We only saw a few signs of a camp near Cache Cave, and a couple of old Huts about 5 miles down the canyon. We stopped to noon about half way down the Canyon. Upon resuming our journey in the afternoon we were gratified to find about 3 miles from the mouth of the Canyon some signs of the fortifications for defence of which we have heard so much. The Canyon upon approaching the River becomes narrower, the bluffs on either side rising to a great height & becoming more abrupt.

The Northern side becomes a perfect wall of rock, which rises in many places

[16]Not to be confused with Fay Worthen.

[17]Legion lieutenant William R. R. Stowell and an Indian who might be the ubiquitous "Cherokee Jim."

perpendicularly some two or three hundred feet above the road. The Southern side however assumes the character of a very steep hill or rather mountain side covered however with grass & here & there with a few bushes. The first indication which we had that we were approaching the fortification was piles of rocks heaped up in the shape of a wall with look holes at regular intervals, which we could now see on every projecting point of the rocks on the Southern side. Shortly after upon turning a bend in the Canyon we found that all the willows in the Cr. Bottom had been cut away & the whole space cleared and a short distance in front of us saw a dam thrown up across the whole breadth of the Canyon. This dam or breastwork was formed of dirt thrown out of a ditch some five feet deep & 10 feet wide. This ditch was filled with water the road crossed it on a temporary bridge. The dam was about four feet high and quite substantial. A sluice way at one end allowed the free passage of the Cr. but this could be easily filled up, thus forming a pond of water in front of the breastwork; about two hundred yards farther on, another breastwork & ditch had been constructed from the creek to a rock near the base of the precipice. Space sufficient for the passage of wagons was however left between the rock & the precipice, & the evident object of this dam was to compel the passage of a train under the precipice which has probably been mined.

About fifty yards farther was another dam & ditch (which the road crossed on a bridge) constructed for the purpose of overflowing the bottom up to the last mentioned dam & thus preventing a [wagon] train from crossing to the opposite side of the bottom & and thus avoid the precipice. About 100 yds farther was the last dam & breastwork across the whole bottom, this would raise the water in the Canyon to a depth of some 6 or 8 ft. It was constructed just above the mouth's [*sic*] of two Canyons or gorges which entered the main canyon directly opposite each other at this point. The earth washed down out of the gorge on the Southern side formed a point of land which extending nearly half way into Echo Canyon obviated the necessity of so long a dam as the first one. A gully washed out down the centre of this point had been dug out and arranged so as to form a breastwork connecting with the dam. Walls of rock were built across the mouth of each of these gorges.

Upon the sides of the steep hills near the gorge on the Southern side, ditches had been dug and embankments thrown up in front at different heights: these commanded the whole fortifications below. But as the upper breastwork commanded completely the one immediately below it, a flanking party by taking possession of the summit of the hill would have complete command of the whole works.

Upon the Southern side every available point or place not protected by nature was fortified with a stone breastwork.[18]

---

[18]Correspondent Browne later erroneously credited Maj. Seth M. Blair, a cavalry officer, as the force behind Echo Canyon's defenses. They were the work of Legion troops supervised by Cols. N. V. Jones and W. B. Pace and Maj. Adam Sharp.

For nearly a mile below these gorges & the last dam the Southern half of the Canyon is elevated by a bench or series of low hills, over this bench the road runs. The Southern half of the gorge in consequence of this bench, becomes a deep glen as the precipice on that side rises from the level of the Cr.

This Glen is filled with willows and cedar trees; in this glen thus protected from the wind the Mormon Army have built their huts or wickeeups. They were constructed by digging a circular hole in the ground, of the required size, over this excavation poles have been placed in the same manner as lodge poles.[19] These were then closely interwoven with willows and finally thatched with straw grass and bark. The doors were formed of a frame work, thatched in the same manner as the hut. Many of them had chimneys of sods or rocks built on the side opposite to the door. A somewhat open spot in the glen some three hundred yards below the last dam had been selected as the site for the headquarters of the Mormon Army & here the huts were built around a square in the centre of which stood a tall pine flag pole. The huts numbered about 150 and could accomodate perhaps 15 men each. The scenery at this point is truly sublime, particularly in the evening when the sun setting behind the high hills throws the bottom of the gorge into a deep shadow light up here & there by some straggling rays, straggling down through some cleft in the mighty walls.

The rocky precipice, rough jagged and broken rising to a towering height on one side, beautifully adorned by cedar [juniper] trees & struggling to hold as it were by every broken spot; on the other side the steep unbroken hillside, swelling up to an elevation which entitles it to the appellation of a mountain, clothed with verdure to its summit; form beautiful contrasts with the shady avenues of willows, wild cherry and sweet smelling shrubs entwined with the beautiful wild hop vine leading across and along the swiftly running stream of crystal water, which enlivens the whole scene with the fitting accompayment, of its sweet gurgling melody.

These fortifications in my estimation would only serve to amuse our brave little army in its progress towards this valley, for a mountain howitzer planted upon the hillside on the Southern side of the canyon would command the whole works, and if a flanking party should gain (and there is nothing to prevent it) the upper of their breastworks on the same side, they would have complete command of all the works below & be at the same time completely protected. Our Army could have routed the whole Mormon force at this point without losing 20 men.[20]

---

[19]Subsequent railroad and highway construction in Echo Canyon obliterated these holes, but similar excavations over which the Utah Expedition's troops pitched their tepeelike Sibley tents are still visible on private ranch land near Fort Bridger. Discovery of the latter in 2013 was by Sgt.-Maj. James F. Martin, U.S.M.C. (ret'd.), a Utah state trooper residing in Tremonton.

[20]Burr's assessment matches that of the U.S. Army troops who later marched through the canyon. The Tenth Infantry's Lieutenant Colonel Smith pronounced these defenses "beneath contempt." Smith to Fanny M. Smith, 7 July 1858, in Mesch, *Your Affectionate Father*, 161. Civilians often viewed these fortifications as formidable. Boy Scouts and trail enthusiasts have preserved some of the stonework defenses.

Upon the banks of the Weber River about a quarter of a mile below the Canyon we found the Mormon Station consisting of some 20 well-constructed log houses, built around a square, and a very substantial corral. We camped a short distance above the ford some three miles below the mouth of the Canyon.[21]

As I rode down I noticed that the banks of the bench upon which the road runs on the side sloping towards the river had been dug out all along so as to give footing & thus form a breastwork.

We remained in camp the next day [5 June] until about three o'clock in the evening when finding that the River was rising rapidly we determined to cross over before it became too deep to ford. Hitching up therefore we crossed over without any difficulty and camped on the opposite side. The boys caught some 4 or 5 fish during the day. At sundown the Gov. arrived with his two ambulances but would not cross the River until his baggage wagons which he had left behind came up. As they did not arrive by dark he camped on that side for the night.

Early the next morning [6 June] the wagon master of his train came up with the news that the tongue of one of his wagons had got broken some 4 miles up Echo Canyon and that they were waiting for some means of repairing it. The Gov. procured a new tongue from the Commissioners and sent it back by Stowell and the wagon master. He then told the Commissioners that he would not ask them to wait for him any longer for him as his train was so heavily loaded that he must necessarily travel slowly. Dr. Forney had crossed over & camped with the Commissioners the evening previous. At about 7 o'clock [Mormon merchant] Harry Lawrence & his party came up to us on their return from the Camp; they reported that the mail arrived the evening before they left camp. Shortly after Porter Rockwell & [Nicholas] Groesbeck rode up with a party of 25 Mormons and a large band of horses & mules. They told us they were on their way from the City to the Platte Bridge to bring up their train which they were obliged to leave there last fall. They left there some 12 or 13 wagons.[22] The Gov's. wagons arrived by 11 o'clock & he started immediately on with them. The Commissioners & Dr. Forney & the mail party in the mean time had started on & I rode on in company with Henry Lawrence & overtook them [that] morning within 8 miles of the summit of the Big Mountain.[23] Resuming our journey after

[21]This infrastructure rose around the relay station constructed by the Hockaday-Magraw mail service and then the B. Y. X. Carrying Company, which eventually morphed into a Pony Express station and the hamlet of Echo City. A major figure in the development of this establishment was James E. Bromley, a sergeant in the Volunteer Battalion's Company A and a veteran of Magraw's Pacific Wagon Road crew.

[22]For Groesbeck's notoriety in running arms and munitions into Utah during the fall of 1857 and Albert Sidney Johnston's concern about his cache at Platte Bridge, see *At Sword's Point, Part 1*, 258–62. The arrival of Groesbeck's party at the Utah Expedition's camp a few days later triggered a near-riot.

[23]When Lawrence reached Salt Lake City, he made a full report of what he had seen while mingling with the federal entourage, and Ferguson, in turn, sent this intelligence to Legion headquarters in Provo. Ferguson to Wells, 6 June 1858, LDS Archives.

resting a short time we crossed the Big Mountain & camped for the night [of 6 June] at the foot of the Little Mountain within 11 miles of the City.

Coming up the East Canyon I noticed at several points along the canyon walls of rock piled up for Breastworks.[24] About five miles from the summit of the Mountain the road turns up a narrow ravine or canyon which it follows to the Summit. At the mouth of this ravine a dam similar to those described in Echo Canyon had been built across the stream and breastworks built on the hill sides. But this is the most foolish attempt at a work of defense that I ever saw or heard of for the hills around are perfectly practible not only for infantry but for dragoons and artillery [to seize]. The only idea which seems to have entered into the heads of the Mormons in the construction of their works of defense was that the army must unavoidably pass up the road, that it is impossible for them to leave it. The scenery here as in Echo Canyon is of the most sublime description. I doubt whether the view from the summit of the Big Mountain can be surpassed in the United States for its severe grandeur & sublimity. The grass along the whole route is most rich & luxuriant.

After meeting our party Porter Rockwell sent two men back on an express to Brigham to inform him of our approach, they passed us by at full speed & intended to go from the Weber River to the City in five hours; the distance is forty miles. After breakfasting the next morning (June 7th) we crossed over the Little Mountain & passing down Emigration Canyon reached the City between 10 and 11 o'clock. Entering the City we were met in the street by Major Gen. George Grant & Major [Brig.] Gen. Wm. H. Kimball who introduced themselves to the Commissioners and escorted them to the Globe Restaurant which had been opened [at Brigham Young's direction] for the purpose of accommodating the party. Arriving at the Globe the carriages were driven into the yard and the animals sent out to pasture. No rooms had been provided for our use & we have to sleep in the carriages & on the back porch of the house, as all houses in the City were abandoned and fastened up.

During the forenoon the Commissioners were visited by Adjt. Gen. Jos. [James] Ferguson, Genl. A. P. Rockwood, Judson Stoddard, Bill Hickman, Robert Burton, and many other leading Mormons, who sat down to dinner with us.

None of the dignitaries were in the City. Every single family in the City had been moved away & there were only a few men left to take charge of the gardens & buildings. All of the stores are closed & there is nothing in the shape of business going on. A few workmen are busily engaged tearing off the roofs off of the buildings in the Temple block which has been used as Public Works. We took a walk during the evening in which we visited the arsenal. I saw in it a brass six pounder [cannon] and an iron 6 pounder, also several cans filled with balls of different sizes which were intended to be used as canister shot.

---

[24]These fortifications are still partly intact and visible.

I am informed that the Presidents [6 April] Proclamation was read in public in this City the evening before we arrived & was received with great surprise and indignation by the people as they had been led to expect through Col. Kane a different expression of sentiment than that found in the beginning of the document. They say that it contains falsehoods and unjust aspersions from the beginning to the end.[25]

There is a regular muster and roll call of the militia of the City at sunrise and sunset every day. At these musters a small band consisting principally of a big drum, performs the Mormon national airs in an eminently Mormon style. Every man has to appear armed and equipped as the law directs, they however do not attempt to drill. On the evening of our arrival in the City an Express arrived from Brigham who is at Provo City to Ferguson & Grant. We also heard that evening that one of the Gov's wagons had upset & broke to peices [*sic*] in the Canyon but that the Mormon wagons returning from the Camp had assisted him and taken up the load of the broken wagon. The morning following (June 8th) we were informed that the Gov. would come in through Parley's Canyon, a longer road but much better than that down Emigration Canyon. Towards noon Ferguson & Grant and one or two others rode out to meet him in that Canyon and a dinner was prepared for him at the residence of Ferronmons [Feramorz] Little at the mouth of that Canyon. Shortly after they left however, the Gov. arrived in the City with his two ambulances having missed the other road & come through Emigration Canyon. He went immediately to Staines where rooms had been prepared for him. His baggage wagons however did not arrive until evening having come through Parley's Canyon.

Towards sundown Ben & Jim Simonds, Ross & Convis arrived in the City. The goods which they had brought in were bought (or taken) from them at the mouth of the canyon by Ferry [Feramorz] Little and sent immediately to Provo. I am told that an order has been issued forbidding all further trade or traffic with the Camp.[26]

---

[25]Ferguson described this scene with disdain: "The [Buchanan] Proclamation is considerable. Quite a jim down [?] Allegiance or a halter [noose], or neither or both. I have nothing to be pardoned for, and do not think I will take it. The Proclamation was read by the boys at 'Retreat' and received with three groans and [a singing of] Doo da. We shall do our best to get things out of the way. I suppose you will be ready for the powder and glad that we send as it will come in quantities large enough to be safe." Ferguson to Wells, 6 June 1858, ibid.

[26]Several of the senior Legion officers in Salt Lake City had become wary of the Delaware Ben Simonds and his eclectic band of tribal free-booters on the Weber River, viewing them with some justification as opportunists aiding the Utah Expedition while professing friendship with Mormons. Accordingly, as the peace commissioners neared Salt Lake City, the Legion took action to prohibit entrepreneurial Latter-day Saints from selling butter and eggs to Simonds to prevent their flow to army quartermasters. Such provisions were instead redirected to the massive Mormon gathering at Provo. Generals Grant and Kimball and Colonels Burton and Jones to Young, 5 June 1858 (including draft Special Rules), LDS Archives. General Ferguson suspected that the army may have engaged Ben to assassinate or kidnap Brigham Young. Ferguson to Young, 21 June 1858, ibid.

Morrell & Jones cannot dispose of the goods which they have brought in, as there are no people here to buy & the men who are here will not pay the prices asked but will only pay the cost of the goods. Jesse Jones did sell his goods to Stoddard at a fair valuation but an hour or so afterwards Stoddard threw up the bargain and refused to take them & Jesse thinks he will have to take them back to Camp.

Morrell had an interview soon after his arrival with Elias Smith the Mormon Postmaster and asked for the delivery of the keys of the P.O. etc., but Smith told him he did not recognize his appointment & made other objections, but finally told him he would take counsel on the subject and give him a definite answer the next day. I am now informed that he has consented to deliver up the office [position] as soon as Morrell can find a room [for a post office]. On the evening of the Gov's. arrival, he & the Commissioners had a long interview with Ferguson and [Col.] Chauncey West who had been deputized for the purpose by Brigham. At 12 o'clock that night the two latter started for Provo and returned from thence the next day by noon bringing the news that Brigham himself would come up & hold a conference with the Commissioners.

I am led to believe that the Mormons insist that the Army shall not enter the valley. The men in the City declare positively that the movement of the Army will be the signal for the burning up of the City. Several of the houses have shavings already piled up in them & everything ready to be set on fire.

They also declare that they never will submit to be ruled by rulers not of their own choice. Wagons heavily loaded are continually leaving the City for Provo loaded with boxes [of wheat] etc., from the tithing office. All of the women have been moved from the City & there is but one or two old hags to be seen.

Although rooms have been fitted up for the Governor & his lady at Staine's no arrangements have been made for their meals as it was thought that Mrs. C would bring her cook with her, the consequence is that she is a little troubled. She dines at the Globe for the present.

Three gentlemen Messrs. H. [Henry] Clarkson, [A. V.] Brookie, & Harvin [James M. Harbin] just arrived have been visiting Brigham. They are from California and are here for the purpose of selling a large tract of land in Col. Kinney's Protectorate of the [Central American] Musquito Country. Their proposals are to sell 300,000,000 [30 million] of acres at ten cents an acre and they are fully authorized by Kinney to make the sale. Brigham however says that he has never violated the constitution or laws of his country & is determined to support that constitution which corrupt demagogues & politicians have violated.

June 10. At noon this morning, Brigham, Heber, Dan'l H. Wells, Geo. A. Smith, Wm. H. Hooper, and some 20 more of the leading men of the Church arrived from Provo. They dined at Brighams mansion. In the evening they visited Gov. Cummings & afterwards the Commissioners. After supper, Brigham Young was serenaded by the Militia band, this compliment has not been extended to the Gentiles. Morrell has made arrangements for a post office in John Kimball's building (the old Surveyor Genl's office) and will probably move into it tomorrow.

Arrangements have been made in the Court Room & everything prepared for a grand convention tomorrow between the Commissioners & the Church leaders. I do not know whether it will be public or not. I understand that the Mormons will insist that the Army shall not enter the Settlements and are willing to make a compromise upon those terms.

I have been well received this far by the Mormons and they have never spoken a word against either myself or my father in my presence or in that of my friends. Morrell however has in some instances been very rudely treated by them.

The second account written in close proximity to the peace commissioners as they traveled from Fort Bridger to Salt Lake was a dispatch to the *Liberty (Missouri) Weekly Tribune* by Owen Hugh O'Neil, a young Irish emigrant who had befriended the newspaper's editor, Robert Miller, while working his way west. At Fort Laramie W. M. F. Magraw hired O'Neil and William Porter Finlay for the Pacific Wagon Road party. When Magraw's engineers went into winter quarters in the Wind River Mountains during October 1857, Finlay joined Magraw's volunteer infantry company. O'Neil elected to remain a civilian at "Fort Thompson" until Magraw and Albert Sidney Johnston ordered that little group to join forces with the army at Fort Bridger in late March 1858. How O'Neil, still a civilian, managed to reach Salt Lake City is unknown.

O'Neil to Miller, 9 June 1858,
O'Neil Letters and Essays, Huntington Library.

We arrived here on the 7th having spent nearly five days on the road. Our journey was retarded by waiting for Governor Cumming, whose progress was made with Slowness and deliberation, worthy the dignity of the governor of all the Utahs and befitting the gravity of his character. ~~He arrived here~~ He overtook us on Weber, where we lay by for a day but as he was not ready or disposed to advance with rapidity, we left him and hastened to salute the holy places of Zion.

On yesterday the Gov arrived here, apparently much fatigued from his trip. One of his wagons broke down and was left between the Big & Little Mountains being replaced by one borrowed from Ben Simonds (I believe). This morning he has recovered from the effects of his exertions on the road, and is as brisk as usual. He is very popular among the Mormons.

The Commissioners, who arrived nearly at the same time with us have as yet had no opportunity of a Conference with the Mormon leaders, as Brigham Young and most of the other principal men have moved to Provo. There is it appears to me very little probability that any arrangement satisfactory at the same time to the Commissioners and the people of the valley can be made. Nearly all the citizens of this place have already moved to Provo, and the few that remain are leaving as fast as conveyance can be obtained. From the best information I can obtain, there now remain in the City, exclusive of the guard, not more than a dozen families, and several of these are moving off today. The night, since the arrival of our party, has been generally devoted to loading wagons which leave the City before day, on the Provo Road.

Wm H Kimbal, Genl Grant, and the other leaders who yet remain here declare that unless the Government offer fair terms of accommodation, they will after the removal of their families and effects set fire to the city and reduce it to ashes. They say that all is now arranged for reducing the city to a heap of ruins, and that if they are compelled finally to leave it they will leave nothing but blackened and smoking ruins to indicate the spot where it stood. They and the whole people are very much displeased with the Presidents Proclamation. They say that it contains charges of crimes which they never committed, and that the judgment of the President has been biased by the misrepresentations of base men whom they have been compelled to drive from their city on account of their vices. Of the character of Judge Drummond they give an awful picture, representing it as too vile almost to be spoken of much less tolerated. Of a few others they speak almost in the same terms, and demand an investigation of the truth of their assertions. From all I can learn there is more truth than poetry in what they say regarding the characters of these individuals. I have since my arrival here seen nothing in the character of the people adverse to good order. All declare themselves willing to submit to the laws but are unwilling to be submitted to the sway of men who make it both a business and a pleasure to interfere with their religious and domestic institutions, and insult them by openly practicing all kinds of immorality.

I hope that this quarrel will not be carried to extremity but that some peaceable accommodation will be effected, for whatever may be said against these Mormons it cannot be denied that their persevering and ingenious industry has worked wonders in this valley, surmounting difficulties which would damp the ardor of almost any other people. They have raised up a city in a short time which for regularity of plan, cleanliness, and the taste displayed in many of its private residences can vie with any place of its age on the face of the globe. . . .

I have just learned that the prospect of a peaceable termination of the Mormon Question is probable. If such is the fact I rejoice at it, and hope that they will be allowed peacefully to pursue the career of improvement which they have so well commenced in this Valley. If they are compelled to abandon this location, I am sure they will burn the City, (who can blame them?) and that this valley will never again be what it now is. So that the government not the Church of L.D. Saints will be the greater losers by the measure. The people who have changed this valley from a wilderness to what it now is can if they get time and peace do still more, and can certainly lose nothing eventually, for they cannot well light on a region naturally more adverse to successful settlement than this was at the time of their first arrival.

An express has arrived from Provo bringing word that President Young will be here tomorrow to confer with the Commissioners. I suppose that he will give the final solution to the question whether war is "to be or not to be." I have many interesting particulars relative to the country to communicate, but as the political issues now pending must be more interesting at present to your readers, I shall ~~defer~~ postpone other matters for a future letter.[27]

Our Present Position a Critical One: The Meetings of 11–12 June

Key to the resolution of the Utah War was the restoration of federal authority in the territory and Mormon acceptance of the army that went with it. President Buchanan's 6 April proclamation of pardon had been printed and would eventually be distributed throughout Utah, but its provisions were of no consequence—literally without effect—until formal acknowledgment and acceptance of these prerequisites by the territory's entire population.[28] The document and Secretary Floyd's instructions to the commissioners were silent on how this was to be done. Seemingly, it was a procedural omission, but rather than reflecting ineptness in Buchanan's draftsmanship, it more likely was an intentional use of ambiguity to permit Messrs. Powell and McCulloch to exercise their judgment on how to proceed as conditions warranted.

[27]Postwar O'Neil traveled to California and became one of the state's early physicians. He married into Santa Barbara's prominent Ortega-Hill family and died of pneumonia in 1875 after venturing into a rainstorm to tend a patient.

[28]Apparently the first copy of Buchanan's proclamation reached Salt Lake City with Maj. Gen. George D. Grant on 6 June, the day before the commissioners arrived. It was immediately read to an outdoor gathering of the few people remaining in Salt Lake City, with highly negative reactions from the group. On 5 June Gen. James Ferguson had delivered another copy to Brigham Young in Provo. Presumably for reasons of control, Young did not distribute this document throughout Utah until 17 June. Church Historian's Office Journal, 6 and 17 June 1858; President's Office Journal, 5 June 1858, both LDS Archives. Those Utahns who kept a copy and passed it on to future generations provided their descendants with a valuable keepsake of the Utah War. By the late twentieth century, the proclamation commanded a four-figure price in the antiquarian book market. The author's copy is now in the collections of the Utah State Historical Society.

Central to the process were two days of meetings ranging between Salt Lake City's Old Council House, the Globe Restaurant, and Brigham Young's office, coinciding with the delivery of Buchanan's message to Congress and the first publication of his proclamation by the *New York Times.* Accompanying Commissioners McCulloch and Powell to these sessions were Governor Cumming and his new traveling companion and ally, Utah's U.S. Indian superintendent Jacob Forney. Powell and McCulloch relegated these two to the role of observers; they apparently had no speaking part in the large-group proceedings and did not attend the smaller side sessions involving only the commissioners, Brigham Young, and the other members of the First Presidency. At the larger meetings, Brigham Young was supported by a delegation that traveled north from Provo on 10 June: members of the Quorum of the Twelve Apostles; and several of Utah's more talented debaters and quicker minds, most notably James Ferguson and Gilbert Clements, who had challenged Alfred Cumming so vigorously in the Tabernacle meeting of 25 April. Oddly present (and deliberately seated next to McCulloch by Brigham Young) was Henry Clarkson, a non-Mormon stranger just arrived from California with three other men seeking to stimulate a mass exodus by selling Young a huge tract of land along the "Mosquito" or Caribbean coast of Nicaragua and Honduras.[29]

Mormon folklore and historiography have tended to characterize these meetings as bargaining sessions, with the result an end to the war via a negotiated settlement. Given that McCulloch and Powell presented a take-it-or-leave-it proposition and were authorized to engage in neither fact finding nor negotiation, it is inaccurate to describe these as give-and-take bargaining sessions. In effect, they were meetings during which, from the Mormon side,

[29]Young possibly intended Clarkson's presence to signal to the commissioners that the Mormons had options for shaping their destiny outside of the United States, although it was fairly well known by the time of the conferences that Young had declined to pursue the offer of Colonel Kinney's Mosquito Coast tract after several weeks of sporadic discussions with Clarkson, John B. Cooper, James M. Harbin, and a Mr. Bookie, a delegation that had traveled to Utah on Kinney's behalf from California after hiring as a guide Brigham Young's returning missionary-nephew, John R. Young. Harbin was then the owner of much of Rancho Rio de Jesus Maria, the 26,000-acre Mexican land grant in Yolo County, California. For the Mormon version of these discussions, see Kenney, ed., *Wilford Woodruff's Journal*, 24–26 May 1858, 5:187–92; Church Historian's Office Journal, 24 May 1858, LDS Archives. The comments attributed to Young during these discussions shed light on his decision not to flee Utah for coastal Central America, and also on whether he ever seriously considered continuing the Move South into northern Mexico. There is no known record of these discussions left by Colonel Kinney's representatives, although after returning to San Francisco Cooper provided a local newspaper with extensive details of the delegation's travels and the tantalizing comment that he had left Stockton on 8 April "as the bearer of private dispatches to Brigham Young." Cooper, "Details of a Journey to Salt Lake, and Return Trip," *San Francisco Daily Alta California*, 12 August 1858, 1/4–5.

there was an exhaustive recitation of grievances against the U.S. government, professions of patriotism and devotion to the U.S. Constitution, denial of wrongdoing, opposition to the garrisoning of the territory, fear of summary executions and judicial murder, and invocation of a citizenry's inherent right to self-defense and selection of their own representatives and administrators. In response to these views, the commissioners urged a focus on the future rather than a preoccupation with past experiences. In unyielding fashion, they explained Buchanan's expectations and demands, emphasizing the federal government's determination to restore federal authority in Utah without religious meddling or further bloodshed, including that of Mormon leaders. The commissioners defended the president's executive prerogative to station the regular army wherever he deemed necessary; occasionally they reacted sternly when they perceived Mormon speakers as disrespectful to the nation's chief executive.

Among the important clarifications that emerged from the productive small-group meetings was an informal understanding that Buchanan, Judge Eckels notwithstanding, had no intent to engage in polygamy prosecutions. *New-York Tribune* correspondent Browne later found something sinister in the absence of any explicit discussion of polygamy at the meetings and reported his belief that this silence was the result of a covert deal struck at the conferences:

> In the letter which I mailed to you on the 19th of June, I stated my belief that secret pledges were given by the Governor and the Superintendent of Indian Affairs to leading Mormons, during the progress of the conferences, upon the subject of polygamy. I will state to you now the name of my informant. It was the Superintendent [Forney] himself. In a conversation on the 16th of June, he asserted that not only were such pledges given, both by the Governor and himself, but that he had assured that any Judge will be removed from office who shall attempt to interfere with the institution of polygamy in this Territory, even if, in the discharge of his official duties, believing polygamy here to be an offense against the law. Since that date, Senator[-elect] Powell has stated to me, speaking both for himself and for Maj. McCulloch, that such pledges, if given at all, were given unknown to the Commissioners.[30]

It also became clear that the reinforced Utah Expedition would at some point soon move deeper into Utah as originally ordered. There was to be no recall order, but the military posts to be established would be sited away from towns.

[30][Browne], "Highly Interesting from Utah," Dispatch, 28 June 1858, *New York-Tribune*, 30 July 1858. What Browne did not mention is that Jacob Forney's position gave him no role in matters of law enforcement or civil-religious matters such as plural marriage.

The discussions did not touch on the Mountain Meadows massacre, presumably because Buchanan's pardon dealt solely with offenses relating to treason. After the meetings of 11–12 June, Ben McCulloch made an informal, somewhat oblique comment about Mountain Meadows that focused on punishing the Indians involved. Attending this session in the Historian's Office was McCulloch, Brigham Young, four apostles, and James Ferguson: "Maj. McCullough said if he had control of an army he would have satisfaction on the Indians south for killing the emigrants. . . . Geo. A. Smith said if the [non-Mormon] emigrants had not killed Indians at first, there would have been no trouble with them."[31] Unstated was the assumption that murders in the territory, such as the Mountain Meadows atrocity, would continue to fall under the purview of the territorial and federal courts in Utah once reconstituted, although in subsequent years defendants charged for a wide range of offenses would seek to avoid prosecution by invoking the presidential pardon of 6 April 1858.

Perhaps least familiar among the records of these meetings were the "minutes" kept by a member of Brigham Young's stenographic staff. Excerpts from this document appear below as the freshest, most spontaneous, least edited account of what took place.

Minutes of Meetings in Salt Lake City, 11–12 June 1858, General Church Minutes, Box 3, Folders 21 and 22, LDS Archives.

11 June 1858

Pursuant to appointment, Prests. Brigham Young, Heber C. Kimball, and Daniel H. Wells, Elders Wilford Woodruff, Geo. A. Smith, John Taylor, Amasa M. Lyman, Ezra T. Benson, Chas. C. Rich, Lorenzo Snow, Erastus Snow, Franklin D. Richards and several other invited citizens met the commissioners in company with Gov. Cumming and Superintendent Forney, who were introduced to the assembly by Pres. Young.

Prest. Young seated them, as follows: Gov. Powell and Maj. McCullough on the stand where the clerk of the Supreme Court [Curtis E. Bolton] sat; Gov. Cumming at Powell's left; Gov. Young, Prests. Kimball and Wells sat on the floor facing the above named gentlemen. Mr. [Henry] Clarkson, from California or Central America, sat at Maj. McCullough's [*sic*] right and Maj. [Jefferson] Hunt took a side seat.[32]

Gov. Young remarked to Gov. Powell that if he wished to have a large meeting he could have one now.

---

[31]Journal History, 16 June 1858, LDS Archives.

[32]Nauvoo Legionnaire Jefferson Hunt, until recently a major general in the California State Militia, had accompanied Clarkson to Salt Lake City.

Gov. Powell replied that if he (Gov. Young) was willing, they would just have a conference of the leading men. "As many of the leading men of your church, however, as you wish."

Gov. Young remarked that the clerks were invited, peradventure, it would facilitate the gentlemen in getting out their report for Pres. Buchanan.

Gov. Young requested [territorial] Marshal Jesse C. Little to ask the gentlemen outside to withdraw until a future time, when Gov. Powell and Maj. McCullough would address them, and also Gov. Cumming if he wished to.

The marshall did as requested.

Gov. Young remarked, "What a pity it is to have so many friends; we naturally do not wish to have our friends withdraw."

Gov. Powell replied, "It materially difficults a person."

Gov. Young informed Gov. Powell and Major McCullough that he had an express from Johnston's camp, stating that he was going to move [toward Salt Lake City].

Gov. Powell assured Gov. Young that it would cost Johnston his commission, if he should move without authority from them. Although they at first denied any power over the army.[33]

Ex. Gov. Powell stated that the object of their mission was to use their best exertions to effect an amicable adjustment of the "Unfortunate difficulties" existing between the General Government and Utah, in which statement, in a few words, Maj. McCullough concurred in.[34]

Gov. Young asked Gov. Powell for his letter of appointment if he pleased.

Gov. Powell replied, that it was a proper question and they would show and read it to them; it was now in their carriage; they had forgotten it.

Gov. Young, in reply to Gov. Powell's remarks, took up the settlement of this country, the reception and treatment of the federal officers for their territory, a few accounts in the president's proclamation and acquitted himself and this people argument[at]ively and conclusively first rate.

Gov. Cumming, at the end of a sentence, began to drop a word. Gov. Powell touched him with his left hand, and said he did not wish Gov. Young interrupted.

Gov. Young said he would pause. But Gov. Cumming not proceed[ing] he proceeded. The gentlemen and Gov. Young kept their seats while speaking.

Gov. Young appealed at the end of a sentence to Gov. Cumming, who, not comprehending his question, was asked by Gov. Young, if he could be kept still, till the halter was put around his neck.

Gov. Cumming replied, surely not (which created a laugh).

---

[33]It is questionable whether Powell would have made such a statement about Johnston in this setting.

[34]During the conferences and the speech making that followed elsewhere in Utah, McCulloch seemed content to let Powell serve as spokesman, either because of his temperament or the residual effects of mountain fever.

"Neither would you, Maj. McCullough," said Pres. Young.

Maj. McCullough said it was not agreeable to hear government spoken against.

Pres. Young answered the Major by saying, "do not mistake me, talking against men (corrupt men) who were in office was not speaking against government; electing a man a president did not make him a despot, a king. I'll thank you, Major, kindly if you will correct me wherein I speak against the government of the U.S."

Pres. Young continued his remarks on the persecution of the saints.

Maj. McCullough replied a little.

Gov. Powell remarked to Maj. McCullough (whispering) that this was not appropriate for religious discussion.

Gov. Young continued telling the delegation that the army should not come in here, etc.

He invited Gov. Cumming to talk when he pleased, he had talked too much, and would pause when any of the gentlemen wanted him to.

Gov. Powell said he would not argue the speech or conversation of Gov. Young. He said it was not his prerogative to talk or discuss on the past, it was the present and the future. If your excellency will allow us, we wish to say that we differ about the wisdom and patriotism of James Buchanan, we believe him sincerely to be a good and patriotic man. Allow me to say that Gen. Johnston's movements are reported to you erroneously. He assured Gov. Young that although he did not control the army, he advised with Gen. Johnston. Says he, "If an American General would take a man and string him up he would be disgraced."

What do you want of us? asked Gov. Young.

Gov. Powell, "We only want you to let the government send troops and to submit to the laws, etc., let the army come in, go through and locate lands [garrisons], protect the inhabitants."

Gov. Young, let me ask of you Gov. Powell, if you justify Missouri in her treatment of our people?

Gov. Powell plead ignorance of the facts.

Gov. Young said, he should be posted on such things. Asked him if he justified Illinois?

Gov. Powell plead ignorance. Unjustifiable ignorance it might be.

Gov. Young referred to Gen. Clark's speech[35] and said he could not be

---

[35]John Bullock Clark commanded the Missouri forces during the Mormon War of 1838 and was charged by Gov. Lilburn Boggs with carrying out the terms of his extermination order. After the Mormon militia surrendered at Far West, Clark addressed the Mormons there (including Brigham Young) on 5 November 1838, telling them that Joseph Smith and others under arrest would be executed; Mormon properties in the state were forfeit; the remaining Mormons must leave the state; and, should he be called again to the scene, "you need not expect mercy, but extermination." Roberts, *A Comprehensive History of the Church,* 1:496–97.

insulted to the heart worse than to be called anything but a true citizen of the United States and have the spirit of 1776 with them. I feel like Lions against those men, the sons of revolutionary fathers, who are trampling the dear bought liberties of their fathers under their feet. I'll guarantee to say that since 1776 when the government sent an army and ventured them in any state or territory, without intimating or notifying the government of that state or territory.

Gov. Powell did not remember whether or not this was the case. Of course we could give you no guarantee, that the judges would act fair and impartially, we don't know that.

Gov. Young related what judges had done, cited bro. Elihu Allen's usage in Missouri, who was kicked out of jail.

J. D. Grant testified to it, being present on the occasion also referred to [Alexander] McRae, Amasa M. Lyman and [John M.] Hockaday. Spoke of Morrill [Hiram F. Morrell] and Hunt's [Garland Hurt's] character of Mr. [William] Craig's appointment to supersede Mr. [George W.] Armstrong [as Indian agent].

1 P.M.

Dr. Forney was requested by Gov. Brigham Young to take a chair by the side of Major McCullough, etc. Mr. Clarkson moved to the left.

Mr. Erastus Snow spoke.

Marshall Little asked Gov. Young if others might come in.

Gov. Young conferred with Gov. Powell, who said anyone Pres. Brigham Young wished to could come in.

Gov. Cumming has not said a word yet.

Mr. Gilbert Clements spoke, corrected Gov. Young in relation to the number of lies [in Buchanan's proclamation].

Gov. Young thought the brethren must have analized the proclamation to find so many.

Erastus Snow said there was one truth in the proclamation, which was like a single pin in the wall, to hang a whole tissue of lies upon.

Gov. Young remarked that these gentlemen were the friends of James Buchanan and believed him to be sincere, and he did not wish them to do or say anything that would not present him in as favorable a light as possible.

Gen. Wells read instructions from Scott to Harney, orders No. 12 and spoke a short time.

Bro. Clawson brought in government documents.

Gov. Young read an aggregate [summary] of his [financial] accounts as superintendent of Indian affairs.[36]

---

[36]This related to Brigham Young's long-standing exasperation over the slow or non-payment of expenses he claimed as Utah's U.S. superintendent of Indian affairs before March 1857. At issue were perceptions by U.S. Treasury Department auditors that some of the reimbursements claimed by Young were for excessive or inappropriate expenses.

John Taylor rose, but the president thought it was too late.[37]

Gen. [Jefferson] Hunt made a few remarks.

Brigham Young, "We want some security for our safety."

Gov. Powell, We have no more security for you than what is contained in the proclamation of the president. Said "I could not go over and investigate all the charges brought against you. How in the name of high heaven could we go and find out the testimony about the murderers of [U.S. Army captain John W.] Gunnison, [territorial secretary Almon W.] Babbitt, etc., etc. I confess it was with a great deal of pleasure I heard the speakers avow their allegiance to the government, but while I do this I must enter my protest, no, not protest, but say that the language used in relation to the Chief Magistrate [President] of our nation. I do not know that I should take exceptions to the immodest words of the speakers, but I wish that the gentlemen who have spoken could have couched their feelings in language more appropriate, but as this is his taste I will not take exceptions."

Mr. Gilbert Clements commenced and made a few remarks on the president's proclamation, when Gov. Young proposed an adjournment.

Meeting adjourned at three twenty P.M. till 5 P.M.

The company from Provo, and a few others dined at Pres. Young's mansion, where John Kay sang "Ocean Shells." Erastus Snow sang "White Canoe." John Kay sang, "To the [land of the] West." Erastus Snow sang, "Wives, children and friends." Wm. C. Dunbar sang, "God will protect us when doing what's right."

During the afternoon and while the singing was going on Prests. Young, Wells and Kimball and Geo. A. Smith, went into the west room of the Globe [Restaurant] (from the dinner table), where they met with Gov. Powell and Maj. McCullough.

Pres. Young had a long conversation with Major McCullough, and then with Gov. Powell, and then with them both together.

Pres. Wells preached Mormonism to McCullough and Elder Geo. A. Smith to Powell. The question whether the army should come through this city and pass to their winter quarters, without molestation or burning; the conversation lasted till very late.

Gov. Young told Powell, how many children he had living and how many dead.

Geo. A. Smith remarked to Powell, that he no doubt understood that Gov. Young had nineteen wives.

Gov. Powell answered, he has so understood from the press.

Gov. Young remarked that was ahead of the truth in relation to the matter. He hardly had a beginning to that. Retired for the night.

In the evening Brigham Young, Jr., Ephraim Hanks, Lot Huntington and

[37]Young may have been unwilling to risk Taylor speaking to the commissioners as he had to Cumming in the Tabernacle on 25 April.

John [Stephen?] Taylor arrived in Provo from Echo Canyon and reported that the U.S. Army had taken John Hoagland prisoner, on suspicion of being connected with the burning of the government trains [in October 1857]. He had a pistol in his belt, which the officers swore was taken at the time of the burning of the trains.[38]

12 June 1858

Gov. Young and Party arrived at the lower room of the Council House at 9:45 A.M.

Gov. Powell and company arrived at 10:15 A.M. pursuant to notice by Marshal Jesse C. Little at the Globe door last evening.

House crowded behind the rails and many invited to front seats.

Gov. Young went out.

Private colloquies held all around the room.

Pres. Kimball preached Mormonism to McCullough and Clarkson.

Bros. John Taylor and Erastus Snow conversed with Gov. Powell until five minutes to eleven, when Gov. Young came in. He immediately called the house to order and gave those who wished liberty to speak.

John Taylor spoke clear, calm, eloquently and good. He was muchly complimented.

Gov. Young called upon Mr. Clarkson, who excused himself, reasonably and gentlemanly.

Geo. A. Smith spoke as follows:[39]

Our present position is, in many respects, a critical one. . . . Mr. Buchanan sends us high minded and honorable gentlemen, they come, the bearers of an executive proclamation, which I have carefully looked at in various ways. My first impression was that the president was determined to exasperate the citizens of this territory by official slanders, charging them with a list of horrible crimes, that would incite them to a rebellion which could never have been produced by any other cause.

This proclamation contains 42 false charges, into which he has refused, up to this time, to make the least inquiry or investigation. . . .

The commissioning of high minded gentlemen authorized to enquire into the state of affairs here and ascertain the facts, was what we had asked for. We expected them to come prepared to make the necessary investigations,

---

[38]A soldier of Bee's Volunteer Battalion, a former teamster, recognized the pistol by the serial number stamped into its frame. Such identification might seem improbable to today's civilians, but soldiers in the U.S. Army still memorize their rifle number.

[39]The length, fluency, and polish of Smith's comments indicate he probably wrote them after the meetings and inserted them in the "minutes" for posterity rather than delivering them in this form extemporaneously. Despite their lack of spontaneity, Smith's remarks are included here to indicate the types of points he made to the commissioners in providing important "cover" to facilitate Brigham Young's uncomfortable, humiliating acceptance of Buchanan's pardon.

and report the truth, which would set us right before the country. But, gentlemen, you tell us you came not to enquire, that it was not your intention to investigate, indeed that you have no power to make inquiries. Then what are you authorized to do? Why, to say to the citizens of the territory of Utah, that the president will not use the national bayonets to interfere with their religion, that he will not deprive them of life, liberty and the pursuit of happiness, that he does not claim such a right and does not intend it. This, gentlemen, as I understand it, is the substance of the message which you have brought us. Am I not right?

This being the case, how does it stand? Simply, in this way. I have left my homes, with my family, kindred and friends, that were not murdered, some five different times. Willingly? Yes! because I was obliged to or fight, and I am afraid to fight. (laughter)

I am a man of peace, and not of war. I accept the pardon. I may have some serious objections to the form in which it is couched and to the forty-two false accusations therein, but what is the position in which it places us before the civilized world, the most detestable of all human beings—the mercenary tool of a tyrant to coerce and murder his own countrymen. But friends, should we throw ourselves in the attitude of defence against the advancing columns of the army it brings on hostilities and bloodshed immediately. Let us drop upon this army and crush it in pieces, and it will not end there. One hundred thousand men would probably come here to exterminate us, and to wipe out the administration's disgrace, and even all this might be a matter of moonshine.

I was in favor of stopping the Army last fall; we gained by that means a winter's quiet. You know a sick patient would pay a large sum of money to physicians to lengthen out a miserable existence a little while, and a man who has as many wives as I have would do a great deal to prolong a happy existence. (Commissioners laugh)

And again our religion forbids the shedding of blood and inspires dread of the consequences; and above all things the shedding of innocent blood. We are informed, upon reliable authority, that there are many in that army that do not thirst for our blood; a portion of the soldiers do not want to kill us, and . . . neither I nor my friends wish to shed their blood, and would not do it except in unavoidable self defence, the crime of shedding the blood of innocent men is worse than half a dozen deaths. Death only closes this mortal career, but to shed innocent blood would dye our garments in worlds to come. . . .[40]

[40]In Mormon doctrine the age of "innocence" is eight; to shed the blood of such children was considered an act with dire consequences in the afterlife. Beneath the surface of Smith's comments was his awareness that a large quantity of such blood was shed at Mountain Meadows by Mormon troops. Hence the title of Bigler and Bagley's documentary history, *Innocent Blood.*

It was with great difficulty that the administration could get a man to come to Utah as governor, whom they considered competent. When Gov. Cumming was appointed, it was boastingly announced by the press generally that a man had been at last found, who could use up Brigham Young effectively, without his knowing it, till after it was done. He seemed to have been considered the hardest case in the country, except Maj. Ben McCullough, and as he could not be induced to accept the governorship and go to Utah, Gov. Cumming was the next choice and his acceptance was hailed with general enthusiasm by our most violent persecutors. I supposed from his name, he was one of the Jackson County [Missouri] mobbers. . . . These sentiments and feelings I had in my breast towards Gov. Cumming; and would have carried them with me to my grave, had he not at length broke out from among this forest of arms and thrown himself into the midst of the settlements unescorted and alone, as a citizen, Governor, and said he was not an enemy and had not come to trample upon the right of American citizens. He showed himself brave, generous, and noble by this act. He declared he did not wish to govern a people, who did not want him, but was ready to fulfill the duties of his office, he desired, and I began to respect him. . . .

I see in Gov. Cumming a manly, free generous spirit. He says, "I come not to govern you as a military despot; but as a fellow citizen." This is right.

What shall we do next? Shall we go out here into the mountains, and raise a mill pond, that will compel us to shed blood? Shall we be found in this position? Or shall we with all its horns and heels swallow the difficulty and say, gentlemen, walk in and fulfill your pledges. We have confidence in you. Should the pledges be violated, what better off would they be, than where they are? This is the best policy we can adopt, if they will do as they should do, and let us alone, they can pass along in safety. . . .

But gentlemen, if Mr. Buchanan actually means, as he says, the citizens of Utah should have the same privileges as other citizens of the United States, all right. . . . Withdraw your armies, and that act would cry louder for peace than a thousand proclamations and promises; it is hard for me to believe that peace is intended, while you point your cannon at our houses and while they remain there, I have good grounds to suspect treachery and foul play. I lack confidence in your words unless your actions correspond.

From my known disposition to avoid personal danger (laughter) my military friends on my left will be but little influenced by the proposals I wish to submit. I propose to say to the army, walk in gentlemen, select your camp grounds and fulfill your orders, if we take this course, in what light will the nations view our position? The result will be that the civilized world will say, the citizens of Utah are disposed for peace, their desires are not to come into collision with the parent government, if they can honorably avoid it; and as to the long list of charges, that have been enumerated against us by Mr. Buchanan in his proclamation the world will say, except a few party friends,

Mr. Buchanan, don't believe them true, or he would not have pardoned them all indiscriminately, or else he does not feel able to punish them, but his mistaken policy dictated that charges grave and serious should be enumerated in his proclamation to ease him down from his awkward position without bursting. Instead of this measure disgracing us in the eyes of intelligent men, it will lift us higher in the scale of humanity. I say then, let us not reject these overtures. Although if we should turn in and put down our foot again and say to the advancing army stop there! they are just as sure to do it as the sun is to rise tomorrow morning; and the next party will stop, if we tell them to; and should volunteers come by thousands, and by hundreds of thousands, their bones will whiten the plains, which will be the only token left to mark the spot where they have been. But who wants to see it?

When I say, walk in gentlemen, fulfill your orders and don't interfere with our gardens, fields and pastures, and I want it perfectly understood that the first man that ravishes or seduces a wife or daughter of mine, I fully intend to blow out his brains. Hundreds with this army came for that very purpose....

But we are told the army are not to be located near the settlements, but in unoccupied places, where grass, water, and timber are convenient, and that they will maintain strict discipline and preserve good order. Let this be done and all will be well.

As I said before, I have full confidence that Mr. Buchanan will not violate the pledges which he has now made to us unless he fully believes that it is for his own interest so to do; and in consequence of the "peculiar" [reduced] condition of the treasury, I believe that his interests will not prompt him to do so, during his administration.

Gov. Powell and Major McCullough complimented Geo. A. Smith, as he went along, as they also did Bro. Taylor.

James Ferguson made a few remarks.

Gov. Young said he had better bring the conference to a close. Gov. Powell proffered to address the people at any time.

Gilbert Clements made a few remarks on the president's proclamation, when Gov. Young proposed an adjournment.

Meeting adjourned till 5 P.M.

The company from Provo and a few others dined at Pres. Young's mansion.

Pres. Young spoke in relation to Gen. Johnston's promising to keep the soldiers from any dense settlement.[41] He said, Gen. Johnston's camp cannot reside in this valley, their cattle are too numerous. Cache Valley is the only valley large enough contiguous.[42]

---

[41]It is unclear whether Young made these and the following remarks at his private dinner meeting or to the reconvened larger group at the Old Council House. The tone suggests the former.

[42]Except for a few camps needed by herders to tend the church cattle grazing there, Cache Valley was unsettled until 1859. The army rejected its use because of its distance from Salt Lake City, high altitude, cold climate, and Shoshone claims, all of which had discouraged Mormon settlement.

Gov. Young would like to hear and would not like to hear the brethren talk. . . . The army attaches [camp followers] would create difficulty with our people. I wish all the United States officers were like Gov. Cumming. As to the gentlemen commissioners, they have no power only to investigate the past but to enquire into the future, if we will submit to the constitution and laws of the United States? We always have and expect to. I have no character, no pride to gratify, no vanity to please. If a man comes from the moon and says he will pardon me for kicking him in the moon yesterday, I don't care about it, I'll accept of his pardon, it don't affect me, one way or the other.

Our necks shall not to be given to the halter [noose]. Col. Johnston said that not a soldier of his army should be quartered in this city. I'm tired of this city. I had not finished my house until I wanted to leave it and build better. I'm a man of enterprize. My duty on this earth is to build up. I call forth the enterprize and the energy of the people. Don't be concerned. We shall live. I could select one thousand of our boys, from 15 to 18, who could whip all the armies that could be sent here. We'll live and prosper. . . .

Brethren, all that ask me if I will sustain constitutional principles, and these principles shall not be surrendered by me, ask if I will submit to constitutional principles? I reply, I will. Will they hang you, Bro. Brigham? Don't be concerned, brethren, we have to do right and God will sustain us; trust in God and keep your powder dry. Don't be afraid of the Indians, if they get friends, they will be friendly and not turn against true friends. I'm not afraid of the Indians. They will kill once in a while. We will bear it. . . .

Go to your business, do right, if the army come. Col. Johnston, I'll venture to say, is a high minded gentleman. I don't ask the commissioners. I want the chief executive of the nation to have his administration made honorable, if possible. I did not vote for him. I would not, if I had an opportunity. . . . We'll do well, don't be frightened. I would have voted for Fillmore [in the election of 1856]. But I won't sustain them in cutting my throat, I'll see him in hell first. I'll not say that I'll see him in heaven but he'll never get there.

Gov. Powell addressed a crowded audience in the Council House at 5 P.M.

At the end of the 12 June session, there was no memorandum of the understandings reached, no ceremonial document signed to signify Mormon acceptance of Buchanan's pardon. In the end, after all of the back-and-forth and posturing, Brigham Young in effect accepted the pardon as tendered. To save face, he characterized the amnesty as offensive and wholly gratuitous, a pardon extended to a people who neither needed nor requested it. Young's comments were a rhetorical fig leaf designed to cover the humiliation of his acceptance. His remarks were akin to a modern presidential "signing declaration," a statement issued when signing into law an unpalatable bill to express distaste for the legislation and probable intent to avoid implementing it. It was a verbal flourish that Lazarus Powell and Ben McCulloch chose to ignore. The process apparently concluded informally on the basis of two verbal comments: George A. Smith's remark, "I am a man of peace, and not of war. I accept the pardon"; and Brigham Young's cavalier man-from-the-moon remark and his assurance, "I'll accept of his pardon." There was an understanding that Albert Carrington would oversee preparation of a memorandum of understanding summarizing the proceedings based on the notes taken by Brigham Young's stenographers, and that Young and the commissioners would certify and send this record to Washington.

Freely and Fully Pardoned: Executing Buchanan's Proclamation

The commissioners immediately couriered letters to Fort Bridger to inform Secretary Floyd and General Johnston of their view of what had transpired. Their report to Floyd informed him, "after the fullest and freest conference with them we are pleased to state that we have settled the unfortunate difficulties existing between the government of the United States and the people of Utah. We are informed by the people and chief men of the Territory that they will cheerfully yield obedience to the Constitution and laws of the United States. They consent that the civil officers of the Territory shall enter upon the discharge of their respective duties. They will make no resistance to the army of the United States in its march to the valley of Salt Lake or elsewhere. We have their assurance that no resistance will be made to the officers, civil or military, of the United States in the exercise of their various functions in the Territory of Utah." Powell and McCulloch added that they were telling Johnston "that he could march his army to the valley whenever he desired to do so. We intend to remain and visit the people and converse with them until General Johnston's army arrives. We think it important that we remain until the army is located in the valley."[43]

The commissioners' letter to Albert Sidney Johnston was essentially the same as the one written to Floyd without most of the background information. For Johnston alone, though, they added the important suggestion "that you issue a proclamation to the people of Utah, stating that the army under

[43]Powell and McCulloch to Floyd, 12 June 1858, "Annual Report of the Sec. of War (1858)," 167–68. The next day, Heber C. Kimball told a Mormon congregation in American Fork that the peace conference was "the damdest operation that he ever saw." Levi Savage Journal, 13 June 1858, 1:123, LDS Archives.

your command would not trespass upon the rights or property of peaceable citizens during the sojourn in, or the march of your army through, the Territory. Such a proclamation would greatly allay the existing anxiety and fear of the people, and cause those who have abandoned their homes to return to their houses and farms. . . . We respectfully suggest that you march to the valley as soon as it is convenient for you to do so."[44]

Alfred Cumming immediately drafted his own proclamation to notify Utahns that the presidential pardon was in full effect. Utah's territorial secretary, John Hartnett, did not arrive in Salt Lake City from St. Louis until 13 June, so Cumming was unable to release this document in legally proper form until the next day. In it the governor proclaimed "that all persons who submit themselves to the laws and to the authority of the federal government are by him freely and fully pardoned for all treasons and seditions heretofore committed. All criminal offences associated with or growing out of the overt acts of sedition and treason are merged in them, and are embraced in the 'free and full pardon' of the President. And I exhort all persons to persevere in a faithful submission to the laws and patriotic devotions to the Constitution and government of our common country. Peace is restored to our Territory."[45]

At first Brigham Young said very little about what had transpired at the Salt Lake City meetings. In the town of American Fork, he commented, "I will say a few words upon those subjects which we feel interested in at the present time. I feel interested in all things that Concern this people. Many want to know what will be the result of this Summers troubles or movements. The hand of God is visible in all things with us. He has brought us to our present position of peace and has hedged up the way of our Enemies."[46] Upon reaching Provo, he simply spoke to his office clerks "about the Providence of God on relation to our preservation, and the favorable aspect of the U.S. Army camping at Cedar Valley, and of the prospect of our returning to the City in reasonable time, also alluded to some of the conversation which took place with the peace commissioners." Lapsing into braggadocio, "President Young remarked that all they wanted was quietly to slide through the City and back out of all their threatenings. The President alluded to a remark he made to McCullogh [*sic*] that if an army of volunteers should come from

[44]Ibid., 119–20.

[45]Ibid., 113.

[46]Kenney, ed., *Wilford Woodruff's Journal*, 13 June 1858, 5:196.

the States for the purpose of using us up. He would send out 50 boys and prevent them coming. . . . Pres. Young remarked that Buchanan would have to be considerably chagrined at the remarks that Congressmen would make to him about the expenses he had put the government to and accomplished nothing."[47]

Beyond the Jordan: Of Timing and Commitments

As he finished his proclamation, Governor Cumming worried about what he saw as a threat to his credibility—the possibility that the assurance he had given to Brigham Young on 11 June about the timing of the army's movement was problematic. Cumming had earlier discussed this subject with Johnston at Fort Bridger, and on 21 May the general assured him, "there will certainly not be any movement of troops for more than 30 days. Before moving the General in Command will publish a proclamation notifying the community that he does not advance with any hostile views, nor will he encamp near any dense settlement, village or City." Cumming immediately shared this information with the Mormons.[48] Nine days later, with the newly arrived commissioners present, a similar discussion took place during which Cumming believed, as he later phrased it, Johnston "pledged himself not to march before the 20th June, at any rate, until he had heard from the Commissioners."[49] Yet on 12 June, without consulting the governor, the commissioners had encouraged Johnston to move toward the Salt Lake Valley immediately and had repeated this advice in their letter to Secretary Floyd. When John Hartnett reached Cumming on 13 June, he relayed Johnston's request that he tell the governor and commissioners he intended to start marching out of winter quarters on 15 June. In fact, even as Hartnett and Cumming met, the Utah Expedition's vanguard was leaving Fort Bridger for a marshaling site on Bear River.

Alarmed, embarrassed, and furious at what he considered a breach of trust and betrayal, Cumming wrote "a formal note to the Commissioners requesting them to inform me substantially their remembrance of this pledge of the General. The gentlemen have deferred answering this note for several

[47]President's Office Journal, 14 June 1858, LDS Archives.

[48]This language (couriered by Cumming to Presiding Bishop Edward Hunter on 25 May) appears to have been a 23 May annotation by Cumming to the bottom of Johnston to Cumming, 21 May 1858, and is found in Church Historian's Office Journal, 26 May 1858, ibid.

[49]Cumming to Cass, 18 June 1858, Hafen and Hafen, eds., *Mormon Resistance,* 325–26.

days."[50] Thus ignored by the commissioners, who had little appetite for an intra-governmental dispute, Cumming accosted Lazarus Powell in the Globe Restaurant on 14 June. Proprietor David Candland recorded the exchange:

> I heard Gov. Cumming ask Gov. Powell for an answer to some note he [Governor Cumming] had addressed to Gov P and the latter pleads business, haste &c, but promised it at some subsequent time perhaps this evening but he Gov C might rest assured he should have it as he Gov C observed by God he would not lose a deal and if Gov P did not furnish it he would have it from some one. I think he said Col Johnson [*sic*]. Gov C was very emphatic and Gov. Powell rather dilatory in feeling I thought. Gov. C said he was bound to be consulted in the march of the troops so as not to infringe on territorial or municipal laws as he was bound to see his constituents protected and he wished the possession of said answer so that if questioned he might produce it and prove to the people he had not played false. Gov P offered to give the word by word of mouth but Gov. C declined it and determined to have it in black & white and he G—d D——d he would not lose his deal.[51]

Cumming took the matter to Johnston directly on 15 June through a letter reciting his understanding of their May discussions. He asked Johnston to "make such disclosures as may be made without detriment to the public service which may enable me to reconcile the apparent discrepancy between my [11 June statement at the conference] and that recently communicated through Mr. Hartnett." Cumming went on to explain, "I stated to President Young that you were pledged not to march until you had received communications from the commissioners or myself, that you had told me that you would issue a proclamation setting forth your intentions. Now it is obvious that, without some explanation on your part, I may be suspected of duplicity in regard to my statement to President Young, and be compelled to resort to some means of defence and explanation. I must, therefore, endeavor to impress upon you the necessity of furnishing me with the desired information to combat the distrust which may otherwise arise in the minds of the people."[52]

---

[50]Ibid.

[51]Douglas K. Candland and Mary Homrighausen Candland, "Documents of David Candland," 14 June 1858, collections of Utah State Historical Society. Powell apparently never wrote the requested letter. For a description of the jousting of the period in Candland's Globe among non-Mormons and between them and Latter-day Saints, see *Harper's Weekly*, 11 September 1858, excerpted in Twila Van Leer, "Gentiles, Mormons clashed over S. L. Valley restaurateur," *Deseret News*, 23 September 1997.

[52]Cumming to Johnston, 15 June 1858, "Annual Report of the Sec. of War (1858)," 114.

Keep the Wax out of My Ears and the Dust out of My Eyes: Spying on Cumming

While Alfred Cumming fumed, his reluctant host at the Staines mansion made a mockery of the hospitality that the governor and his wife accepted in good faith. After successfully probing the couple for the substance of the secret instructions that Buchanan had given to his peace commissioners, William C. Staines rifled their papers and then, with great pride, reported all of this to Brigham Young in Provo plus the details of Cumming's angry 15 June letter to Johnston even before the general received it. Such inside information facilitated Young's ability to exploit, if not aggravate, the growing rupture between Cumming and Johnston while dealing more confidently with commissioners Powell and McCulloch.

To the Cummings and Kane before them, the Staines mansion was a seductive oasis of elegance, luxury, and calm after arduous treks and months of frontier tenting in extreme weather. In reality, the house was a warren of intrigue to ensnare unwary as well as vulnerable guests. The house and its owner-host were components of the Mormon intelligence-gathering web that a month earlier and two thousand miles to the east Albert G. Browne's mother had described as featuring "a spider with eyes on all sides, [which] is the *horror of horrors* . . . I have the same shuddering at the information they receive by their spies, that I have at the movements of a six eyed spider in close proximity to an unconscious, fearless child."[53]

Staines to Young, 17 June 1858, LDS Archives.

Not knowing w[h]ether you are a[c]quainted with the following Itams [*sic*] I have taken the liberty of givin[g] you such information as I have up to this date.

As for the instructions the commissioner had they were: to investigate matters here, but in no wise interfere with what Gov Cummings had done, And as he had acted as investigating committee[e] they do not think it nescery [*sic*] to do any more.

This chatt I had with Mrs Cummings, after this the Gov handed me a letter informing him of thir coming while in my hand he wished to look at it to see if it was the right one. Mrs Cummings being presant remarked that

[53]Sarah Cox Browne to Sarah Ellen Browne, 18 May 1858, Browne Family Papers, Schlesinger Library. For examples of a Brigham Young nephew monitoring and reporting on activities of Indian agent Garland Hurt and even a low-level fellow-Mormon, see Phineas W. Cook to Hosea Stout, 1 February 1857, and Cook to Young, 29 September 1858, both LDS Archives.

it was for the other was a much longer com[muni]cation, and she knows, for by the bye, she is the *Gov private secratry.*

Yesterday while he was absent from his Room I paul pry like[54] steped in, saw a letter directed to Col Johnson dated June 15th 1858, stating the promise or pledge he (Cummings) had made to this people as to the time of the moveing of the Troops, and Johnson is[s]uing a Proclamation which he had promised him he would do, also what you said at Conferance on Friday last that you had been informed that Johnson would move sooner than had been stated by the Gov, and the answer Cummings gave at that time that he as[s]ured you it was not so &c&c

But the Verbal Message he rece[i]ved thru Mr Hartnett the secertary That he should move on the 15th Inst satisfied him that what you stated was correct and he wished him to explain why it was that he should do so untill he (Johnson) should have heard from him or the Commissioners. W[h]ether he intends sending this letter or not I am not able to say. He informed me Yesterday that Judge Eckels and Dr Hurt was to leave Camp Scott on th 15 Inst with a detachment of Troops for the city.

He ask Gov Powell ~~for a~~ to write him a note and state in that the confersation Johnson and they had about moving the Troops and the time of moving. I overhe[a]rd this chatt and Powell after the Gov Damned them from [?] a Inaallok [? macllok?] &c &c all a few times said he would write but he has not done so up to this date and the Old Gentleman is mad about it. He thinks some of the Officers wish to make him trouble and he swares he will not be humbuged by them: he will resign his officer first. I shall endeavor to keep the wax out of my Ears and the dust out of my eyes, the Lord being my helper. Ever praying for Your welfare and the Prosperity of Zion.

PS if you have any Council for me I shall be glad to rece[i]ve and obey the same.

Surprise That Unease Is Felt: General Johnston Responds

Unaware of this brewing storm, on 14 June, General Johnston complied with the commissioners' request that he issue a proclamation from Bear River to soothe Utahns' anxieties. In doing so, Johnston expressed "surprise that uneasiness is felt by the people as to the treatment they may receive from the

[54]A reference to John Poole's 1825 London stage farce, *Paul Pry*, centering on the euphonious lead character, "a comical, idle, meddlesome and mischievous fellow consumed with curiosity . . . an interfering busybody who conveniently leaves behind an umbrella everywhere he goes in order to have an excuse to return and eavesdrop." "*Paul Pry* (play)," *Wikipedia*, accessed 10 November 2014, http://en.wikipedia.org/wiki/Paul_Pry_(play). The play was highly popular, running for a half-century in various countries, including Staines's native England and the United States beginning in 1826.

army." Noting that his honor and orders from the War Department precluded bad behavior, he assured the commissioners, "if no obstruction is presented to the discharge of those duties there need not be the slightest apprehension that any person whatever will have cause of complaint against it. The army will continue its march from this position on Thursday, 17th instant, and reach the valley in five days. I desire to encamp beyond the Jordan on the day of arrival in the valley."[55] Johnson's public statement assured "those citizens of the Territory who, I learn, apprehend from the army ill treatment, that no person whatever will be in anywise interfered with or molested in his person or rights, or in the peaceful pursuit of his avocations; and should protection be needed, that they will find the army (always faithful to the obligations of duty) as ready now to assist and protect them as it was to oppose them while it was believed they were resisting the laws of their government."[56]

General Johnston sent this message—what he called "a few remarks it was thought desirable I should publish"—to the governor on 16 June. The next day, Cumming acknowledged its receipt and undertook to circulate the document. He cautioned Johnston about the need for extreme care during his march to avoid damage to abandoned homes and grazing lands, adding a warning that "the introduction of a mass of hired [civilian] followers of your camp would cause unnecessary irritation." The governor continued in this vein: "In short, with a full knowledge of the condition of affairs in the Territory, whilst I desire that you should continue your march as soon as you are in possession of such facts as will enable you to select and occupy suitable camps, yet it is my duty to protest against your occupation of positions in the immediate vicinity of this city or other dense settlements of the population. Should you resolve to act in opposition to my solemn protest, you may be assured that it will result in disastrous consequences, such as cannot be approved by our government."[57]

Upon receiving this most recent protest from Cumming, Johnston realized that he had ignited a controversy threatening to spill into Washington. Aside from the governor's bruised ego, if the tempest ignited Brigham Young's sensitivities, it had the potential to unwind the still-fragile acceptance of Buchanan's pardon—Cumming's "deal"—and revitalize the Move South. Responding from a new bivouac at Yellow Creek, the general accepted

[55]Johnston to Powell and McCulloch, 14 June 1858, "Annual Report of the Sec. of War (1858)," 120–21.
[56]Statement by Albert Sidney Johnston, 14 June 1858, ibid., 121.
[57]Johnston to Cumming, 16 June 1858, and Cumming to Johnston, 17 June 1858, ibid., 115–16.

responsibility for flawed communications, and, uncharacteristically, provided Cumming with an explanation of his decision-making.

Johnston to Cumming, 19 June 1858,
"Annual Report of the Sec. of War (1858)," 116–17.

Your letter of the 15th instant was received to-day. At the conference with the commissioners at your tent—it being understood that I could not commence the march from Fort Bridger before the arrival of the supplies, and that the preparation for the march, depending upon their arrival, could not probably be made before the 15th or 20th instant, and understanding from them that they believed before that time they would be able to ascertain the result of their mission—*I did say,* as represented by you, that "I would delay the march of the troops until I heard from them"; but by no means did I intend to give to what I said the binding force of a pledge, should it be in confliction with a good military reason for pursuing a different course, nor did I suppose the commissioners and yourself so understood it. As I used the language asserted by you to President Young, the distrust, if any is incited, should rest upon me; and I now disclaim any intention of misleading any one.

The instructions of the President to the commissioners were positive that the army should occupy the Territory of Utah, and my orders do not allow the discretion of making delay, unless reasons should be offered for so doing which should appear to me sufficiently cogent.

It was not foreseen by me that the supplies would arrive as soon as they did, and that the grass in every direction within convenient reach would be so rapidly consumed. The last circumstance alone made it necessary to move; and had it been expedient to halt, marching as slowly as it is necessary to do on account of the very large train indispensable at this distance from the source of supply, it I thought could easily be made known to me. It was designed by me, and I so informed you, that I would give notice of my march from Fort Bridger. But as commissioners were appointed to confer directly with the people, I did not deem a formal notice necessary, and thought the message sent by [way of] Mr. Hartnett would subserve every purpose.

I have the honor also to acknowledge the receipt of your excellency's letter of the 17th instant. I beg leave to say in reference to the subjects mentioned that, in the execution of my orders, I have only to select suitable military sites for posts; such as are healthy and have good water, plenty of wood and grass.

It is not essential to a good selection that it should be contingent to a city or near any settlement, nor would it be desirable to those in command. In marching through any part of the Territory the greatest care will be taken that no one is improperly treated or injury to their property sustained.

The commissioners I understand intend to meet the army at the camp we expect to make between the two [Big and Little] mountains. I would be

> glad, if you can do so, if you will make the visit with them, and to receive the information you have of different parts of the valley, which I am sure will be valuable to me.[58]

Missing from this explanation was Johnston's desire to enter the city in triumph before preemption of the limelight by the arrival of General Harney and fresh troops who had not experienced the rigors of a winter along Blacks Fork. Harney was expected to arrive at Fort Bridger by mid-June. For the Utah Expedition to have been eclipsed at this point would be intolerable not only for Albert Sidney Johnston but his entire command.

Why such an upset over the timing of Johnston's move toward the Salt Lake Valley? The matter of a week or so either way could easily seem of little consequence. Governor Cumming, of course, was distraught over his potential loss of personal credibility, but from the Mormons' standpoint, there were far more important issues involving governmental trust.

Scarred by earlier persecution in Missouri and Illinois by both civilian mobs and uniformed state militias, Mormons lacked trust in the commitments and goodwill of governments and politicians, including a feckless U.S. government. The undisciplined Utah sojourn of the U.S. Army's Steptoe Expedition during 1854–55 compounded the existing damage to the fabric of Mormon-federal relations. It was an imbroglio that reached into Brigham Young's own family with a force that disturbed his sleep three years later.[59] Apostle Smith filled his speech at the conference of 12 June 1858 with warnings that the credibility of the Buchanan administration and its army were on trial in Mormon eyes. Reflecting this skepticism, the Nauvoo Legion continued to move out of Salt Lake City to caches in the south large quantities of gunpowder and the machinery to continue fabrication of firearms.

The ability of the Utah Expedition to fulfill Johnston's assurances was a test and crucial indication of what Utah's future in the American Union might be like. Uncertainty about the army's behavior would prolong the Move South for another three weeks after Brigham Young's acceptance of James Buchanan's pardon. In many respects the absence of sustainable trust, and the paucity of leaders on both sides to nurture it, would impede the full development of positive Mormon-federal relations for the rest of the century and beyond.

---

[58]Cumming did not accept this invitation, although the commissioners did.

[59]MacKinnon, "Sex, Subalterns, and Steptoe," 227–46.

A Great Deal of Interesting Conversation: The Commissioners' Walk-About

With the commissioners' decision to remain in Utah until the arrival and "settlement" of the Utah Expedition, how did they spend their time? Their activities mixed business and pleasure, not unlike those of Kane and Cumming a month earlier. There were meetings with large, skeptical groups of Mormons in Provo and Lehi to explain the agreements and provide assurances about the army's behavior while advising a return home from the Move South. The commissioners indulged in excursions to the Great Salt Lake and met with a few old friends from Texas and Kentucky, including Maj. Seth M. Blair, whom General Wells ordered up from Fillmore for the occasion. Blair recorded that "upon the rect of his letter I immediately repaired to this [Salt Lake] city but mett the Commissioners at Provo City who felt well to me & especially McCullough with whom I had many very interesting conversations while at Provo & this city. I remained with him 10 days."[60] Finally, there was constant interaction in small groups with Brigham Young and his most senior colleagues. Although not engaged in formal fact-finding, the commissioners were inevitably immersed in daily dispensations of the Mormon point of view as well as episodic explanations of LDS religious beliefs provided by apostolic tutors. George A. Smith and his clerks recorded brief glimpses into these interactions, intertwined as they were with notations of ongoing military preparations and receipt of an early account of the prior year's Mountain Meadows massacre.

Church Historian's Office Journal, June 1858, LDS Archives.

15 June

Prest's Young & Kimball, G. A. Smith John Taylor, W. Woodruff, A. Carrington, J. C. Snow, and Thomas Carter had an interview, with Major [Gov.] Powell & McCullough in the historians [office].

Maj. McCullough said, he thought it would be the best policy, for Col Johnson to send the main body of his Army down the Weber Canon, or some other rout[e] to Cach[e] Valley and not come through all the settlements with so large a number of animals. If I had fruit trees in this country I would not have one of them destroyed for the best animals they have in the army!

---

[60]Blair Journal, 6 July 1858, Blair Papers. Blair later recorded a conversation between him, the peace commissioners, and Nauvoo Legion brigadier Peter W. Conover while visiting the latter's home in Provo: "I [asked] 'What would YOU have done, Peter, Ha. Ha. What would YOU have done?' 'Why we would have killed the last son-of-a-gun of 'em if they [the army] had tried to come in [to Salt Lake city inappropriately.]' . . . The men just straightened themselves back in their chairs and laughed to think that such a few should think such a thing." Ibid., fall 1858.

Gov. Powell, Maj. McCullough, Mr. Clarkson & Geo A. Smith went with Elder Taylor to his camp and took supper with him: during the conversation, McCullough said, the Mormons had better go to [blank] and establish a new republic; for the Damned Christians will keep on persecuting you.

G.A.S. said, it would not be many years before the Mormons could go where they pleased as any other religious bodies do; all Sects are persecuted at first; and as soon as the Constitution of the U.S. is respected, we will go to Jackson Co. and build our Temple, on Woodsons farm.[61]

16 June

G.A.S. had a great deal of interesting conversation with Gov. Powell, during their excursion to the Lake.

At 5 P.M. Gov. Powell, addressed a large assembly of the citizens of Utah Co. He tried to act a Comedian he is by no means an eloquent speaker.

17 June

At about noon, Commissioners Powell & McCullough, Geo. A. Smith and John Taylor, started for Lehi City it is expected that Maj. McCullough, will address the people in the evening.

Gov. Young presented Gov. Powell with a set of Mormon books.

18 June

Geo. A. Smith and John Taylor returned from Lehi at 3 P.M. Gov Powell addressed the people of Lehi on Thursday in front of Bp [David W.] Evan's house. He spoke after the same manner as at Provo he read a proclamation from Col. Johnson in which he says, "and should protection be needed, that they will find the Army (always faithful to the obligations of duty) as ready now to assist and protect them, as it was to oppose them while it was believed they were resisting the laws of their Government."

Mother Jones called upon the Commissioners and told them that Prest. Buchanan's Proclamation was nothing but a pack of lies; for she knew that no officer of the government had been mistreated.

In the evening G.A.S. called upon Prest Young and staid until 10 P.M. talking over matters. The Militia officers of Utah have received orders to send as many men to the City to take care of their property as will be necessary while the U.S. Soldiers are passing through; and to be on hand if their services are needed.

19 June

Jacob Hamblin called and had conversation with G.A.S. in regard to the Santa Clara Indians gave an account of the Massacre at Mountain meadows.[62]

---

[61]A reference to the Mormon belief in Independence, Jackson County, Missouri, as the location of Zion and the religion's millennial gathering place.

[62]Hamblin's latest biographer concludes that during this visit to Salt Lake, Hamblin told both George A. Smith and Brigham Young that the massacre was the work of Mormons, not just southern Paiutes. He was instructed to suppress this fact and, in so doing, participated in the church's long-term cover-up of who had been responsible for the atrocity. Compton, *A Frontier Life*, 123–25. See also Bagley, *Blood of the Prophets*, 211–12.

20 June

In the forenoon, Geo. A. Smith was at the President's Office reading news that had just arrived by eastern mail, and brought to this City by Gen. W. H. Kimball, who reported that Gov Cumming had written a very sharp letter to Col Johnson accusing him of breaking his plighted faith,—that he would not move his Army until the 23rd and that he would send in a proclamation, before moving, to notify the people but when the said proclamation arrived it was dated at Bear river, June 14, 40 miles on his way in. Also remonstrating against camping his Army near S. L. City stating that it would be an imposition upon the people.

21 June

D. B. Huntington reports that the Indians are very much disappointed, that peace was restored; they expected to come in here, and while the Mormons and Soldiers were fighting, they would have a chance to rob and plunder.

Correct as Far as I Can Recollect: A First Draft of History

For the commissioners, the principal upset during this generally pleasant interlude was a dispute over the official record of the meetings of 11–12 June, a document with serious implications for their reputations as well as the outcome of their mission. When Albert Carrington, editor of the *Deseret News*, presented Powell and McCulloch with a draft transcript of their conference remarks, the commissioners were shocked at what they considered a breach of trust because of the document's gross misrepresentations and omissions. Ben McCulloch was especially vexed and said so in blunt terms that tested Capt. James H. Simpson's earlier description of his "deep substratum of caution, that will, no doubt, prevent his doing anything rash."[63]

Thus braced, Carrington beat a hasty retreat and reported to Brigham Young while the commissioners plumbed the depths of their memories to reconstruct what they believed to be an accurate version of their extemporaneous remarks in the Council House sessions.[64] What unfolded during the rest of June and into early July was harbinger to the mistrust, parsing of phraseology, and conflicting interpretations that plagued Mormon-federal relations until President Joseph F. Smith's second manifesto on polygamy in 1904.

---

[63]"S" [Simpson], Dispatch, 26 April 1858, *Buffalo (N.Y.) Courier*, 4 May 1858, 2/2.

[64]For an example of Ben McCulloch's corrections to the Mormon draft of his conference remarks, see undated ms. in Ben and Henry Eustace McCulloch Family Papers, Center for American History, University of Texas at Austin.

On 3 July 1858, with the commissioners' departure looming, Carrington admitted failure in obtaining the text of the other speakers' conference remarks, material essential to the assembly of a comprehensive record and report. Not wishing to hazard another encounter with Ben McCulloch, Carrington broke the news to Lazarus Powell.

Carrington to Powell, 3 July 1858,
Carrington Collection, Marriott Library, University of Utah.

In reply to your note of the 1st inst., it gives me pleasure to have an opportunity to inform you that with the utmost diligence on my part, so far as press of other public duties would permit, I have been unable, even at this late date, to procure, from the Reporters and speakers at the conferences held in the Council House in this city, June 11th & 12th, a full transcript of the notes then taken by the Reporters present.

In the conversational part of the reports as furnished by the reporters, I and still am unable to furnish you a copy of the notes of President Brigham Young's share in the conversation, for, up to this date, he has not had an opportunity to revise them; and his speech, on the 12th, is still in the hands of the Reporter.

So far as omissions of what you said are concerned, the Reporters alone are in fault, for you have been furnished a strictly correct copy of their reports to me.

In addition, permit me to remark that, in my estimation, it would be highly improper for me to take the liberty to furnish copies of the remarks and speeches made by others at the time in question, until after the speaker shall have had the privilege of revision, for, aside from a breach of what is deemed a proper courtesy, such a course would subject you to a waste of time in examining reports more than likely to be materially altered by the speakers.

In case the full report of those conferences is ever published by us, I cheerfully give you Governor, my assurance that a copy each, as prepared for publication, will be forwarded to you and your colleague, Major McCulloch for your suggestions, and the revisions of your several portions of the reports, and wait a reasonable time for answers from yourself and McCulloch ere it is set up in type.[65] Such a course is in strict accordance with our invariable practice, and gives all parties that equal and fair chance for self-representation which we so much admire.

Faced with this shortfall, the commissioners fell back on the text of a long status report of their mission they had sent to Secretary Floyd a week

[65]Brigham Young never authorized a published, comprehensive record of the June conferences, although various accounts of what transpired found their way into internal church documents, which, in turn, became foundational to accounts of the 11–12 June sessions published by Mormon historians during the twentieth century.

earlier.[66] Largely from their retained copy of this document, the commissioners quickly fashioned a narrative summary, and later on 3 July obtained Brigham Young's consent to its phrasing. From this irregular, ragged process emerged the official record of the understandings reached in Salt Lake City. Tellingly, the report dealt exclusively with prospective Mormon behavior, making reference to acceptance of the pardon only in connection with a single past offense: "the burning of the army trains and driving off the cattle from the army last fall." The commissioners left for Washington the next day and submitted it to the Buchanan administration through Secretary Floyd on 24 August 1858.

Had Brigham Young and the community for which he spoke actually accepted James Buchanan's pardon and the proclamation that offered it? Governor Cumming, of course, proclaimed on 14 June that they had done so, but a more accurate answer is "sort of." Historian Norman F. Furniss argued that "the peace arranged by Powell and McCulloch, with the help of the fussy governor, was in reality an armed truce, for it left two hostile factions wrestling with each other for control of the Territory."[67] As a practical matter there was little in which Brigham Young could take solace. Notwithstanding all of the Buchanan-like distinctions and hedge words in the document he signed ("correct as far as I can recollect at present"), Young was no longer cloaked in the dignity (and salary) of Utah's governorship. Although still the territory's de facto ruler, the president of the United States had supplanted him as Utah's governor unceremoniously and without formal notification while installing a less-than-accomplished successor whose appearance and flaws prompted ridicule. Seeing Alfred Cumming in Utah's gubernatorial chair reminded Brigham Young of what had been and what could not continue. An occupying army and entourage more than twenty times the size of the fractious Steptoe Expedition was on Young's doorstep, and the uncertain legal implications of both Mountain Meadows and plural marriage lingered as existential threats to the church over which he still presided.

Powell and McCulloch to Floyd, 24 August 1858, "Annual Report of the Sec. of War (1858)," 175–77.

We have enclosed herewith a copy of a paper containing a concise statement of what was said in the conference held in Great Salt Lake City on the 11th and 12th of June last, which is certified by ex-Governor Brigham Young, as correct.

---

[66]Powell and McCulloch to Floyd, 26 June 1858, "Annual Report of the Sec. of War (1858)," 168–72.
[67]Furniss, *The Mormon Conflict*, 211.

We have the honor to be, very respectfully, your obedient servants.
L.W. Powell,
Ben McCulloch

Commissioners to Utah

In the conference held in Great Salt Lake City, on the 11th and 12th of June, 1858, L. W. Powell and Ben McCulloch, commissioners to Utah, and ex-Governor Brigham Young and others, touching difficulties between the United States government and the people of the Territory of Utah, Governor Powell in behalf of the commissioners, said in substance, as follows:

He stated the object of the mission, and distinctly made known the views and intentions of the President concerning the people of Utah. He stated that the commissioners had no power to make any treaty or compact with them. The object of the mission was to make known to the people of Utah the policy the President intended to pursue towards them, and to induce them to submit quietly and peaceably to the authority of the United States.

He stated that it was the determination of the President to see that the authority of the United States be maintained in Utah, and that the Constitution and laws of the nation should be enforced and executed in this Territory; that the President would send the army of the United States to the valley of Great Salt Lake, in such numbers, at such times, and to such places in the valley or other parts of the Territory, as he might think the public interest demanded, and retain it there as long as he should think the interest of the United States required him to do so.

That such military posts would be established in the Territory of Utah, and in the valley of Great Salt Lake as the Secretary of War should think necessary to protect the emigration to and from the Pacific, prevent Indian depredations and to act as a *posse comitatus* to enforce the execution of civil process should it be necessary. He said that the object of the President in sending a portion of the army to Utah, was to enforce the execution of the laws, and protect the civil officers of the government in the exercise of the duties of their offices, that in the event the inhabitants of the Territory quietly and peaceably submitted to the execution of the laws of the United States, and would peaceably receive the officers of the government appointed for Utah, and permit them without resistance to exercise the various functions pertaining to their respective offices, there would be no necessity for the army to be used to enforce obedience to the civil authority. If they should refuse to receive in a peaceable manner the officers of the government, or should in any way resist the execution of the laws of the United States within the Territory, the President would employ if necessary the entire military power of the nation to enforce unconditional submission and obedience to the Constitution and laws of the United States.

If the civil officers of the Territory were peaceably received and no resistance made to them in the discharge of their official duties, the army then in the Territory, or such portion of it as might hereafter be sent there, would only be used to protect emigrants and inhabitants from Indian depredations.

We stated that it was not the intention of the President, in sending a portion of the army to the Territory to deprive the people of Utah of any of their constitutional rights, but to see that the authority of the United States was respected, the civil officers protected and obedience yielded to the Constitution and laws, as enjoined by the President in his proclamation; should they quietly and peaceably submit to the authority and laws of this country, the army would be used as promptly to protect them in all their constitutional rights as it would be to compel obedience to the authority of the United States.

We called their attention to the proclamation of the President which had been distributed among them.

We stated that the President, in order to avoid the effusion of blood, and to cause them to return to their allegiance to our common country, had deputed the commissioners to make known to them the designs and intentions of the government, and the policy that would be pursued towards the people of Utah, which we had now done. We stated that the President asked nothing of them but what it was their duty as good citizens to perform, and that we trusted our mission would result in the restoration of peace, quiet, and order in the Territory.

We further stated that the commissioners had no power to give an order to the army, but that we had conferred with General Johnston, and that his army would not march to the valley of Great Salt Lake until he received information from us; that we did not know where General Johnston would make his permanent posts when he arrived in the valley of Salt Lake. General Johnston, however, told us that it was not his intention to station his army in or very near one of their large cities; that such a location would be calculated to demoralize the army; that he wished to make his permanent posts where wood, water, and grass were abundant. Governor Young expressed a desire that the commissioners would investigate certain charges that had been made against the people of Utah, to wit: as to whether the Mormons had killed Lieutenant Gunnison's party and Colonel Babbit, and burned the records and library of the federal court, and the truth of the charges made by Judge Drummond and others. The commissioners declined to go into the investigation desired for the reason that such an investigation was not within their instructions, and that it was impossible for them to do so if they desired it, for want of evidence and time.

Ex-Governor Young and others state that they were, and had ever been attached to the Constitution and government of the United States, and desired to live in peace and quiet under the government; they denied all the charges that had been made against them, except the burning of the army trains and driving off the cattle from the army last fall; that they admitted, and for that they accepted the President's pardon; they claimed that they were more ardently attached to the Constitution of the United States than others who made charges against them. Upon the President's views and intentions being made known, as set forth herein, it was agreed that the officers, civil and military, of the United States should peaceably and without resistance enter the Territory of Utah, and discharge, unmolested, *all their official duties.*

GREAT SALT LAKE CITY, JULY 3, 1858.

I have examined the foregoing statement of the substance of what was said in the conference held at Great Salt Lake City, Utah Territory, on the 11th and 12th of June, 1858, by Governor Powell and Ben McCulloch, commissioners to Utah, and ex-Governor Young and others, touching the difficulties that existed between the United States government and the people of Utah; the statement in writing examined by me is contained in six pages, hereto attached, and is, in substance a correct synoptical statement of what was said in said conference; the above is correct as far as I can recollect at present.

BRIGHAM YOUNG.

CART BEFORE THE HORSE: FROM THE SUBLIME TO THE RIDICULOUS

As the parties wrangled over how best to describe what had occurred during the conferences of 11–12 June, John Jaques of Springville, one of the multiple poets in Utah inspired to write about the war, sat down to lampoon the commissioners' work. He ended his poem with a bit of advice:

A hint we would be giving,
Which may be of much use
To great novicial rulers,
And save good folks abuse—
Buchanan had avoided
Much guilt and keen remorse,
If he'd not sent to Utah
The cart before the horse.[68]

Owen Hugh O'Neil, the Irish refugee from the Pacific Wagon Road project, had a quite different, more favorable view of the commissioners'

[68]Jaques, "The Mormon Question," 28 June 1858, *Deseret News,* 21 July 1858, 4/1. Other excerpts from this poem and a discussion of its literary context appear in Alford, "Latter-day Saint Poetry and Songs of the Utah War," 1–28.

work. O'Neil had observed them in action (to the extent possible), as well as the fruits of Mormonism. Upon returning to Fort Bridger a few days after these meetings, O'Neil again shared his impressions with Robert Miller, the Missouri newspaper editor to whom he had written on 9 June. That O'Neil did so in such positive fashion after spending part of the winter in Fort Bridger's hotbed of anti-Mormonism, and for a paper published at the center of the Mormon War of 1838–39, makes his perspective unusual.

"O.H.O." [O'Neil], "From the Utah Army," Dispatch, 26 June 1858, *Liberty (Mo.) Weekly Tribune*, 23 July 1858, 2/4.

About a week ago I returned to this place after making a trip to the City of the Saints, which I found deserted, the inhabitants all having moved to Provo, fifty miles South, preparatory to a final departure from the Valley, should the troops enter it with hostile intentions. I reached Salt Lake at the same time with the commissioners, Gov. Powel [*sic*] and Maj. McCulloch, whose conference with the Mormon leaders, as I doubt not you are aware, ended in the unconditional surrender of Brigham and his confederates to the majesty of the law, and the authority of the federal officers.

Too much cannot be said in praise of the Commissioners, by whose unflinching firmness, enlightened candor, and dignified demeanor, the justice, dignity and honor of the country are well illustrated. They have, with equal boldness and truth, shown these people the true line of distinction between the rights of territories and those of the federal Government, (a subject which they, appear to have entertained, hitherto, erroneous opinions,) and have thus rendered the country a service that cannot be too highly appreciated, by bringing back to allegiance, a body of subjects,[69] who, whatever may be their faults have certainly wrought wonders in the midst of the Mountain wilderness which they inhabit, bringing to a state of productiveness, by means laborious but ingenious, a soil naturally most barren. In fact, Powel by his great knowledge of man, legal ability, eloquence and good old *Kaintuck* [Kentucky] fire, humor and earnestness, that goes straight to the point, no matter who is in way; and McCulloch with his devil-may-care, soldierly frankness, which lets out the plainest truths, in the plainest, (but gentlemanly) terms, and a lip that when he smiles fits *tight* over the teeth; great and varied conversational power, and an eye that says as plainly as eye can speak, "who touches my country touches me, if you have any objection let us fight it out," have made a most favorable and wholesome impression on these misguided people. They are particularly fitted for the mission on which they have come, as much so, as others who have been sent to Utah are unfitted by their follies and vices to govern any people, or maintain the dignity of a government.

[69]O'Neil's use of "subjects" rather than "citizens" betrays his origins under a monarchy, albeit one he detested.

The result of the conference will probably be that the people will return to Salt Lake City, and not burn it, as they at first threatened, and had made preparations to do, and that the valley will again smile with peace and abundance.

The army has marched from this place for the Valley, which it has probably reached by this time.[70] No opposition to its progress will be made.

A permanent post had been [formally] established at this point and is now under the command of Col. [William] Hoffman, 6th Inf'y.[71]

I have not space to say anything about the appearances of the country between here and the Valley but that the scenery is magnificent. You may hear from me again by next mail—until then farewell.

If Owen Hugh O'Neil was impressed with the peace commissioners' conduct, Lemuel Fillmore perceived them as indispensable to restoration of federal authority in Utah. Two weeks after O'Neil wrote to his publisher-friend in Missouri, Fillmore sent his view of the commissioners to James Gordon Bennett's newspaper in Manhattan.

[Fillmore], "Utah Affairs," Dispatch, 10 July 1858, *New York Herald*, 9 August 1858, 8/2–3.

There is but one way to get along with the miscreant Saints—that is by a course of unyielding, unchanging, unmitigated firmness. . . . I don't believe they ever intended to fight, but merely frightened us by their loud talking and bragging. In the conference with the Commissioners the Mormons carried high heads, demanded concessions and compromises, boasted that they could whip the army, defamed, slandered and abused the President, insulted the Commissioners, held the most vulgar and heinous language. But while a torrent of beastly and disgusting words were issuing from the throat of [Apostle Erastus] Snow, Commissioner McCulloch interrupted him with this remark, "You say that every word in the President's proclamation is a lie. Read that, last paragraph used, which says the army shall enter the valley; if that is a lie, there is no need of your getting into such a passion over it; but I tell you, sir, that the army shall come in, and no power here can prevent it." The manner of the Commissioner convinced every Mormon present that what he said was a firm and unyielding fact. They immediately (as one of the parties present expressed it) "hung their heads like whipped dogs." From that hour they submitted. . . . We absolutely need strong, able, fearless, determined and united civil officers—men like the Commissioners, who cannot be fooled, cowed, or bribed.

[70]The Utah Expedition marched through Salt Lake on the day O'Neil wrote.

[71]Hoffman would soon be superseded in command at Fort Bridger by Brevet Lt. Col. E. R. S. Canby, Tenth Infantry, with Hoffman returning to his command at Fort Laramie.

As Fillmore's competitor A. G Browne had predicted, Ben McCulloch and Lazarus Powell were indeed agents of the U.S. government, "secure from being Steptoed." In describing to Kane his dealings with the commissioners two months after they left Utah, Brigham Young was as opaque as he was flippant: "We strenuously insisted upon the *peace War* Commissioners investigating the charges which President Buchanan alleged in his Proclamation against us. [It] was in vain; they had 'no power,' 'no time,' 'not authorized'; 'it was utterly impossible.['] 'They only came to bring the Proclamation, and explain the views of President' as therein set forth: as though that *precious document* did not sufficiently explain itself. A footman, postman, or boy could have done the errand as well; but it matters not, they are evidently disappointed in the main errand, and foiled in the other; neither of them will ever be President for not accomplishing peace or war in Utah."[72]

Eventually word of the army's and even the Mormons' contempt for the pardon that the peace commissioners had proffered on Buchanan's behalf flowed to the Executive Mansion. William Weeks of Provo wrote the president to complain that when he had invoked the document's protection from the insults of Capt. James H. Simpson, the Bible-toting army officer "spoke with contempt of said pardon, stating that the Secretary of War had pronounced Brigham Young the greatest imposter of the age and that he should soon die. He made many other threats similar to the foregoing which were both insulting and ungentlemanly. Such abuse is of daily occurrence at his office." Weeks asked, "now, sir . . . as President of the Nation, where in the name of God I or this people shall go for protection, if there is nothing real or substantial in the Pardon granted by your Excellency."[73]

---

[72]Young to Kane, 10 September 1858, LDS Archives.

[73]Weeks to Buchanan, 14 January 1859, ibid.

Chapter 17

"The Most Beautiful Place I Ever Saw"

The Army Arrives

A few hours brought us to the City but it was like entering a Graveyard, silence reigned supreme. If a plague had threatened it instead of us, it could not have depopulated it more. What rank fanaticism it is for Mormons to follow a corrupt humbug and desert so much property.

Pvt. Charles A. Scott, Fourth U.S. Artillery, 26 June 1858

With the arrival of men, animals, and supplies from Fort Union and Fort Laramie, Albert Sidney Johnston saw no need to wait for General Harney's six columns from Fort Leavenworth. The Utah Expedition began its march out of Fort Bridger on 13 June, overriding Johnston's assurance to Governor Cumming that he would remain in winter quarters until the last week in June. The change was one of the general's few missteps in prosecuting the war.

As Johnston later explained to Cumming, he had his reasons. First, the arrival of Colonels William Hoffman and W. W. Loring's battalions, along with their supplies and animals on 8–11 June, removed the impediments to an advance: a lack of transportation and provisions. Second, this influx of thousands of draft animals, beef cattle, and sheep, together with the army herds driven in from Smiths Fork, placed an unsustainable strain on the grazing capacity of the Bridger Valley. Third, further delay increased the danger ahead in crossing the rapidly rising Bear and Weber Rivers.

There were also unstated factors behind the speed with which Johnston moved. The faster he accomplished his mission, the sooner Johnston could expect reassignment or a long leave of absence. Smarting under the War Department's decision to supersede him with first Persifor Smith and then Harney, Johnston perceived, as his son phrased it, "this was a practical way of saying that, though he was good enough for a winter campaign, the Government preferred some one else to do its summer fighting."[1] A new command elsewhere would enable Johnston to visit Louisville and the family he had seen only briefly in August 1857. Such a change would also permit him to leave an onerous command arrangement in an isolated, hostile environment. Finally, the June arrival of two battalions of unfamiliar troops plus hundreds of their camp followers created a combustible mix of veteran campaigners and newcomers who sapped Camp Scott's deteriorating discipline. With the Utah Expedition edgy from a winter in tents and on short rations, this influx plus continued inactivity posed nightmarish risks. Meanwhile, Charley Hart's clarion call to "take a tap, pard" wafted through Fort Bridger's whiskey-soaked gambling dens.

A more subtle indicator of morale problems than the volume of courts martial, card games, and drunken gunplay was the garrison's negative reaction to the prospect of no fight with the Mormons. Aggravating this disappointment was the corrosive belief that Washington politicians had betrayed the Utah Expedition. The dramatic coming and going of Thomas L. Kane, the brazen hovering of Nauvoo Legion patrols, and the surprise arrival of commissioners bearing an unthinkable presidential pardon—all were to U.S. soldiers proof positive of hugger-mugger at the highest level of their government.

Adding to this disillusionment was awareness that the unloved "Mad Bear" would soon supersede the expedition's well-respected commander. Most intolerable of all was the prospect that General Harney and his staff of rear-echelon popinjays might deprive Johnston's threadbare veterans of their rightful credit for a successful campaign, if not their fantasized share of restless Mormon women. By mid-May Johnston had received word that Winfield Scott "doubts whether you will have sufficient numbers to force the passes to Salt Lake and establish yourself in that valley before you receive the larger part, if not the whole, of the reinforcements now under [Harney's] orders to join you." In saying so, the general in chief made clear that "he has equal confidence in your judgment, discretion, zeal, and gallantry" and that his concern was to relieve Johnston of any misimpression that "your

[1] Johnston, *The Life of Gen. Albert Sidney Johnston*, 229.

instructions impose upon you the necessity of advancing so soon as the season and the receipt of means of transportation for your present force will permit."[2] As Alfred Cumming put it indiscreetly to the Nauvoo Legion's adjutant general, "the haste of Johnston is occasioned by the supposition that Genl. Harney is advancing and he wants all the glory himself."[3]

While Johnston's forces left behind the boredom of garrison life, Brigham Young was preparing for the worst. Arms, munitions, machinery, refugees, and even cannibalized roofs continued streaming south. Mormon couriers, scouts, and spies plied the trails between northeastern Utah and Provo. In the political arena, Young completed plans for the next phase of his ongoing joust with federal authority—a campaign to bring about the recall of objectionable Buchanan appointees activated in tandem with divide-and-conquer tactics to undermine the cohesiveness of any federal officers who survived the recall effort.

In mid-June the Utah War was about to morph from an armed confrontation with active military campaigning on both sides to an enduring, unresolved political, legal, and cultural struggle that would outlive Brigham Young, James Buchanan, and Albert Sidney Johnston. With uncanny timing, the shift began on 26 June 1858 in the midst of the Utah Expedition's march through a Salt Lake City deserted and ready for the torch.

A Place Abreast of Lewis and Clark: Recognizing Captain Marcy

When Capt. Randolph B. Marcy reported to General Johnston's headquarters on 9 June, he received the hero's welcome he deserved. With the successful completion of his mission to New Mexico, the Army of Utah had the battery horses, dragoon mounts, and mule teams essential to the expedition's forward movement. Unable to promote Marcy, Johnston honored him as best he could by assigning him to his personal staff as the Army of Utah's inspector general. That Johnston reassigned Marcy from the Fifth Infantry at a time when the regiment desperately needed officers—even a second lieutenant of marines—reflects the depth of the general's gratitude.

With Marcy's assignment to Johnston's staff, his Company D remained under the command of its senior officer present, 2d Lt. Henry Brevoort

[2]McDowell to Johnston, 2 April 1858, "Annual Report of the Sec. of War (1858)," 67.

[3]Ferguson to Young, 21 June 1858, LDS Archives.

Bristol, an officer commissioned from civil life only a year earlier. Of the total of thirty-four officers authorized for the Fifth Infantry's ten companies and regimental staff, only sixteen (47 percent) excluding Marcy were present for duty, compared with twenty-nine (85 percent) in the Tenth. Half of the Fifth's companies could muster only one commissioned officer, whereas all of the Tenth's had more than one, and six of its ten companies had all three of their officers present. In recognition of Marcy's leadership, General Scott recommended his promotion by brevet to major. Incredibly Floyd never sanctioned this honor, presumably because Scott's language was so indirect that Floyd missed his intent or Buchanan chose not to send such a nomination to the Senate when the war's origins and prosecution were so controversial. The army succeeded in promoting Marcy to the substantive grade of major in 1859, but in a nonsensical way: transferring the service's foremost western explorer to an open slot in the paper-intensive paymaster's department.

Correspondent Browne shared General Johnston's enthusiasm about Marcy, reporting,

> There is another officer in the army of Utah who has distinguished himself in a similar manner. I refer of course to Capt. Marcy, whose safe return to his regiment I recorded yesterday. There are few experienced mountaineers who would not have shrunk from the undertaking which he imposed on himself last November—to penetrate to New-Mexico at the dead of Winter, through the heart of the Rocky Mountains, over a route part of which the foot of a white man never traversed before. In the annals of American exploration, that expedition and his return journey deserve a place abreast of the achievements of Lewis and Clarke [*sic*] and of Fremont. Their value, simply as contributions to the geographical knowledge of the mountain region which lies between the waters of the Colorado and those of the Arkansas, is far from insignificant, and is enhanced by consideration of the fortitude, both moral and physical, which was demanded of the Captain and his comrades.[4]

All the Home We Had: Leaving Camp Scott

While Johnston and Browne celebrated Captain Marcy's arrival in their own way, this news and the release of Johnston's long-anticipated marching orders triggered an alcohol-fueled spree that filled Fort Bridger's guardhouse and hospital tents. Even Chief Justice Eckels emerged from the celebration

[4] [Browne], "Later from the Utah Army. The Troops Moving on Salt Lake. Arrival of Captain Marcy," Dispatch, 12 June 1858, *New-York Tribune*, 7 July 1858.

bruised. It was a bacchanalia that Captain Phelps recorded with a mixture of amazement and disgust: "The order is out for the move. . . . Several drunken soldiers of the 10th Infy got into a row against Judge Eckels at his [quarters] today. One of them struck him and the Clerk of Court several times. The Judge has some womenfolk at his establishment who are probably at the bottom of the affair.[5] Some of the Volunteers have been drunk and noisy. A Lieut. and a Corporal of Capt. [Daniel] McLaughlin's [B] Company fired pistols at each other to-night & the Lieut. was hit in the side."[6]

In a vivid description of the army and its preparations on the eve of the vanguard's march, correspondent Simonton again railed against James Buchanan's pardon.

"S" [Simonton], "Interesting from Utah. Preparations for the March on Salt Lake City. Arrival of Col. Hoffman and Capt. Marcy. Provisions Plenty and Transportation Ample," Dispatch, 12 June 1858, Camp Scott, Bridger's Fort, U.T., *New York Times*, 8 July 1858, 1/5–6 and 2/1–6.

My next communication will be dated on the march towards Salt Lake—for the present week has brought in all the supplies and troops for which the army of Utah have been postponing its advance. . . . This gives us over 5,000 animals of all kinds, which will furnish abundance of transportation . . . there is nothing to be done now but pack up and be off towards Zion. . . .

The week has been one of busy preparation for the march and yesterday the whole army rejoiced when the following order, directing the movement, was issued:

Head-Quarters, Department of Utah,
Camp Scott, U.T., June 11, 1858.

General Orders No. 28.—The troops will march from this Camp in three divisions, in as many consecutive days, commencing with the First Division, and moving in the order of their number.

Special instructions with regard to advanced, flank and rear guards will be given immediately after the execution of the preliminary movement herein directed.

---

[5]Later in the summer of 1858 Judge Eckels's involvement with women entered into Mormon efforts to smear him and bring about his recall. The instrument for this effort was a letter allegedly signed by the judge and found on the road to Camp Floyd, wherein he described his efforts to find a "bed partner" for 2d Lt. Clarence E. Bennett of the Tenth U.S. Infantry. Eckels to Bennett, 12 August 1858, Yale Collection of Western Americana, Beinecke Library.

[6]Phelps Diary, 11 and 12 June 1858, Phelps Papers, NYPL.

The following will be the order of march, subject to an additional change on leaving Muddy Creek:

1. Division composed of the Second Dragoons, Phelps's Battery, and the Volunteer Battalion; to advance to the Muddy and await the arrival of the Second Division.

2. Division composed of the Fifth Infantry, Reno's Battery, and Company "B," Seventh Infantry.

3. Division composed of the Tenth Infantry, and Col. Loring's [composite] Battalion.

The morning after the arrival on the Muddy of the Second Division, the First and Second Divisions (Reno's Battery and "B" company, Seventh Infantry excepted,) forming one division, will continue the march.

Reno's Battery, Company "B," Seventh Infantry, and the Third division, now constituting the Second, will continue the march on the second day. The Head-Quarters will be with the Second Division as far as the Muddy; beyond that with the advance.

By order of Brevet Brigadier-General A.S. Johnston.

F. J. Porter, Ass't Adjt.-General.

Detailed orders have also been issued to the force comprising the First Division, directing them to take up the line of march to-morrow, the 13th inst. It will be seen that the route to be pursued is not designated in the orders, being kept from publication here, at present, from motives of military precaution.

Lieutenant W. [William] D. [Duncan] Smith's squadron of dragoons [Company E] left camp yesterday morning with pack mules, to escort Capt. [John] Newton, of the engineers, who goes to reconnoiter the road and examine the condition and report. He is expected also to go to the Bear River, ascertain whether or not the bridge over it is still standing, and if not to select a suitable place for throwing across another. Gen. Johnston has had several strong portable bridges made here in camp, which will be carried along in the advance of the army, and used if occasion requires. The route which the army will take is not absolutely settled yet, but unless I am much mistaken, it will avoid the Canyons. . . .

It is now nine days since the Peace Commissioners and Governor Cumming left the Camp for Salt Lake City, but [we] are yet without any intelligence as to the result of their conferences, with the people of the Valley; but that fact will not retard the movements of the army for an hour now that it is ready to advance. . . .

The evidences accumulate that Brigham Young never dreamed of armed resistance to the United States, and that his impudent braggadocio has always been his reliance for maintaining his influence over his own people, as well as for deterring the present, as he has former National Administrations, from persisting in an effort for his subjection to law. He now seems likely to avail himself of the tendered pardon, covering his retreat as well as may be. You will remember how defiantly, a few months ago, he [was].... Well, the Army is here, just about to march into the city—the President's proclamation says they *shall* go in, and Brigham will accept it with all its conditions, without a blow. Had no pardon been tendered, the result would have been the same, except that Brigham and the other leaders most deeply involved in crime, would have tried to evade the law by keeping out of the clutch of its ministers. A month or two of firmness on the part of the President would have effectually wiped out the stain which the Mormon theocracy has fastened upon the National escutcheon, and that with little shedding of blood except upon the traitors' scaffold. The pretence that a universal pardon was necessary, in order to save the effusion of innocent blood, and the punishment of the least guilty with the leaders in the rebellion, is puerile; for the President would always have had it in his power to pardon the lesser offenders in detail, while making terrible examples of those whose superior intelligence and position among the Saints have enabled them to bring about a state of affairs so lamentable.

I do not believe, however, that the pardon will prevent ultimate collision between the troops and the Saints. On the contrary, its tendency will be to encourage and provoke collisions.... The lenient course of the Executive is well calculated to embolden the Mormons when thus followed up to venture upon resistance, especially when some sudden element of excitement is thrown in as a torch to light the flame. It is the general belief of those here who have had longest experience among the Saints that the volunteered pardon has created the only probability of armed collision, but this effect will not be immediately developed....

In my last I noticed the statement, made upon Mormon authority, that Colonel Thomas L. Kane was rebaptized in the Mormon Church, and received his endowments upon his arrival in the Valley from California. I have heard since then that Governor Cumming denies the statement very emphatically, although how he should be possessed of this negative sort of knowledge in respect to a matter which was not subject of discussion until after the Colonel started for the East, I can not well understand. I give him, however, the benefit of the governor's disclaimer, which has had little effect upon opinion here....

The intelligence of the death of General Smith did not surprise us, for it has long seemed evident that his days were numbered. His decease leaves a Brigadier Generalship vacant, and the universal expression of hope by this army is that it will be conferred upon Brevet Brigadier General Johnston, who combines military genius of a high order, with unflinching courage and great caution. In view of the possible future of the Utah question, it is eminently desirable that a man of those qualities and eminent rank should be in command of the military forces here—one who will risk nothing rashly, precipitate no conflict, yet never shrink from whatever duty presents itself for

> accomplishment. Such a man is General Johnston, whose soldierly qualities, unfailing equanimity, and unaffected urbanity, challenge the admiration and love of his entire command.

After bivouacking overnight at Muddy Creek, the army's vanguard (with Simonton in tow) proceeded to Bear River, where it paused to wait for the two divisions departing Fort Bridger at staggered intervals. The last unit to leave winter quarters was the Tenth Infantry, which marched on 15 June. The commander of Company H, Capt. Albert Tracy, found leave-taking an unexpectedly bittersweet experience:

> We have been here now about seven months, and despite the weariness and dreariness, the privations and discomforts at every hand, it was difficult to say we have not, in a sort, become attached to the locality. It has been for us all the home we had for the time. This morning, then, to view the long area of chimney-stacks, roof-poles, and other relics and debris of a deserted camp, there rises in us a feeling really akin to sadness. The appearance as presented at large, was a not unfit resemblance to the ruins of an ancient town, in a wood-cut. On the other hand, and in view of everything in the future, we are certainly not ill-satisfied to quit a locality like this—one into which we were forced both by stress of circumstances, and the imbicility [*sic*] that looked more after its immediate personal comfort, than the grandeur and success of an expedition which might have brought lasting and honorable reputation. Wherefore at the sound of the bugle, and with all things braced and stayed for the mountains, we fell in for the last time in line, at old Camp Scott—the very name of which remains now but a written sign and record.[7]

High Water as Well as Hell: Regrouping on Bear River

At Bear River Johnston received first word from Messrs. Powell and McCulloch about the conferences. On 14 June he drafted a statement intended to reassure Utahns as the commissioners had urged. Over the next several days at Bear River, amidst torrential rains and high water, Johnston grazed his animals on spring grass, marshaled his forces, and realigned the order of march. On 16 June, the general sent army headquarters his only report during the march.[8]

---

[7]Alter and Dwyer, eds., "The Utah War Journal of Albert Tracy," 15 June 1858, 16–17.

[8]The best account of the army's march between Bridger and Salt Lake City is Tracy Journal, 15–26 June 1858 (with accompanying sketches), ibid., 17–28, summarized in Bigler and Bagley, *The Mormon Rebellion*, 321–23.

Johnston to McDowell, 16 June 1858,
"Annual Report of the Sec. of War (1858)," 117–18.

I have the honor to report that the march of the army of Utah commenced on the 13th instant. . . . The march will be resumed to-morrow in the order directed by my order of this date herewith. The march to the valley will be made in five days. . . .

Captain [John] Newton, of the engineer corps, was detached yesterday with an escort of an officer and thirty men, and the most experienced guide of the mountains, James Bridger, to examine thoroughly the country from this point to the head of Muddy creek, which flows into Bear river.—(See map.) I believe the elevated table land between this and the western end of Cache valley can be ascended by easy gradations, and that the opposite side can be descended into Cache valley without difficulty. If a good road should be found practicable, as I expect, I would respectfully suggest that the commander of the forces here may be authorized to order its construction immediately. The only communication [transit] between important districts should not long be allowed to continue through long and difficult canyons easily obstructed. The health of the troops continues excellent.

As Johnston regrouped for his push on the Salt Lake Valley, what was his actual strength absent the massive reinforcements en route across the plains? In launching the Utah Expedition on 28 May 1857, General Scott had specified a force of 2,500 troops; it was a size that was conceptual rather than an actual headcount at any time during the campaign. By year-end, large-scale desertion, normal discharges, and the diversion of some detachments to other duty (partially offset by the recruitment of Bee's volunteers) had taken a toll, diminishing the expedition's strength to 1,428 men, 43 percent below the level of 2,500 most frequently used by historians to describe Johnston's force.[9] Spring 1858 brought further personnel turbulence and with it more ambiguity as to the size of the command with which the general was to execute the most crucial phase of the war. The Army of Utah's next bimonthly muster and inspection was scheduled to take place on 30 June, but with the churning of troops through Fort Bridger and the acceleration of his scheduled movement, a cautious Johnston needed a current and precise understanding of his troop strength. Before leaving Bear River on 19 June, Johnston ordered such a head count, providing a picture of the Utah Expedition's size at an important juncture in the campaign.[10]

[9]Lt. Col. Sherman L. Fleek to MacKinnon, e-mail message of 5 November 2013.

[10]Field Return of the Army of Utah, Camp on Bear River, U.T., 18 June 1858, Transmitted by Johnston to Cooper, Letters Received, Records of the Adjt. Gen., RG 94, NARA.

Johnston's total strength at Bear River was 2,381 men excluding two companies of the Sixth Infantry and First Cavalry left behind to garrison Fort Bridger as well as civilians.[11] Among these auxiliaries were perhaps as many as eighty women working as company laundresses, many of them the wives of non-coms.[12] Perhaps the most revealing insights provided by these returns was the weakened condition of the desertion-prone Fifth Infantry (only 55 percent the size of the more stable and better led Tenth Infantry), the importance of the Volunteer Battalion (13 percent of the total command even after the April discharge of its six-months men), and the significant size of Colonel Loring's composite battalion drawn from reinforcing units based in New Mexico and Kansas, which accounted for another 24 percent of Johnston's aggregate troop strength. One quarter of Colonel Cooke's dragoons remained dismounted in June, whereas the troopers of the First Cavalry and Mounted Rifles, who had not experienced the punishing November march of Cooke's regiment, were all mounted.

In the final days on Bear River, Johnston revised his itinerary. Originally the general planned to leave the Mormon Trail, bypass the unknown dangers of Echo Canyon with a climb to what he thought were tablelands to its north, loop to unsettled Cache Valley, and then enter the Salt Lake Valley from the north (rather than east) via the relatively easy road from Fort Hall. But at the last minute some unrecorded factor changed his mind and prompted him to abandon this more complex, potentially roadless plan in favor of a more direct, substantially shorter route along the Mormon Trail and through Echo Canyon. Presumably the decisive factor was one of Jim Bridger's scouting reports, although Echo Canyon's unflooded, undefended condition reported by Ben Ficklin (who had just returned through it from Salt Lake) probably contributed to the change in route.[13]

[11]A few days after this roll call, Captain Phelps recorded a virtually identical number of 2,380. Phelps Diary, 20 June 1858, Walker draft typescript, 3.

[12]Army regulations allowed a maximum of four laundresses per company. With a total of forty-two companies enumerated at the camp on Bear River, and assuming that half of them had earlier dropped their laundresses at an established post (as had the Second Dragoons at Fort Laramie in November 1857) or left them behind in Kansas and New Mexico, this would indicate an estimated total of eighty such women on the final march to Salt Lake City. For this aspect of the Utah Expedition, see Godfrey, "Housewives, Hussies, and Heroines," 157–78.

[13]For insight into the unsuitable, daunting terrain that Johnston originally considered as a route to the Salt Lake Valley, see Captain Newton's log of his 222-mile trek during 15–25 June between Bear River, Ogden's Hole, Cache Valley, and East Canyon in Newton to Porter, 17 July 1858, "Annual Report of Sec. of War (1858)," 202–206.

Rejoicing in Green Peas and Strawberries: In the Eye of the Storm

When a footloose and fast-moving James Simonton arrived in Salt Lake City on 17 June, having left the army soon after its arrival at Bear River, he described the nation's biggest settlement between St. Louis and San Francisco. It was, in military terms, an open city. A few excerpts of another gargantuan Simonton dispatch appear here.[14]

"S" [Simonton], "Important from Utah. A Week Later from Salt Lake City," Dispatch, 19 June 1858, *New York Times*, 19 July 1858, 1/1–4.

When I mailed my letter of the 12th inst., I did not expect to date my next from this city. But here I am in "Zion," in full view of "Jordan," having had some little experience of the fact that "Jordan is a hard [road] to travel," or, at all events, that the road towards it fully justifies the declaration of the negro melody. . . .

On Thursday morning, the 17th inst., I left the remainder of our party at daylight, and pushed on towards our destination in company with Mr. Ficklin, an express-rider who had overtaken us. The rain continued to fall in heavy showers, as we ascended the Big Mountain. I should before have noticed the fact that the soil of the canyons through which we had been passing for a day or two had much improved in quality, supporting a heavy growth of shrubbery, amid which the wild-rose—here in full bloom, though in sight of "eternal snows"—was gratefully prominent. Descending the Big [Little] Mountain, whose summit was enveloped in clouds, we struck into Emigration Canyon, by which opening, at last, we passed the last spire of the Wasatch range. And now burst upon our view, as we came out upon the high bench overlooking the Valley of Great Salt Lake, one of the most enchanting landscapes. For days we had been imprisoned among the mountains, whose rugged grandeur and sublimity had almost become tiresome. Suddenly, as we emerged from the fastnesses, the great valley lay out before us, with its teeming fields of grain, and other quiet evidences of refined civilization. The change is sudden and striking, forcing the most practical mind to the observation of contrasts which under other circumstances would be noticed only by the artist.

Great Salt Lake City certainly possesses a charming location. Its site is directly under the mountains, which come down in very steep ridges to a great bench or plateau, overlooking the bottom of the valley. Indeed the city,

[14]Simonton used large portions of David A. Burr's early June description of Echo Canyon and its fortifications, as did Browne.

which sits upon this sloping bench, comes to within a mile or two of the mountain's base, where Emigration Canyon opens upon the plain, while the northeastern corner of the settlement is scarcely a quarter of a mile from the cliffs. The traveler coming out of Emigration Canyon first looks down upon the broad streets of Great Salt Lake some twenty or twenty-five [fifteen] miles distant, although it appears to be not more than a quarter of that distance. As he rides on a little further, the city itself, with its neat buildings, luxuriant shade-trees and teeming gardens, gradually appear, until at last the whole city lays out before him at a glance, with all its streets as plainly marked as though it were a map lying upon the table before him. On the bosom of the distant lake rests a great island [Antelope] from which rises another mountain, lofty almost as those which we have just passed; while to the northward and southward the valley spreads out far as the eye can reach, without a hill to obstruct the view. West of the city, running through the centre of the valley, the Jordan courses its way.

But I must defer for the present any further description of the city and its surroundings, and proceed with some account of the conferences between the civil officers and the people of the Valley, which have resulted in a quiet and peaceable settlement of all existing difficulties—at least, for the present. But first let me say that we found this city of six miles square almost entirely deserted. From many of the houses the roofs had been torn: in scarcely one of them was a window-sash remaining. All had been removed, and the windows boarded up, in anticipation of the coming of the Gentile army. In house after house straw and other combustibles are piled up, ready for the incendiary torch, to be applied by the two or three men left here to guard the city and to burn it the moment the Prophet should give the signal. I do not believe there are five hundred persons in town to-day, although its population, under ordinary circumstances, cannot be far from twelve thousand. All had gone southward, in obedience to the order of Brigham Young, whose power and influence over the people is evidently as absolute as the Emperor of Russia's is over his serfs. I have conversed confidentially with several parties here, who say that many of the people were unwilling to go, and were painfully solicitous about the safety of their homes, being unwilling to sacrifice them; but few of these had the courage to hesitate in implicit obedience to the order of the Prophet when he bade them to move.

I have asked others, who seem to be unshaken in the Mormon faith, what was the motive for the destruction of their city. Their reply is that they knew nothing of the intentions of the President, having heard nothing from him until the arrival of the Commissioners, and that they supposed the army was to come into the Valley, as the mob assailed them at Nauvoo, to drive them out and take possession of their property. In the anticipation of such a consummation as this, they preferred to leave ruins behind them, determined that if they were to [be] despoiled of their homes, strangers should not enjoy them. There is little doubt that the head men of the Church have inculcated these ideas into the people, and have thus wrought them up in the pitch of fanatical fury which so nearly led to the ruin of this fine city; but that Brigham and his chiefs knew they were misleading the people must be evident to every intelligent man who remembers that they have had a mail regularly throughout the year by the way of California, and that Dr. Bernhisel, their delegate at Washington, cannot have failed to apprise them of the views and purposes of the Executive in sending out the army to support the civil authorities.[15]

Mr. Morell [Hiram F. Morrell], the Gentile Postmaster, whose commission the Mormons have heretofore refused to recognize, came in with the Peace Commissioners and again demanded the keys of the Post-Office. [Elias] Smith, the Mormon Postmaster, at first refused the demand, then pretended to assent, and offered part of the mail keys, retaining duplicates. These Morell refused, until at last he concluded to yield, and gave up the whole of them. He refused, however, to let him have any office furniture, and succeeded in making a reasonable pretext for leaving a Mormon clerk in the office for the present, to act as a spy upon its operations. Morell seems to be peculiarly obnoxious to the people here, but for what reason I do not know. He certainly appears to be a faithful and energetic officer. They are also greatly incensed against Dr. Hurt, the Indian Agent, who has given abundant evidence of his title to the respect of his fellow-men. His offence consists in having written private letters (which became public subsequently) exposing some of the iniquities of Mormondom. He is not the man, however, to be frightened from his post, and will probably let the assassin's knife remove him rather than retire from his position. . . .

The brethren have the greatest possible horror of bringing their women in contact with the army—a horror which clearly establishes the fact that the women of this valley are shockingly wicked and untrustworthy, or else very unhappy and discontented. My own brief observation satisfies me that the latter view is the true one.

Time and space fail me to give you any adequate description of this beautiful though deserted city. . . . It is well understood now that the citizens of this place will return at an early day. Indeed the heads of families are already beginning to come back, but they say that they will keep their families south until after the army leave this vicinity. The river Jordan, which bounds the city on the west, will enable Gen. Johnston to enforce whatever orders he may deem advisable to prevent his men from straying into the city and annoying its people, and the probability is that they will soon be quite satisfied with his arrangements to that end. . . .

[15]Young received no mail from Bernhisel during the winter via the Panama-California or any other route.

Your correspondent is living at the Globe Restaurant, already referred to, rejoicing in green peas and strawberries for dinner, and sleeping on the floor of the back porch at night, rolled up in a pair of Mackinaw blankets. Be assured, however, that a man just off the plains and exchanging his never varying fried bacon for such a diet as above noted, considers himself quite above quarreling with a bed of the hardest plank.

A Knight or Two: Romantics on Horseback

While Latter-day Saints continued to trek south and their leaders prepared for an uncertain future, some of the Legionnaires left behind in Salt Lake City found ways to pursue their love lives while performing their military duties. Usually these arrangements were surreptitious; occasionally they were ingenious. Historians have bypassed wartime romance, focusing instead on polygamy as a dry policy issue enlivened with head counts and stereotyped patriarchs in pursuit of teenage brides. Lost in the process is a feel for a vibrant society in which only a minority practiced plural marriage, with most Utah couples—polygamous or otherwise—engaged in loving, sometimes even whimsical, relationships akin to the rest of Victorian America.

The correspondence and reminiscences of Pvts. Henry Clark Jackson and John T. McDonald, both in the small Nauvoo Legion detachment guarding Salt Lake City, provide a glimpse of this human side of the Utah War.

Henry Jackson had been campaigning with the Legion since October 1857, when he rode as part of Maj. Lot Smith's raid on the Utah Expedition's supply trains. Through a letter written in mid-June 1858, one sees a bit of the relationship between Private Jackson and his overburdened refugee-wife as she cared for their sick children.[16] Revealed also is Henry's view of his comrades' connubial visits from wives adventuresome enough to outwit General Wells's sentries.

Pvt. Jackson to Ann Oades Jackson, 15 June 1858, Roylance Collection, LDS Archives.

I Sit Down in hast[e] this Evening to Write you a few lines as I know you will like to hear from me once in a while and as I like to keep you posted up in the news of the day. I did Exspect to come to see you to leave this city on thirsday morning next and per[h]aps I may but it is a little doubtfull with me at this time as the [federal] troops will be hear in a very Short time

[16]More of the Jacksons' correspondence appears in *At Sword's Point, Part 1*, 363–65.

> they Left Bridger yesterday morning and their fore runers Camped on the Weber river last knight to put a Bridge across so as to make it passable for the troops. All teames will now be stoped from traveling until all is passed By this place. I Supose you have heard that peace is made at preasant and will likely Continue for a Little while I ham [*sic*] well at preasant and am Doing first rate. I hope you and the Childeren are well and comfortable. Pleas tell them father rem[e]mbers them and will Come to see them Soon as possabal. I hope you receved my not[e] of Sunday morning about Keeping the Cattle with you until further orders from Me. I in Close with this note letter from Crowle also one for Sister Mcintosh. Pleas Send me a line. Let me know how you are Situated if you want any thing that I can get for you. Rem[em]ber me [to] the folks also to Bro Stephenson if you see him. We have to keep guard to keep the Sisters from Coming back to the Town for some is so allfired Simple that they will Come to town to see their Dear Husbands Spend a Knight or two & then return. Mrs Rowley Came Last fryday and had to return on Sunday before sun rise for the guard was after strainge[r]s. Well as I ham in a hurry I must Close wishing well and hope you will be happy and take good care of your Self. I remain your Husband By the Bonds of the new & Everlasting Covenant.

In 1892 John McDonald, age 61, described his life since immigrating to the United States in 1832 with his family, converting to Mormonism in Pennsylvania and moving to Utah by way of Nauvoo. At the outbreak of the Utah War, McDonald was twenty-seven years old, a bachelor cabinet maker and Legionnaire. After campaigning in the Wasatch, he returned home but resumed active service in the spring of 1858 with the Move South and the need for troops to guard Salt Lake City and prepare it for incineration. McDonald's account of the somewhat unusual way in which he married mid-campaign appeared five days after his death at age 80.

John T. McDonald, "Personal Reminiscences of Early Days in Nauvoo and Utah," 1 January 1892, *Deseret Evening News*, 20 August 1910, 20/1–7.

News of Johnston's Army.

> I was color bearer in the Flying artillery and went up into Big Cottonwood canyon with President Brigham Young and many of the Saints and spent the 24th of July, 1857. While we were there the news came that Johnston's army was coming to wipe us out but they did not do it. I was next called upon to go into the mountains to help watch Johnston's army and see that they did not do any harm. I stayed in the mountains about a month, riding nearly

day and night. Our company was discharged; but we did not get much rest, for I was called to help guard the city.

It was about this time that I first saw my wife, Amelia Cropland, at the home of Mrs. Hardy, where she was living.[17] It was the first night she had been there, and when I opened the door she was sitting with her back to me and I had not seen her face; but I had a very strange feeling as I passed her and something told me that that girl would be my wife. We soon became acquainted.

Romantic Wedding, Wife in Man's Clothes

But a few weeks passed when every soul in Salt Lake was called upon to leave their homes, and move south. My wife's mother was a widow and she had to go with the rest and take my intended bride with her. I didn't like the idea much as I was called to stay and help guard the city; if the army came we were to burn every house to the ground and destroy everything in the shape of improvements. Two or three days before my wife and her folks went south we were engaged and I followed in a few days after they left and found them at Pleasant Grove, about 40 miles south of Salt Lake City. My mother-in-law found shelter with William H. Adams and married him afterwards. My wife and I did not like the idea of being separated so I got two or three days' furlough and went south to see her. On my way down I passed Col. J. C. Little with a drove of sheep and I knew he would get to Pleasant Grove next day so I told my mother-in-law that I was going to meet the colonel and get him to marry Amelia and me, so we both jumped on the same old white horse and rode towards the city until we met Col. Little.

Married on Horseback.

We met him somewhere opposite Lehi on the main road. We rode up to the colonel and told him we wanted him to marry us. He tried to make excuses but it was of no use so he asked us to get down off our horse but we told him: "No, we do our sparking on the old horse. We were engaged on him and now we want to be married on him." So the colonel told us to join hands and he performed the ceremony and married us. I would say here that Col. Little was the second bishop in the Church at that time. We had a very pleasant wedding. There were quite a number present. There were the colonel and one of his sons, a boy, and Richard Atwood, his clerk, and about 300 head of dirty sheep. The sheep seemed to enjoy the wedding very much as it gave them time to rest a little and eat grass.

As soon as we were made man and wife we thanked the bishop and started back to Pleasant Grove on the dead run, a distance of about seven miles. We stayed in Pleasant Grove that night and started for Salt Lake City the next

[17]Records give her maiden name as Eleanor Amelia Crossland, born in England in 1840.

morning. When we arrived in the city we met my father and mother just starting to leave the city so they gave us the keys of the old house and we went to house keeping. But I had to attend to rollcall morning and evening and my wife did not like to stay alone so I used to dress her in my Spanish suit of pants and jacket and take her with me on our old white horse. I passed her off for my cousin from the south. She made a splendid boy. The only thing that I was afraid of was that she was too good looking for a boy but I fixed her up good and I don't think any one ever suspected her of being a girl.

LITERAL OBEDIENCE.

Our next trouble was that every Friday the council was to see that there were no women left in this city and as I was always a great hand to obey counsel I used to get my wife on behind me on my horse and answer rollcall in the afternoon about 6 o'clock and then we would strike out for Pleasant Grove in the night. When we got out of the city I always let my wife ride in the saddle and I rode behind her. We generally got into Pleasant Grove about 1 o'clock at night and went to bed and had a good nap then up in the morning, got our breakfast, and started back to the city so as to be in time to answer to rollcall.

We rode to Pleasant Grove and back 13 times while I was detained in the city on guard. It was a long dreary ride of a dark night 36 or 37 miles and not a house on the road after you left the city until you got to American Fork, a distance of about 35 miles. . . . My mother-in-law used to tell me that I would be the death of her daughter but she is alive and likely to be for some time to come.[18]

THE DEVIL'S CHOICE FLOCK: MORMON STRAWS IN A JUNE WIND

Between the peace conferences and the army's arrival, Brigham Young took steps in his complex strategy for shaping postwar Mormon-federal relations. He had already begun the process of intimidating Alfred Cumming and alienating him from General Johnston and Judge Eckels. Part of this plan was to align Indian superintendent Forney with Cumming rather than the Johnston-Eckels faction and, indeed, by the time of the meetings with the peace commissioners, Forney had in some way bonded with not only the governor but Bill Hickman. If politics makes for strange bedfellows, few pairs were as unlikely as this Pennsylvania physician–Indian superintendent, who had gone west to strengthen his lungs, and one of Utah's most notorious ecclesiastical assassins. What remained to be done was to remove the

[18]Amelia Crossland McDonald died in 1918, eight years after her husband.

army, manage the scandal over Mountain Meadows, secure statehood, and arrange the recall of most of Cumming's colleagues. Under this plan, the latter were to be demonized and then replaced with Utahns or, failing that, with sympatico non-Mormons.

The need for a sea change in Utah's federal appointees had been on Brigham Young's mind for years. It flowed inevitably from Utah's territorial status, the advice that he had dispensed to President Pierce about presidential appointments, and the mantra of Mormon grievances against the U.S. government recited at great length and with regularity.[19] The thought resurfaced with the names of office holders targeted for recall in Young's 8 May 1858 letter to Governor Cumming and again in his conference with Commissioners McCulloch and Powell.

As June unfolded, Young chose the familiar medium of a petition to Washington as the next step in making the case for recalling appointees. In considering this move, Young understood the need for care, given the disastrous backlash in Washington with the arrival in March 1857 of a prolix, aggressively phrased memorial from Utah's legislative assembly. Young needed to resolve several tactical issues to shape such a document: to whom should it be addressed; the petition's length and tone; who should sign it; which appointees should be targeted for removal and why; who should the presumed Mormon successors be; and what part in this gambit should Cumming and Kane play?

Had Kane been in Utah, he would have sought the role of strategist, if not draftsman, for such a petition. In his absence Brigham Young turned to Brig. Gen. James Ferguson, an attorney, actor, and talented editor-writer. With Young in Provo after the conferences, it fell to Ferguson to deal with Alfred Cumming in Salt Lake City once Young determined that the governor was to be key in facilitating a favorable reception in Washington for such a petition.

The crucial last step—transformation of Mormon skepticism about governmental trustworthiness into at least resigned acceptance of the U.S. Army—hinged on two factors controlled by Albert Sidney Johnston: the discipline of his troops; and the sites selected for the garrisons to be established in Utah. For help in influencing Johnston's actions and decisions, Young turned to Alfred Cumming at the same time he worked through Ferguson to inveigle the governor into an active role with the recall petition.

---

[19] *At Sword's Point, Part 1*, 46–47.

YOUNG TO CUMMING, 18 JUNE 1858, LDS ARCHIVES.

Since the Commissioners, Ex-Governor Powell and Major McCulloch, disclaim any control, except advisory, over the movements and acts of Gen'l Johnston and his command; and since it is well understood by all that the passing and camping of those troops through and in close proximity to our settlements would unavoidably cause a great destruction of property, particularly should they camp immediately west of the river Jordan, so near our chief city, we trust, in the exercise of the high functions of your office, for the welfare both of the people, whose Chief Executive you are, and of the Government whose general interests in Utah are confided to your oversight, that you will exercise your power and influence with Gen'l Johnston to take such a course both in marching and camping, with the troops under his command that, in accordance with his Proclamation of June 14th, "no person whatever will be in *any wise* interfered with or molested in his *person* or *rights.*"[20]

Commissioners Powell and McCulloch have publicly declared *all* 'difficulties' settled, and the people of Utah, in accordance with the happy adjustment of the past, have withdrawn all opposition to the movement of United States troops, so they but move within the inhibitions of the Constitution and respective of the person, rights and property of all, and now the courtesy we expect from so high a toned and gallant a soldier as Gen'l Johnston is said to be, to say nothing of a mutual and gentlemanly understanding, would firmly enjoin upon Gen'l Johnston and his command a line of conduct the most strictly in accordance with the Constitution and laws of our common country and the laws of this Territory, and every way becoming the army of a "great, free and enlightened Nation."

Governor, I have offered these suggestions in all frankness and candor, confidently trusting that you, in common with myself and all loyal and good citizens, will use every precaution in your power, both as a citizen and our Chief Magistrate, to prevent any collision between the citizens and the army, and to carefully guard against everything that may give rise to such collision, lest the happy results just budding from an "amicable and honorable" agreement be nipped by conduct that will cause every lover of our Republic to mourn for rights and liberty trampled in the mire.

Since the "adjustment of difficulties," many citizens wish to return to the care of their fields and property, as soon as it may be prudent so to do; but if their meadows, grazing lands, fields, gardens, &c., be laid waste by the marching and camping of troops, it is obvious that they can have, to say the least, but little desire to return to homes desecrated by those who

[20]For an example of the damage and troop behavior Young dreaded, see the postwar havoc created by one of the Utah Expedition's regiments, the poorly led Seventh Infantry, while marching through the new town of Denver in 1860 en route from Camp Floyd, Utah, to Fort Garland, New Mexico. Richardson to Editor, 19 July 1860, in Barry, ed., "Albert D. Richardson's Letters," 41–42.

profess and have agreed to abide that usage which alone comports with the high character which should mark every person claiming to be an American citizen, whether civilian or soldier.

YOUNG TO CUMMING, 19 JUNE 1858, LDS ARCHIVES.

Your favor of the 17th, inst. with accompanying memoranda reached me by the hands of Genl. Grant and Col. Burton yesterday, for which please accept my thanks.

During the term of my executive administration in the Territory I considered it my duty to forbid the entrance of Troops into our settlements looking upon it as an infringement of the peoples rights.[21] However true it is that the peace has been publicly declared by Commissioners appointed by the President of the United States, which your own straight forward constitutional course, aided by the praiseworthy exertions of our mutual and excellent friend Col. Thos. L. Kane had already nearly consummated. Yet the recent date of that announcement and the embittered feelings which it is well known have existed for some time past with the unwise and uniformed make it equally apparent that the close proximity of encampments of Troops near our settlements instead of extending the amicable relations which we are all anxious to establish would rather tend to create difficulties if not provoke a collision.

For these reasons do the people of the Territory rely upon you to exercise not only your extensive personal influence but your unquestioned Gubernatorial authority to prevent the encampment of any large body of troops even temporarily in any place to infringe upon the grazing lands, fields, or gardens of the citizens. By this course I think you will see at once that the best interests of the General and Territorial Governments will be the most fully subserved. I am aware that your position is a most difficult one, for transpiring events lead me to believe that the arrival and movements of the Commissioners instead of aiding you in the legitimate and peaceful discharge of your official duties have rather been calculated to embarrass and perplex your position through the advance upon their arrival of Genl. Johnston some two weeks previous to the time of his pledge. Indeed their only apparent business here was to ask permission for the troops to pass through this as through other Territories, to constitutionally establish certain posts that might be deemed necessary for the protection of Emigration (to neither of which had any objections ever been made) and to ask the people to accept the proffered pardon of Prest. Buchanan.

Permit me to assure you, Governor that any service you may at any time need in the constitutional discharge of your official duties will be always most promptly accorded and to the fullest extent; but it cannot reasonably

[21]While governor, Young may have considered this his duty, but he never took such action.

be expected that the people will return to their deserted homes, while large bodies of troops are camped in their immediate suburbs.

Trusting that you may enjoy in time to come, the happy satisfaction of having fully and successfully accomplished your important and embarrassing mission, and enjoy the rewards of your labors in peace.

P.S. Mr. F[eramorz] Little who accompanies Genl. Ferguson to the city will see Mr. Ficklin concerning contracts for hay, wood, Lumber &c. for the Army. Any assistance you can render Genl. Ferguson in obtaining signatures from your friends to the petition which he bears with him as well as your own signature would be esteemed a favor.

Cumming to Young, 21 June 1858, LDS Archives.

Your several favors 16th 18th and 19th inst. were duly received, and have occupied my serious attention. Pray accept my sincere thanks for your kindness and consideration for me, personally as well as officially.

By reference to the enclosed copy of my note to General Johnston, dated 17th June, you will, I trust, perceive that your wishes and suggestions have been, for the most part, anticipated, so far as any action is concerned.

I have not received an answer to my note, but feel assured that our wishes will have due influence with General Johnston.

In any event, however, be assured that I will not abate any necessary effort to effect the object you refer to, and what I so earnestly desire to accomplish.

Ferguson to Young, 21 June 1858, LDS Archives.

Bro. C[hauncey] West's family being sick (or a part of them) he is anxious to visit them and bears this and the enclosed handed to me by Gov. Cumming. I reached here [Salt Lake City] at 11 P.M. the evening I left Provo. Bros Little and Felt staid at the Mill. On the hill this side the dug-way we met Messrs Kimball, Hooper & Ficklin. Br. Little arranged at once with Ficklin to furnish 50 cords Wood at $15.00 at their camp (then supposed to be contemplated at or near the Jordan Bridge.) From the brethren there, on informing them of the petition I had with me, I learned that the Governor (A. C.) and Secretary [John Hartnett] would both stick right for [U.S. Marshal Peter K.] Dotson and [U.S. Attorney John M.] Hockaday and that there was no use in trying to remove them. In fact that they were not after all the worst of men. I told the brethren I would await further instructions from you previous to acting upon the petition. I left your letter for Gov. Cumming at his house on the night of my arrival. (He was abed.) yesterday I spent some two or three hours with him of which visit the following are the results communicated to me, of course, *confidentially*.

He showed (or rather read) me the [17 June] letter to Genl Johnson, of which he tells me he has to day enclosed you a copy, which answers a portion of your letter [delivered] by me. He showed me a letter from Judge Eckels directing Dotson to take a posse of civilians and proceed to the Indian camp at Bear R. to purchase beef & &c (?). This was the time that you remember when Eph[raim Hanks] was after them. The Governor as good as informed me the object of the visit was for a far different purpose than the purchase of provisions.[22] In fact, I cannot drive from me the impression I have had for weeks and that has made me so infernal vexed at times, that negociations [*sic*] were entered into (or about to be) with Ben Simonds to assassinate or kidnap you.[23]

Gov. C. further showed me a letter addressed to him on the *25th May*, calling for a military posse to arrest *"Brigham Young and 66 others"* and that letter was signed officially by that good man P. K. Dotson. Cumming took a very politic course in the matter. First he asked Gen. Johnson if he had such a posse in readiness (stating to him the purpose of it) Johnson answered him that he had not. He then addressed a letter to Dotson asking him if he had met any resistance in the service of his processes [writs]; what right *he* had to say the Territory was in a state of Rebellion, and informing him that in no case would he call on the military until he had failed to procure the necessary aid from the people &c &c. He showed me the correspondence between him and the Commissioners in which he corners them concerning the premature advance of Johnston. I can assure you there is not very heartfelt sympathy between them. Powell is every day and almost every minute soaping the Camp-poets [newspaper reporters] fishing for puffs. [Seth M.] Blair rambles around with the Texian [McCulloch] handsomely in search of camp-grounds for the Army and keeps him employed. I am inclined to think Brown[e] has rather given Felt the cold-shoulder.[24] I saw them only once at the table together. I shall recommend Southern air [Provo] to him (I hope the Hotel is ready)

The Devil has the most particularly choice flock here I ever saw. Santa Fe and Grand R. Gamblers, Dick James & [Indian agent C. L.] Craig (hand in hand) accompanied by the little painter Landon's wife from Camp (Scott) Correspondents without end. Miner and the little gray-bearded lawyer (Smith) [Charles Maurice Smith] a la Craig and James. Both puppies or scrubs and well matched. But I cannot tell you all. Suffice it to say that *Frank*

---

[22]For the federal description of this little expedition of civilians under Dotson's leadership, see Eckels to Dotson, 21 April 1858, and Dotson to Eckels, 27 April 1858, Microfilm Pub. M12, State Dept. Territorial Papers, Utah Series, 1853–73, Reel 1 (1853–59), NARA. When Cumming became aware of this foray upon his return to Fort Bridger on 16 May, he removed Washington J. McCormick as acting territorial secretary for his participation and berated Dotson for asserting that Utah was still in a state of rebellion. Cumming to Dotson, 25 May 1858, Cumming Papers, Duke University.

[23]There is no documentary or other support for Ferguson's speculation about a plot to murder or abduct Young, a very different circumstance than attempting to arrest him pursuant to a judicial writ.

[24]Nathaniel Felt, a mid-level Mormon leader, and correspondent Browne were both from Salem, Mass.

McNeill of the 5th Infantry and the filibustering Col. Fabin [Henry C. Fabens] are in the group. McNeill looks surly. He is bent on mischief.[25]

I shewed the Petition to Gov. C. He is perfectly willing to endorse all the removals, even Dotson and Hockaday. He suggests that the petition be for the removal of the incumbents, and simply a *recommendation* for the appointment of such individuals as you want. The petition should be accompanied by *another document* stating the reasons as, for instance, Judge Eckels:—expressing himself in very vindictive and bitter terms against the people previous to his arrival in the Territory; calling a Camp-jury (probably excusable as a Camp-regulation) and indicting the people before it; acting as Judge, Prosecutor and Clerk &c &c. Dotson: for a disposition generally manifested to bring the people into collision with the military, by refusing to serve or attempt to serve any process without first calling upon the military &c &c. The other reasons as well as reasons for the removal of others you are already aware of.

This A.M. I saw Gov C. again and chatted with him on the policy of issuing a Proclamation relative to the general pardon and also recommended him to include a warning against in-comers trespassing upon the property of absentees and to call upon the civil officers and people of the Territory to enforce the Territorial Laws.[26] I shall keep on the track and endeavor to furnish you a copy of the Proclamation previous to publication. The flags were flying before I knew it yesterday. Gov. C. hinted he would like a flag at his house. At Sunset (the usual time of lowering flags) I requested Genl West to lower the two flags, and this morning gave the Govr the benefit of one. The other on the Tithing Store will be rehoisted when it is thought best by you.[27] When I came to see them flying yesterday it was too much of a relief to the general gloom that otherwise pervaded the City.

A new arrival states that the Sappers & Miners had commenced the bridge over Weber this morning.[28] They will probably be in in four days. Gov. C. says he thinks that the haste of Johnston is occasioned by the supposition that Genl Harney is advancing and he wants all the glory himself. I had thought that the presence of the Mayor would be very proper to take chief control in the city, and the withdrawal of all the militia. The most to be dreaded now would be a brawl among the Army exiles provoked with some of our people by drink or otherwise. If this can be avoided and such peddlers as Savage can be kept at home, I think there will be no tumble. Dr [Franklin D.] Richards house

[25]Frank E. McNeil and Col. Henry C. Fabens were civilians imprisoned in Salt Lake without charges during the winter, and they later sued Brigham Young. McNeil was not an officer of the Fifth Infantry but was believed by some Mormons to have been a guide for the regiment during 1857. He was subsequently murdered.

[26]Cumming had done all of these things a week earlier on 14 June.

[27]An example of the level of detail for which Young's subordinates sought his counsel.

[28]Probably volunteer troops from Magraw's Company A, not Company A of Engineers, a regular unit from West Point which had not yet reached Bridger.

is occupied by the Commissioners and the great Clarkson & his [Nicaragua] party. By whose permission I know not. Is it intended that the detail should be furnished with provisions? Some very good men among them having been long on service are not able to purchase. I just learn that Bros Hooper & Kimball have arrived and bro. Hooper says the name of Dotson is to remain untouched [in the petition]. I shall do nothing till I hear from you as the interesting items of this letter may throw new light on this black character.

Gov C will forward the petition accompanied by an official letter from himself recommending the grant of the petition, which will be better than ever [even] his signature to the petition. The Correspondence between himself, Dotson & Johnson relative to your arrest has been forwarded to the Department. All is well. God bless you.

FERGUSON TO YOUNG, 24 JUNE 1858, LDS ARCHIVES.

Since the departure of Bros Hooper & Wm H. Kimball, Col [J. C. Little?] has seen Mr [Charles A.] Perry [sutler to the Tenth U.S. Infantry]. He will camp his wagons in the city and abide contentedly the issue of events. He wishes (and it is supposed others will also) to turn his oxen into a herd. Col Little wishes me to ask you concerning the propriety of the grantees of the herd ground in Rush Valley occupying immediately their old range with the herds of the Merchant trains, having in view (if practicable) the exclusion of the Army. He would like an answer by Bro. William [Kimball].

I have just returned from a lengthy chat with Gov. Cumming. He says it is in his opinion, the better plan to let the merchants wiggle, and not open any stores for the present. They are, he says, all [army] Sutlers and at present their proper place is with their Regiments.[29] L. K [Livingston Kinkead] & Co are Sutlers to the 2d Dragoons. [C. A.] Perry & Co to the 10th Infantry. Radford to the 5th and G & G. [Gilbert and Gerrish] to the Quarter Masters Department. When the Army has squatted down, Gov. C. says he will go down and see you and talk with you about the merchants and other matters and learn your wishes. There is a young man here, D Kavanagh from New Mexico, who has a small stock of goods that he wants to sell out by bulk and return. Gov. C. says that the great sweat of the merchants to open [the sale of] their goods is caused, he presumes, by the impression that the sutlers of the contemplated reinforcements are on the way and with large stocks and will not be able to return on the recall of the troops. They of course want to open at present big prices to head those that are coming. Of these facts I think the brethren were not apprized when they left. Hence I thought it best as also did Bro. George [Grant] and Bro. Little, that you should know all the facts. I think there will be no fires of any moment.

[29]During the Mexican-American War, Cumming had been a sutler, so he would have firm opinions on the subject.

Remarks had been made among the riff-raff & some of the Camp-poets that the people kept their houses closed by your dictation. I dropped in upon the Times Correspondent [Simonton] as he was writing and informed him that although the present movements were the result of combined [community] action as were all the acts of this people, yet there was no coercion, and every man was at liberty to make such use of his house and property as he pleased and that you in no case interfered; I requested him to make the statement in his letter [dispatch], and also to state that this people demanded or claimed an authorized investigation of the charges made against them, which had never yet been granted. He pledged me his word that he would make the statement with pleasure.[30] I am in hopes that we will be able to control that portion of the News world at least partially in our favor. All is well. A little excitement boils occasionally but with the blessing & favor of the Almighty it will blow over and produce good results. Praying my Father in Heaven that the Holy Spirit which has ever directed you to guide in safety the affairs of His Kingdom may continue with you and Bros Heber [Kimball] & Daniel [Wells] and all his Servants till the world shall be made to bend to the rule of Heaven, I am Obediently Yours in Christ.

Young to Ferguson, 25 June 1858, LDS Archives.

Your favors of yesterday and to-day are before me. Inform Col. Little and Co. to take herds from the Merchants as you suggested and proceed immediately to the occupying of the herd ground.

Captain Hooper will see Mr. Kavanagh.

Inform John Bolwinkel that he should by all means be constantly found at the [my] Office.

Instruct Col. Little not to be responsible for [government] stock especially against Indians.

I remain as ever your brother in Christ

P.S. You can show the other letter of even [this] date to Gov. Cumming.

Young to Ferguson, 25 June 1858, LDS Archives.

Your favor of yesterday is before me. It has been my feelings to let the Merchants look out for themselves for the present and wait until others come in, and inasmuch as they are of the Army, of course, that is the place for them.—Moreover we wish to have the privilege of waiting until we can see who will do the best by us, before we rent our buildings. We do not wish to be forced into measures because there are a few bayonets behind. We shall wait until they are cached [sheathed].

I would be glad to share with you this hope of being fairly and honestly

[30]Simonton made no such statements in his next dispatch dated 26 June. Ferguson was doomed to disappointment in thinking that he could influence Simonton's coverage.

represented by the "news world" but that is too unusual to expect. If any one should attempt to extend even tardy justice unto us through that channel it would indeed be marvelous in our eyes.

We wish to know if Gov. Cumming has published his [14 June] proclamation, and wishes us to circulate through the Territory, and if so we will print it in the "Deseret News." Are there any alterations from the copies we have?

We think the orders to halt ten days are ominous of good.[31] Peradventure Col. Johnston may also have received similar orders to await the issue of transpiring events, if so we trust that he will so far respect them as not to proceed on his march until further advices.

Be pleased to give my best respects to Gov. Cumming, and say to him I shall, when the proper time arrives, be happy to see him in Provo.

An Approaching Army: Mormon and Gentile Reflections at the Brink

As the Utah Expedition's buglers sounded reveille in the Wasatch foothills above Salt Lake City, a few non-Mormons and Latter-day Saints arose on Saturday, 26 June, to compose their thoughts before the army arrived. Elizabeth Cumming closed a letter written the night before to Thomas L. Kane from the comforts of the otherwise deserted Staines mansion. Correspondent Simonton rolled out of his Mackinaw blankets on the back porch of the Globe Restaurant to generate a long dispatch before dashing off to cover not the army's arrival but what he considered an even bigger story—Brigham Young's Sunday discourse in Provo. In Spanish Fork, a week after delivering her second child, Margaret Webster Adams described her new life in Mormon Utah for her Presbyterian brother in Scotland, stressing her defiance and a willingness to sacrifice everything if Brigham Young touched a match to his Sebastopol strategy. Meanwhile, in Provo, Young remained calm rather than incendiary, spending that important Saturday tending to his own correspondence while preparing to receive couriered reports on the army's approach and passage through Salt Lake City from Gen. James Ferguson.

Mrs. Cumming was less intent on sharing her reactions to the army's approach than venting her indignation over reporters' preoccupation with the peace commissioners' activities while both criticizing and marginalizing her husband's efforts.

[31] It is not clear to which federal orders Young refers.

Elizabeth Cumming to Kane,
25 June 1858, Kane Family Papers, BYU.

I enclose for your perusal *one of many* attacks on my husband. Is it, or is it not, well to notice them? The one I send, has been extensively copied—Towards yourself, it is wanting in respect & courtesy, but it accused him of direct *falsehood*—It appeared, first in the St. Louis Republican of 25th May (Daily) and again in the 26th May (Tri-weekly)—the Republican has long been considered one of the leading papers, not only of St. Louis, but of the West generally—and from its usual candor and prudence has held a deservedly high place among newspapers—"H.C.P." Henry Clay Pate, a well known contributor. (I believe, now, an editor at Westport,) formerly of St. Louis, introduces the article in question, giving it an additional force, as not being anonymous. In St. Louis, we lived long enough to have become acquainted with nearly all the leading people there, which makes the reports in question more important.

The gentlemen Commrs arrived here at the same time with ourselves. We have been here a little more than a fortnight. The inhabitants are nearly all at Provo—waiting until the army shall have passed through the City—and until all becomes quiet again. The army arrives here tomorrow. Several of the leading Mormons, whom I have seen, shake their heads and say "We *hope* all will be well" but look anxious. The army [is] encamped about two miles west of the city—across the Jordan—for the present.[32]

You will see published accounts of the [peace] conference here, after the arrival of the commissioners. Several of the Mormons, President Young among them, took occasion to say that Govr Cumming had already arranged this matter with them, with the exception of the offering a *pardon,* which pardon the gentlemen Commrs had brought with them, and which they, (the Mormons) received. They did not receive it in a very humble way, by the bye. "We are pardoned for having been rebels. We deny that we have been such—but—we receive the pardon—" &c.

Five reporters from the east are here—New York Times, Tribune & some other leading papers have their letter writers here—We see nothing of them. I have twice been informed that they are engaged all this week in writing for the leading eastern papers, under *proper* direction—matter to be sent by tonight's mail, that the representations to be made are to this effect, "that Col. Kane and Govr Cumming had been to Salt Lake City, and had been well received, and that some negotiations had been entered into, but that nothing was *really* accomplished, until the Commissioners arrived."

I am acquainted with the Commissioners, and believe them both to be highly honorable men, who would only allow to be said, just what they

[32]As a newcomer to Salt Lake City, Mrs. Cumming is confused. On 25 June the army camped in the foothills and canyons above and east of the city.

believed themselves, but I have reason to believe differently from this statement—I have seen several of the leaders in the Church, & *they* have told me that the matter was as much settled as it now is, before the Commrs arrived. Here is the question again, is it well to notice what these reporters say?

A great deal more of the same sort is being said and done—with which I will not trouble you. You know how my husband feels about these matters. He says, "Truth always comes out," and so do I believe too. Yet I think that Truth may sometimes be *helped* up out of her well, with advantage both to herself and others. What you said to me about this, when you left the Camp [on 16 May], has lain in my mind, and has induced me to send this letter to you.

Mr. Staines, in whose house we are, till another is made ready for us, said to-day, "I wish Col. Kane knew some things."[33] "Why do you not write and tell him, Mr. S.?" "Oh, I have been hoping to hear from the Colonel, I had rather hear from him first."

I like Mr. Staines, so far as I am yet acquainted with him. Gen. Wm. Kimball, too, makes a very agreeable impression upon my mind.

We have often thought of you upon your return journey. You seemed so unwell the day you left us [at Bridger], that Mr. Cumming was very uneasy about you. I trust you arrived at your home in safety, and found all your loved ones well. Please present my regards to Mrs. Kane, with whom I feel almost acquainted, so often have I heard you speak of her.

I remain your friend
E. W. Cumming

P.S. I was requested to write a postscript to the above note without having seen a word of its contents.

As I am very busy I will say "good evening"—hoping that you have quite recovered from the fatigues of your long journey and are now in the enjoyment of security and friends.

Your friend
A. Cumming

If Elizabeth Cumming momentarily put the army out of mind, reporter Simonton wholly ignored it in his dispatch. With the eastbound mail leaving town at 8:00 A.M., several hours before the Utah Expedition's expected arrival, Simonton completed a near-encyclopedic review of virtually every aspect of current events in Utah other than Albert Sidney Johnston's movements. Not surprisingly, Simonton had become aware of the Mormon petition

[33]It is impossible to know what Staines meant by this comment, though it is tempting to interpret it as an allusion to what he perceived as Alfred Cumming's bad behavior.

taking shape with Governor Cumming's involvement, and so that was one of the subjects on which he commented with some heat after interviewing Seth M. Blair, San Houston's friend whom Brigham Young was considering as Utah's next chief justice.

"S" [Simonton], "View of Mormon Affairs,"
Dispatch, 26 June 1858, *New York Times*,
3 August 1858, 1/4–6, 2/1–3.

Already the Mormon leaders here are at work to get rid of a portion of the federal officials sent among them. Major S. M. Blair told me that they had already petitioned for the removal of Judge Eckles [*sic*], Postmaster Morril [*sic*] and Indian Agents Hurt and Craig. Eckles has excited their hostility by his official course in Camp Scott last winter, where he had the unparalleled impudence to hold the Mormons to be traitors, and to indicate his disposition to execute upon them the laws against treason and sedition. The other officials mentioned have been among them before; and of course as they drove them out by force, it is annoying and humiliating to find them back again. Dr. Hurt certain is a most honorable and excellent gentleman, loved and respected by all who know him, and one who has proven his patriotism within a year past by desperate public service, in which he has sacrificed comfort and health, and it is to be feared, has even cut short his life [by his winter mission]. We shall see now whether justice or the Mormons are strongest in their influence over the Administration of James Buchanan.

Governor Cumming, who seems to have been taken into full communion by the brethren, evidently sympathizes with them in their kind intentions toward his brother officials, and will, doubtless, exert his influence in support of the petitions of removal, which, I am inclined to think, he forwards by this mail. The President, however, will be apt to await the return of the Peace Commissioners before he acts upon the petitions; and I am greatly in error if they do not see, what every other "Gentile" here sees clearly, that it is the Governor who should be removed from a position which he is utterly unfit to fill. His official intercourse with the Mormons here is making smooth sailing for himself at the present; but it will assuredly, in time, complicate the difficulties which cannot be avoided. Firmness and dignity are required in the Governor, but Cumming substitutes for these vulgar familiarity. Besides, he is naturally excitable, and notoriously gets steam up to an alarming point over the whisky-jug. He is not the man for the position, and should be replaced forthwith by some one who will command respect for himself and so be better able to exact respect for the Government he represents. He is, withal, vain as a boy of 13, and offensively imagines himself the embodiment of all that is great and grand.

There can be no question that former Administrations have sent some appointees here, justly obnoxious to the people; and it is of the highest importance that those who, in future, are sent to preside over them should be unobjectionable men in all respects. Probably the best mode of dealing with this people would be to repeal the organic act [of 1850] altogether, and then appoint some such man as Gen. Johnston both civil and military Governor. Blair, and others of the most influential men in this community, do not hesitate to say, even to-day, that they will be d—d if they will submit to have Morell, Eckles & Craig administer the Post Office and other offices of the Government here. They demand, too, "as a right," a share of the offices for themselves as well as the appointment of men to *all* of the offices, whom they shall approve, and he adds that there are a thousand who will jump when he gives the word. I suggest that Mr. Buchanan send his nomination here for confirmation [by Brigham Young], rather than to the Senate of the United States. It is rumored that Blair rather expects to be appointed to Judge Eckles' place; and if he fails to get it, I should not be surprised if Dr. Bernhisel is requested to resign, to give the Major a chance to go to Congress.

MARGARET WEBSTER ADAMS (SPANISH FORK, U.T.) TO GEORGE ADAMS (SCOTLAND), 26 AND 27 JUNE 1858, LDS ARCHIVES.

No doubt you have heard a great Deal about the war Between the united States Government and the Mormons, there was two thousand 5 hundred Soldiers sent against us in the fall of [18]57 to Exterminate the Mormons or kill them of[f], But the Mormons have keep them at Distance all winter, until an investigating Committee was sent from the Congress of the united States to investigate the Mormon Difficulty, they did so and finding that they were an honest industrious upright and law abiding people and the charges laid to them is intirly groundless have removed their troops, if the troops had insisted to come in to Salt Lake the Mormons would have Burned it up, ~~made a massacre of it~~, and then flown to the mountains, for they will have the Privaloge of worshiping god according to the dictates of their o[w]n Conscience, in spite of all the nations upon the Earth, and the whole population of the Territory amounts to about 60 thousand and they were willing to do the above Mentioned, we have a good house with 3 rooms & a sellar and we felt first rate about burning it up & all our property and leaving the desolation to our Enamies to Inherit. . . .

We Believe also Plurality of wives as the ansients servants of God practised Bro George it is nothing to see a man having 5 or 6 wives hear and maintains them respectable & provides for them, But here you cant see any prostitutes nor women Walking the streets working their living by it, and filling up the measure of their days in abominations upon the Earth. In the letter I wrote Thomas [I] Informed him of my marriage. I was married to a young man from Edinburgh His name Hugh Adams In July 23, /55 had a fine son Born May 11 /56 in this spanish Fork City 60 miles south of Great Salt Lake City. Gave Birth to another fine Son June 19th /58. Seven days previous to this time the first Boy's Name Hugh James Adams the second is Orvel Ferdinand Adams Bro George My Husband follows the line or ocupation of Farming we raise all that we make use of, tho scarce or less that is with us no clothing and money, we have a currant [currency] of paper money, but that don't go, No further than the Territory, so it make it acward with regard to mailing letters. If this letter comes to hand I will give you a better discription of things in our next for we are not sur[e] if it reaches you. . . .

No more at present But remains your Loving and Affectionate Brother & sister, Hugh & Margaret Adams.

This leaves us Sabbath 27 [26] of June /58

I Believe you would like for us to tell a little more about the war, time will not permit at present, Suffice it to say the troops of the united States, could have been all used up, and not a man left to tell the tale in 3 hours had not the Mormons Extended the arm of mercy, the Lord is merciful in all his ways and his goodness engurith [*sic*] forever, so you se[e] the Salvation that our Enimies have been in. When you write and want information about anything mention it and we will answer according to our ability.

And what of the man with whom Elizabeth Cumming, James Simonton, and Margaret Adams were so preoccupied that morning? Brigham Young was perhaps the coolest of them all, but a bit wistful. Overnight he had given up the forlorn hope that Albert Sidney Johnston would decide "not to proceed on his march until further advices" and had reconciled himself to the likelihood of the army's arrival in Salt Lake City that day. From the distance of Provo he wrote to Warren S. Snow, bishop of Manti, to describe the scene the army would encounter: "We have about four hundred at the City but not a soul will be seen when the troops enter, unless they commence committing depredations when they will spring up on every side. It is a dismal sight to see the deserted City, windows and doors all boarded up, and not a woman to enliven the scene." Young then paused and added a thought to be shared later that day by every U. S. soldier descending from the Wasatch foothills and canyons to the City of the Saints: "the trees and vegetation make a beautiful outside appearance, in this respect it never looked better." Anticipating the question that was on the bishop's mind, he added, "the government having conceded and granted us our rights for which we were contending and granted a general amnesty for the past, we have agreed not to interpose any further obstruction to the advance of the troops, conditioned that they shall not encamp in or near any city or dense settlement, and will moreover not molest any person in their property or person." Before moving on to discuss Indian affairs and a British-American maritime dispute, Young provided Snow with a thought that aptly captured the character of the territorial-federal conflict then nearing the close of its military phase: "they gloat over it as having obtained a good victory, we consider them badly whipped; they think they are preserving the dignity and consistency of the Government but more especially their party, which we admit is rather at the expense of our feelings but we get the substance."[34]

Houses a Strange Sight to Many of Us: City Passage

While the civilians in the valley below him waited, Gen. Albert Sidney Johnston shook off a blinding headache, marshaled his headquarters staff and Judge Eckels, and began the descent from the Wasatch foothills to Salt Lake City. The Utah Expedition's troops and their civilian camp followers snaked behind Johnston for ten miles, raising powdery dust clouds that nearly suffocated the dragoons of the rear guard.

After nearly a year of anticipating the event, large numbers of people on both sides of the Utah War commented on the army's passage through Salt Lake City, although few were eyewitnesses. By the time the army reached the city, most newspaper reporters had stuffed their dispatches for the day into the departing 8:00 A.M. eastbound mail. What these journalists later wrote from Provo to describe the march-through, was essentially a re-creation based on second- or third-hand accounts rather than their own eyewitness reporting. Most Mormons were absent from the city because of the Move South, and much of the Nauvoo Legion's rear guard had moved out of Salt Lake's center to hidden positions in City Creek Canyon to form a small firing party rather than a collection of diarists. The Utah Expedition's troops were preoccupied with the challenges of the march—the largest concentration of American troops on the move since Winfield Scott's triumphant 1848 entrance into Mexico City. The command's officers, sergeants, and provost

[34]Young to Snow, 26 June 1858, LDS Archives.

THE UTAH EXPEDITION'S MARCH THROUGH SALT LAKE CITY, 26 JUNE 1858

This image, made fifteen years after the event, was the first (and most enduring) depiction of the army's march through a city deserted and ready for the torch. The publisher contrived the image by superimposing a military formation on an 1860 C. R. Savage photo of Brigham Young's houses and office. Johnston's enforcement of strict discipline for this march did much to ease Mormon anxieties as the military phase of the war ended. Contrary to LDS folklore, during this passage Colonel Cooke of the Second Dragoons did not doff his hat out of respect for his former troops in the Mexican War's Mormon Battalion. *Engraving from T. B. H. Stenhouse's* Rocky Mountain Saints *(Salt Lake City, 1873).*

marshal focused on enforcing General Johnston's order that troops and camp followers remain in-ranks without exception, and that teamsters and drovers were to manage the command's thousands of wagons and animals so as to prevent property damage. Not only had Utahns never seen such a force, its enormity captivated the army.

Hanging in the balance with the army's conduct was Brigham Young's willingness to terminate the Move South, deactivate a Legion that he led but technically no longer commanded, and accept the presence of federal troops in the territory. As Apostle George A. Smith had stressed during the peace conferences two weeks earlier, the orderliness with which Johnston's command entered the Salt Lake Valley was to be a first test of the Buchanan administration's ability to fulfill its commitments. This issue, along with the site selection for the Utah Expedition's long-term garrison and the disposition of General Harney's even larger six-column brigade would determine the resolution of the Utah War's military phase.

Albert Sidney Johnston succeeded admirably in managing this march but wrote virtually nothing about his command's passage through Salt Lake City. Rather than generate a report upon camping along the River Jordan, he waited for several days and then simply informed army headquarters, "I found the city abandoned, except by a few persons engaged in guarding the property and keeping the gardens in good order."[35] Perhaps the cumulative impact of fatigue, poor health, a pressing need to relocate his command, and anticipation of General Harney's arrival had dampened whatever inclination Johnston otherwise had to describe his campaign's climax.

If Johnston chose not to record his impressions, several of his subordinates provided fresh, vivid descriptions of the march. Three of the most interesting came from West Pointers native to such diverse locations as South Carolina, Vermont, and New York: Brevet 2d Lt. Samuel Wragg Ferguson, Company G, Second Dragoons; Capt. John W. Phelps, commander of Light Battery B, Fourth Artillery; and 2d Lt. John Van Deusen Du Bois, Company K, Regiment of Mounted Riflemen. Albert G. Browne, Jr., of Massachusetts was probably the sole newspaper correspondent in Salt Lake City to witness this eleven-and-one-half-hour spectacle. Multiple treks back and forth across the Great Plains and Rockies had at last brought Browne to the modest observation post he staked out on a Salt Lake street corner for the *New-York Tribune* that June morning. Unlike his competitors, Browne considered the army's march-through the day's biggest story.

Lieutenant Ferguson and Captain Phelps had not seen a town, let alone slept indoors, since leaving the Missouri River. Lieutenant Du Bois's year of unremitting Indian warfare in New Mexico left him unfamiliar with comforts greater than field bivouacs, small army posts, or the rough accommodations of an occasional isolated rancho. All marveled at the dramatic first view of "civilization" as they broke free of the mountains above the

[35]Johnston to McDowell, 28 June 1858, "Annual Report of the Sec. of War (1858)," 121–22.

city and marched into the empty town. Salt Lake City prompted Johnston's troops to think anew of the homes and families they had left behind in Europe or America's Atlantic Coast.

The newly commissioned Ferguson had received his introduction to frontier brutality and the swaggering Second Dragoons at General Harney's Fort Leavenworth office. He toughened under the superb leadership of Colonel Cooke as he shared the ordeal of the Second's push from Fort Laramie to Camp Scott (the longest winter march in American military history) and six months of isolated patrolling through the frigid valleys of Henrys and Smiths Forks. With a vista of the Salt Lake Valley and the incandescent heat of early summer shimmering below him, Samuel Wragg Ferguson was no longer a "shavetail." He had hardened into a threadbare, seasoned campaigner so dusty that he was unrecognizable even to friends. With this initiation into army life behind him, Ferguson would receive the surrender of Fort Sumter at the beginning of the Civil War, rise to be a Confederate brigadier, and ride with Pres. Jefferson Davis on a last break for freedom at the war's end.[36]

Memoirs of S. W. Ferguson, Typescript, 9–10, Heyward and Ferguson Family Papers, Southern Historical Collection, Wilson Library, University of North Carolina at Chapel Hill.

In the spring, we marched to the Valley of the Great Salt Lake a distance of a little more than a hundred miles. The route was through two deep canons, along the beds of the narrow streams which flowed through them, but which were then dry. The black dust was well nigh intolerable; as we brought up the rear, we had the full benefit of it all. Our hair and beards were so matted that one could not recognize his best friend at a distance of a few yards. We took all possible precautions against ambuscade and attack, while passing through these defiles, but no Mormons showed themselves. When we debouched into the open country, whence Salt Lake City, distant eighteen miles could be seen, a green oasis in a desert of gray alkali and sage brush, the regiment was halted, formed in line and the [company] guidons, which had been brought in the wagon to this point, distributed.

While this was doing, a squadron of Mormon Cav[a]lry splendidly mounted and gaily caparisoned, with silver [saddle and bridle] trimmings, under the command of a namesake of mine [Adjt. Gen. James Ferguson], galloped up and around our little band of dirty old soldiers mounted on

[36]A more polished version of this account appears in Ferguson, "With Albert Sidney Johnston's Expedition to Utah, 1857."

the few horses that had survived the march. Deep were the muttered curses I could over hear; how welcome would be the order to fire; to charge would have been a farce, for they could gallop away from our scarecrows. After all our hardships and sufferings, we were not to fight; a peace commission had arrived a few days before, and all the punishment the Mormons received, was to have several millions of gold spent in their midst, by the Government.

We marched through Salt Lake City, in the most perfect order, as on dress parade; every man and officer in his place; crossed the River Jordan by an excellent bridge and camped on the farther bank. Previous to our coming, the entire population of the city had been removed, by order of Brigham Young, not a woman was allowed to remain, most of the houses had doors and windows boarded up, and the place looked desolate. As we marched through, a few villainous looking men at the street corners, scowled at us. After camping for some time on the bank of Jordan, we marched to the foot hills about fifty miles, and established Camp Floyd.

Captain Phelps's diaries are among the richest but least published of the Utah War's primary sources. On 26 June he struggled to execute his battery's descent into Salt Lake Valley over rough trail with gun carriages, limber chests, and caissons for a dozen brass howitzers (the "Twelve Apostles"), plus an iron forge and tons of explosives. Phelps managed this challenge with disciplined artillerymen, as well as a few veteran battery horses teamed with a complement of untrained, half-wild New Mexico mules and horses trailed north by Captain Marcy. Once bivouacked across the River Jordan, Phelps recorded what he had just seen upon emerging from Emigration Canyon and marching into and through Salt Lake City.

Phelps Diary, 26 June 1858, Walker Draft Typescript, 8–9.

It was about half past ten a clear day as we debouched from the Canon. A blue smoky haze hung over the valley, while on our left, houses here and there glistening white in the morning sun. Far on our right the [Great Salt] lake at length gleamed in the distance. Presently the city itself, began to make its appearance, close under the descent down which our route lay.

On entering the streets we noticed that they were very wide, at least [blank] feet: borders on each side with small runs of water which are brought down from the streams in the mountains immediately east of the town by ditches they are set [bordered] along their course with young cotton wood trees the house[s], are generally built of adobes. . . . Many of the houses had no windows in their casements, which were frequently closed up with boards. The streets were nearly desolate: some few men were seen here and there, but not one single woman made her appearance. Persons could be occasionally seen peering stealthily from the windows: but almost all of the inhabitants have gone to Provo(st)—a town fifty miles to the south of us. . . .

Our route led by Brighams house which is a large white edifice decorated with a beehive on its top and the figure of a lion on its front facing the street. A little below this house and on the same side of the street we noticed the American flag flying. It was at the residence of our Governor (Cummings) who occupies (in part at least) the house of Elder Staines a Saint rejoicing in three wives.

Our long column of troops and wagons have been passing thro town all day. The rear of the column is now, as I write 6:30 P.M. Just winding out of town to cross the Jordan on the left [west] bank of which we are encamped. The grass is all burnt up and we have such fuel as is bought from the mormons.

It strikes [me] on entering the valley, after crossing over so many high hills, that this is a peculiarly isolated region of the globe, and the only one, perhaps in which an isolated sentiment as Mormonism could take root and grow. Mormonism is, in fact, the growth of a waste region of the United States, and all attempts by Brigham or others to transplant it to other soils will prove abortive. Many of the Mormons, it is said, have personal defects, such as lameness, shabismus [eye defect], hump-backs etc.—to think of such men reveling in women! Why should not a system be popular that can this [thus] compensate for the blemishes of nature? While I write subject to repeated interruptions, the sun is setting behind the distant mountains in the NW. And the city, which lies right before me, is responding to his adieu by the shimmer of all the glass window panes which it probably has. Mixed up with its young trees of fresh green resdure [verdure] and lying scattered along the base of the mountain ridges east of the valley, it looks beautiful.

We arrived at this point at about 1 P.M.—distance [marched today] 15.27 miles.

A few days later the captain wrote to his younger sister, Eunice Phelps Hickman of West Chester, Pennsylvania, from the army's subsequent camp along West Creek, a tributary of the Jordan.[37]

"Wolcott" [Phelps] to "Eunice" [Phelps Hickman], 30 June 1858, Phelps Papers, NYPL.

At length, after traversing the hills and vallies that intervene in the one hundred and thirteen miles that separate Great Salt Lake City from Fort Bridger, we emerged from the last valley or Cañon—Emigration Cañon—on the morning of the 26th inst; and the Great Valley, the end and destination of our march for one long year, lay before us "misty and wide." The smoky

[37]Mrs. Hickman died at age 43, six months after her brother wrote this letter. The original is in Phelps Papers, NYPL; a photostatic copy is in the Hamilton Gardner Collection, Utah State Historical Society.

curtains of the morn were not yet drawn up; and houses here and there, a strange sight to many of us, were shining whitely in an early sun. Around us on all sides were mountain barriers whose summits gleamed white and cold with snow, and along whose flanks could be traced by the eye the ancient high water mark of the lake [Bonneville]. Presently the lake itself could be discerned far to our North West, whither it has retreated.

The skirts of lofty mountains are generally broad and of a regular, gentle slope; and it was down such that our route lay. Gradually the famous city itself began to make its appearance beneath us, at the point where the slope begins to merge with the plain. Its broad streets could be seen running to the westward from us, dotted sparsely along their course with houses and young trees. We crossed several of the ditches which bring down irrigation-water from the mountains; for it is so dry in the valley that nothing would grow without irrigation. Every street has a small ditch on each side through which sufficient water is constantly running to irrigate all the little fields of the town. The houses have an acre of land—more or less—attached to each, and the vegetation, consisting of a variety of young trees recently planted, wheat, barley, garden vegetables, flowers etc, was looking very green and thriving. The soil is good; and the Jordan which runs along the western limits of the town, could furnish water enough to irrigate a great many acres. The water could be easily pumped up by wind-mill power, judging from the force of the wind which has prevailed (from the South West) since we have been here.

The houses are generally built of adobes or unburnt bricks, and some of them have considerable pretensions in the way of architecture. While the small and often unenclosed fields shew but little distinction between the Latter-day-Saints, the edifices, on the contrary, are as different in style and costliness as they are in any other city.

I can say but little of Brigham's house, having paid but little attention to it. I noticed, however, that it was quite palatial in its appearance. Upon its top was a bee hive, and upon the fence next the street thro' which our march lay, the image of a lion crouchant as large as life. This house, the principal sacred edifices and the "Deseret Store" with the sign of a bee hive, are all or in part surrounded by a massive stone wall reinforced with buttresses of the reformed Egyptian architecture. A more wretched domiciliation of the religion, law and government of a new empire could not be conceived; it shews the darkling meanness, cunning and ignorance of the mind that originates, leads and controls Mormonism. It is like the stream of Jack Sly in the play; and to think of an immortal soul resorting to such a work-shop to seek and gain eternal life.[38]

---

[38]Reference to a character in the play *The Candidates*, by eighteenth-century American playwright Robert Munford.

The streets were nearly deserted, and the doors and windows of many of the houses closed up. A few men were seen here and there, and occasionally some one could be detected peering furtively from a window; but an air of stillness and desolation reigned in the streets of this abused daughter of Zion, for the inhabitants—almost all the men and all the women—had left their domiciles and withdrawn to Provost [*sic*]—a town fifty miles to the south. Had the emperor of Russia, or the Sultan of Turkey, effected as much by an effort of *his* will—had either unpeopled a whole city at once, we should have considered him a monster. The fault, however, in this case, lies with the people, and shews what a set of trifling slaves their crimes and follies have made them.

Our Camp for several days was on the opposite bank of the Jordan, and not far from the city, and as we looked out towards it from time to time, observing over what a large space its now tenantless houses were scattered, and being thus reminded how very few Mormons it really once contained—probably not six thousand;—when, reverting from this view of things to the far eastward where three hundred millions of Christians are fermenting, as it were, with all that is great, progressive and grand in humanity under the leaven of their doctrines, and perceiving how few dregs had spilt over into this remote, isolated valley whose very freedom and isolation are enough to beget extravagances of any kind, we thought that it is highly creditable to the human race that it should have eliminated and worked out from its bosom so little badness as it has.

We find a great change in the temperature since descending from the greater altitude of Fort Bridger. The mercurial column is about two inches higher here than at the latter place. The thermometer, yesterday, rose to 100 degrees; and as a gale of wind prevailed at the same time from the S.S.W. filling the air with dust, and, moreover, as the grass was burnt up and pasture for our some 4000 animals scarce, we withdrew, yesterday, to this place, which is on a small thread of water, on the flanks of the mountains in the western part of the valley, and about eighteen miles from town. Our general, in the meantime, has gone in search of more permanent stations for the troops. Now and then a Mormon comes into camp with trout, cured with salt, from Lake Utah, with potatoes, cheese etc. for sale; but when one considers the apparently scant resources of the valley in this way and reflects how hard it would be to supply the troops now here and those which are to arrive with provisions from the States, our position, quiet as it now is, does not seem to be unattended with difficulties.

It is said that many of the Mormons are desirous of coming back from Provost to re-occupy their houses; but on the other hand it is rumored that they are on their way still farther south, to White Mountain, which is three hundred miles from here.

> In our march here from Fort Bridger, among high hills and deep vallies, we crossed two principal streams and some of their tributaries. These two streams are of about the same size—say about twenty or thirty yards wide and three feet deep, and both, by a devious course to the northward, finally enter Salt Lake. They are the Bear and Weber rivers, and it is along the former that the great rail-road will run.[39] By following its course, which is a hundred miles longer, but on the direct route to Oregon, all the high, dividing ridges which we crossed would be avoided.

Phelps limited this letter to descriptive comments, but when he wrote on the same day to his old friend J. Watts de Peyster, who was a New York militia general and member of the Hudson River Valley's Dutch aristocracy, he vented the frustrations common among his brother-officers and their troops: "After a year's pursuit of the Mormons as an enemy, to arrive in their capital and find it abandoned, with no evidence of opposition or resistance any where, leaves the expedition almost without an object and wholly without interest."[40] As the summer unfolded, Phelps's anger would rise with Utah's oppressive heat and dust.

Lt. John Van Deusen Du Bois wrote to his mother in Hudson, New York, on the day he passed through Salt Lake City. Although he proclaimed the town "the most beautiful place I ever saw," he had little positive to say about the people who built it. Instead he spent more than half of his letter ranting about Mormons, the perceived coopting of Governor Cumming, and the Buchanan administration's feckless conduct of the war. These were views acquired quickly from brother-officers during his several days at Fort Bridger. In this sense, the tone of Du Bois's letter matched the opinions John Wolcott Phelps shared with General de Peyster a few days later.

2d Lt. John Van Deusen Du Bois to Mother, 26 June 1858, Hammond, ed., *Campaigns in the West*, 116–17.

> You will see by the heading of my letter that I write you from the city of the Mormons. We came through Echo Canyon & found the fortifications as described but all deserted. it is a very narrow gorge in which brave men might make a desperate [stand] using the country around with its hills and canons for their light troops, but I do not think they could have resisted by the defenses in the canon—although much blood would have been shed

[39]Because of sectional wrangling in Congress, this issue was undecided in 1858 and would remain so until the Civil War permitted selection of the central route through Utah.

[40]Phelps to de Peyster, 30 June 1858, Phelps Papers, NYPL.

had they attempted it. We found the city entirely deserted, the windows & doors boarded up & not so much as a dog to bark at us. Some few men hung around the place to take care of the gardens. One hotel [the Globe] was open.

We camped on the "other side of Jordan." Salt Lake City is the most beautiful place I ever saw, Brigham Young's house is a magnificent place, twice as large as the "Hudson House" [hotel] on the ground, two stories high, magnificently furnished, surrounded by gardens with grapes, peaches, & all kinds of fruit & by a high wall built of stone. The city is twice as large as Hudson, is laid out with perfect regularity; the streets fifty yards wide, bordered by trees and on each side of every street runs a little stream of water. Each house stands in the middle of a large garden, peas, potatoes, lettuce & all vegetables are in profusion but the Mormons have orders not to sell to us.

The Governor is becoming a Mormon rapidly. Everyone is disgusted with him. He seems to truckle to Mormondom and cultivate intimate relations with Brigham Young. Just think of it—Mrs. Cumming & one of Brigham's wives are on calling terms. Isn't it a disgrace to the American ladies? The President and all the authorities have failed lamentably. All the murders & robbers have been pardoned and now roam around unmolested. Brigham's power is stronger than ever, and we have been conquered as surely by the Washington weakness as we would have been by the sword. The army is disgusted. It feels its degradation and asks nothing more now except a Mormon General to command it. We certainly have the most cowardly government on the globe. Any strength can bully it & only the weak tribes of Indians dares it ever to show it power. Millions will be paid by the people of the east for this grand humbug. The Mormons are all at Provo as impertinent as ever & do not hesitate to say that the Governor is on their side. We made a great mistake in allowing Territories to make their own laws. They are men now before they can walk.

I am anxious only to go back to New Mexico. We will be on the road before this letter reaches you. . . . I wish . . . to get by a house fire again. By the way, the Mormons put up ice for every family & not a drop of liquor of any kind is allowed in the city.[41]

In Deathlike Silence: Watchmen on the Tower

Few Nauvoo Legionnaires left firsthand accounts of the Utah Expedition's march-through, although some, like Pvt. John T. McDonald, eventually

[41]It is possible that alcohol as well as hard campaigning played a role in Du Bois's medical problems after the Civil War. In 1876 he retired from the army as a colonel, and in 1879 he died prematurely in Hudson at age 46.

recorded what they remembered of the event as much as a half-century later. In McDonald's case, he was preoccupied on 26 June 1858 with the need to keep his bride-in-disguise out of harm's way while carrying out his military responsibilities:

> The day the army entered the city I expect my wife was the only woman left in it. The city guards were all ordered to go up City creek canyon until after the troops had passed through the city and myself with the rest. I was in a fix. I did not know what to do with my wife. I had only one horse and I could not take her up in the mountains. I could not get another horse in time to get her out of the city so I put her on my horse dressed her in my riding suit, stuck my bowie knife in her leggings and started her off for Pleasant Grove on the dead run. But by the time she got ready to go the troops were in the center of the city and she had to ride within a block of the advance guard. She was pretty badly scared. She rode to Pleasant Grove in less than five hours. She had to ride straddle in the saddle nearly all the way and she was badly used up when she got there. I followed as soon as the troops had passed.[42]

The best Mormon account is Brig. Gen. James Ferguson's letter that was immediately couriered to Brigham Young in Provo. Ferguson provided Young with the closest thing to what today would be called a "real time" narrative of the Utah Expedition's passage through Salt Lake City. He also shed light on the disposition of the Mormon petition to President Buchanan and Governor Cumming's role in forwarding it.[43] Ferguson's message provides the wherewithal to challenge a staple Mormon folktale of the war—that as Col. Philip St. George Cooke led the Second Dragoons through the city, he removed his hat as a gesture of respect for the Mormon Battalion, which he had commanded during the Mexican-American War.

James Ferguson (Salt Lake City) to Young (Provo),
26 June 1858, LDS Archives.

> I have given to Mr. Simonton of the "N.Y. Times" [and] "London Times" & Mr. [Lemuel] Fillmore of the [New York] "Herald" letters of introduction to you.[44] They will stop at Lehi to night and most probably attend preaching tomorrow morning at Provo. I think they are rather disposed to

[42]McDonald, "Personal Reminiscences," *Deseret Evening News*, 20 August 1910, 20/1–7.

[43]This study bypasses a fascinating, firsthand account of Johnston's march-through by Legionnaire Peter Sinclair because of its problematic association with convicted document forger Mark Hoffman. Peter Sinclair Journal, 26 and 27 June 1858, MS 6716, LDS Archives.

[44]Simonton was sending dispatches to both the *New York Times* and *London Times* as well as to the *San Francisco Evening Bulletin*.

do the fair thing (no doubt to accommodate their own policy).[45] [Commissioner] Powell has carried *Brown*[*e*] in his pocket till this morning and has now transferred him to *Hust* [Hurt?] who with [Abel?] Gilbert & the Lawyer [Charles Maurice] Smith for his right wing and [Indian Agent C. L.] Craig & Dick James for his left, together with a numerous staff of like vagabonds, stands aloof under the shades of the locust trees watching the interesting progress of events. Genl Johnston and staff (including Capt. Marcy) passed the Governor's residence at 1/2 past 10 this A.M. The 10th Infy passed your residence for the West at 1/2 past 11. Coll Alexander (mounted) at the head of his Column doffed his Cap as he passed the very small [non-Mormon] crowd that stood at the corners watching his march.[46] A large train of Supply wagons followed in his rear. And then came two or three apostate wagons (I know not who). The Light Battery [Phelps] followed. All went along very quietly. The Provost Marshall [Lt. Cuvier Grover] is on duty and the strictest orders have been given to permit no one to leave the line of march for a moment. The 4th[47] 5th Infy, the Heavy Battery [Reno] and the Dragoons are now advancing. Each Regt or Detachment brings in its rear its own baggage & supply wagons. Mr Livingston & Mr Bell arrived about 8 this A.M.[48] They wanted to go to Provo this evg. I requested them to remain till Monday. They will then go to see you. Gilbert is the only noisy man among the Merchants, and is generally supposed to be *crazy de facto*. There is no excitement in town to day. Mr. [McNeil and] Craig will go down to night with Mr Simonton. He carries you a letter of introduction from Capt. [William H.] Hooper. I had quite an assault last evg from McNeill. He seemed determined on a row. I parried it off. Powell was watching and thought I was rather cool in the affair, which I believe I was, with hard trying. McNeill was drunk.

---

[45]When two months later Ferguson read Fillmore's and Simonton's published dispatches, he must have been bitterly disappointed at their hypercritical tone. In a letter introducing Fillmore to Brigham Young, Ferguson had described the reporter as a man "disposed through the columns of the *Herald* of which he is the acknowledged correspondent, to give us a fair and honorable representation." Ferguson to Young, 26 June 1858, LDS Archives.

[46]For the implications of Colonel Alexander's hat-doffing vis à vis later Mormon belief that it was Colonel Cooke who had done so, see MacKinnon, "Case of the Cat in the Hat," in "'Not as a Stranger': A Presbyterian Afoot in the Mormon Past," 5–21. Not only did Colonel Cooke refrain from such a public display of respect on 26 June, the Fifth Infantry's commander, Lt. Col. Carlos Waite, also chose not to do so, although First Counselor Heber C. Kimball had been his childhood school chum and playmate in upstate New York. During early August both Cooke and Waite paid brief courtesy calls on Brigham Young as they started east on furlough. Both officers spoke warmly in Young's office of their long-ago relations with Mormons, but the pleasantries exchanged excluded anything to support the later Mormon folklore attributing to Cooke an overt gesture as the Utah Expedition marched through Salt Lake City six weeks earlier. Collier, ed., *The Office Journal of President Brigham Young*, 8 and 9 August 1858, 1–2.

[47]The Fourth U.S. Infantry was not part of the Utah Expedition; Ferguson probably meant Bee's Battalion of U.S. Volunteers, an infantry unit.

[48]Howard Livingston and William Bell of the mercantile firm of Livingston & Kinkead.

For your favors of yesterday I am much obliged. I showed your letter (as requested) to Govr Cumming. He wishes the [gubernatorial] Proclamation [of 14 June] published in the "News."[49] There is no alteration. I enclose you a copy of the Petition. Govr C. forwarded it [in today's mail]. I omitted the mention of Surveyor General [David H. Burr], as there was no one to remove and Bro [Seth M.] Blair seemed positive that Daval (of Texas) would get the appointment anyhow. Mr Bell, on good authority says that he believes all the reinforcements will be ordered back and a great portion of the present Army of Utah sent to Oregon.

Govr. C. advises the postponement of any return of families to the City at present. His advice in this is verbal and I think he wishes it to be confidential. He is anxious above all things to avoid any difficulty between our people and the army followers.

All is well. God is with us. And the wrath of man will yet be compelled to contribute to His praise and honor.

God be with you Yours obtly in Christ

P.S. [Merchant William] Bell intimated to me confidentially that Eckels talked of resigning. I took the liberty as you see in the Petition of giving the President's proclamation a dig. I could not help it. Bros. Hooper & William Kimball have just dropped in and send their kind regards confirming all I say. George [D. Grant] Robert [T. Burton] and the boys are doing well keeping the lads in the back ground & helping. The Mayor, City Marshall and Recorder are doing all they can and are sustained by Govr. C.

Neither as breezy nor as immediate as Ferguson's letter was the powerful account published sixty-two years later by John R. Young, who in 1858 was Brigham Young's twenty-one-year-old nephew. In his memoirs, John Young claimed to have been among the Legion's "watchers" detailed to monitor the army's movement through Salt Lake. As he recalled the event, "I sat with the guards in the upper room of the Lion House, and saw that army in death-like silence march through the deserted streets of the dead city, a few of the officers with uncovered heads, as if attending a funeral. To us western mountain boys, the solemnity of the march was oppressive; and glad relief came to our strained feelings, when we [later] saw the soldiers' camp fires kindled on the 'other side of Jordan.' "[50]

---

[49]Cumming's proclamation announcing implementation of Buchanan's pardon appeared without comment in "A. Cumming, Governor of Utah Territory," *Deseret News*, 7 July 1858, 3. Ferguson mentioned it here in response to a question in Young to Ferguson, 25 June 1858, LDS Archives.

[50]Young, *Memoirs of John R. Young*, 115. Young's imagery matched that of Lt. Col. Charles F. Smith, Tenth U.S. Infantry, who told his daughter, "It was [like] treading the deserted streets of a city of the dead." Smith to Fanny M. Smith, 7 July 1858, in Mesch, *Your Affectionate Father*, 162.

Conclusions

There is always an easy solution to every human problem—neat, plausible, and wrong

H. L. Mencken, 16 November 1917

The Utah Expedition's passage through Salt Lake City marked the end of the Utah War's active military phase. Immediately thereafter, the territory's armed confrontation with the U.S. government took on a new, political character during a dramatic period of Southern-style "Reconstruction" that stretched into the first decade of the twentieth century. A comprehensive examination of this long postwar political struggle lies outside the scope of *At Sword's Point,* but a long study of this character does call for summary conclusions about the meaning of what took place during 1857–59, especially with respect to the Utah War's character, leaders' accountability, the conflict's winners and losers, and the significance of their struggle.

Defining the Utah War: What Was It?

As this study defines it, the Utah War was the armed confrontation over power and authority between the civil-religious hierarchy of Utah Territory led by Gov. Brigham Young and Pres. James Buchanan's administration. At the heart of the conflict was the disconnect between the two leaders' radically different philosophies of governance. Young viewed Utah as a millennially focused theocracy operating under his prophetic, authoritarian leadership. The U.S. government dealt with Utah as one among multiple federal territories intended to function under republican principles, as a ward of Congress through a federally sworn governor appointed by the president and supervised by the U.S. secretary of state.

The war did not abruptly well up in the spring of 1857 because of a single critical incident. Instead, it arose from a ten-year accumulation of issues, with Mormon-federal relations steadily deteriorating after the 1847 Mormon arrival in the Salt Lake Valley. The failed attempt to replace Young as governor during 1854–55 was emblematic of both the tensions involved and the fecklessness of Presidents Millard Fillmore and Franklin Pierce in dealing with them. By Buchanan's inauguration, virtually every area of contact between Utahans and the federal government had become a contest of wills, with conflicts over administrative or departmental matters aggravated by such emotional issues as the LDS church's 1852 polygamy announcement, the Republican Party's 1856 adoption of an anti-polygamy presidential platform plank, perceptions that Brigham Young was seeking Mormon independence outside the Union, and a series of unprosecuted murders.

The catalyst for Buchanan's decision-making at the end of March 1857 was the administration's receipt of a series of complaints from Utah's federal appointees, depicting Utah as a violent territory led by a disloyal, out-of-control governor prone to incendiary rhetoric that was disrespectful of the U.S. government. To the Mormon side, such provocative language was simply part of its assertion of Utah's constitutional rights in the face of congressional and executive behavior perceived as colonial, corrupt, and ineffective.

By the early spring of 1857, Buchanan had given up on retaining Brigham Young. His embryonic plan was to reassert federal authority by superseding Young with a non-Mormon successor who was to be escorted west by a large military expedition. This force would serve as a posse comitatus in support of the territory's governor, federal judges, and U.S. marshal. Within weeks, news that virtually all of Utah's federal appointees except Young had fled the territory—the second such exodus in less than six years—seemed to validate Buchanan's decision. By the early fall of 1857, the conflict was on its way to becoming the country's most extensive and expensive military action during the period between the Mexican-American and Civil Wars—one that ultimately pitted Utah's large militia against almost one-third of the U.S. Army.

Another way to define the Utah War is to recognize that indeed it was a violent conflict, notwithstanding the enduring, pernicious myth that it was bloodless. Even some of the war's non-Mormon participants were either insensitive to or unaware of the violence involved. In 1859 former newspaper correspondent Albert G. Browne, Jr., wrote from Boston to Fort Bridger's Judge William A. Carter to reminisce that "we fought the Utah war together—the sole bloodshed in which appears to have been that of several thousands of oxen."[1] Obscured in the process—sometimes deliberately—was the enormity of the Mountain Meadows massacre, the nation's greatest incident of organized mass murder of unarmed civilians until the 1995 Oklahoma City bombing. This atrocity, combined with losses from the attack on Fort Limhi, the murder of the Aiken party, the death of ammunition trader Richard E. Yates, and a plethora of other individual wartime killings produced approximately 150 deaths on both sides of the Utah War. These were casualties roughly equivalent to those in Utah's eastern neighbor, "Bleeding Kansas."

Understanding the war's geopolitical scope as well as its carnage is essential to grasping its character. Rather than a confrontation confined to Washington, D.C., and Utah's Wasatch Front, the war was a sprawling affair that was a regional, national, and international conflict.

In terms of troop sourcing, the Utah Expedition drew regular units from posts in Florida, Minnesota, New Mexico, Kansas, Texas, and California, as well as individual soldiers from recruit depots in New York, Pennsylvania, and Kentucky. If one also considers the massive volunteering efforts during early 1858, virtually the entire country was involved. Both the federal and Mormon sides benefited from an influx of British deserters and veterans from the Crimean War, as well as the enlistment of civilian adventurers from a wide variety of other international locations.

Geographically, both the Nauvoo Legion and Utah Expedition operated not only in Utah—a territory seven hundred miles wide—but ranged through parts of adjacent Oregon, California, Nebraska, and New Mexico. Because of speculation about a mass Mormon exodus from Utah to the Pacific Coast (and perhaps beyond) and the ambiguous destination of the Move South, the war alarmed the governments of Russia, Great Britain, the Sandwich Islands, Mexico, and the Netherlands. President Buchanan's covert consideration of plans to link the Utah War to Manifest Destiny potentially expanded this already formidable scope to northern Mexico and Spanish Cuba.

[1]Browne to Carter, 22 October 1859, Carter correspondence, Marriott Library, University of Utah.

Because of enduring controversies enveloping the Utah War's historiography, an understanding of what the conflict was not is almost as important as grasping what it was. Despite immediate (and long-lasting) Mormon complaints of religious persecution, the Utah War was not a federal attack on the LDS church or its religious tenets. As unpopular as the polygamy issue was across the country, in the non-Mormon world of 1857 there was no U.S. statute barring the practice of plural marriage until 1862. Although flawed as an executive, James Buchanan was too experienced a lawyer and politician to cross this constitutional line. He disavowed religious persecution repeatedly, especially in his 8 December 1857 annual message to Congress, the instructions he gave to Governor Cumming on 30 July 1857, and his 6 April 1858 presidential proclamation of pardon. For Buchanan, the issue in Utah was restoration of federal authority, not eradication of Mormonism.

If the Utah War was not a religious crusade, neither was it the product of the multiple conspiracy theories perceived by Brigham Young and others. At the war's onset, Young branded the conflict a contractors' fight intended to benefit the administration's commercial friends; during the Civil War, he came to see it as the product of a proto-Confederate plot in Buchanan's cabinet designed to weaken the defenses of the U.S. government by scattering its army and draining the Treasury. Conspiracy theorists among Buchanan's political enemies perceived the war as a diversionary thrust by which the president tried to shift the public's focus away from the divisive slavery issue in Kansas. All of these theories lack substance and credibility, although the notion of a Kansas diversion remains especially seductive for some historians.

There is no evidence that the conspiracy theorists of the past 150 years have accurately assessed Buchanan's Utah decision-making in the spring of 1857. This is not to say that the president was incapable of such deviousness. To the contrary, there is reason to believe that once the need arose in mid-November 1857 to reinforce the Utah Expedition, continued armed confrontation in the Rockies and Great Basin did provide a field for presidential manipulation. This opportunity led to Buchanan's scheming in early 1858 to open a second front through a major thrust from the Pacific Coast to force Brigham Young out of Utah and into Mexico. Realistic or not, it was a plan devised by Buchanan to scratch two presidential itches: resolution of the Mormon problem, and pursuit of American Manifest Destiny through the acquisition of Cuba via Mexico. In assessing the president's billiardslike machinations and the likelihood of their linkage to the Utah War's prosecution, timing is everything.

Finally, one must ask if the Utah War was essentially a rebellion or a conflict of a less serious character. The most recent narrative history of the war, Bigler and Bagley's *The Mormon Rebellion,* addresses this question in its very title as well as its point of view. On the other hand, a respected earlier study by Norman F. Furniss avoided that title in favor of a more neutral one, *The Mormon Conflict.* This definitional issue is a vital one, not just a matter of semantics. As discussed earlier, President Buchanan used the term "rebellion" in a variety of confusing ways, beginning with the mixed signals in his December 1857 annual message to Congress and ending with the more definitive assertion in his 1858 message that "at the commencement of my administration [Utah] was in a state of open rebellion." It was a shift in language, signaling at bare minimum the existence of deeply flawed presidential communication skills.

On balance, I believe that when Buchanan made his initial decisions about Utah in the spring of 1857, he faced a serious problem of territorial control and gubernatorial insubordination. It was a situation fully warranting Buchanan's decision to replace Brigham Young, but not yet one constituting rebellion. General Scott had used the term "rebellion" in his operational orders for General Harney on 29 June 1857, but a month later Secretary Cass's parallel instructions to Cumming avoided the word.

The events that unfolded in the territory during September–October 1857 changed all this, especially Brigham Young's illegal proclamation of martial law, his restrictions on travels of civilians in and around Utah, his theft and destruction of federal property, and his authorization of lethal force against the Utah Expedition.[2] By mid-September 1857 Young had

[2]Technically it could be argued that a general officer of the Legion, Brigadier James Ferguson, directed the use of lethal force a month earlier than did Young. In mid-August 1857 Ferguson provided these instructions, loaded with euphemisms for killing, to a commander in northern Utah, Maj. Samuel Smith: "It is reported an armed force from Oregon is coming to invade this Territory from the North, simultaneously with those coming from the East,—You will therefore take immediate measures to know if such should be the case before they come upon us. Before they arrive in the settlements they must be met and repulsed. They must not be permitted to come into this territory. . . . Get the Indians to watch, and send out yourself a hundred or two miles a few men to find out. . . . Remember our mode of warfare is to destroy our enemies without losing our own men; waylay them, stampede their animals, cut off their patrolling parties, burn the grass and lay waste the country before them, separate them from their baggage if possible and burn it and them until they are utterly destroyed and wasted away and your own men all this time comparatively safe." What these orders set in motion was Major Smith's arrest of the civilian Aiken party near Fort Box Elder and its subsequent assassination by Legion officers Porter Rockwell and Bill Hickman. Ferguson to Samuel Smith, 12 August 1857; Young and Wells to Colonels Cummings and Burton, 25 September 1857, Nauvoo Legion Letterbook, LDS Archives.

crossed a Rubicon of sorts. In so doing, he changed the character of Utah's dispute with the U.S. government from a series of provocations to armed rebellion, a term that Albert Sidney Johnston used thereafter. All of this negative gubernatorial leadership produced a tone to Utah's society that made possible the killings at Mountain Meadows and elsewhere.

Seeking to describe this scene as it unfolded during the course of 1857–59, I have most frequently used the term "armed confrontation." As with the matter of how to characterize Buchanan's intense plotting about Mexico and Cuba, the appropriateness of the labels that one uses to characterize the overall Mormon-federal conflict—especially rebellion—depends upon the timing of the actions involved. What had not been a rebellion in March 1857 became one seven months later; the conflict that began soon after Buchanan's inauguration was not the result of one or more conspiracies, although by year-end 1857 the president was engaged in solitary scheming to further Manifest Destiny that today opens him to perceptions of such behavior.

In April 1858 the editor of the Mormon newspaper in Liverpool recognized the importance of this timing issue and used it to argue that "Congress should not have called upon the Administration [in January] for information as to whether the people of Utah *are* in rebellion; but it should, with the stern spirit of justice, have demanded information as to whether the people of Utah *were* in rebellion at the time that Government dispatched an expedition to subdue that people by military force." Stepping over the true nature of the Utah Expedition's orders in the spring of 1857, the role of free agency and personal responsibility implicit in Brigham Young's behavior, and the fratricide committed by his Nauvoo Legion during the fall (including at Mountain Meadows), the editor concluded Buchanan's actions had driven "the people to the attitude of self-defence and indignant protestation against being made the victims of extermination and wholesale slaughter." Under this perverse chain of logic, Old Buck, if not the devil, made them do it.[3]

Before leaving matters of definition, it is appropriate to ask whether this conflict—rebellion or not—was truly a war. For a variety of reasons, including its frustrations over the political character of the conflict's outcome, the institutional army as well as some military historians have avoided this term in favor of descriptors like "campaign" or "expedition." To me, these labels fall short in conveying the importance of what took place while seeming

[3] "Buchanan's Report on the Utah Rebellion," Editorial, *Millennial Star* (Liverpool), 3 April 1858, 214.

to exclude the fact that there was a Mormon as well as federal involvement. Admittedly there were neither pitched battles by massed troops nor a congressional declaration of war, but this guerrilla conflict did involve two clearly opposing sides fielding substantial armed forces, occasional exchanges of gunfire, significant (in one case even unprecedented) atrocities, the involvement of more than a dozen Indian tribes, indictments for treason and murder, a presidential pardon for an entire territory, economy-busting military expenditures, a massive flow of refugees, and bloodshed comparable and contemporaneous to that in Kansas. When one considers also the alarm and defensive actions of six foreign governments, as well as the size of the Utah Expedition and Nauvoo Legion and the scope, range, and character of their operations, war is an appropriate, common-sense term to use. This is how we speak of the West's nineteenth-century Indian conflicts; why should Utah be different? To avoid the word "war" to describe the armed confrontation between the Nauvoo Legion and Utah Expedition during the late 1850s is to exchange plain-spokenness for the type of indirection that would later dub the Korean War of 1950–53 a police action.

Leaders' Accountability

Who bore what responsibility for starting, prosecuting, and ending the Utah War? Because of its decade-long gestation period, the conflict's origins involved multiple leaders on both sides. Their overt acts and misjudgments led to missed opportunities for mid-course corrections as Mormon-federal relations deteriorated. Salt Lake City's Beehive House as well as Washington's Executive Mansion and Capitol Hill were all culpable in the onset of the Utah War, but it would be a mistake to assume that the responsibility should be distributed equally among them.

Within a year of nominating Brigham Young as Utah's first governor and superintendent of Indian affairs, the sensational 1851–52 affair of the "runaway officials" prompted President Fillmore to revisit this appointment by insisting that Thomas L. Kane justify his influential endorsement of Young in 1850. In doing so, Kane and then Fillmore again supported an appointment flawed from the beginning. It was an arrangement that concentrated the power of multiple overlapping offices in a territorial executive whose prime allegiance was to his religious role rather than to the federal government he swore to serve. Compounding Fillmore's misjudgments was President Pierce's fecklessness in not appointing an even-handed governor to succeed Young when his term ended in the fall of 1854. Beset by personal demons of alcohol and family tragedy, as well as the political uproar unleashed by his approval of the Kansas-Nebraska Act, Pierce was embarrassed by Colonel Steptoe's decision to decline Utah's governorship. Deciding to avoid the political risk of sending another nomination to the U.S. Senate, Pierce left Young in office on a de facto basis through the mechanism of a day-to-day continuance. With this uncourageous approach to troubled territorial leadership, Franklin Pierce left resolution of the Mormon problem to his successor.

As Presidents Fillmore and Pierce grappled with the leadership controversy in Utah, they continued to appoint other officers for the territory who lacked the requisite character, tact, and judgment. Contemporaneously, Congress aggravated this shortfall by neglecting its responsibility to oversee the acts of Utah's legislative assembly as provided by the territory's 1850 Organic Act. Even more serious was Congress's short-sightedness in failing both to provide the right of preemption for Utah's residents and to remedy this early mistake when repeatedly petitioned to do so by settlers desperate to acquire title to the property upon which they squatted and toiled without federal sanction. This land issue constituted one of the most explosive and unnecessary territorial-federal pinch points during the long run-up to the Utah War.

Eventually Congress did sever the office of superintendent of Indian affairs from the territory's governorship, but this salutary change came only in the closing days of President Pierce's administration. Consequently, Young's successor in this role, Superintendent Jacob Forney, did not reach Utah until November 1857, and then only under the auspices of the U.S. Army. By the time James Buchanan took office, serious damage in Indian relations had already occurred amidst accusations that Latter-day Saints had long fostered an unhealthy distinction in the tribes between settlers and non-Mormons while subverting Indians' allegiance to the United States. These were distinctions that Brigham Young argued occurred naturally but were aggravated by emigrants' abusive behavior toward Indians en route to the Pacific Coast.

Notwithstanding the contributions by successive presidents and Congress to the deterioration in territorial-federal relations, their acts and omissions paled in comparison to the long-term impact of the negative leadership exercised by Brigham Young. Young's 8 May 1853 public discourse advocating summary execution for thieves, his provocative role in the violence of the February 1857 Ambrose-Betts affair, and his five-week abandonment of Utah for a foray into Oregon Territory—all rendered him unfit to continue as a territorial governor. After years of presidential neglect, it fell to James Buchanan to confront the controversies surrounding Utah's supreme leader. He did so in the spring of 1857.

If President Buchanan acted appropriately in superseding Brigham Young, his decision to do so without formal notification and by appointing Alfred Cumming was seriously flawed. Compounding this misjudgment was Buchanan's acquiescence in Secretary Floyd's selection of General Harney as the Utah Expedition's initial commander, a role for which Harney was as ill-suited as Cumming, Floyd, and even General Scott were for theirs. That the administration then drafted instructions to Harney and Cumming that ran to cross purposes aggravated these leadership shortfalls, as did Buchanan's subsequent silence on whether the Utah Expedition's reinforcements were to be regular or volunteer troops. James Buchanan did not blunder in replacing Brigham Young, but he surely faltered in executing his decision.

Secretary of War John B. Floyd's contribution to the war was that of an enabler rather than a cabinet officer challenging or tempering Buchanan's misjudgments about the campaign. At the same time Floyd overrode, if not ignored, General Scott's military judgment while encouraging a continuation of the dysfunctional, self-imposed exile of "Old Fuss 'n' Feathers" in New York. All of this Floyd did with a lax, perhaps corrupt, administrative style that at year-end 1860 led to his resignation in a scandal over the financing of the Utah Expedition and an indictment for malfeasance in office. Small wonder that, after a conflicted session with Floyd in April 1858 Capt. Montgomery C. Meigs, an army engineer, noted, "he seemed to be in a good humor, but he is one of the men who, I doubt not, can smile and smile and cut your throat. I have no confidence in him. I know that he does things which in my view of morality are dishonest. . . . [I do not know] whether he has a perverted moral sense or none at all."[4]

Responsibility for transforming into a rebellion this jointly created, conflict-ridden relationship between Utah Territory and the U.S. government rested solely with Brigham Young. That in the midst of this transformation a battalion of Young's militia and its Indian auxiliaries committed the

[4]Meigs, *Capitol Builder*, 20 April 1858, 611.

Mountain Meadows massacre was an event for which he also was culpable, although I am not persuaded that Young overtly ordered the atrocity. In this sense my view is akin to Young's most recent non-Mormon biographer, who concludes, "there is no satisfactory evidence that Young ordered the massacre."[5] If this were a jury trial rather than a documentary history, it seems to me that on this issue a Scotch verdict of not proven would be a more appropriate assessment of Young's conduct than one of guilty or not guilty. I realize that this view is more nuanced than the blunt, succinct essays titled "Brigham Young Did It" and "No He Didn't" published in 2003 by historians Will Bagley and Ronald W. Walker.[6]

Shortly after returning home from Utah, Thomas L. Kane provided his brother Pat with an account of his experiences. This material included a reference to wrongdoing by Brigham Young that was as enigmatic as it was brief. Would that we could determine whether Kane meant Young's role in the Mountain Meadows tragedy in calling him a "sheep" that "went astray at one time" and identifying the timing of his lapse as "a certain day last fall." Tom Kane rarely criticized Mormons and virtually never discussed Brigham Young's short suits. Did these cryptic comments to a brother who was his closest confidant refer to an appalling massacre on 11 September 1857, Young's proclamation of martial law four days later, or some other misstep that took the then-governor of Utah and his flock across what I have called a Rubicon to rebellion? We will never know Kane's meaning, but that does not mean one cannot speculate.[7]

What is clear to me is that ten years of Young's negative leadership, capped by his September 1857 authorization for tribal raids on emigrants' cattle, established a climate of violence and provocations in Utah that made the massacre possible, if not probable. The subsequent conspiracy to conceal what happened, while vilifying the victims, deprived them and their survivors of justice for centuries. In this cover-up, Brigham Young was complicit—and more so than the other leaders who followed him into this shameful obfuscation.

What responsibility did Thomas L. Kane bear in all this? Kane, of course, entered the Utah War in mid-conflict. After tentative, unsuccessful attempts

[5]Turner, *Brigham Young, Pioneer Prophet,* 280.

[6]Bagley and Walker in "Did Brigham Young Order a Massacre?" *True West,* 1 April 2003.

[7]Kane to R. P. Kane, undated ms., "In Re Mormons" File, Thomas Leiper Kane Papers, APS.

to stay Buchanan's hand during the spring and fall of 1857, he withdrew from Mormon affairs but then returned to the fray at year-end in an attempt to preclude further bloodshed. For reasons rooted in his complex psyche and family history, Kane undertook a mission to Utah wholly on his own initiative and at a personal cost that he could ill afford. He did so without presidential support other than two letters of introduction provided by Buchanan that essentially wished Kane well while making clear that he was not a government agent. Contrary to Kane's later assertion that Buchanan had verbally empowered him to recommend executive pardons for deserving Mormons, there is no evidence that the president had done so, and none was granted on an individual basis other than in the case of William R. R. Stowell, in which Kane was uninvolved.

At the heart of the president's post-Christmas meeting with Kane and James C. Van Dyke was Buchanan's desire to maintain what I have called plausible deniability—the ability to distance himself from Kane's mission should it fail or turn controversial. It was consistent with Buchanan's leadership style that he withheld from Kane (as well as Congress and General Scott) his contemporaneous plans to purchase Cuba from Spain or to acquire it by force after stimulating a mass Mormon exodus into northern Mexico by opening a second front against Utah from the Pacific Coast.

Once into Utah, Kane pursued his mission with a combination of courage, secretiveness, and collaboration with Young that would have enraged Buchanan had he realized it. While ingratiating himself with Brigham Young and Alfred Cumming, Kane needlessly destroyed his relationship with Albert Sidney Johnston. Under these circumstances, though, Kane brought off his signal contribution to resolving the standoff in Utah: inducing Cumming to travel with him to Salt Lake City without army support. From this high-profile gesture much else followed, including Kane's subsequent campaign to preserve Cumming's political viability by arguing that his trek to Salt Lake City constituted a noble, heroic devotion to duty warranting his indefinite retention as governor.

Notwithstanding the significance of the Cumming-Kane journey to Salt Lake City, the fact is that several other crucial events leading to the war's resolution fell into place without Kane's involvement or even presence. Foremost among these were the peace commissioners' discussions with Brigham Young and their proffer of Buchanan's proclamation of pardon. Unaware of what

Kane was doing other than the fact that he had reached Utah, the president had unilaterally launched a strategy independent of Kane by which the active phase of the Utah War indeed came to an end without further bloodshed.

If Thomas L. Kane deserves credit for managing Alfred Cumming's travel to Salt Lake City and Brigham Young's technical acceptance of him as the territory's governor, Kane could also behave less admirably. At times his penchant for manipulation was extreme to a fault, as Kane himself was aware. As early as 1850 he confessed to Young that he was struggling to lose "almost entirely the natural love for intrigue and management once a prominent trait of my character," but two years later he admitted a lack of success in the effort to his father-in-law: "I am by nature unscrupulous, a low animal cunning, a natural proneness to even unnecessary intrigue and artifice, are among the inherent defects of my character."[8]

A prime example of this behavior in 1858 was the cynical way in which he positioned Cumming for intimidation—a fish delivered by Kane and to be cooked as Young chose. Kane stoked the Cumming-Johnston enmity by masking his discussions with the governor about foregoing an army escort to Salt Lake City and by confining courier service between the two officers to Mormon messengers, an exclusivity that Kane knew infuriated Johnston. At the same time, Kane sowed the seeds for a split among Buchanan's other appointees by alienating Cumming from Eckels while criticizing the judge to congressional leaders and Buchanan. Kane also encouraged an alliance between Cumming and Superintendent Forney to add to the burgeoning Cumming-Young affinity. This divide enabled Young to keep Utah's federal establishment in turmoil for years.

Complementing this duplicity and divisiveness was Kane's manufacture of the myth of conflicting war and peace factions atop the Mormon hierarchy. Here was a fiction that cast Brigham Young in the counterintuitive role of the Utah Expedition's protector, standing in opposition to a Nauvoo Legion and Standing Army led by a shadowy faction of unnamed aggressors barely under Young's control. Louis Bertrand, the French journalist and Mormon convert, knew Brigham Young personally and was in Utah during the war. In assessing the way Young ruled the territory, Bertrand thought about the Old Testament and commented, "the authority of Moses was constantly

[8]Grow and Walker, eds., *The Prophet and the Reformer*, 76.

challenged by the descendants of Jacob while he was yet alive. That of Brigham over modern Israel is sovereign and limitless."[9] Brother Bertrand had it right.

Kane's success in convincing Cumming and Fay Worthen of the war-peace story and then using them to merchandise it to the nation's newspaper editors, as well as Secretary Cass, Speaker Orr, Senator Mason, and President Buchanan, permitted the latter to declare victory prematurely. With this announcement in place, the president reduced the army's presence in Utah during the summer of 1858, and then abandoned support for many of his appointees to the territory during 1859 in a way that largely undercut his initial resolve to restore federal authority in Utah.

Finally, there was Kane's notable lack of interest during 1857–58 (and thereafter) in obtaining justice for the 120 victims of the Mountain Meadows massacre and their 17 child-survivors. For Kane, Mountain Meadows was a blind spot inconsistent with his lifelong reputation as a humanitarian. In that insensitivity and the cover-up that it facilitated, he shared culpability with other leaders on both sides, including Brigham Young, George A. Smith, Alfred Cumming, Albert Sidney Johnston, and even James Buchanan.

Alfred Cumming's principal contribution to resolution of the Utah War's active phase was his courageous trek to Salt Lake City without military escort to assert his claim to Utah's governorship. A fact that is overlooked today is that he did so while fearful that he may have been infected with rabies. Once ensconced in Salt Lake City, Cumming compromised himself by serving as a fig leaf for the notion that federal authority had been fully restored in Utah and that Brigham Young was abiding by the less-than-clear understandings reached with Commissioners Powell and McCulloch. Cumming's indiscretion in sharing the instructions issued to him and the commissioners by the Buchanan administration, as well as his betrayal of the confidences of Mormon dissidents seeking federal protection, signaled ethical lapses and future trouble for the Mormon-federal relationship. At one point in the spring of 1858, the Legion's senior officers became aware that Cumming intended to undertake a Mountain Meadows fact-finding trip to southern Utah, but this journey and inquiry never happened. The theory that Cumming changed his plans because he struck an accommodation with

[9] Homer, *On the Way to Somewhere Else,* 113.

Young on 24 April is intriguing but as yet unproven. For whatever reasons, Utah's governor, like Kane and others, turned a blind eye to the massacre, although later a visually impaired Judge John Cradlebaugh did not.

Clouding the matter of Cumming's behavior and decision-making was his fondness for alcohol, an affinity about which many in Utah gossiped, including army troops, Young, and Kane. It was an important issue rather than a harmless peccadillo. At stake was the question of whether James Buchanan had selected an officer in poor health with impaired judgment for an arduous position in the midst of a distant, complex environment calling for stamina, tact, consummate good judgment, and effective leadership. The overwhelming evidence is that Cumming was a well-intended but under-powered governor whom many of his new constituents mocked. Within weeks of arriving in Utah, one New York reporter wrote, "Indeed, in both Governor and Secretary the Administration has been peculiarly unfortunate, as time will eventually show. Surely Mr. Buchanan might find men to fill Federal offices who would be a credit rather than a disgrace to the country—men of whom it could not be said, as it is of the Governor, that he is 'a whisky barrel in the morning, and a barrel of whisky at night.' "[10] How, if at all, Brigham Young used his awareness of Cumming's untoward advances on the Staines mansion's female servants is unclear.

Of all the senior leaders involved in the Utah War, Albert Sidney Johnston was the one least open to perceptions of serious culpability. Ordered to Washington from Texas without an awareness of whether his new assignment would be to pacify Kansas or command the Utah Expedition, Johnston then rushed toward Utah, superseding the indecision and misjudgments of Col. Edmund B. Alexander to lead his troops to the shelter of Fort Bridger. He did so with a strength of leadership and willingness to share hardship that earned him the admiration of his troops as well as a promotion by brevet. If Johnston later became aware of Winfield Scott's failed attempt to subordinate him to Brevet Maj. Gen. John E. Wool, Johnston possessed the self-confidence to ignore this strange gambit, just as he dealt maturely with the War Department's subsequent decisions to supersede him first

[10]Unsigned dispatch [probably Simonton], 4 August 1858, *New York Times,* 28 August 1858. In 1855 an army officer at Fort Benton estimated Cumming's weight at nearly three hundred pounds and described his inability to descend a hill without the help of an Indian squaw, who placed him on a blanket and carried him down. Bradley, "Affairs at Fort Benton," 277.

with Brevet Maj. Gen. Persifor F. Smith and then with Harney. Johnston's handling of the Utah Expedition's march through Salt Lake City and his decision on the location of Camp Floyd drew plaudits from even Brigham Young. They were demonstrations of leadership supportive of all that Kane, Cumming, and the peace commissioners had done to reassure Young about the intentions of the U.S. government.

There were, of course, those who, along with Brigham Young, Thomas L. Kane, Sam Houston, and James Buchanan, criticized Johnston for his November 1857 rejection of eight hundred pounds of salt proffered by Young. This decision by a commander in the field was a minor matter, albeit one loaded with symbolism that opened Johnston to attacks by distant armchair critics. If Albert Sidney Johnston deserved criticism, it was over his handling of two issues more important than the salt imbroglio or the timing of his march toward Salt Lake City: determining the facts of the Mountain Meadows massacre, and the use of tribal allies to support the Utah Expedition's operations.

A fairly accurate account of the massacre had reached Johnston on the Sweetwater River as early as the third week of October 1857 with the arrival of Indian Agent Garland Hurt and his Ute guides. A month later, Johnston was at Fort Bridger with Hurt and the new leaders of Utah's criminal justice system: Governor Cumming, U.S. Attorney Hockaday, U.S. Marshal Dotson, and Chief Justice Eckels. There is no sign that these military and civilian officers discussed their responsibility to investigate what was clearly a major atrocity executed in their jurisdiction with Mormon complicity, if not instigation. That Johnston never mentioned these or any other killings to General Scott, Adjutant General Cooper, or Secretary Floyd strikes a twenty-first-century analyst as a disengagement uncharacteristic of Johnston. It is likely that in the wilderness of northeastern Utah, Albert Sidney Johnston viewed reports of the Mountain Meadows massacre as unverified, the responsibility of the administration's civilian departments, or an unwelcome distraction from his main mission. If so, it was a judgment that neither added distinction to Johnston's reputation nor squared with his subsequent compassion in providing services withheld by Brigham Young: a Christian burial for the massacre's victims, as well as an armed escort and comfortable eastbound transportation home for their child-survivors.

As with Johnston's disinterest in who had done what at Mountain Meadows, his willingness to use the tribes of northeastern Utah and perhaps southeastern Oregon to support the Utah Expedition is puzzling. It was a tactic at odds with the army's then-cultural taboo against recruitment of such auxiliaries. Johnston's dispatch of Ben Ficklin's party to the Flathead country in late December 1857, and the mission of Garland Hurt to the Uintas' winter encampment a few weeks later, were provocative moves that opened the colonel to Mormon perceptions of army scalp hunting. In April 1858, when news of the Bannock and Northern Shoshone raid on Fort Limhi reached Johnston, together with Mormon accusations of army responsibility, his denial—bolstered by a supportive affidavit from W. M. F. Magraw and Jim Bridger—lacked credibility. Both men were Johnston's subordinates, and each had had well-known personal conflicts with the Mormons. Johnston's abrupt cancellation of plans to engage Chief Washakie's Shoshones to operate and defend the Green River ferries—an arrangement never disclosed to army headquarters—smacked of a commander eager to abandon an ill-conceived alliance once it became controversial in the wake of the Fort Limhi massacre. It was in this volatile arena of Indian affairs that Johnston, like Brigham Young, strayed into problematic tactics.

Even as the general marched through Salt Lake City on 26 June, Young continued to flog the notion of a murderous connection between Johnston, Hurt's visit to the Uintas, and the loss of Mormon lives and herds. To Bishop Warren Snow he confided, "General Johnston should send a messenger and notify his famous Indian allies that their amiable services can be dispensed with. It appears that the plan was for them to come in ahead and get located in the midst of the settlements, and then when the men were drawn away to fight the troops, butcher the women and children. Christian civilized warfare. O how we do admire it."[11]

A Conflict Irrepressible or Preventable?

Given the foregoing, it is appropriate to ask a variation of the question that has preoccupied Civil War historians for decades: was the armed confrontation in Utah inevitable—an irrepressible conflict—or was it avoidable? In 1860 Brigham Young reportedly delivered a discourse in which he characterized the Utah War's clash between Mormonism and its enemies as of

[11]Young to Snow, 26 June 1858, LDS Archives.

the "irrepressible" kind, but from the context it is unclear if he used this label in its modern historiographical sense.[12] In 1886 historian Edward W. Tullidge wrote of an "irrepressible conflict" in the 1850s between Governor Young and Utah's non-Mormon federal appointees, but Tullidge's phrasing may have been influenced by the language of the ongoing debate among historians over the Civil War's preventability.[13]

Surely before James Buchanan took office, Brigham Young, Millard Fillmore, Franklin Pierce, and congressional leaders had it within their power to alter the flow of events to mitigate the steady deterioration in Mormon-federal relations that would await "Old Buck" on 4 March 1857. These officers failed in this responsibility—not because such mid-course corrections were impossible, but rather because their worldview and limited leadership skills caused them to falter before the challenge.

In Utah, after decades of persecution elsewhere, Brigham Young was in a position of power so distant from federal supervision that he acted and spoke without inhibitions. In the process, he lost sight of the fact that he was not solely a private citizen or religious leader, but was also a sworn federal official with so many overlapping roles—governor, superintendent of Indian affairs, militia commander—that he was responsible for the protection of every person in Utah, irrespective of background or status. So imperious had Young's behavior grown by 1857 that his most recent biography is titled *Brigham Young: Sovereign in America.*[14]

Aggravating Young's shortsightedness and negative leadership was the proclivity of successive presidents and the U.S. Senate to send inappropriate officers to governmental positions in a territory that above all others required first-rate talent. The steady flow of neophytes, hacks, alcoholics, and opportunists to Salt Lake City fueled Brigham Young's contempt for the U.S. government and stimulated his proclivity for autocratic, provocative behavior. The absence of an army post in Utah, at a time when every other frontier state and territory on its periphery had such a military presence,

[12]"From Utah," Dispatch, 24 August 1860, *New York Times,* 20 September 1860, 5/2. The newspaper reporter described Young's remarks as part of a discourse delivered in Salt Lake City's Bowery on 19 August 1860, but the definitive transcript of Young's preaching that Sunday and on ones bracketing that date does not include such a discussion. Van Wagoner, ed., *Complete Discourses of Brigham Young,* 12, 19, and 26 August 1860, 3:1628–38.

[13]Tullidge, *The History of Salt Lake City and Its Founders,* 139.

[14]Mason, *Brigham Young: Sovereign in America.*

meant the federal government that had sent them west left Utah's underpowered civilian officials vulnerable to gubernatorial intimidation. During the Fillmore administration, the imbroglio of the "runaway officials" was a warning signal unheeded; in Franklin Pierce's administration, the expiration of Young's term in September 1854 presented an opportunity lost. The dynamics were such that Brigham Young never dealt with strong, able, incorruptible representatives of the U.S. government whom he could neither intimidate nor compromise until confronted by Lazarus Powell, Ben McCulloch, and Albert Sidney Johnston in June 1858.[15]

The cumulative effect of these preventable but unresolved conflicts, plus the politicization of the polygamy issue in 1856 and the determination of most territorial appointees to flee Utah in the spring of 1857, made Buchanan's removal of Brigham Young both necessary and probable. Nonetheless, this move alone need not have touched off a Mormon rebellion. Buchanan could have handled the change in leadership without provoking Young into crossing the Rubicon as he did in September–October 1857, and Young, under pressure, could have responded nonviolently.

For his part, Young had started 1857 by expressing to Kane the belief and hope that President-elect Buchanan was a leader with whom he could work. What Young then failed to do was to reach out to Buchanan by communicating with him in writing or in person. Later, well after the die was cast, Buchanan told Delegate Bernhisel that the Utah War could have been avoided if he and Young had met face to face for two hours. Perhaps in today's era of rapid transportation, electronic communications, and displays of shuttle diplomacy, such a session would have been possible, but in the spring of 1857 a meeting between Young and Buchanan would have been problematic for reasons of logistics as well as culture.

Prior to the Civil War, presidents of the United States rarely left Washington, and during his term Buchanan did so only occasionally to visit summer resorts in the mountains of Pennsylvania. Although he had traveled extensively in Europe as minister to Russia and Great Britain, Buchanan never saw the United States west of Pittsburgh. Brigham Young, in turn, was averse to leaving Utah because of his morbid fear of arrest and assassination; fundamentally he never left the intermountain West once he returned to Salt Lake City from his second trip across the plains in 1848.

[15]Perhaps the sole exception was Indian Agent Garland Hurt, who had arrived in Utah during 1855.

Yet if Brigham Young declined to resolve Utah's problems by meeting with the president in Washington or elsewhere, say in St. Louis or New Orleans, he was willing to travel long distances for other purposes, even in the stormy weather of a western spring. During April–May 1857, Young traveled nearly a thousand miles over a five-week period to visit the Mormon outpost at Fort Limhi, Oregon Territory. Had he invested an equivalent amount of time and energy to meet with Buchanan or a member of his cabinet in an accessible location, Young's departure from Utah's governorship might have been smoother and less confrontational. Put bluntly, Young was temperamentally unable to do what an ailing Thomas L. Kane later accomplished in making the round-trip trek between Philadelphia and Salt Lake City during January–June 1858.

Technically, then, the Utah War was preventable, but the ingrained sense of self and the stunted communications behavior of James Buchanan and Brigham Young prevented them from reaching out to one another to air grievances, seek common ground, and modify behavior. The month that Franklin Pierce took office in 1853, Young sent him a long letter of commentary about Utah affairs, including the future of the territory's governorship. Young never did likewise or communicated directly with James Buchanan, insisting instead on using Delegate Bernhisel and Thomas L. Kane as intermediaries or proxies. Buchanan reciprocated this standoffishness, although in 1859, when war threatened to erupt between Great Britain and the United States over a border incident in the Pacific Northwest, the president did not hesitate to send an aging, virtually immobile Winfield Scott to the San Juan Islands by steamer to negotiate a successful resolution of the conflict. Perhaps Buchanan did so then because of what he had learned from the lack of face-to-face diplomacy with Brigham Young during the Utah War. If so, the lesson came too late to help Utah, and Brigham Young, supremely self-confident and unrestrained in his isolation, was unwilling to make the effort to engage Buchanan directly during 1857–58.[16]

For Brigham Young and James Buchanan, preventing the Utah War would have been difficult but possible.

[16]During the 1840s Scott had been instrumental in negotiating a settlement with Great Britain in the Aroostook War, the dispute over the Maine–New Brunswick border. It is interesting to contemplate what, if anything, a Scott-Young meeting in San Diego might have accomplished in the spring of 1857. Kaufman and Soares, "'Sagacious Beyond Praise'?" 57–82.

Winners and Losers

The Utah War had no winners; there were only losers. Mormon folklore has long portrayed the Utah Expedition's uncomfortable winter, spent amidst the charred ruins of Fort Bridger on short rations, as a circumstance forced upon it by a victorious Nauvoo Legion. The fact is that what drove Johnston's decision to bivouac at Bridger, rather than to press on to Salt Lake City in November 1857, was severe weather, deep snow, and a massive loss of animals rather than a triumph of Mormon arms or strategy.

Similar attempts to characterize the Move South as a carefully devised public-relations gambit and military tactic overlook this thrust's improvised, ad hoc nature as a desperate response to federal pressure from all directions. The Move South had a devastating economic and family impact on a Mormon population already burdened by daunting requirements to support the Nauvoo Legion and the Standing Army of Israel; it did so just as Utah's settlers should have been engaged in spring planting. Notwithstanding the welcome cash infusion associated with the building of Camp Floyd, it took Utah years to recover from the disruptions and dislocations associated with the Move South. Brigham Young's contemporaneous dispatch of expeditions to locate large oases of refuge in the White Mountains and along the Colorado River were equally failed gambits driven by Young's need for action and his imperfect grasp of the region's geography and the realities of Mojave hostility.

By the same token, Mormon characterizations of Brigham Young's meeting with Buchanan's peace commissioners as negotiating sessions, during which hard bargaining by Young extracted favorable terms from the U.S. government, missed the point of what happened. Commissioners Powell and McCulloch controlled these discussions in unyielding fashion and extended Buchanan's pardon on a federally dictated take-it-or-leave-it basis. What took place amidst Mormon bluster and bravado during the second week of June 1858 (and thereafter) was, in effect, Brigham Young's humiliating acceptance of terms drafted by James Buchanan in Washington and preprinted by an army field press in Kansas. As Captain Marcy had so aptly put it from the distance of New Mexico, "the Mormons . . . will not give us a fight, it is all gas as sure as you are born . . . the Mormons boast a great deal of what they intend to do, but they do not execute their boasts."

Unquestionably the greatest war loss sustained by the Mormon side was the enduring stain to the LDS church's reputation caused by its members' involvement in the Mountain Meadows massacre and subsequent cover-up. It is an albatross that still burdens the church notwithstanding quantum enhancements to its image during the intervening 150 years. Accompanying this disastrous episode was the damage to Brigham Young's personal reputation as the supreme leader on whose watch such an appalling atrocity occurred, a blow dwarfing even his removal as governor and indictment (but not trial) for treason as well as murder.

Although James Buchanan succeeded in his goal of replacing Brigham Young as Utah's governor, the restoration of federal authority that he sought was flawed and delayed. This shortfall was a product of Brigham Young's intimidation of Governor Cumming and success in engineering a split in Utah's federal establishment, as well as of Buchanan's premature acceptance of Young as a positive, continuing influence in the territory.

Buchanan too suffered a loss of personal reputation as a result of the war, falling victim to a successful Mormon campaign to ridicule him as a blunderer who initiated a military campaign that Mormons believed never should have occurred.

If any individuals emerged as heroes from the Utah War, my candidates are Capt. Randolph B. Marcy of the Fifth U.S. Infantry and Maj. Howard Egan of the Nauvoo Legion.

In the case of Marcy's trek to New Mexico and back, the character of his leadership under arduous circumstances and the value of his success to the Utah Expedition's mission are obvious. General Scott's public commendation of Marcy and his private recommendation for promotion to major by brevet—the only such nomination during the war other than Johnston's—speak volumes about the general in chief's view of this feat. Why Secretary Floyd failed to act on Scott's recommendation and why the general declined to persist in the matter (as he had done to secure Johnston's brevet), remains one of the war's mysteries.[17]

---

[17]Floyd's (and perhaps Buchanan's) unwillingness to brevet Marcy in 1858 was consistent with his earlier decision not to promote Harney and Philip St. George Cooke despite a favorable recommendation inherited from Jefferson Davis, his predecessor, on which President Pierce had refused to act. As Davis left the War Department on 3 March 1857, he attributed Pierce's decision to "his general objection to entering into the [controversial] question of Brevet promotions." There is no sign that Floyd or Buchanan had a similar aversion to brevet promotions, and, of course, they authorized one for Johnston in 1858 retroactive to November 1857. Notwithstanding this mixed, confusing record on brevets, Floyd and Buchanan promoted Harney and Cooke in regular fashion to substantive grades later in 1858 in the wake of General Smith's death, and they also did so for Marcy in 1859 when a regular opening occurred in the paymaster's department, enabling them to advance Marcy to major. Davis, memorandum to war dept. files, 3 March 1857, *The Papers of Jefferson Davis,* 6:111–12.

On the surface, Howard Egan might seem an unlikely hero. He was, after all, the defendant in one of Utah's first murder trials in 1851 and a prominent member of Brigham Young's inner circle of rough operatives dubbed the "b'hoys." But in Howard Egan's case, still waters ran deep, and he served the Mormon side of the war in important, hazardous assignments ranging from acquiring gunpowder in California to escorting Thomas L. Kane first to Fort Bridger and then to Philadelphia. That Egan did so dependably and without the flamboyance of homicidal peers like Porter Rockwell and Bill Hickman may have been what prompted Brigham Young to select him repeatedly for such independent assignments. During the Utah War, no Nauvoo Legion officer traveled as extensively and alone across unfriendly territory as did Egan. Emblematically, as Major Egan waited for weeks at the Kanes' home to courier dispatches to Brigham Young during June 1858, Elizabeth Kane was so captivated by his dignified, rough-hewn demeanor that she insisted on photographing him. Egan's postwar role in operating the Pony Express west of Salt Lake City is well known; historians need to understand as thoroughly his remarkable exploits during 1857–58.[18]

The War's Significance

Above all else, the war changed Utah forever, altering its Mormon-to-gentile population balance while propelling the territory from its cultural isolation, stimulating the establishment of independent newspapers, and signaling the need to complete transcontinental telegraph and rail lines, as indeed took place in or near Salt Lake City during 1861 and 1869. Utah, of course, never took on the secular flavor of society in California, but with the arrival of the Utah Expedition and its thousands of soldiers and camp followers, the Salt Lake City and Utah of December 1858 were on their way to becoming far more cosmopolitan places than the controlled, isolated Kingdom in the West to which Brigham Young returned from Fort Limhi on 28 May 1857, the day on which Winfield Scott announced formation of the Utah Expedition.

Among the war's immediate byproducts was Brigham Young's judgment that the Civil War was not a Mormon fight. While understandable in view of what had taken place during 1857–58, Young's decision to opt out of that

[18]We may hope that historian William G. Hartley's pending biography of Egan will provide such an understanding.

conflict differentiated Utah from every other American state and territory, while prolonging national doubts about its support for the Union until the Utah National Guard's active participation in the Spanish-American War. With Utah's contribution to the Union Army limited to a single cavalry company that served for only ninety days, it fell largely to a brigade of California volunteers and a regiment of Confederate parolees, rather than Mormon troops, to protect the territory during and immediately after the Civil War. Meanwhile President Abraham Lincoln struggled to finance the war with the Treasury and national credit worthiness ravaged by the enormous cost of James Buchanan's Utah conflict.[19]

Among the least examined of the Utah War's impacts was its likely diminishment of James Buchanan's appetite for dealing decisively with Southern secession during the winter of 1860–61. Three years earlier "Old Buck" had been politically and militarily embarrassed when a territorial-federal dispute morphed unexpectedly into a dramatic Mormon rebellion with wide-ranging implications. In December 1857 the president told Congress, "This is the first rebellion which has existed in our Territories; and humanity itself requires that we should put it down in such a manner that it shall be the last." Buchanan did not carry this resolve forward in his dealings with South Carolina and the disaffected sister states as the nation slid toward the bloodbath of disunion on his watch.[20] Whether and how this experience early in Buchanan's presidency affected his handling of the secession crisis at the end of his administration warrants serious examination. Such a study lies beyond the scope of *At Sword's Point,* although it is tempting to hypothesize such a connection to encourage further study.[21]

While the Utah War's military phase ran its course in late June 1858, the *New York Herald*'s on-scene correspondent turned flippant. Chocked by dust clouds and beset with the inconvenience of an empty city, reporter Lemuel Fillmore dismissed the conflict with a quip: "Thus was peace made—thus was ended the 'Mormon war,' which, *mirable dictu,* was much less sanguinary and direful than the 'Kansas war,' and may thus be summarily historized:—killed, none; wounded, none; fooled, everybody."[22] As a Kansas realtor in

[19]Flaherty, "Exhausted Condition of the Treasury," 245–47.

[20]Buchanan, "First Annual Message to Congress," 8 December 1857, Moore, ed., *Works of James Buchanan,* 10:129–63.

[21]MacKinnon, "Prelude to Armageddon," 78.

[22][Fillmore], "How Peace Was Made," Dispatch, 19 June 1858, *New York Herald,* 19 July 1858, 1/6, 2/1–6.

search of adventure, Fillmore had just arrived in Salt Lake City and was perhaps the reporter least qualified to make such a pronouncement. A month later he was on an eastbound stage, returning home to Kansas in the wake of a knife fight in a Provo hotel over slavery rather than Mormonism with rival correspondent James W. Simonton, who, in turn, soon left the territory for San Francisco.[23] When published anonymously in New York, Fillmore's offhand comment circulated widely and stuck. No one then and few people today realize who wrote this assessment—one still used to trivialize the war, ridicule its leaders, and trowel over unpleasant complexities such as 120 bodies indifferently buried at Mountain Meadows.

In its own way, Lemuel Fillmore's catchy dispatch started the long, undeserved obscurity from which the full story of the Utah War is still emerging. Viewed in the light of documentary discoveries and rigorous analysis, it is the tale of an unprecedented territorial-federal conflict worth understanding, one with continental and even international sweep. Rooted in a long-simmering political dispute over governance and provocative rhetoric, it morphed into armed confrontation, rebellion, and war. Along the way, the Utah War became a farrago of bloodshed, recriminations, damaged reputations, economy-busting costs, Manifest Destiny, geographical discovery, diplomatic anxieties, and personal epiphanies for a vast array of heroes, villains, and ordinary folk.

To understand the conflict is to probe a dark but significant chapter of the convoluted, even quirky, development of America's fastest growing religion, as well as the West's secular Sagebrush Rebellion as it still plays out under Mormon leadership in places such as Grand Staircase–Escalante, Utah; Bundyville, Nevada; and Harney County, Oregon. As with the Spanish Civil War eighty years later, the Utah War became a proving ground for the men, materiel, tactics, and weapons used in a gigantic conflict soon to follow. Small wonder that it was a war which Capts. George B. McClellan, William Tecumseh Sherman, and P. G. T. Beauregard were as eager to enter as Lt. Col. Robert E. Lee was anxious to avoid. Students of Mormonism, the frontier, and antebellum America need to seize the opportunity to join "Cump" Sherman and Thomas ("Doctor Osborne") Kane at the rail of the S.S. *Moses Taylor*—steaming west toward Mormon Utah to pursue their shared hopes for redemption.

---

[23]For conflicting accounts of this brawl and which reporter was stabbed, see Robert Burns, affidavit, 28 June 1858, and George A. Smith, Church Historian's Journal, 28 June 1858, both in LDS Archives.

Epilogue

Taken together it was one of the most wretched spectacles that I ever witnessed. What a mixture of dust, Mormonism, jurisprudence, whiskey and filibusterism! And to be met with here in the Rocky Mountains!

Capt. John W. Phelps, 29 June 1858

Although Albert Sidney Johnston remained on duty in Utah for another twenty months after the long march through Salt Lake, he never revisited the city. Neither was he destined to meet Brigham Young. In early July 1858, as the Move South reversed course, the two leaders moved along opposite shores of Utah Lake in different directions—literally and metaphorically.

First Encounters: Mutual Misery and Bitterness

While General Johnston and President Young never crossed paths, their followers did. The federal troops marching toward Cedar Valley encountered returning refugees in the thousands. Their tattered condition drew ridicule from some soldiers, but most were shocked. The scene was so stark that even Maj. Fitz John Porter expressed compassion, although he continued to be hostile to Mormon leaders. At this point in the war, Porter had seen enough of Utah. While collecting his thoughts at a dusty camp near Utah Lake, he fantasized about reassignment, the best route for returning east, and the pleasures of his comfortable home and waiting bride in Manhattan.

"From Incidents of the Utah Expedition of 1859 to 1860, Under Genl. A. S. Johnston," 9 July 1858, 25–26, Porter Papers, lc.

While we were at our former camp B. Young had given permission to his followers to return to their homes & when we marched a singular spectacle was presented of a population returning to their homes in one direction by the side of the army from which they had been forced by their leaders to flee moving in the other and yet without fear and with perfect safety. With such consideration extended towards them they could but believe we were belied [maligned]. We met thousands of people on that day women and children, driving their animals and carts, bare footed and almost naked. Often did I see the poor women & children hold up one foot to relieve it from the burning sands and stones. For hundreds of miles had they been forced to travel, at first through snow ice mud & water & now over the barren desert. This migration has been going on for several days & has not yet ceased nor will it for 3 or 4 weeks. These poor people have nothing to clothe themselves with, but little to eat & nothing to procure the necessaries of life with. Their crops have been neglected & their supplies scarce. No matter what they produce they must give one tenth to the Church. I fear there will be much suffering from cold & hunger this winter. B. Young has been cruel to his people & merits a severe punishment.

As for the war it is now at an end, tho' this people are not conquered and never will submit to the authority of the U.S. Government so long as the present rulers are left among them. As for [military] honors there is no longer any to be reaped here & [I] should be glad of the chance of returning. I look for Gen. Harney to come & for Gen. Johnston to be relieved & my hope is I will be permitted to return with him. I would like much to return by way of California & land in N.Y. from the [Panama] steamer. The long & dreary route from here to Leavenworth is fearful & I would prefer taking the desert route to California, to bear additional fatigue, than pass over a route I know so well. However I shall try & take all things patiently & wait for what turns up.

One of the Utah Expedition's surgeons, Dr. A. Roberts Bartholow, viewed the army's trailside encounters as an opportunity for scientific observation. What he saw among the refugees confirmed the prejudices that he had developed at Camp Scott without ever having met a Mormon: "For many days a vast dust cloud . . . marked their progress. On foot, on horseback, in wagons, with cattle and horses and all the movable paraphernalia of their farms, the Mormon host journeyed northward. On our way to the post of Camp Floyd, we passed through the whole concourse. This gave us such an opportunity as could not occur again of seeing the material of which the

Mormon nation is constituted. Their appearance and opinions were so at variance with the rest of mankind, that the first impression made on our minds was that the Mormon people is a congress of lunatics."[1]

After passing thousands of ill-clad, weary, unwashed, and undernourished Mormons, Bartholow filled his quarterly "sanitary" reports to the surgeon general as well as his medical lectures with devastating descriptions of Latter-day Saints. Like Captain Phelps, he saw them not as hard-scrabble refugees but as a distinct species of humans—grotesque in physical appearance and behavior because of years of polygamy and isolation in Utah. It was the sort of prejudice used to demonize as sub-human the Irish Catholics flooding into America's Atlantic ports since the 1840s famine. When published, Bartholow's assessments shocked the nation, spawning similar papers from other physicians while confirming the biases of laymen already scandalized and prepared to believe the worst. It was another legacy of the Utah War plaguing the Mormon image well into the twentieth century.[2]

Not all of the encounters between southbound soldiers and returning refugees were civil, even when there were fraternal lodge ties in common. An artillery officer described one roadside dispute between Masons that almost came to blows: "A Mormon in high standing in Church and state was met by one of our volunteer officers the other day who had known him some fifteen years ago when they were both steamboat captains on the upper waters of the Mississippi. The Mormon had left that region without paying some of his debts and especially to the volunteer officer; and hence our officer bestowed upon him some pretty thoroughly selected epithets, assuring him that they had been carefully chosen. The Mormon made a considerable show about satisfaction and fighting, but at length told the Volunteer imploringly that—'*the matter ought to be taken in a Masonic* sense!'—'No!' replied the Volunteer, 'we are ordered by the chief lodge of the United States not to hold any intercourse with your Mormon lodges!' "[3]

If returning Mormons were exhausted and miserable, so too were the Utah Expedition's troops and camp followers. Capt. John W. Phelps had a trailside encounter with an entourage of bedraggled civilians consisting of Utah's chief justice; a family of British apostates under his personal protection; a Ute

[1]Bartholow, "The Physiological Aspects of Mormonism," 194.

[2]Bush, "A Peculiar People," 61–62, 66.

[3]Phelps to Charles Phelps, 11 July 1858, Phelps Papers, NYPL.

girl, whom the judge had cast in the role of servant-mascot; and a vengeful Nicaraguan freebooter then in the process of suing Brigham Young for false imprisonment. He recorded: "Being in a hurry to buy some potatoes which an apostate Mormon had brought forward for sale I only noticed 1st that the clouds of dust that diminished the sun had made the Judge as black as the rest of us. 2nd. That he arose to meet me, and while offering a bottle of whiskey for our consolation introduced to us 'Col. Fabers [Fabens] of the Nicaraguan Army' which he said had been kept a prisoner in Salt Lake City all winter. Taken together it was one of the most wretched spectacles that I ever witnessed. What a mixture of dust, Mormonism, jurisprudence, whiskey and filibusterism! And to be met with here in the Rocky Mountains!"[4]

Virtually all of the Utah Expedition's troops harbored negative views of the society that surrounded them, as well as of the Buchanan administration that had ordered them to Utah. As early as their departure from Camp Scott, many soldiers believed that the president had truckled to unpunished traitors while denying them the glory of a military resolution to the Mormon problem.

In early July 1858 Capt. Randolph B. Marcy's positive attitude was an exception to this pessimism. Marcy assumed that he would soon return home on furlough and sensed that what also awaited him was national acclaim and possible promotion. Accordingly, Marcy's first letter to his wife after arriving in Salt Lake City was filled with thoughts of love and even whimsy rather than the frustration and anger expressed by so many of his comrades-in-arms such as Captain Phelps, Capt. William Duncan Smith, Second Dragoons, and 2d Lt. George Dashiell Bayard, First U.S. Cavalry.

Capt. Marcy to Mary Marcy, 5 July 1858, Hollon Transcriptions.

Since I wrote you last we have entered the polygamous city of the Mormons and passed to the other side of Jordan. We are now about 20 miles from the city and will move tomorrow to a place about 40 miles distant where we find a better camp. When we pass[ed] through the City it was almost wholly deserted and looked most desolate, but within a few days the Mormons have been returning with their numerous wives and the place has (I am told) resumed its usual appearance, but I have not been there since. I shall endeavour to pay my Friend Brigham Young a visit before long, as he invited me last fall, and if perchance he should take it into his head to invite me to tarry over night

[4]Phelps Diary, 29 June 1858, Walker draft typescript, 14.

with him, what would you advise me to do?[5] I am afraid after being so long virtuous to trust myself among so many pretty women, as many of them must necessarily be in a very suffering [neglected] condition, and it would be a severe tax upon my virtue if any of them should make an attack upon it. I think therefore upon reflection that I should decline the invitation. I have seen but very few Mormon women and those are old and ugly. I presume they have thus far trusted none others in our neighborhood. One of the Elders remarked to a gentile a few days since that if the Army was allowed to mix with their people that every woman in Salt Lake City would be [pregnant] within a month. If that is the case, they must indeed be a virtuous community and they must entertain a very favorable opinion of military men. I have no doubt that the army would be very glad to go into female society once more, but I hope they are not so bad as the Elder would make them.

I received a letter since my return [from New Mexico] written by Genl. Scott's aid[e] which is highly flattering to me and will I presume gratify you. . . . This is I think the most complimentary notice that I have ever seen give[n] to an officer by Genl. Scott and I feel amply compensated for all I went through. Genl. Johnson has given me the best position in his power and told me that he would be glad to do anything to advance my interest at Head Quarters.

There seems to be a very general appreciation of my services throughout the Army and all congratulated me without jealousy.

I shall make an effort to go home in a few weeks and I presume I shall have no difficulty. If anyone goes I certainly shall. I would walk or crawl a long distance to see my dear family again, but I must wait patiently until the time comes and when I get home I expect to see more pleasure than I ever have before. Give ten thousand kisses to our sweet children and tell them how devotedly I love them and imagine yourself in my arms for a short time. . . .

P.S. I omitted an important part of Genl. Scott's letter. Here it is: "The Genl. in Chief has commanded to be forward[ed] this day to the War Dept. a copy of the foregoing letter endorsed as follows: 'Respectfully submitted for the information of the Secretary of War and I beg to add that in my opinion Capt. Marcy has again richly earned by gallantry and good conduct the rank of Major by Brevet.' "[6]

If Captain Marcy was cheerful, Captain Phelps was angry. Gone were May's pleasant dreams of Phelps's interactions with Queen Victoria at the Court

[5]Marcy did not meet Brigham Young until later in the summer. He refers playfully to the offer of accommodations in Salt Lake City tendered to the Utah Expedition's officers and ladies via Apostle John Taylor in the fall of 1857.

[6]Despite Scott's recommendation, Marcy remained a captain until promoted to the substantive grade of major in the paymaster's department in 1859.

of St. James. By July he realized that he was stuck for the indefinite future in an inhospitable territory distant from friends and family on the Atlantic Coast. On 19 July he wrote to General de Peyster to muse again that the Utah Expedition was a year old, likening its inactivity to "being sheathed in the valley as the useless sword is in its scabbard." The next day Phelps used this metaphor again as well as a variation on the theme of inactivity in ranting to both his sister Eunice and her husband, U.S. representative John Hickman: "The army is thrust into a hot, dusty valley about thirty-five miles South West of the City, like an old sword into its scabbard for which there is no longer any use . . . [the army is] like a pair of boots [thrust] into a dark closet, being worn out in its long march from Leavenworth through heat, dust, snow and politics. Never did an army come to a stranger finale than this. Resistance has been withdrawn from it suddenly as to take away its breathe."[7]

Capt. William Duncan Smith, commander of the Second Dragoons' Company E, echoed Phelps's emotions in writing from Camp Floyd to his brother in Manhattan. Such was Smith's discomfort over an injured foot and bitterness over the conduct of the Utah War, he took little solace in his promotion a month earlier after languishing for twelve years as a lieutenant.

Smith to N. Wallace Smith, 22 July 1858, Gratz Collection, HSP.

I most heartily congratulate you, my dear fellow, and sister Julia, upon the addition to your family. The child will no doubt open to you both a thousand points of enjoyment which were before sealed. Do not forget to teach the little thing, as soon as it can appreciate the institution, that it has a soldier uncle who takes an interest in its welfare.

The public journals has, no doubt, given you, long before this time, accounts of our march from "Bridger's Fort" to this place. The march was made with the same [*illegible*] as would have been observed had hostilities actually existed consequently the Dragoons as usual, had plenty of work to do.

We passed through Salt Lake City without stopping, and encamped about a mile from there on "The Jordan." Only the officers were allowed to visit "*the City*," by request of the Civil Authorities—this I believe. We stayed in that camp for a few days—then marched eighteen miles to "Mill Creek," where we halted for two, or three days, including the 4th of July—then marched about twenty five miles south, to Utah Lake—then to this point,

[7]Phelps Diary, 2 May 1858, Phelps to de Peyster, 19 July 1858; Phelps to Eunice Phelps Hickman and Phelps to John Hickman, both 20 July 1858, all Phelps Papers, NYPL.

head of "Cedar Valley," about twelve miles. We have been here since about the 8th instant I think.[8]

While in camp near the City a horse trod upon my left foot, from which injury I suffered much pain, but of which I did not complaint to Surgeon [Edward N. Covey] until several days after our arrival in this camp. Upon examination he pronounced one of my toes "broken." Since then I have walked with a crutch, but I think the injured part is now nearly well. It was my usual luck, but I am glad it was no worse.

Salt Lake City is a pretty place, covering a large extent of ground, but not containing, *under the most favorable circumstances,* a population of fifteen thousands. Of course I speak of my own opinion. It speaks well for the industry, energy, perserverance [*sic*], and good management of the Mormons. This I say in order to give the *Devil* his due.

All the other settlements, I have seen, are but caricatures of what are generally esteemed even as towns. The country is miserable. The soil is light, very little rain falls, consequently clouds of dust are constantly rising, which blind, choke, and render cleanliness impossible, and life almost unendurable. We are all completely disgusted by the policy which has been pursued by the administration, or by some other Civil Authority. The army is now like a party which remains here by the permission of the Mormons. We are fifty miles from the City, and by request of the Civil Authorities, (it is understood), are not allowed any freedom. There is no intercourse between us and the people, and our camp is, as it were, among a people hostile to us, with whom we have had to be on our good behavior. There is no considerable settlement near to us. It would have been a blessing to the mass of the Mormons, and to our country, had we been allowed to fight the infernal rebils. The matter is no nearer to a settlement than it was this time last year. Next to a fight with them, the policy is to put a military force near, (within cannon range) to their largest towns,[9] so as to hold them in subjection to the laws, for I maintain, without fear of contradiction, that, by their existing union of church and laws, Brigham Young is still the tru Governor of Utah; and the United States will soon see this assertion proven by events. Gov. Cumming has been completely duped by Brigham and the leading Mormons. We are no nearer civilization and the comforts of life, than we would be were we on the plains. Some provisions are brought in by the Mormons, but they charge such fabulous prices that our pay will not allow indulgence in their use.

Mr. Bill [William Bell], of whom you spoke, is connected in business, I think with Livingston, Kinkaid & Co. who are Sutlers to our regiment. That firm has a good standing with the officers, and with the Mormons.

---

[8]This was "Old" Camp Floyd or the "Upper Camp."

[9]This was done in October 1862 with the establishment of Camp Douglas on the bench overlooking Salt Lake City.

It is likely that Bill may do something for your claim, but my idea is, that law will be very loose out here, except for the benefit of the Mormons, until other than Mormon juries can be obtained. If I should have a chance of being of any service to your friend Rosevelt, I will, of course, avail myself of it.[10]

Remember me kindly to Mr. Rosevelt, and express my thanks to him for his kind offer of service.

I have now the grade which will probably stick to me until I end my professional and eart[h]ly career together—unless by some good fortune I should be appointed a Pay master in the Army. You have probably heard long before this of my promotion, through regular regimental succession, to the grade of Captain. My weary and *unusual* waiting of twelve years took away all pleasure from its announcement. The pay is, however, increased to fifteen, or sixteen dollars more a month. To show you how Army life goes; I had to pay about one hundred dollars "to wet my commission"—fifty for a basket of champayne, and the use [rest?] in sundries. It is a rule of service which knows no exception among honorable men. . . .

Heaven only knows when the 2 Dragoons will get out of the country or where it will next move to, as it is the marching regiment of the service. But, in any event, I am going to save as much as possible in order to go on leave at the first opportunity. . . .

I long very much to see you all, and I cherish fondly the idea of having my longing gratified by the end of the year. Write as often as you can. Kiss the little one for me and give my best love to sister Julia.[11]

2D LT. GEORGE DASHIELL BAYARD
(CAMP ON NORTH PLATTE, FIVE MILES ABOVE ASH HOLLOW, N.T.)
TO MOTHER (WOODBURY, N.J.), 2 AUGUST 1858,
LIFE OF GEORGE DASHIELL BAYARD, 135–37.

We have got thus far on the *back track.* I always had a presentiment that we should [would] never go to Utah.

We left Fort Laramie on our return, on the thirtieth ult. [July], and will probably reach Kearney [*sic*] on the fifteenth of this month, and [Fort] Riley, (unless stopped by orders) by the twenty-eighth or twenty-ninth. I hope as you saw the orders in the papers for our return, that I shall find plenty of letters awaiting my arrival. I am anxious to hear from you all, as I have not heard since the nineteenth of June. We are all glad of the countermarch, for all accounts we receive describe Utah as the most miserable place on the face of the earth, and the people there the most wretched. I received a letter

[10]Possibly a reference to Manhattan's Judge James J. Roosevelt, a friend of James Buchanan.

[11]A typescript of this document is in Letters from Camp Floyd Collection, MS 191, Marriott Library, University of Utah. During the 1970s historian-archivist Everett L. Cooley intended it for publication.

from Dr. Corey [*sic*] dated "Camp Floyd, Cedar Valley, July twenty-second." He is very much disgusted.[12]

The government have made more than a *failure*. They have acceded virtually, to every demand made by the Mormons. The troops are removed far from the towns, while the civil officers are in fact powerless, Brigham remaining as omnipotent as ever.

The administration has disgraced itself and acted most culpably. After making immense contracts for all sorts of supplies, and after a great display and flourish of trumpets, they have backed down from every position they assumed. Of what use are our judges there? The juries are Mormon and will convict no one without the permission of Brigham. Our Governor is a mere figurehead, while Brigham's word is respected as gospel. This is the ridiculous conclusion of the great expedition to conquer the Mormons!

By the time we reach Fort Riley, the summer will be over, and nothing will have been accomplished. We have had a tedious march to Laramie, and will have as tedious a march back again, and *that* is the whole story.

If our illustrious masters at Washington, knew in what estimation their wisdom is held in the army, they would, doubtless, feel a little indignant, but not more so than we are, on account of their blundering.

Christian A. Madsen, a thirty-six-year-old Mormon convert recently arrived from Denmark, saw things differently.[13]

Madsen (Salt Lake City) to Brother Widerborg (Denmark), 25 July 1858, *Skandinaviens Stjerne*, 15 October 1858.[14]

The American troops are now on their way back to the United States. I don't know what the conditions of the peace treaty are, but Brigham has said that if the United States does not abide by them, there will be trouble. The States have to withdraw from the "Mormon War" without losing face. Because of the mercy of the Lord, they got off without being punished for their injustice. The entire army, including Cumming and others, can thank Brigham Young that they are still alive today. The young lions of Zion were not bloodthirsty, but they were justifiably indignant and wanted to punish this great injustice as a testimony to the world that the Lord had delivered the army into the hands of God's people and that, according to Brigham

[12]Asst. Surg. Edward N. Covey. In 1859 assailants shot and wounded Covey and several army companions in Salt Lake City, an attack for which there were no arrests.

[13]A month earlier, Enoch B. Tripp, a Legion officer guarding Salt Lake City before the Utah Expedition's arrival, wrote a longer but similarly Mormon-centric account of the war's origins, prosecution, outcome, and meaning to his "absent friends" in Maine. Tripp to parents, 20 June 1858, Tripp journal, 20 June 1858, 15–18, LDS Archives.

[14]English translation from Hale, ed., *Danes in North America*, 194–204.

Young, for a few days a third of our boys were ready to wipe them off the face of the earth.

There are a lot of heathens here these days, especially people who belong to the army. They are orderly and don't disturb the peace or harm anyone. The merchants are unhappy, though, because when the troops leave, the profitable trade will be over.

Yet not all of Utah's Danish converts were as hostile to the Utah Expedition as Madsen. The Fourth Artillery's Captain Phelps encountered one such immigrant, a teenager with whom he quickly established a rapport: "A boy, a Dane, who says that his father died in Denmark—that his mother has married a Mormon and is at Fort [blank] on her way [with the Move South] to White Mountain which is some 300 miles south of this, wishes to become a soldier in my company." Groping for a way to describe the lad's itinerant mother, Phelps fell back on his years of campaigning in Florida and journalized, "what an alligator she must be to leave her eggs thus around the world! Were she not alive I would enlist the boy and save him from Mormonism."[15]

In the months that followed, General Johnston contented himself with commanding the army's department of Utah from Camp Floyd, the enormous adobe post built by cash-starved Mormon laborers in Cedar Valley, forty miles southwest of Salt Lake City.[16] He saw it mushroom into Utah's second biggest settlement and the nation's largest garrison. Johnston's friends in St. Louis and Louisville speculated that he might succeed General Scott or even President Buchanan. As the army's indispensable man in Utah, Johnston received neither furlough nor reassignment despite his repeated requests for both. The general came to view Camp Floyd and his assignment there with a distaste akin to Lieutenant Ives's reaction to his brief sojourn at Fort Yuma. Johnston told his daughter, "I have . . . no hopes of escapeing from this infernal region—It is to me worse than any imagined horrors of a Siberian exile. . . . the [mountain] scenery which is sublime and magnificent preserved

---

[15]Phelps Diary, 29 June 1858, Walker draft typescript, 12.

[16]There were two posts officially named Camp Floyd. The first, a short-lived cantonment of tents later dubbed "Old Camp Floyd" or "the Upper Camp," was established on 8 July 1858 at the north end of Cedar Valley at the mouth of West Canyon. Sixty days later, the need for a more extensive water source and additional land led to abandonment of this site for a second, adobe-built establishment ("the Lower Camp") about ten miles farther south in Cedar Valley adjacent to the hamlet of Fairfield. It is the latter installation to which most historians refer in using the term "Camp Floyd." Four first-rate related studies are: Bylund, *In Search of Johnston's Army*; Nielson, *Roll Call at Old Camp Floyd, Utah Territory*; Moorman and Sessions, *Camp Floyd and the Mormons*; and Alexander and Arrington, "Camp in the Sagebrush."

its novelty to me for a long time but that is now gone & it has resolved itself into a huge prison wall, a barrier to cut me off from all those I love."[17] He sat on the steps of his adobe headquarters, smoking a pipe, thinking of his family in Kentucky, watching the sand storms his sarcastic troops dubbed "Johnsoons," and relishing the strains of his favorite soldiers' song played nightly by one of the garrison's bands.[18]

Finally, on 1 March 1860, General Johnston cantered out of Camp Floyd heading for California and a new command. Johnston's journey home produced one of the eeriest scenes of the Utah War. As the general and his sixty-dragoon escort rode across the rim of the Great Basin near the killing field of Mountain Meadows, Major Porter realized they were being shadowed by a heavily bearded horseman with a dog perched behind the saddle in signature fashion. The outrider was Orrin Porter Rockwell, Brigham Young's bodyguard. Rockwell's solitary vigil more than three hundred miles from Salt Lake City sent an unmistakable message to the departing general about the real locus of power in Utah Territory. As Fitz John Porter described the scene, "it was a warning. We were at once on our guard and our party, somewhat separated . . . was halted and united."[19] Johnston's death came not at Porter Rockwell's hands but in 1862 at the battle of Shiloh, Tennessee, while serving as the Confederacy's senior field general.

While Johnston rusticated at Camp Floyd, his chief adversary, Brigham Young, struggled with a brief period of depression, fear of lynching, and self-isolation. Initially Young seemed relieved, albeit wistful, at how the Utah Expedition had comported itself while marching through Salt Lake City. The day after, he wrote Ferguson, "we are truly gratified with the quiet manner in which the passage of the Army through the city as well as the orderly demeanor of our brethren which, however, we expected as a matter of course. We should be sorry indeed if any of our men, men who profess to be saints, and brethren should demean themselves to bring disgrace upon themselves or reproach upon the fair fame of our beloved city."[20] What followed this satisfaction was Young's unhappy realization that his role and the condition of the territory had begun to change in unattractive ways beyond his control.

[17]Johnston to Henrietta Preston Johnston, 15 August 1859, quoted in Roland, *Albert Sidney Johnston*, 236.

[18]Ware, *The Indian War of 1864*, 250–51.

[19]Porter, A Characteristic (Mormon) Conspiracy, Porter Papers, LC. Upon sensing danger, Rockwell's dog would silently lick his master's face.

[20]Young to Ferguson, 27 June 1858, LDS Archives.

By the end of July, though, he had shaken off the mood that Winston Churchill would later call the "Black Dog." Young rebounded to shape the early phases of what would become a long-term, legal campaign of Mormon resistance against the federal establishment. It was an active leadership role distinct from the formal governance of the territory—one that Alfred Cumming understood and accepted until his own departure for Georgia and a rendezvous with obscurity on the eve of the Civil War. Young continued this resistance until his death from natural but mysterious causes at age 76 in 1877, years after he escaped the consequences of Utah War–related federal indictments for treason in 1857 and murder in 1871.

Although Albert Sidney Johnston, Brigham Young, and Alfred Cumming emerged from the Utah War with varying degrees of reputational damage, the conflict's most prominent casualty was President Buchanan. It could be argued that Buchanan deserves credit for doing what President Pierce was too feckless to accomplish: restoring federal authority in Utah through a sea change in gubernatorial leadership. But in doing so, Buchanan's presidential skills failed both him and the nation. During the opening months of his administration, Buchanan performed six important presidential responsibilities poorly: selecting his most senior Utah War appointees; gathering intelligence; using military advisors; communicating effectively; managing the war's financing; and demonstrating constancy of purpose.

Two other factors worked to undercut any interpretation of Buchanan's Brigham Young policy as necessary and justified: a successful Mormon campaign to ridicule the Utah War as a presidential blunder compounded by proto-Confederate plotters in his cabinet; and widespread public revulsion over Buchanan's perceived responsibility for the Civil War's carnage. Over more than 150 years, these twin forces of ridicule and revulsion degraded Buchanan's image to that of a corrupt pro-Southern dough face presiding ineptly over the nation's slide into the bloodbath of disunion.

Small wonder that Washington, D.C., lacked a memorial to honor Buchanan until Herbert Hoover's administration, and that his grave in Lancaster, Pennsylvania, stands neglected in a declining cemetery. It is a scene quite unlike the elaborate Victorian memorial created for Albert Sidney Johnston near the Texas statehouse in Austin. To this day, the Commonwealth of Pennsylvania remains unwilling to honor Buchanan in the U.S. Capitol's Hall of Statuary as one of its most prominent native sons, although the states of Utah and Texas long ago placed statues there to honor Brigham Young and his Utah War ally, Sam Houston.[21]

Warfare by Other Means: Utah's Reconstruction

Subsequent to the Utah Expedition's arrival, there were episodic incidents of what Shakespeare's stage directions called alarums and excursions, but the days of blood letting and armed confrontation were largely over. In abandoning these tactics as well as the Sebastopol strategy and its Move South, Young shifted to different actions. What unfolded, with Thomas L. Kane's long-distance counsel, was a broad campaign of political manipulation, local intimidation, lobbying, and public relations. If Carl von Clausewitz, the great military strategist, had postulated that "war is merely the continuation of politics by other means," what took place in Utah during the last half of 1858 and subsequently was the converse of this concept. After 26 June armed confrontation morphed into a continuum of non-military but still contentious legal, image, and political struggles as well as occasional gunfire of the sort that struck down Sgt. Ralph Pike, Surgeon Edward Covey, and merchant Jack Mendenhall on the streets of Salt Lake City. The *New York Herald*'s Utah correspondent described the early stages of this transformation two weeks after the Utah Expedition marched through Salt Lake City, noting that "we do not now head our articles 'the Mormon war' but we may yet have to so do, for the Mormon and Gentile war is just commencing. It will at first be in accordance with the forms of law, but may not end so."[22]

The opening gambit in this campaign was already in motion by the time Johnston reached Salt Lake City and even then was playing out in James Buchanan's Executive Mansion as well as at the editorial offices of several Manhattan newspapers.

In this early stage of the strategy, Thomas L. Kane was the prime mover. Young's anxiety over keeping Kane's linkage to Mormonism covert, as well as the global scope of his ambitions, shows in his operating instructions to Horace S. Eldredge, his business agent in St. Louis, as Eldredge prepared

[21]A recent assessment of the Utah War's impact on Buchanan's presidency and its image is MacKinnon, "Prelude to Armageddon," 46–85. In 2015 Buchanan's latest biographer, Prof. Jean Baker, commented, "he was terrible." Gail Collins, "Hillary Versus History and, Now, Our James Buchanan Moment," Op-Ed, *New York Times*, 3 January 2015, A16/5.

[22][Lemuel Fillmore], "Utah Affairs," Dispatch, 10 July 1858, *New York Herald*, 9 August 1858, 8/3.

to travel east and eventually succeed Bernhisel as Utah's territorial delegate in Congress. Young admonished Eldredge, "let your intercourse with Col. Kane be confidential, and move about from place to place without attracting more than necessary notice; as also Brother [George Q.] Cannon, not that we think you or he is apt to make any unnecessary display, but simply as a caution to be wise and discreet, and while you with our good friend [Kane], move the whole world no one will know who has done it." Cannon lowered his profile while operating in Kane's hometown by masking the fact that Young had appointed him president of the Philadelphia Mission as well as the newest member of the Quorum of the Twelve Apostles.[23]

Few glimpses into Kane's postwar impact are as vivid as the dramatic about-face in the editorial voice of Horace Greeley's *New-York Tribune* following Kane's visit to Manhattan immediately after he returned from the White House. Theretofore, Greeley had had little to say about the Utah War, seemingly content to deal with that subject through front-page publication of the news dispatches provided by his field correspondent, A. G. Browne, Jr. During 1857–58 Browne's reporting had hardly been impartial, filled as it was with anti-Mormonism, contempt for Brigham Young, admiration for General Johnston, dismay over Governor Cumming's sympatico relations with the Latter-day Saints, and occasional advocacy of extreme measures such as the summary execution of senior Mormon leaders. Browne's dispatch of 3–4 June from Camp Scott appeared in the *Tribune* on 1 July and was consistent with his earlier views.

Two days after publication of that piece, the newspaper printed an unsigned editorial headed "The Rebel Army" that veered sharply from the tone of its own correspondent's reporting. Sensing that "perhaps there is something in the air of Utah that stimulates treason," the editorial asserted that a cabal of federal appointees at Camp Scott, led by Judge Eckels and abetted by Albert Sidney Johnston, was undercutting Cumming. The editorial also criticized Ben McCulloch and Lazarus Powell, asserting that "they harmonize completely, were are told, with Judge Eckels and Gen. Johnston, and, not content with upsetting and overriding the Governor, are resolved to upset and override the President too" with respect to his proclamation of pardon. Greeley's harshest words were reserved for the Utah Expedition's

---

[23]Young to Eldredge, 20 October 1858, LDS Archives. See also Young to Cannon, 7 September 1858, ibid., for instructions on influencing the press and interfacing with Kane.

soldiers, accusing them of "rancorous and ferocious feelings against the Mormons," as well as "an air of offended dignity at the idea that the Peace Commissioners had arrived to snatch their hated victims from their revengeful grasp." He argued that if U.S. troops must be stationed in Utah, "they ought to be some fresh corps, and not a body of men filled with such hatred and prejudice."[24]

Given the proximity of this editorial's appearance to Kane's New York visit, the fact that he left Philadelphia intent on visiting Manhattan newspaper editors, and the consistency between the piece's phrasing and the content of Kane's Mormon-related correspondence during March–May 1858, it is reasonable to assume that the abrupt shift in the *Tribune*'s editorial position reflected Kane's influence. Most telling of all was the close ten-year relationship between Kane and Horace Greeley, a connection that resulted in collaboration between the two men on a wide range of philanthropic, reform, and political causes. Small wonder, then, that when Greeley brought out his annual almanac for 1859, it included an account of the Utah War highly sympathetic to the Mormon side and closer in tone to an essay Kane might write than the long study that the *Tribune*'s own war correspondent (Browne) produced for the *Atlantic Monthly* later that year. As Greeley saw Kane's contribution, "what an army of the United States, at an expense of millions of dollars, failed to do, was done at his private charges [expense] by a single energetic man of straightforward intentions and sound judgment. By a few days of friendly converse, he subdued the Mormons. The 'Lion of the Lord' was tamed."[25]

The next step in the strategy unfolded in the West: the Mormon petition to President Buchanan seeking recall of many of his political appointees. That Governor Cumming transmitted the petition to Secretary of State Cass for Young as the army approached Salt Lake City presaged drama and intrigue in Mormon-federal relations during the balance of the nineteenth century.

In sending this document to Cass, Cumming wrote: "I have the honor of transmitting a petition from citizens of this Territory requesting the President to remove from office Chief Justice Eckels[,] Post Master Morrell[,]

---

[24][Greeley?], "The Rebel Army," Editorial, *New-York Tribune,* 3 July 1858, reprinted in *Millennial Star* (Liverpool) 20 (31 July 1858): 493–94. Greeley's rival, Henry J. Raymond of the *Times,* had executed a similar editorial about-face just before Kane reached home.

[25]Grow and Walker, eds., *The Prophet and the Reformer,* 88n25; Greeley, "Utah and the Mormons," *The Tribune Almanac and Political Register for 1859,* 42.

Indian Agents Hurt and Craig. All the gentlemen whose names are mentioned in the Petition are unusually obnoxious to the People of this territory and in my opinion ought to be promptly removed from their respective offices."[26]

As a matter of strategy, the accompanying petition was not signed by Cumming but included the signatures of sixty prominent church, Nauvoo Legion, and business leaders unidentified by title. Among the signatories were Brigham Young, William A. Hickman, and John Flack, all of whom would be indicted by a federal grand jury in 1871 for the murder of Utah War ammunition trader Richard E. Yates. The petition urged Buchanan to replace Judge Eckels with Seth M. Blair, Morrell with William H. Hooper, and Hurt and Craig with Richard R. Hopkins and non-Mormon merchant John B. Kimball. For each appointee targeted for removal, the document included an explanatory paragraph, crafted by James Ferguson, which set forth their offenses. The petition reserved the most extensive and florid commentary for Judge Eckels and Indian Agent Hurt.[27]

No action was taken on these recommendations, and there is no trace of this document in federal records. The *New York Times* did not publish its full text, but instead summarized it, as did correspondent Browne in the *Tribune.*[28]

Faced with the failure of this petition to produce results, Young persevered. Fifteen months later, although no longer governor, he sent Utah's new delegate to Congress a petition-like memorandum setting forth a new slate of nominees (with multiple, prioritized alternates) for each position in the territory except Governor Cumming's. This effort also failed, but Young pressed on.[29]

Integral to the June 1858 petition was a Brigham Young sub-strategy best described as divide and conquer. This thrust was intended to pit against one another a group of Mormon-friendly federal appointees (Governor

[26]Cumming to Cass, 26 June 1858, Cumming Papers, Duke University.

[27]Petition: Citizens of Utah to James Buchanan, 25 June 1858, Thomas L. Kane Papers, Yale Collection of Western Americana, Beinecke Library. After finalizing the petition, Young realized that it lacked the signatures of the territory's most prominent non-Mormon businessmen and wrote Ferguson, "it would be well to have [Howard] Livingston and [William] Bell and perhaps some others also to sign it, or a similar petition, at least, asking for the same objects, and stating that in their opinion it should be granted." This tactic echoed the petition Young engineered in December 1854 for Colonel Steptoe, his officers, and Utah's leading gentiles to sign urging President Pierce to reappoint him as governor. The 1858 gambit failed. Young to Ferguson, 27 June 1858, LDS Archives.

[28]"From Utah, Mormon Memorial to the President," *New York Times,* 11 August 1858, 3/4; [Browne], "Highly Interesting from Utah. The Army at Salt Lake City," Dispatch, 28 June 1858, *New-York Tribune,* 30 July 1858.

[29]Young to William H. Hooper, 16 September 1859, LDS Archives.

Cumming, superintendent of Indian Affairs Forney, and the soon-to-arrive U.S. attorney Alexander Wilson) and a cadre of officials viewed as "anti" (General Johnston, Indian Agents Hurt and Craig, U.S. Marshal Dotson, Postmaster Morrell, and the three federal judges led by Chief Justice Eckels). On the day the Utah Expedition marched through Salt Lake City, Young described to Mormon leader Warren S. Snow the early workings of this sub-strategy: "Governor Cumming and Superintendent Forney still appear desirous of doing the right thing which rather holds such men as Hurt, Dotson, and their companions in check. We trust that all matters will go right and a collision avoided."[30] Most important to creating this alignment was the marginalization of Cumming, an officer vulnerable to Young's blandishments by virtue of vanity, alcoholism, and perhaps blackmail. Almost immediately after attorney Wilson arrived in Utah in November 1858, he was suborned through a combination of alcohol and bribery.

Kane outlined part of the broader Mormon strategy of resistance in a letter for Young dictated to Elizabeth Kane on 18 July 1858 soon after returning home from Washington and New York and while recovering from another of his physical collapses.

KANE TO YOUNG, 18 JULY 1858, LDS ARCHIVES.

> We have news from Utah of the reception of the Commissioners and Army and the temperate conduct of your people. There is no longer need therefore to detain Mr. [Howard] Egan to be the bearer of despatches calculated to meet an emergency. I have already called off my thoughts from the past, and commenced directing them upon the future.—Cumming is to be sustained; part at least of the road to hell is paved with good intentions of enforcing a peace policy; the horse leeches have begun to nasty the beds [with manure] they have been crawling over; the temporary influence of the army—(always odious to the nation in healthy times when it interferes with politics) this factitious influence, based almost entirely upon the distribution of jobs, will quite fade away before winter:—in a word, from present prospects, I see no reason why you also should not begin now to look to the great matter of the future, and devote all your energies to the task of securing the recognition of Utah as a State.

[30]Young to Snow, 26 June 1858, ibid. For a description of this split among federal appointees and how it impeded territorial affairs such as the investigation of the Mountain Meadows massacre, see comments attributed to attorney Wilson during a 25 January 1859 meeting in the Staines mansion between him and a Mormon delegation comprised of George Peacock, Warren S. Snow, and J. C. Little as set forth eighteen years later in Peacock to David O. Calder and George Reynolds, 4 April 1877, ibid.

I remember that we fully talked over the measures to be taken with this view, and I will therefore only advert to two of them—to which I think, immediate attention should be given:

1. A *general Investigation* should be demanded by the people of Utah, that the country may be authoritatively informed of the falsity of the charges and the iniquity of the proceedings against them &c. This you may afterwards press or not, as circumstances indicate. But meantime Gov. Cumming should be led to examine into as many matters as possible and send home a favorable report upon them. It may be worth while to get what contradictions &c. you can out of the other civil officers.

2d. Consummate the arrangement with the Press.[31]

I close by offering you my sincere congratulations on the wisdom of the course you have pursued. It is additional[ly] apparent to me since my return. The unanimity with which our [Eastern] people were prepared to carry on the Mormon War was frightful—not, you will understand, that they particularly desired to wage a "war of extermination"—but they were prepared to *vote supplies* to any amount, while the miscreants *in* Utah carried on the work: and thus, like the frantic crowd rushing for a narrow passage, driving the foremost before it, and declaring itself innocent of the trampling done by them—we should have been responsible for any amount of outrage and violence committed in our name. It appears that your enemies themselves supported the President's proposal to send the Commissioners and [pardon] proclamation, so certain were they that these would be too late, and that the Administration would be thus *set right* and the Country united on extreme measures, without a chance of their losing their Holy War.

But I see that the reaction has set in. I wish no better proof of it than this latest figure [scene], which is a contest who shall have the *credit* (mark the change of strain) of the pacification of Utah—Johnston or the Peace Commissioners. Of course the Army, having the greatest number of hired liars at command, will win (until the truth itself is told at last). The reaction has commenced however, I say. You must not take Dr. Bernhisel or Gov. Cumming's authority on this, until they have opened as many other so styled *hopeless* fights as I have. It will be a work of Time, as I told you, to obtain your State Sovereignty—but Time will do the work. Let us save [continue] the Territorial Organization this winter for the future basis and I am confident I see my way to daylight.

I am an ill man, I regret to say—quite an ill one. But you have known me worse, and I intend to live, and what is more intend to give you months of my time between this and Christmas to lay the guns, and order on the assault.

---

[31]Upon receipt of Kane's advice, Young accelerated his covert thrust to use T. B. H. Stenhouse in New York to influence, if not bribe, newspaper editors.

As for the ~~last~~ late War—it will end for good with the withdrawal of the present forces from the Basin.—Get them out quietly—let me have a few sound facts and arguments spread before the nation, and, my word for it, you have seen your last soldier marched across the plains—have heard your last forever of all such wickedness and folly.

How much I would like to write to you all, my friends, I know you must be aware, I know you are aware also how affectionately I remain Your friend to serve you.

Thomas L. Kane, Accompanying Memorandum, 1858.

Colonel Kane.—Says Buchanan's is certainly the most corrupt administration he has ever had to [deal] with. The old man fears colkado [habitual timidity] to[o] much to love him but this he considers a most Salutary State of mind, though he is anxious the administration shall get a dead fall in Pennsylvania [elections] this Autumn. Yet Colonel Kane is now an avowed supporter of the administration and will probably continue to be so until congress meets [in December 1858].

He has found the most liberal Sentiments so far, among Some of his old republican friends but he perceives that it is of more importance we should prepare for this diffusion which must arise, on Utah formally asking for admission as a State.[32]

Colonel Kane would have the people of Utah show themselves to be quiet and orderly and well disposed; that the new batch of officials may be made to fill the public prints with contradictions of slanders against the mormons exposures conspiracies against them and so forth but all the while they should seem to exspect [*sic*] an examination to be made on the part of the nation into the charges against them and a change of policy on the part of the administration upon the facts being known let the Deseret News and public speakers avoid language of abuse during this time of apparent expectation a good occupation for the news would [be] the contradiction of the camp lies one by one not touching however upon the more pinching matters of history, till they [*sic*] sky grows somewhat clear the contractors and speculators should be handled without gloves and every fact relative to loss of cattle stated and of waste and so forth to the country what was with Utah. Costs it will be useful also to laugh good humordly at the army and tell the whole truth of their achie[ve]ments last fall and other matters to counteract the mistatements of which they were the modest authors that their columns at Bridger terfied [*sic*] the mormons into submission; but your aim should be to earn a good character and give your friends occasion to say if popular agitation should hereafter arise among you such was Utah for so long a season when she was hopefully exspecting that justice would be done her.

[32] Utah again sought statehood in 1862 and multiple times thereafter but was unsuccessful until 1896.

> Back up Cumming and humor the officials but get out of them and even the officers if it costs nothing written and signed all the true statements that you can if they come properly then better leave off pressing for the commission of enquiry but you must demand it at this time if Cumming will demand why you are not to be trusted to carry your own mail and get the [Washington] departments into hot water with him about a number of minor questions. It will serve a good purpose but of course Brigham Young will keep a dignified Silence and seem proudly above attending to trifles manifestation of discontent especially when the time comes for them he will leave to turbulent persons whom his patriotic efforts become daily less efficient to control perhaps your known adherents will be able to take a conspicuous part in over coming the factious elements in the Legislature but the mistake must no longer be commited of offering the mormons as a unit to be the mark [target] of the malice of their en[e]mies and Young and a few friends shouldering every thing and dividing distributing responsibility among others.

A month after Kane shared these thoughts with Brigham Young, Ben McCulloch wrote to his friend Seth Blair from Washington to offer his own comments about Utah's future.

McCulloch to Blair, 27 August 1858,
Church Historian's Office Journal, 2 October 1858, LDS Archives.

> I am glad to hear everything is getting on quietly in Utah. How long do you think it will last? I must confess I entertain fears regarding their long continuance. The prejudices of mankind are so great against each other, when they differ on religious subject, that there is no calculating on what they will do. Consequently, if asked, I would express myself as I did in Utah; viz., that it would be better for all parties, for the Mormon people to remove to some other country. However, this is a matter that they alone must determine. One word as to [federal] government officials in Utah; I don't think this administration will remove any of its appointees, until they have given them a fair chance to show whether they are honest and competent. This is the opinion of your friend.

Seth Blair's reaction to McCulloch's comments was that "this was a fair admission on the part of the peace commissioners that it was a religious war, and that the Mormon religion could not be protected by the government."

In many respects, what followed the Utah Expedition's march through Salt Lake City was nearly a half-century of "Reconstruction," a period resembling the South's agony during 1865–76, only longer. In Utah, as in the eleven states of the Confederacy, there was to be the arrival of political carpetbaggers, the mass appearance of deputy U.S. marshals, and the ebb and flow of army units in response to Washington's attitude toward Utah.

In the immediate wake of the Utah War, Brigham Young's decision to opt out of the Civil War had serious political consequences. During the 1860s a politically defenseless Utah lost six huge areas from its western and eastern regions to create or enlarge the territories of Nevada, Colorado, Nebraska, Dakota, and Wyoming. In this sense, Utah Territory was less successful than a defeated Texas, which during its period of Reconstruction forestalled the creation of a State of Coyote from her western region.[33]

If during the first twenty years of this period Brigham Young was able to parry congressional attempts to obliterate Utah as a political entity, he and his successors failed to stop two of the greatest threats of the Reconstruction era: federal pursuit of accountability for Mountain Meadows, and a legal onslaught against the practice of plural marriage.

With respect to the Mountain Meadows massacre, only one person—John D. Lee, a Nauvoo Legion major and Brigham Young's religiously adopted son—was tried, convicted, and executed. During the twenty-first century, Latter-day Saint religious leaders as well as historians of varied backgrounds have shed much light on who, in addition to Lee, did what at Mountain Meadows while memorializing the victims and reconciling with their descendants. In 2011 a collaboration of such interested parties, including the LDS church, succeeded in having the U.S. Department of the Interior designate Mountain Meadows a national historic landmark. Notwithstanding these efforts, the atrocity continues to stain the reputation of a church that long ago left behind the provocative rhetoric and violent actions of its early leaders.

Bolstered by passage of the first federal anti-polygamy statutes and swelling national indignation, the campaign against plural marriage began in earnest after the Civil War, with President U. S. Grant using subjugation of the South as a model for his Mormon policy. When in December 1867 U.S. senator Aaron Cragin of New Hampshire introduced a bill severely limiting the power of the LDS church, Nauvoo Legion, and Mormon juries hearing polygamy cases, Brigham Young lost control of his temper and language. To Utah's territorial delegate in Congress, Young vented, "I have a proposition

[33]Furniss, *The Mormon Conflict*, 204–34; Bigler and Bagley, *The Mormon Rebellion*, 326–64; MacKinnon, "'Like Splitting a Man Up His Backbone,'" 100–24.

to make to Cragan [*sic*] and [Senator Ben] Wade [of Ohio] and all such men. When my old nigger [servant] has been dead one year, if they wash their faces clean they may kiss his ass. I hold all such men in the greatest contempt and fear not their wicked deeds."[34] Although Cragin's bill failed, the future was to become even more perilous. Vigorous prosecutions would continue in various ways until Utah gained statehood in 1896. In 1890 and 1904 church presidents issued manifestos that, in effect, disavowed the practice of plural marriage. Although state polygamy prosecutions atrophied after the first half of the twentieth century, public controversy over who engages in the practice and with what religious affiliation continues unabated in Utah and neighboring states. Today, this still-intense interest stems not from national anti-Mormonism but rather from a combination of curiosity, the prominence of a defiant Fundamentalist (but not LDS) polygamy movement, the titillation of an anything-goes American entertainment and media culture, and a sea change in legal as well as social attitudes about the related issue of same-sex marriage.

Accompanying these changes in attitude about Mountain Meadows and polygamy has been a positive shift in public views of Mormonism generally. Today Mormonism is arguably one of America's fastest growing religions, with more than fifteen million members worldwide. For decades, Americans have chosen Mormons among others for the most senior leadership roles in the country's universities, businesses, foreign service, and military organizations, as well as in gubernatorial statehouses, Congress, and the president's cabinet. In 1857–58 Brigham Young pitted himself against an expeditionary force led by West Pointers, but at least four consecutive generations of his direct descendants served with distinction in army ranks ranging from private to general officer, many with commissions from the U.S. Military Academy. During the presidential campaigns of 1968, 2008, and 2012, three Latter-day Saints—all descendants of Utah War veterans—entered the contest as aspiring standard bearers of a Republican Party that in 1856 had called for the eradication of polygamy as one of the "twin relics of barbarism."[35]

---

[34]Young to Hooper, 4 January 1868, LDS Archives.

[35]Mormon presidential candidates were George Wilcken Romney (1968), Willard Mitt Romney (2008 and 2012), and Jon Meade Huntsman, Jr. (2012), former governors of Michigan, Massachusetts, and Utah, respectively.

The War's Impact on Individuals: Heroes and Villains-in-Waiting

What happened after 1858 to the war's participants less prominent than Albert Sidney Johnston, Brigham Young, Alfred Cumming, and James Buchanan? What was the fate of the campaign's other Latter-day Saints, non-Mormons, American Indians, Hispanos, black slaves, Anglos, European nobleman, women, mountaineers, explorers, reporters, dandies, illiterates, Ph.D.s, rogues, soldiers, and civilians? For most, the Utah War was the defining experience of their life. They then receded into an anonymity garnished with personal memories of the Move South, riding with Lot Smith, or surviving the Utah Expedition's brutal march to the charred remains of Fort Bridger.

For a few other people on both sides, the Utah War was a foundational experience if not an epiphany. From this background, they sprang into a panoply of well-known adventures both heroic and tragic, often in connection with the Civil War, in which dozens of Utah veterans served as general officers and Medal of Honor recipients. Most cases of post-1858 prominence or notoriety for such people are remembered somewhere in Utah, the American West, or Europe as well as among the enormous cadre of Civil War enthusiasts. What has been largely lost is an awareness of the linkage of such post-1858 adventures to the Utah War and vice versa.[36]

The prime example of a Utah War villain-in-waiting was William C. Quantrill, the Civil War's most notorious guerrilla. Chief among those troops later known for more positive adventures were Charles H. Wilcken and John Jerome ("Johnny") Healy. After deserting from the Fourth U.S. Infantry in October 1857, Private Wilcken crossed into Mormon lines and converted. He became bodyguard, coachman, nurse, and pallbearer to Brigham Young's two presidential successors (John Taylor and Wilford Woodruff), as well as an adopted son of Apostle George Q. Cannon. He is little remembered outside Utah for these dramatic experiences of the late nineteenth century or for his family standing as the forebear of George Wilcken Romney and Mitt Romney.

---

[36]An extensive account of the Utah War's impact on the subsequent personal development of its most noteworthy participants, as well as discussion of the multiple societal forces unleashed by the conflict, appear in MacKinnon, "Prelude to Civil War: The Utah War's Impact and Legacy" in Alford, ed., *Civil War Saints*, 1–21; and "Epilogue to the Utah War: Impact and Legacy," 186–248.

Then there was Private Healy, a native of Cork, Ireland, who served as a teenaged dragoon with the Utah Expedition after filibustering in Nicaragua with Gen. William Walker. Following the Utah War, Healy drifted north to Montana's earliest gold strikes; co-founded Alberta's notorious whiskey-trading post, Fort Whoop-Up; and became sheriff of Montana's Fort Benton during the 1870s. While a Montana newspaper reporter, Healy coined the informal but enduring motto of the Royal Canadian Mounted Police: "They always get their man." By 1882 Healy had moved further west to establish a successful trading post at the foot of Alaska's Chilkoot Pass, gateway to the Klondike. During the subsequent gold rush, he became a transportation magnate on the Yukon River as agent for Chicago's Cudahy family, as well as the model for the Jacob Welse character in Jack London's first novel, *A Daughter of the Snows.* Former private Healy died of cirrhosis of the liver in San Francisco in 1908, penniless and exhausted after a failed effort to promote a railroad link between Siberia and Alaska beneath the Bering Straits.[37]

Other than Lorenzo Snow and Joseph F. Smith, the Nauvoo Legionnaires called postwar to become the fifth and sixth prophets of the LDS church, no soldier on either side of the Utah War rose higher than Theodore Schwan, a German immigrant to New York who had enlisted during the conflict in the Tenth U.S. Infantry's Company K as a fifteen-year-old. Between 1857 and 1916 Schwan held every rank from private to major general, receiving the Medal of Honor for Civil War heroism and commanding brigades at the turn of the century in Cuba and the Philippines. In the latter campaign Schwan was a comrade-in-arms to Brigham Young's West Pointer grandson, Richard Whitehead Young.

Among those other participants with striking adventures after the Utah War was Thomas L. Kane, but reflecting the continuing public controversy over the Utah settlement and Kane's role in it, President Buchanan barely acknowledged Kane's mediation of the conflict. During his June 1858 visit to the White House, Kane had told the president that he did not intend to seek public recognition for his efforts; Buchanan took Kane at his word and all but ignored him. On 17 November 1858 Eli K. Price, a mutual friend and prominent Pennsylvania Democrat, wrote to Buchanan: "As one of the many friends of Col. Thos. L. Kane, I sympathised much in his expedition

[37]For Healy's extraordinary adventures on both sides of the U.S.-Canadian border, see Tolton, *Healy's West.*

to the Mormons; and rejoiced that you were enabled to end that trouble without blood shed. Fearing the pressure of important matters might occasion [your] forgetfulness of what some of us believe it would be a pleasure to you to do, I write this note to say how much it would gratify Mr. Kane's friends to find his service noticed in your Annual Message. He has not felt at liberty to defend himself against misrepresentations, nor can we advise him to do so while it might prejudice any public interest." Thus pressured, Buchanan drafted a single sentence three weeks later in which he simultaneously recognized and disavowed Kane, telling Congress that "I cannot, in this connection, refrain from mentioning the valuable services of Colonel Thomas L. Kane, who, from motives of pure benevolence, and without any official character or pecuniary compensation, visited Utah during the last inclement winter for the purpose of contributing to the pacification of the Territory." In publishing his reminiscences ten years later, Buchanan again limited discussion of Kane's role to a repetition of the same sentence. It was presidential appreciation of a stripe described in early 1858 by Pat Kane and Buchanan's disaffected friends as "Buck all over."[38]

Within a week of Buchanan's 1858 annual message, Kane shook off his vow of anonymity and disengagement from Utah affairs and accepted an invitation to lecture at the New-York Historical Society, beginning to gather materials from which to deliver there an address in defense of Alfred Cumming.[39] It was a speech designed to outmaneuver a president both skeptical about the governor's effectiveness and politically pressured to remove him as a Brigham Young puppet. Once delivered in Manhattan on 21 March 1859 and publicized nationally, Kane's laudatory lecture made it virtually impossible for Buchanan to recall Cumming.[40]

Thomas L. Kane died in 1883 with his reputation intact. Beyond the world of Utah and Mormonism, historians remember him for philanthropy and distinguished service as a Union Army general. True to form, at the beginning of the Civil War, Kane abruptly left his family to recruit a regiment of

---

[38]Price to Buchanan, 17 November 1858, accessed 17 April 2014, http://natedsanders.com/Eli-K-Price-Autograph-Letter-Signed-to-President-lot13885.aspx, copy in author's possession; "Second Annual Message of the President," 6 December 1858, Moore, ed., *The Works of James Buchanan,* 10:245, and Buchanan, *Mr. Buchanan's Administration,* 238.

[39]Kane to H. H. Cumming, 18 December 1858, Thomas L. Kane Collection, American Historical Manuscripts Collection, New-York Historical Society.

[40]MacKinnon, ed., "*The Executive of Utah.*"

Pennsylvania riflemen and seek an active field command. He would challenge a superior officer to a duel and suffer serious illnesses as well as war wounds. They were are all experiences trying to Elizabeth Kane and reminiscent of her husband's dramatic Utah mission. Yet if Thomas's Civil War experiences were an ordeal for Elizabeth, her father sensed both greatness and divine guidance awaiting Kane, speculating that it would be connected to his Utah mission. Four months into the war Elizabeth reminded her husband of Mr. Wood's prophecy: "I can't help thinking that he is destined to make his mark on these times, that Utah journey . . . may all have been the Master's preparations for a work He had on hand for him to do."[41] At Gettysburg, his last battle before resigning his commission, Kane fought alongside and against a surprising number of other generals whom he had met in Utah as junior officers. Years later, Utah memorialized Kane in the name of one of its southernmost counties and with a handsome statue placed in the state capitol's rotunda. Kane's family did not comply with his wish that his heart be buried in the Salt Lake Temple; instead he lies intact beneath a Presbyterian chapel erected in his honor in Kane, Pennsylvania, a structure later acquired by the LDS church and is now a museum.

To the end, Kane believed the story that he worked so hard to sell to the Buchanan administration, Congress, and the American public—that during the winter of 1858 an unappreciated Brigham Young had risked his own standing among belligerent Mormons to avoid bloodshed and protect the U.S. Army's Utah Expedition when he supposedly had the power to destroy it. In 1860 Kane was still at it, writing to Sen. Richard Mason of Virginia and President Buchanan to describe a Mormon faction that he called "the more excited of the Utah zealots, whose longing for a war with the United States is even now kept under [check] by Young and Company with considerable difficulty."[42]

In September 1877, returning east from Young's funeral, Kane's train entered the familiar splendor of Echo Canyon. As the cars swayed and the cliffs passed, Kane once again reached for his diary. There he recorded jumbled thoughts about Brigham Young, bloodshed, and prosecution of the Utah War, but nothing about his own role in ending the conflict or the recent execution by firing squad of John D. Lee:

---

[41]Elizabeth to Thomas, 25 August 1861, Box 21, Fd 1, Kane Family Papers, BYU.

[42]Kane to Mason, 20 April 1860, enclosure to Kane to Buchanan, same date, James Buchanan Papers, HSP.

> Coming back on Weber & Echo—The truth upon the Echo fortifications &c—[Young] had assumed the responsibility of ordering the first blood shed himself. The man who sheds blood before he has my order his blood be on his own head. And he (?) was quite the man at some last moment to have, himself, loosened a mass of rock prepared for his lever as if upon the heads of an advancing foe, disregarding his last warning. It was expected by numbers that he would do this from some commanding height where his prophetic figure would be seen cutting against the sky. But this would have been merely as a signal. The best proof of his determination to put off shedding blood is found in his forbidding cavalry attacks. He had a fine body of well-fed horse to bring upon our poor crowbaits, and it was the expectation of an attack from them which first sent the word of alarm that reached [Secretary] Floyd.
>
> But he said, "No. Do nothing but assail their transportation" (November 1857). After that when it was plain they would not and could not take up towards Fort Hall [Oregon Territory]—they could not move anywhere he said, "Use no unnecessary violence whatever." About the same time he said, "They seem bent on starving themselves to death."[43]

What Thomas L. Kane also had a right to remember during that last eastbound passage through Echo Canyon was the key contribution he had made twenty years earlier to a controversial but peaceful resolution of the Utah War. By September 1858 Kane was still unemployed, financially strapped, and disgusted with James Buchanan—a combination of forces under which his physical ailments morphed into mental depression. The blues had also struck Brigham Young immediately after the Utah Expedition's march through Salt Lake City. It was a low from which Kane's alarmed father-in-law pulled him with a perceptive reminder of both his accomplishments and the courage he had mustered in facing adversity on a grand scale:

> Perhaps the depression is only what ought [to] have been expected after the high strung enthusiasm which carried you so triumphantly through your Mormon mission. You attained your object of preventing bloodshed fully. Therefore thank God for having been the instrument in His hands of effecting that good. Think how much you have had to go through during the last 10 months, including as they do very extraordinary illness and your father's death. Who would have ventured to prophecy in September 1857,

[43] "Thomas L. Kane's Account of His Journey to Salt Lake City, 30 August 1877–17 September 1877," original recopied in hand of Mrs. Kane, Kane Family Papers, BYU. In 1877 Kane was still probably unaware of Young's authorization for the use of lethal force in October 1857 and his directive that the Legion's troops were to target the Utah Expedition's officers and guides.

> that you could have passed through the trials you have since undergone and been alive to tell the tale. Yet God has spared you & for some good end.[44]

The reality was that, despite all of the illness along the way, hyperactive involvement in the Utah War had been a tonic and worthy challenge for Thomas L. Kane. As Thomas was departing for his Utah mission in January 1858, his younger brother John had tried to explain to his unsettled family that inactivity in Pennsylvania was ruining Kane: "Tom is never so well as when exposed to what would kill most men of his build, and that hard life in open air (no matter how hard) always agrees with him better than the most tranquil of sedentary existence. . . . He is too great a man to occupy himself with trifles." Two months later an exhausted Kane provided his own self-assessment, after surviving what he called "the magical storm," his wilderness ordeal in the snow to find General Kimball at Quaking Aspen Hill: "This is the discipline adapted for my nature, and I should have more of it. I should live in the stone fortress on the rocks of the moon." For Thomas L. Kane that storm, like the war itself, "compelled an active struggle with the danger it threatened. It was a grand & solemn enactment productive of the highest poetical impression."[45]

A complete, accurate understanding of this extraordinary territorial-federal conflict still beckons those interested in the history of Mormon Utah, the American West, and even international relations in a wide range of unlikely places. For nearly sixty years, the conflict has remained as colorful an episode as I have ever encountered. It is one during which my grandfather was born and a war my grandchildren now seek to understand in their own way.

[44] William Wood to Kane, 22 September 1858, Kane Family Papers, BYU.

[45] *At Sword's Point, Part 1*, 511–12; Kane, "Diary II (1858)," 28 March 1858, 8 and 8A.

Bibliography

This bibliography has separate sections for secondary sources (books, articles and book chapters, and unpublished works), published primary sources, unpublished primary sources, and newspapers.

Abbreviations

APS	American Philosophical Society, Philadelphia
Beinecke Library	Yale Collection of Western Americana, Beinecke Rare Book and Manuscript Library, Yale University, New Haven
BYU	Brigham Young University, Provo, Utah
HSP	The Hist. Society of Pennsylvania, Philadelphia
LC	Library of Congress, Washington, D.C.
LDS Archives	Church History Library and Archives, The Church of Jesus Christ of Latter-day Saints, Salt Lake City
NARA	National Archives and Records Administration, Washington, D.C.
NYPL	New York Public Library, Astor, Lenox and Tilden Foundations
RG	Record Group
SLC	Salt Lake City

Secondary Sources: Books

Aird, Polly. *Mormon Convert, Mormon Defector: A Scottish Immigrant in the American West, 1848–1861.* Norman, Okla.: Arthur H. Clark, 2009.

Alford, Kenneth L., ed. *Civil War Saints.* Provo and S.L.C.: Religious Studies Center, Brigham Young University, and Deseret Book, 2012.

Arrington, Leonard J. *Great Basin Kingdom: An Economic History of the Latter-day Saints 1830–1900.* Cambridge, Mass.: Harvard University Press, 1958.

Bagley, Will. *Blood of the Prophets: Brigham Young and the Massacre at Mountain Meadows.* Norman: University of Oklahoma Press, 2002.

Baley, Charles W. *Disaster at the Colorado: Beale's Wagon Road and the First Emigrant Party.* Logan: Utah State University Press, 2002.

Barba, Preston Albert. *Balduin Möllhausen, the German Cooper.* Philadelphia: Publications of the University of Pennsylvania, *American Germanica* 17, 1914.

Beidleman, Richard G. *California's Frontier Naturalists.* Berkeley: University of California Press, 2006.

———. "The 35th Parallel: Whipple and the Naturalists, 1853–1854," *California's Frontier Naturalists.* Berkeley: University of California Press, 2006, 256–70.

Bigler, David L. *Forgotten Kingdom: The Mormon Theocracy in the American West, 1847–1896.* Spokane, Wash.: Arthur H. Clark, 1998.

Bigler, David L., and Will Bagley. *The Mormon Rebellion: America's First Civil War, 1857–1858.* Norman: University of Oklahoma Press, 2011.

Bitton, Davis. *George Q. Cannon: A Biography.* S.L.C.: Deseret Book Company, 1999.

Blaine, James G. *Twenty Years of Congress: From Lincoln to Garfield: With a Review of Events Which Led to the Political Revolution of 1860.* 2 vols. Norwich, Conn.: Henry Bill Publishing Company, 1884 and 1886.

Brooks, Juanita. *The Mountain Meadows Massacre.* Norman: University of Oklahoma Press, 1962.

Burns, Robert I., S.J. *The Jesuits and the Indian Wars of the Northwest.* New Haven, Conn.: Yale University Press, 1966.

Bylund, Duane A. *In Search of Johnston's Army: Old Camp Floyd and West Creek as Seen through the Eyes of a Relic Hunter.* New York: Iuniverse, Inc., 2009.

Casebier, Dennis G. *The Mojave Road.* Norco, Calif.: Tales of the Mojave Road Publishing Company, 1975.

Chaky, Doreen. *Terrible Justice: Sioux Chiefs and U.S. Soldiers on the Upper Missouri, 1854–1868.* Norman, Okla.: Arthur H. Clark, 2012.

Chittenden, Hiram Martin. *History of Early Steamboat Navigation on the Missouri River: Life and Adventures of Joseph LaBarge.* 2 vols. New York: Francis P. Harper, 1903.

Collins, Michael L. *Texas Devils: Rangers and Regulars on the Lower Rio Grande, 1846–1861.* Norman: University of Oklahoma Press, 2008.

Compton, Todd M. *A Frontier Life: Jacob Hamblin, Indian Missionary and Explorer.* S.L.C.: University of Utah Press, 2013.

Connelley, William Elsey. *Quantrill and the Border Wars.* Lawrence: Kansas Heritage Press, 1992.

Crocheron, Augusta Joyce. *Representative Women of Deseret: A Book of Biographical Sketches, to Accompany the Picture Bearing the Same Title.* S.L.C.: J. C. Graham, 1884.

Crosby, Caroline Barnes, Edward Leo Lyman, Susan Ward, and S. George Ellsworth, eds. *No Place to Call Home: The 1807–1857 Life Writings of Caroline Barnes Crosby, Chronicler of Outlying Mormon Communities.* Logan: Utah State University Press, 2005.

Cumming, Joseph Bryan. *A Sketch of the Descendants of David Cumming and Memoirs of the War between the States.* Augusta, Ga.: Privately printed, 1925.

Curtis, George Ticknor. *Life of James Buchanan, Fifteenth President of the United States.* 2 vols. New York: Harper & Bros., 1883.

Cutrer, Thomas W. *Ben McCulloch and the Frontier Military Tradition.* Chapel Hill: University of North Carolina Press, 1993.

Derr, Jill Mulvay, and Karen Lynn Davidson, comps. and eds. *Eliza R. Snow: The Complete Poetry.* Provo and S.L.C.: Brigham Young University Press and University of Utah Press, 2009.

Ecelbarger, Gary W. *Frederick W. Lander: The Great Natural American Soldier.* Baton Rouge: Louisiana State University Press, 2000.

Ettinger, Amos Aschbach. *The Mission to Spain of Pierre Soule, 1853–1855: A Study in the Cuban Diplomacy of the United States.* New Haven, Conn.: Yale University Press, 1932.

Furniss, Norman F. *The Mormon Conflict, 1850–1859.* New Haven, Conn.: Yale University Press, 1960.

Gammon, C. L. *The Great Mormon War of 1857 and 1858.* N.p.: 3312 Publishing, 2013.

Gates, Zethyl. *Mariano Medina: Colorado Mountain Man.* Boulder, Colo.: Johnson Publishing, 1981.

Goetzmann, William H. *Army Exploration in the American West, 1803–1863.* New Haven, Conn.: Yale University Press, 1959.

———. *Exploration and Empire: The Explorer and the Scientist in the Winning of the West.* New York: Alfred A. Knopf, 1966.

Gray, William H. *History of Oregon, 1792–1849, Drawn From Personal Observation and Authentic Information.* Portland: Harris & Holman, 1870.

Grow, Matthew J. *"Liberty to the Downtrodden": Thomas L. Kane, Romantic Reformer.* New Haven, Conn.: Yale University Press, 2009.

Hale, Frederick, ed. *Danes in North America.* Seattle: University of Washington Press, 1984.

Haley, James L. *Sam Houston.* Norman: University of Oklahoma Press, 2002.

Hirshon, Stanley P. *The White Tecumseh: A Biography of William T. Sherman.* New York: Wiley, 1997.

Hollon, W. Eugene. *Beyond the Cross Timbers: The Travels of Randolph B. Marcy, 1812–1887.* Norman: University of Oklahoma Press, 1955.

Holzer, Harold. *Lincoln and the Power of the Press.* New York: Simon & Schuster, 2014.

Hunter, Milton R. *Brigham Young the Colonizer.* Independence, Mo.: Zion's Printing and Publishing, 1945.

Johnson, Forrest Bryant. *The Last Camel Charge: The Untold Story of America's Desert Military Experiment.* New York: Berkley Caliber, 2012.

Johnston, Joe. *Necessary Evil: Settling Missouri with a Rope and a Gun.* St. Louis: Missouri Hist. Museum Press, 2014.

Johnston, William Preston. *The Life of Albert Sidney Johnston: Embracing His Services in the Armies of the United States, the Republic of Texas, and the Confederate States.* New York: D. Appleton and Co., 1878.

Josephy, Alvin M., Jr. *The Nez Perce Indians and the Opening of the Northwest.* New Haven, Conn.: Yale University Press, 1965.

Klein, Philip S. *President James Buchanan: A Biography.* University Park: Pennsylvania State University Press, 1962.

Larsen, Marlin Kent. *The Forgotten Son: William Henry Kimball.* Hyrum, Utah: Downs Printing, 2011.

Leland, Joy, ed. *Frederick West Lander: A Biographical Sketch (1822–1862).* Reno, Nev.: Desert Research Institute, 1993.

Leslie, Edward E. *The Devil Knows How to Ride: The True Story of William Clarke Quantrill and His Confederate Raiders.* New York: Random House, 1996.

Lyman, Edward Leo. *Amasa Mason Lyman, Mormon Apostle and Apostate: A Study in Dedication.* S.L.C.: University of Utah Press, 2009.

———. *San Bernardino: The Rise and Fall of a California Community.* S.L.C.: Signature Books, 1996.

MacKinnon, William P. *Predicting the Past: The Utah War's Twenty-First Century Future.* Leonard J. Arrington Mormon History Lecture Series, No. 14. Logan: Utah State University Press, 2009.

Madsen, Steven K. *Exploring Desert Stone: John N. Macomb's 1859 Expedition to the Canyonlands of the Colorado.* Logan: Utah State University Press, 2010.

Mason, David Vaughn. *Brigham Young: Sovereign in America.* New York: Routledge, 2014.

Maxwell, John Gary. *The Civil War Years in Utah: The Kingdom of God and the Territory That Did Not Fight.* Norman: University of Oklahoma Press, 2016.

May, Robert E. *Manifest Destiny's Underworld: Filibustering in Antebellum America.* Chapel Hill: University of North Carolina Press, 2002.

———. *The Southern Dream of a Caribbean Empire, 1854–1861.* Gainesville: University of Florida Press, reprinted 2002 from same title, Baton Rouge: Louisiana State University Press, 1973.

McGavin, E. Cecil. *U.S. Soldiers Invade Utah.* Boston: Meador Publishing, 1937.

McGill, James W. *Rediscovered Frontiersman: Timothy Goodale.* Independence, Mo.: Oregon-California Trails Assn., 2009.

Merrill, George F. *The First One Hundred Years of American Geology.* New York: Hafner Publishing, 1969, facsimile of 1924 edition.

Moorman, Donald R., with Gene A. Sessions. *Camp Floyd and the Mormons: The Utah War.* S.L.C.: University of Utah Press, 1992; reprinted 2005.

Mumey, Nolie. *The Life of Jim Baker, 1818–1898: Trapper, Scout, Guide and Indian Fighter.* Denver: World Press, 1931.

Nelson, Jack William. *Forgotten Pathfinders: Along the North Branch of the Old Spanish Trail, 1650–1850.* Grand Junction, Colo.: Self published, 2003.

Nielson, Roger B. *Roll Call at Old Camp Floyd, Utah Territory: Soldiers of Johnston's Army at the Upper Camp, 8 July to 8 September 1858.* Springville, Utah: Self published, 2006.

Olliff, Donathon C. *Reforma Mexico and the United States: A Search for Alternatives to Annexation, 1854–1861.* Tuscaloosa: University of Alabama Press, 1981.

Pelzer, Louis. *Augustus Caesar Dodge: A Study in American Politics.* Iowa City: State Historical Society of Iowa, 1909.

Perez, Louis A., Jr. *Cuba in the American Imagination: Metaphor and the Imperial Ethos.* Chapel Hill: University of North Carolina Press, 2008.

Peskin, Allan. *Winfield Scott and the Profession of Arms.* Kent, Ohio: Kent State University Press, 2003.

Peterson, Jesse G. *A Route for the Overland Stage: James H. Simpson's 1859 Trail Across the Great Basin.* Logan: Utah State University Press, 2008.

Poll, Richard D. *Quixotic Mediator: Thomas L. Kane and the Utah War.* Ogden, Utah: Weber State University Press, 1985.

Quist, John W., and Michael J. Birkner, eds. *James Buchanan and the Coming of the Civil War.* Gainesville: University Press of Florida, 2013.

Rice, William B. *The Los Angeles Star, 1851–1864: The Beginnings of Journalism in Southern California.* New York: Greenwood Press, 1969.

Roberts, Brigham H. *A Comprehensive History of the Church of Jesus Christ of Latter-day Saints, Century I.* 6 vols. S.L.C.: Deseret News Press, 1930.

Roberts, Ralph S. *Bishop David Evans and His Family.* Lehi, Utah: The Bishop David Evans Family Assn., 1972.

Roland, Charles P. *Albert Sidney Johnston: Soldier of Three Republics.* Lexington: University of Kentucky Press, 1964; reprinted 2001.

Rowan, Steven W. *The Baron in the Grand Canyon: Friedrich Wilhelm von Egloffstein in the West.* Columbia: University of Missouri Press, 2012.

Schindler, Harold. *Orrin Porter Rockwell: Man of God, Son of Thunder.* S.L.C.: University of Utah Press, 1983.

Scroggs, William O. *Filibusters and Financiers: The Story of William Walker and His Associates.* New York: MacMillan, 1916.

Sehlinger, Peter J. *Kentucky's Last Cavalier: General William Preston, 1816–1887.* Lexington: Kentucky Hist. Society, 2004.

Shuler, Jack. *The Thirteenth Turn: A History of the Noose.* New York: Public Affairs, 2014.

Stenhouse, T. B. H. *The Rocky Mountain Saints: A Full and Complete History of the Mormons, From the First Vision of Joseph Smith to the last Courtship of Brigham Young . . .* New York: D. Appleton and Company, 1873.

Stickles, Arndt M. *Simon Bolivar Buckner: Borderland Knight.* Chapel Hill: University of North Carolina Press, 1940.

Stocqueler, J. H. *The British Soldier: An Anecdotal History.* London: Wm. S. Orr and Company, 1857.

Stott, Clifford L. *Search for Sanctuary: Brigham Young and the White Mountain Expedition.* S.L.C.: University of Utah Press, 1984.

Thompson, Jerry. *Civil War to the Bloody End: The Life and Times of Major General Samuel P. Heintzelman.* College Station: Texas A&M University Press, 2006.

Tidball, Eugene C. *Soldier-Artist of the Great Reconnaissance: John C. Tidball and the 35th Parallel Pacific Railroad Survey.* Tucson: University of Arizona Press, 2004.

Tolton, Gordon E. *Healy's West: The Life and Times of John J. Healy.* Victoria, B.C.: Heritage House, 2014.

Tullidge, Edward W. *History of Salt Lake City and Its Founders.* S.L.C.: Star Printing, 1886.

Turner, John G. *Brigham Young, Pioneer Prophet.* Cambridge: Belknap Press of Harvard University Press, 2012.

Van Wagenen, Michael Scott. *The Texas Republic and the Mormon Kingdom of God.* College Station: Texas A&M University Press, 2002.

Vibart, Col. Henry Meredith. *Addiscombe, Its Heroes and Men of Note.* Westminster, U.K.: Archibald Constable and Company, 1894.

Walker, Ronald W. *Wayward Saints: The Godbeites and Brigham Young.* Urbana: University of Illinois Press, 1998.

———. *Heroes and Hero Worship: Brigham Young and the Utah War.* Leonard J. Arrington Mormon History Lecture Series, No. 20. Logan: Utah State University Press, 2015.

———, Richard E. Turley Jr., and Glen M. Leonard. *Massacre at Mountain Meadows.* New York: Oxford University Press, 2008.

Wallace, Edward S. *The Great Reconnaissance: Soldiers, Artists and Scientists on the Frontier, 1848–1861.* Boston: Little, Brown and Company, 1955.

Wight, Jermy Benton. *Frederick W. Lander and the Lander Trail.* Bedford, Wyo.: Star Valley Llama, 1993.

Wilson, Mark R. *The Business of Civil War: Military Mobilization and the State, 1861–1865.* Baltimore: Johns Hopkins University Press, 2006.

Woodward, Arthur. *Feud on the Colorado.* Los Angeles: Westernlore Press, 1955.

Woodward C. Vann, ed. *Mary Chestnut's Civil War.* New Haven, Conn.: Yale University Press, 1981.

Zobell, Albert L., Jr. *Sentinel in the East: A Biography of Thomas L. Kane.* S.L.C.: Nicholas G. Morgan, Sr. Publisher, 1965.

Secondary Sources: Articles and Book Chapters

Aird, Polly. "'You Nasty Apostates, Clear Out': Reasons for Disaffection in the Late 1850s," *Journal of Mormon Hist.* 30 (Fall 2004): 129–207.

Alexander, Thomas G. "Carpetbaggers, Reprobates, and Liars: Federal Judges and the Utah War (1857–58)," *The Historian* 70 (Summer 2008): 209–38.

———. "Conflict and Fraud: Utah Public Land Surveys in the 1850s, the Subsequent Investigation, and Problems with the Land Disposal System," *Utah Hist. Qtly.* 80 (Spring 2012): 108–31.

——— and Leonard J. Arrington. "Camp in the Sagebrush: Camp Floyd, Utah, 1858–1861," *Utah Hist. Qtly.* 34 (Winter 1966): 3–21.

Alford, Kenneth L. "Latter-day Saint Poetry and Songs of the Utah War," *Mormon Hist. Studies* 12 (Spring 2011): 1–28.

Allen, Curtis R. "Soldiers into Saints: Saints into Soldiers," *Utah Genealogical Assoc. Crossroads* 4 (December 2008): 171–78; expanded version published as "William Ashton: Handcart Pioneer and Five-Year Foot Soldier," www.tellmy storytoo.com/pdf/handcart pioneerandfootsoldier2.pdf, accessed 17 November 2012.

Ambacher, Bruce. "George M. Dallas, Cuba, and the Election of 1856," *The Pennsylvania Magazine of Hist. and Biography* 97 (July 1973): 318–32.

Austerman, Wayne R. "Parker Burnham: An Expressman of Old El Paso," *Password* 27 (Spring 1982): 5–14.

———. "The Brash Reinsman: Ben Ficklin's Adventures," *Virginia Cavalcade* 33 (Winter 1984): 114–25.

Bagley, Will, and Ronald W. Walker. "Did Brigham Young Order a Massacre?" *True West Magazine* 50 (April 2003): 31–34.

Ball, Durwood. "Filibusters and Regular Troops in San Francisco, 1851–1855," *Military Hist. of the West* 28 (Fall 1998): 161–83.

Ballenger, T. L. "Colonel Albert Sidney Johnston's March through Indian Territory in 1855," *Chronicles of Oklahoma* 47, no. 2 (1969): 132–35.

Barney, Ronald O. "The Mormons Captured during the Utah War in 1857," *The Pioneer* 29 (July–Aug. 1982): 8–9.

Barrett, Gwynn. "Walter Murray Gibson: The Shepherd Saint of Lanai Re-Visited," *Utah Hist. Qtly.* 40 (Spring 1972): 142–62.

Beeton, Barbara. "James Hervey Simpson in the Great Basin," *Montana The Magazine of Western History* 28 (Winter 1978): 28–43.

Beidleman, Richard G. "Up the Colorado River with Ives and the Naturalists," *California's Frontier Naturalists.* Berkeley: University of California Press, 2006, 294–306.

Bigler, David L. "Mormon Missionaries, the Utah War, and the 1858 Bannock Raid on Fort Limhi," *Montana The Magazine of Western Hist.* 53 (Autumn 2003): 30–43.

———. "The Aiken Party Executions and the Utah War, 1857–1858," *Western Hist. Qtly.* 38 (Winter 2007): 451–70.

———"The Crisis at Fort Limhi, 1858," *Utah Hist. Qtly.* 35 (Spring 1967): 121–36.

Binder, Frederick Moore. "James Buchanan and the Earl of Clarendon: An Uncertain Relationship," *Diplomacy and Statecraft* 6 (July 1995): 323–41.

Bohl, Susan. "A War on Civilians: Order Number 11 and the Evacuation of Western Missouri," *Prologue: The Journal of the National Archives* 36 (Spring 2004): 44–51.

Bordewich, Fergus M. "A Cajoling, Bullying Manipulator," review of Harold Holzer's *Lincoln and the Power of the Press,* in *Wall Street Journal,* 18–19 October 2014, C6/1–5.

Brackett, Col. Albert G., "Albert Sidney Johnston," *United Service: A Monthly Review of Military and Naval Affairs* 4 (November 1890): 460–65.

Bradley, James H. "Affairs at Fort Benton from 1831 to 1869," *Contributions to the Hist. Soc. of Montana* 3 (1900): 201–87.

Briggs, Robert H. "The Utah War," chapter 3, *The Fate of the Mountain Meadows Militiamen* (monograph pending publication, copy in editor's possession).

Britsch, R. Lanier. "Another Visit with Walter Murray Gibson," *Utah Hist. Qtly.* 46 (Winter 1978): 65–78.

Bush, Lester E., Jr. "A Peculiar People: 'The Physiological Aspect of Mormonism 1850–1975,'" *Dialogue: A Journal of Mormon Thought* 12 (Fall 1979): 61–83.

Carter, D. Robert. "Guard Quarters: A Den of Dereliction," *(Provo) Daily Herald,* 26 June 2005, B2.

Clarke, Henry S. "W. C. Quantrill in 1858," *Kansas Hist. Collections* 7 (1901–1902): 218–23.

Compton, Todd M. "'In & through the roughefist country it has ever been my lot to travel': Jacob Hamblin's 1858 Expedition across the Colorado," *Utah Hist. Qtly.* 80 (Winter 2012): 4–21.

Cortada, James W. "An Elusive Cuba," *Spain and the American Civil War: Relations at Mid-Century, 1855–1868,* in *Transactions of the American Philosophical Society* 70, Part 4 (July 1980): 21–30.

Cravath, Jay. "Iretaba: Mohave Chief and American Indian Diplomat," *The California Territorial Qtly.* 103 (Fall 2015): 24–32.

Crocheron, Augusta Joyce. "Reminiscences of General Kane," *The Contributor* 6 (1884–85): 475–77.

Crouch, Barry A. "A 'Fiend in Human Shape'? William Clarke Quantrill and His Biographers," *Kansas History* 22 (Summer 1999): 143–56.

Cuthbertson, Gilbert. "Shepherd Was Name to Fear in Border War Era," 9 September 1965, *Kansas City (Mo.) Times,* 140.

Davis, W. N. "Western Justice: The Court at Fort Bridger, Utah Territory," *Utah Hist. Qtly.* 23 (April 1955): 99–125.

De Bruhl, Marshall. "In Search of Sam Houston," *Prologue* 27 (Spring 1995): 6–15.

Dickson, Ephriam D., III. "Crazy Horse: Who Really Wielded the Bayonet that Killed the Oglala Leader?" *Greasy Grass* 12 (May 1996): 2–10.

———. "On the Trail of Captain Simpson's Illusive Photographer, 1858–59," *Fort Douglas Vedette: Newsletter of the Fort Douglas Museum Association* 34 (Summer 2009): 3–6.

———. "'Shadowy Figures About Whom Little is Known': Artists of the Simpson Expedition, 1858–59," *Utah Hist. Qtly.* 83 (Fall 2015): 270–89.

Dorrance, William H. "Scorched Earth Plans for O'ahu," *The Hawaiian Journal of Hist.* 33 (1999): 159–69.

Evans, Max J. "William C. Staines: 'English Gentleman of Refinement and Culture,'" *Utah Hist. Qtly.* 43 (Fall 1975): 410–20.

Flaherty, Jane. "'The Exhausted Condition of the Treasury' on the Eve of the Civil War," *Civil War Hist.* 55 (July 2009): 244–77.

Foster, Robert L. "During the Winter of 1857–58, Captain Randolph B. Marcy Led a Desperate 634-Mile March to Secure Supplies," *Wild West* 17 (February 2005): 62–65.

Fox, Ruth May. "The Echo Canyon War," *Improvement Era* 35 (July 1932): 530, 552–53.

Gaede, Frederick C., and James S. Hutchins, "The Military Art of Albert Tracy," *Military Collector and Historian* 48 (Spring 1996): 17–25.

——— and Michael F. Bremer. "Albert Tracy Revisited," *Military Collector and Historian* 56 (Spring 2004): 56–58.

Godfrey, Audrey M. "Housewives, Hussies, and Heroines: The Women with Johnston's Army," *Utah Hist. Qtly.* 54 (Spring 1986): 157–78.

Goetzmann, William H. "The Topographical Engineers and the Western Movement," *The Brand Book, New York Posse of The Westerners* 4 (1958): 77–81, 90–91.

Gorenfeld, Will. "The Taos Mutiny of 1855," *New Mexico Hist. Review* 88 (Summer 2013): 287–319.

Gould, James Warren. "The Filibuster of Walter Murray Gibson," *Annual Report for 1959*. Honolulu: Hawaiian Hist. Soc., 1960: 7–32.

Greeley, Horace. "Utah and the Mormons," in *The Tribune Almanac and Political Register for 1859*. New York: H. Greeley & Co., 1859.

Grow, Matthew. " 'I Have Given Myself to the Devil': Thomas L. Kane and the Culture of Honor," *Utah Hist. Qtly.* 73 (Fall 2005): 345–64.

Hafen, LeRoy R. "A Winter Rescue March Across the Rockies," *The Colorado Magazine* 4 (January 1927): 7–13.

Hamilton, Lt. W. R. "History of the Mormon Rebellion, 1856–57," *United Service: A Monthly Review of Military and Naval Affairs* 4 (July–December 1890): 1–22, 183–91, 272–82, 380–89, 446–59, 587–95; and 5 (January–April 1891): 65–71, 148–61, 264–68, 342–48.

Hartley, William G. "The Miller, the Bishop, and the 'Move South,' " *BYU Studies* 20, no. 1 (1979): 99–105.

———. "Dangerous Outpost: Thomas Corless and the Fort Limhi/Salmon River Mission," *Mormon Hist. Studies* 2 (Fall 2001): 135–62.

Houston, Alan Fraser, and Jourdan Moore Houston. "The 1859 Lander Expedition Revisited: 'Worthy Relics' Tell New Tales," *Montana The Magazine of Western Hist.* 49 (September 1999): 50–71.

Huett, Wil. "A Man Called Mary Anne," *True West* (November 1991): 42–45.

Hunter, Leslie Gene. "The Mojave Expedition of 1858–59," *Journal of the Southwest* 21 (Summer 1979): 137–56.

Jenson, Andrew. "Walter Murray Gibson: A Sketch of His Life and Adventures, in Two Chapters," chapter 1, *Improvement Era* 4 (November 1900): 5–13.

Jones, Zachary R. " 'Wars and Rumors of Wars': United Kingdom Latter-day Saints and the Crimean War, 1853–1856," *Mormon Hist. Studies* 14 (Spring 2013): 29–43.

Kaufman, Scott, and John A. Soares, Jr. " 'Sagacious Beyond Praise'? Winfield Scott and Anglo-American-Canadian Border Diplomacy, 1837–1860," *Diplomatic History* 30 (January 2006): 57–82.

Klein, Philip Shriver. "Bachelor Father: James Buchanan as a Family Man," *The Western Pennsylvania Hist. Magazine* 50 (July 1967): 199–214.

Langellier, John P. "The William Lee Diary Account of the James H. Simpson Expedition, 1858–59," *Annals of Wyoming* 59 (Fall 1987): 36–47.

Leavitt, Francis Hale. "Steam Navigation on the Colorado River," *California Hist. Soc. Qtly.* 22 (March 1943): 1–25.

LeCheminant, Wilford Hill. "A Crisis Averted? General Harney and the Change in Command of the Utah Expedition," *Utah Hist. Qtly.* 51 (Winter 1983): 30–45.

Lowry, Thomas P. "Boys in the Bag," *Civil War Times* 36 (August 1997): 50–53.

MacKinnon, William P. "125 Years of Conspiracy Theories: Origins of the Utah Expedition of 1857–58," *Utah Hist. Qtly.* 52 (Summer 1984): 212–30.

———. " 'Like Splitting a Man Up His Backbone': The Territorial Dismemberment of Utah, 1850–1896," *Utah Hist. Qtly.* 71 (Spring 2003): 100–24.

———. "Epilogue to the Utah War: Impact and Legacy," *Journal of Mormon Hist.* 29 (Fall 2003): 186–248.

———. "Loose in the Stacks: A Half-Century with the Utah War and Its Legacy," *Dialogue: A Journal of Mormon Thought* 40 (Spring 2007): 48–53.

———. "Sex, Subalterns, and Steptoe: Army Behavior, Mormon Rage, and Utah War Anxieties," *Utah Hist. Qtly.* 76 (Summer 2008): 227–46.

———. "Buchanan's Thrust from the Pacific: The Utah War's Ill-Fated Second Front," *Journal of Mormon History* 34 (Fall 2008): 226–60.

———. "'Who's in Charge Here?': Utah Expedition Command Ambiguity," *Dialogue: A Journal of Mormon Thought* 42 (Spring 2009): 30–64.

———. "The Utah War, 1857–1858," in W. Paul Reeve and Ardis E. Parshall, eds., *Mormonism: A Historical Encyclopedia*. Santa Barbara, Calif.: 2010, 120–22.

———. "Hammering Utah, Squeezing Mexico, and Coveting Cuba: James Buchanan's White House Intrigues," *Utah Hist. Qtly.* 80 (Spring 2012): 132–51.

———. "'Not as a Stranger': A Presbyterian Afoot in the Mormon Past," *Journal of Mormon Hist.* 38 (Spring 2012): 1–46.

———. "Fitz John Porter's Letter," Letter to Editor, *Journal of Mormon Hist.* 38 (Summer 2012): vii–ix.

———. "Presidential Billiards Revisited," Letter to Editor, *Journal of Mormon Hist.* 38 (Fall 2012): vii–x.

———. "Prelude to Armageddon: James Buchanan, Brigham Young, and a President's Initiation to Bloodshed," in *James Buchanan and the Coming of the Civil War,* John W. Quist and Michael J. Birkner, eds. Gainesville: University Press of Florida, 2013, 46–85.

———. "Into the Fray: Sam Houston's Utah War," *Journal of Mormon Hist.* 39 (Summer 2013): 198–241.

———. "Rooted in Utah: Civil War Strategy and Tactics, Generals and Guerrillas," in *Civil War Saints,* Kenneth L. Alford, ed. Provo and S.L.C.: Religious Studies Center, Brigham Young University, and Deseret Book, 2012, 385–97.

———. "Vita: Albert Gallatin Browne Jr., A Brief Life of an Early War Correspondent: 1832–1891," *Harvard Magazine* 111 (November–December 2008): 48–49.

———. "Rest of the Story," Letter to Editor, *Dialogue: A Journal of Mormon Thought* 42 (Summer 2009): xviii–xix.

———. "And the War Came: James Buchanan, the Utah Expedition, and the Decision to Intervene," *Utah Hist. Qtly.* 76 (Winter 2008): 22–37.

———. "'Take a Tap, Pard': The Utah Expedition as Finishing School for Civil War Hard Cases," in Kenneth L. Alford, ed., *Civil War Saints.* Provo and S.L.C.: Religious Studies Center, Brigham Young University, and Deseret Book, 2012, 393–96.

Madsen, Steven K. "The Old Spanish Trail: John N. Macomb's 1859 Expedition to the Canyonlands of the Colorado," *Overland Journal* 29 (Fall 2011): 87–107.

Martin, Ann Frederick. "Miguel Alona: The Hero of Cochetopa Pass," in *The Hispanic Contribution to the State of Colorado,* Jose de Onis, ed. Boulder, Colo.: Westview Press, 1976, 79–90.

May, Robert E. "Young American Males and Filibustering in the Age of Manifest Destiny: The United States Army as a Cultural Mirror," *The Journal of American Hist.* 78 (December 1991): 857–86.

McClellan, Richard D. "Not Your Average French Communist Mormon: A Short History of Louis A. Bertrand," *Mormon Hist. Studies* 2 (Fall 2000): 3–24.

Miller, David H. "Baron von Egloffstein and the First Published Images of Grand Canyon," in *A Rendezvous of Grand Canyon Historians: Ideas, Arguments, and Third-Person Accounts: Proceedings of the Third Grand Canyon History Symposium, January 2012,* Richard D. Quartaroli, comp. and ed. Flagstaff, Ariz.: Grand Canyon Hist. Society, 2013, 171–77.

———. "The Ives Expedition Revisited: A Prussian's Impressions," *Journal of Arizona Hist.* 13 (Spring 1972): 1–25.

———. "The Ives Expedition Revisted: Overland into Grand Canyon," *Journal of Arizona Hist.* 13 (Autumn 1972): 177–96.

Miller, Jeremy. "The Long Draw: On the Trail of an Artistic Mystery in the American West," *Harper's* (January 2012): 50–59.

Moody, Marshall D. "Kit Carson, Agent to the Indians in New Mexico, 1853–1861," *New Mexico Hist. Review* 28 (January 1953): 1–20.

Morgan, Edwina. "Brigadier General Thomas Williams," *Michigan Genealogist* (Summer 2007): 13–18.

Murphy, Lawrence R. "Cantonment Burgwin, New Mexico, 1852–1860," *Arizona and the West* 15 (Spring 1973): 5–26.

Musser, Joseph B. "Walter Murray Gibson—Oceanic Adventurer," *United States Naval Institute Proceedings* 52 (September 1926): 1709–32.

Nelson, Jack. "Marcy's Ordeal along the North Branch of the Old Spanish Trail," *Spanish Traces* [Old Spanish Trail Assn.] 6 (Spring 2000): 28–30.

———. "The North Branch of the 'Old Spanish Trail' from 'Touse North to the Winty,' 1600–1850," *Journal of the Western Slope* 11 (Fall 1996): 1–43.

Nicholson, John. "Some Incidents in the Life of Nelson A. Empey," *Improvement Era* 8 (1904–1905): 16–22.

Oakes, Amy. "Diversionary Spectacle: The U.S. Government's Expedition to the Utah Territory, 1857–1858," *Diversionary War: Domestic Unrest and International Conflict.* Stanford: Stanford University Press, 2012, 100–29.

Parks, Donald. "The Army of the Mormon War, 1857–1858," *Journal of America's Military Past* 29 (Fall–Winter 2002): 74–89.

Parshall, Ardis E. "'Pursue, Retake & Punish': The 1857 Santa Clara Ambush," *Utah Hist. Qtly.* 73 (Winter 2005): 64–86.

Perry, Benjamin Franklin. "Alfred Cumming," *Reminiscences of Public Men, by Ex-Gov. B. F. Perry.* Philadelphia: John D. Avil & Co, 1883, 290–96.

Pinney, Marie. "Charles Becker: Pony Express Rider and Oregon Pioneer," *Oregon Hist. Qtly.* 67 (September 1966): 213–56.

Poll, Richard D. "The British Mission During the Utah War, 1857–58," in *Mormons in Early Victorian Britain,* Richard L. Jensen and Malcolm R. Thorp, eds. S.L.C.: University of Utah Press, 1989, 224–42.

———. "The Move South," *BYU Studies* 29 (Fall 1989): 65–88.

———. "Thomas L. Kane and the Utah War," *Utah Hist. Qtly.* 61 (Spring 1993): 112–35.

Potterf, Rex M. "John W. Dawson, Herodotus of Fort Wayne," *Old Fort News* 32 (Summer 1969): 1–14.

Renner, Richard Wilson. "Ye Kort Martial: A Tale of Chicago Politics, Theater, Journalism and Militia," *Journal of the Illinois State Hist. Soc.* 66 (Winter 1973): 376–86.

Robinson, John Cleveland. "The Utah Expedition," *Magazine of Amer. Hist.* 11 (January–June 1884): 335–41.

Rogers, Brent M. "A 'Distinction Between Mormons and Americans': Mormon Indian Missionaries, Federal Indian Policy, and the Utah War," *Utah Hist. Qtly.* 82 (Fall 2014): 250–71.

Rolph, Daniel N. "Kentucky Reactions and Casualties in the Utah War of 1857–58," *The Journal of Kentucky Studies* 4 (September 1987): 89–96.

Ryan, Garry David. "Camp Walbach, Nebraska Territory, 1858–1859: The Military Post at Cheyenne Pass," *Annals of Wyoming* 35 (April 1963): 5–20.

Sadler, Richard W. "The Spencer-Pike Affair, " *Utah Hist. Qtly.* 76 (Winter 2008): 79–93.

Sawin, Mark Metzler. "A Sentinel for the Saints: Thomas Leiper Kane and the Mormon Migration," *Nauvoo Journal* [subsequently *Mormon Hist. Studies*] 10 (Spring 1998): 17–27.

Seifrit, William C. "Charles Henry Wilcken: An Undervalued Saint," *Utah Hist. Qtly.* 55 (Fall 1987): 308–21.

Shengold, David. "From the Other Shore: Aleksandr Herzen on James Buchanan," *Slavic Studies* 51 (Winter 1992): 758–66.

Smart, William B. "Oregon and the Mormon Problem," *Reed College Bulletin* 26 (January 1948): 41–62.

Smith, Melvin T. "Colorado River Exploration and the Mormon War," *Utah Hist. Qtly.* 38 (Summer 1970): 207–23.

Snow, Jerry. "Getting History Right," in *A Rendezvous of Grand Canyon Historians: Ideas, Arguments and First-Person Arguments: Proceedings of the Third Grand Canyon History Symposium, January 2012,* Richard D. Quartaroli, comp. and ed. Flagstaff, Ariz.: Grand Canyon Hist. Society, 2013, 167–70.

Stowers, Robert E., and John M. Ellis, eds. "Charles A. Scott's Diary of the Utah Expedition, 1857–1861," *Utah Hist. Qtly.* 28 (April and October 1960): 154–76, 388–402.

Taft, Robert. "The Pictorial Record of the Old West: Heinrich Balduin Möllhausen (Part VI)," *Kansas Hist. Qtly.* 16 (August 1948): 225–44.

Thompson, Jerry D. "When Albert Sidney Johnston Came Home to Texas: Reconstruction Politics and the Reburial of a Hero," *Southwestern Hist. Qtly.* 103 (April 2000): 453–78.

Trowbridge, John Townsend. "An Early Contributor's Recollections," *Atlantic Monthly* 100 (November 1907): 582–93.

Unattributed, "Albert Gallatin Browne," *Report of the Harvard Class of 1853, 1849–1913, Issued on the Sixtieth Anniversary for the Use of the Class and Its Friends.* Cambridge, Mass.: [Harvard] University Press, 1913, 46–51.

Van Wagenen, Michael Scott. "Sam Houston and the Utah War," *Utah Hist. Qtly.* 76 (Winter 2008): 66–78.

Walker, Ronald W. "Buchanan, Popular Sovereignty, and the Mormons: The Election of 1856." *Utah Hist. Qtly.* 18 (Spring 2013): 108–32.

———. "The People Are 'Hoggafed or Humbugged': The 1851–52 National Reaction to Utah's 'Runaway' Officers." *Journal of Mormon History* 39 (Fall 2013): 1–43.

———. "Thomas L. Kane and Utah's Quest for Self-Government, 1846–51," *Utah Hist. Qtly.* 69 (Spring 2001): 100–19.

——— and Matthew J. Grow. "The Affair of the 'Runaways': Utah's First Encounter with the Federal Officers, Part I." *Journal of Mormon History* 40 (Winter 2014): 1–52.

Wells, Eugene T. "Kirk Anderson's Trip to Utah, 1858," *Missouri Hist. Society Bulletin* 18 (October 1961): 3–19.

Westwood, Howard C. "President Lincoln's Overture to Sam Houston," *Southwestern Hist. Qtly.* 88 (October 1984): 125–44.

White, David A., comp. "Alfred Cumming, 1856, Indians on the Upper Missouri," *News of the Plains and Rockies, 1803–1865,* 3:415–36.

———, comp. "Randolph B. Marcy, 1858 [Ft. Bridger To New Mexico And Return, 1857–58]," *News of the Plains and Rockies 1803–1865,* 4:183–211.

Secondary Sources: Unpublished Works

Allen, Curtis R. "The Tragedy of Jesse Wharton." Unpublished essay in editor's possession, courtesy of Mr. Allen, Centerville, Utah.

Bailey, Maj. Travis R. "A Victorious Defeat: Mission Command Failure in the 1857 Utah War." Unpublished master's thesis, School of Advanced Military Studies, U.S. Army Command and General Staff College, Fort Leavenworth, Kans., 2016.

Fehr, Kregg M. "Mules, Mormons, and Marcy: A Study of the Mormon War and the Significance of Captain Randolph Barnes Marcy's Relief Expedition to New Mexico." Wichita Fall, Tex.: Unpublished master's thesis, 1993, Department of History, Midwestern State University.

Flake, Lawrence R. "George Q. Cannon: His Missionary Years." Provo, Utah: Unpublished doctoral dissertation, 1970, Department of Church Hist. and Doctrine, BYU.

Ismert, Martin E. "Quantrill-Charley Hart?" Unpublished paper presented at the Posse of the Westerners of Kansas City, 13 October 1959. William Clarke Quantrill Research Collection, McCain Library, University of Southern Mississippi, Hattiesburg.

Jones, Shirley Greenwood. "Brigham Young's Rhetoric: A Critical and Cultural Analysis of Key Sermons in Five Rhetorical Events." S.L.C.: Unpublished doctoral dissertation, 1942, Department of Communications, University of Utah.

Keele, Reba Lou. "A Doctrinal Group Counterattacks: An Analysis of the Oral Rhetoric of the Mormons in the Utah War, 1855–1859." Lafayette, Ind.: Unpublished doctoral dissertation, 1974, Department of Speech, Purdue University.

Lindell, Jennifer. "Mormons and Native Americans in the Antebellum West." San Diego: Unpublished master's thesis, 2011, Department of Hist., San Diego State University.

Lord, Theodore Akerly. The Utah Expedition, draft chapter in unpublished biography of Fitz John Porter, Fitz-John Porter Papers, MSS 36590, Box 66, Manuscript Division, LC.

MacKinnon, William P. Heroes and Hard Cases. Unpublished paper presented at 48th Annual Conference, Mormon Hist. Association, Layton, Utah, 7 June 2013.

———. Pawns, Opportunists, and Scapegoats: The Utah War and Tribal Manipulation. Unpublished paper presented at 57th Annual Utah State History Conference, S.L.C., 18 September 2009.

Peterson, Charles S. "A Historical Analysis of Territorial Government in Utah under Alfred Cumming, 1857–1861." Unpublished master's thesis, Department of History, BYU, 1958.

Van Wagenen, Michael. Mormons in Texas. Unpublished address, 49th Annual Conference, Mormon Hist. Association, San Antonio, Tex., 5 June 2014.

Published Primary Sources

Ackley, Richard Thomas. "Across the Plains in 1858," *Utah Hist. Qtly.* 9 (October 1941): 190–228.

Aird, Polly, Jeff Nichols, and Will Bagley, eds. *Playing with Shadows: Voices of Dissent in the Mormon West.* Norman, Okla.: Arthur H. Clark, 2011.

Alexander, E. P. *Military Memoirs of a Confederate: A Critical Narrative.* New York: Charles Scribner's Sons, 1907.

Alexander, Edward Porter, and Gary W. Gallagher, ed. *Fighting for the Confederacy: The Personal Recollections of General Edward Porter Alexander.* Chapel Hill: University of North Carolina Press, 1989.

Alter, J. Cecil, and Robert J. Dwyer, eds. "The Utah War Journal of Albert Tracy," *Utah Hist. Qtly.* 13 (January, April, July, October 1945): 1–128.

Anderson, Kirk. Letters to *Missouri Republican,* August–September 1858, Eugene T. Wells, ed. "Kirk Anderson's Trip to Utah, 1858," *Missouri Hist. Society Bulletin* 18 (October 1961): 3–19.

Barnes, James J., and Patience P. Barnes, eds. *Private and Confidential: Letters from British Ministers in Washington to the Foreign Secretaries in London, 1844–67.* Selinsgrove, Penn.: Susquehanna University Press, 1993.

Bartholow, A. Roberts. "The Physiological Aspects of Mormonism, and the Climatology, and Diseases of Utah and New Mexico," *The Cincinnati Lancet and Observer* 10 (April 1867): 193–205.

Bayard, Samuel J. *Life of George Dashiell Bayard, Late Captain, U.S.A., and Brigadier-General of Volunteers, Killed in the Battle of Fredericksburg, Dec. 1862.* New York: G. P. Putnam's Sons, 1874.

Beehrer, George W., and Julie Beehrer Colyer, ed. "Freighting Across the Plains: True 1858 Experiences of George W. Beehrer from His Diary and Related to a Friend," *Montana The Magazine of Western History* 12 (Autumn 1962): 2–17.

Bigler, David L., and Will Bagley, eds. *Innocent Blood: Essential Narratives of the Mountain Meadows Massacre.* Norman, Okla.: Arthur H. Clark, 2008.

Brooks, Juanita, ed. *On the Mormon Frontier: The Diary of Hosea Stout, 1844–1861.* 2 vols. S.L.C: University of Utah Press and Utah State Hist. Society, 1964.

[Browne, Albert G., Jr.] "The Utah Expedition: Its Causes and Consequences," *The Atlantic Monthly. A Magazine of Literature, Art, and Politics* 3 (March–May 1859): 361–75, 474–91, 570–84.

———. "The Ward of the Three Guardians." *Atlantic Monthly* 39 (June 1877): 697–703.

———. Unsigned dispatches of various dates 1857–58, *New-York Daily Tribune.* Clippings of many of these dispatches subsequently annotated by the reporter are included in his personal scrapbook, Special Collections, J. Willard Marriott Library, University of Utah, S.L.C.

Buchanan, James. *Mr. Buchanan's Administration on the Eve of the Rebellion.* New York: D. Appleton and Company, 1866.

———. *The Utah Expedition: Message Transmitting Reports from the Secretaries of War, of the Interior, and of the Attorney General, Relative to the Military Expedition Ordered into the Territory of Utah.* 35th Cong., 1st sess., 1857–58, H. Ex. Doc. 71, serial 956.

——— and John Bassett Moore, ed. *The Works of James Buchanan, Comprising his Speeches, State Papers, and Private Correspondence.* 12 vols. New York: Antiquarian Press Ltd., 1960.

Burr, David A. Dispatches of various dates 1857–58 (signed "A.B.C."), *New-York Daily Times.*

———. Unsigned dispatches for various dates 5 January–27 May 1858, *New-York Daily Tribune.* The Browne scrapbook (see above) contains clippings of many of these reports as well as hints from Browne as to his substitute's identity.

Clay-Clopton, Virginia, and Ada Sterling, ed. *A Belle of the Fifties: Memoirs of Mrs. Clay, of Alabama, covering Social and Political Life in Washington and the South, 1853–66.* New York: Doubleday, Page & Company, 1905.

Collier, Fred L., ed. *The Office Journal of President Brigham Young, 1858–1863, Book D.* Hanna, Utah: Collier's Publishing Company, 2006.

Cooper, John B. "Details of a Journey to Salt Lake, and Return Trip," *San Francisco Daily Alta California,* 12 August 1858, 1/4–5.

Cumming, Elizabeth Wells Randall. *The Genteel Gentile: Letters of Elizabeth Cumming, 1857–1858,* ed. by Ray R. Canning and Beverly Beeton. S.L.C.: Tanner Trust Fund, University of Utah Library, 1977.

Dallas, George Mifflin, and Julia Dallas, eds. *A Series of Letters from London Written During the Years 1856, '57, '58, '59.* 2 vols. in 1. Philadelphia: J. B. Lippincott, 1869.

Dallas, Susan, ed. *Diary of George Mifflin Dallas: While United States Minister to Russia, 1837–1839, and to England, 1856 to 1861.* Philadelphia: J. B. Lippincott, 1892.

Davis, Jefferson, and various editors. *The Papers of Jefferson Davis: 1808–1889.* 14 vols. Baton Rouge: Louisiana State University Press, 1971–2015.

Dickson, Ephriam D., III. *A Sojourn in Zion: The 7th U.S. Infantry in Utah Territory, 1858-1860* (forthcoming).

Du Bois, John Van Deusen. *Campaigns in the West, 1856–1861: The Journal and Letters of Colonel John Van Deusen Du Bois with Pencil Sketches by Joseph Heger,* George P. Hammond, ed. Tucson: Arizona Pioneers Hist. Society, 1949; reprinted, Arizona Hist. Society, 2003.

Egan, Major Howard. *Pioneering the West, 1846 to 1878: Major Howard Egan's Diary*, ed. and comp. by William M. Egan. Richmond, Utah: Howard R. Egan Estate, 1917.

Ekins, Roger Robin, ed. *Defending Zion: George Q. Cannon and the California Mormon Newspaper Wars of 1856–1857*. Spokane, Wash.: Arthur H. Clark, 2002.

Farmer, James E., and Dale F. Giese, ed. *My Life with the Army in the West, memoirs of J. E. Farmer, 1858–1898*. Santa Fe, N.Mex.: Stagecoach Press, 1967.

Ferguson, Samuel Wragg. "With Albert Sidney Johnston's Expedition to Utah, 1857," George W. Martin, ed., *Collections of the Kansas State Hist. Society* 12 (1911–12): 303–12.

Finlay, William Porter. Dispatches of various dates 1857–1858 (signed "W.P.F."), *Saint Louis Leader.*

Fillmore, Lemuel. Unsigned dispatches of various dates 1858, *New York Herald.*

Floyd, John B. "Report of the Secretary of War, 6 December 1858," *Message from the President of the United States,* House Exec. Doc. 2 (35-2), serial 942.

Godfrey, Donald G., and Rebecca S. Martineau-McCarty, eds. *An Uncommon Common Pioneer: The Journals of James Henry Martineau, 1828–1918.* Provo, Utah: Religious Studies Center, Brigham Young University, 2008.

Goodell, Joatham, and David L. Bigler, ed. *A Winter with the Mormons: The 1852 Letters of Joatham Goodell.* S.L.C.: University of Utah Tanner Trust Fund, 2001.

Gove, Jesse A. *The Utah Expedition, 1857–1858: Letters of Capt. Jesse A. Gove, 10th Inf., U.S.A., of Concord, N.H., to Mrs. Gove, and Special Correspondence of the New York Herald*, edited by Otis G. Hammond. Concord: New Hampshire Hist. Soc., 1928.

Grow, Mathew J., and Ronald W. Walker, eds. *The Prophet and the Reformer: The Letters of Brigham Young and Thomas L. Kane.* New York: Oxford University Press, 2015.

Hafen, LeRoy R., and Ann W., eds. *Mormon Resistance: A Documentary Account of the Utah Expedition, 1857–1858.* Lincoln: University of Nebraska Press, reprinted 2005 from *The Utah Expedition, 1857–1858: A Documentary Account of the United States Military Movement under Colonel Albert Sidney Johnston, and the Resistance by Brigham Young and the Mormon Nauvoo Legion.* Glendale, Calif.: Arthur H. Clark, 1958; reprinted 1982.

Hamilton, Henry S. *Reminiscences of a Veteran.* Concord, N.H.: Republican Press Assoc., 1897.

Hawthorne, Nathaniel. *Our Old Home.* Boston and New York: Houghton, Mifflin, 1907.

Healy, John J. *Life and Death on the Upper Missouri: The Frontier Sketches of Johnny Healy.* Ed. by Ken Robison. Great Falls, Mont.: n.p., 2013.

Heintzelman, Samuel P. "Report on Southern California Indians," dated 15 July 1853 in Franklin Pierce, *Message of the President of the United States, Transmitting Report in Regard to Indian Affairs on the Pacific.* H. Ex. Doc. 76 (34-3), 1856–57, serial 906, 34–53.

Henson, Margaret Swett, comp., and Donald E. Willett, ed. *The Texas That Might Have Been: Sam Houston's Foes Write to Albert Sidney Johnston.* College Station: Texas A&M University Press, 2009.

Holmes, Kenneth L., ed. and comp. *Covered Wagon Women: Diaries & Letters from the Western Trails 1840–1890.* 11 vols. Glendale, Calif., and Spokane, Wash.: Arthur H. Clark, 1983–93.

Homer, Michael W., ed. *On the Way to Somewhere Else: European Sojourners in the Mormon West, 1834–1930.* Norman, Okla.: Arthur H. Clark, 2006.

Houston, Samuel. Floor remarks, U.S. Senate, 25 February 1858, *Congressional Globe* (35-1), 1858, 873–75.

Huseman, Ben W. *Wild River, Timeless Canyons: Balduin Möllhausen's Watercolors of the Colorado.* Fort Worth, Tex.: Amon Carter Museum, 1995.

Hyde, John, Jr. *Mormonism: Its Leaders and Designs.* New York: W. P. Fetridge & Co., 1857.

Ives, Lt. Joseph C. *Report upon the Colorado River of the West.* Washington: Government Printing Office, 1861. Printed as Senate Exec. Doc. 90 (36-1), serial 1058.

———. Preliminary Report of First Lieut. J. C. Ives, Topographical Engineers, 1 November 1858, to Capt. A. A. Humphreys, Topographical Engineers, in Charge of the Office of Exploration and Surveys, "Report of the Sec. of War [1858]," 608–19.

Johnson, Andrew, LeRoy P. Graf, and Ralph W. Haskins, eds. *The Papers of Andrew Johnson.* 16 vols. Knoxville: University of Tennessee Press, 1967–2000.

Johnson, George Alonzo. "The Steamer General Jesup: The First Steamship to Explore the Colorado River," *Qtly. of the Soc. of California Pioneers* 9 (June 1932): 108–18.

Jones, Rev. John William. *Life and Letters of Robert Edward Lee: Soldier and Man.* New York and Washington: Neale Publishing Co., 1906.

Kane, Thomas Leiper. *The Mormons: A Discourse Delivered before the Historical Society of Pennsylvania, March 26, 1850.* Philadelphia: King and Baird, 1850.

Kenney, Scott G., ed. *Wilford Woodruff's Journal, 1833–1898.* 9 vols. Midvale, Utah: Signature Books, 1983–85.

King, Pauline, ed. *The Diaries of David Lawrence Gregg: An American Diplomat in Hawaii, 1853–1858.* Honolulu: Hawaiian Hist. Society, 1982.

Langley, Harold D., ed. *To Utah with the Dragoons and Glimpses of Life in Arizona and California, 1858–1859.* S.L.C.: University of Utah Press, 1974.

MacKinnon, William P., ed. *At Sword's Point, Part 1: A Documentary History of the Utah War to 1858.* Norman, Okla.: Arthur H. Clark, 2008.

———. *"The Executive of Utah": Selected Utah War Documents and Commentary Relating to Thomas L. Kane's Lost Lecture in Defense of Governor Alfred Cumming, New-York Historical Society, 21 March 1859.* Norman, Okla.: Arthur H. Clark, 2016.

Manning, William Ray, ed. *Diplomatic Correspondence of the United States: Inter-American Affairs, 1831–1860.* Washington: U.S. Department of State and Carnegie Endowment for International Peace, Division of International Law, 1939.

Marcy, Randolph B. "Expedition Across the Rocky Mountains," in *Thirty Years of Army Life on the Border.* New York: Harper & Brothers, 1866.

———. "Guides, Hunters and Trappers" (chapter 2 of "Big Game Hunting in the Wild West"), *Outing: An Illustrated Monthly Magazine of Recreation* 11 (November 1887): 133–41. Also available at http://ezine.nitroexpress.info/NickuduFiles/Vintage/Shorts6132.pdf, accessed 21 December 2013.

———. "Ramblings in The West," *Harper's New Monthly Magazine* 76 (February 1888): 397–405. Also available at http://www.legendsofamerica.com/we-ramblings.html, accessed 5 April 2013.

———. *The Prairie Traveler. A Hand-Book for Overland Expeditions.* New York: Harper & Brothers, 1859.

McLemore, Clyde, ed. "Ficklin's Expedition to the Flathead Country in 1858," *Frontier and Midland: A Magazine of the West* 16 (Autumn 1935): 66–69.

Meigs, Montgomery C., and Wendy Wolff, ed. *Capitol Builder: The Shorthand Journals of Montgomery C. Meigs, 1853–1859, 1861.* Washington, D.C.: Government Printing Office, 2001.

Mesch, Allen H. *Your Affectionate Father, Charles F. Smith.* N.p.: privately printed, 2016.

Möllhausen, H. B. "Over the Santa Fe trail Through Kansas." John A. Burzle, transl., and Robert Taft, ed. *Kansas Hist. Qtly.* 16 (November 1948): 337–80.

Möllhausen, Heinrich Balduin. *Reisen in die Felsengebirge Nord-Amerikas bis zum Hoch-Plateau von New-Mexico, unternommen als Mitglied der im Auftrage der Vereinigten Staaten ausgesandten Colorado-Expedition [Journeys into the Rocky Mountains of North America as far as the High Plateau of New Mexico undertaken as a Member of the Colorado Expedition by Commission of the United States Government].* 2 vols. Leipzig: H. Costenoble, 1861.

Morehead, Charles R. "Morehead's Recollections" (Appendix C). In *War with Mexico, 1840–1847: Doniphan's Expedition and the Conquest of New Mexico and California,* by William E. Connelley. Topeka, Kans.: Crane & Company, 1907, 600–22.

Nevins, Allan, and Milton Halsey Thomas, eds. *The Diary of George Templeton Strong: 1835–1875.* 4 vols. New York: Macmillan, 1952.

O'Neil, Owen Hugh. Dispatches of various dates 1858 (signed "O.H.O."), *Liberty Weekly Tribune* (Clay County, Mo.).

Osborn, William J. Unsigned dispatches of various dates 1858, *Washington, D.C., Union.*

Palmer, James, and Fannie Palmer Gleave, ed. *James Palmer's Travels and Ministry in the Gospel, 1820–1905.* S.L.C.: Utah Publishing Company, 1963.

Richardson, Albert D., and Louise Barry, ed. "Albert D. Richardson's Letters on the Pike's Peak Gold Region, Written to the Editor of the Lawrence *Republican,* May 22–August 25, 1860," *Kansas Hist. Qtly.* 12 (February 1943): 14–57.

Roberts, Madge Thornall, ed. *The Personal Correspondence of Sam Houston.* 4 vols. Denton: University of North Texas Press, 2001.

Sharswood, George, ed. *Report of the Seventeenth Annual Meeting of the American Bar Association Held at Saratoga Springs, New York, August 22, 23, and 24, 1894.* Philadelphia: Dando Printing and Publishing Company, 1894.

Sibley, Marilyn McAdams, ed. "Robert E. Lee to Albert Sidney Johnston, 1857," *Journal of Southern Hist.* 29 (February 1963): 100–107.

Simonton, James W. Dispatches of various dates 1858 (signed "S"), *New-York Daily Times.* Contemporaneously he was sending unsigned reports to several other newspapers in the United States and United Kingdom, most notably San Francisco's *Evening Bulletin.*

Simpson, J. H. *Report of Explorations across the Great Basin of the Territory of Utah.* Washington, D.C.: Government Printing Office, 1876.

———. Dispatches of various dates 1858 (signed "S"), *Buffalo (N.Y.) Courier.*

Thorndike, Rachel Sherman, ed. *The Sherman Letters: Correspondence between General and Senator Sherman from 1837 to 1891.* New York: Charles Scribner's Sons, 1894.

Tracy, Brevet Col. Albert, U.S.A. "Lo—With an Attachment," *The United Service: A Monthly Review of Military and Naval Affairs* 8 [New Series] (October 1892): 378–80.

Tracy, A., U.S.A. "The Humors of Outpost. A Relic of Old Fort Bridger," *Army and Navy Journal,* 25 December 1869. Included in Tracy Scrapbook, WA MSS S-2596, Yale Collection of Western Americana, Beinecke Library, New Haven, Conn.

Turley, Richard E., Jr., and Ronald W. Walker, eds. *Mountain Meadows Massacre: The Andrew Jenson and David H. Morris Collections.* Provo and S.L.C.: Brigham Young University Press and University of Utah Press, 2009.

Van Wagoner, Richard S., ed. *The Complete Discourses of Brigham Young.* 5 vols. S.L.C.: The Smith-Pettit Foundation, 2009.

Wallace, Sarah Agnes, and Frances Elma Gillespie, eds. *The Journal of Benjamin Moran, 1857–1865.* 2 vols. Chicago: University of Chicago Press, 1948.

Ware, Capt. Eugene F. *The Indian War of 1864.* New York: St. Martin's Press, 1960.

White, David A., comp. *News of the Plains and Rockies, 1803–1865.* 8 vols. Spokane, Wash.: Arthur H. Clark, 1996–2001.

Williams, G. Mott. "Letters of General Thomas Williams, 1862," *The American Hist. Review* 14 (January 1909): 304–28.

Windle, Mary J. *Life in Washington, and Life Here and There.* Philadelphia: J. B. Lippincott & Company, 1859.

Winther, Oscar Osburn, ed. *A Friend of the Mormons: The Private Papers and Diary of Thomas Leiper Kane.* San Francisco: Gelber-Lilienthal, Inc., 1937.

Xantus, John. *Letters from North America.* Teodore Schoenman and Helen Benedek, transl. and ed. Detroit: Wayne State University Press, 1975.

Young, John R. *Memoirs of John R. Young, Utah Pioneer 1847, Written by Himself.* S.L.C.: Deseret News, 1920.

Zwinger, Ann, ed. *John Xantus: The Fort Tejon Letters, 1857–1859.* Tucson: University of Arizona Press, 1986.

Unpublished Primary Sources

Beauregard, P. G. T. Letter, 9 February 1858, to John Slidell. HM 24506, Mormon File, Manuscripts Department, Huntington Library, San Marino, Calif.

Blair, Seth M. Papers. Private collection of Mr. John B. Bond, Roy, Utah.

Boos, Theodore. Typescript memoir, My Life in the Army. Yale Collection of Western Americana, Beinecke Library, New Haven, Conn.

Browne Family Papers. Schlesinger Library, Radcliffe Institute, Harvard University, Cambridge, Mass.

Browne, Albert G., Jr. Letter, 22 October 1859, to William A. Carter. William Alexander Carter Correspondence, 1859–1872, Accn 2496, Special Collections and Archives, J. Willard Marriott Library, University of Utah, S.L.C.

Buchanan, James. Papers. Collection 91, HSP.

Burr, David A., and David H. Burr. Burr Family Papers. Special Collections, Krock Library, Cornell University. Photostats of much of this material also in the Burr Collection, American Antiquarian Society, Worcester, Mass.

Burr, David A. Letter to Messrs. [Albert G.] Brown[e] & [James W.] Simonton, 9 April [June] 1858. Burr Family Papers (see above); typescript in Mortimer Rare Book Room, Neilson Library, Smith College, Northampton, Mass.

Candland, David. Documents of David Candland. Typescript (1967), Utah State Hist. Society, SLC.

Carrington, Albert. Letter to Lazarus W. Powell, 3 July 1858. Carrington Collection, MS 0549, Special Collections, J. Willard Marriott Library, University of Utah, SLC.

Carson, Christopher ("Kit"). Correspondence, 1854–1867. Vault MSS 513, L. Tom Perry Special Collections, Harold B. Lee Library, BYU.

Carter, William Alexander. Correspondence, 1859–1872. Accn 2496, Special Collections and Archives, J. Willard Marriott Library, University of Utah, S.L.C.

Carter, William A. Typescript (letters 1857–1859). Manuscript Division, William L. Clements Library, University of Michigan, Ann Arbor.

Cooke, Philip St. George. Cooke Family Papers, 1855–1871. Acc. 23896, Library of Virginia, Richmond.

Cumming, Alfred. Papers, 1792–1889. David M. Rubenstein Rare Book and Manuscript Library, Duke University, Durham, N.C., microfilm copy at Utah State Hist. Society, S.L.C.

Cumming, Capt. Alfred. Letters. Papers of Hammond, Bryan, and Cumming Families, Special Collections, South Caroliniana Library, University of South Carolina, Columbia.

Davis, Jefferson. "Jeff Davis's Speech. The Grey-Haired Statesman Pays a Tribute to Sidney Johnston," unsigned dispatch, 7 April 1887, *Fort Worth (Tex.) Daily Gazette*, 8 April 1887.

Dickerson, Capt. John H. Letter, 16 April 1858, to W. A. Gordon. Manuscripts Department, Bancroft Library, University of California, Berkeley.

Douglas, Stephen A. Papers. Special Collections Research Center, University of Chicago Library.

Evans, Frank. Collection. MS 1251, Fds. 11, 13, 14, 16–18, LDS Archives, S.L.C. (Largely photostats of holographic Kane correspondence in possession of Kane family before dispersal to collections of APS and BYU.)

Ferguson, Samuel Wragg. Memoirs of S.W. Ferguson, No. 2754-z, undated typescript, Heyward and Ferguson Family Papers, Southern Hist. Collection, Wilson Library, University of North Carolina at Chapel Hill.

Gardner, Hamilton. Papers, 1942–1960. Mss B-113, Utah State Hist. Society.

Gatlin, Richard C. Papers. #3868, Southern Hist. Collection, Wilson Library, University of North Carolina at Chapel Hill.

Hamblin, Jacob. Diaries and reminiscences. Typescript, LDS Archives.

Haskell, Thales H. Thales Hastings Haskell, Pioneer—Scout—Explorer—Indian Missionary, 1847–1909. Typescript assembled and written by Albert E. Smith, S.L.C., 1963, Special Collections, Sherritt Library, Southern Utah State University, Cedar City.

Heintzelman, Samuel P., Journal, 1856–1860. Samuel Peter Heintzelman Papers, 1822–1913, MSS25676, Manuscript Division, LC.
Hunt, Henry Jackson. Papers, 1841–1978. Journal for May–August 1858. MSS26864, Box 1, Manuscript Division, LC.
Ives, Lt. Joseph C. Letters. Special Collections, Lied Library, University of Nevada–Las Vegas; typed transcriptions in private collection of Mr. Kenneth M. Ives, Nokesville, Va.
Johnston, Albert Sidney, and William Preston Johnston. Papers (including original of Porter Diary for 21 October 1857–30 April 1858). Louisiana Research Collection, Tulane University, New Orleans.
Journal History of the Church of Jesus Christ of Latter-day Saints, LDS Archives.
Kane, Thomas L., and Elizabeth W. Papers. L. Tom Perry Special Collections, Harold B. Lee Library, BYU.
Kane, Elizabeth W. Journal. Thomas L. and Elizabeth W. Kane Papers, BYU.
———. Mother of the Regiment. Typescript, Thomas L. and Elizabeth W. Kane Papers, BYU.
———. History of Kane County [Pennsylvania]. Typescript, Thomas L. and Elizabeth W. Kane Papers, BYU.
Kane, Thomas L. Collection, Pennsylvania State Archives, Harrisburg, Pa.
———. Papers. Stanford University Libraries, Stanford, Calif.
———. Papers. Thomas Leiper Kane Collection, APS.
———. Papers. Thomas L. Kane Collection, American Hist. Manuscripts Collection, New-York Historical Society.
———. Papers. WA MSS 279, Box 1, Fds. 3-6, Yale Collection of Western Americana, Beinecke Library, New Haven, Conn. Transcriptions in editor's files.
Lane, Joseph. Papers, 1835–1906. Manuscript Collections, Lilly Library, Indiana University, Bloomington.
Lord, Theodore Akerly. The Utah Expedition, draft chapter for unpublished Porter biography. Fitz-John Porter Papers, MSS 36590, Box 66, Manuscript Division, LC.
Lyman, Amasa M. Collection. LDS Archives.
Macomb, John N., and Ann Minerva ("Nannie") Rodgers Macomb. Letters. Rodgers Family Papers, 1740–1987, MSS38125, Series I, Boxes 4 and 6, Manuscript Division, LC.
Mansfield, Col. Joseph K. "Army of Utah," draft memorandum, ca. January 1858. Joseph K. F. Mansfield Papers, Middlesex County [Conn.] Hist. Society.
Marcy, Randolph B. Letters. Typed transcriptions, W. Eugene Hollon Papers, UM35, Box 33, Ward M. Canaday Center for Special Collections, University of Toledo [Ohio]. (Originals in George B. McClellan Papers, Manuscript Division, LC.)
McClellan, George B. Letters. Typed transcriptions, W. Eugene Hollon Papers (see above).
McCulloch, Benjamin. Letters. Ben and Henry McCulloch Family Papers, Center for American History, University of Texas at Austin.
Newberry, John Strong. Letters. Spencer Fullerton Baird Papers, 1833–1889, Record Unit 7002, Box 30, Fd 17, Smithsonian Institution Archives, Washington.
Oades, Ann Jackson. Letters. Ward Jay Roylance Collection, LDS Archives.

O'Neil, Owen Hugh. Letters and essays. Huntington Library, San Marino, Calif.

Ouseley, Sir William Gore. Dispatches 1857–1858, to Lord Clarendon. Clarendon Deposit, Bodleian Library, Oxford University. Significant excerpts from these reports may be found in Barnes and Barnes, *Private and Confidential* (see above).

———. Dispatch no. 14, 25 January 1858, to Lord Clarendon. F. O. 15/98 ff. 36-39, Records of the Foreign Office, British National Archives, Kew. The text of this report may be found in MacKinnon, "Presidential Billiards Revisited" (see above).

Park, John Wesley. Park Brothers Papers. MS 94–28, Special Collections, Wichita State University Libraries, Wichita, Kansas.

Phelps, John Wolcott. Papers. Mss Col 2399, Manuscripts and Archives Division, NYPL.

———. Diaries, 1857–1858. NYPL; typed transcriptions in Hamilton Gardner Papers, Utah State Hist. Society.

———. Diaries, 1858. Originals and typed transcriptions, private collection of Jeffrey N. Walker, Esq., S.L.C.

———. Letters, Series 6:1857–1858. Herbert S. Auerbach Collection on Mormons and Indians, 1808–1935, Manuscripts Division, Dept. of Rare Books and Special Collections, Firestone Library, Princeton University.

Pitchforth, Samuel. Diary, 1857–1868. Typescript, Mor M270.1 P68d, Brigham Young University Library.

Porter, Fitz-John. Papers. MSS 36590, Box 53 (holograph drafts for multiple unpublished articles, including: An Incident of Army Life Among the Mormons during the Utah troubles of 1859 [*sic*] to 1860; and A Characteristic [Mormon] Conspiracy; as well as Diary in Utah by Maj. F. J. Porter, Extracts from the Diary of Maj. Fitz-John Porter A.A.G. while acting with Genl. Albert Sidney Johnston in the Utah Expedition, copied by permission of Col. Wm. Preston Johnston by John R. Anderson. Decr. 1876 [original in Louisiana Research Collection, Tulane University]); and Box 66 (The Utah Expedition, draft chapter for unpublished Porter biography by Theodore Akerly Lord), Manuscript Division, LC.

Rollins, James S. Papers. C1026, Fd. 49, State Hist. Society of Missouri, Columbia.

Royle, William Henry. Papers, letters to his mother, 1858–1860. MsSC 211A, Washington State Hist. Society, Tacoma.

Ryan, George E. Personal Correspondence. Collection No. 364, Ryan Family Papers, The American Catholic Hist. Research Center and Archives, The Catholic University of America, Washington.

Scott, Winfield. Letter, 11 February 1858, to William Preston. Wickliffe-Preston Papers, 63M 349, University of Kentucky Library, Lexington.

———. Papers. William L. Clements Library, University of Michigan, Ann Arbor.

Sherman, William T. Papers, Ohio Hist. Society, Columbus.

Simpson, James Hervey. Dispatches (signed "S"), various dates Spring–Summer 1858. *Buffalo (N.Y.) Courier.*

Smith, Capt. William Duncan. Letter, 22 July 1858, to N. Wallace Smith. Confederate

Generals, Gratz Collection, Cube 5, Box 16, HSP. Typescript in Letters from Camp Floyd, MS 191, Special Collections and Archives, J. Willard Marriott Library, University of Utah, SLC.

Smith, George A. Church Historian's Journal. LDS Archives.

Smith, Persifor Fraser. Papers. HSP.

Squires, John Fell. Autobiography in Notes of Interest to the Descendants of Thomas Squires by His Son. Typescript, LDS Archives.

Thomas, Sarah C., comp. "Elias Smith's Journal." Typescript 1984, Utah State Hist. Society, SLC.

Tracy, Albert. Papers, 1843–1893. Mss Col 3020, Manuscripts and Archives Division, NYPL.

———. Scrapbook, Drawings, Letters, and Poems, 1843–1892. WA MSS S-2596, Yale Collection of Western Americana, Beinecke Library, New Haven, Conn.

Tripp, Enoch B. Journal, vol. 4, 17 March 1858–30 September 1866. MSS 2032, Box 3, Fd 4, L. Tom Perry Special Collections, Harold B. Lee Library, BYU.

Under secretary of state (British) for foreign affairs. Memo, "Contemplated Emigration of Mormons from Utah to the Sandwich Islands," 8 June 1858. Found in Rear-Admiral Robert L. Baynes, commander Pacific station (Peru), to sec. of Admiralty board (London), 22 July 1858; ADM 1 (Correspondence and Papers of the Admiralty, and Ministry of Defence, Navy Dept.), Box 5694, Bundle Y, Item 156, British National Archives, Kew.

U.S. Army. Records of Office of the Chief of Engineers. RG 77, NARA.

———. Records of the Quartermaster General. RG 92, NARA.

———. Records of the Office of the Adjutant General. RG 94, NARA.

———. Records of Headquarters, Department of Utah. RG 98, NARA.

———. Records of Headquarters. RG 108, NARA.

———. Records of the Judge Advocate General. RG 153, NARA.

———. Records of the Dept. of the Pacific. RG 393, NARA.

U.S. Dept. of the Interior. Records of the Bureau of Indian Affairs, RG 75, NARA.

———. Records of the Pacific Wagon Road Office, RG 48, NARA.

U.S. Congress. Records of the House of Representatives.

Williams, Laurence A. Correspondence. Martha Custis Williams Carter Papers, MS 6, Tudor Place Foundation, Washington, D. C.

Williams, Thomas. Correspondence. MSS 6769, L. Tom Perry Special Collections, Harold B. Lee Library, BYU.

———. Correspondence. Boxes 3 and 4, Williams Family Papers, Burton Hist. Collection, Detroit Public Library.

———. Thomas. Correspondence. In Henri Folmer, ed., Letters of Major Williams, Johnston's Expedition, 1858–1859, undated typescript, McCracken Research Library, Buffalo Bill Hist. Center, Cody, Wyo.

Wool, John E. Letters and telegrams. John Ellis Wool Papers, State Library of New York, Albany.

Young, Brigham. Correspondence. Brigham Young Collection, LDS Archives.

———. A Series of Instructions and Remarks by President Brigham Young, at a Special Council, Tabernacle, March 21, 1858. Typescript, LDS Archives. This may be found in Van Wagoner, ed., *The Complete Discourses of Brigham Young*, 3:1411–21 (see above).

Zobell, Albert Levi, Jr. Collection. MS 6102, Reel 12, Box 21, Fds. 10 and 11, LDS Archives, S.L.C. Access courtesy of Mrs. Albert L. Zobell, Jr. (Largely typed transcriptions of photostatic Kane correspondence in Frank Evans Collection.)

Newspapers

Alta California (San Francisco, Calif.)
Congressional Globe (Washington, D.C.)
Courier (Buffalo, N.Y.)
Daily Evening Bulletin (Philadelphia)
Daily Tribune (Chicago)
Daily Union (Sacramento, Calif.)
Deseret News (S.L.C.)
Eagle (Poughkeepsie, N.Y.)
El Paso Herald (El Paso, Tex.)
Evening Bulletin (San Francisco)
Fort Worth Daily Gazette (Fort Worth, Tex.)
Gazette (Santa Fe, N.M.)
Liberty Weekly Tribune (Clay County, Mo.)
Millennial Star (Liverpool, U.K.)
Missouri Republican (St. Louis)
National Intelligencer (Washington, D.C.)
New York Herald (Manhattan)
New-York Daily Times (Manhattan)
New-York Daily Tribune (Manhattan)
Republican Advocate (Batavia, N.Y.)
Saint Louis Leader
Skandinaviens Stjerne (Copenhagen)
Sun (Pittsfield, Mass.)
The Mountaineer (S.L.C.)
Valley Tan (S.L.C.)
Washington Union (Washington, D.C.)

Index

"A.B.C." (pseudonym). *See* Burr, David Auguste
Adams, George, 584–85
Adams, Margaret Webster, 584–85
Adams, Samuel, 370
Adams, William H., 570
Aiken party executions, 75n18, 251–52, 485–86, 508, 601, 603n2
Alaska, 37, 646
alcohol and drunkenness: Cumming's problem with, 30, 282, 282n21, 420–21, 621, 639; Du Bois's problem with, 595n41; Ives Expedition, 120n9; James Ferguson's death from, 77–78; Kimball's problem with, 350; Magraw's problem with, 109, 111n46; Nauvoo Legion and, 325–26; peace commissioners' problems with, 507; Salt Lake City ban on, 595; and Seventh U.S. Infantry, 485; Utah Expedition and, 221, 486–87, 509, 556, 558–59; Wilson's problem with, 639; Young contempt for, 615, 639; Young's ban on, 326
Alexander, Edmund B.: captivity of Stowell, 353n13; commander of Utah Expedition, 37, 147, 159; doffs hat to Mormons, 597, 597n46; leadership in Utah War, 612
Alexander, Edward Porter, 490
Alexander II (tsar of Russia), 37
Alona, Miguel, 45, 47, 48n20, 49, 52nn22–24, 53, 56n22
American Indians: attack on Fort Limhi, 93, 187n1, 237–43, 269; conversion to Mormonism, 56, 128–29, 231n27; Mormon alliances, 40, 55–59, 143–44, 148–54; Mormon Indian policy, 80n30, 312; Nauvoo Legionnaires disguised as, 75, 75n18, 216; viewed as Lamanites, 66, 128n24, 316. *See also names of specific tribes and Indian people*
American Revolution, 336n54
Andrew, John A., 98n22
anti-Mormonism: Houston assault on, 269–71; Kane encounters with, 188, 191n5, 194, 200, 202n29; newspaper bias, 494, 636; reaction to Mountain Meadows, 144, 316; settler fear and apprehension, 34, 449; U.S. congressional bias, 443n48; Utah Expedition bias, 282, 288, 288n34, 552; volunteer military forces, 245–46, 255–56. *See also* Mormonism
Antonio (teamster), 491
Appleton, John, 189–90, 190n3
Arapahoe Indians, 61
Armstrong, George W., 105, 528
Arrington, Leonard J., 169n27, 246
arson, Young's threats of, 83–84, 143–44. *See also* Sebastopol (scorched-earth) policy
Aspen, Uintah County, Wyo., 348n1
Atlantic Monthly, 96, 100

Babbitt, Almon W., 14, 371n41, 529
Bagley, William Grant "Will," 13–15, 23, 315, 324, 608
Baird, Spencer F., 124, 133n35
Baker, Jim, 45, 48n20, 49, 51
Bannock Indians, 80n30, 85, 151n13, 213, 237, 237n38, 269, 316, 614
Barnard, Ezra, 187n1, 237
Barry, William F., 482
Bartholow, A. Roberts, 624–25
Battalion of U.S. Volunteers. *See* U.S. military units
Bayard, George Dashiell, 626, 630–31
Beale, Edward Fitzgerald, 129–30, 146–47, 147n5
Beale's Crossing, 125n20, 129–30, 343

Bean, George Washington, 19, 311n49, 315, 388n6
Beardsley, George Austin, 22, 302
Bear River, 41, 74, 254, 349, 374, 513, 537, 540, 546, 555, 560, 562–65, 576
Beauregard, Pierre Gustave Toutant, 169–71, 259, 263–64, 622
Beaver, Utah Terr., 311
Becker, Charles W. "Charlie," 72, 75, 253, 353, 353n12
Bee, Barnard E., 44, 88, 108, 273, 281n19, 474n16, 486–87, 563, 597n47
Bee's Volunteer Battalion. *See* U.S. military units
Beehrer, George W., 490–91
Bennet, James Arlington, 37, 406, 406n37
Bennet[t], James F., 89, 89n3
Bennett, Clarence E., 559n5
Bennett, James Gordon, 387, 443, 553
Bennett, John Cook, 37, 258–59, 259n30, 264, 264n44
Bennion, John, 247n3
Bennion, Samuel, 247n3
Benson, Ezra T., 160–62, 194, 231–32, 312, 330
Bernhisel, John M.: as congressional delegate, 231, 231n26; dispatches from Washington, 19, 162, 177, 502; instructions from Young, 81–84, 441–44; intelligence-gathering role, 92n9; and Peace Commission, 384, 407–9; relationship with Buchanan, 180–82, 182n57, 198n20, 393–98, 616–17; relationship with Kane, 189–90, 200–201, 502–3; replacement as congressional delegate, 584, 636; rescinds the Utah charter, 71, 71n9
Bertrand, Louis Alphonse, 75–77, 277
Bielawski, Casimir, 116
Bigler, David L., 22, 229, 246
Bigler, Jacob, 22, 252
Bigler, John, 257n27
Bigler, William, 257, 257n27, 264, 501
Big Mountain, 516–17, 565
Black, Jeremiah S., 402
Blackfeet Indians, 281, 346
Blacks Fork of the Green River, 31–32, 253, 292n43, 485, 543
Black Warrior affair (1854), 218, 218n7
Blair, Seth Millington: credit for Echo Canyon defenses, 514n18; letter to Sam Houston, 266–69; meeting with peace commissioner (Ben McCulloch), 544, 544n60, 576, 598; member of Texas Rangers, 265; recall of federal appointees, 583–84, 638; Utah War as religious war, 642
Blake, George A. H., 126, 129–30, 130n30, 146–47, 147n5, 209, 216–17, 311
"Bleeding Kansas," 31
Boggs, John, 156
Booker, C. K., 116
Bordewich, Fergus M., 459n68
Bowen, David Davis, 327, 329
Bowman, Andrew W., 47–48
Box Elder County/Military District, 251, 320, 603n2
Bridger, Jim "Old Gabe," 36, 99, 164, 563–64
Bridger's Pass, Nebr. Terr., 18
Bringhurst, Samuel, 312n8
Bristol, Henry Brevoort, 557–58
Britain. *See* Great Britain
Brocchus, Perry E., 430n18
Broderick, David, 261
Bromley, James E., 516n21
Brooks, Jo, 100, 100n27
Brown, Edgar, 253–55, 279, 298
Brown, Homer, 187, 210n50, 251–52
Browne, Albert Gallatin, 43, 73–75, 75n17, 88, 103–7, 110, 187n1, 316, 473, 507, 509, 524, 524n20, 554, 558, 588, 601. See also *New York Tribune*
Browne, Sarah Cox, 92n9, 102–3
Browning, Robert L. (U.S. marine), 20, 37, 478–79
Buchanan, James: creation of Peace Commission, 393, 396–97; decision to intervene in Utah, 30, 32, 159–60, 601–3; and Elizabeth Craig, 416–18; honoring the memory of, 634–35; Houston ambivalence toward, 2; inauguration as president, 29–30, 159; Kane, communications from, 91–92, 210–11, 221–22, 224–28, 236–37, 239, 278, 289–93, 491, 491n47; Kane, minimal recognition of, 646–47; and Manifest Destiny, 174–76, 184–85; messages to Congress, 32, 42, 146n7, 154–55, 159–60, 404n36, 468, 523, 602–3; minister to Russia, 616; negotiations for end of war, 384, 392–96; proclamation of pardon, 398–404, 468, 493–94, 523; reinforcement of Utah Expedition, 159–60; territorial acquisition, 14, 172n30, 175–86, 399–400, 420, 604, 609; as U.S. minister in London, 218n7
Buckner, Simon Bolivar, 259, 262–64

buffalo (bison), 52n24, 111, 207, 280n13, 412, 478

Buffalo (N.Y.) Courier, 467, 470, 479, 481–84, 495. *See also* Simpson, James Hervey "S"

Bull, Johnny, 491

Bulwer-Lytton, George, 98n22

Burbank, Augustus Ripley, 449

Burbank, Daniel Mark, 449n57

Burns, Anthony, 96

Burr, David Auguste "A. B. C." 97, 97n19, 253–54, 279–81, 284–85, 292n40, 510n10, 512–20. See also *New York Times*

Burr, David H., 97, 451, 512, 598

Burton, Robert Taylor, 248, 251–52, 435n26, 446, 517, 518n26, 574

Butterfield Overland Mail Trail, 147n7

B. Y. X. Carrying Company, 265n49, 516n21

Cache Valley, 533n42, 564, 564n13

Cairook (Mojave chief), 128, 130

California: Aiken party murders, 486; anti-Mormon hatred, 32, 144, 188, 190, 194, 275, 316–17; arrival of Kane, 83, 194–203, 363n28; formation of volunteer forces, 80n29, 154–57, 180, 255–62; Ives Expedition, 114–19, 126; Kane departure for, 32; Kane leaves for Utah, 207–13; Kane in San Bernardino, 194–207; Nauvoo Legion raids, fears of, 143–54; and opening two-front campaign, 160–62, 175, 280, 356n21; Pacific Rail Road Survey, 120n10; passage of emigrants to, 406, 439, 450n60; Rancho Rio de Jesus María, 523n29; Scott's relocation to, 167–71, 299; supplying arms and munitions to Mormons, 31, 158–59, 336, 620; supplying troops to Utah Expedition, 601; Warner's Ranch, 144n2; Young's arson threats, 83–84, 143–44. *See also* San Bernardino, Calif.; San Francisco, Calif.

California's Chimney Peak (aka Picacho Peak), 112

Calkin, Asa S., 81, 228–29, 330–32

Calkin, Lizzie, 332

Calkin, Marietta S., 330–32

camels, U.S. Army use of, 129, 129n28, 146–47

Camp Barnard, Volunteers, 302

Camp Floyd, Utah Terr., 79n27, 91, 262, 289, 351n5, 479, 481, 490n44, 590, 613, 618. *See also* Old ("Upper") Camp Floyd

Camp Scott, Utah Terr.: arrival of peace commissioners, 412–15; departure of Kane and Cumming, 376, 385–86; described, 111, 290–93, 485–91, 556; determining the location of, 21–22; expedition sent to rescue Marcy, 93–94; imprisonment of Stowell, 326; Johnston promotion to general, 26, 174; Kane's arrival, 275–88, 293–98, 355–56, 404; Marcy's return, 62; Mormon attacks, planned/anticipated, 77, 106, 298; Mormon refugees/spies, 84, 87–92; non-coms' Christmas ball, 14; relocation to Blacks Fork, 253, 253n18, 358; troop strength/reinforcements, 474, 474n16, 511, 556, 589; Utah Expedition departure for Salt Lake City, 558–62

Camp Walbach, Nebr., 18, 475n18

Canada, 186, 617n16, 646

Candland, David, 449

Cannon, George Quayle, 388, 645

Carrington, Albert, 217, 535, 544, 546–47

Carroll, A. J. "Captain Iron," 116, 131

Carson, Christopher "Kit," 13–14, 36, 40, 57–61

Carson Valley, Utah Terr., 31, 90n4, 149, 153, 403–4, 404n36, 479

Carter, Thomas, 544

Carter, William A., 488–89, 601

Cass, Lewis, 103–4, 175, 178, 190n3, 308, 401–4, 419, 437–38, 450, 637–38

"The Cat and the Old Rat" (children's story), 427n15

Cayuse Indians, 148, 151, 152

Cedar Valley, Utah Terr., 79, 408n42, 536, 623, 632, 632n16

Chandler, N. A., 156

Chappuis, Gaston, 76, 76n20

"Charley Hart" (alias). *See* Quantrill, William Clarke

Cheyenne Indians, 61, 75, 94, 475, 488

Cheyenne Pass, Nebr. Terr., 475n18

Chicago Daily Tribune, 403, 471. *See also* "Junius" (pseudonym)

Child, Warren G., 248–49

Cincinnati Times, 258

Civil War, American: Beardsley's service, 302; Buchanan and crisis leading to, 185, 634; burning of Richmond, 336n54; capture of Fort Sumter, 589; causes/preventability of, 614–17, 634; conspiracy theories, 602; death of Albert Sidney Johnston, 633; Du Bois's service, 595n41;

Civil War, American *(continued)*:
formation of Zouave units, 263n42; Jefferson Davis and, 169n27; Kane's service, 212, 214, 294, 647–48; Knowlton's service, 464n80; Lot Smith's service, 464n80; Marcy's service, 45–47; McClellan's service, 62n46; officer appointments/volunteer regiments, 169–71, 245–46, 263–64, 645; Quantrill's Raiders, 14, 36, 310n1, 487–90, 645; railroad route through Utah, 594n39; Reconstruction period, 643; Robinson's service, 278n9; Samuel Wragg Ferguson's service, 589; Schwan's service, 646; U.S. Army in New Mexico, 485n30; U.S. Army in Utah, 466n84; Utah as opting out, 620–22, 643; Van Vliet's service, 408n43; Young's views on, 185, 602, 620–21, 643

Clapp, Hannah Keziah, 421–22

Clarendon (Lord). *See* Villers, George (Earl of Clarendon)

Clark, Frances Swan Kimball, 199–200, 203–7

Clark, George Sakerman, 203–4, 205n36, 208, 211n51

Clarke (Captain), 365

Clarke, Newman S., 130, 133, 143–50, 152–54, 159, 163, 194–95

Clements, Gilbert, 429–32, 523, 528–29, 533

Clinton, Jeter, 394

Cobb, Howell, 402, 417

Collins, James L., 57–58

Colorado River, Ives Expedition along:
assignment of Ives's mission, 18, 113–14; described by Möllhausen, 112, 121–22, 123–24, 127–30, 134–37; final report by Ives, 114–15, 132–33; Grand Canyon discovery, 36; Ives's letters to wife, 124–25, 132–33, 140; Mojave hostilities, 139–41; Mormon intelligence-gathering, 125–27, 134–39; planning and organization, 116–22; reaching the head of navigation, 130–32; rivalry with Winder and Johnson, 122–23; support of Utah War effort, 123

Colorado River, Lyman Expedition along, 388–92

Compton, Todd, 343

Conover, Peter W., 336, 544n60

Cooke, Philip St. George: anti-Mormon rhetoric, 288; commander of 2nd Dragoons, 91, 100, 564; myth of doffing hat to Mormons, 587, 596–97, 597n46; promotion, 619n17; relationship with Johnston, 288

Cooper, John B., 344, 523n29

Cooper, Samuel, 35, 174n37, 261, 261n36, 613

Cottonwood Camp, 210

Cottonwood Wash (Emery County, Utah), 21

Covey, Edward N., 631, 631n12

Cox, William I., 125–26, 145, 161

Cradlebaugh, John, 105n36, 292, 452n62

Craig, C. L., 456, 576, 583–84, 597, 638–39

Craig, Elizabeth Church, 37, 416–18

Craig, William, 528

Crazy Horse (Sioux chief), 44, 44n12

Crimean War, 66–68, 368n35

Crocheron, Augusta Joyce, 203, 203n32

Crocheron, George W., 203

Cropland (Crossland), Eleanor Amelia, 570–71

Crosby, Caroline Barnes, 203–4, 207–8

Crow Indians, 108

Cuba: *Black Warrior* affair, 218, 218n7; Buchanan's desire to acquire, 14, 159, 175–86, 399, 420, 601–4, 609; impact of Utah War, 28, 262–63; Preston as U.S. minister to Spain, 172n30; Spanish-American War, 646

Cumming, Alfred: appointment as Utah governor, 30–31, 377n33, 422; arrival in Salt Lake City, 376–78; assessing his role and competence, 14; described, 421–22, 507; dispatches to Washington, 436–37; dog bite, 347, 358, 611; dueling challenge, 294n47; first meeting with Young, 378–81; fondness for alcohol, 30, 282, 282n21, 420–21, 612, 639; indiscretions with women, 465–66; and Move South, 325n34; pencil sketch of (1855), 346; relations/communications with Kane, 299–300, 305–8, 347–48, 419–20, 503–4; relations/communications with Young, 420–21, 433–36, 455–57, 539–40, 573–75; relationship with Johnston, 281; relocation to Salt Lake City, 347–48, 354–57, 363–64, 370–76; remarks at April 25 Tabernacle meeting, 423–32

Cumming, Elizabeth Wells Randall, 306, 370–72, 465, 580–82, 585

Cumming, R. W., 422

Cumming, William, 294n47

Cunningham, Andrew, 229, 242, 389

Dallas, George Mifflin, 317
Dame, William H., 19, 68–69, 208–9, 217, 224, 311, 311n5, 392. *See also* White Mountain Expedition
Daniels, Joseph, 147–48, 149n9
Danites, 42, 74n15, 90–91
Daughter of the Snows, A (London), 646
Davis, Jefferson, 163, 166, 169n27, 173, 263, 263n42, 294n45, 397n25, 589, 619n17
Davis, Nathan, 78, 337
Delaware Indians, 94, 242, 376, 518n26
Denver, Colo., 573n20
Denver, James W., 57–58, 94–95
Derry, Charles, 323n32, 325n34
Deseret, Utah Terr., 126, 198, 206, 388n6
Deseret News, 81, 107, 273n62, 332, 336, 395, 546, 580, 641
Deshler, James, 89, 89n3
Devereaux Mansion. *See* Staines Mansion
Diaz, Porfirio, 343
Dickerson, John H., 40, 165n16, 347, 365, 370, 469
Dodge, Caesar Augustus, 176
Dotson, Peter K., 96n16, 465, 575–78, 613, 639
Douglas, Stephen A., 258
drunkenness. *See* alcohol and drunkenness
Du Bois, John Van Deusen, 588, 594–95, 595n41
dueling (code duello): Cumming-Johnston challenge, 294n47; Davis-Johnston challenge, 294n45; Huston-Johnston challenge, 294n45; and Kane during the Civil War, 648; Kane-Johnston challenge, 293–94, 370, 416; Mowry challenge, 508n5; and William Cumming, 294n47; Young's dream about, 508
Dunyon, John L., 84
Dutch East Indies, 28, 37, 72, 177, 182n57, 198n20, 392–93, 394n19

Earl, Jesse J., 287n31
Earl, Wilbur J., 287n31
Eaton, N. J., 172–73, 173n32
Echo Canyon, 649; as Nauvoo Legion headquarters, 70; Cumming-Kane passage through, 376n50, 432n19, 511; defenses/fortifications, 79–80, 162, 340, 349, 512–19, 594–95; fears of Indian attack, 316; Legion soldier desertion, 328–29; location/troop strength, 296, 373, 378n57; reinforcement/resupply, 251–54; Utah Expedition passage, 564–65
Eckels, Delana R.: as acting Utah chief justice, 77, 90n4–91, 104–5, 292–93; appointment of territorial officials, 366–67, 371n41, 577; assaulted at Fort Bridger, 485–87, 509, 558–59; communications with Buchanan, 96n16, 103; judicial review of polygamy, 383–87, 425n12, 454, 524; Mountain Meadows investigation, 613; relationship with Cumming, 450–51, 510n10, 571, 610, 636–39; relationship with Kane, 285–86, 304–5; rumors of resigning, 598
Eckelsville, Utah Terr. (now Wyo.), 82, 87, 90n4
Egan, Howard, 248, 276, 315n18, 336, 372, 449, 464n80, 495–96, 502–3, 619–20, 639
Egloffstein, Baron Friedrich Wilhelm von, 116, 120n10
Eldredge, Horace S., 92, 265n50, 635–36
Ellerbeck, Thomas, 78, 337, 337n56
Emery County, Utah, 21
"Essay on Man" (Pope), 351n5
Ewing, Hugh, 261–62
Ewing, Thomas, 262
Explorer (steamboat), 112, 116–18, 123–28, 128n25, 130–32, 138, 138n44

Fabens, Henry C., 577, 626
Fallon, Christopher, 176, 183, 185, 399
Faulkner, Charles J., 470
Feldman, Henry, 72–75, 95, 98n23, 253, 353, 353n12
Ferguson, James: assessment of Nauvoo Legion, 77–80, 168, 168n23, 246–47; Buchanan Proclamation, 518, 518n25, 522n28; criticism of Move South, 337; death, 77; intelligence-gathering, 510–11, 586–98; Mountain Meadows order, 26; negotiations for end of war, 522–35; recall of federal appointees, 572, 575–80, 638; relationship with Kane, 441, 441n44; use of force against Utah Expedition, 603n2
Ferguson, Samuel Wragg, 588–90
Feud on the Colorado (Woodward), 122
Ficklin, Benjamin Franklin "Ben," 37, 75n17, 88, 108, 187n1, 237–38, 416, 564–65, 575, 614
Fillmore, Lemuel, 487n40, 553, 596–97, 597n45, 621–22. See also *New York Herald*
Fillmore, Millard, 265, 534, 600, 605–6, 615–16
Fillmore, Utah, 311, 336, 544

Finlay, William Porter, 14, 17–18, 88–91, 108n43, 259, 268n54, 520
First Presidency, 71, 217, 251, 254n20, 273, 313, 459n68, 461, 499, 523. *See also* Quorum of the Twelve Apostles
Flathead Indians, 88, 108, 237n38, 238, 416, 614
Fletcher, Jack W., 46n16
Florence, Nebr., 464n80–465
Florida, 260, 475, 601, 632. *See also* Seminole Wars
Floyd, John B.: awarding military contracts, 410n44, 492n49; Colorado River expedition, 115; declaration of martial law, 302n61; instructions to Peace Commission, 401–7, 412–15, 522–23; launching a two-front campaign, 159–60, 164–67; Mountain Meadows investigation, 317; promotion of Heintzelman, 263–64; promotion of Johnston, 173–74; promotion of Marcy, 558, 619, 619n17; recognition of volunteer regiments, 245–46, 257; reports on army operations, 44n11, 54; resignation as secretary of war, 607; Utah Expedition, changing command, 469–73; Utah Expedition, financing scandal, 607; Utah Expedition, Harney named commander, 607; Utah Expedition, reinforcements, 57n34
Floyd, William, 147n3
Forney, Jacob, 90, 93, 105, 108–10, 285, 434n22, 510n10, 513, 516, 523–25, 571, 606, 610, 639
Forsyth, John, 175–77, 183
Fort Benton, Mont., 646
Fort Boise, Ida. Terr., 151
Fort Box Elder, Utah Terr., 603n2
Fort Bridger, Utah Terr. (now Wyo.): arrival of Kane, 225–29, 234, 237–40, 275–88, 295–306, 348–51; Browne at, 98n22; Canby as commander, 553n71; Cumming at, 377, 420–23, 465; Cumming-Kane departure, 383, 388, 438; designated a permanent post, 79n27; disciplinary problems, 291, 485–91, 509, 556, 558–59; Hoffman as commander, 553n71; Kane's return home, 441–44, 464–65; Marcy Expedition to New Mexico, 19, 38–39, 44–45, 47, 49–54, 65, 114; Marcy's return from New Mexico, 60–63, 95; Mormon refugees/spies at, 87; Nauvoo Legion attacks, 14, 31–32, 67, 77, 94, 229–30, 267, 450; Peace Commission arrival and stay, 410–11, 520–22; relocation of Camp Scott, 253; Utah Expedition arrival and overwintering, 31–32, 69, 339n59, 618; Utah Expedition departure for Salt Lake City, 537–43, 555–64
Fort Clara, Utah Terr., 119, 126, 209, 389
Fort Defiance, N.Mex. (now Ariz.), 55–57, 59, 147
Fort Hall, Ore. Terr. (now Ida.), 150–52, 194, 312, 564, 649
Fort Kearny, Nebr., 477, 482, 484, 630
Fort Laramie, Nebr. Terr. (now Wyo.): arrival of Peace Commission, 410–12, 468–69, 493–94; arrival of Utah Expedition, 31, 69, 476–77; Hoffman as commander, 553n71; Kane's return home through, 298n55, 365–66; Mormons employed at, 91n6; Mormon territorial claims, 71, 71n9; Nauvoo Legion attack, 67, 77, 94; resupply of Utah Expedition, 99n26, 103, 473–74, 555
Fort Leavenworth, Kans. Terr.: arrival and death of Persifor Smith, 471–72; Cumming's travel through, 373n46, 397, 451; expedition resupply, 103; formation of Utah Expedition, 30, 162; Harney's column departs from, 478, 555; Morrison's column departs from, 482; Peace Commission travel through, 407, 412; photograph, 480; reinforcements and resupply for Utah Expedition, 407, 468, 469–70, 473–74, 474n16, 490; Utah Expedition communications, 95, 99n26
Fort Limhi, Ore. Terr. (now Ida.): attack by Indians, 93, 187n1, 237–43, 269; attack as pivotal event in Utah War, 316n19; building/construction, 229; casualties from attack, 85n43, 213; decision to reinforce mission, 31, 229; evacuation/abandonment, 80n30, 150–51, 151n13, 253; and Mormon Indian policy, 312, 316, 316n19; research concerning, 22; Young's 1857 visit, 153, 344, 359n25
Fort Massachusetts (renamed Garland), N.Mex. Terr. (now Colo.), 55, 58–59, 72n13
Fort Pierre, Nebr. Terr., 281
Fort Riley, Kans. Terr., 630–31
Fort Simcoe, Wash. Terr., 149
Fort Supply, Utah Terr. (now Wyo.), 31, 229, 238n39, 267
Fort Tejon, Calif., 116, 121, 129, 146–47
Fort Thompson, Dak. Terr. (now Wyo.), 108, 108n43, 110, 520

Fort Union, N.Mex. Terr., 103, 555
Fort Vancouver, Wash. Terr., 150
Fort Walla Walla, Wash. Terr., 148, 150, 152, 165, 196
Fort Whoop-Up, Alberta, Canada, 646
Fort Yuma, Calif., 114, 116–26, 130, 132, 147, 149, 391
Fox, Jesse, 434
Freemasonry, 625
Frémont, John C., 52, 120n10, 558
Frémont Expedition of 1853–54, 120n10, 558
French, Charley, 491
Furniss, Norman F., 603

Garland, John, 39, 49, 56–61, 280n16, 472, 474n16
Garnett, Richard B., 150n12
Garnett, Robert S., 149–50, 150n12
Gee, Sol, 108
General Jesup (steamboat), 119, 122–23, 125, 128–30, 146–47
Gentles, William, 44, 44n12
Gerrish, Abel, 254
Gerrish, William, 109, 240, 287n32, 358
Gibbs, George, 148, 148n11
Gibson, Walter Murray, 37, 177, 182n57, 198n20, 394n19, 399
Gila River, 116, 144n2, 344
Gilbert, Abel, 353, 374, 375–76, 376n50, 420–21, 511, 511n14, 597
Gilbert & Gerrish (sutlers), 90, 109, 240, 254, 353, 513, 578
Globe Restaurant and Coffee House (Salt Lake City), 234n32, 340, 379n58, 517, 523, 538, 568, 595
Godbe, William S., 211n51
Goodale, Jenny (Shoshone), 36, 44n11, 45
Goodale, Timothy, 45, 49, 65
Gove, Jesse A., 40, 283
Grant, George D., 316n19, 445–46, 517–18, 518n26, 521, 574
Grant, Ulysses S., 643
Great Britain: Buchanan as minister to, 616; impact of Utah War on, 28, 317, 601; intelligence-gathering on Mormon exodus, 178–79; Mormon colonies/missions, 153, 330, 332; Royal Navy deployment, 37, 179, 184; South Africa Kaffir Wars, 18; supplying arms and munitions, 31; U.S. border disputes, 617, 617n16
Great Eastern (steamship), 126, 126n22
Greeley, Horace, 636, 637. See also *New York Tribune*
Green River, 19, 32, 56, 95, 98–99, 99n25, 117, 305n65, 316, 349, 614
Green River County, 221, 225, 232n28, 253, 292, 385
Greenwood, A. B., 317
Greenwood, George, 327, 445n51
Groesbeck, Nicholas, 325n34, 336, 516, 516n22
Grover, Cuvier, 87–88, 91, 282, 294
Grow, Matthew J., 19, 279n80, 294, 296, 356, 462
Gunnison, John W., 439
Gwin, William M., 261, 272

Hamblin, Jacob: Colorado River exploration, 343; diaries and reminiscences, 137–39; monitoring Ives Expedition, 79n28, 118–20, 126, 136–37; report to Young on Mountain Meadows, 545, 545n62
Hamilton, Henry, 145–46
Hamilton Gardner Papers, 282–83
handcart emigration, 91n6, 251, 324
Hanks, Ebenezer, 197–98, 200–203
Hanks, Ephraim K., 248, 529–30, 576
Harker, Joseph, 247n3
Harmon, Nicholas Groesbeck, 325n34
Harmony, Utah, 317, 433
Harney, William S.: anti-Mormon rhetoric, 288, 288n34; arrival at Fort Bridger, 543, 555, 588; command of Utah Expedition, 30, 165n16, 396, 469–73, 607; criticism of Scott's leadership, 79n25, 167–68; declaring martial law, 221, 221n12, 302n61; Johnston named commander in place of, 32, 35; Johnston replaced as commander by, 403, 556–57, 613; march west from Fort Leavenworth, 473–75, 478–84; promotion, 619n17; relationship with Cumming, 281, 346; replacement of Smith, 57n34, 472–73; strategy and tactics, 159, 173, 173n31
Harney County, Ore., 622
Harris, John, 478
Harris, McGee, 247n3
Harrison, George "Beefsteak," 91n6
Haskell, Thales, 135–39, 209
Haslam, James, 187n1
Hatch, Ira, 120, 137, 209, 209n48, 389, 389n7
Hatch, John Porter, 56n30

Hawaii, Kingdom of (aka Sandwich Islands): British naval protection, 37, 184; impact of Utah War, 28; Mormon colonies/missions, 153, 215, 229–30; rumors of Mormon exodus to, 392–93; sinking of U.S.S. *Levant* near, 478
Hawaii, Territory of, 336n54
Hawkins, Leo, 426, 426n13
Healy, John Jerome "Johnny," 645–46
Heintzelman, Samuel P., 164, 259–60, 263–64
Henrys Fork Valley, 87, 589
Hickman, Eunice Phelps, 591–94, 628
Hickman, John, 245, 628
Hickman, William Adams "Bill": formation of Standing Army companies, 14, 248; member of Nauvoo Legion, 486, 517, 638; military troop movements, 253–54; support of Young's Standing Army, 247, 247n3; vigilantism and executions, 508, 571, 603n2, 620
Hill, George Richard, 333
Hockaday, John M., 97, 97n19, 100, 104–6, 110, 451, 528, 575, 577, 616
Hockaday-Magraw mail service, 292n42, 412, 516n21
Hoffman, Mark, 26, 596n43
Hoffman, William, 484, 488, 553, 553n71, 555, 559, 630
Holbrook, Joseph, 249
Holt, Joseph, 402
Holzer, Harold, 459n68
Homer, Michael W., 76, 76n20
Houston, Margaret, 271–73
Houston, Sam: Blair friendship, 583; Blair letter to, 264–68; connection to Utah War, 264–66; honoring memory of, 635; Johnston relationship, 236, 264, 269, 613; McCulloch friendship, 396–97, 506; and Mormonism, 2, 27, 36, 246; and Peace Commission, 384, 393, 509; Senate speech on Utah War, 269–73
Hudson, N.Y., 594–95, 595n41
Hudson River/Valley, 167, 594
Hudson's Bay Company, 17, 152, 152n14
Humbert, Charles J., 73n14
Humboldt, Alexander von, 117, 120, 140
Humphreys, Andrew A., 117, 122–23, 132–33, 139, 482n29
Hurt, Garland, 60n41, 90n5, 93–94, 105–6, 317, 380, 456, 567, 613–14, 616n15, 638–39
Hyatt (Iats) Indians. *See* Mojave Indians
Hyde, Orson, 217, 285, 380

Ibapah Valley, 311
Illinois: anti-Mormon views, 449n57; formation of volunteer units, 259n30, 262–63; memories of Mormon persecution, 152, 221, 292, 310, 527, 543; Mormon exodus from, 183
Independence, Mo., 342n64, 545n61
intelligence-gathering: Bernhisel collection in Washington, 162, 265n50, 394, 458; Buchanan and "plausible deniability," 33; double-crossing and lying, 242n50; honey-pot entrapment of Cumming, 381, 466, 539–40; Ives Expedition, 164; Mormon network for, 30, 49, 65, 125–30, 198, 312, 316, 376, 388, 510, 561; Peace Commission, 493–94; returning captives as source for, 72–75, 75n17; Utah Expedition, 95, 148, 253–54, 303. *See also* spies/spying
international impact of Utah War, 17, 28, 113, 184–85, 259, 601, 622
Iretéba (Mojave), 128
Irwin, Joseph C. "Doc," 287n32
Isaac (Paiute chief), 389
Ives, Cora M. Semmes, 115, 123–25, 130–34, 140
Ives, Joseph Christmas: assignment of Colorado River exploration, 18, 113–14; expedition planning and organization, 116–22; expedition's shift to military mission, 159; Grand Canyon discovery, 36; letters to wife, 124–25, 132–33, 140; report on Colorado River mission, 112, 114–15. *See also* Colorado River, Ives Expedition along

Jackson, Alden A. M., 203, 206
Jackson, Ann Oades, 568–69
Jackson, Caroline, 203
Jackson, Henry Clark, 568–69
Jackson County, Mo., 342, 342n64, 545n61
James, Dick, 576, 597
James, Jesse, 487n40
James, Richard W., 449
Jaques, John, 551
Jesup, Thomas S., 119n6
Johnson, George Alonzo, 119, 119n6, 122–23, 125, 127n23, 129–31, 133
Johnston, Albert Sidney: anti-Mormon rhetoric,

35, 268n35; captivity of Stowell, 353n13; commander of Utah Expedition, 32, 147, 159, 397n25, 467–69, 555–56, 612–13; death at Shiloh, 633; declaring martial law, 302n61; dueling challenges, 293–94, 294n45, 370, 416; honoring memory of, 634; Indian relations, 239–40, 316; leadership and reputation, 54n26, 339n59, 556, 634; leadership in Utah War, 269–71, 288–89, 612; and Mountain Meadows massacre, 613–14; orders Marcy Expedition, 39–40, 45, 50–51; and peace process, 403–6, 415–16; postwar responsibilities, 632–33; proclamation of presidential pardon, 535–39; promotion to general, 26, 171–74, 469–73, 619, 619n17; protecting Marcy Expedition, 93–101; reinforcing the Utah Expedition, 49, 56–57, 60, 60n41, 71; relationship with Cumming, 364–65, 457, 539–43, 571–75, 636; relationship with Kane, 26–27, 281–88, 293–94, 298–305, 370, 609–11; relationship with Sam Houston, 2, 246, 264–67, 271–73; relationship with Young, 616, 623–24; replacement as expedition commander, 163–66; reports to McDowell, 95, 107–8; Stowell capture and treatment, 326, 353n13. *See also* Utah Expedition

Johnston, William, 106

Jones, Henry, 216

Jones, Nathaniel V., 248, 514n18

José (Mojave chief), 127

"Junius" (pseudonym), 471. See also *Chicago Daily Tribune*

Kane, Elisha Kent, 190–93, 211n52–212, 222, 306, 306n69, 357, 365, 441

Kane, Elizabeth W.: correspondence from Thomas, 194–95, 440; and death of Thomas, 647–48; departure of Thomas to Utah, 187, 191–93; diary accounts of, 20, 27; feelings about Buchanan mission, 33–34, 400–401, 492–93; finances and living arrangements, 195n11, 306n70; journal entries, 204–6, 440, 462, 463–64, 501–2; as physician and photographer, 192n7, 620; return of Thomas from Utah, 495–96, 501–2

Kane, Harriet "Little Harry," 192–93

Kane, John K. (judge), 33–34, 195–96, 211n52, 440

Kane, John K., Jr., 193, 650

Kane, Penn., 648

Kane, Robert Patterson "Pat": assists Elizabeth, 192; letters from Thomas, 210–12, 222–24, 276–77, 280n13, 285–86, 304–5, 348, 350n4–351, 369–70, 502–3, 608; meeting with Buchanan, 400, 491, 491n47, 647

Kane, Thomas L. (aka Dr. A. Osborne), 282–83, 507, 648; arrival in California, 194–203, 363n28; arrival at Camp Scott, 281–84; arrival at Fort Bridger, 275–79; arrival in Salt Lake City, 212–16; challenging Johnston to duel, 293–94; Civil War service, 212, 214, 294, 647–48; criticism of Buchanan, 494–95; death of father, 435–36, 440–41; departs home for Utah, 187–91, 262, 622; departs Utah for home, 441, 457–58, 461–65, 495–97; dueling challenges, 293–94, 370, 416, 648; image and behavior, 279–80, 293–94; leaves California for Utah, 203–12; letters home to family, 195–96, 366–69, 439–40; letters to Pat Kane, 211–12, 222–24, 276–77, 280n13, 285–86, 304–5, 351, 369–70; meeting with General Kimball, 348–52, 355–57; recognition by Buchanan, 646–47; and Reconstruction period, 635–42; relations/communications with Cumming, 299–300, 305–8, 347–48, 419–20, 503–4; relations/communications with Young, 29–30, 219–20, 232–33, 240–41, 250–52, 295–97, 352–55; relationship with Johnston, 284–85; reports to Buchanan, 91–92, 210–11, 221–22, 224–28, 236–37, 239, 278, 289–93, 296, 300–304, 359–63, 491, 491n47, 497–503; role and mission, 14, 26–27, 32–34

Kane, William Leiper, 193, 213

Kansas-Nebraska Act of 1854, 81, 606

Kansas Territory: "Bleeding Kansas" murders, 31, 601, 605; and civil unrest, 393, 401, 469, 621–22; formation of Utah Expedition, 30, 612; Fort Leavenworth, 480; Indian alliance with Mormons, 75; Indian alliance with Utah Expedition, 94–95; Quantrill raid on Lawrence, 310n1, 487–90; slavery, 602; statehood attempt, 272, 470; supplying troops to Utah Expedition, 601; Utah Expedition reinforcement, 60n41, 160, 162, 169, 171, 316, 408n41, 420, 473, 564; Young's arson threats, 83–84

Kay, John, 342, 449, 529
Kelly, Henry Brooke, 105, 105n37
Kentucky, 256–57, 474n16, 601
Kimball, Heber C., 203–4, 217, 378–79, 401, 433, 440, 446, 448n54, 466, 525, 529–30, 544, 579, 597n46
Kimball, John B., 446, 448, 448n54, 520, 638
Kimball, Mary Ellen, 440, 461
Kimball, William H.: commander of the Standing Army, 248; and Move South, 318n25, 352–53; officer in Nauvoo Legion, 350; relationship with Kane, 296–99, 301, 306, 315n18, 348–50; relocation of Cumming to Salt Lake City, 353–63, 373–74, 378–81
Kingham, George S., 240
Kinney, Henry Lawrence "Colonel," 344, 519, 523n29
Kirkham, Ralph W., 148
Klassen, Jacob S., 250n11
Klikatat Indians, 149
Klondike gold rush (1896–99), 646
Knight, Samuel R., 137–39
Knowlton, John Quincy, 464n80

Lamanites (aka American Indians), 66, 128n24, 316
Lander, Frederick W., 109n45, 264, 264n45
Las Vegas, N.Mex. Terr. (now Nevada): evacuation of the Mormon mission, 31; Ives Expedition approach to, 138; Kane en route to Utah, 188, 207–10; lead mining and smelting, 208; Spanish Trail route to Utah, 118, 130–31
Lawrence, Henry, 458, 510, 516, 516n23
Leavitt, Dudley, 120, 137
Lecompton Constitution (Kans.), 470
Lee, Custis, 471
Lee, Jem, 167
Lee, John D., 317, 643, 648
Lee, Robert E., 279, 471, 482n28, 622
Lee, William H. F. "Rooney," 36–37
Leroux, Antoine, 124n19
Lewis, Tarlton, 329–30
Lewis and Clark Expedition (1804–6), 558
Liberty (Missouri) Weekly Tribune, 520, 552–53
Lincoln, Abraham, 269, 406n37, 459n68, 507, 621
Lion House (Salt Lake City), 234, 284, 598
"Lion of the Lord," 505, 637
Little, Feramorz, 518, 575
Little, J. C., 78, 526, 528, 530, 570, 578–79, 639n30
Little, Lewis Henry, 485
Little Soldier (Dakota Sioux), 242
London, Jack, 646
Loring, William Wing, 61, 62n45, 486, 555, 560, 564
Los Angeles, Calif., 121, 158, 194, 197n17. *See also* San Pedro, Calif.
Los Angeles Star, 124n19, 145–46, 196
Luck, William, 249
Lyman, Amasa M.: Colorado River expedition, 14, 19, 126–27, 242n49, 311, 343, 384, 388–92; at Council meetings, 217, 525, 528; evacuation of San Bernardino colony, 143–45, 199–200, 202n31; excommunication from church, 389n8; and Major Blake, 129–30, 146–47, 209, 216–17; reporting on Kane-Young meeting, 216–17; restoring Las Vegas lead mining, 208
Lyman, Edward Leo, 19, 202n31
Lyman, Francis Marion, 389n8
Lyman, Rhoda Ann, 207, 280n13

Macomb, John N., 19, 55
Madsen, Christian A., 631–32
Magraw, W. M. F., 108–11, 156, 286n30, 302, 358, 487, 520, 614
Majors, Alexander, 474, 490
Mansfield, Joseph K. F., 171n29
Marcy, Mary Ellen "Nellie," 39–43, 47, 48–50, 62, 62n46, 63–64
Marcy, Mary M., 41–42, 626–28
Marcy, Randolph B.: anti-Mormon rhetoric, 288n34; autobiography, 46–47, 52n23; Civil War service, 46–47; family fears over safety, 41–43; *Harper's* magazine article, 50–54; leadership and reputation, 43, 339n59, 619; letters to family, 49–50, 62–63, 626–27; passage through Salt Lake City, 626–28; promotion, 558, 619n17, 627n6; relationship with McClellan, 260; reports on New Mexico trek, 47–48; return from New Mexico, 557–60; in Seminole Wars, 42n6; and Utah War, 61–65, 72–76, 87–88, 93–103, 113–14, 420, 474, 474n16. *See also* New Mexico
Marcy's Volunteers, 45
Martineau, James Henry, 209, 217, 242n49, 329–30

Mason, Richard M., 65, 77, 91, 250, 611, 648
Mathews, Joseph, 211n51
Matthews, William I., 144
Maxwell, Lucien, 63n47
May, Charles A., 484
Mayfield, John, 205n36, 208, 211n51
McBride, George, 237, 239
McClellan, George B.: Civil War service, 47; letters to Marcy family, 41–43, 63–64; marriage to Nellie Marcy, 62n46; return to army service, 41, 259–60, 622
McCormick, Washington J., 96n16, 292n42, 367n33, 371n41, 465, 576n22
McCulloch, Ben: army service, return to, 259–60, 397, 397n25; Confederate Army service, 506; described, 396–97, 506–7; friendship with Blair, 265, 267–68, 68n54; friendship with Houston, 265, 267–68, 268n54, 273; relationship with Kane, 404, 410, 419; relationship with Young, 508, 539; service as peace commissioner, 264. *See also* Peace Commission
McDonald, John T., 568, 569–71
McDowell, Irwin, 85, 107–8, 289n36, 563
McNeill, Frank, 576–77, 597
McRae, Alexander, 528
Medina, Mariano "Marianne," 45, 47, 48n20, 49, 187n1
Mémoires d'un Mormon (Bertrand), 76
Mencken, H. L., 599
Mexican-American War: capture of Mexico City, 148n9, 586; Cooke's service, 596; Cumming's service as sutler, 578n; Garland's service, 472; McCulloch's service, 397, 505–7; Mormon Battalion, 77, 82, 183, 378n55, 587, 596; Persifor Smith's service, 470; Totten's service, 472; U.S. military commitments, 2, 467; veterans, volunteering for Utah War, 155–56, 257; Williams's service, 475
Mexico: destination in Move South, 341–44, 523n29; flight of Mormon refugees, 14, 183; impact of Utah War, 28; relating to Utah Expedition second front, 175, 184–85, 395n20, 602; rumors of Mormon exodus, 392–93, 436, 436n31, 601; territorial acquisition by U.S., 175, 179–86, 386, 604, 609; U.S. annexation of Texas, 183. *See also* New Mexico
Miller, David H., 18, 46n16, 47n18, 52n24, 121, 121n11, 124
Miller, James T., 237, 239
Miller, Robert, 552
Mills, Edward T., 211n51, 389
Mills, Samuel C., 101, 279, 480–81
Mills, William Gill, 384, 387–88
Minnesota, 601
Missouri: Cumming's background in, 422, 427–28, 431–32, 532; forces in Mormon War of 1838, 527n35; formation of volunteer units, 255–56; location of Zion, 342n64, 545n61; Mormon persecution, 152, 221, 292, 310, 543; orders for Mormon "extermination," 268n55; response to Quantrill raids, 310n1, 487n40; Young's arson threats, 83–84
Mitchell, Armistead H., 155–56
Mojave Indians (aka Hyatts, Iats): and Ives Expedition, 139–41; massacre of Rose Baley party, 125n20, 343; meeting with Ives Expedition, 127–29; meeting with Lyman Expedition, 390–91; and Mormons, 119–20, 126–27, 134, 137–39, 618
Möllhausen, Carolina, 139
Möllhausen, Heinrich Balduin: diary entries of, 18–19, 113; diary entries, Colorado River, 127–29, 134–36; diary entries, Fort Yuma, 120–24; encountering Mojave hostilities, 139–40; painting of *Explorer* (Ives Expedition), 112; participation in Ives Expedition, 116–17; return to Prussia, 140–41
Monticello (Jefferson home), 507
Moon, Hugh, 326
Moore, John B., 19
Morehead, Charles R., 100n29, 187n1
Mormon (newspaper), 387
Mormon Conflict, The (Furniss), 603
Mormon History Association, 23, 675
Mormon Rebellion, The (Bigler and Bagley), 603
Mormon Trail, 188, 348n1, 564
Mormonism: dealing with non-Mormons, 31, 83, 125, 289, 371, 446–48, 520, 620; difficulties in leaving the faith, 444–46; doctrine and beliefs, 66; location of Zion, 61, 66, 202, 342n64, 520, 545n61; proselytizing and Protestant hostility, 152–53; Reformation of 1856, 328. *See also* anti-Mormonism; polygamy

Morrell, Hiram F., 108, 301–2, 451, 456, 510, 513, 519–20, 528, 567, 637–39
Morrison, Pitcairn, 479, 482–85
Morton, William H., 54, 54n26
Mosquito Coast. *See* Nicaragua
Mountain Meadows massacre: described, 31; impact on LDS image/reputation, 643–44; Indian role in, 55, 93, 391n12, 545n62; investigation, 309, 433–35; orders for, 26; settler demands for protection, 144–46; whites disguised as Indians, 75n18. *See also* Nauvoo Legion
Mountaineer, The (newspaper), 77
Move South: announcement/instructions for, 309–10, 318–24; evacuation of Salt Lake City, 505, 569, 586; movement of infrastructure, 336–41; movement to Mexico, 341–44, 523, 523n29; planning of, 182–83; question "where," 341–45, 601; question "why," 310–18, 384, 432–33, 468, 618; recollections of, 14, 26, 330–35; refugee hardship and suffering, 21, 36, 436–38, 494–95, 568–69, 623–26; refugees returning home from, 623–26; resistance to, 324–30; response of Cumming to, 440, 444–46, 457; response of Kane to, 352–58; termination of, 588, 623, 635
Muddy Creek, 28–29, 162, 295, 351n7, 376, 503, 560, 562–63
Mullan, John, 164–65
Mullins, Francis "Frank," 21
Murdock, John R., 464n80
myth/perception of war-peace split, 241, 255, 341, 359, 364, 416, 447, 449–55, 496

Nauvoo, Ill., 200, 203, 208n45, 343, 428, 566–67, 569–71
Nauvoo Legion: attack on Fort Laramie, 67, 94; attack on Forts Bridger and Laramie, 67; attack on Utah Expedition, 196, 231n26, 287n32, 309–10; characterization of military actions, 605, 618; desertions/capture, 326, 329, 485; disciplinary problems, 325–26, 486; intelligence-gathering, 56, 56n31; Kane relationship to, 295; military capabilities and weakness, 77–80, 168; mobilization and harassment actions, 31–32; monitoring Utah Expedition, 216; operations outside Utah, 601; prisoners, capture/release of, 72–75; raids in California, 143–46; response to Fort Limhi attack, 316n19; restoring Las Vegas lead-mining effort, 208; role in Move South, 325–28, 337, 586, 618; submitting to military service, 446; training and tactics, 68; U.S. amnesty program, 510n10; and Utah Expedition passage through Salt Lake City, 595–98. *See also* Echo Canyon; Fort Limhi; Mountain Meadows massacre; Standing Army of Israel
Navarupe (Mojave), 128
Nebraska Territory: Blackfeet treaty negotiations, 281; Camp Walbach, 18, 475n18; Kane return home through, 341, 464n80; Mormon-Indian relations, 66; Mormon "scorched-earth" policy, 66, 68; Nauvoo Legion actions in, 31, 601; U.S. Army route through, 159, 221n12, 483; Utah territorial losses to, 643; Young's arson threats, 83–84, 84
Nelson, Jack W., 46n16
Nephi, Utah, 14, 210n50, 252, 315, 334–35
New Mexico: accounts of Marcy's winter survival, 45–54; arrival of Marcy Expedition, 55; call for volunteers, 43–45; Cochetopa Pass, 47–49, 52, 52n24; Johnston's communications with Marcy, 95–101; Kit Carson as Indian agent, 57–60; and Marcy trek, 26–27, 38–41; protecting Marcy mission, 93–95; rumors of Mormon-Indian alliance, 55–56, 94–95; supplying troops to Utah Expedition, 601. *See also* Marcy, Randolph B.; Mexico; Taos, N.Mex.
New York: army headquarters, 95, 98n21, 99n26, 104, 106, 148, 171; enlistment of army troops, 54n26, 72, 601; formation of volunteer forces, 257; Kane departure from, 32, 187, 189–91, 262; transfer of troops to California, 160
New York Herald, 82, 201, 266–68, 384, 387, 394, 487n40, 500, 553–54, 621, 635. *See also* Fillmore, Lemuel; Stenhouse, T. B. H.
New-York Historical Society, 1859 Kane lecture at, 647
New York Times, 61–62, 323n32n385–86, 411–15, 422, 459, 468–69, 491–97, 523, 559, 565–68, 583–84, 638. *See also* Burr, David Auguste; Simonton, James "S"
New York Tribune, 73, 81–82, 90–97, 101–3, 284–85,

411–13, 459, 512–13, 581, 636–38. *See also* Browne, Albert Gallatin; Burr, David Auguste
Newberry, John Strong (Dr.), 19, 116, 120, 120n9, 124, 133n35, 141
Newton, John, 560
Nez Perce Indians, 148–49, 151, 237n38
Nicaragua (Mosquito Coast), 344, 523, 578, 626, 646
Nordmann, Carl F., 259
Nullification Crisis (1832–33), 198, 198n21

Oat-sen-a-wantz (Mojave chief), 390–91
Old ("Upper") Camp Floyd, 21, 629n8, 632n16. *See also* Camp Floyd, Utah Terr.
Old Council House (Salt Lake City), 523, 533n41
Olliff, Donathan, 182
O'Neil, Owen Hugh "O. H. O.," 520–22, 522n27, 551–53
On the Mormon Frontier (Brooks), 313
Orr, James L., 450–55
Osborne (Dr. A.) (pseudonym). *See* Kane, Thomas L.
Osborne, Anthony, 363n28
Ouseley, Sir William Gore, 17, 25, 159, 177–86, 357, 417
Owen, John, 487

Pace, W. B., 514n18
Pacific Wagon Road, 88–89, 108–9, 264n45, 516n21, 520
Paiute (Piede) Indians, 55, 93, 130, 145, 389–90, 391n12, 545n62
Parowan, Utah, 118, 208–9, 211n51, 217, 311, 329, 329n46, 336–37, 343, 384, 388
Pate, Henry Clay, 581
Paul Clifford (Bulwer-Lytton), 98n22
Peace Commission, 404–7, 410–16; appointment of Powell and McCulloch, 221n13, 264, 273, 396–98, 400–407; arrival in Salt Lake City, 505–7, 510–11, 581–82; authority to pardon, 398–404, 467–68, 493–94, 502, 535–37, 538–41; congressional call for creation of, 393; creation by Buchanan, 396–97; criticisms of, 385, 551–54, 576, 636; and end to war, 522–35, 544–54, 562, 571–74, 611, 616–20; journey to Utah, 410–16, 481; reporting on Move South, 324–25, 25n34; reporting on Salt Lake City discussions, 546–51. *See also* McCulloch, Ben; Powell, Lazarus W.
Peacock, George H., 116–17, 132, 137n43, 187n1, 639n30
Peck, Robert Morris, 488–90
Pend d'Oreille Indians, 237n38
Pennsylvania: burial of Buchanan, 634; burial of Thomas Kane, 648; Civil War "Bucktail Rifles," 214, 647–48; court martial of Sumner, 164; formation of volunteer forces, 257; Kane land ownership, 192n8; recruitment of army troops, 474n16, 601; Whiskey Rebellion of 1791, 198, 198n21, 393, 413; Wyoming Valley, 239, 239n41
Phelps, John Wolcott: on army discipline, 486–87, 559–60; description of Kane, 282–83; diaries and reminiscences, 20; observation of returning refugees, 623–26, 632; presidential pardons, 509–10; reinforcement of Utah Expedition, 255–56; Salt Lake City arrival, 588, 590–94
Phelps, William Wines, 438
Philippines, 646
Pickett, William, 199–201
Pierce, Franklin, 30, 152, 177, 218, 218n7, 393, 498–99, 499n56, 600, 615–17, 619n17, 634, 638n27
Pike, Ralph, 44, 44n12, 635
Pitchforth, Samuel, 315
Plitt, George, 392, 400
Poll, Richard D., 19–20, 190n4, 201, 202n29, 221n13, 296, 314–15, 330
Polydore, Henrietta, 96, 96n16
polygamy: constitutional protection of, 418; Cumming attitude toward, 435; impact on LDS image/reputation, 644; Joseph F. Smith manifesto of 1904, 546; Judge Eckels's charges/opinion, 383–87, 454, 524; Mormon image in practice of, 568, 625; national furor over, 30, 232, 602; politics and public relations, 255–56, 387, 494, 600, 616; prohibition/prosecutions, 524, 643–44; protecting women from non-Mormon men, 567; Young defense of, 643–44. *See also* Mormonism
Pony Express, 507, 516n21, 620
Poole, David, 487
Pope, Alexander, 351n5

Porter, Fitz John: adjutant to Johnston, 90, 99, 101, 288–89; advice to McClellan, 260; anti-Mormon rhetoric, 42n7, 268n55, 288–89; departure from Utah, 633; diary entries, 87, 94–95, 242n50, 278, 286–88, 297–98, 364–65, 420; feelings toward Kane, 279, 282, 286n30, 289, 375; observations about Cumming, 282, 282n21, 363–64; reputation and abilities, 279; Utah Expedition incidents, 623–24; on Utah War origins, 35
Powell, John W., 241, 297
Powell, Lazarus W.: described, 396–97, 507; relationship with Kane, 419; relationship with Young, 508. *See also* Peace Commission
Pratt, Parley, 465
Preston, William, 171–73, 183
Price, Eli K., 646–47
Provo, Utah, 231, 253, 309, 315, 317–18, 321–22, 325–26, 329, 329n46, 337–42, 419–20, 433, 440, 478–79, 518–23, 544–45, 552, 580–81
Pugmire, Jonathan, 340–41
Putnam, Haldimand Sumner, 482

Quaking Aspen Hill, 348, 348n1, 350, 375–76, 513
Quantrill, William Clarke (aka "Charley Hart"), 14, 36, 487–90, 490n44, 645
Quitman, John A., 171, 263
Quorum of the Twelve Apostles, 71, 102n31m210, 217, 307, 313, 319, 369, 389n8, 523, 636

Radford, John D. "Jack," 287n32, 587
Rafael Swell (near Cottonwood Wash), 21
railroad surveys/construction, 115, 148n11, 164, 193, 236, 515n19, 646
Rancho Rio de Jesus Maria (California), 523n29
Raymond, Henry J., 494–95
"Red the Missourian" (teamster), 491
Reformation of 1856, 328
Rich, Charles C., 202n31, 217, 525
Richards, Franklin D., 525, 577–78
Richards, Henry P., 247
River Jordan, 110–11, 541, 565–67, 573, 581, 590–93
Robinson (Sergeant-Major), 485
Robinson, David C., 116, 131, 135
Robinson, John Cleveland, 278, 278n9, 281, 297
Robison, Lewis, 315, 315n18
Rockwell, Orrin Porter: formation of Standing Army companies, 14, 248; member of Nauvoo Legion, 276, 486, 516–17; military troop movements, 253–54; vigilantism and executions, 466n84, 508, 603n2, 620; as Young bodyguard, 633
Rockwood, A. P., 78, 248, 517
Romney, George Wilcken, 645
Romney, Willard Mitt "Mitt," 645
Rowberry, John, 312, 312n8
Rupe, Jim, 100n29
Rush Valley, Utah Terr., 190, 316, 408, 408n42, 578
Russell, Majors and Waddell (freight contractors), 474, 490–91
Russia, 37, 228–29, 336, 566, 616
Russian strategy, Young's. *See* Sebastopol (scorched-earth) policy
Ryan, George E., 478

"S" (pseudonym). *See* Simonton, James; Simpson, James Hervey
Sagely, Redmond B., 156
Salmon River Mission. *See* Fort Limhi, Ore. Terr.
salt: army resupply, 39, 51, 89, 133, 136; Young's offer to Johnston, 234–36, 241, 271, 286–87, 354, 395
Salt Lake City: arrival and activities of Kane, 215, 449–51; arrival of Cumming, 373–77, 444–49, 465–66; arrival of Peace Commission, 505, 507, 510–11; arrival of Utah Expedition, 543, 580–86; building and settlement, 152; described, before Utah Expedition arrival, 565–68; infrastructure destruction, 68, 309; infrastructure relocation, 336–39, 343; Kane departure, 457–60; passage of Utah Expedition, 586–98; River Jordan, 110–11, 541, 565–67, 573, 581, 590–93, 595; shooting of Utah Expedition soldiers, 631n12. *See also* Staines Mansion
Salt Lake Valley: arrival of the Mormons, 152, 600; movement of Utah Expedition to, 537, 540–43; Utah Expedition arrival, 31
San Bernardino, Calif.: evacuation of Mormon colony, 31, 126, 135, 144–45, 149–53, 468; Frances Clark service to LDS church, 462; Kane arrival on Utah mission, 194–205; Kane departure for Utah, 206–13; Spanish Trail route to

Utah, 161n4, 188; U.S. Army reinforcement of, 146–47
San Francisco, Calif.: departure of Ives Expedition, 116–17; evacuation of the Mormon colony, 31, 153; fear of Nauvoo Legion attack, 143–44, 157; Kane arrival on Utah mission, 191n5, 195–97, 212; organization of volunteer companies, 155–56; Scott's planned relocation, 130, 133; vigilante committees, 262n37
San Francisco Daily Alta California, 157, 196–98
San Pedro, Calif., 116, 160, 188, 194. *See also* Los Angeles, Calif.
Sandwich Islands. *See* Hawaii, Kingdom of
Sargent, Charles H., 257–58
Schreiber, Robert, 259
Schwan, Theodore, 646
Scott, Charles A., 555
Scott, Mary, 48
Scott, Winfield: changes Utah Expedition command, 162–67; communications with Floyd, 289n36; creation of Utah Expedition, 563, 603; dispatches from Johnston, 95–100, 106; Harney criticism of, 79n25; leadership and capabilities, 607; negotiates settlement of Aroostook War, 617n16; negotiates settlement of Utah War, 617; opposition to two-front campaign, 160–62; promotion of Johnston, 171–74; recognition/promotion of Marcy, 46, 558, 619–20; reinforcement of Utah Expedition, 57, 177, 183, 272n60, 467, 474n16; relationship with Buchanan, 609; relocation to California, 167–69, 179–80, 299; replaces Johnston as expedition commander, 468, 469–73, 612–13
Sebastopol (scorched-earth) policy, 66–69, 242, 310, 314, 321–23, 325n34, 336n54, 342, 580, 635. *See also* arson, Young's threats of
Seminole Wars, 42n6, 156, 368. *See also* Florida
Sharp, Adam, 514n18
Shays's Rebellion (1786–87), 198, 198n21
Shepherd, George, 487, 487n40
Sherman, John, 185, 261–62
Sherman, William Tecumseh "Cump," 34, 184–85, 189, 259, 261–62, 264, 622
Shoshone Indians (aka Snakes), 80n30, 85n43, 95, 105, 109, 148, 151n13, 213, 237, 237n38, 269, 305n65, 307, 316, 533n42, 614
Simonds, Ben (Delaware), 242–43, 376, 378, 518n26, 520, 576
Simonds, Jim (Delaware), 518
Simonton, James "S," 383, 397n27, 468, 473, 487n40, 493, 512–13, 562, 580, 582, 596–97, 622. See also *New York Times*
Simpson, James Hervey "S," 397, 467, 472, 472n10, 478–85, 490, 505, 546, 554. See also *Buffalo (N.Y.) Courier*
Sinclair, Charles E., 105n36, 292, 452n62
Sinclair, Peter, 26, 596n43
Skandinaviens Stjerne, 631–32
"Skloom" (Yakama chief), 149
Skull Valley, 316
slavery/slave-related violence, 96, 175, 185, 256–57, 262, 488n42, 602, 622
Slidell, John, 169–71, 263
Smith, Anne Elizabeth Cumming, 370–72
Smith, Charles Maurice, 293n44, 576, 597
Smith, Edmund Kirby, 482n28
Smith, George A., 39, 68, 69, 162n6, 224, 231, 240, 248, 273, 311, 313–14, 329, 379, 384, 387–88, 421, 439, 448, 455, 466, 535, 544–45, 545n62, 587–88, 611
Smith, Hyrum, 215
Smith, Joseph, Jr., 2, 31, 259n30, 264, 342n64, 527n35
Smith, Joseph F., 215
Smith, Joseph Lee Kirby, 482
Smith, Lot: beginning military activities, 253; leadership in Nauvoo Legion, 248; raids on Utah Expedition, 41, 87, 121n12, 159, 177, 255, 470, 487; reward for capture, 378; service in Civil War, 464n80
Smith, Melvin T., 217
Smith, N. Wallace, 626–31
Smith, Persifor Frazer, 57n34, 159, 261, 469–73, 556, 613
Smith, Samuel, 251–52
Smith, Thomas L., 238
Smith, William, 37, 259n30
Smith, William Duncan, 560, 626, 628–30
Smiths Fork Valley, 498, 555, 589
Smithsonian Institution, 141, 148n11
Snow, Eliza Roxcy, 438
Snow, Erastus, 525, 528–30, 553
Snow, J. C., 544

Snow, Lorenzo, 525, 646
Snow, Warren S., 585–86, 614, 639, 639n30
Sohon, Gustavus, 346
Solomon Creek, Kans. Terr., 488
Southern Emigrant Trail, 144n2
Spanish-American War, 621, 646
Spanish Civil War, 622
Spanish Trail/Old Spanish Trail, 114n1, 118, 129–34, 134n38, 137–38, 161n4, 188, 342, 391–92
Spencer-Pike Affair, 44, 44n12, 635
spies/spying, 67, 88–92, 135–36, 285–86, 394, 445. *See also* intelligence-gathering
Squires, Harry, 333
Squires, John Fell, 14, 333–35
Squires, Thomas, 334
S.S. *Moses Taylor*, 34, 262, 622
Staines, William C., 14, 235, 381, 445, 463, 582, 591
Staines Mansion: construction and lodging, 235; Cumming's lodging and lechery, 340, 376–78, 429, 445, 465–66, 580, 612; lodging for Kane, 216, 234n32, 284, 376–78, 463; spying on Cumming, 539–40; spying on visitors, 381, 539. *See also* Salt Lake City
Standing Army of Israel: adoption of name, 69n6; attack on Utah Expedition, 254–55; creation/formation, 67, 69–72, 162, 216, 229, 245–46, 318, 468; criticisms of, 79n25, 250–53, 610–11; evacuation of Fort Limhi, 238; financial and manpower burden, 246–50, 324, 327, 618; Kimball as commander, 350; research on, 14, 22, 27; officers and organizational structure, 229–30, 296, 350; operational activities, 240, 242, 253–55, 309; role in the Move South, 318–24; termination, 309–12, 323n32–324, 443n47. *See also* Nauvoo Legion
State of Deseret, 70–71
Stenhouse, T. B. H., 83, 378n57, 384, 387–88, 432n19, 458–60, 640n31. See also *New York Herald*
Steptoe, Edward J., 68, 143, 150–52, 152n14, 408n42, 499n56, 606, 638n27
Steptoe Expedition of 1854–55, 19, 31, 507–8, 543, 548, 554
St. Louis Republican, 449–50
Stoddard, Judson, 517, 519
Stott, Clifford L., 19, 217
Stout, Hosea, 313–15, 325n35, 328–30, 445–46
Stowell, Cynthia Jane Park, 21, 326
Stowell, William R. R., 293n44, 326, 353n13, 510n10, 513, 516, 609
Strong, George Templeton, 167
Struggles, J., 157
Sumner, Edwin V., 164, 475, 480, 484, 488–90

Tanner, Joseph Smith, 205n36, 211n51
Taos, N.Mex., 63, 65, 100, 377. *See also* New Mexico
Taylor, John, 34, 69, 201, 217, 264, 387, 426–32, 432n19, 459, 525, 529–30, 544–45, 645
Taylor, Joseph, 293n44, 353n13
Taylor, Paul H., 116
Taylor, Zachary, 173
Texas: army exploration of Red River, 42n5; Civil War Reconstruction, 643; hopes for an LDS colony, 2, 345; memorial to Johnston, 634; supplying troops to Utah Expedition, 601; U.S. annexation, 182–83. *See also* Houston, Sam
Texas Rangers: Blair as member, 256, 267; McCulloch as member, 273, 397, 403, 506–7; reputation and abilities, 268n54; veteran volunteers for Utah War, 155–56
Texas Revolution, 182, 265, 267, 294, 397, 506–7
35th Parallel Pacific Railroad Survey (1853–54), 115
Thirty Years of Army Life on the Border (Marcy), 46–47
Thomas, George H., 124n19
Thompson, Jacob, 80–81, 108–10, 358, 402
Thompson, Mathew (aka John, Nathaniel, James), 90–91
Tipton, John, 120n9, 132, 139n37
Toanob (Paiute), 391n12
Tooele City/Valley, 312, 316, 342, 419, 434
Totab (Mojave chief), 391, 391n12
Totten, Joseph G., 472
Toucey, Isaac, 402, 478
Tracy, Albert, 562
treason: Cumming accused of, 422–23; indictment of Stowell, 510n10; indictment of Young and others, 32, 81–82, 90n4, 107, 287n32, 398, 450, 619; presidential pardon, 398–99, 401–4, 411–14, 525, 536
Turley, Richard E., Jr., 23, 434n22
Twiggs, David E., 470

Udall, David, 333–35
Uhler, James M., 21, 43, 44n11, 636–38

Uintah Indians, 87, 93–95, 238–39, 305n65
Union Pacific Railroad, 97, 348n1
U.S. Army Department of the East, 163
U.S. Army Department of the Pacific, 146, 159, 163
U.S. Army Department of the West, 469
U.S. Army Department of Utah, 469–70, 632
U.S. Department of the Interior, 104, 643
U.S. Department of State, 190n3, 492
U.S. Marine Corps, 20, 37, 478–79
U.S. Military Academy. *See* West Point
U.S. military units: Bee's Volunteer Battalion, 44, 88, 108, 273, 474n16, 486–87, 563, 597n47; California volunteers, 154–57; First Cavalry, 474n16, 480, 488–90, 564, 626; First Dragoons, 146; First Infantry, 263; Fifth Infantry, 19, 20, 21, 42n6, 44, 88, 90, 150n12, 278, 294n45, 474n16, 478, 479, 557–58, 560, 564, 577, 577n25, 597, 597n46, 619; Fourth Artillery, 18, 20, 474n16, 476n19, 555, 588; Fourth Infantry, 597n47, 645; Illinois Regiment of Volunteers, 262–63; Kentucky volunteers, 256–57; Mormon Battalion, 77, 82, 183, 378n55, 587, 596; New Jersey volunteers, 302; Ninth Infantry, 150n12, 169n25; Ohio Volunteers, 257–58; Pennsylvania volunteers, 214, 257; Regiment of U.S. Mounted Riflemen, 61, 148n11, 474n16, 477, 564, 588; Second Artillery, 162, 164, 474n16, 482; Second Cavalry, 173n22, 397n25, 471, 474n16; Second Dragoons, 87, 162, 253, 279, 474n16, 477, 560, 564n12, 578, 587–89, 596, 626, 628; Seventh Infantry, 162, 474n16, 478–79, 483, 485, 485n30, 560, 573n20; Sixth Infantry, 162, 474n16, 484, 488, 553, 564; Tenth Infantry, 43–44, 54, 54n26, 55, 72–75, 87, 89n3, 91, 101, 105n37, 282n21, 294n45, 298, 474n16, 485, 509, 558–59, 560, 562, 564, 578, 597, 646; Tenth Iowa Infantry, 264n44; Third Artillery, 154, 194, 196, 474n16, 475; Third Dragoons, 73n14; Third Infantry, 48, 61, 264n44, 474n16, 477
U.S.S. *Levant*, 478
Utah Expedition: announcement of formation, 30; arrival at Fort Laramie, 31, 69, 476–77; departure for Salt Lake City, 555–59; desertions/capture, 32, 72, 88, 120n9, 196n13, 487, 510, 563–64; encounters with returning refugees, 623–26; entry into Salt Lake City, 580–95; entry into Salt Lake Valley, 543, 550, 555–57, 562–64; leadership and discipline, 485–91, 556; march to Salt Lake City, 559–64; Mormon intentions and strategy, 75–80, 107–8; Mormon spying, 87–92, 135–36; Nauvoo Legion attack, 367; passage through Salt Lake City, 586–98; planning second front, 143–44, 146, 159–60; politics and military glory, 280; protection from Mormon attack, 253–55; refusal of beef and flour, 240, 242n50, 276, 298, 359; refusal of salt from Young, 234–37, 395, 613; reinforcements, 49, 56–57, 60, 60n41, 474n16; resupply, 98, 99n26, 103, 467, 473–74, 555; termination of military operations, 599; U.S. Marine presence, 20; use of camels, 129, 129n28, 146–47; views on Mormon society, 626–31. *See also* Johnston, Albert Sidney
Utah Expedition, 1857–1858, The (Hafen and Hafen), 18
Utah State Historical Society, 23, 675
Utah War: assigning responsibility, 605–14; avoidable or inevitable, 614–17; causes of, 599–605; congressional investigation, 392–93; congressional reports by Buchanan, 491–93; criticism of Buchanan, 494–95; Fort Limhi attack as pivotal event, 316n19; identifying winners and losers, 618–20; impact on LDS image/reputation, 644; international reach/impact, 17, 28, 113, 184–85, 259, 601; origins, 29–34; postwar notoriety, 645–50; reconstruction period, 635–44; research on, 13–15; significance, 620–22; war-peace split, myth/perception of, 241, 255, 341, 359, 364, 416, 447, 449–55, 496; Young's war strategy, 65–68
Ute Indians: alliance with Mormons, 13–14, 39–40, 55, 59–60, 60n41; Carson as Indian agent, 57–59; conversion to Mormonism, 231–32; making peace with Navajo, 55–56, 60; and Mountain Meadows massacre, 317, 613; naming of Cochetopa Pass, 52n24; protecting Marcy Expedition, 93; raiding white settlements, 134–35, 144, 307, 316

Van Dyke, James C., 33–34, 201, 609
Van Ettan, E., 464n80
Van Vliet, Stewart, 84, 89n3, 111, 236, 264, 341–42, 383, 392, 395, 407–10, 10n44, 458, 486
Van Wagoner, Richard S., 233–34, 249–50

Victoria (queen of England), 37, 627–28
Vigilance Committees (vigilantism), 145–46, 154, 199–202, 262n37, 466n84
Villers, George (Earl of Clarendon), 17, 25, 159, 177–84

Wagner, David, 491
Walker, Robert J. (governor of Kansas), 401, 469
Walker, Ronald W., 433–34, 462, 590–91, 608
Walker, William, 646
Wallace, William A. "Yo Mismo," 196–98
Walla Walla Indians, 148, 151
War of 1812, 336n54, 472
Ward of the Three Guardians, The (Browne), 96–100
Warner, Juan José (formerly Jonathan Trumble), 143–46
war-peace split, myth/perception, 241, 255, 341, 359, 364, 416, 447, 449–55, 496
Warren, William S., 143–44, 389
Washakie (Shoshone chief), 90n5, 109
Washington, George, 167n21, 336n54
Washington National Tribune, 488–90
Washington Union, 400
Watts, Baldwin "Baldy," 187n1, 237
Watts de Peyster, J., 594
Weber County, 320
Weber River/Canyon, 239, 242, 376, 513, 516–18, 518n26, 544, 555, 569, 577, 594, 649
Weller, John B., 154–55
Wells, Daniel H.: commander of Nauvoo Legion, 32, 85n44; creation of Standing Army, 60–72, 229–30; investigation of Mountain Meadows, 433–34; member of First Presidency, 217–18, 254; presence at Council meetings, 217, 525, 528–29; relationship with Kane, 463–64; relationship with Young, 340; role in the Move South, 325–26, 329, 337–40
West (General), 248–49
West, Chauncey W., 328, 464n80
West, Lewis A., 464n80
Western Standard (newspaper), 388
West Point/West Point graduates, 89n3, 97n18, 101, 115, 150n12, 162, 260, 282, 408n40, 475, 490, 588, 644, 646
Whipple, Amiel Weeks, 115, 119n6, 120, 128
Whiskey Rebellion (1791–94), 198, 198n21, 393
White Mountain Expedition, 217, 242, 311, 388, 435, 468. *See also* Bean, George Washington; Dame, William H.
White Mountains, 19, 341, 392, 618, 632
Wilcken, Charles H., 645
Wilford Woodruff's Journal (Kennedy, ed.), 71–72, 217–19
Williams, Lawrence A., 99, 101
Williams, Mary Neosho "Moodie," 472, 475–78
Williams, Thomas, 18, 210, 472, 475–78
Willie, James G., 250n11, 251
Wilson, Alexander, 639
Winder, William A., 122–23, 125
Wind River Mountains, 99, 108, 520
Wingate (Mr.; pseudonym), 83–85, 276
women, 559n5; accompanying Marcy Expedition, 44n11; army laundresses, 564n12; and Cumming's lechery, 465–66; divorce, 90n4; Indian intermarriage with Mormons, 238n39; Legionnaire connubial visits and marriage, 568–71; prostitution, 216; protected from contact with non-Mormon men, 567; response to Move South, 330–32; role in Utah War, 189, 203–4, 368, 368n36; sexual abuse/sexual liaisons, 466, 466n84, 559n5; venereal disease, 391
Woodruff, Wilford, 34–35, 66, 220n10, 225, 259n30, 266, 313, 318, 377, 434–36, 448, 525, 544, 645. See also *Wilford Woodruff's Journal*
Woodward, Arthur, 122
Wool, John E., 163–67, 171–72, 468, 469–70, 612
Worthen, Lafayette Shaw "Fay," 22, 426n13, 446–51, 463, 464n80, 611
Worthen, Sam, 513
Württemberg, Duke Paul Wilhelm von, 120

Yates, Richard E., 303n63, 350, 508, 601, 638
Yell, Archibald, 156
"Yo Mismo" (pseudonym). *See* Wallace, William A.
Yost, Samuel M., 58–60
Young, Brigham: announcement of Move South, 309–10; assassination/kidnap attempt on, 518n26; ban on alcohol, 326; banishment of James Young, 508–9; calls war council, 70, 312–15; cedes governorship to Cumming, 421, 435, 468; contempt for alcohol, 615, 639; creation of Standing Army, 68–71, 247, 318;

early war strategy, 65–68, 71–72; fears of California invasion, 144, 156–58; indicted for treason, 32, 81–82, 90n4, 107, 287n32, 398, 450, 619; "Lion of the Lord," 505, 637; mobilization of Nauvoo Legion, 31; Mormon territorial claims, 71–72; Mountain Meadows massacre, 607–8, 649; pardon by Buchanan, 220–22, 543; philosophy of governance, 30; postwar Mormon-federal struggle, 635–44; and recall of federal appointees, 455, 557, 559n5, 572, 582–83, 637; Reformation of 1856, 328; relations/communications with Cumming, 420–21, 430–36, 455–57, 573–75; relations/communications with Kane, 219–21, 352–53, 461–65; relationship with Buchanan, 222, 616–17; relationship with Sam Houston, 2; responsibility for confrontation and war, 607–8; scorched earth policy, 68–69, 310; superintendent of Indian Affairs, 109, 528n36, 605; superseded as governor, 30–31; support of U.S. territorial expansion, 185–86; threats of arson, 83–84, 143–44; treason indictments, 287n32. *See also* First Presidency

Young, Ebenezer Russel, 459

Young, James Valentine, 508–9, 509n6

Young, Jemima Angell, 509n6

Young, John R., 523n29

Young, Joseph Angel, 217, 240–41

Young, Levi Edgar, 332–33

Young, Mary Ann Angell, 509n6

Young, Richard Whitehead, 646

Young, Zina Huntington, 330

Younger, Cole, 487n40

Zion, location/significance, 61, 66, 202, 342, 342n64, 520, 545n61

The Editor

William P. MacKinnon's interest in the Utah War and the American West began at Yale during his undergraduate years as a history major in the late 1950s studying with Professors Howard R. Lamar and David M. Potter and Curator Archibald Hanna. In 1960 he earned a B.A. degree magna cum laude from Yale and was elected to Phi Beta Kappa. MacKinnon has remained active in the university's affairs as an Associate Fellow of her Davenport College and board member of the Yale Library Associates, a group that he chaired during 2000–2004.

As an independent historian over the past half century, MacKinnon has written articles, essays, and book reviews on Utah's violent territorial period as well as on the U.S. Army's western campaigns that have appeared in more than thirty scholarly journals and encyclopedias. He became involved with the Arthur H. Clark Company's Kingdom tn the West series in 1996 upon beginning what became his two-volume documentary history of the Utah War, *At Sword's Point.* This body of work has brought him recognition by the Utah State Historical Society as an elected Fellow and Honorary Life Member and by the Mormon History Association as its president during 2010–11. Both organizations have also honored him with multiple awards for his articles and books. Over the years MacKinnon has been selected to deliver lectures endowed to honor prominent Mormon historians, including those memorializing Leonard J. Arrington and Juanita L. Brooks. In 2013 MacKinnon was elected sheriff (presiding officer) of the Santa Barbara Corral of Westerners International.

Parallel to his career as a historian, MacKinnon has worked as a business executive and management consultant since his graduation from the Harvard Business School with an M.B.A. degree in 1962. During the next twenty-five years, he was a financial and human resources executive with General Motors Corporation in New York and Detroit, including service during 1982–87 as vice president in charge of GM's corporate Personnel Administration and Development Staff. Since 1988 he has been president of MacKinnon Associates, a strategy consulting firm providing counsel on organizational and management issues to boards, CEOs, and other senior officers.

MacKinnon's third career has been in public and community service—including volunteer leadership roles as board chairman of Children's Hospital of Michigan and trustee of the Detroit Medical Center—at such educational institutions as the Birmingham, Michigan, School Board, Kettering University, the University of Virginia's Darden School, and the U.S. State Department's Overseas Schools Advisory Council. MacKinnon served during 1962–68 in squadrons of the New York Air National Guard following active duty with the U.S. Air Force.

He currently resides in Santa Barbara, California, with wife, Patricia, to whom *At Sword's Point* is dedicated.

Kingdom in the West Series

The role of the Church of Jesus Christ of Latter-day Saints in the settlement of the American West has been a subject of controversy and fascination for 170 years. Kingdom in the West: The Mormons and the American Frontier explores the story of the Mormon people and their part in the wider history of the American West.

1. *The Pioneer Camp of the Saints: The 1846 and 1847 Mormon Trail Journals of Thomas Bullock,* edited by Will Bagley. 1997.
2. *Forgotten Kingdom: The Mormon Theocracy in the American West, 1847–1896,* by David L. Bigler. 1998.
3. *Scoundrel's Tale: The Samuel Brannan Papers,* edited by Will Bagley. 1999.
4. *Army of Israel: Mormon Battalion Narratives,* edited by David L. Bigler and Will Bagley. 2000.
5. *Defending Zion: George Q. Cannon and the Mormon California Newspaper Wars of 1856–1857,* edited by Roger Robin Ekins. 2002.
6. *Fort Limhi: The Mormon Adventure in Oregon Territory, 1855–1858,* edited by David L. Bigler. 2003.
7. *Gold Rush Saints: California Mormons and the Great Rush for Riches,* edited by Kenneth N. Owens. 2004.
8. *On the Way to Somewhere Else: European Sojourners in the Mormon West, 1834–1930,* edited by Michael W. Homer. 2006.
9. *Doing the Works of Abraham: A Documentary History of Mormon Polygamy,* edited by B. Carmon Hardy. 2007.
10. *At Sword's Point, Part 1: A Documentary History of the Utah War to 1858,* edited by William P. MacKinnon. 2008.
11. *At Sword's Point, Part 2: A Documentary History of the Utah War, 1858–1859,* edited by William P. MacKinnon. 2016.
12. *Innocent Blood: Essential Narratives of the Mountain Meadows Massacre,* edited by David L. Bigler and Will Bagley. 2009.
13. *Playing with Shadows: Voices of Dissent in the Mormon West,* edited by Polly Aird, Jeff Nichols, and Will Bagley. 2011.

14. *Dale Morgan on the Mormons: Collected Works, Part 1, 1939–1951,* edited by Richard L. Saunders. 2012.
15. *Dale Morgan on the Mormons: Collected Works, Part 2, 1949–1970,* edited by Richard L. Saunders. 2013.

Series subscriptions are welcomed. Manuscript proposals of a documentary nature may also be submitted. Address inquiries to the publisher:

THE ARTHUR H. CLARK COMPANY
2800 Venture Drive
Norman, Oklahoma 73069-8218
(405) 325-5609